A Dictionary of
Economics

SEE WEB LINKS

Many entries in this dictionary have recommended web links. When you see the above symbol at the end of an entry go to the dictionary's web page at http://www.oup.com/uk/reference/resources/economics, click on **Web links** in the Resources section and locate the entry in the alphabetical list, then click straight through to the relevant websites. Additional web links are available in an appendix.

John Black was a Fellow and Tutor in Economics at Merton College, Oxford, and then Professor of Economic Theory at the University of Exeter. His many publications include *The Economics of Modern Britain, Essential Mathematics for Economics* (with J. F. Bradley), and *Housing Policy and Finance* (with D. C. Stafford). He is now an Emeritus Professor of the University of Exeter.

Nigar Hashimzade is Professor of Economics at the University of Reading. She undertakes research in economics and econometrics. Her publications include papers in *Economic Theory* and *Econometric Theory*, and she has contributed to *Essays in Dynamic General Equilibrium Theory* (2005).

Gareth Myles is Professor of Economics at the University of Exeter and a Research Fellow of the Institute for Fiscal Studies. His main research areas are public economics, labour economics, and microeconomics. His publications in these areas include the textbooks *Public Economics* (1995) and *Intermediate Public Economics* (2006).

A Dictionary of
Economics

THIRD EDITION

JOHN BLACK
NIGAR HASHIMZADE
GARETH MYLES

OXFORD
UNIVERSITY PRESS

OXFORD
UNIVERSITY PRESS

Great Clarendon Street, Oxford OX2 6DP

Oxford University Press is a department of the University of Oxford.
It furthers the University's objective of excellence in research, scholarship,
and education by publishing worldwide in

Oxford New York

Auckland Cape Town Dar es Salaam Hong Kong Karachi
Kuala Lumpur Madrid Melbourne Mexico City Nairobi
New Delhi Shanghai Taipei Toronto

With offices in

Argentina Austria Brazil Chile Czech Republic France Greece
Guatemala Hungary Italy Japan Poland Portugal Singapore
South Korea Switzerland Thailand Turkey Ukraine Vietnam

Oxford is a registered trade mark of Oxford University Press
in the UK and in certain other countries

Published in the United States
by Oxford University Press Inc., New York

British Library Cataloguing in Publication Data

Data available

Library of Congress Cataloging in Publication Data

Data available

Typeset by SPI Publisher Services, Pondicherry, India
Printed in Great Britain
on acid-free paper by
Clays Ltd, St Ives plc

ISBN 978-0-19-923705-0

1 3 5 7 9 10 8 6 4 2

Contents

Preface to the Third Edition

This dictionary aims to provide a convenient source of reference for a wide audience. Students taking a first course in economics and non-specialist readers of journals such as *The Economist* will find clear descriptions of fundamental concepts. For more advanced students and professional economists the dictionary includes entries on technical concepts written in a more formal style. The dictionary continues to include many useful definitions relating to personal finance, investments, and financial markets.

The main changes to the dictionary reflect the development of economics as a discipline since the second edition was produced. It is now commonplace for economic arguments to draw on concepts from game theory. This has led to the inclusion of more entries that deal with standard games and solution concepts for games. Econometrics has become an integral part of economics, so this edition includes a comprehensive range of new entries that reflects this fact. These entries generally provide a technical definition and a brief explanation of the application of the concept.

AAA rating *See* TRIPLE-A RATING.

abatement cost The cost of securing a reduction in pollution. The abatement cost can be quoted as a cost per unit or the total cost of achieving a given target. The marginal abatement cost should be equated to the marginal benefit to determine the efficient reduction in pollution. The concept of abatement cost applies to pollution caused by the production activities of firms and the consumption activities of consumers. *See also* EXTERNALITY.

ability and earnings *See* EARNINGS FUNCTION.

ability to pay The principle that any *tax should fall on those who can afford to pay. The government requires tax revenue to pay for *public goods and *income redistribution. Taking account of ability to pay means that tax payment should increase with the income or assets of taxpayers. The main objections to the ability to pay criterion are that it is hard to measure ability to pay, and that taxing income reduces the incentive to work. However, the collection of taxes from those who cannot afford to pay is unpopular, expensive, and sometimes impossible. Ability to pay is an alternative to the *benefit principle under which only those who benefit from any given public expenditure should be taxed to pay for it. Given the scale of taxes necessary to run a modern society, use of the ability to pay criterion for taxation seems inevitable.

abnormal profit *See* SUPERNORMAL PROFIT.

absolute advantage The ability to produce an output using fewer inputs than other producers. With only one type of resource, such as hours of work, a producer with lower inputs has an absolute advantage. When there are many factors of production absolute advantage means that the *production set for one producer is everywhere outside that of another. Absolute advantage gives no guidance on what to do with resources, which are best employed where their *comparative advantage is greatest.

absorption The total of expenditure on real goods and services, by consumers, investors, and the government. Absorption is the use of output: it excludes exports and includes imports. This is contrasted with *production, which includes exports and excludes imports. The absorption approach to *devaluation looks at its effects on various forms of expenditure, and points out that devaluation can only improve the balance of payments on current account if production increases relative to absorption.

abstinence Refraining from, or at least postponing, consumption which could have been undertaken immediately. Where the funds not being spent arise from current income, abstinence is thus the same as *saving; but the term also covers refraining from running down past savings or spending windfall gains.

accelerated depreciation The right to *write off capital goods for tax purposes faster than the rate at which they would normally be depreciated. This is intended to encourage *investment, as it enables a company to defer its taxes when it invests. Under accelerated depreciation a firm's profits net of *depreciation, and thus its tax liabilities, are lower than they would have been under normal depreciation. Once the capital goods are written off, profits net of depreciation become higher than they would have been under normal depreciation, and the tax bill rises again.

accelerator A model relating *investment to changes in *output. The accelerator model asserts that firms invest more when output is rising and less when it is falling. The argument is that a rise in *demand leads some firms to produce more and leads them, and other firms, to expect that demand will rise further. The rise in output raises the ratio of output to *capacity, and the expectation of further rises in demand makes firms believe it would be profitable to have more capital equipment. Accelerator-type models help explain empirically observed variations in both *fixed investment and *investment in stocks and work in progress.

acceptance Adding one's signature to a *bill of exchange, thereby accepting *liability to pay the bill at *maturity if the original signatory fails to do so. Acceptance of a bill of exchange by an institution of high financial standing, such as a *merchant bank, makes the bill safer to hold and thus easier to sell. The acceptor is taking a *risk, and makes a charge for this.

accepting house A financial firm that is willing to accept *bills of exchange, that is, to guarantee that they will be paid on the due date. An accepting house uses its financial reputation to earn a fee for acceptance, and its specialized knowledge of financial markets to avoid taking too many risks of accepting bills where it is actually going to have to honour its *guarantee. The principal London accepting houses form the Accepting Houses Committee.

accession countries Countries applying to join the *European Union (EU). The countries that are currently linked with future membership are Croatia, Bosnia, the Republic of Macedonia, Turkey, Montenegro, Serbia, and Albania. Accession country is also used to refer to a country that has recently joined the EU, including Cyprus, the Czech Republic, Estonia, Hungary, Latvia, Lithuania, Malta, Poland, Slovakia, and Slovenia.

accommodatory monetary policy A policy of allowing the supply of money to expand in line with the demand for it. If the *demand for money rises because of sustainable real growth in the economy, accommodatory monetary policy is desirable, and failure to expand the *money supply obstructs real growth. If, however, the cause of rising demand for money is a temporary, unsustainable surge in real activity, *inflation in prices and wages, or both, accommodatory monetary policy allows these excesses to continue too long. When obvious *excess demand or high inflation eventually forces a shift to a more restrictive monetary policy, this will have to be severe and may cause a serious *depression.

account(s) A statement about activities over some period. Accountability is the obligation to produce such a statement: the directors of companies are accountable to their shareholders, and in the UK ministers are accountable to Parliament for the activities of their departments. Accounts take various forms:

1. A statement of the relations between two parties: a *bank account records the deposits, borrowing, and withdrawals of a customer. Firms keep accounts of the goods and services provided to customers: goods provided on account are supplied on credit, and an account rendered is a demand for payment for goods and services supplied.

2. A systematic summary in money terms of the activities of a business over some period, usually a year. The two main statements in such accounts are the *profit-and-loss account and the *balance-sheet. A profit-and-loss account shows receipts and payments, and the profit or loss made during an accounting period. A balance-sheet lists the *assets and *liabilities of a firm on specified dates, at the start and the end of an accounting period. Accountants are producers and *auditors of accounts: they are often required to be professionally qualified, where the accounts have to be credible to creditors, law courts, and the tax authorities. Firms' accounts have to be certified as accurate by professional auditors.

3. National income and expenditure accounts are surveys of the economic activities of a nation. They include analysis of the production of goods and services, the distribution of incomes, and the expenditures of investors, consumers, and the government. In the parts of national income accounts related to transactions with the rest of the world, the *current account records sales and purchases of goods and services, property incomes and transfers, and the *capital account records sales and purchases of assets, including both real *foreign direct investment, inwards and outwards, and financial transactions, sales and purchases of securities abroad, and the making and repayment of international loans. *See also* APPROPRIATION ACCOUNT; BANK ACCOUNT; CAPITAL ACCOUNT; CHECKING ACCOUNT; CURRENT ACCOUNT; CURRENT (BANK) ACCOUNT; DEPOSIT ACCOUNT; MERCHANDISE ACCOUNT; PROFIT-AND-LOSS ACCOUNT; UNIT OF ACCOUNT.

accounting *See* COST ACCOUNTING; CREATIVE ACCOUNTING; INFLATION ACCOUNTING; MANAGEMENT ACCOUNTING.

accounting period The period of time, normally a year, to which a set of company accounts refers.

accounting profit The level of profit calculated using standard accounting principles. Accounting profit is equal to sales revenue less the explicit costs of a firm's operation, such as input costs, depreciation, interest, and taxes. In contrast, the calculation of *economic profit also includes the normal return to capital as a cost.

accounts payable The part of a firm's *liabilities, as shown in its *balance-sheet, consisting of bills received from suppliers on which payment is due but has not yet actually been made.

accounts receivable The part of a firm's *assets, as shown in its *balance-sheet, consisting of bills sent to customers on which payment is due but has not yet actually been received.

acquisition (company) Expansion of a *company through the purchase of other businesses. If these are unincorporated, terms are agreed with the owners. If the other business is a public company, its *shares are bought. Where some, but not all, of the shares of another company are bought, special rules govern the treatment of existing shareholders who do not wish to sell their holdings. *See also* REVERSE TAKEOVER.

actuarially fair odds *See* FAIR ODDS.

actuary An expert who uses statistical records to predict the future. An actuary uses records of the occurrence of uncertain events, such as death at given ages, or fire, theft, and accidents to cars, to predict how frequently similar events are likely to occur in the future. These predictions take account of observed trends in health or crime, as well as past facts. Actuarial expertise enables *insurance companies to write policies with an expectation of making profits, but not with complete reliability.

adaptive expectations The principle that the future values of an economic variable can be calculated using its past values and a margin of error. Under adaptive expectations people learn from their experience, in a predictable way. For example, if the current inflation rate is higher than had been expected people revise their expectations for the future inflation rate upwards.

adjustable peg A system where countries stabilize their *exchange rates around *par values that they retain the right to change. Under this system a country undertakes to intervene in the foreign exchange market to keep its currency within some margin, for example 1 percent, of some given exchange rate parity, the 'peg'. The country retains the right to adjust the parity, that is, to move the peg. This was more or less the case under the *Bretton Woods system in the 1950s and 1960s. This system provides opportunities for *speculators at times when it appears that the peg is going to have to move, but has not yet done so.

adjusted *R*-squared A version of the *coefficient of determination (*R*-squared) adjusted for the degrees of freedom. While *R*-squared will never decrease when adding a variable to the regression, adjusted *R*-squared will rise or fall, depending on whether the contribution of the new variable to the fit of the regression more than offsets the correction for the loss of an additional degree of freedom. Adjusted *R*-squared can also be negative.

adjustment *See* CYCLICAL ADJUSTMENT; PARTIAL ADJUSTMENT; SEASONAL ADJUSTMENT.

adjustment costs The costs of making changes in the economic *variables one controls. Any economic agent, whether an individual, a firm, or a government, has *preferences which determine what the optimal levels of the variables under their control would be, if they were free to make a fresh start in setting them. When actual levels differ from these optimal levels, adjustment costs must be considered.

If adjustment costs are lump-sum, or increase proportionally or less than in proportion to the changes made in any one period, it will pay to make at once any change that is worth making at all. If adjustment costs increase more than proportionally to the size of the change, however, it pays to adjust only gradually. In adjusting its labour force, for example, a firm may find that small increases present no recruitment problem, and small decreases can be accommodated by *natural wastage because of retirements and other voluntary departures, whereas rapid recruitment poses serious selection and training problems, and rapid decline involves *redundancies, which are expensive and damaging to morale. *See also* MENU COSTS.

adjustment programme A package of policy measures designed to cure *balance-of-payments problems. Adoption of a satisfactory adjustment programme is frequently made a condition of assistance from the *International Monetary Fund. Curing balance-of-payments problems requires decreasing *absorption relative to production. This can be approached via reducing absorption, by cutting government spending, and/or increasing taxes. It can also be approached via increasing production by using resources more efficiently; this often involves increased use of the market mechanism and *devaluation of overvalued currencies.

administered price A price set by some form of administrative process, rather than adjusting to clear a market. The levels of and changes in administered prices often require the consent of the government or of some official regulatory body. Administered prices may be maxima, as in the case of *rent controls, or minima, as with *minimum wage laws and some agricultural policies.

administration The situation of a *company in financial difficulties whose affairs are put into the hands of an administrator by court order. The object of administration is to enable the company to survive as a going concern or, if that proves impossible, to get a better price for its assets than immediate *liquidation would produce.

ad valorem tax A tax proportional to the price of the object being taxed. This can be contrasted to a *specific tax which is levied at a rate per unit of quantity, independent of the price. Ad valorem taxes have the advantageous feature that their real value is not eroded by *inflation.

advance corporation tax (ACT) The system by which UK companies deducted income tax at source when distributing *dividends to their shareholders. With a tax rate of $100t$ percent, companies paid the Inland Revenue $£t/(1 - t)$ for every £1 distributed to shareholders. These payments were treated as a payment on account of the company's own *corporation tax. ACT was abolished in 1999.

advances Bank loans to their customers. These may be *unsecured loans, but are often secured by the bank holding stocks and shares or *life insurance policies owned by the borrower.

advantage *See* ABSOLUTE ADVANTAGE; COMPARATIVE ADVANTAGE.

adverse selection The tendency for a *contract to attract the types of agents that are least profitable. For example, if an insurer offers *health insurance without any medical examination, the expectation is that people with poor health prospects are likely to accept it, while people with better health prospects, who can get better terms from a more selective insurer, will reject the unconditional contract. In trying to be non-selective, adverse selection causes the worst risks to select themselves. Adverse selection is a consequence of *asymmetric information: agents know their own type (private information) but this is unobservable (no public information). Contracts that could be offered if agent types were observable cannot be offered when types are unobservable, and this can result in *market failure.

adverse supply shock An unexpected shift of the supply curve to the left, i.e. a reduction in the quantity supplied for any given price. This could result from natural disasters such as floods or earthquakes; from human, animal, or plant diseases; or from major political upheavals such as war or revolution. To oil importers, the sudden price increases imposed by the *Organization of Petroleum Exporting Countries in the 1970s appeared as adverse supply shocks. Such a shock reduces the *real income an economy can produce even at full employment of its available resources. Supply shocks are used as a modelling device in macroeconomics to represent aggregate economic risk.

advertising Activity designed to sell products. It seeks to attract the attention of potential customers, inform them of the existence and attributes of a product, and persuade them to start or continue to buy it. It works via the media, that is, newspapers, television, or the internet; by shop displays, posters, or mailshots; or through the actual design of products themselves and their packaging. While there is a logical distinction between informative and persuasive advertising, psychologically these are extremely difficult to distinguish. Political, charitable, and religious bodies, and the government, advertise, as well as commercial organizations.

Advisory, Conciliation and Arbitration Service (ACAS) A UK *quango providing facilities for conciliation, arbitration, and mediation in *industrial disputes.

after-sales service The provision of services after goods have been sold which make them more useful to customers. This can include advice on and training in the use of the product; routine maintenance, servicing, and repairs in the event of breakdown; provision of materials and spare parts; replacement under *warranty in the event of failure of the goods supplied; and updating if the product is developed further. Customers' expectations of cheap and efficient after-sales service are of great importance in making products competitive, and lack of customer confidence in the quality and price of after-sales services may make products unsaleable. *See also* COMPETITIVENESS.

after-tax income The income remaining to an individual or a company after *direct taxes have been paid. The calculation of after-tax income takes no account of the liability to *indirect taxes when the income is spent.

age–earnings profile A graph showing the mean earnings of workers at various ages. Such profiles can be drawn up for all workers, or for specified groups of workers, for example manual workers, professional workers, etc.

agency cost *See* AGENCY THEORY.

agency problem The difficulties encountered when a principal delegates a task to an agent. The agency problem arises when the principal and the agent have different objectives and there is *asymmetric information and an *incomplete contract. The asymmetric information prevents the principal from perfectly monitoring the agent, and the incomplete contract makes it impossible to determine what will occur in all possible contingencies. The principal cannot therefore ensure that the agent always chooses the action the principal would wish to see chosen. *Agency theory determines how contracts can be designed to ensure that these problems are best mitigated.

agency theory The theory of the contractual relationship between a principal and an agent. Agency theory analyses the issues that arise when a principal delegates a task to an agent but there is *asymmetric information and an *incomplete contract. The basis of the analysis is that the principal and the agent have different objectives. For example, the owner of a firm (the principal) may wish to maximize profit but the manager of the firm (the agent) aims to maximize a utility function that is increasing in income but decreasing in effort. The first-best contract would make the reward a function of effort and be designed to induce the efficient effort level in every circumstance. The agency problem arises when there is an asymmetry of information such that the principal cannot observe the effort level of the manager and hence cannot condition the contract upon it. Instead, the contract has to be conditioned upon an observable and verifiable quantity such as the level of profit. This prevents the contract from ensuring that the efficient level of effort is always supplied. The design of the contract has to take into account incentive effects and the allocation of risk between the principal and the agent. It is often assumed that the principal is *risk-neutral and the agent *risk-averse, in which case, putting incentive effects to one side, all of the variability in pay-off should fall on the principal. Such a contract does not provide any incentive for the agent, so leading to the balance of risk sharing and incentives. The need to provide an incentive to the agent makes the expected profit of the principal lower than that with the first-best contract that could be used with no asymmetry of information. This is the agency cost of implementing a second-best contract in the presence of asymmetric information. Agency theory has found many applications in economics. Two illustrative examples are the consequences of the separation of control between shareholders and managers, and the delegation of taxation and *public good provision to states within a federation.

agglomeration economies The *external economies of scale available to individuals or firms in large concentrations of population and economic activity. These arise because larger markets allow wider choice and a greater range of specialist services. Agglomeration economies are believed to explain the tendency of conurbations to contain an increasing share of the population of many countries.

aggregate demand The total of intended or *ex ante attempts to spend on final goods and services produced in a country. In a *closed economy aggregate demand is the sum of consumption, investment, and government spending on goods and services. In an *open economy in addition to this it includes export demand and excludes imports. A rise in aggregate demand is a necessary condition for an increase in real output. It is not a sufficient condition, however, unless an economy has spare *capacity to produce the goods and services demanded. If the goods demanded are available only as imports, these rise; if the extra goods are not available at all, inflationary pressure is created.

aggregate demand schedule A diagram showing for each level of *national income the total level of aggregate demand in an economy that would result from it. *Internal balance in the economy requires that aggregate demand be equal to national income.

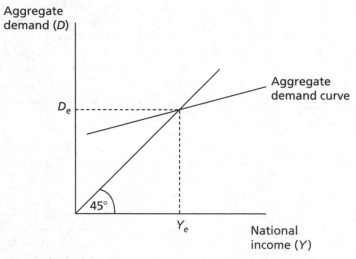

Aggregate Demand Schedule

aggregate production function *See* PRODUCTION FUNCTION.

aggregate supply The total amount of real goods and services that the enterprises in an economy are willing to provide at any given ratio of prices to wages. This can be increased by greater *productivity due to increases in the volume of productive equipment or improvements in technical knowledge or the quality of the labour force. Whether actual output equals aggregate supply depends on two conditions. First, there must be sufficient aggregate demand to match the supply: if there is not, output is demand-constrained. Second, there must be a sufficient supply of labour to satisfy firms' demand for it: if *real wages are low, aggregate supply by firms may require more employment than the labour supply forthcoming at these wages, in which case output is constrained by labour shortages. In an economy where firms do not act competitively, the concept of aggregate supply is not applicable: firms in markets characterized by *imperfect competition do not have supply curves. *See also* DEMAND-DETERMINED OUTPUT.

aggregation The process of summing individual values into a total value. Aggregate demand is the sum of demand from individual economic agents, and the aggregate capital stock is the sum of capital held by individual firms.

aggregation problem **1.** The conceptual difficulties encountered when an aggregate value is used to represent the total of individual values. Consider an economy with many firms, each of which uses inputs of capital and labour to produce output. Two forms of aggregation problem can arise. First, any attempt to sum the quantities of capital used by individual firms to arrive at an aggregate quantity of capital has to confront the issue posed by different types of capital. For instance, the number of metal presses used by a car manufacturer cannot just be added to the number of computers used by a software developer. Second, even if all firms use the same type of capital, it is generally not possible to aggregate the firms into a single representative firm using the aggregate stock of capital. For this to be possible it has to be the case that one extra unit of aggregate capital produces the same additional output as one extra unit of capital for an individual firm. This is only true if all firms have access to the same *constant returns to scale production technology.
  2. The erroneous interpretation of observed association between two variables at the aggregate level as evidence of association at the individual level. This is also known as the *ecological fallacy.

agricultural protection The use of *tariffs and trade controls on agricultural products to raise their prices in a country and thus to increase its farmers' incomes. This may be desired to slow down the tendency for the share of agriculture in total income and employment to decrease. It may also aim at increasing self-sufficiency in foodstuffs and agricultural raw materials in the interests of national security. Agriculture is protected in most industrial countries, particularly those of the European Union and Japan. Agricultural protection in advanced countries hinders economic growth in *less developed countries, most of which are net exporters of agricultural products.

aid Economic assistance from one country to another, the recipient typically being a *less developed country. Aid is usually intended either to provide humanitarian relief in emergencies, to promote economic development, or to finance military expenditure. Aid may take the form of outright gifts of money, which may be tied to purchases from the donor, or untied and available for expenditure anywhere. It may take the form of *soft loans, on terms easier than those available to the borrower in the world capital market. Aid may also be given in kind, including food, plant and equipment, military supplies, or technical assistance. Bilateral aid is given directly by a donor to a recipient country; multilateral aid is channelled through an international organization, without direct contact between donors and particular recipients. *See also* GRANT IN AID; TIED AID; UNTIED AID.

Aid to Families with Dependent Children (AFDC) A US federal welfare programme, originally set up in 1935, that enabled states to use federal grants to provide financial support for poor children. AFDC was replaced in 1996 by *Temporary Assistance to Needy Families.

Aitken estimator This is more commonly known as the *generalized least squares estimator.

Allais paradox An example of choice under uncertainty where the outcome for most experimental subjects violates the axioms of *expected utility theory. In the first experiment subjects are requested to choose between winning £1 million for sure and a gamble in which the prizes are £1 million with probability 0.89, £5 million with probability 0.10, and nothing with probability 0.01. Most experimental subjects would choose the option of £1 million for sure. In the second experiment the choice is between two different gambles. For the first gamble the prizes are nothing with probability 0.89 and £1 million with probability 0.11. The second gamble has prizes of nothing with probability 0.90 and £5 million with probability 0.10. Most subjects choose the second gamble. These typical choices violate the independence axiom of expected utility theory: if the first option is chosen in the first experiment then the first option should also be chosen in the second experiment. The Allais paradox and other similar examples have motivated the search for alternatives to expected utility theory. *See also* ANOMALIES; BEHAVIOURAL ECONOMICS; DECISION THEORY; PROSPECT THEORY.

Almon distributed lag A version of a restricted lag model in which the lag coefficients are parameterized as polynomial functions. This model allows the capture of delayed or non-monotonic impact of lagged variables upon the dependent variable and is used mostly for relatively short time series with long lags. The major drawback, common for restrictive functional forms, is the induced autocorrelation.

almost sure convergence (convergence almost everywhere, convergence with probability one, strong convergence) A random variable x_n converges to a constant c almost surely if the probability of observing a sequence that does not converge to c vanishes for n large enough. Formally, as n goes to infinity, lim Prob$[|x_i - c| > \varepsilon$ for all $i \geq n] = 0$ for all $\varepsilon > 0$. Almost sure convergence implies *convergence in probability.

alpha stocks The most actively traded securities in the *Stock Exchange Automated Quotation System. About 100 securities came into this category when it was in official use by the London Stock Exchange. These were shares of companies with high turnover and high *market capitalization. Alpha stocks had numerous *market-makers, and immediate publication of transactions in them was required. They were part of a system of categorization that also included beta, gamma, and delta stocks which were those of smaller companies, and less intensively traded.

altruism Selfless concern for others. Standard economic analysis assumes decision-makers are motivated by self-interest. This assumption is inconsistent with many observed economic choices such as contributions to charities that do not provide any direct benefit to the donor. The concept of altruism has been invoked to explain these observations. It is questionable whether altruism can be incorporated in an economic framework since, if there is any increase in utility from an act of altruism, the act cannot be purely selfless.

amalgamation *See* MERGER.

American Economic Association (AEA) The American Economic
Association was first organized in 1885 and incorporated in 1923. The main
purposes of the association are the encouragement of economic research, the issue
of publications on economic subjects, and the organization of the US job market for
economists.

(⊕) SEE WEB LINKS

• The home page of the AEA with membership information and links to publications.

**American Federation of Labor and Congress of Industrial
Organizations (AFL–CIO)** The main US labour federation. The name results
from the amalgamation in 1955 of two associations, the AFL representing mainly
craft unions, and the CIO representing mainly industrial unions. The AFL–CIO
operates mostly at the political level: wage and other industrial bargaining is carried
out by its member unions. It is the US equivalent of the UK's *Trades Union
Congress (TUC).

amortization The building up over a period of a fund to replace a productive
asset at the end of its useful life, or to repay a loan. In the case of a loan, the amount
required for amortization depends on the interest rate that can be earned on the
accumulated fund. In the case of replacement of physical assets, the amount
needed depends not only on the interest rate, but also on the expected lifetime of
the asset and on the rate of inflation, which affects the expected cost of replacement.

analysis of variance A statistical technique based on decomposing the total
*variance of some characteristic of a population into parts correlated with other
characteristics, and *residual variation. In particular, analysis of variance is used to
test whether sections of a population appear to differ significantly in some property.
For example, if y_i is the personal income of individual i, analysis of variance can be
used to test whether there are significant regional differences in mean income. The
total variance of the population is decomposed into the part due to differences
within regions, and the part due to differences between regional means. The larger
the proportion of total variance due to differences between group means, the more
likely it is that the groups are systematically different, whereas the higher the
proportion of total variance due to within-group variance, the more likely it is that
apparent differences between group means arise from sampling error.

animal spirits The term used by John Maynard Keynes (1883–1946) to convey
the idea that major investment projects are usually undertaken not on the basis of
careful calculation of the profits they are expected to make, but on the strength of
'hunches' of *entrepreneurs that, beneath the uncertainties that would make a
rational and cautious person delay a decision, there is an opportunity to be grasped
by whoever has the courage to try.

announcement effect The effect of an announcement of a change in policy,
even before it is actually put into effect. For example, a promise by the government
to reduce taxes next year may lead to an immediate increase in consumer spending.
Policy announcements can produce such effects only if the policy-maker has
credibility.

annual general meeting (AGM) A meeting of the voting *shareholders of a company, or the members of an association, at which the officers report on the last year's activities, and accounts are submitted for approval. AGMs normally elect the chief officers and directors of companies, and the chief officers and committee members of associations. In the UK, company AGMs appoint the company's *auditors. Companies are required by law to hold AGMs, and associations are usually required to do so by their constitutions.

annualized percentage rate of interest (APR) A rate of interest that allows comparison between loan contracts with different terms and payment structures. The APR is defined as the rate of interest that equates the present discounted value of funds received to the present discounted value of payments made. Assume a loan contract provides £120 now (time 0) and £120 in two years' time, and is repaid with five biannual payments of £50 beginning six months from now. The APR, denoted by r, is then defined as the solution to

$$\frac{120}{(1+r)^0} + \frac{120}{(1+r)^2} = \frac{50}{(1+r)^{0.5}} + \frac{50}{(1+r)^{1.0}} + \frac{50}{(1+r)^{1.5}} + \frac{50}{(1+r)^{2.0}} + \frac{50}{(1+r)^{2.5}}.$$

The APR in this case is $r = 0.082$ (8.2 percent). Where a loan is repaid in instalments and the nominal interest rate is expressed as a percentage of the original capital, the APR may be considerably higher than the nominal interest rate. In the UK lenders are legally obliged to inform borrowers of the APR on mortgage, credit card, or other loans.

annual report and accounts An annual report on a company's or other organization's activities during the last *financial year, and *accounts covering this period. The annual report is normally presented by the chairman at the *annual general meeting of shareholders or members, and the accounts are presented by the treasurer. These form a major source of information on companies and other organizations. Copies of the annual report and accounts are usually sent to shareholders and members, either in full or in summary form.

annuity A contract by which a financial institution such as an *insurance company agrees to provide a regular income for the remainder of the holder's life. The name annuity arises from annual payments, but the payments can in fact be of any agreed frequency. The recipient will be a named person; it is also possible to contract for full or reduced payments for life to surviving spouses or other dependants. The payments may be fixed in money terms, or *index-linked. Annuities enable the recipients to spend their capital as well as their income without the danger of running out of funds before they die.

anomalies Economic choices that cannot be explained by the application of standard choice theory based on the *axioms of preference. Anomalies have been identified in empirical data and controlled experiments. Examples of anomalies include under-saving for retirement and purchasing lottery tickets with an expected return that is negative. The identification of anomalies has led to the development of *behavioural economics and the rejection of *expected utility. *See also* ALLAIS PARADOX; EXPERIMENTAL ECONOMICS; PROSPECT THEORY.

anticipated inflation *See* EXPECTED INFLATION.

anti-competitive practice Any practice that reduces the degree of competition in a market. Anti-competitive practices include *price fixing, *dumping, regulations, and monopolization. Both governments and firms can be responsible for anti-competitive practices.

anti-dumping action The procedure by which complaints of *dumping are investigated and the case for the imposition of anti-dumping duties is assessed. Anti-dumping actions are processed by importing countries. A tariff commission or similar body investigates whether dumping has occurred, and whether it is causing injury to the domestic industry. Given the lack of any agreed definition of dumping, and the probable lack of impartiality in national tribunals judging cases between domestic complainants and foreign suppliers, the threat of anti-dumping actions has an all-round protectionist effect.

anti-dumping duty A *tariff imposed to protect domestic producers of a good against competition from *dumping of imports. Such duties are imposed only after investigation of complaints by domestic producers. As it is difficult to define dumping, and there is no internationally agreed procedure for deciding when it has occurred, the threat of anti-dumping duties is a general obstacle to the expansion of international trade.

anti-pollution measures Policies to reduce or eliminate *pollution. These include taxation, quantitative restriction, or prohibition of activities causing pollution; *zoning regulations to locate polluting activities where they will do the least harm; and support for research into the effects of pollution and the discovery of methods of production with fewer harmful *by-products. Education of industrial firms and the general public can both increase voluntary avoidance of pollution, and generate political support for compulsory methods of reducing it, either by taxation or controls. *Incentives to avoid pollution can also be given by imposing legal liabilities on polluters either to compensate particular victims, or to pay for the general costs of cleaning-up operations.

antitrust The US term for policies designed to restrict monopoly and promote competition. The Antitrust Division of the US Department of Justice and the *Federal Trade Commission are the main agencies for antitrust policy. The name comes from the US use of trusts to describe large firms formed by amalgamation. US antitrust measures frequently work by making practices such as *price discrimination illegal. The very name embodies an anti-monopoly position. This can be contrasted with UK terminology, where the *Monopolies and Mergers Commission, now replaced by the *Competition Commission, was given discretion to judge whether any particular monopoly or merger was harmful. *See also* MONOPOLY POLICY.

applied microeconomics A range of specialized areas of study within *microeconomics, such as *industrial organization, *labour economics, *public economics, *health economics, and *urban economics.

apprenticeship A system by which firms take on workers, typically young ones, for an initial period of employment during which they spend part of their time training. *Training for apprentices may be provided by formal instructional courses, either within the firm or at outside institutions, by learning on the job under the supervision of experienced workers, or in both ways. At the end of their training, apprentices receive some form of formal vocational qualification. Apprentices are frequently paid less than fully qualified workers, and are not guaranteed a job at the end of their training.

appropriation account An account showing what has been done with the total funds available to a company or other organization. This shows the division of total funds between tax payments, real investment, external loans, purchase of securities, retention of cash balances, and distribution to shareholders.

appropriation bill A US federal legislative bill authorizing expenditure. This has to be approved by both houses of Congress.

a priori Literally translated from Latin: from what is before. In the economic literature it is used to indicate that a claim is true on the basis of earlier reasoning or on the basis of empirical evidence.

arbitrage Buying a good or asset in one market where price is low, and simultaneously selling in another market where price is higher. This does not involve taking any *risk. Arbitrage tends to prevent the price of the same good or asset in different markets from moving further apart than a margin equal to transaction costs. Interest arbitrage is borrowing in a market with lower interest rates and simultaneously lending in a market with higher ones. *See also* NO ARBITRAGE.

arbitrage pricing theory (APT) A theory of asset pricing that assumes *arbitrage ensures equilibrium and that asset prices are explained by a set of underlying factors. The fundamental assumption of APT is that investors will arbitrage away any excess return so that the market will be in equilibrium. This ensures that the expected returns of all assets are linearly related to the fundamental factors that correlate the returns on different assets. The coefficients in the linear relationship are called the factor loadings, or the asset's sensitivities to the factors; they reflect the extent to which the asset is exposed to the risk of each factor. These risk factors generalize the *beta coefficient of the *Capital Asset Pricing Model.

arbitrageur A person or company who undertakes a set of transactions involving buying in one market and selling in another, where the prices are known simultaneously. Thus, although a profit can be made if the prices are different, an arbitrageur takes very little *risk. The term arbitrageur is also used to describe those who buy and sell companies or parts of companies at pre-arranged prices, again taking very little risk. An arbitrageur is contrasted with a *speculator, who buys and sells in markets where the prices are not known simultaneously, so that beween purchase and sale the speculator is at risk.

arbitration A system for settling disputes by submitting them to the judgement of a mediator acceptable to both parties. An arbitrator may be an independent individual, or a committee, often containing nominees of both parties with an independent person in the chair. Arbitration is often used in commercial and labour disputes, as it is usually quicker and cheaper than legal or *industrial action. It may be binding, where both parties are obliged by law or by contract to accept the results. Even when it is not binding, the parties may well accept the result rather than face the delays, costs, and risk involved in resort to legal or industrial action. *See also* PENDULUM ARBITRATION.

arc elasticity The ratio of the proportional change in one variable to the proportional change in another, as measured between two points over a discrete range. Arc elasticity is distinguished from *point elasticity, which is the limit approached by arc elasticity as the two points move closer together.

arm's-length price The price that two unrelated parties would agree for a transaction conducted in the absence of duress. If the good involved in the transaction is traded on a competitive market then the equilibrium price is the arm's-length price. If the good is not traded, such as an intermediate input transferred between two subsidiaries of a single firm, then the arm's-length price is intended to reflect the equilibrium price that would emerge if it were traded.

Arrow–Debreu economy A model of the economy that incorporates consistent decision-making by individual consumers and firms. The Arrow–Debreu model was the culmination of a research programme to demonstrate the *existence of equilibrium in a *competitive economy. Adam Smith (1723–1790) identified how the 'invisible hand' of competition implied the efficiency of economic activity. It was soon realized that this observation had limited value without a corresponding formal model of the competitive economy. A formal model needed to derive market demand from the utility maximization of consumers and market supply from the profit maximization of firms. An equilibrium would then consist of a set of prices that ensured demand was equal to supply for all goods simultaneously. Léon Walras (1834–1910) developed such a model to the point of demonstrating that the number of relative prices was equal to the number of independent demand–supply equations but could not prove the existence of a simultaneous solution to his equations. The contribution of Kenneth Arrow (*b.* 1921) and Gerard Debreu (1921–2004) was to specify a competitive model for which they could prove the existence of an equilibrium. Their analysis provided final settlement of the existence question. It also introduced many new tools to economists (specifically, the role of convexity arguments, the use of correspondences, and the value of fixed point theorems in equilibrium arguments). In addition, Arrow and Debreu also formalized Adam Smith's efficiency argument in the two *Fundamental Theorems of Welfare Economics. The Arrow–Debreu economy has been generalized to include dated commodities (goods available at different times) and *contingent commodities (goods available in different states of the world). This allowed the model to address economic issues concerned with time and uncertainty. These extensions provided, among many uses, the basis for the formal development of the theory of finance. *Arrow–Debreu state prices are now a basic tool for the valuation of financial instruments. The analysis of Arrow and Debreu set new standards of rigour in economics, and the Arrow–Debreu economy remains the foundation of much formal modelling in economics and finance. *See also* EDGEWORTH BOX; EXISTENCE OF EQUILIBRIUM; GENERAL EQUILIBRIUM.

Arrow–Debreu state price The price of a unit of consumption in a future state of the world. *See also* ARROW–DEBREU ECONOMY.

Arrow's impossibility theorem The theorem provides a proof that no perfect process exists for aggregating individual rankings of alternatives into a collective (or social) ranking. An example of an aggregation process is *majority voting but the *Condorcet paradox shows how this can fail to produce a useful outcome. A perfect process is defined as one that satisfies a set of desirable axioms. The basis of Arrow's theorem is a set of axioms that a collective ranking must satisfy. One of several equivalent ways of expressing these axioms is the following. *Independence of irrelevant alternatives*: adding a new option should not affect the initial ranking of the old options, so the collective ranking over the old options should remain unchanged. *Non-dictatorship*: the collective ranking should not be determined by the preferences of a single individual. *Pareto criterion*: if every individual agrees on the ranking of the options, so should society. Hence, the collective ranking should coincide with the common individual ranking. *Unrestricted domain*: the collective choice method should accommodate any possible individual ranking of options. *Transitivity*: if option *A* is preferred to option *B* and *B* to *C* in the social ranking then *C* cannot be preferred to *A*. The theorem proves that there is no aggregation process that simultaneously satisfies these five axioms. *See also* COLLECTIVE CHOICE; INTERPERSONAL COMPARISONS; VOTING.

A-share An *ordinary share in a company which, while it receives the same dividends as other ordinary shares, does not give its holder any voting rights. A-shares are issued to enable the group controlling a company to raise capital from outside without parting with *control. Because A-shareholders are excluded from control, these shares generally trade at a lower price than voting ordinary shares in the same company.

Asia-Pacific Economic Cooperation (APEC) An association of nations around the Pacific rim aiming at the creation of a Pacific free-trade area. APEC was set up in 1990; it has 21 members, including Australia, Canada, Chile, China, Indonesia, Japan, Malaysia, Mexico, New Zealand, Singapore, the US, and a number of small Pacific states. It aims at creating a free-trade area for its industrialized members by 2010, and its less developed members by 2020. When complete this will cover a large percentage of world trade.

assembly line A device moving a good being produced, for example a car, past a sequence of workers or machines. As it passes each work-station, a particular task is performed. Tasks may include adding components, working on components already in place, or checking the work of earlier stages. Assembly-line production allows *economies of scale, by keeping down the time needed to move workers or machines from one task to another.

asset motive The incentive to hold money as a *store of value. If prices are expected to be stable, money is a poor store of value as it earns little or no return. When *inflation is expected, money does even worse as a store of value. If prices fall, however, money is an attractive asset, and if any chance of falling prices is anticipated, this can prompt a desire to hold money as an asset. In the *IS–LM model of *Keynesian economics consumers can hold savings in money or in bonds. Money is a safe asset whereas bonds are risky. The relative proportions of the two assets in savings will depend on a consumer's degree of risk aversion. If highly risk-averse a large proportion will be held in money.

asset prices The prices of assets, including land and buildings, productive equipment, and *securities. As assets can be sold again, their present prices are strongly influenced by *expectations about their future prices, and by the interest rate at which future values are discounted. As stocks of assets are very large compared to any one period's new asset creation, asset prices are anchored much less firmly than goods prices to costs of production. It is common for asset prices to vary widely over quite short time periods; the large differences between the maximum and minimum prices of individual shares reported within any one year is a typical observation.

assets Possessions of value, both real and financial. Real assets include land, buildings, or machinery owned. Financial assets include cash and securities, and credit extended to customers. The assets side of a company's *balance-sheet includes both real and financial assets. Asset management is managing for others, for a fee, their portfolios of real or financial assets. *Asset-stripping is selling off the assets of companies. Assets is also used in a metaphorical and usually favourable sense to describe things that cannot actually be owned, as in the phrase 'a company's best assets are the skill and loyalty of its employees'. *See also* CURRENT ASSETS; INTANGIBLE ASSETS; LIQUID ASSETS; PORTFOLIO; TANGIBLE ASSETS.

asset-stripping A pejorative description of the process of dividing up the assets of a company in cases where the total value of the parts when separated is greater than their value when combined. Examples could include selling off unused or under-utilized land or buildings, or selling off activities where heavy investment carries tax allowances which the company cannot use to other companies whose large present profits make the tax allowances valuable to them. A more favourable description of asset-stripping activities is corporate restructuring. Advocates of corporate restructuring argue that asset-stripping is only profitable because the assets were being inefficiently used, or simply neglected, in the first place.

Assisted Area A UK region made eligible for special government assistance to encourage investment because of persistently above-average *unemployment. Development Areas are eligible for more help than Intermediate Areas. Grants for these areas are also available from the European Union through the European Regional Development Fund. Although special help for Assisted Areas has been available under various schemes since the 1930s, regional differences in unemployment have been very persistent.

asymmetric information A situation where some participants in an economic transaction have access to more, or better, relevant *information than other participants. For example, an insurance company may not know whether an individual driver is good or bad, but the individual knows how often they drive when tired or after drinking alcohol. In this case the driver possesses more information than the insurance company. The demonstration that a *competitive equilibrium is *Pareto efficient assumes symmetric information. Economic agents need not be fully informed but they must be equally informed (or equally uninformed). For example, a competitive equilibrium is efficient if there is uncertainty about future asset returns provided no agent has superior information. Asymmetric information is a source of *market failure. Agents with superior information will attempt to gain advantage from this, and inefficiency will result. *See also* ADVERSE SELECTION; AGENCY THEORY; MORAL HAZARD; PRINCIPAL–AGENT PROBLEM.

asymptotic distribution A distribution used to approximate the true finite sample distribution of a *random variable.

asymptotic theory A theory of the limiting behaviour of estimators and functions of estimators, their distributions and moments, as the sample size approaches infinity. The results of asymptotic theory are used as approximations in finite sample inference, when the true finite sample properties are unknown.

Atkinson index A measure of *income inequality. Define the equally distributed equivalent income, M_{EDE}, as the level of income that if given to all households generates the same level of *social welfare as the current income distribution. If the marginal utility of income falls with income then M_{EDE} is less than the mean level of income, μ, whenever there is income inequality. The Atkinson index, A, is then defined by $A = 1 - \frac{M_{EDE}}{\mu}$. A higher value of A represents greater inequality. *See also* GINI COEFFICIENT; LORENZ CURVE.

auction A sale where the price is fixed by an auctioneer who invites bids, and awards the article being auctioned to the highest bidder. In an *English auction the highest bid is publicly announced at each stage, and other parties are given a chance to make higher bids. In a sealed-bid auction the bids are not publicly announced: each bid is submitted sealed, and a time limit is set at which the auctioneer opens the bids and awards the article to the highest bidder, without further bids being invited. In a *Dutch auction the auctioneer announces a decreasing series of prices, and the article is awarded to the first bidder. In any of these types of auction there may or may not be a reserve price, which is the lowest bid the seller will accept; this may or may not be published. The auctioneer normally charges the seller and possibly also the buyer a fee calculated as a percentage of the realized price. *See also* FIRST-PRICE AUCTION; SECOND-PRICE AUCTION.

auctioneer **1.** In practical usage, the auctioneer manages the bidding process in an *auction.
   2. As a theoretical construct, the auctioneer is a fictitious device to explain the determination of equilibrium prices in a *competitive economy in which no firm or consumer has price-setting power.

audit The process of checking *accounts. Auditors check whether the accounts of a company, private trader, or association are complete and consistent, whether they agree with other records of purchases, sales, and inventories, and whether they comply with legal requirements and professional standards. *Companies are legally required to have their accounts externally audited, and many other bodies are required to do so by their own constitutions. Many companies and other organizations employ internal auditors, to check the accuracy and completeness of their internal bookkeeping. The audit provides a safeguard against both fraud and incompetence in accounting. *See also* EFFICIENCY AUDIT.

auditor A person or accountancy firm employed to check the *accounts of a company, private trader, or association. Auditors check whether accounts are complete and consistent, and whether they are in agreement with other records of purchases, sales, and inventories. They may certify that accounts present a 'true and fair view' of a company's finances, or they can 'qualify' them, that is, add adverse comments. The auditors of UK companies are elected by the *annual general meetings of the companies' shareholders, and are required to be professionally qualified accountants. Other bodies such as charities are required to have their accounts audited, but their auditors are often unpaid. Many companies and other organizations also employ internal auditors, to check on the accuracy and completeness of the firms' internal bookkeeping, as a safeguard against both fraud and confusion in accounting.

augmented Dickey–Fuller (ADF) *See* DICKEY–FULLER TEST.

augmented Phillips curve *See* PHILLIPS CURVE.

autarchy The absence of trade. For any economy autarchy refers to the situation in which there is no internal trade. For an open economy autarchy can also refer to the absence of external trade. The term is also applied to the policy aim of reducing a country's dependence on foreign trade, for example by *tariffs and *quotas, even when foreign trade cannot be entirely eliminated.

authorized capital The nominal value of the *shares a company is empowered to issue. Companies often extend their authorized capital in advance of actual issue of new shares. This allows the timing of capital issues to be fixed in the light of the firm's need for new capital and the state of the capital market, and allows *share options to be exercised.

autocorrelation (serial correlation) A measure of the linear relation between the value of any item in a *time series and those coming before or after it. First-order autocorrelation refers to the relation of each item to those immediately before or after. Positive autocorrelation means that deviations from the mean tend to persist from period to period; negative autocorrelation means that deviations from the mean tend to be reversed. Many economic time series, such as *unemployment or the inflation rate, show positive autocorrelation.

autocorrelation coefficient In time series, the correlation between a random variable and its lagged value.

autocorrelation function (ACF) A sequence of the *autocorrelation coefficients of a *covariance stationary time series process as a function of the lag length.

autocovariance In time series, the covariance between a random variable and its lagged value. Since it depends on the units of measurement of the underlying variable, it is often more convenient to divide it by the variance and use the resulting *autocorrelation coefficient instead.

autocovariance function A sequence of autocovariances of a *covariance stationary time series process as a function of the lag length.

automated econometrics An approach in empirical econometrics where model evaluation and selection is performed by a computerized algorithm according to pre-programmed decision rules. The algorithm largely mimics the general-to-specific approach to econometric modelling.

automatic stabilizers *See* BUILT-IN STABILIZERS.

automation Production by machinery without the need for immediate human intervention.

autonomous consumption That part of *consumption which does not depend on current income. If aggregate consumption, C, is given by $C = a + bY_d$, where Y_d is *disposable income, a can be regarded as autonomous consumption. $a > 0$ because even those with no income need to consume to live, and can finance expenditure by running down assets or borrowing. The level of a is influenced by total assets held, expectations of future income or acquisitions of assets through legacies, and social conventions about minimum acceptable standards of living.

autonomous investment The part of *investment which is not explained by changes in the level of output. This includes investment in public services, which are determined by government policy, investment to exploit new technical knowledge or geographical discoveries, and considerable amounts of replacement of existing capital as it wears out.

autoregressive conditional heteroscedasticity (ARCH) model A time series model in which the random error is conditionally heteroscedastic with respect to its past realizations. This model is used to describe volatility clustering, i.e. a pattern observed in many financial data where large and small forecast errors appear to occur in clusters. The simplest form is ARCH (1),

$$y_t = \beta x_t + \varepsilon_t$$

where $\varepsilon_t = u_t \sqrt{\alpha_0 + \alpha_1 \varepsilon_{t-1}}$ and u_t has a standard normal distribution.

autoregressive integrated moving average (ARIMA (p, d, q)) model A univariate time series model, in the most general form given by

$$\Delta^d y_t = \mu + \gamma_1 \Delta^d y_{t-1} + \ldots + \gamma_p \Delta^d y_{t-p} + \varepsilon_t - \theta_1 \varepsilon_{t-1} - \ldots - \theta_q \varepsilon_{t-q}$$

where $\Delta^d y_t$ is the dth difference of y_t. This is a generalization of the autoregressive moving average (ARMA (p, q)) model used to describe a non-stationary process that becomes stationary after being differenced d times. When d is a fraction the process is sometimes referred to as an autoregressive fractionally integrated moving average, or ARFIMA process.

autoregressive moving average (ARMA (p, q)) model A univariate time series model that encompasses autoregressive and moving average models, and in the most general form is given by

$$y_t = \mu + \gamma_1 y_{t-1} + \ldots + \gamma_p y_{t-p} + \varepsilon_t - \theta_1 \varepsilon_{t-1} - \ldots - \theta_q \varepsilon_{t-q}.$$

autoregressive process A model of a time series as a function of its own past values and a *random error. *See also* AUTOREGRESSIVE INTEGRATED MOVING AVERAGE MODEL; AUTOREGRESSIVE MOVING AVERAGE MODEL.

average cost Total cost of production divided by quantity produced. Average *fixed cost necessarily decreases with output. Average *variable cost may decrease with output up to the point where limits to *capacity become a constraint, after which it tends to rise. If average variable cost rises faster than average fixed cost falls, this produces a *U-shaped average cost curve. Where a firm has multiple products average cost can be defined only if it is possible to attribute particular costs to particular products.

average cost pricing The policy of setting prices so as just to cover average costs, allowing the producer to *break even. While this is not a profit-maximizing policy (except when there are constant returns to scale so average cost is equal to marginal cost), it may be a policy followed by a government-controlled firm, or for a private but non-profit-making body. *Marginal cost pricing is the first-best pricing policy for a producer operating in the public interest but this requires any losses to be financed without imposing deadweight costs elsewhere in the economy. Average cost pricing, where goods are sold at the lowest price consistent with covering average costs, ensures there are no losses to be financed, so can be a *second-best optimum.

average tax rate Tax liability as a proportion of the tax base. *See also* MARGINAL TAX RATE.

Averch–Johnson effect The observation that whenever the profit to capital ratio of a company is regulated it has an incentive to over-invest in capital. This results in an inefficiently high level of capital accumulation.

avoidable cost That part of the cost of any output that could be saved by not producing it. Some costs are clearly not avoidable, for example capital costs. Other costs might on first inspection appear to be avoidable, but may actually not be. For example, ceasing production would save on fuel, materials, and labour; but fuel and materials may be bought on long-term contracts, and employees laid off may be entitled to pay in lieu of notice. Thus these costs, too, may not be avoidable in the short run.

axiom A sentence or proposition that is not proved or demonstrated but is used as a starting point for deducing other conclusions. When used in economics, an axiom is any initial assumption from which other statements are logically derived. In this use, an axiom is not necessarily a self-evident truth but is instead a formal statement used in further deduction.

axioms of preference A set of assumptions that characterize rational preferences. The standard axioms are *completeness* (given any two options x and y then either x is at least as good as y or y is at least as good as x), *transitivity* (if x is at least as good as y and y is at least as good as z, then x is at least as good as z), and *reflexivity* (x is at least as good as x). Preferences that satisfy these axioms can be represented by a set of *indifference curves that do not cross. This represents the starting point for the standard theory of choice.

backdoor The conduct of monetary policy through channels that are not publicly observable.

backwardation A situation in which the futures price (or forward price) of a commodity is lower than the *spot price. *See also* CONTANGO; FORWARD AND FUTURES.

backward-bending supply curve A *supply curve for a good that shows reduced supply at higher prices. A backward-bending labour supply curve can result from the *income effect of a higher wage rate dominating the *substitution effect.

backward induction The process of solving multi-stage decision problems by finding the optimal choice in the final stage conditional on earlier choices, and then working back to the beginning taking one stage at a time. Backward induction can be applied to single-agent finite dynamic programming problems. It can also be used to solve for the *Nash equilibrium in multi-stage games.

backward integration The expansion of a firm's activities to include the production of inputs formerly bought in from outside. Examples include a firm manufacturing its own components, mining its own mineral requirements, generating its own power supplies, or even growing food for its own works canteen. Backward integration may be pursued to improve the quality or reliability of inputs, or to increase a firm's monopoly power by denying access to inputs to actual or potential rivals.

bad debt *Debt whose repayment is known to be impossible or unlikely. Failure of the borrower to make payments of principal or interest on the due dates is evidence that a debt should be suspect, but a debt can become bad even before the payments are actually due if the debtor is known or believed to be insolvent. If payments are delayed, creditors who think that ultimate payment is likely may be willing to formally *reschedule debts, or merely to wait for payment without any formal agreement. At what stage bad debts should be 'written off', that is, the creditors should cease to record them as assets in their accounts, is a matter of judgement. Institutions with numerous debts owing to them may make provision for losses without specifying which particular debts they regard as being uncollectable.

bad debt provision A statement in the accounts of a creditor of the extent to which it expects to have to write off bad debts, that is, to cease to record them as assets in its accounts. A firm with bad debts must at some stage decide to write them off. If it has numerous debtors, each of doubtful solvency, it is possible to make a 'bad debt provision', naming an amount by which it expects to have to write off bad debts, without the need to specify on which particular debts hope has been abandoned.

'bad money drives out good' *See* GRESHAM'S LAW.

balance *See* EXTERNAL BALANCE; INTERNAL BALANCE; INVISIBLE BALANCE.

balanced budget Equality between total government receipts and expenditure. There is thus no need to borrow and thereby increase the *government debt. The UK government operates under the *golden rule that the budget need not balance every year but current receipts and expenditure should be balanced on average over an economic *cycle.

balanced budget amendment A proposal to compel the US government to balance its budget by a consitutional amendment forbidding further government borrowing. Such an amendment would remove the discretion to allow a deficit to deal with a *depression in activity or a political crisis requiring increased military spending. Also, short-run fluctuations in the budget position cannot be avoided because of the dependence of revenue on fluctuations in the level of activity. There is also certain scope for *creative accounting, or the creation of off-budget but government-controlled special funds so that a balanced budget is not enforceable.

balanced budget multiplier An argument in *Keynesian economics that a rise in government spending on real goods and services combined with an equal rise in taxation, leaving the budget deficit or surplus unaltered, must increase the national product by exactly the amount spent. The basic national income identity gives $Y = C + I + G$. Assume I is fixed and that the consumption function is $C = a + b(Y - T)$, where T is income taxation. Then $Y = a + b(Y - T) + I + G$, and variations in Y, T, and G must satisfy $dY = b(dY - dT) + dG$. If the budget is balanced, then $dT = dG$ and hence $dY = dG$, which is the balanced budget multiplier.

balanced growth path An equilibrium in which major aggregate economic variables, such as output and the capital stock, grow at the same rate over time, and the real interest rate is constant. This reflects historic observations of the long-term stability of interest rates and capital-to-output ratios in developed countries. In development economics, balanced growth path refers to simultaneous and coordinated expansion of several sectors of an economy, also known as a *big push. This is in contrast to the concept of unbalanced growth, in which a large investment in one sector of a developing economy generates, through backward and forward linkages, the scope for expansion in other sectors.

balance of payments **1.** An overall statement of a country's economic transactions with the rest of the world over some period, often a year. A table of the balance of payments shows amounts received from the rest of the world and amounts spent abroad. The *current account includes exports and imports, that is, visible trade, and receipts from and spending abroad on services such as tourism. It also includes receipts of property incomes from abroad and remittances of property incomes abroad, and receipts and payments of international transfers, that is, gifts.

The *capital account of the balance of payments includes inward and outward *foreign direct investment, and sales and purchases of foreign securities by residents and of domestic securities by non-residents. The third element in the balance of payments is changes in official *foreign exchange reserves.

2. The difference between total receipts and expenditure in any category of payments. Overall payments, including changes in foreign exchange reserves, must balance by definition, but this is not true for any one category of payments. The balance of payments on current account is the difference between total receipts and expenditures on current account: if receipts exceed spending, there is a current account surplus, and if spending exceeds receipts there is a current account deficit. The balance of payments on capital account is the difference between receipts and expenditures on capital transactions with the rest of the world. Receipts come from the sale of securities or real capital assets to non-residents; expenditures are on loans to non-residents or purchase of real assets abroad. Changes in foreign exchange reserves are equal to the sum of the current and capital account surpluses. A balance-of-payments problem or crisis means that the balance-of-payments situation is not sustainable. This may be because foreign exchange reserves are being run down, or because they are being maintained, but only by borrowing abroad at a rate that cannot continue for long before foreign lenders become too worried about the safety of their loans to provide any more. A *balance-of-payments crisis differs from a problem only in the speed at which exhaustion of exchange reserves or borrowing capacity is approaching: a problem calls for action at some time, a crisis for immediate action.

balance-of-payments crisis An unsustainable *balance of payments. This means that *foreign exchange reserves are falling rapidly, or are being maintained only by a level of foreign borrowing leading to difficulties in obtaining further loans. A balance-of-payments crisis may be ended by improving the balance of payments on current account, via a recession in domestic activity, or by *devaluation. It may alternatively be ended by changing policies so as to prevent *capital flight and induce inward capital movements. It may also help if a foreign loan can be obtained to allow time for the current account balance to improve.

balance of trade The excess of visible exports over visible imports. This is a major, but far from the only, component of the balance of payments on *current account.

balance-sheet A statement of the money values of the *assets and *liabilities of a firm or any other organization at some moment, particularly the end of a *financial year. Assets can include money, securities, land, buildings and other capital equipment, stocks and work in progress, and amounts due from debtors. Liabilities include secured and unsecured debts. The excess of assets over liabilities is the *net worth of the firm; for a solvent firm this is positive, and is treated as a liability of the firm to its shareholders, so that the balance-sheet by definition balances. Any firm whose liabilities exceed its assets is insolvent. It should be noted that not all items on a balance-sheet are equally reliable. The value of cash held and that of amounts due from debtors are certain, and the value of easily traded securities and commodities is reliably known, though liable to change rapidly; but the value of real assets such as land, buildings, and equipment, and that of securities which are not readily traded, are matters of estimation. A balance-sheet, which shows the state of affairs at a moment in time, is contrasted with a *profit-and-loss account, which shows flows over some period such as a firm's financial year.

balances with the Bank of England Balances held at the *Bank of England by UK commercial banks. Most payments by cheque involve the customers of different banks: the bank whose customer makes a payment has to transfer money to the bank whose customer receives it. This is done through the bank *clearing system. Most of these payments are mutually offsetting, but the small residual of payments due to or from each bank at the close of the daily clearing is settled by the transfer of bankers' balances with the Bank of England.

balancing item An entry in a set of *accounts to cover the discrepancy between two different figures for the same item. This is used when two methods of measurement produce different results for figures which should by definition be the same if both methods were completely accurate. Statisticians include a balancing item, or statistical adjustment, rather than changing one figure to agree with the other, when they do not know which, if either, is correct.

bank A financial institution whose main activities are borrowing and lending money. Banks borrow by accepting *deposits from the general public or other financial institutions. Bank loans are an important source of finance for firms, consumers, and government. *Commercial banks may be all-purpose or specialized. Investment banks specialize on loans to firms; merchant banks on financing capital market transactions and international trade; and savings banks on collecting and lending the savings of numerous, mostly small-scale, savers. *Central banks supervise the banking system and control the *money supply. In the US the central bank is the Federal Reserve; in France the Banque de France; and in the UK the Bank of England. There are also international banks. The World Bank, or *International Bank for Reconstruction and Development, is an investment bank at the international level. The nearest international equivalent to a central bank is the *International Monetary Fund. The *European Central Bank conducts monetary policy in the *Eurozone. The *European Bank for Reconstruction and Development is a European investment bank, similar to the World Bank at a European level. *See also* CLEARING BANK; INVESTMENT BANK; JOINT-STOCK BANK; MEMBER BANK; MERCHANT BANK; OVERSEAS BANK.

bank account An account with a bank, held by an individual, firm, or government. Bank accounts are used by holders to conduct their transactions, either by providing cash when it is needed or by transferring balances to other people as ordered by cheques, direct debits, or electronic transfers. Money in an account may be instantly available, as in a current account (UK) or a checking account (US); or notice of withdrawal may be required, as in a deposit account (UK) or a time account (US). An account may be in credit, when the bank owes the customer money, or overdrawn, in which case the customer owes the bank money. Current accounts normally earn little or no interest, and may be liable to charges; interest is paid at somewhat higher rates on deposit accounts, and interest at considerably higher rates is charged on *overdrafts, which may also incur extra charges.

bank deposit *See* DEPOSIT.

Bankers Automated Credit System (BACS) The system by which depositors instruct their banks to make payments to named accounts, without the need to use a cheque. BACS is widely used for payments of dividends and wages.

banker's draft A cheque issued by a bank and sold to a customer. This may be acceptable to a third party who would not accept the customer's cheque for the amount, which may be too large to be covered by any bank card. The bank's credit is better than that of the customer, and a banker's draft is unstoppable. The equivalent of the banker's draft in the US is the certified check.

Bank for International Settlements (BIS) An international bank based in Basel, founded in 1930 to coordinate payments of reparations after the First World War. Its possible role as the principal international bank was taken over after 1945 by the *International Monetary Fund. The BIS has acted as trustee for the *Organization for Economic Cooperation and Development and the European Monetary Agreement, and as a clearing-house for *European Currency Units. It sets capital adequacy ratios for European banks, and compiles statistics on international debt. Most European central banks are members of the BIS, as are those of Canada, Japan, and the United States.

(⊕) SEE WEB LINKS

• The official website of the Bank for International Settlements with links to working papers and economic statistics.

banking The provision of payments facilities, credit, and capital to individuals, firms, and the government. Retail banking is the provision of payments, savings, and credit facilities in relatively small quantities to large numbers of individual or small business customers. Investment banking is the provision of credit and capital in larger quantities to relatively large businesses. Universal banking combines these functions in the same banks, as for example in European countries including Germany. In the US and the UK the functions are largely separate: in the US through the *Glass–Steagall Act of 1933, and in the UK through voluntary choice by the banks. The argument against universal banking is that mistaken investments may impair the solvency of banks responsible for the payments system. Modern banking is increasingly adding further functions, including stockbroking and *portfolio management, mortgage finance, and insurance, to these traditional activities. *See also* BRANCH BANKING; FRACTIONAL RESERVE BANKING; RELATIONSHIP BANKING; RETAIL BANKING; WHOLESALE BANKING.

banking system The network of institutions responsible for providing banking services. This consists of two parts. First, there are the actual banks providing services to the general public; these may be universal banks, or specialist institutions dealing with particular types of banking business. These range from 'high street' banks, with numerous branches dealing with many small clients, to merchant banks specializing in financing capital market transactions or foreign

b

trade. Second, there are higher-level institutions, which are not involved in direct contact with the general public. These are *central banks, which act as bankers for other banks and the government, and are responsible for monetary policy and macroeconomic management of the monetary system; and bank regulatory bodies, which supervise other banks and check their probity, *liquidity, and solvency. These higher-tier functions can be combined in the same institution, as with the *Bank of England for the UK, or separated, as in Germany.

bank loan A loan from a bank to an individual or firm. Bank advances for large amounts or for business purposes are normally made against *security, for example the title deeds of buildings or life insurance policies. Bank overdrafts or personal loans for small amounts are often unsecured, if the customer is regarded as a good risk.

bank note Paper money issued by a bank. The issue of notes in most countries is either entirely confined to or subject to strict control by the *central bank. A bank note was originally a promise to pay coin on demand; this tradition is preserved by the form of words used on Bank of England notes in the UK.

Bank of Credit and Commerce International (BCCI) A large international bank that operated in many countries, whose collapse in 1991 with a multi-billion pound shortage of funds provoked widespread suspicion of false bookkeeping and money-laundering, and widespread concern about the adequacy of supervision arrangements for international banks.

Bank of England The UK *central bank. Originally founded in 1694 as a private bank to lend to the government and manage the *national debt, by the 19th century it had developed into a central bank. In 1844 the Bank Charter Act formalized its status. Its main functions were controlling the *money supply, through the Issue Department, and acting as a banker for the government and other banks, through the Banking Department. The bank came under formal government ownership when it was nationalized in 1946. The Governor and Directors are now appointed by the government. The Bank of England administered *exchange controls until these were abolished in 1979, and advised the government on *monetary policy until 1997, when it was made independent. It holds the national *foreign exchange reserves, in the Exchange Equalization Account, and manages the national debt. It is also responsible for supervision of the banking system, and acts as *lender of last resort in financial crises.

bank rate Until 1972 the rate at which the *Bank of England used to *rediscount first-class bills for its customers. When this system was in operation many other interest rates were specified in terms of their margin above bank rate. It directly affected other interest rates only when the market needed to borrow from the Bank of England, but changes in bank rate were announced as a means of informing the *City of the Bank of England's views on what commercial interest rates should be.

bank regulation The application to banks of public controls stricter than those on businesses in general. This is justified by concerns that bank failures may disrupt the rest of the economy in a way that other business failures do not. Banks provide most of the *money used in a modern economy, and lend on a large scale. If a bank is managed irresponsibly, taking excessive risks and holding too small reserves, this is liable to cause a *bank run by its customers if they suspect it of being illiquid or insolvent. If one bank defaults on its obligations, this is liable to undermine other banks or financial institutions. Most countries therefore empower either their *central bank or some other public institution to supervise banks, laying down rules for their lending and reserve holding, and monitoring the banks' accounts to check that the rules are being obeyed. In many countries the central bank acts as *lender of last resort, to prevent banks that are illiquid from defaulting. It is more important to safeguard banks' *solvency than their *liquidity; a solvent bank should be able to borrow liquid assets when it needs them, but no amount of liquidity can save a bank once it is known to be insolvent. Bank regulators have in the past also been concerned with restraining banks' use of monopoly power.

bank run A situation when the customers of a bank lose confidence in it and all try to withdraw their money. The inability of a bank to provide customers with their money upon request causes inconvenience and often results in a panic, swiftly spreading to affect other banks. To avoid this danger, most countries have public bodies which supervise banks, to prevent their getting into difficulties, and *central banks to rescue them if they do. *See also* FINANCIAL CRISIS.

bankruptcy A legal arrangement to deal with the affairs of individuals unable to pay their debts. Bankruptcy proceedings may be started by the insolvent debtor or by unpaid creditors. The assets of a person adjudged bankrupt by a court are taken over by an official receiver and sold, the funds being used to repay creditors so far as possible. Those who have become bankrupt cannot accept credit without warning the lender that they are an undischarged bankrupt, and also face various restrictions on their future activities: in the UK, for example, they cannot be directors of companies or Members of Parliament. *See also* CHAPTER 11 BANKRUPTCY.

bargaining The process of negotiating the terms of a trade. Bargaining occurs in formal economic contexts (for example between a firm and a union over the wage rates) and in informal settings (for example within the family over the allocation of domestic chores). It is also of major importance in the political process. Economic theory provides both positive and normative perspectives on bargaining. The positive theory represents bargaining as a game of strategy and attempts to predict the outcome. The most influential analysis in this literature is the Rubinstein bargaining model that analyses the outcome of a bargain between two impatient individuals. The Rubinstein model assumes bargaining takes the form of alternate offers of how to share a surplus. The equilibrium solution shows that the share obtained by each party is determined by their relative degree of impatience. The normative theory of bargaining has focused on the characteristics of a desirable outcome from the bargaining process. The Nash bargaining model is founded on a set of axioms that describe desirable properties for the outcome of two-person bargaining. Only one outcome satisfies these axioms: the bargain must maximize the product of the gains to each party from the bargain. The concept of bargaining is also central to the resolution of externality problems described by the *Coase theorem.

bargaining power The ability to obtain a large share of the possible joint benefits to be derived from any agreement. Bargaining power is partly dependent on the losses that failure to agree is likely to cause to the various parties to a negotiation. In the absence of agreement, each party has a fall-back position: the less uncomfortable this is, and the longer any party can afford to stay in it, the stronger is their bargaining power. A party with a very uncomfortable fall-back position and an urgent need for an agreement has very little bargaining power. Bargaining power is increased by unity, financial reserves, and a reputation for toughness, and is decreased by division, shaky finances, and a reputation for being willing to compromise. *See also* BARGAINING.

barriers to entry Laws, institutions, or practices which make it difficult or impossible for new firms to enter some *markets, or new workers to compete for certain forms of employment. Barriers to entry may take various forms. The law may confer *monopoly rights on existing firms, or impose qualifications for licences for new operators which are so obstructively administered as to make new entry difficult. Existing firms may have monopoly control over essential inputs, sites, or technical know-how, protected by *patents or commercial secrecy. If the capital required for new plants is very large, this restricts the number of possible entrants. The fear of *price wars by existing firms may deter some new firms from trying to enter an industry. In some markets sheer gangsterism is used to discourage entry. Barriers to entry are often higher against foreign firms or individuals than against nationals: the *European Union tries to prevent this so far as EU residents are concerned, with varying success. *See also* STRATEGIC ENTRY DETERRENCE.

barriers to exit Obstacles that make it costly for a firm to exit a market. Barriers to exit intensify competition in a market because incumbent firms have little choice but to 'stay and fight'. Examples of barriers to exit include the costs involved with writing off assets, redundancy payments, penalties for terminating contracts, and the loss of reputation and goodwill.

barter The exchange of one type of good or service for another, without the use of money. This developed to allow society to take advantage of the *division of labour and the gains from *specialization. Barter, however, is often inconvenient: a person who has goods of one type and wants goods of another has to find somebody who wishes to make the opposite exchange, either for their own use or as a professional intermediary. The use of precious metals as a medium of exchange, and the subsequent development of *money, avoided this inconvenience. Barter is nowadays only used when the monetary system has broken down, in countries subject to civil disorder or *hyperinflation, or internationally by countries with inadequate supplies of foreign exchange.

barter economy An economy in which goods are directly exchanged for other goods without the use of a *medium of exchange.

Basel Agreement The Basel Agreement of 1988 established international risk-based capital adequacy standards for banks operating in signatory countries. The agreement set standards for international banking practice in order to establish a level playing field for competition in international banking.

baseline A projection of how the economy will develop if existing *trends and policies continue unchanged. *Models of the economy may be based on theory, *econometrics, or some combination of these. Before it is possible to calculate the effects of changing any aspect of nature, technology, or economic policy, it is necessary to construct a baseline projection. This tracks the future of the economy if present levels or trends in natural phenomena, technology, and economic policies continue unchanged. Any calculation of the predicted effects of changes in nature, such as oil discoveries, changes in technology, such as the introduction of new materials and advanced production techniques, or changes in official policies such as tax rates, tariffs, or interest rates is then conducted in terms of the predicted departure of the economy from the baseline projection.

base money *See* MONETARY BASE.

base period The period whose data are identified with the index of 100 (sometimes 1) in constructing an *index number. In the UK, for example, in 2007 official data on national income aggregates, year 2003 was used as the base period. *Base-weighted or Laspeyres index numbers derive their weights from base-period data, whereas *current-weighted or Paasche index numbers do not.

base rate 1. The rate of interest used by *commercial banks as a basis for charging for loans. Most borrowers pay a premium over base rate, whose size depends on how risky loans to them are considered to be, and what *collateral they can provide.
2. An informal term for the rate at which the Bank of England lends to *discount houses (this corresponds to the *minimum lending rate that was abolished in 1981). The rate at which the Bank of England lends governs interest rates elsewhere in the banking system.

base-weighted index A weighted average of prices or quantities, where the weights used are the quantities or the prices of the base period. Where p_{ij} and q_{ij} are the prices and quantities of N goods, $i = 1, 2, \ldots N$, in period j, and t labels the latest period and 0 the base period, the base-weighted or Laspeyres price index is given by

$$P_B = (\Sigma_i p_{it} q_{io}) / (\Sigma_i p_{io} q_{io})$$

and the base-weighted or Laspeyres quantity index is given by

$$Q_B = (\Sigma_i p_{io} q_{it}) / (\Sigma_i p_{io} q_{io}).$$

basic rate The rate of income tax that applies to all taxable non-saving incomes above a lower limit, below which a starting rate is payable, and below an upper limit, above which a higher rate is payable; the basic rate in fact applies to most UK taxable income. In 2008–9 it was 20 percent. This was previously called the standard rate.

basis point A commonly used unit of measurement of changes or differences in interest rates. It is defined as 1 percent of 1 percentage point, so that a 50 basis points rise in the *rate of interest means a rise by 0.5 percentage points.

batch production A method of production where output emerges in discrete quantities. It is often used when there is a requirement that a certain quantity of a product should be of a uniform pattern and quality, but the required characteristics differ between different orders.

battle of the sexes A two-player game that illustrates the gains that can be obtained from coordination and the difficulties of achieving coordination. A typical description of the game involves a husband and a wife who must choose between spending an evening at the opera and an evening at a football match. The husband prefers football to opera and the wife opera to football. Both prefer to be together than to attend separate events. This information is summarized in the pay-off matrix.

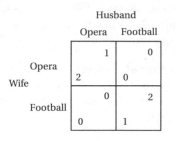

The game has two *Nash equilibria in pure strategies, {Opera, Opera} and {Football, Football}, and a *mixed strategy equilibrium in which the players randomize between playing strategy {Opera} and strategy {Football}. The interesting feature of the game is that all the equilibria can be criticized. In the pure strategy equilibria one of the players receives a pay-off consistently lower than the other even though the underlying game is symmetric. In the mixed strategy equilibria there will be a positive probability that the players fail to attend the same event. The players can both gain if they adopt a random device (such as tossing a coin) to correlate their choices.

Baumol's law The assertion that over time the public sector will increase as a proportion of the economy. The basic hypotheses driving this result are that the public sector (i) is labour-intensive relative to the private sector, and (ii) cannot increase productivity by substituting capital for labour. For example, hospitals need a minimum number of doctors per patient. The labour market links public and private sector wages, so wage increases in the private sector become cost increases for the public sector. If public sector and private sector output remain in the same proportion, public sector expenditure must rise as a proportion of total expenditure.

Bayesian econometrics An approach to estimation and inference in *econometrics in which the uncertainty about the value of an unknown parameter is expressed in terms of a probability distribution. This is in contrast with the classical approach in which parameters are fixed in repeated samples. In the

Bayesian framework data is treated as a fixed set of additional information used in updating the prior beliefs of the analyst about the distribution of the parameters. The revised beliefs, or the posterior distribution of the parameters, given the current data, are obtained from the prior distribution using *Bayes theorem. Therefore, the prior distribution of the parameters and the *likelihood function of the data must be fully specified for estimation to proceed.

Bayesian inference An approach to *hypothesis testing that involves making an assessment of which of two hypotheses, the null (H_0) or the alternative (H_1), has a higher probability of being correct. First, prior probabilities of each of the hypotheses being correct, $P(H_0)$ and $P(H_1)$, are assumed, and the prior odds ratio, $P(H_0)/P(H_1)$, is formed. Then, based on the prior density functions and the likelihood functions of the data conditioned on each of the hypotheses, the prior odds ratio is modified to form a posterior odds ratio. In contrast to the classical approach, it is not necessary to accept or reject each hypothesis. If needed, such a decision can be made by minimizing the expected loss from making a wrong decision, using some specified loss function, where the expectations are calculated with respect to the posterior probabilities on each hypothesis.

Bayes theorem A relationship between the conditional and the marginal probabilities of random events. Let $P[A]$ denote the marginal probability of A and let $P[A|B]$ denote the probability of A conditional on B. Bayes theorem states that $P[A|B]=P[B|A] \times P[A]/P[B]$.

BBB The *Standard and Poor rating of securities which are regarded as being of medium riskiness.

bear A trader who expects prices to fall. A trader on a stock or commodity market who believes that prices are more likely to fall than to rise will sell now any shares they own, in the hope of being able to buy them back more cheaply when their price has fallen. In extreme cases bears speculate by selling forward shares or commodities that they do not actually hold, hoping to be able to buy them cheap before delivery is due. *See also* BULL; SPECULATION.

bearer bond A *security where the person or organization holding the certificate of title is entitled to receive any interest and redemption payments. Such securities have no central register of holders; the owners are thus at considerable risk of loss by theft or accident. Bearer bonds are attractive to anybody seeking to remain anonymous in order to avoid taxation, controls on capital movements, or legal checks on the laundering of money derived from criminal activities. They are therefore illegal in some countries, including the UK.

bear market A stock market in which prices are expected to fall. A widespread belief that prices are more likely to fall than to rise, at least in the immediate future, leads investors to sell shares or defer purchases. *See also* BULL MARKET.

before-tax income The income of an individual or company before deduction of *direct taxes.

beggar-my-neighbour policy A policy that seeks benefits for one country at the expense of others, or tries to cure an economic problem in one country by means which tend to worsen the problems of other countries. (Some authors use the term 'beggar-thy-neighbour': the meaning is identical.) The term was originally devised to characterize policies of trying to cure domestic depression and unemployment by shifting effective demand away from imports on to domestically produced goods, either by the use of *tariffs and *quotas on imports, or by *competitive devaluation. Beggar-my-neighbour policy has also taken the form of reducing domestic inflation through *currency appreciation. This improves the terms of trade and thus reduces cost-inflationary pressure in the appreciating country, but tends to increase *cost inflation in the country's trading partners.

behavioural economics An approach to economic analysis that incorporates psychological insights into individual behaviour to explain economic decisions. Behavioural economics is motivated by the observation of *anomalies that cannot be explained by standard models of choice. It provides an explanation for the anomalies by introducing human and social cognitive and emotional biases into the decision-making process.

behavioural equation *See* STRUCTURAL EQUATION.

behavioural theories of the firm Theories of firm behaviour based on considering the objectives of individuals and groups within firms. In contrast to orthodox models of the firm based on the assumption of *profit maximization, with some allowance for risk aversion, behavioural models consider the motives of managers and other groups within the firm. In small firms a preference for an easy life, or desire to remain one's own master, may limit ambition. In larger firms, pursuit of managerial perquisites, or empire-building based on love of power or prestige, may lead to maximization of turnover rather than profits. It is also argued that lack of information leads firms into choices based on *satisficing.

below-the-line Items following but not part of the *profit-and-loss accounts of firms or the income sections of *national income accounts. For firms below-the-line items indicate how profits are used, or how losses are financed. In national income accounts they are capital account transactions. In both cases below-the-line items refer to changes in the form in which assets are held, and not to transactions giving rise to *income.

benefit(s) *See* DEFINED BENEFIT; FRINGE BENEFITS; HOUSING BENEFIT; MARGINAL BENEFIT; MEANS-TESTED BENEFITS; SICKNESS BENEFIT; SOCIAL SECURITY BENEFITS; SUPPLEMENTARY BENEFIT; UNEMPLOYMENT BENEFIT; UNIVERSAL BENEFIT.

benefit principle The principle that the cost of public expenditures should be met by those who benefit from them. This is an alternative to the *ability to pay principle. The benefit principle faces several difficulties in application. There may be groups judged as needy of government support because they do not have the earning power to be self-sufficient. By definition, the benefit principle cannot be applied in this case. Benefits may also be very difficult to measure, especially for non-excludable *public goods where there is no revelation of preferences.

benefits in kind Government provision of goods and services to those in need of them. This is an alternative to providing citizens with monetary incomes sufficient to meet their needs via the market. Governments wishing to provide for the basic needs of their citizens, including subsistence, housing, education, and medical services, have to choose between these two methods. Providing income is supported by the argument that people vary in their individual tastes and needs, so that any available resources will be more efficiently used in providing goods and services that they choose for themselves. There are, however, various arguments in favour of benefits in kind. In the case of medical and educational services, the tasks of assessing and meeting needs are closely connected. Housing, medical services, and education are often regarded as *merit goods: improved housing, health, and education are supposed to benefit society at large as well as the individual recipient. There is the possibility that if those in need of services for themselves, and more particularly for their children, were given money to pay for them, they might prefer to spend some or all of it on different commodities. As an attempt to combine the merits of market provision of services with the advantages of benefits in kind, it has been proposed that, for example, education should be supplied by the state issuing parents with *vouchers, which could be spent only at educational institutions, and would not otherwise be tradable.

benefits system The system of provision in cash and in kind of sufficient income and services to maintain minimum standards of welfare among a country's residents. This system has to support those unable to provide for themselves because they are too old or young to work, or are disabled, ill, or simply unable or unwilling to obtain work. Such a system is necessarily expensive: choices which have to be made about it are between payments in cash and provision of *benefits in kind; between *universal benefits and *means-tested benefits; between unconditional benefits and benefits conditional on work or training; and between benefits as of right and benefits at the discretion of officials.

Benelux A customs union of Belgium, the Netherlands, and Luxembourg, set up in 1948. The Benelux Customs Union contributed to the foundation of the *European Economic Community, which all three members joined when it was formed in 1958.

Bergson–Samuelson social welfare function *See* SOCIAL WELFARE FUNCTION.

Bertrand competition *Competition between two or more firms in an industry with product price as the strategic variable. This encourages the use of price-cutting as a form of competition. If the products produced by the firms are *perfect substitutes, in the *Nash equilibrium of the price-setting game, price equals *marginal cost. The market equilibrium is then efficient even though the number of competing firms is limited. Bertrand duopoly is the special case of a market with two sellers engaged in price competition.

best-fit line A straight line on a scatter plot that represents a linear relationship between two sets of data in the best way as measured by some criterion, e.g. the *least squares criterion.

best linear unbiased estimator (BLUE) The estimator that in the class of
linear unbiased estimators has the smallest variance. Under the conditions of
*Gauss–Markov theorem the *least squares estimator is BLUE.

beta coefficient A measure of how variations in the return on a particular
share correlate with variations in the return on a market index. The beta coefficient
is used as a summary of the riskiness of an asset. If r_{it} is the return on asset i from
time $t - 1$ to time t, and r_{It} is the return on the market index, β_i is calculated by
finding the best fit to

$$r_{it} = \alpha + \beta_i r_{It} + \varepsilon_t$$

so the beta of asset i is defined by $\beta_i = \frac{\sigma_{iI}}{\sigma_I^2}$, where σ_I^2 is the *variance of the return on
the market index representative of the market and σ_{iI} is the *covariance between the
return on asset i and the return on the index. In the special case of the *Capital Asset
Pricing Model the index I is the market portfolio. Beta is used as a measure of risk
because the variance of return for asset i is

$$\sigma_i^2 = \beta_i^2 \sigma_I^2 + \sigma_{\varepsilon i}^2$$

where $\sigma_{\varepsilon i}^2$ is the part of the variance unexplained by the index. $\beta_i < 0$ means that r_i
moves opposite to the market on average; a zero or low value of β_i means that the
asset has mainly *idiosyncratic risk, independent of overall market movements; a
positive value of β_i means that r_i moves on average with the market.

beta stocks Shares in the second rank for frequency of trading on a *stock
exchange. On the London Stock Exchange, before the system was replaced in
1991 by Normal Market Size, there were about 500 beta stocks, compared with
about 100 *alpha stocks, the most frequently traded category, and over 3000 gamma
and delta, or less traded, stocks.

between-groups estimator An estimator of the vector of the parameters in
a linear regression model with panel data, computed as an *ordinary least squares
(OLS) estimator using time averages of the data for each cross-section unit
(group means). It is consistent when OLS on the pooled data is consistent, but
is inefficient relative to *generalized least squares. *See also* PANEL DATA;
WITHIN-GROUPS ESTIMATOR.

Beveridge curve A graph depicting the relationship between unemployment
and the job *vacancy rate. When the vacancy rate is plotted on the vertical axis and
unemployment on the horizontal the curve slopes downwards as a higher rate of
unemployment occurs with a lower rate of vacancies. An inward move depicts
increased efficiency in the labour market as any level of unemployment is sustained
with fewer vacancies.

Beveridge Report A report on social security, prepared by Sir William
Beveridge during the Second World War, and published in 1944 as *Full Employment
in a Free Society*. This was widely regarded as the basis for the creation of the post-
war *welfare state in the UK.

bias of an estimator The expected value of the difference between the estimator and the true value of the estimated parameter.

bid *See* HOSTILE BID; TAKEOVER BID.

bid–ask spread (bid–offer spread) The difference between the price that can be obtained for an immediate sale of an asset (the bid price) and the price that has to be paid for an immediate purchase of that asset (the ask price). The spread is the profit margin for the dealer.

big bang 1. A shorthand expression for the view that reforms should be carried out as rapidly as possible. This is contrasted with the view that major changes should be made gradually. These views clash in countries undertaking *liberalization or *structural transformation. The argument for rapid change is that it creates a sufficiently large group who have gained from change to make it politically irreversible, whereas gradual change encourages opposition, because the losers often suffer before the gainers benefit.
   2. The major change to trading practice that took place in 1986 when fixed commissions were abolished in the *City.

big four A term that was used to describe the four largest UK 'high street' banks, namely Barclays, Lloyds, HSBC (formerly the Midland), and NatWest.

big push A doctrine in *development economics according to which the development of a poor country occurs on the basis of a synchronized expansion in many sectors. In normative terms, it implies that the government has to plan how to spread new capital investment across many sectors. In positive terms, it implies that the capital formation necessarily occurs through balanced growth.

bilateral monopoly A market situation with a single buyer (a monopsonist) facing a single seller (a monopolist). This could arise where a single supplier firm faces a single government purchaser, for example the Ministry of Defence, or where a single trade union faces a single employer, for example a nationalized industry. Under bilateral monopoly, price and quantity are decided by bargaining between the two parties.

bilateral trade A situation where trade between any two countries has to balance, or any imbalance has to be financed by credits arranged directly between the two countries. This is contrasted with *multilateral trade, which requires only that trade with all other countries combined should either balance, or be financed by overall credit from other countries. Bilateral trade has the disadvantages of *barter at the national level. It is more efficient to be able to run surpluses with some trade partners and deficits with others, and to be able to finance any overall surplus or deficit with loans to or from any other country. For a country with a *convertible currency, bilateral surpluses or deficits on either current or capital account are of no importance; only overall or multilateral balances matter.

bill A short-dated security, usually maturing in under a year. *Treasury bills are issued by the UK government; trade bills are issued by firms to obtain short-term finance more cheaply than borrowing from the banks; *bills of exchange are issued by private firms to finance foreign trade. A bill specifies its *maturity, for example 91 days from the date of issue, and the currency in which it is to be repaid. Bills carry no explicit interest; the interest on bills is provided by issuing them at a *discount to their redemption value. Bills can be traded before maturity; while their market price is subject to change with changes in the rate of interest, because of their early maturity dates large interest changes are needed to move bill prices very far. For example, a bill maturing in 6 weeks will be reduced in price by only 0.58 percent by a rise in short-term interest rates from 5 to 10 percent a year. Bills are thus regarded as *liquid assets.

billion (bn, b.) One thousand million ($= 10^9$) in the US and modern British system. A billion was a million million ($= 10^{12}$) in the traditional British system but this is no longer in use.

bill of exchange A short-dated security issued to finance foreign trade. The customer pays an exporter not in cash but with a bill payable usually in 3 or 6 months. This can be sold in the discount market to provide immediate cash for the supplier. If the customer is not well known, a bill can be made more marketable by *acceptance by a merchant banker, who adds a signature to the bill guaranteeing payment, should the issuer default.

bimodal distribution A distribution with two distinct peaks, with a dip between. An example is the empirical distribution of human death rates per 1000 population, which are higher in infancy and in old age than in the years between.

binary choice models *See* DISCRETE CHOICE MODELS.

binomial distribution The distribution of the number of occurrences of a random event as the result of making a number of independent drawings, with a known and constant probability of the event occurring each time. If the probability of the event (for example 'heads' throwing a coin, or '6' throwing a die) each time is p, and the probability of non-occurrence is $(1 - p)$, the binomial distribution gives the probability of exactly r occurrences in n independent tries, where the r satisfies $0 \le r \le n$. This probability is given by

$$p^r(1 - p)^{n - r} {}_nC_r$$

${}_nC_r$ denotes the number of ways of choosing r objects out of n

$$_nC_r = n!/[r!(n - r)!]$$

where $r!$ denotes 'r factorial', defined as $0! = 1$ and for $r > 0$

$$r! = r(r - 1)(r - 2)\ldots(2)(1).$$

biological interest rate The rate of interest that ensures the optimal allocation of goods between generations. In an *overlapping generations economy with no capital and no storage the optimal allocation, or the *golden rule, is achieved when the interest rate is equal to the rate of population growth (hence the name 'biological').

black economy *See* HIDDEN ECONOMY.

black market Trading which violates *rationing or *price control laws, usually both. Black markets can by definition exist only when governments attempt to control prices or ration quantities.

Black Monday 19 October 1987, the day on which world stock markets collapsed. In New York the *Dow Jones index fell by 23 percent, and significant falls occurred in London and other major stock markets worldwide. The collapse started widespread fears of a worldwide *depression, which did not in fact occur.

Black–Scholes equation An equation used to value financial *options. The Black–Scholes equation is based on a model of equilibrium in financial markets with continuous trading. That is, asset prices potentially change at every instant in time. The model assumes that there is a risk-free asset and that all excess returns are eliminated by *arbitrage. The method of Black–Scholes is to develop a partial differential equation that the price of every option must satisfy. This equation states that the value, V, of an option must satisfy

$$\frac{\partial V}{\partial t} + \frac{1}{2}\sigma^2 S^2 \frac{\partial^2 V}{\partial S^2} + rS\frac{\partial V}{\partial S} - rV = 0$$

where S is the value at time t of the underlying asset, r is the risk-free rate of return, and σ^2 is the variance of the return on the underlying asset. The value of a particular option is found by solving the partial differential equation using as boundary conditions the characteristics of that option.

Blair House Agreement An agreement on the liberalization of international trade in farm products concluded in November 1992 between the *European Community (EC) and the US. It included cuts in the volume of subsidized food exports.

blue book A UK government publication (so called from the colour of its cover), the annual *United Kingdom National Accounts*, published by the UK Office for National Statistics (formerly the Central Statistical Office), that provides data on UK national income and expenditure, both in the aggregate and by sectors. Before 1983 it was entitled *National Income and Expenditure*.

blue chip The equity shares of large and reputable companies. Such companies normally have high *market capitalization, and a liquid market in their shares.

board of directors The governing body of a company, which appoints the company's officers. Most *company directors are elected by shareholders at general meetings of the company, but a board may be given powers of co-option. Boards include executive directors, employed by the company full-time or for a major portion of their time, and may include non-executive directors. These usually either have suitable commercial experience, or are selected because they have titles or hold offices which make the company look respectable. Directors are normally paid fees for their services to a company.

bond A security with a *redemption date over a year later than its date of issue. Bonds may be issued by firms, financial institutions, or governments. They may have a fixed redemption date, have an option for the borrower to repay at any date over a period, or even be perpetuities. They may carry fixed interest, or interest variable with notice or linked to some financial index. Their interest and redemption payments may be specified in money terms, or *index-linked to a suitable price index. Finally, they may vary in the degree of risk attached to them. Government bonds are called 'gilt-edged', or 'gilts', and are generally regarded as very safe. Well-established firms issue 'investment-grade bonds', which are also regarded as safe, while financially adventurous firms issue *junk bonds, where there is recognized to be a non-negligible danger that the borrower may default. When bonds have a long time to *maturity, their market price is sensitive to changes in current and expected interest rates, which control the *present discounted value of future redemption and interest payments. A rise in interest rates lowers present discounted value; thus even bonds which are extremely safe, in the sense of absence of risk if held to maturity, suffer from variations in their market value as interest rates change. This liability to price fluctuations diminishes as redeemable bonds approach maturity. *See also* BEARER BOND; GRANNY BOND; PREMIUM BOND.

bond-rating agency An agency specializing in assessing the creditworthiness of governments, municipalities, and corporations issuing bonds. *Standard and Poor and *Moody's are leading US bond-rating agencies.

bonus A payment to a firm's employees additional to their normal pay. Bonuses may be linked to performance, of either the whole firm, a specified section of it, or the individual recipient. Bonuses provide *incentives to employees, both to exert themselves and to stay with the firm rather than looking for a better job elsewhere. Bonuses differ from normal pay in that there is no obligation to repeat them, and they are not pensionable. They are normally taxable.

bonus issue An issue of additional *shares in a company to existing shareholders, in proportion to their holdings. This is distinguished from a *rights issue, where existing shareholders are offered first option on new shares, at a preferential price, but only get them if they pay for them. Bonus issues bring in no cash to the company, and are made as a gesture of confidence, and a signal of a probable rise in *dividends.

book value The value which is put on assets in a firm's *accounts. This may be the original purchase price, or a revised figure based on a periodic revaluation. It is contrasted with trying to value assets at their current market prices. Book value is often used when the assets are non-marketed, so that regular revaluation would be expensive and unreliable, or where the assets are marketed but their price is volatile, so that 'marking to market' would produce very variable valuations. *Balance-sheets using book values may conceal either large hidden reserves or undeclared losses in a firm.

boom A period of optimism, high economic activity, and relatively low unemployment. In booms prices rise faster than usual, and primary commodity prices increase relative to those of industrial products.

bootstrap A computer-intensive technique of re-sampling of the data to obtain the sampling distribution of a statistic. The initial sample is treated as the population from which samples are drawn repeatedly and randomly, with replacement. These bootstrapped samples are used to compute a statistic, and the resulting empirical distribution of this statistic is interpreted as an approximation to the true sampling distribution.

Borda count A system of voting in which each voter ranks the alternatives. Assume there are n alternative choices available. Each voter submits a ranking of these alternatives. The first choice of each voter is given n points, the second choice $n - 1$, and so on. Any alternative not included in the ranking is awarded 0 points. The points awarded to each alternative are then summed across voters and the alternative with the most points in total is chosen. Borda voting always selects a winning alternative (or tied alternatives) but the outcome can be affected by the introduction of alternatives that cannot win. *See also* COLLECTIVE CHOICE; MAJORITY VOTING.

borrowing Incurring debts to finance spending. This is done by individuals, firms, and governments. Borrowing is desirable when the benefits from using borrowed money are greater than the interest costs. This may be because of urgent need for individual spending or sudden falls in income, or favourable investment opportunities for firms. Similarly, governments borrow to spend when borrowing is less costly than taxation; too much borrowing causes *debt service to become burdensome. Countries borrow when they want to invest more than they save. This is worthwhile if investment is very productive; however, too much borrowing leads to balance-of-payments problems. *See also* FOREIGN CURRENCY-DENOMINATED BORROWING.

bottleneck The effective *constraint on the maximum speed or level of an activity. Its use in economics is a physical analogy to the maximum rate at which a liquid can be poured through the neck of a bottle. In production, transport, or administration, the effective constraint is often a shortage of some specific form of labour or some particular piece of equipment. A major role of efficient *management is to observe and remedy bottlenecks as they arise, or still better to foresee them and take action in time to prevent them from emerging.

bottom line The profit or loss on an activity. The expression derives from the custom in drawing up *accounts of showing the profit or loss at the foot of the statement.

bounded rationality The argument that there is a finite limit to the amount of information the human brain can hold and process. Teamwork and computers can vastly increase the amount of information that can be collected, and the calculations that can be performed, but using the information and understanding the implications of the calculations are still subject to severe limits. Bounded rationality casts doubt on the model of rational economic choice as considering all possible alternatives and choosing the best, or *optimization. The theory of *satisficing assumes that individuals and organizations consider only a relatively small number of alternatives, and frequently stop searching once they find

a tolerable course of action, rather than seeking the best possible. *See also*
BEHAVIOURAL ECONOMICS.

Box–Cox transformation A transformation for time-series data of the form

$$x_t = \frac{y_t^\lambda - 1}{\lambda}$$

where x_t is the transformed series, y_t is the original series, and λ is a number
between 0 and 1. It is often used to stabilize the variance of the time series. $\lambda = 0$
corresponds to the logarithmic transformation, and $\lambda = 1$ is a mean reduction.
The optimal λ can be estimated from the data, simultaneously with other
parameters in a completely specified time series model for y_t.

Box–Jenkins approach A method of identification, estimation, and diagnostic
checking of *autoregressive integrated moving average (ARIMA) models. First,
sample *autocorrelation coefficients and *partial autocorrelation coefficients are
used to specify a tentative ARIMA model. Next, the parameters of the tentative
model are estimated. Finally, diagnostics tests are performed, e.g. by analysing
the residuals. If the model is rejected a new identification is specified and the
process is repeated.

boycott A refusal to trade with the person, company, or country boycotted. The
name comes from a 19th-century Irish land agent unpopular with his master's
tenants. A boycott may involve refusal to buy goods and services from somebody, or
to sell to them. A secondary boycott extends this to anybody who does not join in
the original boycott. While it is hard to make a boycott completely effective, as trade
can usually be conducted secretly or indirectly, this involves delay, expense, and
inconvenience. A boycott is thus an effective form of pressure on individuals, firms,
or countries whose conduct or opinions are widely disapproved of.

***BP* curve** A curve depicting balance of payments equilibrium in the *IS-LM*
model. The *BP* curve is drawn on the same diagram as the *IS* and *LM* curves and
shows combinations of *Y* (*gross domestic product) and *r* (the interest rate) at which
the overall balance of payments is in equilibrium. This means that the current and
capital account balances of payments sum to zero. As higher *Y* tends to produce a
current account deficit, and higher *r* tends to produce a capital account surplus, the
BP curve is upward sloping. If international capital mobility is high, the *BP* curve is
flatter than the *LM* curve.

Brady Plan An agreement in 1989 by which Mexico's external debt was
restructured. The plan was suggested by, and named after, the US Secretary of
the Treasury. It involved a mixture of debt reduction and 'new money' in the form
of credit extensions from creditors who chose not to reduce their exposure.

brain drain A pejorative description of the tendency for talented people from
poor countries to seek employment in richer ones. Sometimes this migration occurs
because, while similar skills are needed in both poor and rich countries, the rich pay
more for them. In other cases the brain drain occurs because the technical and
economic backwardness of poorer countries means that job opportunities there are

limited or non-existent. It is also possible that the brain drain is encouraged because of tendencies in poorer countries to fill such good jobs as there are on a basis of family connections, political influence, and corruption, while on average richer countries, though subject to some of the same problems, tend to fill posts on a more meritocratic basis.

branch banking The banking system under which *banks are allowed to have branches. Branch banking in some countries, including the United States, has sometimes been restricted to reduce the monopoly power of banks.

brand A name used to identify the maker or distributor of a good. A brand was originally a mark burned on the hide of an animal to identify its owner, or on the person of a convicted criminal to warn the public of their character. In some cases a brand name is that of the original maker, which has been retained by a new owner after the originator ceased to be an independent firm. Brand names benefit producers and distributors, as they facilitate *advertising and building up a reputation for a product or range of products. Branding may benefit consumers where it is difficult or impossible to discover the quality of a good by inspection before actual purchase. If the maker is easily identified, then a good which fails to give satisfaction in use will not be bought again. Producers and distributors know this, and have a strong incentive to maintain quality, and to make amends if they have failed; this incentive is weaker with unbranded goods where responsibility is hard to trace.

brand loyalty The tendency for consumers to prefer familiar names. Consumers frequently buy brands they have used before, or seen widely advertised, in preference to unbranded products or unfamiliar names. Brand loyalty is a form of *satisficing behaviour: actions which have produced satisfactory results in the past are repeated unless something goes wrong. This makes it difficult for new suppliers to enter a market, even if their product is, in fact, just as good or better, and as cheap as or cheaper than established branded products. Brand loyalty may be rational for consumers, however, unless the cost of unsuccessful experiments with new brands or unbranded products is low. It may even be rational to prefer more widely advertised brands, on the argument that the seller would be wasting money advertising a product unless it was good enough for people to be likely to make repeat purchases.

brand recognition The idea that the name of a brand is recognized by consumers, and conveys favourable product information.

Brandt Report The report of an Independent Commission on International Development Issues, chaired by Willy Brandt, former German Chancellor. The report, on steps to promote North–South cooperation, was published in 1980 as *North–South: A Program for Survival*. It included pleas for a reduction in Northern protectionism.

break-even The ratio of output to *capacity just sufficient to allow a business to cover its costs. Output below the break-even level means losses; only if output is on average above the break-even level will a firm make profits. Demand is usually subject to random fluctuations, and equipment sometimes fails, so capacity must exceed the average level of demand to avoid having to turn away too many customers at times of peak demand. Failure to satisfy demand not only loses immediate revenue, but decreases future demand, as customers who feel they cannot rely on the good or service being available seek alternatives. Firms thus have a strong incentive to hold adequate capacity, but this has to be paid for.

break-up value The sum a business could realize by ceasing operation entirely and selling off its *assets. For most firms break-up value is below value as a going concern, so they stay in business. If a firm's break-up value exceeds its value as a going concern, it is economically rational to close it down and sell off the assets. Many types of asset do not have liquid markets, so the process of closing down takes time, during which asset values may change. It may thus be very difficult to estimate a firm's break-up value, which makes closing it down a risky venture.

Bretton Woods **1.** The venue of a conference held in 1944 to discuss the new international monetary arrangements to be set up after the Second World War. This led to the creation of the *International Monetary Fund and the *International Bank for Reconstruction and Development (or World Bank).
   2. Shorthand for the *international monetary system resulting from the conference. This involved pegged exchange rates, to be altered only in the event of fundamental disequilibrium. The Bretton Woods system lasted until 1971, when it gave way to a system of *floating exchange rates.

Breusch–Pagan test In a linear regression model, a test of the null hypothesis of *homoscedasticity against the alternative hypothesis that the variance of observation i has the form $\sigma_i^2 = h(z_i{'}\alpha)$, where h is a function common for all i, z_i is an $(S \times 1)$ non-stochastic vector with first element equal to one, and α is an $(S \times 1)$ vector of unknown coefficients. The test can be conveniently performed by (1) estimating the original regression by *ordinary least squares (OLS) and (2) regressing squared OLS residuals on $Z = (z_1, \ldots, z_N)$. The test statistic is $\eta = NR^2$, where N is the sample size and R^2 is the coefficient of determination from the second regression. Under the null hypothesis H_0, η is asymptotically $\chi_{(S-1)}^2$; this result does not depend on the function h.

broad money A relatively broad definition of money. This applies to definitions such as *M2, which includes building society deposits, or *M3, which includes interest-bearing bank deposits. It does not apply to *M0 or *M1. Broad money measures of the *money supply tend to be less stable relative to *gross domestic product than more narrow measures.

broker A person or company who does not trade as a principal, but puts buyers and sellers in touch with one another. Stockbrokers do this for stocks and shares, commodity brokers for commodities, insurance brokers for insurance policies, and shipping brokers for tramp and charter shipping. Brokers are able to charge *commission for this service because of their specialized knowledge of the markets.

brokerage The fee, normally a small percentage of the price, charged by a broker for the service of putting buyer and seller in touch with one another.

Brownian motion A *Gaussian process with independent non-overlapping increments. It is named after Robert Brown (1773–1858), a botanist who in 1827 first observed under a microscope the random movement of pollen or dust particles floating in water. The name is used both for this phenomenon and for the mathematical model that describes it; the latter is also known as the Wiener process.

bubble A cumulative movement in the price of an asset whose price is high mainly because *speculators believe it will rise still further. Such speculative behaviour can force prices to rise for some period on a path that is eventually realized to be unsustainable; at some point a bubble will burst, but it is hard to predict when this will happen.

budget A statement of a government's planned receipts and expenditures for some future period, normally a year. This is usually accompanied by a statement of actual receipts and expenditures for the previous period. The annual budget statement in the UK is a statement of the government's financial plans made in Parliament by the Chancellor of the Exchequer. The word budget originally meant the contents of a package; the budget is so called because it brings all the government's tax and spending plans together. A budget surplus means that total government receipts exceed total spending; a budget deficit means that spending exceeds receipts; and a balanced budget means that receipts and spending are equal. All calculations concerning budget surpluses and deficits depend on the definition used. Items which could on some definitions be regarded as part of the budget but are in fact excluded, for example government-guaranteed borrowing by other bodies, are termed off-budget items. *See also* BALANCED BUDGET; BUDGET CONSTRAINT; UNIFIED BUDGET.

budget constraint The limit to expenditure. For any economic agent, whether an individual, a firm, or a government, expenditure must stay within limits set by the ability to finance it. The finance may come from income, from assets already held, or from borrowing; loans will be obtainable only if lenders believe that they are sufficiently likely to be repaid. The budget constraint thus says that the *present discounted value of total present and future expenditure cannot exceed the present discounted value of present wealth plus future income. Spending can only exceed income plus present wealth to the extent that it is possible to borrow. *See also* HARD BUDGET CONSTRAINT; INTERTEMPORAL BUDGET CONSTRAINT; SOFT BUDGET CONSTRAINT.

budget deficit The excess of a government's total expenditure over its income. This has to be met by borrowing, which increases government debt. Budget deficits can be calculated for any level of government—central, local, state in federal countries such as Germany or the United States—or for general government, which is all these levels combined. It is important to distinguish whether the deficit is calculated including as expenditure the nominal or the real interest on government debt: conventional measures of the budget deficit use nominal interest, but an *inflation-adjusted budget deficit would include real interest only. The *cyclically adjusted budget deficit is what the budget deficit would be if the existing tax and spending rules were maintained but national income rose or fell to its normal level; this can only be estimated.

budget line A graph showing what combinations of quantities of two goods can be afforded by a consumer with a fixed total amount to spend. If each good is available in any quantity at a fixed price per unit, the budget line is a straight line with a slope equal to the relative price of the two goods.

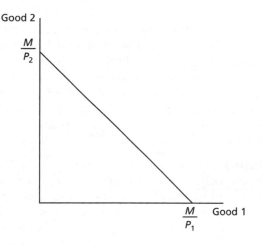

Budget Line

budget surplus The excess of a government's total income over its expenditure. This can be used to repay government debt. Budget surpluses can be calculated for any level of government—central, local, state in federal countries such as Germany or the United States—or for general government, which is all these levels combined. *See also* BUDGET DEFICIT.

budget year The fiscal year used by the US federal government. This runs from 1 October to 30 September in the following year. It corresponds in concept to the UK fiscal year, which, however, runs from 6 April to 5 April in the following year.

buffer stock A stock of a commodity held for the purpose of stabilizing its price. If price is liable to fluctuate, because of variations in supply, demand, or both, a buffer stock operator can limit price rises by selling stocks and can limit price falls by buying stocks. This can be done either at the discretion of the manager, or in accordance with a pre-announced maximum selling price and minimum buying price. The price can only be kept within these limits if the prices set are consistent with long-run market conditions. If the minimum price is too high, stocks will tend to accumulate indefinitely, until the buffer stock runs out of funds; if the maximum price is set too low, stocks will run out during periods of high price. Successful stabilization requires that a buffer stock is provided with sufficient funds to be able to hold enough stocks to deal with periods of high demand, and not run out of funds during low price periods. With a selling price above the buying price, a buffer stock is bound to make a trading profit, but it has to meet storage, interest, and administrative costs. Whether it can break even after meeting these costs depends on having a sufficient margin between its buying and selling prices, and on judging correctly which market price changes represent short-run fluctuations to be stabilized, and which reflect changes in long-run market conditions, to which it must in time adapt.

building and loan association A US cooperative institution providing mortgage finance for home owners. This is the US equivalent of a UK building society.

building society A UK financial institution, whose main activity is accepting deposits from the general public to finance *mortgage lending on private housing. Building societies are the largest single source of mortgage finance. They also engage in some lending on commercial properties, and in other financial activities. Some provide current account facilities, including cheques and electronic transfers, for their depositors. Building societies have recently been permitted to transform themselves into companies, and several have done so, while others have chosen to remain mutuals. *See also* DEMUTUALIZATION.

built-in stabilizers Any features of the economy that tend to limit economic fluctuations through routine behaviour, without the need for specific decisions. The government's *budget provides an important example. If national income falls, the application of given direct and indirect tax rates cuts revenue automatically; if unemployment rises, the application of given benefit rules ensures that income maintenance payments rise. This raises the budget deficit, and limits the fall in incomes. Similarly, when national income rises the budget deficit falls. The advantage of built-in stabilizers over deliberate policy measures is that they operate automatically and immediately. The disadvantage of built-in stabilizers is that they can only diminish fluctuations and cannot eliminate them completely. Any further *stabilization requires deliberate changes in policies.

bull A trader who expects prices to rise. A trader on a stock or commodity market who believes that prices are more likely to rise than to fall will buy shares, in the hope of selling them at a profit when the price has risen. In extreme cases bulls speculate by contracting to buy forward shares or commodities for which they cannot afford to pay, hoping that when prices rise they will be able to borrow the cash needed for settlement. A bull market is a market dominated by bulls, in which for some time prices tend to rise persistently. *See also* BEAR; SPECULATION.

bullion *Gold held in bulk, usually in the form of gold bars. Bullion is largely held by central banks, as part of their countries' *foreign exchange reserves.

bull market A stock market in which prices are expected to rise. A widespread belief that prices are more likely to rise than to fall, at least in the immediate future, leads investors to buy shares or defer sales.

Bundesbank The German *central bank. The Deutsche Bundesbank, with headquarters in Frankfurt-am-Main, had until 2002 a constitutional duty to protect the value of the Deutschmark, and acquired a formidable reputation for financial caution and monetary stability. Since the introduction of the Euro the Bundesbank has been a participant in the *European System of Central Banks.

bundle of goods A collection of specified quantities and qualities of various types of goods and services. A *price index is constructed by measuring changes in the total cost of buying a given bundle of goods, whose composition depends on the purpose of the index.

bundling The marketing of related products as a single unit. The price of the bundle is set at less than the sum of the prices of the separate items. Bundling is an example of second-degree *price discrimination and is employed to increase profit by extracting additional *consumer surplus.

burden *See* DEBT BURDEN; TAX BURDEN.

Bureau of Economic Analysis (BEA) The branch of the US Department of Commerce which assembles and publishes the US national income accounts.

(⊕) SEE WEB LINKS

• The Bureau of Economic Analysis provides access to official US economic data.

business **1.** All forms of industrial and commercial profit-seeking activity. The business cycle refers to fluctuations in the aggregate level of economic activity, and the *Business Expansion Scheme in the UK used 'business' in this sense.
   2. The firms conducting these activities.
   3. The ownership/management side of firms, as opposed to their ordinary employees; this group is often referred to as the business community.

business cycle The fluctuation of economic activity around the long-term growth path. A cycle involves a period of above-trend growth of output (recovery and prosperity), and a period of below-trend stagnation or decline (contraction or recession). Cycles of various lengths have been identified. The shortest cycle is the Kitchin inventory cycle (3–5 years). Next follows the Juglar fixed investment cycle (7–11 years)—this is the standard economic cycle. The Kuznets infrastructural investment cycle is even longer (15–25 years). The longest cycle usually identified is the Kondratieff wave (45–60 years). *See also* ENDOGENOUS BUSINESS CYCLE; POLITICAL BUSINESS CYCLE; REAL BUSINESS CYCLE.

business ethics The study of what standards businesses should observe in their dealings over and above compliance with the letter of the law. This covers questions such as fair dealing with their labour force, customers, suppliers, and competitors, and the impact of their activities on the environment, public health, and animal welfare. If a good reputation helps to gain and retain business, ethical conduct need not necessarily conflict with profit, but there are bound to be cases where it does. Particularly difficult questions of business ethics arise in multinational firms, where practices such as gifts to officials, which are essential to doing business at all in some countries, are regarded as criminal in others. *See also* CORPORATE GOVERNANCE.

Business Expansion Scheme (BES) A UK fiscal device intended to encourage investment of *venture capital in new businesses. This operated from 1981 to 1994, when it was replaced by the *Enterprise Investment Scheme. Investment under the BES was encouraged by tax concessions; it is not clear how many businesses coming into the scheme were really new, and how far it benefited businesses which would have been started in any case even without the scheme, or whether it encouraged *creative accounting to enable businesses which were already in existence to participate.

business rate A UK tax on business premises, levied to finance local authorities. The rate per pound of valuation at which business rates are levied used to be decided by the local authorities themselves, but it is now set at a common national level, the *uniform business rate. The valuation of premises for rating purposes is decided by a District Valuer.

buyer A person who buys things, usually for money. In their role as a consumer everybody is a buyer, but firms employ specialist buyers. In the case of goods which vary in quality, design, or specification, or where suppliers are difficult to track down, a buyer is a highly skilled expert whose services are vital to the firm.

buyer's market A market in which conditions are better for buyers than for sellers. This occurs, for example, when sellers are numerous and under pressure to raise money quickly, while buyers are scarce and can afford to wait. In such a situation it is likely that prices will be unusually low and that conditions of sale will be unusually favourable for buyers.

buy-out Change in *control of a company through its previous shareholders being bought out by new owners. These may already be connected with the firm: in a *management buy-out the firm is bought by its existing managers. A buy-out may alternatively be undertaken by outsiders. Finance may come from the purchasers' own resources, or from loans; in a *leveraged buy-out part of the price is raised by fixed-interest loans.

bygones Past events which play no part in rational present decision-making. For a firm, bygones include *sunk costs and past operating profits and losses, except to the extent that these play a part in forming present expectations.

by-product A good produced in the process of the production of some other good. Sale of a by-product makes production more profitable than if it had to be thrown away, or was costly to dispose of. For example, tar and other heavy fractions are the by-products of oil refining for petrol. The term by-product is used where one good (petrol) would be produced for its own sake even if the other (tar) were useless. This is distinguished from *joint production, which is profitable only if both goods can be sold.

cabotage **1.** The transport of goods within a country. In the US and some other countries this is required to be carried out by domestic carriers. Such a restriction is a form of *protectionism.

2. A right to transport goods within a country granted to a foreign carrier.

Cairns Group A coalition of nineteen countries that export agricultural goods. The Cairns Group was formed in 1986 to exert pressure to ensure that the liberalization of agricultural trade remained a high priority in trade talks. The members of the Cairns Group are Argentina, Australia, Bolivia, Brazil, Canada, Chile, Colombia, Costa Rica, Guatemala, Indonesia, Malaysia, the Philippines, South Africa, Thailand, and Uruguay.

(⊕) **SEE WEB LINKS**

• Information on the activities of the Cairns Group and on trade negotiations related to agriculture.

calibration Identification of the numerical values of the parameters in an economic model by (1) using for some parameters the values obtained in other empirical and theoretical studies, (2) using informed judgement to make a best guess of the values for other parameters, (3) simulating the model, and (4) fine-tuning the parameter values by matching the model predictions with empirical observations. This procedure is most often used in the assessment of *business cycle models.

call money Money lent in the London money market, repayable at very short notice. This is a highly *liquid asset for UK banks and other financial institutions. Because of transaction costs it is practicable to lend money on these terms in large amounts only.

call option A contract giving the holder the right, but no obligation, to buy a fixed number of units of an asset on (or before) some future date (the exercise date) at a pre-arranged price (the strike price). A European call option can be exercised only at the final exercise date. An American call option can be exercised at any time up until the exercise date. A call option will never be exercised if the *spot price of the asset is below the strike price in the contract.

Cambridge equation The formulation of the *quantity theory of money as $M = kPY$. Here M is the demand for money balances, P is the price level, Y is the level of real national income, and k is a parameter reflecting economic structure and monetary habits, namely the ratio of total transactions to income and the ratio of desired money balances to total transactions. The Cambridge equation is a modified form of the *quantity equation, $MV = PT$, with $k = T/(VY)$, where V is the *velocity of circulation and T is the real volume of transactions.

CAP *See* COMMON AGRICULTURAL POLICY.

capacity The maximum output of goods and services a firm or an economy is capable of producing. *See also* EXCESS CAPACITY; SPARE CAPACITY.

capacity utilization Actual output as a percentage of *capacity.

capital **1.** Man-made material resource used or available for use in production, for example machinery. This is also referred to as physical capital.
2. Material or financial wealth, accumulated by an individual or a company, that can be used to generate income. *See also* HUMAN CAPITAL.

capital account Transactions which do not involve income or expenditure, but change the form in which assets are held. Receipt of a loan, for example, is not income, but an exchange of cash now for a promise to repay, usually with interest, in the future. In a country's *balance of payments, the capital account is a record of international exchanges of assets and liabilities.

capital accumulation The process of increasing the stock of *capital. This is one of the main sources of *economic growth in the short and medium run. Whether capital accumulation can raise long-run growth is not obvious. Some empirical studies suggest that it plays a minor or no role in economic growth, while others find that it has a significant positive effect on the long-run growth rate.

capital adequacy Possession by a firm of sufficient capital for the business it is doing. This matters to the firm itself: if it is under-capitalized, a small adverse shift in circumstances can impair its solvency. Capital adequacy therefore matters to a firm's creditors. In the case of banks and other financial institutions, it also matters to the regulatory authorities, whose concern is that the failure of particular firms might cause a general financial panic. The level of capital adequacy is defined by the Basel Committee of the *Bank for International Settlements.

capital allowances Deductions of investment expenditure from a firm's taxable *profits. This encourages investment, since for any given level of gross profits, the more investment a firm does, the less tax it has to pay.

capital appreciation An increase in the prices of the assets owned by an enterprise. When increases in the value of land, buildings, equipment, or stocks are merely proportional to general *inflation in the economy, it is argued that they do not increase the real value of a business. They should therefore not be included in its profits for tax purposes, or in the national income accounts.

Capital Asset Pricing Model (CAPM) A model of equilibrium in financial markets that generates very precise predictions about the structure of returns on risky assets. The CAPM assumes the infinite divisibility of assets, no transaction costs, and no taxes. It also assumes that all investors have a one-period investment horizon, hold the same expectations about asset returns, have *mean-variance preferences, and are able to borrow and lend at a risk-free rate of interest. Under these assumptions the equilibrium of the financial market is described by the Capital Market Line (CML) and the Security Market Line (SML). For every efficient portfolio, p, the CML states that

$$\bar{r}_p = r_f + \left[\frac{\bar{r}_M - r_f}{\sigma_M}\right]$$

where r_f is the risk-free interest rate, $\bar{r}_p$ is the expected return on the portfolio, $\bar{r}_M$ is the expected return on the market portfolio, and σ_M the standard deviation of the return on the market portfolio. The SML applies to individual assets and requires that, in equilibrium, the expected return on asset i satisfies

$$\bar{r}_i = r_f + \beta_i\left[\bar{r}_M - r_f\right].$$

The *beta coefficient of asset i, β_i, is interpreted as a measure of the riskiness of the asset and is defined by $\beta_i = \frac{\sigma_{iM}}{\sigma_M^2}$, where σ_{iM} is the covariance of the return on asset i and the return on the market portfolio.

capital-augmenting technical progress *See* TECHNICAL PROGRESS.

capital consumption In national accounts, the amount by which gross investment exceeds net investment, i.e. the same as *replacement investment. Loss of value of capital equipment is due to use, ageing, or *obsolescence. Part of the value of the capital stock owned by an enterprise is lost in any period through wear and tear in use. The passage of time also reduces its expected remaining useful life; and it may become obsolete through advances in technology or changes in factor prices.

capital deepening An increase in *capital intensity in production, when the capital input grows faster than the labour input, and therefore the capital per worker (or per hour of labour) increases. *See also* CAPITAL WIDENING.

capital expenditure Expenditure by a company which cannot be treated as a *cost in calculating its profits. It thus has to be paid for either out of post-tax income, or by raising external finance. Capital expenditure may be on creating new capital goods, or, more often, on buying them from outside suppliers. It also includes the purchase of existing businesses, and of patents and trademarks.

capital flight Large-scale and sudden movements of capital from a country, by residents or foreigners. The causes of capital flight include concern with public disorder or persecution leading to personal danger to its owners, possibility of confiscation, drastically increased taxation, or rapid inflation leading to a loss of value by the country's currency.

capital formation The process of adding to the stock of real productive equipment of an enterprise, either by constructing it, or, more often, by buying it from outside suppliers.

capital gain An increase in the value of assets. This is the difference between their present value and the price at which they were purchased. If the general *price level is stable, real and nominal capital gains are equal. If there is general inflation of prices, capital assets show real gains only if their prices increase proportionally faster than the general price level, and assets with constant money values suffer real capital losses.

capital gains tax (CGT) A tax on increases in the value of assets. CGT is usually only collected on the realization of gains by sale or bequest; to tax unrealized capital gains would require regular valuations of all assets. In the UK capital gains tax has been levied since 1965. Only gains over some minimum sum each year (£9200 in tax year 2007–8) are liable to tax, and until recently it was levied only on proportional gains greater than the rise in the *retail price index (RPI) since an asset was acquired. Certain forms of assets, including the main residence of any taxpayer, are exempt from UK capital gains tax.

capital gearing *See* GEARING.

capital goods Goods intended for use in production of other goods or services, rather than for final consumption. Some goods, such as power stations and oil-drilling equipment, can only be capital goods. Many goods can be used for either production or consumption: cars, for example, may be used for business purposes or privately, and furniture may be used in private homes or for business purposes in hotels and restaurants. *See also* FINAL GOODS.

capital inflow *See* CAPITAL MOVEMENTS.

capital intensity The ratio of capital employed to other factors in production, usually labour, in which case it is measured as the ratio of the total value of capital equipment to the total amount of labour hired.

capitalism The economic system based on private property and private enterprise. Under this system all, or a major proportion, of economic activity is undertaken by private profit-seeking individuals or organizations, and land and other material means of production are largely privately owned. Under capitalism parts of the economy may be in public ownership. The government may impose certain regulations on the activities of the private sector regarding public health and safety, enforcement of competition, and protection of the environment. Such regulation is, however, typically negative: the rules lay down what individuals or firms may not do, but initiative about what is done within these rules is decentralized.

capital issues The main way in which new *shares come into existence. Money to fund newly floated companies, or to finance the expansion of existing ones, can be obtained by selling newly issued shares to the public. New issues are regulated by the stock exchange; in particular, firms are required to provide potential investors with a *prospectus giving information about the business's past results and forecasts of its future prospects.

capitalist A person whose income, or a significant proportion of their income, comes from the ownership of capital.

capital–labour ratio The ratio of capital to labour employed in a process, a firm, or an industry; the same as *capital intensity.

capital levy *See* CAPITAL TAX.

capital loss A fall in the price of an asset. A capital loss is incurred when the price of an asset falls below what was paid for it, and is realized when an asset is sold for less than it cost. Sale at a lower price means a nominal capital loss; a real capital loss is incurred if an asset rises in price less than in proportion to general inflation since it was acquired, and is realized if it is sold for less than its purchase price adjusted for inflation. Capital losses are sometimes allowed as deductions in calculating liability to tax; usually capital losses on some assets can be offset only against capital gains on others.

capital market The *stock exchanges and other institutions where *securities are bought and sold. The securities concerned include both shares in companies and various forms of private and public debt. The capital market allows firms, governments, and countries to finance spending in excess of their current incomes. It also enables individuals, firms, and countries to lend to others savings they cannot employ as profitably themselves. Some transactions in capital markets involve the sale of newly issued shares and debt instruments, but the vast majority occur in *secondary markets, where existing shares and debt instruments change ownership. The lack of an efficiently organized capital market may create an obstacle to the efficient use of savings, and thus to overall economic development.

capital mobility The extent to which capital can be shifted between different uses, and in particular between different countries. This is restricted in various ways. Capital in use may be entirely sunk, or it may be possible to withdraw it from its present use only gradually, as existing equipment wears out. Capital mobility is hindered by *asymmetric information: investors do not have sufficient information, or sufficient confidence that such information as they have is reliable, about opportunities in different industries or foreign countries. International capital mobility is frequently limited by government controls, in both capital-importing and capital-exporting countries. *See also* PERFECT CAPITAL MOBILITY.

capital movements Movement of capital between countries. Capital outflow (or outward capital movement) is the movement of domestically owned capital abroad; capital inflow (or inward capital movement) is the movement of foreign-owned capital into a country. Capital movements may take the form of *foreign direct investment, that is, investment in real capital assets, the purchase of shares, or long- or short-term loans. All such movements form part of the capital account of the balance of payments. *See also* SHORT-RUN CAPITAL MOVEMENTS.

capital outflow *See* CAPITAL MOVEMENTS.

capital–output ratio The ratio of the capital used in a process, a firm, or an industry to output over some period, usually a year. This ratio for any process depends on the relative cost of different inputs. Where *technology makes alternative techniques feasible, firms usually choose the cheapest, so capital–output ratios tend to be high when capital is cheap relative to other inputs. For a firm or an industry, the capital–output ratio will depend on the mix of different outputs produced and different processes used. The capital–output ratio can be measured as an average ratio, comparing total capital stock with total output, or as a marginal ratio, comparing increases in capital used with increases in output. Both average and marginal capital-output ratios are taken to refer to normal levels of working: when output is abnormally low during a *recession, the average capital–output ratio is unusually high, but the marginal capital–output ratio is unusually low.

capital reserves Part of the net assets of a company in excess of the share capital originally contributed by shareholders. Capital reserves may arise from the sale of new shares at a price above their par value, from retention of profits, from the revaluation of assets, or from capital gains made by a company. Normally, capital reserves are not distributable as dividends; this is in contrast to revenue reserves, which are available to maintain dividends in years of low current profits.

capital stock **1.** The total value of the physical capital of an enterprise, including *inventories as well as fixed equipment. This can be measured in various ways: historical cost is what the equipment originally cost to buy; written-down value is historical cost of equipment minus deductions for ageing and wear and tear in use; replacement cost is what it would cost to replace existing equipment with equivalent new items. Any of these may or may not be adjusted for inflation since the equipment was first acquired. The capital stock of an industry, region, or country is the sum of the capital stocks of enterprises in it.
2. The number of shares, including both common stock and preferred stock, that a company is authorized to issue by its corporate charter.

capital stock adjustment A theory of investment based on the *capital-output ratio. The model assumes that firms have a target capital–output ratio. If at any time actual capital stock is less than is implied by this ratio, the firm invests so as to close part of the gap during the next period. Partial adjustment is assumed, taking account of both uncertainty and costs of adjustment. Thus if Y is output and the desired capital–output ratio is a, the target capital stock is $K^* = aY$, and if the actual capital stock K is not equal to K^* then investment is $I = b(K^* - K) = b(aY - K)$, where $0 \leq b \leq 1$. As with the *accelerator model, a rise in Y increases K^* and thus leads to investment.

capital tax A tax on individuals or companies based on the value of their capital. An alternative name for this is a capital levy. Such a tax requires capital to be valued, and would be difficult to collect if it could not be paid out of income received from the capital over some short period. Most countries have thus chosen to tax either income from capital, or realized capital gains, or capital transfers, rather than capital itself.

capital transfers Transfers of assets between individuals, by gift or bequest, where the recipient regards the receipt as an addition to their capital rather than part of their income. In the UK these were subject to the *capital transfer tax, with small amounts allowed to be exempt. The capital transfer tax was replaced by the *inheritance tax in 1986.

capital transfer tax (CTT) A tax on capital transfers from one person to another by gift or bequest. Governments have two motives for using a capital transfer tax rather than a *wealth tax if they want to tax capital. First, it is argued that a CTT is less discouraging to saving than a wealth tax. A CTT is less likely than a wealth tax to be resented, and thus avoided or evaded by taxpayers. Second, a wealth tax involves the regular identification and valuation of assets. When capital is transferred, particularly by inheritance, the legal procedures involved make it easier to identify assets, which have to be valued in any case for probate purposes.

capital widening A situation when the capital stock grows at the same rate as the labour force, so that the capital–labour ratio remains constant, while the aggregate output continues to grow. *See also* CAPITAL DEEPENING.

CAPM *See* CAPITAL ASSET PRICING MODEL.

carbon tax A proposed tax on the use of fuels that emit carbon dioxide (CO_2). This is an example of a Pigouvian tax, designed to correct a negative externality, in this case the excess accumulation of CO_2 in the atmosphere which may have negative effects on world climate.

cardinal utility A *utility function that can be subjected to a positive affine transformation without altering the implied preference order. A positive affine transformation applied to the initial utility function U generates the transformed utility function $U^* = a + bU$, where $b > 0$. The utility function U is cardinal if the functions U and U^* represent the same set of underlying preferences. An example of cardinal utility is an expected utility function. *See also* INTERPERSONAL COMPARISONS; ORDINAL UTILITY.

carry forward losses The right to deduct past losses from present profits in calculating liability to tax. Most tax systems collect taxes from companies and unincorporated businesses which make profits, but do not make payments to firms making losses, presumably because it is believed that the fraudulent production of apparent losses would be too easy. This asymmetry in the treatment of profits and losses tends to discourage investment. To minimize this discouragement firms are allowed to carry forward losses. This means that if a firm has made a loss in one period, if and when it returns to profit it will be allowed to deduct the loss carried forward in calculating its *taxable income. It may thus pay a profitable business to acquire another business whose main asset is previous losses which can be carried forward for tax purposes.

cartel A formal or informal agreement between a number of firms in an industry to restrict *competition. Cartel agreements may provide for setting minimum prices, setting limits on output or capacity, restrictions on *non-price competition, division of markets between firms either geographically or in terms of type of product, or agreed measures to restrict entry to the industry. Cartels suffer from problems of enforcement, which make them liable to break down. So long as the other members of a cartel comply with the terms of a cartel agreement, it is usually beneficial for any one member to cheat, for example by giving secret price discounts or covertly exceeding quota limits on output. Enforcement of cartel agreements is made more difficult if governments regard cartels as undesirable, and make the existence of the cartels or the policies they follow either illegal, or lawful but not legally enforceable. The *Organization of Petroleum Exporting Countries is the most famous cartel of recent times. *See also* INTERNATIONAL CARTEL.

cash Literally, notes and coin; the word cash is used in economics mostly as a synonym for money in general. *See also* CASH DISCOUNT; CASH FLOW; CASH LIMITS; CASH RATIO.

cash discount A discount for prompt payment. Where goods are commonly sold on credit, it is often possible to obtain a reduction in price for prompt payment, in notes and coin, by direct debit, by cheque backed by a bank guarantee card, or by electronic transfer. Sellers are willing to offer cash discounts because immediate payment saves them both delay in receiving their money, and possible administrative costs or loss through default involved in credit sales or deferred payment.

cash flow Cash flow is the amount of cash received less the amount spent by a business or a household for a given accounting period. For a business, this is recorded in a cash flow statement that shows all sources and uses of cash from one period to the next and serves as a measure of the short-term financial health of the business. A major responsibility of the finance director of any business is to forecast its cash flow, on both current and capital account, and to ensure that the timing of receipts and payments is such that money is always available to meet any payments that have to be made. *See also* DISCOUNTED CASH FLOW.

cash limits Limits set on overall expenditure in cash terms. In particular, the use of cash limits in the public sector aims at more efficient use of government expenditures. When any government or business organization forms its spending plans, it provides its managers, who are responsible for spending, with budgets. These budgets may be specified in real or in nominal terms. The objection to budgeting in *real terms is that it leaves managers with no incentive to shop around for the best value for money in their purchases, or to resist price increases when they bargain with contractors and wage increases when they negotiate with trade unions. With cash limits, if the managers make bad bargains or are weak in wage negotiations, they will get fewer real goods and services for their departments. The disadvantage of cash limits is that if prices or wages change for reasons which are beyond the managers' control, the level of real spending will be higher or lower than the budgetary authorities intended.

cash ratio A ratio of cash or cash equivalent holdings to total liabilities of a company, bank, or other financial institution. High cash ratios are supposed to guard against the collapse of such institutions should public confidence in their ability to repay deposits fall.

catch-up In the context of economic growth this is the convergence in income per capita across countries through knowledge and technology spillovers from developed to less developed countries.

categorical variable A variable whose values are alphanumerical codes for different categories of observations or for different qualitative outcomes, which may or may not be ordered or ranked: for example, sex (male/female coded as M/F), preferred mode of transportation (cycle/bus/taxi coded as 1/2/3), opinions from a survey (say, 'strongly opposed', 'opposed', 'neutral', 'support', 'strongly support' coded as 0/1/2/3/4). When used in a regression they are recoded as 0/1, or dummy variables, with value 1 for a particular observation if it belongs to a given category and 0 if it does not.

causality (in Granger's sense) *See* GRANGER CAUSALITY.

caveat emptor Literally translated from Latin: let the buyer beware. This summarizes the principle that the buyer has to bear the risk of quality of their purchase. Considered as a legal principle, this is inconsistent with much modern legislation and many regulations designed to promote public health and safety by protecting buyers, who cannot reasonably be expected to be experts on all the products they purchase.

Cecchini Report A report on the gains expected as a result of the *'1992' programme for unifying the European Community's internal market. The report was published in 1988 as *The European Challenge, 1992*.

ceiling In trade cycle theory this is the maximum level of aggregate real output the economy can attain during the expansion, which corresponds to full employment. *See also* FLOOR.

ceiling price The highest legally permitted price of a good or service, typically intended to make basic commodities affordable for low-income consumers. An alternative price control policy is market intervention using a *buffer stock.

censored sample A sample in which observations on the dependent variable are missing or reported as a single value for a known set of values of independent variables. For example, if the demand for concert tickets in a certain concert hall is measured by the number of tickets sold, the true demand is not observed whenever some concert is sold out: in all such cases the same total number of tickets sold is reported. *See also* TOBIT MODEL.

census An official inquiry concerning the number and characteristics of the population of a given area. Censuses are normally carried out by official bodies, by means of questionnaires, reply to which is compulsory. In the UK censuses are normally held every ten years; the most recent was in 2001. Information is collected on personal characteristics such as age, sex, family status, and occupation; censuses may also collect information on other topics such as housing conditions, mobility, language, ethnic grouping, or religion.

(⊕) SEE WEB LINKS

• The guide to data from the UK 2001 census.

census of production A systematic survey of productive enterprises, normally carried out by an official body with powers to compel firms to reply to questionnaires. Information is typically collected from enterprises on topics such as the nature of their products, the quantity and types of inputs used, the number and types of employees, and value added. The results of censuses of production can be used to draw up *input–output tables for the economy.

central bank A bank which controls a country's money supply and monetary policy. It acts as a banker to other banks, and a *lender of last resort. In some countries, including the UK, the central bank is also the main regulator of other banks.

central bank independence Independence of the central bank from immediate short-run control of its aims and operations by the government. This includes independence in personnel issues, such as appointments of board members, and in the choice and control of instruments that affect inflation. Because central banks typically operate on a longer time scale than politicians, an independent central bank is expected to be better for monetary stability, while governments can sometimes be tempted into inflationary policies, for example, by boosting spending and employment or cutting interest rates to gain popularity in the short run.

central government The highest level of government in any country. Federal countries, such as Germany or the United States, have central, state, and local government, whereas unitary countries have only central and local government.

Central Limit Theorems (CLT) A number of results in statistical theory concerning the limiting distribution, under certain conditions, of the (properly scaled) sample average of random variables or random vectors, as the sample size increases to infinity. For example, the Lindeberg–Lévy CLT states that if $x_1, \ldots, x_N$ are independent, identically distributed random vectors with mean vector μ and covariance matrix Σ, then $\sqrt{N}\bar{x}$ converges in distribution to a normal random vector with mean μ and covariance matrix Σ—here

$$\bar{x} = \frac{1}{N} \sum_{i=1}^{N} x_i.$$

central planning The operation of an economy through centralized decision-taking whereby the decisions are taken at the centre and orders issued to enterprises concerning their production and investment plans. While in theory such a system should allow the use of all resources in an economy in the public interest, without wasteful duplication of effort, the amount of information required to achieve efficiency is too great, and the incentives to supply the centre with reliable information are too poor. As a result, centrally planned economies, such as those of the former Soviet Union and other Eastern European countries, were not able to perform as well as a decentralized system based on *competition between independent decision-takers, and had to abandon central planning in the late 1980s in favour of the *market economy.

Central Statistical Office The UK government department responsible up to 1996 for publishing many major UK statistical sources. These include the *National Income Accounts, Economic Trends,* and the *Balance of Payments Accounts.* In 1996 it was merged with the Office of Population Censuses and Surveys to form the *Office for National Statistics.

certainty equivalent The certain outcome which would confer a utility level equal to the *expected utility of entering a gamble. *See also* RISK PREMIUM.

certificate of origin A document certifying that a good was produced in a given country. Such certificates are necessary in *free-trade areas, where the members do not have uniform external tariffs. They are needed to confine duty-free entry to goods produced in member countries, to avoid goods from non-members being imported to the free-trade area via members with low external tariffs and re-exported to members with higher external tariffs.

CES *See* CONSTANT ELASTICITY OF SUBSTITUTION.

CET *See* COMMON EXTERNAL TARIFF.

ceteris paribus Literally translated from Latin: other things being equal. This means that other things which could change are for the moment being assumed to remain constant. The ceteris paribus assumption is made in economic reasoning to focus attention on the effect of changes in a limited set of variables of interest.

CGT *See* CAPITAL GAINS TAX.

chairman The member of a committee or *board of directors elected or appointed to preside at its meetings. The chairman frequently has a casting vote.

Chancellor of the Exchequer The UK's chief finance minister. The Chancellor is a member of the cabinet, and is in charge of *HM Treasury, the UK ministry of finance. The Chancellor is responsible for overall supervision of monetary and fiscal policy, is the government's principal economic spokesperson, and presents the *budget to parliament.

chaos theory A theory that describes the behaviour of deterministic nonlinear dynamic systems characterized by sensitivity to initial conditions. Sensitivity means that small differences in starting positions for the system result in large differences in the positions of the system achieved after a finite length of time.

Chapter 11 bankruptcy A chapter of the US bankruptcy law by which a firm can apply to the courts for protection against all creditors while it is reorganized so as to enable it to pay its debts; the debtor usually proposes a plan of such reorganization. The argument for such a provision is that it gives better results for creditors as a whole than allowing firms to be forced into *liquidation by any one creditor.

Chapters 12, 13 Chapters of the US bankruptcy law that apply to family farmers and fishermen, and private individuals respectively. The provisions of these chapters allow reorganization under supervision of the bankruptcy court with the intention of rehabilitation. This is in contrast to a Chapter 7 filing that involves *liquidation.

characteristics theory A theory of demand that views each good as a bundle of characteristics. The theory assumes that consumers do not obtain utility from goods directly but from the characteristics they contain. The characteristics contained in individual goods are aggregated into the total quantity of characteristics consumed. The theory is able to explain how changes in the specification of products and the introduction of new products affect demand. *See also* HEDONIC PRICING.

chartist A jargon name for a trader in the financial markets who uses recurring patterns in the behaviour of market variables over time to forecast their movements in the future. The name comes from the use of charts or graphs to show the past behaviour of variables such as share prices. There is a large body of empirical evidence that past asset prices do not help to predict current prices, which leaves the methods of chartists without any empirical justification.

cheap money The maintenance of low interest rates during a period of *depression to encourage investment. This policy was followed in the UK during the 1930s and 1940s. It was not very successful in stimulating investment in the 1930s, except in housing. While cheap money may have been a necessary condition for recovery, it was not a sufficient one: it was described at the time as 'trying to push on a string'. In the post-war period of widespread excess demand, cheap money merely worsened the problems which had to be tackled by *rationing and *price controls.

checking account An account with a US commercial bank which can be drawn on without notice, in cash or by writing a cheque. Until recently such accounts paid no interest. The UK equivalent is a *current account.

cheque A written order by a customer to a bank to pay cash, or to transfer money on deposit to another account. It is convenient but not legally compulsory to use a form provided by the bank for this purpose. Cheques will not normally be honoured by the bank unless the customer has a sufficient credit balance or an agreed *overdraft facility. Cheques were once convenient and very widely accepted; but they are not *legal tender, and there is no compulsion to accept them. An increasing number of businesses are not accepting cheques as the credit card becomes more ubiquitous.

Chicago Board of Trade (CBOT) A leading *futures and *options on futures exchange that was founded in 1848. The original purpose was to help the agricultural industry manage risk through the trade of agricultural commodities such as corn, wheat, oats, and soybeans. Over time futures contracts were introduced on non-storable agricultural commodities and non-agricultural products. There are currently over 3600 members who trade 50 different futures and options products. *See also* CME GROUP.

(⊕) SEE WEB LINKS
• Information about the CBOT and the products traded on the exchange.

Chicago Mercantile Exchange (CME) Founded in 1898 for trade in *futures contracts on agricultural commodities. The exchange introduced the first financial futures contracts in May 1972. *See also* CME GROUP.

(⊕) SEE WEB LINKS
• Information about the CME and the products traded.

Chicago School The collective name for the economists affiliated with the University of Chicago in the 1970s who believed in self-interest as the explanation of all economic actions, the merits of free markets, the futility of and possible harm from government attempts to control the economy, and the importance of the money supply in determining inflation.

chicken A two-player game that illustrates the potential costs of conflict. The game considers two drivers who head directly at each other on a narrow road. Each driver aims to hold their nerve and continue straight while forcing the other driver to swerve (to 'chicken out' of the conflict). If both head straight a crash is inevitable. This information is summarized in the pay-off matrix.

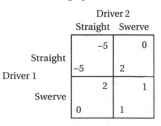

The game has two pure-strategy *Nash equilibria, {Swerve, Straight} and {Straight, Swerve}. The difficulty for the players, and the interesting feature of the game, is that the players have no method for determining which of these equilibria will apply in any particular play of the game. The players benefit from anti-coordination (two players using different strategies), but the game has no mechanism to achieve this. An alternative is to play the mixed strategy equilibrium because this is symmetric between the players. However, there is then a positive probability that the worst outcome, {Straight, Straight}, will occur.

chief executive The officer of a company or other organization responsible for seeing that decisions on principles by the *board of directors are actually implemented in day-to-day operations. The chief executive is frequently also chairman or president of a company; opinion is divided as to whether these offices are better separated or combined. The US term for this is chief executive officer (CEO).

child benefit A state payment towards the cost of maintaining children. In the UK this is paid to the parent or guardian with custody of a child, or to the mother in two-parent households.

Child Tax Credit A UK means-tested *tax credit paid to eligible families with responsibility for one or more children aged under 16. *See also* WORKING TAX CREDIT.

Chinese walls The requirement that financial firms prevent transfers of information between staff who are dealing with different clients, which could lead to conflicts of interest or to *insider dealing. For example, if department A is advising clients with funds under management to buy or sell shares in company B, it should not know what advice department C is giving to B on a takeover bid that will affect its share price.

chi-square distribution A continuous distribution, denoted $\chi^2_{(n)}$, described by the density function

$$f(x) = \frac{1}{\Gamma(n/2)2^{n/2}} x^{\frac{n}{2}-1} e^{-x/2}, 0 \le x < \infty, \ n = 1, 2 \ldots .$$

The parameter n is termed 'the degrees of freedom'. This distribution can be derived from the normal distribution and arises in econometrics as the distribution of sums of certain random variables. In particular, if z is a standard normal random variable then z^2 has $\chi^2_{(1)}$-distribution, and if $z_1, \ldots, z_n$ are independent standard normal random variables then the sum $z_1^2 + \ldots + z_n^2$ has $\chi^2_{(n)}$-distribution. A $\chi^2_{(n)}$-random variable has mean n and variance $2n$. This distribution is used for hypothesis testing in many econometric applications.

chlorofluorocarbons (CFCs) (freon) Non-toxic chemicals widely used as coolants in refrigeration and air conditioning, and as propellants in aerosols. It has been discovered that their effect in the stratosphere is to deplete the *ozone layer, posing a worldwide threat to health through admitting increased solar radiation. An international agreement to reduce their use was reached in the *Montreal Protocol in 1987; since then emissions of CFCs around the developed world have largely ceased.

choice of technique The choice of method of production where more than one method is possible. A technique is a set of inputs capable of producing a given output or set of outputs. If more than one set of inputs can produce the outputs, a choice of techniques must be made. A profit-maximizing firm prefers the technique for which the total cost of inputs is the lowest.

cif *See* COST, INSURANCE, AND FREIGHT.

circular flow of income In *Keynesian economics this is a simple model of a static economy, based on the assumption of a one-period lag between income and expenditure. If there were neither *injections of new purchasing power into this flow nor *leakages out of it, total income in each period would be equal to the spending arising from incomes in the previous period, and total income would remain constant over time. Injections of new purchasing power not derived from last period's income can be made by investment, government spending, or exports. Leakages from the circular flow, by which this period's income does not lead to incomes next period, are caused by saving, tax payments, or imports. If injections and leakages are equal, incomes will be constant; if injections exceed leakages, incomes rise over time; and if leakages exceed injections, incomes fall.

CITES *See* CONVENTION ON INTERNATIONAL TRADE IN ENDANGERED SPECIES.

City The City of London financial district, or 'square mile'. This area includes the *Bank of England, the *London Stock Exchange, *Lloyd's, and the headquarters of many UK banks, insurance companies, and other financial institutions. It also contains branches of many foreign and international banks and financial institutions. 'The City' is also used to stand for the people working there in the financial sector.

City Code The City Code on Takeovers and Mergers. This was originated in 1968 by a takeover panel under the auspices of the *Bank of England. It lays down a code of conduct for *takeovers and *mergers; the objective is to ensure that all investors are given equal access to full information and fair advice. The code is not actually law, but bears a similar relation to correct City practice as the Highway Code does to safe driving.

claimant A person applying for any benefit from the state. Benefits, for example unemployment, sickness, or disability benefit, need to be claimed for two possible reasons. In some cases the person has a clear legal right to the benefit, but the civil servants administering the *benefits system need to be informed of the facts. In other cases payment of the benefit is discretionary: in this case the claimant has both to establish the facts and to convince the administrator that he or she has a good case for receiving the benefit. Claimants' associations exist to help claimants to understand what benefits they are entitled to, or eligible to apply for, and to advise them on the procedures for claiming these benefits.

classical dichotomy The view in *classical economics and *neoclassical economics that real variables in the economy are determined purely by real factors and not by monetary factors, and nominal variables are determined purely by monetary factors and not by real ones. This view is rejected by Keynesian and monetarist economics, mainly through the argument of *sticky prices: if prices fail to adjust in the short run, an increase in the money supply raises aggregate demand and thus alters real macroeconomic variables.

classical economics The economic analysis of the 18th and 19th centuries associated with Thomas Malthus (1766–1834), John Stuart Mill (1806–1873), David Ricardo (1772–1823), and Adam Smith (1723–1790). Classical economics represents the genesis of modern economic analysis; it provided lasting insights into the efficiency of competition, the process of growth, and the theory of value.

classical model A model of the economy in which it is assumed that prices, wages, and interest rates are flexible, so that in equilibrium all markets clear. In such an economy factors are fully employed, and the growth of output depends on the growth of available factor supplies.

classical unemployment Unemployment caused by wages being too high relative to productivity, so that the firms in an economy cannot profitably employ all the labour on offer at these real wages. This type of unemployment can be reduced by a policy aimed at reducing the real wage rate, e.g. tax policies, or by improving productivity, e.g. through education and training.

Clayton Act A US act of 1914 extending federal antitrust law. It forbade price discrimination, tying arrangements and exclusive dealing, and the acquisition of another corporation's stock where this led to monopoly or decreased competition. The act allowed triple damages to those injured by breaches of antitrust law. Labour unions and agricultural associations were exempted from antitrust actions.

Clean Air Act Legislation setting standards for atmospheric pollution. In the US this requires the *Environmental Protection Agency to set air quality standards for pollutants, and to issue guidelines for control of emissions.

clean floating exchange rate *See* PURE FLOATING EXCHANGE RATE.

clearing The system for settling payments due from one bank to another. There are numerous *commercial banks, and in most transactions settled by a transfer of bank balances from buyer to seller, the two parties hold accounts with different banks. The inter-bank clearing process is an arrangement to reduce the amount of funds which needs to be transferred to settle all these payments. All the cheques are sent to a *clearing-house, where the amounts payable to and from the customers of each bank are added up. Each bank then needs to make a payment to other banks only if total payments by its customers exceed total payments to them, and the bank need receive a payment only if the total receipts of its customers exceed their total payments. The actual settlement is normally done daily, by the transfer of balances held by the various banks with a central bank.

clearing bank A bank which is a member of the *clearing-house. Most large banks in the UK are clearing-house members; banks which are not members have to use a clearing bank as their agent to get their cheques cleared.

clearing-house An institution where claims by various banks against each other are offset. This greatly reduces the need for transfers of funds between banks, as each bank need only remit the net excess of its gross payments out over gross payments in, or receive the net excess of payments in over payments out.

cliometrics The application of quantitative methods to the analysis of economic history.

close company A company with very few members. In the UK a close company is one with five or fewer participants or directors, or one where five or fewer participants or directors would be entitled to more than 50 percent of the assets in the event of *winding up.

closed economy A form of *autarchy; an economy without contacts with the rest of the world by means of trade and movement of capital and labour. Examples of economies that existed as autarchies during certain periods in their history are Japan between the 1600s and the 1850s, Spain in the 1940s and 1950s, Albania in the late 1970s to mid-1980s, and currently North Korea; however, in almost all such cases some trade with neighbouring countries took place. A model of a closed economy is used in many theoretical applications as an abstraction, when the introduction of the outside trade, as well as the movement of capital and labour, may complicate the analysis without affecting the main issue under consideration.

closed shop The requirement that all workers of certain grades in a given business or establishment belong to a recognized *trade union.

closing prices Prices in a stock or commodity exchange at the end of a day's trading.

club An institution formed to supply an excludable *public good. The defining feature of a club is that it can exclude non-members from the use of its facilities. Exclusion permits a price to be charged for membership which allows efficient provision of the public good by the club to its members. The concept of a club has wide application, from the analysis of sports clubs to the study of international organizations such as NATO. *See also* SAMUELSON RULE; TIEBOUT HYPOTHESIS.

Club of Rome A global think tank involving natural scientists, economists, business people, senior civil servants, heads of state, and former heads of state. The basic premise of the club is that 'each human being can contribute to the improvement of our societies'.

( ) SEE WEB LINKS
• The official website of the Club of Rome.

clustering The tendency of firms in certain industries to concentrate in areas where there are other firms of a similar type. This enables them to use the services of related industries providing inputs of goods and services, and possibly to gain from the training provided by other firms in a cluster by poaching their skilled labour force. This is held to explain the tendency of industries to concentrate in particular areas, for example Silicon Valley in California, with a high density of electronics and computer-based industries, and the M4 corridor in England. Economic development agencies often aim at the creation of new clusters; this is sometimes difficult to achieve, as it involves simultaneous investment in various industries and forms of technical education.

CME Group The exchange that provides the widest range of *futures and *options products. CME Group was formed in 2007 through the merger of the *Chicago Board of Trade and the *Chicago Mercantile Exchange.

( ) SEE WEB LINKS
• The home page of CME Group.

coalition A group of individuals or firms who have separate objectives, but combine to adopt strategies or advocate policies. A coalition government is one relying on the support of two or more political parties. A coalition may be unstable and eventually dissolve or collapse with the emergence of new situations or policy issues that have different impacts on its members, whenever the members of the coalition are interested in exploring the possibility that an alternative alliance might enable them to achieve more of their own objectives.

Coase theorem The argument that *externalities can be corrected by the market. Formally, the theorem states that in a competitive economy with symmetric information and zero transaction costs, the allocation of resources will be efficient and invariant with respect to legal rules of entitlement, or *property rights. The implication of the theorem is that there is no need for policy intervention with regard to externalities except to ensure that property rights are clearly defined and protected.

Cobb–Douglas function A functional form, named after its originators, that is widely used in both theoretical economics and applied economics as both a *production function and a *utility function. Denote aggregate output by Y, the input of capital by K, and the input of labour by L. The Cobb–Douglas production function is then given by

$$Y = AK^{\alpha}L^{\beta}$$

where A, α, and β are positive constants. If $\alpha + \beta = 1$ this function has constant returns to scale: if K and L are each multiplied by any positive constant λ then Y will also be multiplied by λ. The Cobb–Douglas production function has also been applied at the level of the individual firm. With this production function, a cost-minimizing firm will spend a proportion α of its total costs on capital and a proportion β on labour. When the Cobb–Douglas function is applied as a *utility function the inputs, K and L, are replaced by the consumption levels of two types of good, say, X and Y. With this utility function a utility-maximizing consumer will spend a proportion α of their budget on good X and a proportion β on good Y. The Cobb–Douglas function can also be extended to include three or more arguments.

cobweb A model used to illustrate the situation in which time lags in the response of one variable (e.g. supply) to a change in another variable (e.g. price) may introduce fluctuations into the economy. The cobweb is also known as the hog cycle following its use in explaining the observed pattern of hog prices. Depending on the parameters of the model, the fluctuations may increase (unstable cobweb), decrease (stable cobweb), or remain constant (trivial cycle) in magnitude

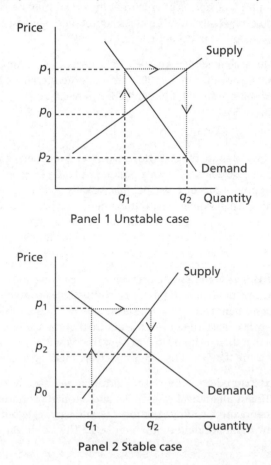

Panel 1 Unstable case

Panel 2 Stable case

Cobwebs

from period to period. The underlying assumption for this kind of behaviour is *adaptive expectations of economic agents (producers in the figure), rather than *rational expectations.

Cochrane–Orcutt procedure A two-step estimation of a linear regression model with first-order serial correlation in the errors. In the first step the first-order *autocorrelation coefficient is estimated using the *ordinary least squares residuals from the main regression equation. In the second step this estimate is used to rescale the variables so that the regression in terms of rescaled variables has no serial correlation in the errors. This is an example of *feasible generalized least squares estimation.

coefficient of determination In a linear regression model, this is the proportion of sample variation in the dependent variable explained by the regression. It is denoted by R^2 and is equal to the squared *correlation coefficient between the observed values of the dependent variable and the values predicted by the estimated regression equation. The coefficient of determination is only meaningful if the regression contains an intercept term.

coefficient of variation The *standard deviation of a random variable as a percentage of its *mean.

coin Money consisting of solid tokens, typically of metal. Coins were originally made of precious metals, usually *gold or silver, and were imprinted with patterns such as the sovereign's portrait to certify that their weight and fineness had been tested and approved. Sovereigns discovered that they could make profits by debasing the coinage, so that the material was of less value than the face value of the coin. This led to the rise of *token money, which does not claim to have intrinsic value. Since the rise of paper money, coinage has been largely used as small change. In a modern economy coins form only a small part of the total money supply. While the material costs are low, the processing costs of minting low-denomination coins mean that they may cost more to produce than their face value.

coincidence of wants When two parties each hold goods that the other party wishes to have. This is the condition for a *barter transaction to be agreed upon. In the absence of money, if an agent wants to trade good A for good B, they have to find another agent willing to trade good B for good A. This is achieved when there is a coincidence of wants. The inconvenience of this led to the rise of professional traders, acquiring goods they did not want for themselves but could exchange again, and to the use of money as a *medium of exchange.

co-insurance The sharing of risk between the insurer and the insured. Co-insurance arises when an insurance policy covers only a proportion of total losses. In such a case the insured does not receive full compensation for any loss so bears part of the risk. This is often desirable since cover for the entire loss may create a *moral hazard: the insured would take too few precautions to avoid the risk, for example of fire or motor accidents.

cointegration Two or more series of non-stationary random variables are cointegrated if there exists a stationary linear combination of these variables.

Cointegrated series 'drift together' at roughly the same rate. More generally, if series X and Y are both integrated of order b, denoted $I(b)$, and $Z = Y - \beta X$ is $I(d)$ with $d < b$ for some constant β, then X and Y are cointegrated with the order of cointegration $(b - d)$; if $(b - d)$ is a fraction then X and Y are fractionally cointegrated.

collateral A valuable article or property pledged as the security for a loan. In *mortgages, land or buildings are used as collateral; share certificates or life insurance policies with a surrender value are used as collateral for *bank loans; in pawnbroking the collateral pledged can be any portable valuable. If payments of interest and repayments of the principal are not made on time, in the last resort the lender can sell the collateral asset. This makes loans with collateral much safer for lenders than loans without collateral. When credit markets are imperfect, because of *asymmetric information, individuals or firms who cannot offer collateral find it difficult and expensive to obtain loans.

collective bargaining The system by which wage rates, hours, and conditions of employment in a firm or an industry are decided by negotiation between *trade unions representing the employees and employers or employers' associations.

collective choice The process of aggregating individual preferences into social preferences in order to make a social (or collective) choice from a set of alternatives. The most frequently encountered collective choice process is *majority voting. Alternatives to majority voting include the *Borda count (if there are n alternatives then each voter's first choice is given n points, the second choice $n - 1$, and so on; the alternative with the most points is chosen) and approval voting (each voter can vote for any number of options; the option with the most votes is chosen). Collective choice also refers to the branch of economics that studies the properties of these processes. Two fundamental results are the *median voter theorem and May's theorem. The latter determines that majority voting is the only process to satisfy a set of desirable conditions when a choice must be made from just two alternatives. When there are more than two alternatives the *Condorcet paradox shows that majority voting can lead to intransitive social preferences. It is then not possible to select a preferred alternative. The failure of majority voting to function perfectly in all circumstances is representative of a general failure of collective choice processes. *Arrow's impossibility theorem proves that there is no perfect collective choice process that can aggregate all possible individual preferences in all circumstances. An alternative perspective views collective choice being made through a *social welfare function that has individual utility levels as arguments. A collective choice is made by confronting the alternatives with the social welfare function and choosing the option yielding the highest level of welfare. If *interpersonal comparisons of utility cannot be made then the construction of a social welfare function faces the same impossibility as any other collective choice process. *See also* PARADOX OF VOTING; VOTING.

Collector of Taxes A UK official responsible for the collection of *direct taxes on individuals and businesses. The collector does not fix the amount payable; this is decided by an *Inspector of Taxes.

collinearity *See* MULTICOLLINEARITY.

collusion Action in concert without any formal agreement. For example, firms may refrain from undercutting each other's prices, or from selling in each other's market areas. Collusion is common when anti-monopoly legislation makes explicit agreements illegal or unenforceable. Its existence is extremely difficult to prove.

command economy An economy operated by *central planning.

commercial bank A bank dealing with the general public, accepting deposits from and making loans to large numbers of households and small firms. Such banks are known in the UK as retail or high street banks. They also provide various services for depositors, including provision of cash and credit cards, storage facilities for valuables and documents, foreign exchange, stockbroking, mortgage finance, and executor services.

commercial bill *See* BILL.

commercial policy The government policies affecting foreign trade. This covers the use of *tariffs, trade subsidies, *quotas, *voluntary export restraint agreements, and other *non-tariff barriers to trade, restrictions on rights of establishment for foreign businesses, and the regulation of international trade in services such as insurance. The issues of commercial policy between governments are often negotiated through the *World Trade Organization or regional groups such as the *European Union or the *North American Free Trade Agreement as well as directly, in bilateral or multilateral agreements. *See also* PROTECTIONISM.

commission A payment for the services of an agent or intermediary in a transaction. This payment can be a fixed amount or an increasing function of the value of the transaction. Commission may be payable by the buyer, the seller, or both; examples of agents working on a commission basis include sales staff, estate agents, stockbrokers, and auctioneers.

commitment A promise by governments or central bankers about future policies. Commitment, sometimes pre-commitment, promises that monetary or fiscal policies will not be changed, or that if policy changes are needed they will take specified forms. This may not be fully credible if in the future a change in the economy creates incentives for the government to renege on their promises. *See also* CREDIBILITY.

commodity A standardized good, which is traded in bulk and whose units are interchangeable. Commodities are mostly the output of the *primary sector, that is, agriculture and mining, or semi-processed products. Because these goods are standardized, commodity markets can trade spot goods by sample, and can trade in *futures and *forward contracts in commodities. *See also* SPOT MARKET; STANDARDIZED COMMODITY.

commodity agreement An agreement among producing countries, or among producing and consuming countries, to regulate the output and price of a particular commodity and/or to provide relevant information, in order to improve the functioning of the global market for this commodity. Producers may agree to limit exports through a quota arrangement, by stockpiling production, or by reducing output or plantings. Such agreements are overseen by the *United Nations Conference on Trade and Development.

Commodity Credit Corporation (CCC) A US federal agency set up in 1933 to provide price support for US farmers. Federal Treasury money is used to lend to farmers on the security of their crops; the loans and accumulated interest can be settled by delivery of the crops at support prices. The CCC sells the resulting stocks later if and when prices rise.

(⊕) SEE WEB LINKS

• The home page of the Commodity Credit Corporation.

commodity exchange *See* COMMODITY MARKET.

commodity market A place or institution through which commodities are traded. *Markets were originally places or buildings, where traders could come together, which facilitated comparisons of price and quality. Non-standardized commodities such as fish and fresh vegetables, which need to be physically inspected, are often still traded in such markets; in other cases names such as the 'Corn Exchange' commemorate former physical centres which have been replaced by systems of traders linked by telephones and computers. Commodity markets include both *spot markets, where goods are traded for immediate delivery, and *forward and futures markets, where prices are agreed in advance for delivery at various dates in the future. Such trading is facilitated by market conventions on the specification and quality of the goods traded, and systems for adjudicating disputes. These are clearly essential for spot trades where the buyers do not physically inspect what they are getting, and even more so for forward and futures trading, where it is impossible to inspect crops which have not yet been grown or minerals which have not yet been mined.

commodity price index A price index of the prices of commodities, mainly agricultural and mineral products traded in bulk. Commodity price indices are used as *leading indicators of economic fluctuations.

common access resource A resource, or good, whose characteristics make it costly to exclude potential consumers from its usage, and which is vulnerable to congestion and overuse. In this sense it is an *impure public good. An example is a lake that can be used by any fisherman, or a field that can be used for grazing by any farmer. The *tragedy of the commons describes the inefficient equilibrium that results from overuse.

Common Agricultural Policy (CAP) The *European Union (EU) policy towards agriculture. This includes a *price support scheme which has led to excess production. As the supported prices are generally above world market levels, there is also an external tariff, and export subsidies are used to enable surplus products to be exported. Various grants to farmers are also available. The CAP absorbs up to two-thirds of total EU expenditure, raises the cost of living for EU consumers, damages non-EU farmers, and created great difficulties in reaching agreement in the *Uruguay Round of world trade talks.

common external tariff The tariff charged on trade with non-members by all countries in a *customs union or *common market. When used with capitals, Common External Tariff normally refers to the external tariff of the *European Union.

common market A fully integrated market area with complete freedom of internal trade, as in a *customs union, and free labour and capital mobility. The European Union is an example of a common market. Full mobility of labour involves the right to reside and accept employment in all member countries, and mutual recognition of professional and technical qualifications, subject to satisfying local language requirements. Full *capital mobility requires lack of exchange controls, and full rights of establishment for firms in all countries.

commons *See* COMMON ACCESS RESOURCE.

common stock The equity capital of a US corporation. Holders of common stock are entitled to attend and vote at general meetings, to receive declared dividends, and to receive their share of the residual assets, if any, if the corporation is wound up. Common stock corresponds to *ordinary shares in UK companies.

Commonwealth The Commonwealth of Nations is a confederation of 53 member nations that were formerly members of the British Empire (Mozambique is the exception), and was formerly known as the British Commonwealth. The appointed head of the Commonwealth is Queen Elizabeth II. The Declaration of Commonwealth Principles issued in 1971 stresses the need to foster international peace and security, democracy, liberty of the individual, and equal rights for all, and also the importance of eradicating poverty, ignorance, and disease; it opposes all forms of racial discrimination.

communism A theory of classless society with common ownership of property and wealth and centrally planned production and distribution based on the principle 'from everyone according to their skills, to everyone according to their needs'.

community charge A UK system of local taxation introduced in 1990 for England and Wales (1989 for Scotland). It consisted of a flat rate charge per adult inhabitant of each local authority, with some exemptions, for example the disabled, and lower rates for low income earners. This tax, nicknamed the poll tax by its opponents, proved to be unpopular and difficult to collect, and was replaced in 1993 by the *council tax, based largely on property values.

community indifference curve In international trade theory, a member of the family of indifference curves representing the tastes of a country, and sometimes the country's well-being. The use of community indifference curves is legitimate as long as the community preferences are well-defined, which requires certain assumptions on the preferences and incomes of the individual consumers.

company A form of organization for a business, with a legal personality distinct from the individuals taking part in it. This has been found essential in organizing large and complex businesses. The formation of companies is controlled by the state. At various times in the UK, companies have been formed by royal charter, act of Parliament, or registration with an official *Registrar of Companies. A company is empowered to own assets, incur debts, and enter into *contracts, and may be sued and taxed. It may or may not have *limited liability for its shareholders: without limited liability shareholders are in the last resort responsible for meeting the company's debts; with it, they are liable only to the extent of any unpaid part of the book value of their shares. Under the UK Companies Acts there are three classes of company: private companies with unlimited liability, private companies with limited liability, and *public limited companies (PLCs). Private companies can place restrictions on the transfer of their shares, and cannot offer them to the general public. All UK companies are required to provide financial information to their shareholders, the Registrar of Companies, and HM Revenue and Customs, the obligations of PLCs being the most stringent. Further obligations on disclosure are required to qualify for listing of company shares so that they can be traded on stock exchanges. A company is governed by a *board of directors, elected at an *annual general meeting of its ordinary shareholders. *See also* CLOSE COMPANY; HOLDING COMPANY; JOINT-STOCK COMPANY; LIMITED COMPANY; MULTINATIONAL; PRIVATE COMPANY; QUOTED COMPANY; SHELL COMPANY; STATE-OWNED COMPANY.

company director A member of a company's *board of directors. Directors may be executive, that is, full- or part-time employees of the company, or non-executive. Non-executive directors are chosen either for their specialized knowledge and experience, or because their title or reputation is thought to confer respectability. The duties of directors are laid down by law, and their qualifications in the UK are laid down in the Company Directors Disqualification Act.

company law The law relating to the formation and operation of *companies. Laws are necessary for the existence of companies, which are artificial persons whose rights and obligations exist only in a legal framework provided by the state. Company law lays down the rights and duties of directors and shareholders, and determines the extent of *limited liability for a company's debts, and the amount of information a company is obliged to provide for its shareholders, the *Registrar of Companies, and the tax authorities.

company taxation The system for taxing company *profits. Two systems are possible. In the classical system the company is taxed as an independent entity; any *dividends have to be paid out of post-tax company income, and are taxed again as the income of shareholders. In the *imputation system, company profits are taxed as though they were the income of shareholders, and dividends are not then taxed again. The argument against the classical system is that it impedes capital mobility between companies, as income left in the company where it is earned is taxed much less than income distributed as dividends and then reinvested in another company. The UK used the imputation system until 1999.

comparability *See* INTERPERSONAL COMPARISONS.

comparative advantage A country is said to have a comparative advantage in production of a good if it has lower *opportunity costs in producing this good compared to another country or the rest of the world. If countries specialize in the production of those goods in which they have a comparative advantage then free trade improves production and consumption efficiency by increasing aggregate output with the same amount of resources and expanding the choice for consumers. *See also* ABSOLUTE ADVANTAGE.

comparative costs *Comparative advantage expressed in terms of costs. The comparative costs of a good are low in a country which has a comparative advantage in producing it, and high in a country with a comparative disadvantage.

comparative statics The analysis of how the *equilibrium position in an economic model would change if the values of the exogenously fixed parameters of the model were altered. Such alterations can involve exogenously given quantities, for example a country's population, or parameters describing behaviour, for example the propensity to save. 'Comparative' indicates that two or more equilibrium states of the economy are being compared. 'Statics' indicates that each state is simply considered as an equilibrium and that transition between equilibria is not analysed.

compensated demand (Hicksian demand) Demand for a good expressed as a function of prices and utility. Compensated demand functions are obtained by the minimization of expenditure subject to the achievement of a given level of utility. Assume there are two goods consumed in quantities x_1 and x_2 with prices p_1 and p_2. Represent the preferences of the consumer by the *utility function $U = U(x_1, x_2)$. The compensated demand functions for the two goods are obtained as the solution to

$$\min p_1 x_1 + p_2 x_2 \text{ subject to } U(x_1, x_2) \geq U$$

where U is the utility level that must be achieved. The structure of the minimization shows that the compensated demand functions can be written in the form $x_i = h_i(p_1, p_2, U)$, $i = 1, 2$. *See also* MARSHALLIAN DEMAND.

compensating variation The amount of additional income needed to restore an individual's original level of utility following a change in the economic environment. For example, the change in the economic environment can be an increase in the price of a good, or the provision of a local park. In the first case the compensating variation will be positive and in the second case the compensating variation will be negative (assuming the consumer enjoys the good and the park). Formally, denote initial prices by p^0, prices after some change by p^1, and initial utility by U^0. Using the *expenditure function the compensating variation, CV, is given by

$$CV = E(p^1, U^0) - E(p^0, U^0).$$

See also EQUIVALENT VARIATION.

compensating wage differential A differential in wages intended to compensate workers for special non-pecuniary aspects of a job. Examples would be extra pay for work with hazardous substances or involving unsocial hours.

compensation for externalities The payment of compensation by those causing adverse *externalities to the victims. There are two different points involved here. The economic benefit of 'making the polluter pay' is that it creates an incentive to avoid creating pollution, unless avoiding it is too expensive to be worthwhile. This internalizes the externality concerned, and makes for economic efficiency, whether or not the charge the polluter pays goes to the victims of pollution. Where these are widely diffused it may be impossible or too expensive to identify and compensate them. Compensating the victims may be appealing on grounds of *equity, but is irrelevant to efficiency. It may indeed create inefficiency: if the victims could have avoided being damaged at low cost by changing their own conduct, getting compensation for actual damage may lead to too little evasive action being taken. On efficiency grounds, if the victims of externalities are compensated at all, it should only be for unavoidable damage. *See also* POLLUTER PAYS PRINCIPLE.

compensation principle The welfare criterion that a change in the economy is beneficial if the gainers could afford to compensate the losers. This is known as the Hicks–Kaldor principle, from its originators. It is subject to the criticism that if the gainers could afford to compensate the losers, but do not in fact do so, and the new distribution of real incomes and structure of relative prices are different from the old, the same criterion could sometimes be passed by a change back to the old situation.

competition **1.** The situation when anybody who wants to buy or sell has a choice of possible suppliers or customers. *See also* CUT-THROAT COMPETITION; POTENTIAL COMPETITION; UNFAIR COMPETITION.
  2. The formal assumption in economic modelling of every agent acting as a *price-taker. *See also* PERFECT COMPETITION.
  3. The notion of two or more economic agents engaged in strategic interaction and pursuing individual gain. *See also* BERTRAND COMPETITION; COURNOT COMPETITION; IMPERFECT COMPETITION; MONOPOLISTIC COMPETITION; NON-PRICE COMPETITION.

Competition Commission (CC) A UK body set up in 1998 to replace the *Monopolies and Mergers Commission and the *Restrictive Practices Court, with the same aims: controlling monopoly and encouraging competition. The CC is empowered to investigate situations of market domination, where an existing firm or group of firms acting in concert has 40 percent or more of a market, and mergers where a proposed merged firm would have more than 25 percent of a market. It can also investigate restrictive practices or illegal collusion referred to it by the *Office of Fair Trading (OFT). The decisions of the CC are only recommendations; where breaches of current laws are concerned, enforcement is dealt with by the OFT; new legislation, or prohibition of rejected merger proposals, is up to the government.

(⊕) SEE WEB LINKS

• The official website of the Competition Commission.

competition policy Government policy to encourage competition. This may be concerned with the structure of industries, or with the behaviour of firms within them. As regards the structure of industries, governments have sometimes favoured monopolies, as with the UK postal service, or regulated entry, as with telephones, television, and public transport, and have sometimes restricted them via monopoly legislation and the setting up of the UK *Monopolies and Mergers Commission, now the *Competition Commission. As regards the conduct of firms, governments have legislated against various practices which were thought to inhibit competition, including retail price maintenance, exclusive dealing, and refusal to supply. In the UK the *Office of Fair Trading is responsible for enforcing these rules. On the other hand, governments have supported self-regulatory bodies, which are sometimes held to operate against competition between firms in their industries and against entrants to them. *See also* ANTITRUST.

competitive advantage An advantage a firm possesses over its competitors. There are numerous sources of competitive advantage, including more efficient production techniques, brand image, consumer loyalty, and location. Possession of a competitive advantage should deliver a firm a higher level of profit than obtained by its rivals.

competitive devaluation Attempts by two or more countries to improve their competitive position relative to the others by devaluing their currencies. For each country, *devaluation gives at least a temporary cost advantage, which improves the competitiveness of domestic firms. They can either maintain their prices in domestic currency and cut their foreign currency prices, or raise their prices in domestic currency and use the revenue gained to improve the quality of their products. Each country only retains the advantage thus gained until the next competitor devalues.

competitive economy An economy in which all economic agents treat prices as given when making economic choices. The analysis of the competitive economy has proved fundamental to the development of the current understanding of how economies function. *See also* ARROW–DEBREU ECONOMY; COMPETITION; FUNDAMENTAL THEOREMS OF WELFARE ECONOMICS.

competitive equilibrium Equilibrium in an economy with competitive markets. It is described by a set of prices and an allocation of commodities such that: each agent maximizes their objective subject to resource and technology constraints, and all markets clear. *See also* EXISTENCE OF EQUILIBRIUM.

competitiveness The ability to compete in markets for goods or services. This is based on a combination of price and quality. With equal quality and an established reputation, suppliers are competitive only if their prices are as low as those of rivals. A new supplier without an established reputation may need a lower price than rivals to compete. With lower quality than rivals, a firm may not be competitive even with a low price; with a reputation for superior quality, a supplier may be competitive even with a higher price than rivals. Similar propositions apply to a country's exports.

competitive tendering The system of purchasing goods or services by inviting bids or 'tenders' and choosing the supplier from among the bids received. Other things being equal, the cheapest tender will be chosen, but purchasers will also be guided by their views on the technical and financial capacity of the bidders to deliver the goods and services reliably. Competitive tendering is also used in selecting applicants to run *franchises or *contracted-out public services.

complementarity A relation between two goods or services in which a rise in the price of one decreases demand for the other, because these goods are often purchased and/or used together, e.g. car tyres and petrol. *See also* SUBSTITUTE.

complementary goods *See* COMPLEMENTARITY.

compliance costs The costs to a firm of complying with laws and regulations affecting the markets it trades in. This may include extra record-keeping, using extra staff to maintain *Chinese walls between departments, and employing compliance officers to monitor the behaviour of other members of staff. Compliance with the requirements of tax authorities imposes significant costs on many businesses.

composite commodity A set of goods whose relative prices do not change, so that they can be treated as a single commodity. The concept of a composite commodity is used as a simplifying device in demand analysis.

compound interest The interest on a loan that itself earns interest in later periods, i.e. the interest due each period is added to the amount outstanding. Thus, at an interest rate of $100r$ percent per period, after 1 period an original loan of A amounts to $A(1 + r)$; after 2 periods to $A(1 + r)^2$; and after N periods to $A(1 + r)^N$. These successive values form a geometric progression with common ratio $(1 + r)$. With continuously compounded interest the amount of loan is an exponential function of time, Ae^{rt}.

computable general equilibrium model A general equilibrium model of the economy so specified that all equations in it can be solved analytically or numerically. Computable general equilibrium models are used to analyse the economy-wide effects of changes in particular parameters or policies.

computerized trading Use of a computer programme to track various pieces of market information, such as share or commodity prices, and to execute specified trades if certain conditions are observed.

concentration The extent to which a market is dominated by a limited number of firms. The commonest ways of measuring concentration are the *N-firm concentration ratio and the *Herfindahl index. *See also* EXPORT CONCENTRATION.

concentration ratio *See* N-FIRM CONCENTRATION RATIO.

concert party A group of investors acting in collusion in stock exchange transactions, for example buying shares to secure a *takeover. This may be done to avoid attracting attention and to evade disclosure requirements.

conciliation Resolving disputes by producing an agreement acceptable to all parties. This function may be performed by the parties themselves, or by a neutral intermediary, such as the UK's *Advisory, Conciliation and Arbitration Service. Conciliation may work by persuading some parties that their demands are impossible, or that the fears of other parties are reasonable. It often works by subdividing the points in dispute, so that compromise can be reached by each side giving way on issues which do not matter much to them in return for gains on points they consider vital. Conciliation may also work by producing verbal formulae that each party accepts on a different interpretation; this, however, does not resolve the real disputes, and may store up trouble for later.

conditional distribution For two jointly distributed random variables X and Y the conditional distribution of Y given X is the distribution of Y when X takes particular values. For discrete random variables it is given by

$$P[Y = y \mid X = x] = P[X = x, Y = y]/P[X = x].$$

For continuous random variables, the conditional density function is given by

$$f(y \mid x) = f(x, y)/f(x)$$

where $f(x, y)$ is the joint density function, and $f(x)$ is the marginal density function of X.

conditionality The practice by which the *International Monetary Fund (IMF) makes its loans conditional on the borrowing country adopting an approved *adjustment programme or policy package. Conditionality is justified on the argument that the IMF has limited total resources, and that there is no point in using them in cases when a country's trade or macroeconomic policies make it unlikely that their balance-of-payments problems can be solved even with an IMF loan.

Condorcet paradox The observation that the preference order resulting from pairwise majority voting can be intransitive. Assume there are three options x, y, and z, and three individuals A, B, and C. Assume the individuals rank the alternatives as follows (preferred option given first): A: x, y, z; B: y, z, x; and C: z, x, y. If a vote is taken over the pair x and y then x will win with a majority of two votes against one. Similarly, y will defeat z, and z will defeat x. The preference order obtained from the voting process is cyclical, and therefore intransitive. The Condorcet paradox was an early example of *Arrow's impossibility theorem. *See also* COLLECTIVE CHOICE.

Confederation of British Industry (CBI) A federation of UK companies, mainly from the manufacturing sector. The CBI was founded in 1965; it collects information from members, and lobbies government on their behalf on matters such as economic policy, tax rules, employment legislation, competition policy, and industrial standards.

(⊕) SEE WEB LINKS

• Information on the CBI and access to publications and reports.

confidence interval An estimation rule that produces with a given probability, when applied to repeated samples, intervals containing the true value of the unknown parameter.

congestion A situation when too many consumers are trying to use the same *impure public good simultaneously, and, as a result, the benefit to each user of this public good is reduced. Examples of impure public goods that may suffer from congestion are parks and roads. Congestion is a negative *externality: while drivers on crowded roads, for example, are themselves inconvenienced, a cost they bear themselves, they also cause delay, higher fuel costs, and a greater chance of accidents to other road users.

conglomerate A business conducting activities in different industries with very little in common. *See also* CONGLOMERATE MERGER.

conglomerate merger A merger between firms which operate in different sectors of the economy. Such a merger offers no economies of scale except possibly in raising finance, but tends to reduce riskiness in so far as the component businesses are exposed to independent sources of fluctuation in profits.

conjectural variation A model of an *oligopoly in which each firm forms expectations about their rival's reaction (or variation) to this firm's potential change in action. Various standard models, such as Cournot, Bertrand, and Stackelberg oligopolies, as well as competition and joint profit maximization, can be derived as particular cases from the first-order conditions of the conjectural variation model for certain values of the parameters.

conservative central banker A central banker with a higher valuation of price stability relative to activity levels than the average for a country's population. Because a conservative central banker can acquire a reputation for anti-inflationary policies, appointing such a central banker may allow a country a more favourable trade-off between employment levels and price stability than could be achieved with a central banker whose preferences coincide with those of an average citizen.

conservative social welfare function A method of evaluating economic changes which puts more weight on reductions in welfare than on increases. The extreme form of this is the Pareto criterion by which nobody must lose, but less extreme forms are common. Policy-makers are well aware that resentment for injuries is more intense and more persistent than gratitude for favours. Many protectionist policies can best be justified on the grounds that they prevent losses by particular groups, regardless of the cost to other people. Where a utilitarian would favour any change which gave a larger gain to a poorer group than it caused losses to a richer one, a policy-maker with a conservative social welfare function might resist it.

consistent estimator An estimator that converges in probability to the true value of the estimated parameter.

consolidated accounts The combined *accounts of all the members of a group of companies. Such accounts show the profits and losses, assets, and liabilities of the group as a whole, netting out any transfers of income and any debts between them. The parent companies of groups are required to produce and file consolidated accounts.

Consols UK government undated securities. The name is short for Consolidated Fund Annuities; the Consolidated Fund is the government's account at the Bank of England into which tax revenues are paid. Consols are redeemable at par at the government's discretion, but the holders have no right to demand redemption. The nominal yields of 2½ or 3 percent are below current interest rates, so the possibility of redemption is remote. As perpetuities, the price of Consols is proportional to $1/r$, the reciprocal of the *long-term interest rate.

consortium A group of companies or banks combining to run a project. This method is used for projects too large or risky to appeal to any one firm on its own. The Channel Tunnel, for example, was constructed by a consortium.

conspicuous consumption Spending on goods and services primarily to display income or wealth, or to attain a certain social status.

constant elasticity of substitution (CES) The property of production or utility functions such that the ratio between proportional changes in relative prices and proportional changes in relative quantities is always the same. A CES function may be written

$$y = k[\delta(x_1)^\rho + [1-\delta](x_2)^\rho]^{1/\rho}$$

where y is output or utility, x_1 and x_2 are inputs, and k is a constant. The ratio of proportional changes in relative quantities to proportional change in relative prices is the elasticity of substitution, $\sigma = 1/(1 - \rho)$; if $1 > \rho > 0$, then $\sigma > 1$ and the goods are good substitutes; if $\rho < 0$, then $\sigma < 1$ and the goods are poor substitutes. The *Cobb–Douglas function is the limiting case corresponding to $\rho = 0$; in this case $\sigma = 1$.

constant prices A common set of prices used to value the output of a firm or an economy in successive periods. Changes in the real activity of an enterprise or an economy are measured by valuing its real inputs and outputs each year at the same, constant, set of prices. The prices used may be those of some particular date, or average prices over a period.

constant returns to scale A property of a function of one or several variables such that a uniform relative change in all of its arguments results in an equal relative change in the value of the function; also referred to as linear homogeneity. For example, a Cobb–Douglas production function exhibits constant returns to scale when the elasticities of all inputs with respect to output sum up to one. Formally, consider the function $f(x_1, \ldots, x_n)$. If the function satisfies the assumption of constant returns to scale then

$$f(\lambda x_1, \ldots, \lambda x_n) = \lambda f(x_1, \ldots, x_n)$$

for any $\lambda \geq 0$.

constrained optimum The solution of a constrained optimization problem at which one or more constraints are binding. Also referred to as constrained maximum (minimum) when optimization involves maximizing (minimizing) the objective function. Assume $f(x)$ is to be maximized subject to the constraints $g_i(x) \geq 0$, $i = 1, \ldots, m$, where $x = (x_1, \ldots, x_n)$. Then the maximum occurs at a *saddle point of the Lagrangian function

$$L \equiv f(x) + \Sigma_i \lambda_i g_i(x)$$

with L maximized for each x_i and minimized for λ_i. The optimum is constrained if, at the saddle point, at least one of the constraints holds as an equality. Examples of constrained optima are the maximization of utility subject to a budget constraint for a consumer who is never satiated, and the minimization of cost subject to a production constraint for a firm employing factors of production with strictly positive prices.

constraint In economics, a condition which has to be satisfied for any economic activity to be feasible. Constraints may arise from facts of nature: for example, a country has only a certain amount of land available. They may arise from human actions in the past: a country's capital stock is predetermined by its past investment, and its working population by its past demographic and immigration policies. Such resource constraints can be gradually changed by human action. Technological constraints may arise from the limits on available technology; this again can be gradually improved on by research and development. Incentive compatibility constraints are imposed on human agents by the need to motivate others. Constraints are usually expressed in terms of inequalities, since while the economy cannot use more of a resource than there is, some can be left unemployed. Economic problems typically take the form of maximizing or minimizing some objective function subject to satisfying a number of constraints, each of which may or may not be effective. *See also* BUDGET CONSTRAINT; LIQUIDITY CONSTRAINT.

consultant An outside specialist hired by an enterprise to advise on particular technical, commercial, or legal aspects of its activities. A person or firm employed as a consultant normally has a reputation for technical expertise and experience. Consultants have no executive authority within the organizations which hire them: their function is to give advice to the management, which will not necessarily act on it. Consultants are often employed in the course of resolving internal disputes in an organization about its best course of action.

consumer A purchaser of goods and services for the personal satisfaction of themselves or other members of their households, as distinct from use to generate further income.

consumer behaviour The way in which consumers choose how to use their incomes. In economic theory it is usually assumed that every consumer is aware of their wants and how to satisfy them and that consumers attempt to maximize the benefits received from consumption of goods and services. Thus, consumers behave so as to maximize their preferences or *utility function. An alternative view is that consumers work partly on a basis of *satisficing, that is, repeating satisfactory purchases until something goes wrong, and partly on a basis of trial and error, to explore their own reactions to products they have not previously tried. This position leaves more scope for *advertising to influence purchases than the view that consumers maximize a fixed utility function subject to known constraints.

consumer borrowing *See* CONSUMER DEBT.

consumer choice *See* CONSUMER BEHAVIOUR.

consumer confidence The degree of optimism of consumers on the current and expected state of the economy. The level of confidence determines their spending and saving decisions. Consumer confidence can be measured through surveys. In the US the Consumer Confidence Index, based on a survey of 5 000 households, is published by the Conference Board, an independent research organization. In the UK, the Consumer Confidence report, based on the survey of 1 000 households, is published monthly by the Nationwide Building Society. Survey questions involve appraisal of current and expected (say, six months ahead) economic and employment conditions and family income.

consumer credit Credit granted to consumers by suppliers of goods and services. This may be granted by the suppliers themselves accepting payment by instalments or on deferred terms, or by the use of credit cards and other systems by which the supplier is paid at once by a credit institution, which then collects payments in instalments from the customer.

consumer debt The amount owed by consumers at any time as the result of past acceptance of consumer credit. The amount of consumer debt rises each month through new purchases on credit, and the addition of interest payable on existing debt; it falls each month through repayments, and the writing-off by creditors of *bad debts which they have given up hope of collecting, where debtors are dead, bankrupt, or untraceable.

consumer durables Long-lived goods bought for final consumption. Their services are expected to be enjoyed over a period longer than that (usually a year) used in national income accounting. Examples are private cars, boats, and domestic items such as furniture and appliances. Footwear and clothing are not normally treated as consumer durables, although they are frequently made to last for several years. House purchase is normally treated as an investment and not as spending on a consumer durable.

consumer expenditure Spending on private consumption. This can be divided into spending on non-durable goods such as food, drink, or tobacco; spending on consumer durables, such as cars and furniture; spending on services, such as travel and entertainment; and spending on housing, either as rent or as the imputed rent enjoyed by owner–occupiers.

consumer goods Goods designed for use by final consumers. These are mostly bought by consumers, but some, such as business cars, are bought by enterprises, and many are exported. Many consumer goods are held in inventories by shops and wholesalers.

consumerism The view that economic life should be organized for the benefit of consumers, rather than producers. Because consumers are individuals while producers are mostly organized in firms, and consumers spread their purchases over a much wider variety of goods and services than most firms produce, consumers are mostly less well informed and less organized than producers. Consumerism takes the view that where the interests of consumers and producers clash, the law should take the side of *consumer protection against firms' profits or their workers' job security.

consumer non-durables Non-durable goods, such as food, drink, or tobacco, designed for use by final consumers. Some of these are in fact used by businesses, for example food for works canteens, and many are exported. Some non-durables such as wine actually have quite long shelf lives: they are non-durable in the sense that they can only be used once when they are finally consumed.

consumer price index (CPI) A price index covering the prices of consumer goods. The UK CPI is the measure of inflation that is used for macroeconomic purposes and it forms the basis for the inflation target. The CPI is also used for international comparisons. *See also* GDP DEFLATOR; RETAIL PRICE INDEX.

consumer protection Laws to protect consumers. These concern minimum health and safety standards, information and labelling requirements, the provision of advice to consumers, and regulation of consumer credit. The principal official US agencies concerned are the Food and Drug Administration and the Consumer Product Safety Council. UK acts protecting consumers include the Sale of Goods Act, the Trade Descriptions Act, and the Consumer Credit Act. UK public corporations also have consumer councils to handle complaints.

consumer rationality **1.** Making choices on the basis of preferences. In this sense a consumer is rational if he always chooses the feasible alternative that he most prefers. The choice of an alternative that is not the best is irrational.
2. Possessing preferences that satisfy a set of *axioms. Let $\succsim$ represent the statement 'at least as good as'. The standard axioms of consumer theory for choice under certainty are: 1. *Completeness*: for any two alternatives x and y either $x \succsim y$ or $y \succsim x$; 2. *Reflexivity*: $x \succsim x$ for any alternative x; and 3. *Transitivity*: for any three alternatives x, y, and z, if $x \succsim y$ and $y \succsim z$ then $x \succsim z$. If a consumer's preferences satisfy these axioms he can be described as rational. This is not the only set of possible axioms, so 'rationality' in this sense is not uniquely defined.

consumer sovereignty The proposition that consumers are the best judges of their own interests. This is the basis for leaving consumption patterns to be decided by the market; consumers face fixed prices of goods and services, which reflect the costs of production, and are left to maximize their own utilities by choosing whatever combinations of goods and services suit them best. As a positive statement, it describes what consumers are permitted; as a normative statement, it prescribes what consumers should be permitted.

consumer surplus The excess of the benefit a consumer gains from purchase of a good over the amount paid for the good. An individual demand curve shows the valuation put by a consumer on successive units of a good. Goods whose value to the consumer is higher than their price are bought; purchasing stops when their marginal utility is equal to their price times the marginal utility of money. Consumer surplus can be measured by the area below the demand curve but above the price. Individual consumer surpluses from purchase of the same good can be aggregated for the market as a whole. Total consumer surplus from purchase of two or more differentiated goods, in general, is not well-defined unless the marginal utility of income is constant.

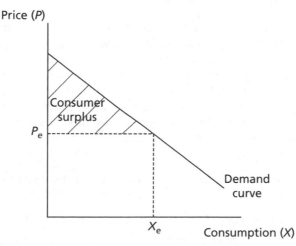

Consumer Surplus

consumption In economics, the final use of goods and services by economic agents to satisfy their needs, as opposed to providing for future production. National income accounting distinguishes private consumption and consumption by government bodies. Private consumption is divided between spending on non-durables, which are goods and services for immediate enjoyment, and spending on durables, such as cars, which are expected to provide services over a number of years. *See also* AUTONOMOUS CONSUMPTION; CAPITAL CONSUMPTION; CONSPICUOUS CONSUMPTION.

consumption externality An *externality that affects the utility level of an agent, or the marginal utility of this agent's own consumption. An example of a negative consumption externality is noise from a neighbour's television or cigarette smoke from someone close; an example of a positive consumption externality is the sight of a well-kept garden.

consumption function A function showing how the consumption of an individual or a country as a whole is determined. Individual consumption is an increasing function of income, for individuals whose income is exogenously determined. For individuals who can choose how much to work, consumption and income are jointly determined, but still tend to rise or fall together. Consumption is also affected by many other factors, including size of dependent family, total assets, and factors affecting 'permanent income', such as job security and pension prospects. Aggregate consumption is an increasing function of the national total of disposable incomes; it is also affected by factors such as total assets, the age distribution of the population, and the distribution of incomes, if the poor tend to save a lower proportion of their incomes than the rich.

consumption goods *See* CONSUMER GOODS.

consumption possibility line *See* BUDGET LINE.

consumption tax *See* EXPENDITURE TAX.

contagion The tendency of investors to doubt the solvency of some firms or countries when others are in trouble. Default by one bank, for example, may trigger a run on other banks, or default on its debts by the government of one less developed country may make it harder for others to borrow, even when there is no objective evidence to justify this. Fears of contagion may force central banks to support institutions in financial difficulties which they would otherwise leave to their fate, or induce the *International Monetary Fund to assist countries whose policies they do not regard as completely satisfactory, to avoid the greater evil of widespread financial collapse.

contango A situation in which the *futures price (or *forward price) of a commodity is higher than the *spot price. *See also* BACKWARDATION.

contemporaneous correlation Correlation between the realizations of two time series variables in the same time period.

contestable market A market that has very low *barriers to entry and exit; in a perfectly contestable market entry and exit are costless. In such a market potential as well as actual competition is a constraint on what the incumbent producers can charge, so that a competitive price is observed even when there is only one seller. Examples of highly contestable markets include low-cost airlines, internet service providers, electricity and gas suppliers, etc. In practice the existence of at least some *sunk costs means that no markets are perfectly contestable.

contingent commodity A good that is available only if a particular event (or 'state of the world') occurs, for example an ice cream delivered only if the sun shines. Contingent commodities form the basis of *general equilibrium models of uncertainty since a financial security can be modelled as delivering a bundle of contingent commodities. *See also* ARROW–DEBREU ECONOMY.

contingent fee A fee payable only if an activity is successful. For example, a UK estate agent only receives commission if a sale is achieved, and some training establishments offer 'no pass, no fee' terms. UK lawyers were previously prevented from charging contingent fees, where they get paid only if they win their client's case, but this was changed in 1998 to allow lawyers to act on a 'no-win, no-fee' basis. US lawyers can work on the basis of contingent fees. Contingent fees permit litigants with limited resources to sue.

contingent liability A liability which will only arise in certain specific circumstances. For example, a guarantee of somebody else's debts will have to be honoured only if they fail to pay up. Insurance companies incur contingent liabilities when they issue fire or accident insurance policies: they will have to pay out only if policy-holders suffer fires or accidents. Contingent liabilities create problems for accountants in valuing businesses, particularly with contingencies whose likelihood is difficult to assess.

contingent market A market for the trade of a *contingent commodity. Many contingent markets do not exist: in some cases this is because too few people would be interested in trading on them to make a market economic to run. In other cases a contingent market cannot be organized because the contingencies themselves, such as the invention of currently unimagined new products, cannot be specified in advance.

contingent protection Instruments of import restriction which are not actually used unless they are thought to be needed, but are available should a domestic industry be threatened by a surge of imports. This includes measures such as *anti-dumping duties. Contingent protection is a disincentive to suppliers from *less developed countries investing in building up markets in industrial countries.

contingent valuation A method used to obtain an economic valuation of a non-market good such as the natural environment. The contingent valuation method is based on the use of consumer surveys. A typical survey would ask either how much a consumer would be willing to pay for a specific environmental feature, or the compensation they would require for the loss of the feature. The method is termed 'contingent' valuation because the survey answers are contingent on a particular description of the scenario.

continuous compounding The charging of interest or discounting of future receipts on a continuous basis. At a rate of $100r$ percent, added annually, after T years a loan will have grown to $(1 + r)^T$ times its original value. If interest is added v times a year, it will grow to $(1 + r/v)^{Tv}$, which is greater the larger is v. As v tends to infinity, $(1 + r/v)^{Tv}$ tends to a limit e^{rT}, where e is the exponential constant. Similarly, if a future receipt due in T years is discounted to find its present value at a continuous rate r, its present value with continuous discounting is e^{-rT} times what is due at the end of the T years.

continuous distribution *See* CONTINUOUS RANDOM VARIABLE.

continuous random variable A random variable is said to be continuous or have a continuous distribution if it can assume any value from a continuous range. The range can be infinite. The cumulative distribution function (cdf) of a continuous random variable is continuous in its domain. *See also* DISCRETE RANDOM VARIABLE.

continuous time The treatment of time in dynamic economic models as a continuous variable. Processes in continuous time are described by differential equations. This is contrasted with the treatment of time as a discrete variable, where processes are described by difference equations.

continuous time process *See* STOCHASTIC PROCESS.

contract A legal agreement between two or more parties, specifying the actions to be taken and payments to be made by each party. A contract may also specify how any dispute over its interpretation will be resolved, for example by arbitration or legal action. Contracts may be contingent, that is, may stipulate that actions shall be taken only in specific circumstances, as for example in insurance policies. The terms permitted in legally enforceable contracts are governed by legislation. *See also* FORWARD CONTRACT; FUTURES CONTRACT; IMPLICIT CONTRACT; INCENTIVE CONTRACT; SERVICE CONTRACT.

contract curve The locus of *Pareto-efficient allocations in an exchange economy. In an *Edgeworth box the contract curve is the set of tangency points between the indifference curves of the two consumers. It is termed the contract curve since the outcome of negotiation about trade between two consumers should result in an agreement (a 'contract') that has an outcome on the contract curve. The competitive equilibrium of an economy is always located on the contract curve.

contracted-out (services) Services paid for by one body, for example a UK local authority, but provided under contract by an outside supplier. This is contrasted with services provided by *direct labour, employed by the authority. Examples of contracted-out services include refuse collection, office cleaning, and the provision of school meals.

contract of employment A contract between an employer and an employee, stating the job description, pay, and conditions. The provisions of the contract can include normal hours of work, arrangements for overtime, holiday entitlement, disciplinary and grievance procedures, period of notice on either side, and any arrangements for redundancy pay beyond the statutory entitlement.

contract theory The study of contracts, with particular emphasis on the design of contracts to provide appropriate *incentives. *See also* IMPLICIT CONTRACT; INCENTIVE CONTRACT; PRINCIPAL–AGENT PROBLEM.

contractual savings Savings made on a regular basis in conformity with a contract. This could be via life insurance policies, or a repayment mortgage. Individuals may adopt these forms of savings as a method of self-discipline. They have the disadvantage that escape from the contract generally involves financial penalties; this may give trouble if income falls, for example through unemployment, or if special needs arise. Continuing with contractual savings does not necessarily mean that an individual is a net saver, as they may be financed by running down other assets, or getting into debt via personal loans or use of credit cards.

contributory pension scheme A pension scheme in which scheme members are required to contribute to the scheme's funds, usually by deduction of a percentage of their pay. Usually under such a scheme the employer also bears part of the cost, whereas under a non-contributory pension scheme the entire cost is borne by the employer.

control (of a company) The ability to win votes at company general meetings. Any person or group holding over 50 percent of the voting ordinary shares can exercise control; in practice control is usually possible with considerably under

50 percent of the voting shares, provided that the other shareholders do not combine.

Convention on International Trade in Endangered Species (CITES)
An international agreement between governments, entered in force in 1975, whose aim is to ensure that international trade in specimens of wild animals and plants does not threaten their survival.

C

( ) **SEE WEB LINKS**
• The home page of the CITES.

convergence (economic) A tendency for two or more economies to become increasingly similar. This may be, for example, in respect of per capita incomes, real growth rates, inflation rates, interest rates, methods of economic organization, or social policies. In the context of economic growth, convergence implies that poorer countries converge in living standards with the richer countries owing to the tendency of the former to grow faster than the latter. Conditional convergence means that the countries may have different levels of per capita income in the long run, but after taking account of the determinants of the long-run per capita income poorer countries tend to grow faster than richer countries. The concept of convergence clubs means that convergence may take place for some subsets of countries, e.g. a group of rich countries alone, or a group of mid-income developing countries. Convergence is predicted by a number of theoretical models of growth; the empirical evidence is ambiguous.

convergence criteria A set of four criteria, laid down for *European Monetary Union by the *Maastricht Treaty of 1993, that had to be met by a member state before it could adopt the Euro. The criteria set limits to divergencies in inflation rates, and changes in exchange rates during the period leading up to union, and set maxima of 3 percent for budget deficits, 60 percent for the ratio of government debt to *gross national product, and 2 percentage points for the excess of the long-term nominal interest rate over that of the three best-performing member states.

convergence in distribution (weak convergence) A sequence of random variables $x_1, \ldots, x_n, \ldots$ with corresponding distribution functions $F_1(x), \ldots F_n(x), \ldots$ converges in distribution (or weakly) to the random variable x with distribution function $F(x)$ if the sequence of the corresponding distribution functions converges to F at all continuity points of F

$$x_n \xrightarrow{d} x \iff \lim_{n \to \infty} |F_n(x) - F(x)| = 0 \iff |F_n(x) - F(x)| < \varepsilon$$

for every $\varepsilon > 0$ starting from some n. The distribution given by $F(x)$ is called the limiting or the asymptotic distribution of x_n. This concept allows the approximation of the unknown distribution $F_n(x)$ of an estimator or a test statistic with a known asymptotic distribution $F(x)$. If $x = \theta$ is a constant the limiting distribution is degenerate, i.e. collapses to a single point. In this case (but not in general) convergence in distribution also implies convergence in probability.

convergence in mean squares A sequence of random variables $x_1, \ldots, x_n, \ldots$ converges in mean squares to a random variable x if $E[x^2]$ and $E[x_n^2]$ exist and the expectation of the squared (Euclidean) distance between x_n and x converges to zero as n tends to infinity: $\lim_{n\to\infty} E[(x_n - x)^2] = 0$. In particular, x can be a constant, $x = \theta$. In this case convergence of x_n to θ in mean squares is equivalent to the convergence of the bias and the variance of x_n to zero as n tends to infinity. Convergence in mean squares implies convergence in probability (the converse does not hold, in general). This is a particular case of convergence in the pth mean (or in L^p norm) defined as $E[x^p]$, $E[x_n^p]$ exist and $\lim_{n\to\infty} E[(x_n - x)^p] = 0$. Convergence in pth mean implies convergence in rth mean for every $r\varepsilon\,(1, p)$.

convergence in probability A sequence of random variables $x_1, \ldots, x_n, \ldots$ converges in probability to a random variable x if for every positive number ε the probability of the (Euclidean) distance between x_n and x exceeding ε converges to zero as n tends to infinity, so

$$x = \text{plim } x_n \iff x_n \xrightarrow{p} x \iff \lim_{n\to\infty} P\big[|x_n - x| \geq \varepsilon\big] = 0 \iff \lim_{n\to\infty} P\big[|x_n - x| \leq \varepsilon\big] = 1$$

for every $\varepsilon > 0$. This means that, if we consider a sequence of probabilities, $P_n = P\,[|x_n - x| \geq \varepsilon]$, then starting from some n_0 each probability in this sequence is arbitrarily small. In particular, x can be a constant. Convergence in probability implies convergence in distribution (the converse does not hold, in general).

convertibility The right to change money into foreign currency. A currency is convertible if holders can change it into foreign currency without permission from the authorities. A fully convertible currency is convertible by any holder, for any purpose. A currency may be convertible for non-resident but not for resident holders. Under current account convertibility holders have the right to convert their currency for any current account purpose, such as trade or foreign travel, but not for capital account purposes such as making loans or buying assets abroad. Current account convertibility requires that the authorities can monitor the use of funds; under full convertibility this is not necessary.

convertible currency *See* CONVERTIBILITY.

convertible debenture A company share which is a *debenture, in the sense that it pays a regular dividend but carries no vote, and the holder has the right at some future date to exchange it for *ordinary shares on pre-arranged terms. This gives the holders relative security during the early years of a venture, while enabling them to participate in the long-run benefits if things turn out well.

convex preferences *Preferences such that a mixture of two equally valued outcomes is at least as good as either of the individual outcomes. If preferences are strictly convex then the mixture is strictly preferred. Formally, assume that outcome x is equally valued to outcome y, and define the mixture z by $z = \lambda x + (1 - \lambda)y$. Then the preferences are convex if z is at least as good as x for any λ such that $0 \leq \lambda \leq 1$. The preferences are strictly convex if z is strictly preferred to x for any λ such that $0 < \lambda < 1$.

cooperation Agreement by two or more individuals, firms, or governments to work together. Cooperation as a method of coordinating economic activity is contrasted with *competition, where individuals, firms, or governments operate independently and sometimes in opposition to each other. All economic systems use some mixture of both mechanisms. Often firms or countries cooperate in some activities, such as research or the setting of industrial standards, while competing in other activities, especially current sales.

cooperative game A strategic game in which groups of players may form coalitions in order to increase the benefits from participation in the game. The players in a particular coalition act cooperatively to promote the interests of the members of that coalition.

cooperative society A business owned by its employees or customers. The Cooperative Wholesale Society in the UK is a cooperative of cooperatives.

coordination failure A situation where activities which could have benefited two or more parties do not take place because they fail to coordinate their plans. In *less developed countries, for example, one might find mineral resources which are not mined because there is no transport to export them, and a railway which is not built because there is no freight for it to carry. If both projects went forward, both would be profitable, but neither is started, because the firms concerned do not know about, or do not trust, each other. The same problem can affect governments: a number of countries may refrain from liberalization of their trade because of worries about the effects on their balance of payments, whereas if they could all agree to liberalize at once, all could benefit.

copyright The exclusive right to reproduce artistic, dramatic, literary, or musical work, or to authorize its reproduction by others. Copyright persists for a finite period after the author's death; it can be sold or inherited. It also extends to films and television, and is one of the main forms of *intellectual property rights.

core 1. A central region in an economy, with good communications and high population density, which are conducive to its prosperity. The core is surrounded by the *periphery, outlying regions, usually with poorer communications and sparse population. At the world level, core countries are characterized by higher development and higher accessibility, in terms of transportation and trade, relative to the periphery.
  2. The set of feasible allocations that cannot be improved upon by a coalition formed by a subset of the consumers in an economy. A coalition can improve upon an allocation if there is some reallocation of the resources within the coalition such that a new allocation is obtained that is at least as good as the old for all coalition members and strictly preferred for some. In an *Edgeworth box the core of the economy is the set of *Pareto-efficient allocations that are preferred by all consumers to the initial endowment point. The 'core convergence theorem' proves that the core of the economy shrinks to the set of competitive equilibria as the number of consumers in the economy increases. The concept of the core can also be applied to *cooperative games.

core inflation A measure of inflation of consumer prices excluding the prices of certain items. This may apply to food, whose prices are subject to seasonal fluctuations, fuel, whose prices are subject to large variations, for example because of actions by the *Organization of Petroleum Exporting Countries, and other seasonal items or items whose prices may be subject to temporary shocks. The use of a measure of core inflation may assist in the production of better forecasts of the long-run inflation. Since 2000, core inflation is the preferred measure of inflation in the US by the Federal Reserve Board; most other countries use the measure of inflation as determined by the *consumer price index.

corner (a market) In a *futures market, to create a situation where other people have between them contracted to deliver more of a good or security than is available. However high a price has to be agreed to obtain such contracts, the holder can make a large profit by forcing the counter-parties who cannot deliver to pay to be released from their contracts. In a commodities market, to buy and hoard a large amount of commodity sufficient for the price to be manipulated. Attempts to create a corner may fail if a high price brings in supplies from unexpected sources.

corner solution In the context of a constrained optimization problem this is a solution that does not change in at least one direction in response to any arbitrarily small perturbation to the gradient of the objective function at the optimum.

corporate equity The net assets of a company after paying all creditors, including debenture and preference shareholders. This is the net amount available for ordinary shareholders.

corporate governance The processes, both formal and informal, through which a corporation is administered and managed. Corporate governance involves the legal requirements imposed upon the corporation, the policies adopted by the corporation, and the informal customs within the corporation. The concept of corporate governance also embodies the interactions between the many parties that can be viewed as stakeholders in the corporation: directors, managers, shareholders, employees, customers, banks, and regulators.

corporate income tax A tax on the profits of firms and corporations, as distinct from taxation of the incomes of their owners.

corporate sector That part of the economy which is conducted by companies working for private profit. *See also* PRIVATE SECTOR; PUBLIC SECTOR.

corporation A collective body carrying out economic activities, able to sue and liable to be sued, and to pay taxes, as an entity distinct from the individuals running or employed by it. A public corporation is a state-owned body; a private corporation is often used as a synonym for a company, but formally not all companies are corporations. *See also* MULTINATIONAL; PUBLIC CORPORATION.

corporation tax The UK system of company taxation. This tax is levied on the trading profits of all companies, with slightly lower rates for smaller companies. The corporation tax was introduced in 1965 with the structure of a classical tax system in which companies were subject to tax on their profits and shareholders were also liable to income tax on the dividends received. The corporation tax was changed to an imputation system in 1973, so that a shareholder receiving a dividend was entitled to an income tax credit representing the corporation tax already paid.

The classical system was reintroduced in 1999, with the abolition of *advance corporation tax.

corporatism A concept of a political economic system in which economic decisions are achieved through negotiation between centralized corporate bodies representing interest groups. In particular, under corporatism wages are determined through collective negotiations between the representatives of employers and workers. An example of a corporatist system is the New Deal in the US in 1933–45. The idea of corporatism as collectivism and social justice without elimination of private property was formulated as an alternative to *socialism.

correlation coefficient A unit-free measure of the degree of linear relationship between two random variables, say, X and Y defined by

$$\rho_{XY} = \frac{Cov(X, Y)}{\sqrt{Var(X)}\sqrt{Var(Y)}}$$

where $Cov(X, Y)$ is the *covariance between X and Y. The correlation coefficient lies between -1 and 1, with $\rho_{XY} = 1$ corresponding to a perfect positive linear relationship, and $\rho_{XY} = -1$ corresponding to a perfect negative linear relationship between X and Y. Positive (negative) correlation means that large values of X are likely to be observed with large (small) values of Y.

corruption The use of bribery to influence the actions of a public official. More generally, corruption refers to obtaining private gains from public office through bribes, extortion, and embezzlement of public funds.

corset A colloquial name for the Supplementary Special Deposits Scheme. This was a UK monetary device used from 1973 to 1980, controlling the growth of bank deposits and interest-bearing eligible liabilities. The scheme was abandoned because the effect of imposing quota limits to the expansion of particular institutions was thought to be anti-competitive.

cost(s) The value of the inputs needed to produce any good or service, measured in some units or numeraire, usually money. *See also* ADJUSTMENT COSTS; AVERAGE COST; AVOIDABLE COST; COMPARATIVE COSTS; COMPLIANCE COSTS; FACTOR COST; FIXED COST; HISTORICAL COST; JOINT COSTS; OPPORTUNITY COST; OVERHEAD COSTS; PRIVATE COST; REAL COSTS; REPLACEMENT COST; SELLING COSTS; SOCIAL COST; SUNK COSTS; TRANSPORT COSTS; VARIABLE COST.

cost accounting The branch of accounting concerned with the costs of economic activities. This includes measuring the costs of activities already carried out, so that their profitability can be assessed, and estimating the likely costs of future activities, to assist management in planning and in tendering for contracts. It is concerned generally only with private costs.

cost–benefit analysis The quantification of the total social costs and benefits of a policy or a project, usually in money terms. The costs and benefits concerned include not only direct pecuniary costs and benefits, but also *externalities, meaning external effects not traded in markets. These include external costs, for example pollution, noise, and disturbance to wildlife, and external benefits such as reductions in travelling time or traffic accidents. Cost–benefit analysis is often used to compare alternative proposals. If the total social benefits of an activity exceed total social costs this can justify subsidizing projects which are not privately profitable. If the total social costs exceed total social benefits this can justify preventing projects even when these would be privately profitable.

cost centre A section of a firm or of an organization that adds to the costs and does not generate profits directly, but contributes to the revenues indirectly. Examples include research and development, customer service, and marketing divisions.

cost curve A curve relating costs to the quantity of a good produced. The total cost curve or schedule shows total costs at each level of output; the average cost curve shows total costs divided by quantity produced; and the marginal cost curve shows the addition to total costs caused by any increase in output. The marginal cost curve thus shows the slope of the total cost curve at any level of output. Any of these curves may be drawn for fixed costs, variable costs, or both combined. Cost curves can be constructed for the short run, in which few inputs can be adjusted, or for the long run, in which all inputs can be adjusted. A U-shaped average cost curve means that at low levels of output average cost falls as output increases, but after some point average cost tends to rise. Short-run average cost curves seem likely to be U-shaped because at low levels of output fixed costs must be spread over few units, while at output levels which are high relative to plant capacity marginal costs tend to be high. Long-run average cost curves may well not be U-shaped.

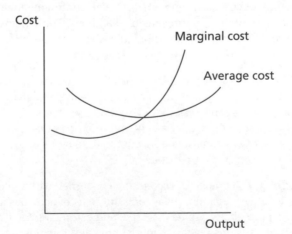

Cost Curves

cost-effectiveness The achievement of results in the most economical way. This approach assesses efficiency by checking whether resources are being used to produce any given results at the lowest possible cost. Cost-effectiveness is most relevant as a concept of efficiency in cases such as the provision of defence, education, health care, policing, or environmental protection, where it is sometimes difficult to measure the monetary value of the results achieved.

cost function The minimum cost of producing a given output level expressed as a function of input prices. Assume there are two inputs capital, K, and labour, L, with cost-per-unit of r and w respectively. Let the production function relating inputs to output, Y, be given by $Y = f(K, L)$. The cost function is obtained from the solution to the minimization problem

$$\min rK + wL \text{ subject to } f(K, L) \geq Y.$$

Solving the minimization provides the factor demand functions $K = K(r,w,Y)$ and $L = L(r,w,Y)$. Substituting these back into the objective gives the cost function

$$C(r,w,Y) \equiv rK(r,w,Y) + wL(r,w,Y).$$

cost inflation In *Keynesian economics inflation due to increases in particular prices or *wage rates being passed round the economy. Increases in costs cause producers to raise prices; increases in prices cause workers to demand higher wages; and increases in wages in one occupation lead to demands for increases in others to restore differentials. The cumulative effect of all these processes leads to a cost-inflationary spiral, which it is extremely difficult to stop. *See also* DEMAND INFLATION; WAGE–PRICE SPIRAL.

cost, insurance, and freight (cif) The value of imports when they enter a country. Cif value is the value of goods when they reach the port of entry to their country of destination: it includes their purchase price in the country of origin, and the freight and insurance costs of shipping them to a foreign port. Cif does not include import duty or costs of transport within the country of destination.

cost minimization The objective of an enterprise to produce its output at the lowest possible cost. It usually refers to the cost of providing goods or services of a specified quality; it does not mean achieving lower costs by cutting standards. Cost minimization is a necessary condition for profit maximization. It does not imply operating at the lowest point of a U-shaped cost curve, unless the market will accept the level of output which this entails. If there are large *economies of scale, the desired output may well be less than the minimum point on the cost curve: what is socially desirable is producing what is wanted at minimum cost, not achieving low average cost via producing things nobody wants.

cost of capital The rate of return an enterprise has to offer to induce investors to provide it with capital. The cost of loan capital is the rate of interest that has to be paid. The cost of equity capital is the expected yield needed to induce investors to buy shares. When a firm uses both methods of raising capital, its cost of capital is the average of the costs of capital raised by the two methods, weighted by the proportion of funds raised in each way. The cost of capital depends on the apparent riskiness of the purpose for which it is to be used, the collateral offered for any loans, and the overall financial soundness and reputation of the borrower.

cost of living index An index of the cost of maintaining a given standard of living. This is found by measuring the total cost of some given basket of goods and services. The composition of the basket has to be changed periodically, to take account of both changes in the proportions of income spent on different goods as relative prices change, and changes in the types of goods and services purchased because of changes in tastes or technology. The main UK cost of living index is the *retail price index.

cost of protection The total cost to an economy of adopting protectionist trade policies. In the short run, this is the cost to consumers of having to buy more expensive domestic products rather than cheaper or better quality imports. This often exceeds the private gains to domestic producers. In the longer run, protection has other costs: among these are the discouragement to technical improvements given by not having to compete with imports, and the diversion of business effort from improving production into *rent-seeking. While in the short run protection may generate employment in the protected production sector, in the long run it cannot cut a country's natural rate of unemployment: it merely diverts labour from potential export industries into import-competing ones.

cost-plus pricing A contract providing that price will equal measured costs plus an agreed percentage mark-up for profit. This procedure is criticized because it gives the producer no incentive to keep down costs; rather, the incentive is to increase costs needlessly, thereby increasing the profit margin also. Cost-plus pricing is often used in government contracts, for example, in military spending, where the customer wants the product urgently and there is great uncertainty about costs. Under these circumstances a cost-plus contract may give a lower expected price than a fixed-price contract, because any fixed price agreed would include a substantial risk premium for the producer.

cost-push inflation *See* COST INFLATION.

cost schedule *See* COST CURVE.

Council for Mutual Economic Assistance (CMEA, COMECON) An international organization of the planned economies of the USSR and its allies. The CMEA was founded in 1949, and included the USSR, Bulgaria, Czechoslovakia, East Germany, Hungary, Poland, and Romania in Central and Eastern Europe, plus Cuba, Mongolia, and Vietnam. CMEA members tended to trade relatively intensively with each other. The organization broke up in 1991, as part of the collapse of both the USSR and the faith in central planning.

council housing State-financed housing for rent, provided in the UK through local authorities. This has for many years been the second largest category of housing in the UK, below owner-occupation but above private rented housing. Council housing is allocated on the basis of need, with priority for factors including number of children, and the quality and degree of overcrowding of present accommodation, with top priority for the homeless. Rents are generally held below a market-clearing level; a large proportion of council tenants in fact receive concessional rents and/or *housing benefit to assist with payment. There are usually waiting lists to obtain council tenancies.

Council of Economic Advisers A US body of three academics appointed
to advise the President on the state of the economy. They assist in the preparation
of the President's annual Economic Report to Congress, and in the formulation
of US government economic policy.

council tax The main UK tax levied by local authorities. Council tax is payable
by the occupants of dwellings at rates depending on their valuation, as assessed
in seven bands by the District Valuer. A reduced rate of council tax is payable by
sole occupants of houses, and some low-income households are exempt. The rate
at which council tax is levied is decided by individual local authorities, subject
to upper limits fixed by the central government.

counter-party The other party in any transaction. For an exporter, the
counter-party is the foreign customer; for a lender, the counter-party is the
borrower. In any transaction, counter-party risk is the risk that the other parties
may fail to fulfil their side of any contract or informal bargain. In many markets,
*market-makers can reduce counter-party risks for both sides by substituting
themselves as the counter-party for both outside buyers and sellers. Outsiders are
left dealing with 'the market', and do not have to worry about the solvency or
honesty of a particular trading partner.

counter-party credit risk The risk when selling goods on credit that the
purchaser may fail to make payments when they become due. Credit for short
periods can be given against a trade bill, which can be discounted, so that the seller
receives cash immediately and passes the credit risk to whoever buys the bill.
For longer-term credits it may be possible to insure the risk, possibly via an
official agency such as the UK *Export Credits Guarantee Department or the US
*Export–Import Bank.

counter-trade A form of international trade in which one country buys goods
and services from another country without money being involved, in exchange for
other goods and services (barter), or for a promise of future purchase of a specific
product (counter-purchase). Another form of counter-trade is buyback, when a
multinational firm accepts from the host country part of the output as a partial
payment for building a plant in this country. An example of counter-trade is the
oil-for-food programme between India and Iraq. Counter-trade often occurs in
military sales and with the countries that lack hard currency, such as the formerly
planned economies of Eastern Europe.

countervailing duty A *tariff imposed to offset the effects of some foreign
policy such as an *export subsidy, which domestic producers claim gives an unfair
advantage to foreign competitors.

countervailing power The use of organizations to protect their members
against monopolistic exploitation by others. Examples include the formation of
cooperatives to protect consumers from suppliers and the formation of *trade
unions to protect workers against monopsonistic employers. The alternative is
control of the monopolists by public regulatory authorities.

coupon 1. The dividends due on a security. With a bearer security, the holder claims payments due by using a physical coupon attached to the documents of title. 2. Tokens, usually paper, used as evidence of entitlement under *rationing schemes.

Cournot competition A form of imperfect competition where all firms simultaneously decide how much to produce. If there are only two firms, it is known as Cournot duopoly. Cournot competition produces an equilibrium with price greater than the competitive price and lower than the monopoly price. The converse holds for the total output. A Cournot equilibrium becomes more similar to the competitive equilibrium the more firms there are, and the better substitutes their products are for one another.

Cournot duopoly *See* COURNOT COMPETITION.

covariance A measure of the degree of linear relationship between two random variables, say, X and Y. The covariance between X and Y is defined by

$$Cov(X, Y) = E[(X - E[X])(Y - E[Y])].$$

Positive (negative) covariance means that large values of X are likely to be observed with large (small) values of Y.

covariance matrix For a vector of random variables $X = [X_1 \ldots X_n]$, a matrix of variances of each component along the main diagonal and covariances between all pairs of components in non-diagonal elements. The covariance matrix is defined by

$$E[(X - E(X))(X - E(X))^T].$$

covariance stationary process (second-order stationary process, weakly stationary process) A time series process y_t for which the first two moments of the joint distributions of its finite subsequences exist and are constant over time: $E(y_t) = \mu < \infty$, $var(y_t) = \sigma^2 < \infty$, $cov(y_t, y_{t+k}) = \gamma_k < \infty$ for all t.

cover 1. The protection against risk which an insurance policy provides for the policy-holder. This may be limited as to the type of risk covered: for example, a motor policy may cover third-party risk only, or extend to protection against fire, theft, and accidental damage. Cover may also be limited in extent, covering losses only above some minimum or below some maximum amount. 2. The ratio of the total profits of a business to its dividend payments. High dividend cover means that dividends are unlikely to be cut if profits decrease, whereas low dividend cover leaves investors exposed to cuts in dividends if a company encounters bad times.

covered interest parity A relationship between interest rates and exchange rates derived from the absence of an *arbitrage opportunity. An investor can either invest in the domestic economy at interest rate r_a per year or invest in a foreign economy at interest rate r_b. The investment abroad requires domestic currency to be exchanged into foreign currency. Let the current exchange rate be e_0 and the *forward exchange rate be e_1. One unit of wealth invested at home yields final wealth a year later of $(1 + r_a)$. Converting the unit into the foreign currency and entering a forward contract to convert back ensures final wealth $(1 + r_b) e_0/e_1$. Both these investments are risk-free (apart from inflation risk) since all values are known at the time of investment. They must therefore have the same return if there is to be no arbitrage. Hence $(1 + r_a) = (1 + r_b)e_0/e_1$, which is the covered interest parity relationship. The same argument can be repeated for investments of different lengths thus linking the *term structure of interest rates to forward exchange rates. *See also* UNCOVERED INTEREST PARITY.

Cowles Foundation The Cowles Commission for Research in Economics was founded in Colorado Springs in 1932. It moved to the University of Chicago in 1939, and to Yale University in 1955, when it was renamed the Cowles Foundation. The major contributions of the Cowles Commission have been in the fields of econometrics and general equilibrium theory. Nine economists have been awarded Bank of Sweden Prizes (Nobel prizes in economics) for work undertaken at the commission.

( ) SEE WEB LINKS

• The home page of the Cowles Foundation.

CPI *See* CONSUMER PRICE INDEX.

crawling peg exchange rates A form of a fixed exchange rate regime that sets limits to the rate of change in the exchange rate, rather than setting the level of the exchange rate to any particular value. A 'crawling peg' could take several forms, among them the following. The authorities could pre-announce a trend rate of movement in par exchange rates by small regular changes in the same direction, for example ½ percent a month. They could retain discretion to change par rates in either direction by up to a low limit, for example 1 percent a month. Alternatively, they could announce that the par rate would be continually adjusted to be equal to the average of market rates over some period of the past, for example a year. In all cases it is assumed that market rates would be held within fixed limits around the par rates by intervention in the market.

creative accounting A practice of using alternative, usually permitted, methods and approaches to accounting for manipulation of accounting figures in order to transform them in a desired way. Examples include the creation of special accounts to which transactions can be relegated so as to appear as off-balance-sheet items, or selling assets and leasing them back, thus exchanging present receipts from the sale for future liabilities in the rentals payable. Creative accounting may be used in shifting receipts between apparent income and apparent capital gains, if these are subject to different tax rates or rules.

creative destruction A model of *economic growth driven by quality-improving innovations that make old technologies or products obsolete. Current innovations exert a positive *externality for future research and development and a negative externality on incumbent producers. This may create disincentives to adopt new technologies and new institutions, which, in particular, can explain why some societies grow more rapidly than others. According to this paradigm, because of vested interests the producers and researchers who specialize in old technologies may create obstacles for the arrival of new innovations that might destroy their *rent. The struggle between the innovative forces and the vested interests of those working with old technologies results in cycles with alternating periods of stagnation and innovative phases. The notion of growth through creative destruction was first introduced by Schumpeter in the 1930s and was extensively developed in the *endogenous growth literature in the 1990s.

credibility The extent to which policy announcements are believed. Policy announcements by monetary or fiscal authorities are credible if it is rational for people to believe that the authorities will in fact carry out their announced policies. Thus, if the authorities have no incentive to deviate from the announced policies in the future, these policies are credible. When there is an incentive to deviate, credibility may be achieved if the authorities have a sufficiently long reputation, or history of holding to their promises. *See also* REPUTATIONAL POLICY.

credible threat A threat that the maker is expected to carry out. A's threat to B is that if B acts in certain ways, A will harm B. This threat is credible only if it is rational for B to believe that A will carry it out; if the threatened action also harms A, the threat will not seem credible to B. This holds unless B believes that A will feel that loss of credibility from failure to carry out the threat is even worse than the direct effects of the action itself. A reputation for ruthlessness or even irrationality thus makes threats more credible.

credit 1. The system by which goods or services are provided in return for deferred rather than immediate payment. Credit may be provided by the seller, or by a bank or finance company. *See also* CONSUMER CREDIT; EXPORT CREDIT AGENCY; HIRE PURCHASE; SUBSIDIZED CREDIT; TRADE CREDIT.
　　2. The reputation for financial soundness which allows individuals or companies to obtain goods and services without cash payment.
　　3. A positive item, that is, a receipt or asset in accounts.

credit control 1. The policy of controlling aggregate demand by means of restriction of access to credit. This may simply mean using monetary policy instruments, that is, the quantity of money and interest rates. It may also involve regulation of particular types of lending, for example hire purchase restrictions, exhortations to banks against lending for speculative purposes, or quantitative limits on lending by particular institutions.
　　2. The system of monetary control adopted in the UK during the 1970s, when banks and other deposit-taking finance houses were required to maintain minimum reserve asset ratios.
　　3. The systems by which commercial organizations seek to ensure that they get paid in reasonable time for goods and services supplied on credit.

credit creation A name for the process by which the banks collectively can make loans in excess of extra *base money they receive. If base money increases, through a balance-of-payments surplus or open market operations by the central bank, this will mostly be paid into somebody's account with a commercial bank. The bank concerned can then lend most of the extra money out, which in turn raises deposits at other banks. Collectively, if banks hold $100n$ percent of their total assets in base money, they can increase loans, and thus total deposits, by up to £$1/n$ for every £1 of extra base money. How close to $1/n$ the credit multiplier actually is depends on the proportion of the total money supply which the banks' customers choose to hold as cash rather than bank balances.

credit crunch *See* CREDIT SQUEEZE.

credit cycle The theory that *business cycles are caused by fluctuations in credit. Booms occur because banks and other lenders become over-optimistic in granting credit. At some stage their mistakes lead to defaults and a loss of confidence, resulting in a depression. During the depression lenders are over-cautious, and bad debts are gradually written off. After a while bankers recover from the shock and start lending again, which leads to a recovery, in the course of which they once again become over-optimistic, leading to the next cycle.

creditor nation A country with positive net foreign assets. Foreign assets include outward foreign direct investment and loans to foreigners. Against this must be offset any external liabilities: inward foreign direct investment, foreign deposits in domestic banks, and ownership of domestic securities. A country is a creditor nation if its external assets exceed its external liabilities.

creditors The balance-sheet item showing debts owing to others. This is divided between payments due in under a year, and other debts.

credit rating An assessment of the probability that an individual, firm, or country will be able and willing to pay its debts. Such an assessment is based on all available information about the subject's total assets and liabilities, exposure to risk, and past record in making prompt payment of interest and principal when due. An individual, firm, or government with a good credit rating can borrow or obtain goods on credit more easily and cheaply than one whose credit rating is poor. *See also* CREDIT-RATING AGENCY.

credit-rating agency A firm which collects information affecting the creditworthiness of individuals or companies, and sells the resulting *credit rating for a fee to interested parties. These include firms considering lending to the individual or company, or providing them with goods or services on credit.

credit rationing Non-price restriction of loans. This takes place when lenders will not make loans to all applicants willing to pay the interest rate demanded, even though they have enough funds for lending. This is likely to occur when the lenders cannot perfectly distinguish between risky and safe borrowers, and when the borrowers have *limited liability on defaulted loans. The lenders may prefer to ration credit rather than raise interest rates to clear the market for loans because of *adverse selection: a higher interest rate would attract borrowers with riskier projects, thus leading to a worse incidence of bad debts and less profitability than a lower interest rate which produces excess demand for loans.

credit restriction *See* CREDIT CONTROL.

credit squeeze A policy package intended to restrain the level of demand by restricting credit. This may include restricting the money supply, raising interest rates, restricting the level of lending by particular banks or other credit intermediaries, or restricting the type of transactions for which credit is available. For example, limits could be placed on the maximum percentage of the price of goods which could be covered by *hire purchase, or the maximum percentage of house prices which could be covered by a mortgage.

credit standing *See* CREDIT RATING.

credit union A financial institution run as a cooperative. A credit union is owned and controlled by its members who are the union's account holders. Only members of a credit union may make deposits or take out loans.

creditworthiness The opinion of potential lenders about the safety of loans to any particular borrower. Credit-rating agencies exist to assess the creditworthiness of firms, banks, and foreign governments; their assessments affect the willingness of banks and other credit institutions to make loans. *See also* CREDIT RATING.

creeping inflation Inflation at moderate rates but persisting over long periods; this is commonly observed in many countries.

critical path analysis The system of planning complex processes whose components take time and have to be carried out in a given sequence, by calculating the longest path of planned activities to the end of the project, and the earliest and latest that each activity can start and finish without making the project longer. A critical path is the sequence that has no spare time, or float, in any of the activities, so that a delay in any component along the path would result in the delay of the entire project; this determines the shortest time in which the project can be completed.

critical value The value of the test statistic for which the test just rejects the null hypothesis at the given significance level. *See also* HYPOTHESIS TESTING.

cross-holding (of shares) The position when two companies each hold shares in the other. If such holdings were of significant size this would make it difficult for either company's shareholders to displace the existing management; if both were majority holdings it would be impossible to vote out either set of directors so long as they agreed.

cross-price elasticity *See* CROSS-PRICE ELASTICITY OF DEMAND.

cross-price elasticity of demand The ratio between the proportional change in demand for a good and the proportional change in the price of a different good. This is calculated assuming that the price of the good itself is constant. Thus if q_x is the quantity of good x, and p_y is the price of good y, the cross-price elasticity of demand is given by

$$\varepsilon_{xy} = \frac{\partial q_x}{q_x} \bigg/ \frac{\partial p_y}{p_y} = \frac{p_y}{q_x}\frac{\partial q_x}{\partial p_y}.$$

If $\varepsilon_{xy} > 0$, x and y are substitutes; if $\varepsilon_{xy} < 0$, x and y are complements.

cross-section data Data for a number of units, such as individuals, firms, industries, or countries, relating to the same time period. *See also* PANEL DATA; TIME-SERIES DATA.

cross-subsidization The provision of a good or service at a loss, which is met by the supplier from profits made on other goods and services. Where the goods and services concerned have joint costs, or are complementary in demand, the extent of any cross-subsidy is difficult to determine.

crowding out The possibility that an increase in one form of spending may cause another form to fall. This could happen in various ways. Suppose for example that government spending on *public works rises. This might use scarce resources, such as skilled engineers, diverting them from alternative investment projects which are thus delayed. Alternatively, if increased demand causes inflation, this might lead to tighter monetary policy, thus cutting other forms of spending. Finally, if private investors dislike increased government debt, a rise in public works might lead to a fall in private investment. Complete crowding out occurs if other spending falls by 100 percent of the rise in public works. Partial crowding out occurs if other spending falls, but by less than public spending rises. It is possible that crowding in may occur, that is, other spending is actually increased, if conditions are such that the Keynesian *multiplier works, or through favourable effects of an overall rise in spending on the confidence of private investors.

CTT *See* CAPITAL TRANSFER TAX.

cum dividend Sale of shares including the right for the purchaser to receive a dividend already declared but not yet paid. *See also* EX DIVIDEND.

cumulative distribution function (cdf) The cdf of a random variable X at point x is the probability that X takes values at or below this point. Hence, $F(x) = P[X \leq x]$. The following properties must hold for any cdf: it is a non-decreasing right-continuous function; it tends to 0 at minus infinity and tends to 1 at plus infinity.

cumulative preference share A share where dividends to the holder must be paid, including any arrears due from previous years, before any dividends can be paid to ordinary shareholders.

currency Another name for money. *See also* CONVERTIBILITY; HARD CURRENCY; OVER-VALUED CURRENCY; SOFT CURRENCY; TRADING CURRENCY; UNDER-VALUED CURRENCY.

currency appreciation A rise in the price of a country's currency in terms of foreign currency. This makes foreign goods cheaper relative to home-produced goods, which tends to increase imports, and it makes home-produced goods dearer abroad, which tends to decrease exports. Currency appreciation is thus generally bad for a country's *balance of trade. Lower import prices, however, tend to reduce *inflation.

currency depreciation A decrease in the value of one currency in terms of other currencies.

currency reform Replacement of a currency by a new one. This may be done for convenience, because inflation has made the value of units of the old currency inconveniently small. Currency reform has also been used to take money out of circulation because the holders wish to avoid bringing the size of their assets to the notice of the tax authorities or the police, by imposing a limit on the amount of new money any individual can obtain.

currency risk The risk that changes in exchange rates will affect the profitability of any activity between the time when one is committed to it and the time when it is carried out. This affects foreign trade, foreign lending, and foreign direct investment. Commitment may arise from a contract, as in export sales or foreign currency loans, or from incurring sunk costs, as in foreign direct investment or setting up foreign distribution systems for exports. It is possible to reduce currency risk by use of forward currency markets, at a cost, but only for relatively short time periods.

currency swap *See* SWAP.

current account Transactions where the payments are income for the recipient. A country's balance of payments on current account includes trade in goods, or visibles; trade in services, or invisibles; payments of factor incomes, including dividends, interest and migrants' remittances from earnings abroad; and international transfers, that is, gifts. *See also* CAPITAL ACCOUNT.

current account deficit An excess of expenditure over receipts on current account in a country's balance of payments.

current account surplus An excess of receipts over expenditure on current account in a country's balance of payments.

current assets Assets turned over frequently in the course of business. These include cash, debtors (other than bad debts), and stocks. Current assets are contrasted with fixed assets, which last some years and are depreciated.

current (bank) account In the UK and many other countries, a bank account requiring no notice for withdrawals. Some banks pay no interest on current accounts; others pay interest that is typically lower than that paid on a *deposit account. The US name for a current account is a *checking account.

current liabilities Debts due to creditors which are payable within the next 12 months. These have to be shown separately in balance sheets from longer-term liabilities.

Current Population Survey (CPS) A monthly survey of households conducted by the Bureau of the Census for the Bureau of Labor Statistics of the US. It provides a comprehensive body of data on the labour force, employment, unemployment, and persons not in the labour force.

(((⊕))) SEE WEB LINKS

• A hub for joint technical papers on the Current Population Survey and data sources between the US Bureau of Labor Statistics and the US Census Bureau.

current prices Measurement of economic magnitudes using the prices actually prevailing at any given time, for example, 2008 *gross domestic product at 2008 prices. This may mean the prices in force at some particular date, for example 1 April, or the average of prices observed over the year; in years of high inflation these could differ significantly. Measurement of economic variables in current prices is contrasted with measurement at constant prices. Comparisons in current prices record nominal and not real differences, whereas comparisons in constant prices record real changes.

current-weighted index (Paasche index) A weighted average of prices or quantities, where the weights used are proportional to the quantities or prices of the most recent period. Where p_{ij} and q_{ij} are the prices and quantities of goods $i = 1, 2, \ldots, N$ in period j, 0 labels the base period, and t the latest period, the current-weighted, or Paasche, price index is given by

$$P_c = \Sigma_i p_{it} q_{it} / \Sigma_i p_{i0} q_{it}$$

and the current-weighted, or Paasche, quantity index is given by

$$Q_c = \Sigma_i p_{it} q_{it} / \Sigma_i p_{it} q_{i0}.$$

Customs and Excise The UK tax authority responsible for collecting *indirect taxes, including customs duties, revenue duties on alcoholic drinks and tobacco, and value-added tax (VAT), until it was merged with HM Revenue in 2005 to form *HM Revenue and Customs.

customs drawback A refund of customs duty collected on imports, paid when they are re-exported.

customs duty A tax on imports, or a *tariff.

customs union A group of countries with free trade between members and a *common external tariff on trade with non-members. These trading rules govern a large proportion of trade, but may exclude particular sectors of the economy, such as agricultural products. *See also* FREE-TRADE AREA.

cuts in expenditure Reductions in government spending. These may refer to changes in actual government spending which have already taken place, or, more usually, to announcements of planned reductions. Cuts in actual spending may be due to the application of unchanged spending rules in changing circumstances: for example, a reduction in unemployment benefits when employment rises during a boom. They may alternatively be due to a change in policy about spending, for example increasing the stringency of tests for eligibility for benefits. Similarly, announced plans to cut spending may be in anticipation of a reduction in the need for it, or an indication of changes in policy. In an inflationary economy, government spending has to rise in money terms if it is to stay constant in real terms; 'cuts' often take the form of money increases smaller than anticipated increases in costs.

cut-throat competition Competition between suppliers of goods or services, by price cutting or otherwise, which is so intense as to endanger the survival of some or all of the competitors.

cycle *See* BUSINESS CYCLE; CREDIT CYCLE; KONDRATIEFF CYCLE; LIFE CYCLE; STOP–GO CYCLE; TRADE CYCLE.

cyclical adjustment The adjustment of figures such as *gross domestic product, government spending, or the budget deficit to show what they would be if total activity was at its trend or normal level. This is usually done in the framework of a particular model showing how these aggregates are related to the level of activity, and a model of the long-run trend in activity; thus, the results obtained using different models may differ.

cyclically adjusted budget deficit A calculation of what the government's budget deficit would be if the economy was at a normal level of activity. This is achieved by assuming that the rules and rates concerning spending and taxes are unchanged. As taxes are an increasing and government spending is a decreasing function of national income, during a slump in activity the cyclically adjusted budget deficit will be smaller than the actual, and an actual deficit may correspond to a cyclically adjusted budget surplus. Such adjustments usually do not take account of the probable effect of changing national income on the interest costs of government debt, nor do they take account of the fact that if the budget deficit is itself a target for government policy, a change in activity rates may be accompanied by discretionary changes in government tax and spending policies.

cyclically adjusted PSBR A calculation of what the *Public Sector Borrowing Requirement would be if the economy was at a normal level of activity. This is usually made by assuming unchanged rules and rates for taxes and government spending.

cyclical unemployment Unemployment during the recession phase of a *business cycle, which can be expected to disappear during the next boom.

data mining Extraction of useful information from large datasets. This is construed in a broader sense than data analysis. While data analysis is focused on estimation and assessment of the existing models, data mining attempts to extract implicit information, by using 'automated' software techniques for finding patterns and regularities, as well as detecting anomalies, in sets of data. This is sometimes referred to as 'knowledge discovery'.

dawn raid A move without notice by one firm to buy a substantial number of the shares of another. There is normally a limit to the number of shares that can be bought without giving notice of a *takeover bid; a dawn raid is often the prelude to a formal bid.

DDD A *Standard and Poor's credit rating indicating that servicing of a security is in default or in arrears.

deadweight burden of taxes The excess of the total harm done by a tax over the actual revenue raised. An indirect tax raises the price of the taxed good to the consumer. The quantity sold falls, as consumers only buy units of the good for which their benefits exceed the tax-inclusive price. There are thus some units where the benefit to the consumer would be higher than the cost of production, but lower than the tax-inclusive price. The *consumer surplus which could have been made on these units is lost; this is the 'triangle of loss'. Similarly, direct taxes are liable to reduce effort, since workers will only exert effort whose cost to them is less than net-of-tax pay. They will not work where the cost to them is less than the pre-tax wage but more than the post-tax wage; the *producer surplus which could have been made on these units is lost. Most taxes produce some deadweight burden: a well-designed tax system seeks to minimize the deadweight burden involved in raising any given total tax revenue.

deadweight debt Debt incurred without leading to the creation of any specific asset from which the cost of debt service can be met. This applies to personal debts incurred to finance consumption, business debts incurred to finance operating losses, and government debt incurred to finance wars or unemployment benefit. This is contrasted with personal debt incurred to finance training which increases earning power, debt incurred by firms to finance profitable investment projects, and government debt incurred to finance education or improvements to infrastructure, which may give no direct return but do increase the economy's tax base.

deadweight loss A measure of the welfare that is lost when the equilibrium in a market is not Pareto efficient. Deadweight loss arises, for example, when a monopoly prices above marginal cost or when the government levies a commodity tax. In the case of monopoly some of the *consumer surplus that would be present if the market were competitive is captured as monopoly profit but some is lost; this is the deadweight loss. Similarly, a commodity tax captures some consumer surplus as government tax revenue but again some is lost.

dealing *See* EXCLUSIVE DEALING; INSIDER DEALING.

dear money High interest rates, which make it expensive to borrow. How high rates need be to constitute dear money depends on the rate of inflation: only interest rates greater than the rate of inflation make borrowing expensive in *real terms. If the central bank is using monetary policy to reduce aggregate demand, dear money and tight money, or difficulty in gaining credit, tend to go together. During a *financial crisis, however, a central bank may seek to make money dear but not tight: the aim is to induce lenders not to increase precautionary balances or call in debts, as holding cash is expensive, while they remain confident that they will be able to obtain credit whenever they need it.

death duties Taxes levied on a person's estate after their death. These may be levied to discourage inherited wealth, or simply as a convenient source of government revenue. In the UK death duties have taken various forms: estate duty was replaced by capital transfer tax, which in turn was replaced by inheritance tax. All these have been extended to include taxes on transfers made before death, as without this death duties would be too easy to avoid.

debenture A secured loan raised by a company, usually with fixed interest and sometimes with a fixed redemption date. Debenture holders have no control over the company so long as their interest is paid and any conditions of the loan are complied with, but if the interest is not paid or the conditions are broken they can take control of the company, and they rank before other shareholders in the event of liquidation. Convertible debentures are debentures carrying a right to convert to equity shares at some future date.

debt Money owed by one person or organization to another. A debt contract states the terms of borrowing: what interest and redemption payments the borrower must make, and what collateral must be provided. Debt contracts stipulate the currency in which payment is due; foreign currency debt is debt where the interest and redemption payments due are in some currency other than the debtor's own. Debt may have interest or redemption payments linked to a price index. *See also* BAD DEBT; DEADWEIGHT DEBT; GOVERNMENT DEBT; NATIONAL DEBT; NON-MARKETABLE DEBT; NON-PERFORMING DEBT; SOVEREIGN DEBT.

debt burden The cost of servicing debt. To an individual or business, this is what they have to pay in interest and redemption payments. If government debt is held externally, payments to non-residents are a real burden on residents. This is increased for the country as a whole if the need for external debt service worsens the country's *terms of trade. Even where debt is held internally by residents, it is usually impossible for the government to finance debt service except by the use of taxes which distort incentives, so that taxation reduces the real wealth of taxpayers by more than the amount the government receives. This *deadweight burden arises from the existence of government debt, even if this is held by residents.

debt-collection agency A firm specializing in the collection of debts on behalf of other firms. Such firms need skills in tracing the addresses of debtors, discovering whether they have concealed assets, and bringing pressure to bear to make debtors who can pay do so. This may involve legal proceedings, or publicity, to make it more difficult for defaulters to obtain credit from other lenders.

debt crisis Inability or unwillingness of major debtors to service their debts, or serious fears of this. A debt crisis occurs if major debtors are unable or unwilling to pay the interest and redemption payments due on their debts, or if creditors are not confident that these payments will be made. This is most likely to happen when debts are large, and interest rates rise or the economy slumps.

debt deflation A situation when spending is depressed because individuals and firms have too much debt. This causes them to reduce spending and limit further borrowing. If debtors have higher spending propensities than their creditors, or if debtors tend to be liquidity-constrained whereas their creditors typically are not, this reduces aggregate demand.

debt for equity A system by which firms or countries with excessive debt exchange part of their debt obligations for equity, held initially by the former creditors. This may be beneficial for both debtors and creditors. The debtors gain from a reduction in *gearing: when the profits of firms or export receipts of countries are low, less of them has to be spent on debt service. The creditors may also expect to gain, if the debtor's recovery prospects are uncertain. Holders of debt will lose if things go very badly for the debtors and they default, while if things go well the creditors do not share in the benefits. Holders of equity get little if things go badly, when the debtors might default anyway, but they do at least share in the benefits if things go well.

debt management The management of the debt of a company or government to keep down its expected cost and ensure that funds are always available when needed. This includes forecasting when net borrowing will be needed, choosing the type of securities to be issued or redeemed, and timing the maturity dates of outstanding debt to prevent excessive concentration of redemption payments at particular dates, which might give rise to difficulties in funding them.

debt neutrality *See* Ricardian equivalence.

debtors The part of the assets shown in a balance sheet consisting of debts due to a firm. Debts due to be paid in the next accounting period have to be distinguished from those due to be paid later.

debt relief An agreement by the creditors of an indebted firm or country to accept reduced or postponed interest and redemption payments from the debtors. This may be in the interest of creditors if they believe they can expect more from debtors making real efforts to pay tolerable bills than from hopelessly insolvent debtors who would be liable simply to default.

debt rescheduling *See* reschedule debt.

debt service The payments due under debt contracts. This includes payment of interest as it becomes due, and redemption payments. Where debt is long-dated, a large proportion of debt service consists of interest payments. Where debt is short-dated, most debt service consists of redemption payments. If an individual, firm, or country has difficulty in servicing debt, the shorter-dated their debts are, the worse their problems.

debt service ratio The ratio of a country's debt service payments to its total export earnings. This is normally expressed as a percentage. The higher a country's debt service ratio, the more likely it is to have difficulty in servicing its debts, either from export earnings or by raising new loans.

decentralization 1. The dispersal of the power and duty to take decisions away from the centre and towards other bodies. Within the public sector this means leaving decisions to local or regional rather than central government. In the private sector it means devolving decisions to divisions or subsidiaries of firms instead of taking them at headquarters. Decentralization may also be pursued by transferring decisions from the state to private bodies such as housing associations, or by breaking up monopolistic companies.

2. The attainment of a chosen economic allocation by the redistribution of initial resources followed by competitive trading. The practical relevance of the decentralization argument depends on the extent to which resources can be redistributed and the absence of market failure. *See also* FUNDAMENTAL THEOREMS OF WELFARE ECONOMICS.

decile Same as 10th percentile, or 0.1th *quantile.

decision theory The analysis of rational decision-making. A rational decision-maker chooses between the available alternatives on the basis of their consequences. If there is certainty each alternative has a known consequence that can be evaluated in terms of the decision-maker's objectives. In most circumstances the objectives can be summarized in a *utility function. Decision theory then describes the conditions under which an optimal choice exists, and provides a characterization of the optimal choice. When there is risk, each alternative generates a probability distribution over possible consequences and the decision-maker has to choose between probability distributions. The choice is made using the decision-maker's *expected utility function. If the probability distribution is unknown then the choice is made under conditions of uncertainty. The decision-maker has to utilize subjective probabilities to assess the consequences of alternatives. The discovery of *anomalies in empirical and experimental investigations of choice situations has brought into question some of the underlying assumptions of decision theory. *See also* ALLAIS PARADOX.

decision tree A graphical representation of the choices in a decision-making process. A tree is composed of nodes, branches, and endpoints. Each node represents a point at which a decision has to be taken. The branches emanating from nodes are the alternatives from which a choice can be selected. Each endpoint of the tree has an associated value which is the pay-off from reaching that endpoint.

decreasing balance depreciation The system of accounting for the depreciation of assets by assuming that they lose a fixed percentage of their remaining value each year until they are finally scrapped, when their remaining value is written off. This results in a steadily decreasing stream of depreciation allowances.

decreasing returns to scale A property of a function of one or several variables such that when all variables change by the same factor the value of the function changes less than proportionally. For example, a production function with capital and labour as two factors has decreasing returns to scale if the output with twice as much capital and labour less than doubles. A function of several variables has decreasing returns to one of its variables if it changes less than proportionally to an increase in this variable, holding other variables constant. Formally, consider the function $f(x_1, \ldots, x_n)$. If the function satisfies the assumption of decreasing returns to scale then

$$f(\lambda x_1, \ldots, \lambda x_n) < \lambda f(x_1, \ldots, x_n)$$

for any $\lambda > 1$.

deductibility The tax concession available in many countries including the US by which certain contributions to charities can be deducted from gross income to arrive at taxable income. The argument for these concessions is that through them the state can encourage donations to worthy causes, by lowering the net cost to individual donors, while decentralizing the decision as to what causes should be supported.

deductibles The part of any insured loss which has to be borne by the insured party. The UK term for this is an excess. The point of making the insured bear the first part of any loss is partly to reduce *moral hazard by making them more careful, and partly to avoid the administrative cost of processing numerous small claims.

default Failure to make payments such as the interest or redemption payments on debt on the due date. Default may be partial or total, ranging from a slight delay in payment accompanied by apologies and promises that payment will soon be forthcoming to total and defiant repudiation. Default is frequently avoided by creditors agreeing to reschedule debt, which they may prefer as it avoids showing bad debts in their own accounts. The main deterrent to default for individuals and firms is that bankruptcy or insolvency makes it difficult to carry on trading. For countries, which as sovereign debtors cannot be made bankrupt, the deterrent to default is that it makes future loans very difficult to obtain.

defence spending Military spending by governments.

deferred share A company share on which dividend payments may be deferred. If this is done, the deferred payments take priority over dividends on any lower-ranking share until they have been paid.

deficiency payment A subsidy paid to farmers when the prices at which certain products can be sold are below a target set by government policy.

deficit *See* BUDGET DEFICIT; CURRENT ACCOUNT DEFICIT; TRADE DEFICIT.

defined benefit A provision of a pension scheme by which the benefits to be received by the pensioner do not depend on the financial performance of the pension fund. Under a defined benefit scheme the risk of poor financial returns on the pension fund is borne by the employer or insurance company running the scheme, and does not affect the pensioner so long as the company remains solvent. *See also* DEFINED CONTRIBUTION.

defined contribution A provision of a pension scheme by which the rules fix the contributions to the scheme by employers and employees. The benefits paid to pensioners are determined by what can be afforded from the pension fund built up by these contributions. *See also* DEFINED BENEFIT.

deflation 1. A progressive reduction in the price level. This would make real interest rates exceed nominal interest rates, which might make it impossible to lower nominal interest rates during a slump sufficiently to make real investment appear profitable. This is known as the *liquidity trap.

2. A reduction in activity due to lack of effective demand. This could be brought about deliberately by the monetary authorities in order to reduce inflationary pressure, or could occur through a collapse in confidence which the authorities were unable to avert. *See also* DEBT DEFLATION.

deflationary gap An estimate of the difference between the level of effective demand required for a normal level of economic activity at any time, and the actual level during a recession. The deflationary gap thus provides an estimate of the amount by which effective demand needs to rise to restore a normal level of activity.

deflator *See* EXPENDITURE-BASED DEFLATOR; GDP DEFLATOR.

degrees of freedom The minimal number of independent characteristics, or variables, required to specify completely the state of the system at a given moment. If there exists a constraint or a set of constraints on these variables, in other words, relationships among the variables, each such constraint reduces the number of degrees of freedom by one. Thus, the number of degrees of freedom equals the number of variables that completely specify the system less the number of constraints imposed on these variables. For example, the number of degrees of freedom for the least squares residuals from a linear regression model with K parameters estimated from a sample of N observations equals $(N - K)$, since in minimizing the sum of squared residuals K first-order conditions are imposed on N data points.

deindustrialization The tendency for the industrial sector to account for a decreasing proportion of *gross domestic product and employment. In advanced countries large improvements in industrial productivity in the 20th century increased real incomes. Consumers and governments have largely chosen to spend these on services, including education, medical care, banking and insurance, entertainment, and tourism. An increasing proportion of economic activity in advanced economies thus consists of services.

deintellectualization The process of 'dumbing down' in education and society in general. It is typified by the current popularity of qualitative degree subjects relative to quantitative degree subjects, and by the replacement of departments of economics by schools of business. Deintellectualization has also led to the growth of 'management speak' as a substitute for reasoned argument.

Delors Report A report proposing a single currency and common monetary policy for the *European Community (EC). The *Report on Economic and Monetary Union in the European Community* was published in 1989. It was produced by a committee chaired by Jacques Delors, the President of the EC, and proposed a progression through monetary convergence to the setting up of a *European System of Central Banks and a common European currency.

demand 1. The desire and ability to acquire a good or service.
   2. The quantity of a good or service that economic agents are willing to buy at a given price. *See also* AGGREGATE DEMAND; CROSS-PRICE ELASTICITY OF DEMAND; DERIVED DEMAND; EFFECTIVE DEMAND; EXCESS DEMAND; INCOME ELASTICITY OF DEMAND; INELASTIC DEMAND.

demand curve A graph relating demand for a good or service to its price. The price of the good is usually shown on the vertical axis and the quantity demanded at each level of price on the horizontal axis. Other factors affecting demand are assumed constant, including incomes, the prices of other goods, and influences such as fashion and the weather. A demand curve may represent the demand of an individual consumer, or of the market as a whole. The demand curve for a good is normally downward-sloping, that is, more is demanded at a lower price. The demand curve may shift if incomes or the prices of other goods alter, or if there are changes in other factors, for example competition from new products. *See also* COMPENSATED DEMAND CURVE; DOWNWARD-SLOPING DEMAND CURVE; KINKED DEMAND CURVE; MARKET EQUILIBRIUM.

demand-deficiency unemployment *See* KEYNESIAN UNEMPLOYMENT.

demand-determined output The situation when effective demand is the only constraint on output. This is likely to be the case only during a deep slump. At most times there are shortages of particular skills or types of equipment which restrict output in some parts of the economy, even when output in other parts is demand-determined. The ability to fill shortages by the use of imports and inward migration of particular types of labour means that an open economy is closer to having its output demand-determined than a closed economy would be.

demand for money The amount of money people wish to hold, or the function determining this. In *Keynesian economics, the main motives for holding money rather than other forms of wealth are the transaction motive (to meet day-to-day needs); the speculative motive (in anticipation of a fall in the price of assets); and the precautionary motive (to meet unexpected future outlays). The main factors that affect demand for money are prices, interest rates, national income, and the pace of financial innovations, as well as expectations concerning inflation.

demand function A function showing how the demand for any good or service relates to underlying variables. The ordinary demand function (or Marshallian demand function) depends on income and prices. The *compensated demand function depends on prices and utility. *See also* AGGREGATE DEMAND; EXCESS DEMAND.

demand inflation Inflation due to excess demand. If resources are not perfectly mobile between different regions and sectors of the economy, demand inflation can occur even if the level of effective demand in the economy as a whole is below the level needed for normal levels of employment. The higher the aggregate level of activity, the larger the proportion of areas and industries which experience excess demand for goods and labour of various sorts, and the more powerful is demand-inflationary pressure. Demand inflation is contrasted with *cost inflation, in which price and wage increases are transmitted from one sector to another. These should be regarded as different aspects of an overall inflationary process: demand inflation explains how inflation starts; cost inflation explains why inflation once begun is so difficult to stop.

demand management The use of monetary and fiscal policy to influence the level of aggregate real effective demand in the economy. Demand management may aim at various targets: a high and stable level of activity and employment; a somewhat lower level, designed to cure inflation; or the balance of payments. The use of demand management was based on the ideas of *Keynesian economics, but the use of fiscal policy to manage demand no longer has a major role in macroeconomic policy.

demand-pull inflation *See* DEMAND INFLATION.

demand schedule *See* DEMAND CURVE.

demarcation The reservation of particular tasks to workers with specialized skills. A demarcation dispute is a protest by a union against other workers performing jobs which are regarded as the preserve of its own members.

demographic transition The reversal of the relationship between income per capita and population growth in an economy from positive to negative in the process of economic development, primarily due to the combination of declining birth and mortality rates and accelerating technological progress.

demographic unemployment Unemployment whose immediate cause is changes in the composition of the labour force. Demographic unemployment can arise if the number of new workers entering the labour force through natural increase or inward migration exceeds the number leaving the workforce through retirement or emigration.

demutualization The conversion of financial or other institutions owned by their members into companies owned by shareholders. Most UK building societies and insurance companies have gone through this process.

Department for Business, Enterprise and Regulatory Reform (BERR) The central purpose of BERR is to help achieve success for businesses in the UK. The department was created in June 2007 when the Department of Trade and Industry was disbanded.

(((⊕))) SEE WEB LINKS

• The official website of the Department for Business, Enterprise and Regulatory Reform.

dependency culture A situation where welfare provision leads many people to depend permanently on state handouts and to drop out of the labour market. Proposals to avoid the development of a dependency culture include placing time limits on welfare handouts, or making receipt of benefits conditional on accepting training or *workfare.

dependency ratio The retired population as a proportion of the working population. The dependency ratio is increasing in many countries and is an important factor in the *pensions crisis.

dependent variable In an econometric model, the variable of interest whose behaviour the model attempts to explain and/or predict; in other words, the variable on the left-hand side of a regression equation. The variables that are used in an econometric model to explain or predict the behaviour of the variable of interest are called the explanatory variables or the independent variables; these are the variables on the right-hand side of a regression equation. A lagged dependent variable can be used as an explanatory variable in a dynamic model.

depletable resources A resource the stock of which decreases whenever the resource is being used and does not increase over the timescale relevant for economic decision-making. Examples include deposits of coal, oil, or minerals. The adjustment speed of depletable resources is so slow that they can be modelled as made available once and only once by nature.

deposit An account with a bank or other financial institution, such as a building society in the UK. Deposits may be on current account (UK), or checking account or sight deposits (US), which bear relatively low rates of interest and can be withdrawn on demand, or deposit accounts (UK) or savings accounts or time deposits (US), which bear higher rates of interest but require notice of withdrawal. *See also* IMPORT DEPOSIT; SPECIAL DEPOSITS; TIME DEPOSIT.

deposit account A deposit with a bank in which the deposit is held for a fixed term or which requires notice for withdrawal, and where interest is paid. This is UK terminology; the corresponding US term is *time deposit. This is contrasted with a current account (UK; in US, checking account) which is repayable on demand and bears relatively low or no interest.

deposit insurance Insurance of the depositors with banks or other financial intermediaries against default by the bank. Usually this is paid for through premiums charged to all banks or funded by a central bank or government.

Depository Institutions Deregulation and Monetary Control Act (DIDMCA) A US act of 1980 which imposed uniform reserve requirements on US commercial banks, savings banks, mutual savings banks, and savings and loan associations, empowered the Federal Reserve to ask for supplemental reserves, and removed some interest rate ceilings. The act was intended to increase competition in US banking.

depreciation (capital) Loss of value of capital goods due to wear and tear, ageing, or *obsolescence. Economic depreciation refers to the changing market value of the capital good. For accounting purposes the value of a capital good is assumed to decrease each year. The amount by which to 'write down' an asset in a balance-sheet can be estimated in alternative ways. Straight-line depreciation assumes that the asset loses an equal amount of its value each year over its expected lifetime, the number of years allowed for write-down depending on the type of asset. Decreasing balance depreciation assumes that the asset loses a constant percentage of the value remaining each year after deducting previous write-downs until it is finally scrapped, when the remaining value is written off. *See also* ACCELERATED DEPRECIATION; DECREASING BALANCE DEPRECIATION; STRAIGHT-LINE DEPRECIATION.

depreciation (currency) *See* CURRENCY DEPRECIATION.

depressed area A region with persistently higher unemployment and lower per capita incomes than the rest of the economy. National governments and the European Union have tried to improve the position of depressed areas by making them eligible for various forms of assistance to increase investment in them and improve their job prospects.

depression A prolonged period of abnormally low economic activity and abnormally high unemployment. This is often accompanied by a tendency for prices to fall, or at least to rise more slowly than usual, and by a fall in the relative prices of primary products as compared with those of industrial products.

deregulation The removal or relaxation of government regulation of economic activities. *See also* FINANCIAL DEREGULATION.

derivative (financial) A tradable security whose value is derived from the actual or expected price of some underlying asset, which may be a commodity, a security, or a currency. Derivatives include futures contracts, futures on stock market indices, *options, and swaps. Derivatives can be used as a hedge, to reduce risk, or for speculation. A derivatives market is a market such as the *London International Financial Futures and Options Exchange on which derivatives are traded.

derived demand The demand for an input to a productive process. This depends on the output of the good or service being produced. Derived demand also depends on the price of the input and the prices of other inputs which are substitutes for or complements to it. If other inputs are good substitutes, the elasticity of derived demand may be high; but if other inputs are poor substitutes, the elasticity of derived demand may be very low, especially if the input accounts for only a small proportion of total costs.

deseasonalized data *See* SEASONAL ADJUSTMENT.

destination principle of taxation A regime of international taxation according to which consumption taxes are levied where products are consumed. The rates of VAT and excise applied are those of the country of final consumption, and the entire revenue accrues to that country's budget. This system ensures production neutrality, since indirect taxes do not discriminate between foreign and domestic producers, and exports are exempt from domestic taxation. The disadvantage is the need for monitoring of cross-border trade flows. *See also* ORIGIN PRINCIPLE OF TAXATION.

deterrents to entry *See* BARRIERS TO ENTRY.

detrending *See* TREND.

Deutschmark (DM) The currency of West Germany, and, after German Economic and Monetary Union in 1990, of the whole of Germany. The DM was replaced by the Euro in 2002.

devaluation For a country with a pegged exchange rate regime devaluation is an officially announced lowering in the value of the domestic currency relative to foreign currencies, usually as a means of correcting balance of payment deficit, at least temporarily. Devaluation and *currency depreciation are similar: devaluation is used for a discrete change in the exchange rate brought about as a matter of policy, whereas depreciation occurs gradually through the working of the foreign exchange markets. Devaluation makes exports cheaper abroad in terms of foreign currency, and imports dearer at home in terms of home currency, and thus tends to improve the balance of trade but at the cost of increased import prices. *See also* COMPETITIVE DEVALUATION.

developing countries *See* LESS DEVELOPED COUNTRIES.

development *See* ECONOMIC DEVELOPMENT.

development aid *See* AID.

development economics The branch of economics devoted to the understanding of the process of economic development. Development economists are particularly concerned with policies to raise the standard of living in *less developed countries.

Diamond–Mirrlees production efficiency lemma A result stating that in a competitive economy with constant returns to scale (or decreasing returns to scale and a 100 percent tax on profits) commodity taxation should not distort the input choices of firms. The policy implication of the lemma is that commodity taxes should be levied on final consumption goods and not on inputs to production. This lemma justifies the use of a *value-added tax system in which producers can reclaim the tax paid on inputs.

Dickey–Fuller (DF) test A test of the null hypothesis that a stochastic process is a *random walk (possibly with drift and/or deterministic trend) against the alternative that it is stationary, under the assumption that the random disturbances in the model are *white noise. An extension which accommodates some forms of serial correlation in the disturbances is the augmented Dickey–Fuller (ADF) test. The test statistics under the null have non-standard distributions and their critical values are tabulated using computer simulations.

diffusion of innovations The spreading of innovations round the economy, and between countries. This may proceed by simple copying of an innovation, possibly under licence, or by modifying and adapting an innovative idea to apply it to related problems elsewhere in the economy. Diffusion of innovations between countries also occurs through *foreign direct investment.

Dillon Round *See* WORLD TRADE ORGANIZATION.

diminishing marginal product The tendency for successive extra units of any input to a productive process to yield smaller increases in output. If one input to a productive process rises, while other inputs are held constant, total output may increase; if it does, the input has a positive marginal product. As successive extra units of an input are applied, however, after a certain point output is likely to rise at a diminishing rate.

diminishing marginal utility *See* MARGINAL UTILITY.

direct investment abroad *See* FOREIGN DIRECT INVESTMENT.

directive of the European Union A legislative act of the European Union that requires member states to achieve a specified outcome but which does not dictate the method of achieving the outcome.

direct labour The use by a UK local authority of its own employees for work such as refuse collection or maintenance of its housing stock. This is an alternative to having such work contracted out to independent firms.

director *See* BOARD OF DIRECTORS; COMPANY DIRECTOR; NON-EXECUTIVE DIRECTOR.

direct tax A tax paid directly by the party on whom the formal incidence falls. Examples are income taxes, capital taxes, and property taxes. In contrast an *indirect tax (for example, *value-added tax) is paid by an intermediary. The distinction is of limited value in analysing economic incidence.

dirigisme Willingness of the state to intervene in the economy, either systematically or ad hoc. This is contrasted with *laissez-faire, in which there is a preference by the state for non-intervention.

dirty floating *See* MANAGED FLOATING EXCHANGE RATE.

discount A reduction in price. A cash discount or a discount for prompt payment is a reduction in price allowed to customers who pay cash, or pay promptly. A security stands at a discount if its present market price is below the price at which it is due to be redeemed. The *present discounted value of payments due to be received at a future date is found by reducing them by a percentage per period, for each period by which the receipt is delayed. Discounting bills of exchange means buying at a reduced price the right to receive payment when it becomes due. *See also* CASH DISCOUNT; QUANTITY DISCOUNT.

discounted cash flow The method of calculating the net present value of a project by adding the *present discounted values of all net cash flows at various future dates. If the net receipts (income less cost) at time t are R_t, and the rate of interest is $100r$ percent, the present discounted value of net receipts at time t is $R_t/(1 + r)^t$, and the discounted cash flow is the sum of these into the future, given by

$$F = \sum_{t=1}^{\infty} R_t/(1+r)^t.$$

A project may have an indefinite life, or it may be expected that for $t > t^*$, $R_t = 0$. Some of the R_t may be negative; this will be the case if construction takes time and there is a running-in period before a new project is expected to make profits. There may also be closing-down costs at the end of a project.

discount house A *City institution specializing in discounting bills of exchange.

discounting the future Placing a lower value on future receipts than on the present receipt of an equal sum. The fundamental reason for discounting the future is impatience: immediate consumption is preferred to delayed consumption. This is referred to as pure time preference. Both individuals and societies are impatient in this sense. Other reasons for discounting the future include the risk that a payment may not in fact be made, the possibility that the person entitled to receive the payment may not be alive to enjoy it, and the expectation that the wealth of the recipient will have increased by the time the payment is due, thus lowering the marginal utility derived from any given sum. *See also* HYPERBOLIC DISCOUNTING.

discount rate The interest rate at which future receipts or payments are discounted to find their present value. If the discount rate is $100r$ percent per annum, the *present discounted value of a payment of A due in T years' time is $V = A/(1 + r)^T$. *See also* TEST DISCOUNT RATE.

discount window Lending by district Federal Reserve Banks to US depository institutions.

discouraged worker A person who drops out of the labour market after a period of unemployment. This follows after they have been unable to get work of a type they regard as suitable for their qualifications, or in some cases to get any work at all. Discouragement may result from recognition that disuse is causing their skills to deteriorate, from fear that employers regard prolonged unemployment as being in itself a bad signal, or from finding unemployment preferable to employment.

discrete choice models A class of regression models in which the dependent variable is a *categorical variable.

discrete distribution *See* DISCRETE RANDOM VARIABLE.

discrete random variable A random variable is said to be discrete or have a discrete distribution if the set of its possible values is discrete, finite, or countably infinite. The *cumulative distribution function (cdf) of a discrete random variable is a step function, continuous from the right. *See also* CONTINUOUS RANDOM VARIABLE.

discrete time The treatment of time in dynamic economic models as a discrete variable. Processes in discrete time are described by difference equations that determine the evolution of the system from one period to the next. This is contrasted with the treatment of time as a continuous variable, where processes are described by differential equations.

discrete variable A variable which can only take certain particular values, for example integers. This is contrasted with a *continuous variable, which can take any value over some interval.

discretionary policy Policy where choices concerning policy measures, their extent, and their timing are entrusted to the judgement of policy-makers. This is contrasted with *rules-based policy, where policy-makers either follow pre-announced rules, or always follow well-defined precedents. The argument for preferring rules to discretion is that if the authorities act at their discretion they may attempt to obtain short-term gain at the expense of long-term losses. For example, a monetary policy authority may exploit the short-run *Phillips curve to secure an immediate increase in output at the expense of a long-term increase in inflation. The main argument for discretionary policies rather than exclusive reliance on rules is that rules can only cope with types of disturbance which were thought of in advance, at least as possibilities. If anything new and unforeseen occurs, such rules will be impossible to apply.

discretionary spending Spending which a government body is empowered but not legally required to undertake. This can include both spending on real goods and services, such as public works, and grants to individuals or organizations. Discretionary spending is contrasted with *mandatory spending programmes, where certain forms of spending are required by law or by the rules governing schemes like pensions or disability benefits.

discriminating monopoly A situation where a monopolist sells different units of output at different prices. There are different degrees of *price discrimination. For example, with third-degree price discrimination a different price is charged in each market. For maximum profit a monopolist sets prices so that at the amounts sold, marginal revenue in each market equals marginal cost. If the elasticity of demand differs across markets, the profit-maximizing price will be higher in markets with less elastic demand, and lower in markets with more elastic demand. Discriminating monopoly is only possible when the monopolist can identify which market each customer belongs to, and where resale between markets is costly or impossible.

discrimination 1. In employment relationships this is the unequal treatment of individuals, through hiring or employment rules or through difference in the conditions of employment, based on prejudice against their race, sex, religion, age, or marital status, as well as union membership or other activities. In many countries such practices are illegal.

2. In international trade this is the treatment of imports on a different basis according to their country of origin. In a free-trade area, customs union, or common market, imports from non-members are subject to tariffs while imports from members are admitted tax-free. Even treating free-trade areas and common

markets as single trading units, it is possible to discriminate between different non-members: there may be preferences in tariffs for goods from particular countries, or special quota arrangements applying to particular sources of imports. Discrimination is contrasted with the principle of *most favoured nation treatment, by which goods from all countries are admitted on the most favourable terms granted to any supplier. While the *General Agreement on Tariffs and Trade and now the *World Trade Organization commit countries in principle to non-discrimination, most world trade is in fact subject to various forms of discrimination.

diseconomies of scale Diseconomies arise when a firm produces beyond the minimum point of the long-run average cost curve. This causes the average cost of each successive unit of output to increase. At the level of the plant, diseconomies may arise from congestion, as more people or machines in the same locality get in each others' way. At the level of the firm, which can have multiple plants, it is harder to see how diseconomies of scale can arise. Very large organizations may require many layers of management, increasing the difficulty of information transmission and motivation.

disembodied technical progress Improvements in technical knowledge that allow more output to be obtained from given inputs without the need to invest in new equipment. Disembodied technical progress is contrasted with embodied technical progress, where the improved technique is built into the new equipment.

disequilibrium A situation in which planned economic actions cannot be carried out. *Ex ante plans for spending and selling, or for producing and consuming, cannot be carried out if they are inconsistent with each other. For example, if the ex ante level of demand for a product exceeds the level of supply then not all demand can be satisfied. Disequilibrium can arise in individual markets, or in the external relations between countries. It produces discrepancies between ex ante plans and *ex post outcomes, which lead to a dynamic process of change. Economic *dynamics studies whether the reactions to disequilibrium tend to reduce its extent or to exacerbate it. *See also* FUNDAMENTAL DISEQUILIBRIUM.

disguised unemployment A situation when workers are involved in an inferior occupation, not fully utilizing their skills, or working less than they are willing to, and therefore continue seeking employment elsewhere. This may occur during recessions, and is also often observed in *less developed countries.

disincentives Economic arrangements which weaken the inducement to undertake a particular action. As examples, high marginal tax rates provide a disincentive to supply effort, and low rates of interest provide a disincentive to save. Disincentives can be used to achieve policy objectives: a high tax on tobacco is a disincentive to smoke, and encourages a healthier lifestyle.

disintermediation Replacement of the use of financial intermediaries by direct contact between the providers and users of capital. For example, instead of savers depositing their money in banks and the banks lending to industry, disintermediation means that industrial firms borrow directly from the general public.

disinvestment The process of reducing the capital stock. So far as fixed capital is concerned, this may be by scrapping, or by non-replacement of capital goods as they wear out. Stocks and work in progress can also be reduced.

dismissal for cause Termination of employment by the employer sacking the worker for unsatisfactory conduct. Grounds for dismissal for cause could include incompetence, failure to obey instructions, absenteeism, dishonesty, drunkenness at work, or breach of health and safety regulations. Dismissal for cause is distinguished from *redundancy, where there is no complaint about the employee, but the employer's need for labour has changed or ceased. A UK employee who disputes the existence or seriousness of the cause cited for dismissal can take a case of wrongful dismissal to an industrial tribunal.

dispersion Scattering or spread of the data points around the sample mean. Commonly used measures of dispersion are the *standard deviation and the sample *coefficient of variation, defined as the ratio of the standard deviation to the sample mean; the advantage of the latter is that it does not depend on the units of measurement.

disposable income Personal income actually available for spending. This is total or gross income less direct tax and social security contributions.

dissaving Decreasing net assets by spending in excess of income. This may be done either by spending money taken from bank balances or the proceeds of selling assets, or by incurring debts. People with positive net assets can dissave relatively easily: even if their assets are not very liquid, they can usually be used as collateral for loans. Individuals with negative net assets find dissaving difficult; lending to them is increasingly risky as their net asset position worsens.

distorted prices Prices of goods and services which do not reflect the true marginal social cost of providing them. Prices may be distorted by monopoly on the part of the sellers, by legal regulation, or by failure to take account of external costs and benefits created by the production of the good concerned.

distortions Any feature of the economy that results in prices failing to reflect marginal social valuations. In a *competitive economy with no *market failure, prices ensure that for any pair of products the marginal rate of substitution of all consumers is equated to the marginal rate of transformation of all producers. Through this process prices reflect social valuations and guide choices to ensure an efficient allocation. When distortions are present this will not be the case. Distortions can be caused by externalities, taxes, or monopoly. The theory of second best attempts to tackle the problem of what to do when some distortions can be reduced, but others cannot be removed.

distribution 1. The shares of income received by different sections of the community. The functional distribution of incomes refers to the shares of income derived from the services of labour, land, and capital. The personal income distribution refers to the relative number of personal incomes of different sizes.

2. The process of moving goods and services from producers to final consumers, via a network of wholesalers and retail shops.

3. A function showing the probability of various possible outcomes of a random experiment. *See also* CONDITIONAL DISTRIBUTION; CUMULATIVE DISTRIBUTION FUNCTION; JOINT PROBABILITY DISTRIBUTION.

distributional equity *See* EQUITY.

distributional weight The relative importance given to different members of a society in the evaluation of *social welfare. As an example, let the utility level of consumer h be denoted U^h and define the *social welfare function

$$W = \sum_{h=1}^{H} \alpha^h U^h.$$

The value of α^h is the distributional weight given to consumer h. The higher is the value of α^h relative to the values for other consumers, the more important is the utility of h in the calculation of social welfare. For the utilitarian social welfare function all the distributional weights are equal and usually normalized to 1. For the Rawlsian, or maximin, social welfare function the distributional weights are equal to 0 for all consumers except the consumer with the lowest utility level who is assigned a weight of 1.

distributive judgement *See* EQUITY.

distributive justice *See* EQUITY.

disturbance term *See* ERROR TERM.

disutility A loss in utility, from consumption of a 'bad'. For example, utility from leisure is often interchanged with disutility from labour.

divergence indicator A measure of how far the exchange rates of currencies of members of the *Exchange Rate Mechanism of the European Monetary System diverged from their agreed central parities with the *European Currency Unit.

diversification 1. A spread of the activities of a firm or a country between different types of products or different markets. The truly single-product firm is highly exceptional and practically all firms are diversified to some extent. The advantage of diversified markets is that a firm or country will be at less risk, as its markets are unlikely all to slump at the same time.

2. The division of an investment portfolio between a range of financial assets. If the assets in the portfolio are correctly selected diversification can reduce risk.

divestment The disposal of part of its activities by a firm. This sometimes reflects the commercial judgement that the activity concerned would be more profitable operating independently or run by another firm. In other cases, divestment is required by anti-monopoly regulators to reduce a firm's monopoly power.

dividend A payment of income by a company to its shareholders. Dividends are so called because a company is legally required to divide any sum available for distribution between its shareholders in proportion to the number of shares held.

Cooperative society dividends are payments to customers who are members, the total sum available being divided between customers in proportion to the value of their purchases. *See also* CUM DIVIDEND; EX DIVIDEND; STOCK DIVIDEND.

dividend control Restrictions on the distribution of dividends by firms. These may be imposed as part of a *prices and incomes policy; they usually take the form of preventing or limiting increases in dividends. If wages are controlled, political considerations may require a balancing restriction on profits. Profits themselves are hard to control. Dividend controls are not fully parallel to wage controls, as undistributed profits are retained by firms and are available for distribution after the controls are relaxed, but they may be the closest parallel the authorities can employ.

dividend cover The ratio of total earnings for equity in a company to dividends paid out. This is usually above 1, as some profits are retained, but it is possible for a company which has built up reserves from past profits to pay dividends for periods when the cover from current profits is less than 1, or even negative.

division of labour The system by which different members of any society do different types of work. This has two advantages: it allows individuals to specialize on types of work at which they have a *comparative advantage, and to acquire specialized skills, both through training and by learning from experience on the job how to work efficiently and avoid mistakes.

divorce of ownership and control of companies *See* CONTROL (OF A COMPANY).

do it yourself (DIY) Tasks carried out within a household which could have been performed by a paid specialist. The term covers mainly decorating, home improvements, and motor repairs. DIY stores sell materials for use in such activities. DIY activities are encouraged by the tax system, which requires employed labour to be paid for out of taxed income, whereas family labour is tax-free.

dollar ($) Several countries use 'dollar' as the name for their national currency. These countries include Australia, Canada, Fiji, Hong Kong, Jamaica, New Zealand, Singapore, and the United States. Any mention of 'a dollar' without qualification normally refers to the US dollar, unless it occurs in a context which implies that it means the local currency.

dollarization The use by a country of a foreign currency (often the dollar) in parallel with, or as an alternative to, the domestic currency.

dollar standard A system of exchange rate management in which other countries peg the exchange rates of their currencies with the US dollar, and hold their *foreign exchange reserves mainly in the form of US dollars. It was argued that the *Bretton Woods exchange rate system operating in the 1950s and 1960s was effectively a dollar standard. More recently the decline of the dominant position of the United States in the world economy has made the adoption of a dollar standard less likely.

domestic credit expansion The part of any increase in the money supply which is not due to a balance-of-payments surplus. The money supply can rise through lending by the banking system to either the state or the private sector. This extra internal bank lending is domestic credit expansion.

domestic product The value of the total product of enterprises operating in a country, regardless of their ownership. This is contrasted with national product, which is the product of enterprises owned by residents, regardless of where they operate. To get from domestic to national product it is necessary to add the profits of enterprises owned by residents but operating abroad, and to subtract the profits of enterprises operating in the country but owned by non-residents.

domestic rates A UK system of local taxation of householders. This operated up to 1990 in England (1989 in Scotland), when it was replaced by the *community charge. Domestic rates were levied on the occupants of houses in proportion to their rateable value, which was assessed by a District Valuer. The rate charged per pound of rateable value was decided by local authorities, subject to 'capping', or maximum limits set by the central government.

dominant firm A firm with a position of strong leadership in its markets. Such a position may be due to large economies of scale, possession of essential patents, or legal restrictions on entry. It is possible for a firm to lose its dominant position, through anti-monopoly action or technical innovations by smaller rivals.

dominant strategy A strategy for one party in a game which gives results at least as good for them as any other, whatever strategy the opponent adopts. If strategy A dominates strategy B there is no point in using B. The determination of the equilibrium of a game can be simplified by recursively eliminating dominated strategies.

domino effect The tendency of one country's accession to an organization, or adoption of a policy, to induce other countries to follow suit. In the case of joining trade blocs, this could be because the bloc benefits members at the expense of outsiders. In the case of policies, if one country gives tax concessions or subsidies to attract foreign investment, this may divert it from other countries, which induces them to offer similar concessions.

dotcom company A name for companies devoted to providing internet access and various activities including sales over the internet. These were emerging in great numbers during the dotcom bubble of the later 1990s that burst in 2001. Dotcoms are now an established feature of the business environment.

double coincidence of wants *See* COINCIDENCE OF WANTS.

double counting An error that occurs when a total is obtained by summing gross amounts instead of net amounts. For example, finding the total product of an economy by adding up the gross sales of each enterprise, without subtracting purchases of inputs from other enterprises, involves double counting. As firms buy large amounts of fuel, materials, and services from one another, simply adding gross outputs results in double, or multiple, counting of output. Double counting is avoided by subtracting purchased inputs from gross output to get *value added for each enterprise. The national product is total value added.

double-dividend hypothesis The claim that a tax levied on an activity causing a negative externality both reduces the externality problem and raises tax revenue, thus allowing other distortionary taxes to be reduced. For example, the introduction of a *carbon tax will decrease carbon emissions and raise revenue, thus permitting a reduction in the rate of income tax or profit tax. The idea of a double-dividend is intuitively compelling, but it has proved difficult to demonstrate in formal models.

double entry bookkeeping The system of keeping accounts in which, as a check on accuracy and consistency, every payment appears twice, in different accounts, once as a credit and once as a debit. Thus a sale appears as a credit for the department making it, and a debit for the customer, while a purchase appears as a debit for the department making it and a credit for the supplier. Double entry books can if desired be represented in a single table, using rows for credits and columns for debits. As a check on double entry accounts, every debit item must have a corresponding credit, and the totals of all credit and debit entries must be equal.

double taxation The collection of taxes on the same flow by two tax instruments. Double taxation of income by two countries can occur when an economic asset earns income in one country but is owned in another. If countries tax both the profits of firms operating in their territories, and the incomes of their residents, double taxation will occur unless there is an agreement between the two countries to prevent it. Double taxation is thought to be undesirable as it hinders international factor mobility. The double taxation of saving refers to the taxation of labour income and the taxation of the interest income that results from saving part of the labour income. The terminology is often used, but it is arguable whether this constitutes double taxation as defined since the two flows are distinct in this case.

double taxation agreement An agreement between two countries to avoid double taxation of the same income. Any income earned in one country by assets whose owner is a resident of the other is taxed only once, at the rate of whichever country has higher tax rates. The absence of such agreements would discourage international investment. As most advanced economies have both inward and outward capital movement, double taxation agreements between them can be mutually beneficial.

Dow Jones (Dow Jones Industrial Average) A leading index of US stock market prices. This is an index of the 30 most widely traded US industrial shares. Dow Jones publications also include indices of transportation and utilities stocks, and a composite index which is an average of all three.

down payment The part of the price of goods sold on hire purchase or instalment credit that has to be paid immediately. When hire purchase controls formed part of UK monetary policy, varying the required minimum down payment was used to influence demand for the goods concerned.

downside risk The risk that the outcome of a project will be below the expected mean return. From the point of view of a lender financing a project, the downside risk is that a project may not yield enough to enable the borrower to repay a loan.

downstream *See* FORWARD INTEGRATION.

downward-sloping demand curve A demand curve showing that the quantity demanded decreases as price increases. Demand curves are normally assumed to slope downwards, which is consistent with the outcome of empirical demand studies. This is not a logical necessity: it is theoretically possible for *Giffen goods to exist. Such goods have a positive income effect that more than offsets the negative substitution effect of a price rise, so producing an upward-sloping demand curve. *See also* LAW OF DEMAND.

drawing rights The right of members of the *International Monetary Fund (IMF) to acquire foreign currency from the IMF in exchange for their own, to an extent proportional to the size of their quota. Drawing rights were extended after 1970 by the creation of *special drawing rights, which enabled members to obtain further amounts of foreign currency.

dual economy An economy in which modern industries, mines, or plantation agriculture exist side-by-side with backward sectors, with little interaction between them. This situation may occur in *less developed countries due to the effects of foreign direct investment with the use of expatriates for skilled work.

duality The idea that there are multiple ways of viewing a single issue. More formally, duality applied to optimization theory states that every maximization problem has a dual minimization problem. Any problem can be transformed into its dual by interchanging constraints and objectives. In consumer theory the problem of maximizing utility subject to a budget constraint is dual to minimizing expenditure subject to achieving a given level of utility. The use of duality provides alternative ways to represent the solution. For example, the *expenditure function and the *indirect utility function are equivalent representations of consumer behaviour.

dummy variable *See* CATEGORICAL VARIABLE.

dumping Selling goods in a foreign country at a price which local producers regard as unfairly low. This may mean selling at less than the long-run average costs of production plus transport costs; charging a lower price in export markets than is charged for comparable goods in home markets; or simply selling at a price with which producers in the importing country cannot compete. *Anti-dumping duties are tariffs imposed in response to alleged dumping.

duopoly A special case of *oligopoly in which there are only two firms. *See also* BERTRAND COMPETITION; COURNOT COMPETITION; STACKELBERG DUOPOLY.

duopsony A market situation with only two buyers. This is the parallel on the demand side to duopoly, which is a market situation with only two sellers.

Durbin's test A test for the first-order serial correlation in errors in the presence of a lagged dependent variable, when the *Durbin–Watson test is not valid. The test statistic is based on *ordinary least squares residuals from the main regression, and under the null hypothesis of no serial correlation has a standard normal distribution.

Durbin–Watson test A test of the null hypothesis of no serial correlation against the alternative of first-order serial correlation in the error term in a linear regression. The test statistic is based on the residuals from the least squares regression, and under the null hypothesis has a non-standard distribution that depends on the values of the explanatory variables. The upper bound and the lower bound on the critical values, that do not depend on the explanatory variables and only depend on the sample size and the number of regressors, are tabulated using Monte Carlo simulations; the Durbin–Watson bounds test uses these bounds rather than the critical values. This test is not valid if the regression contains the lagged dependent variable among explanatory variables or there is no intercept; it cannot be used to test for higher-order serial correlation; it is inconclusive when the value of the test statistic falls between the upper bound and the lower bound of critical values.

Dutch auction An auction that begins with a high price that is lowered until either a purchaser is willing to accept the price or a minimum reserve is met and the item is withdrawn from sale. *See also* AUCTION.

Dutch disease The effect of an increase in one form of net exports in driving up a country's exchange rate, which handicaps the sale of other exports and impairs the ability of domestic products to compete with imports. The name comes from the supposed effects of natural gas discoveries on the Netherlands' economy.

duty/ies *See* ANTI-DUMPING DUTY; COUNTERVAILING DUTY; CUSTOMS DUTY; DEATH DUTIES; ESTATE DUTY; EXCISE DUTY; STAMP DUTY.

dynamic equilibrium An equilibrium in an intertemporal setting, that is, when economic agents make their choices for more than one time period. The characterization of the dynamic equilibrium depends on the set-up of a particular model. For example, in a competitive economy with an infinitely lived consumer characterized by a utility function and a time discount factor, a short-term (single-period) production technology, and a bounded sequence of initial endowments for each period, the Walrasian equilibrium is described by a bounded production path and a bounded price sequence such that the consumption path is feasible in every period and maximizes the discounted stream of utility subject to the single aggregate (over time) budget constraint, and the production path maximizes short-run profit. In this case the single budget constraint implies the assumption of complete markets, i.e. at time zero there is a forward market for every commodity for every day, or an asset (such as money) is available to transfer purchasing power over time.

dynamic inconsistency A situation in which the optimal plan of a decision-maker made at one point in time is no longer optimal later in time. This can occur in game theory when a player wishes to change a chosen strategy during the play of the game. For example, a government may find it optimal to announce tight monetary policy to convince workers to accept low pay rises. Once low pay rises have been accepted the government may find it preferable to implement a loose monetary policy to boost output. Dynamic inconsistency also arises in *behavioural economics where it is often termed 'time inconsistency'. A decision-maker that is time inconsistent can be viewed as being formed from many different 'selves'. Each self represents the decision-maker at a different point in time. Time inconsistency arises when the sequence of choices made by the separate selves are different from the choice planned by the initial self.

dynamic inefficiency Arises when the equilibrium of an intertemporal economy is not *Pareto efficient. The allocation of consumption needs to be efficient across commodities at each point in time and between consumption and saving. In a dynamically inefficient economy there is excessive saving which leads to excessive capital accumulation. Dynamic efficiency is characterized by the *golden rule. *See also* OVERLAPPING GENERATIONS ECONOMY.

dynamic programming A method for solving intertemporal optimization problems. Dynamic programming exploits the fact that at any point in time the maximized pay-off for the decision-maker can be written as the maximized value of the sum of current pay-off and discounted value of future pay-offs. *See also* OPTIMIZATION.

dynamics The study of how economies change over time. Change may occur as a result of exogenously determined factors, and endogenously as individuals, firms, and governments react to observed disequilibria. Dynamics is contrasted with *comparative statics, which is concerned with how changes in exogenous factors or behavioural assumptions will alter equilibria. Dynamics is concerned with the questions of whether, in what manner, and how rapidly an economy will approach any new equilibrium.

early retirement Retirement before the legally established retirement age. Some workers choose to take early retirement in order to enjoy more leisure. For other workers early retirement can be imposed by an employer as an alternative to redundancy.

earmarking A linkage between a particular tax and a particular type of state expenditure. In the UK, for example, television licence revenue goes to support the British Broadcasting Corporation. In contrast, the revenue from the Road Fund Licence is not assigned to building and maintaining roads. *See also* HYPOTHECATION.

earned income Income received in return for work. This is distinguished from unearned income, which is income from property, such as rent, dividends, or interest.

earnings The pay of the employed labour force. Earnings include payment for overtime and bonuses, as well as basic pay. They are distinguished from wage rates, which refer to normal time working only and exclude bonuses. Earnings normally rise faster than wage rates when economic activity increases, and fall relative to wage rates when economic activity declines. *See also* TRANSFER EARNINGS.

earnings (company) The part of the profits of a company available for equity shareholders, after deducting debenture interest. Companies may distribute these earnings in dividends, pay tax, or retain them to expand the business. Share prices are believed to depend strongly on company earnings. *See also* RETAINED EARNINGS.

earnings function The relationship between earnings in the labour market and the human-capital stock accumulated by an individual. The standard hypothesis is that individuals make a sequence of positive net investments in *human capital over the life cycle so that earnings increase over time.

earnings per share The amount of company earnings available per ordinary share issued. These earnings may be distributed in dividends, used to pay tax, or retained and used to expand the business. Earnings per share are a major determinant of share prices.

East Asian tigers Four East Asian economies, namely Hong Kong, Singapore, South Korea, and Taiwan, whose incomes and trade have grown extremely rapidly in the period since the 1950s.

easy fiscal policy A policy of cutting taxes, increasing government spending, and accepting the resulting budget deficits and increases in government debt. Such a policy is likely to be advocated when the economy is depressed but it imposes future costs on the economy when government debt has to be serviced and repaid.

easy monetary policy A policy of having low interest rates and easy access to credit, to stimulate real economic activity. Such a policy is likely to be adopted in times of depression, when investment and employment are both below normal. A danger of easy monetary policy is that entrepreneurs may be tempted by easy credit to start up businesses which are viable only with very low interest rates, but are not sufficiently profitable to pay the normal interest rates which are likely to be restored when the economy recovers.

ecological fallacy An erroneous interpretation of observed association between two variables at the aggregate level as an existence of such association at the individual level. High sample correlation at the aggregate level between two variables weakly correlated at the individual level, referred to as the ecological correlation, is caused by the removal of individual variation by the aggregation (the aggregation problem).

e-commerce The practice of advertising and selling goods and services over the internet. This has rapidly become established as a standard business practice.

econometric model A representation of an *economic model in the form of a statistical equation or a set of equations that makes it possible to use statistical methods of data analysis for estimation and inference, such as testing the model assumptions, estimating the model parameters, and computing forecasts.

econometrics A discipline that develops mathematical and statistical methods, applies them to the estimation of economic models, and conducts quantitative analysis of the behaviour of economic data. Econometric theory mainly deals with establishing the statistical properties of estimators and the development of tests, while applied econometrics uses statistical methods to test and evaluate economic theories, and to forecast future values of economic variables.

economically active population The number of people during a specified time period who supply labour for the production of goods and services as defined by the United Nations System of National Accounts.

Economic and Social Research Council (ESRC) A UK *quasi-autonomous non-government organization (quango) set up to fund research and postgraduate training in economics and other disciplines in the social sciences. The ESRC was previously called the Social Science Research Council.

(⊕) **SEE WEB LINKS**
• The home page of the ESRC.

economic development An economic transformation of a country or a region that leads to the improvement of the well-being and economic capabilities of its residents.

economic efficiency A general term for making the maximum use of available resources. Economic efficiency in this sense is purely descriptive, and does not provide a precise definition or test. *Pareto efficiency is a formalization of the concept of economic efficiency that provides a method of testing for efficiency.

economic geography A discipline that studies spatial aspects of economic activities. One of the main areas of research in economic geography is *globalization and its effect on economic activities across countries.

economic growth Persistent increase in per capita aggregate output and in the aggregate physical capital per worker at a non-diminishing rate in an economy. Economic growth has been empirically observed in both developed and *less developed countries for over a hundred years, with the growth rate of output per worker differing substantially across countries. Other *stylized facts related to economic growth are the observations of a constant rate of return to capital, a nearly constant ratio of physical capital to output, and nearly constant shares of labour and physical capital in national income. Economic growth is also characterized by structural transformation, such as the shift from agriculture to industry and services, urbanization, the shift from home work to employee status, an increasing role of formal education, an increased role for foreign trade, decreased reliance on natural resources with technological progress, and the growing importance of government. Early theories of growth were based on capital accumulation but have the major shortcoming that the long-run per capita growth rate was determined entirely by exogenous technological progress. Endogenous growth theories have identified several channels through which continuing growth can occur without the need to appeal to exogenous progress. These channels include *learning by doing, human capital as a source of non-diminishing returns to investment, technological advance as a result of intentional research and development activity, and the diffusion of technology. Endogenous growth theory emphasizes the role of governmental actions, in particular the provision of infrastructure services and the protection of *intellectual property rights. The latest growth theories focus on the differences in the long-run levels of aggregate output per worker across countries and the role of the quality of institutions, or *social capital.

economic imperialism Domination of the economies of colonies by their rulers, or of politically independent countries by foreign or multinational companies.

economic indicators A collection of statistical information about the economy. The most commonly used country economic indicators include the *gross domestic product, output by sectors, private consumption, retail sales volume, employment, unemployment, average earnings, investment, productivity, inflation, producer input and output prices, current account, volume of trade in goods and services, exports, imports, public debt, and interest rates.

economic man A person who makes rational decisions in order to achieve their most preferred outcome given the constraints upon choice. The model of economic man is very specific in its view upon the process of choice, but it achieves generality by placing no restrictions on the nature of *preferences or on constraints upon choice.

economic model A theoretical construct designed to analyse the behaviour of economic agents using quantitative and logical methods. A model can be formulated verbally and/or in the form of equations and/or diagrams, and is composed of a list of variables that characterize the economic agents and the economic environment under consideration, and a list of assumptions about their interaction. A model assigns objectives to economic agents and specifies constraints on choices. An economic model is always a simplified representation of the real world, and the choice of the degree of simplification is dictated by the focus of the research and the availability of relevant information.

economic planning A component of public policy that controls economic activity. It can involve the use of direct controls, such as rationing and price, rent, and wage limits, or indirect controls, such as monetary and fiscal policy. *See also* ECONOMIC POLICY.

economic policy The set of controls used by the government to regulate economic activity. Economic policy can be broadly classified into three areas: fiscal policy (issues related to taxation, government spending, and public deficit), monetary policy (interest rates and inflation), and trade policy (tariffs and trade agreements). *See also* ECONOMIC PLANNING.

economic profit The difference between the revenue received from the sale of an output and the opportunity cost of the inputs used. *See also* PROFIT.

Economic Recovery Tax Act of 1981 US legislation enacted in 1981 'to encourage economic growth through reductions in individual income tax rates, the expensing of depreciable property, incentives for small businesses, and incentives for savings, and for other purpose'. The act is credited with a major reduction in tax rates, but the revenue and growth effects are disputed.

economic rent A payment for the services of an economic resource above what is necessary for it to remain in its current use. Economic rent can result from monopoly power, network effects, political decisions, and star power. Unimproved land, which is valuable purely on account of its location, commands a rent based on its value to the user. Nobody had to be paid to make it, so rent paid to a landlord is economic rent. In the case of land which has been improved, however, for example by drainage, part of the rent is a necessary incentive for the improvements. If landlords knew that no rent could be charged, the land would not be improved.

Economic Report of the President An annual report written by the Chairman of the *Council of Economic Advisers that reviews the economic situation in the US.

economics A social science that studies individual and group decisions on how to use scarce resources to satisfy their wants and needs. *See also* BEHAVIOURAL ECONOMICS; DEVELOPMENT ECONOMICS; ENVIRONMENTAL ECONOMICS; INDUSTRIAL ECONOMICS; INSTITUTIONAL ECONOMICS; INTERNATIONAL ECONOMICS; KEYNESIAN ECONOMICS; LABOUR ECONOMICS; MARXIAN ECONOMICS; NEOCLASSICAL ECONOMICS; NEW CLASSICAL ECONOMICS; NORMATIVE ECONOMICS; POSITIVE

economic sanctions   132

ECONOMICS; SUPPLY-SIDE ECONOMICS; TRANSACTION COST ECONOMICS; URBAN
ECONOMICS; WELFARE ECONOMICS.

economic sanctions *See* TRADE SANCTIONS.

economic statistics Data related to the economic activity of individuals and
entities, such as firms and governments. *See also* ECONOMIC INDICATORS.

economic system The part of the social system composed of institutions and
customs related to the production, distribution, and consumption of goods and
services. Important characteristics of an economic system are the property rules and
the degree of *economic planning: examples are traditional, capitalist, socialist, and
mixed systems.

economic theory The part of economic research that focuses on the
construction of *economic models and the development of mathematical methods
appropriate for their analysis. It is usually contrasted to applied economics, which
deals with the empirical applications, such as quantitative data analysis and
practical policy recommendations.

economic union An international agreement with provisions for a common
market and the harmonization of certain *economic policies, particularly
macroeconomic and regulatory policies. An example is the European Union.

economies of scale The factors which make it possible for larger organizations
or countries to produce goods or services more cheaply than smaller ones.
Economies of scale which are internal to firms are due to *indivisibilities and the
*division of labour. If specialized equipment comes in units of some minimum size
a larger total output makes it more economic to use. The division of labour means
that it is possible with a larger workforce to restrict the range of tasks performed by
each individual worker. Also, in a larger firm the breakdown of any particular piece
of equipment, or the absence of any individual worker, causes less disruption to
production. Against these sources of economies of scale have to be set the
increasing difficulty of coordinating and motivating people in larger organizations.
How large a firm can become before the problems of scale outweigh the economies
varies widely between different industries. Economies of scale which are external
to firms, but operate at the national level, arise from similar causes; there is scope
for more specialist services in a large economy than in a small one.

economies of scope The benefits arising from carrying on related activities.
These are similar to economies of scale, but whereas with economies of scale
cost savings arise from carrying out more of the same activity, with economies of
scope cost savings arise from carrying out related activities. Specialized labour,
equipment, and ideas used in one activity are often also useful in related activities.
Given the prevalence of multi-product firms, much of what is normally referred to
as economies of scale is in fact economies of scope.

economy The system of activity connected with the production, trade, and
consumption of goods and services of a region, country, or other (not necessarily
geographic) area. *See also* CLOSED ECONOMY; DUAL ECONOMY; FREE-MARKET

ECONOMY; HIDDEN ECONOMY; MARKET ECONOMY; MIXED ECONOMY; OPEN
ECONOMY; PLANNED ECONOMY.

Edgeworth box A graphical device for depicting resource allocation in a two-consumer, two-good economy. The width of the box corresponds to the economy's endowment of good 1 and the height of the box to the endowment of good 2. The bottom-left corner of the box is the origin for consumer 1 and the top-right corner is the origin for consumer 2. An allocation of the endowment between the two consumers is represented by a point in the box. Adding the consumers' preferences to the box allows *Pareto-efficient allocations to be determined. Introducing prices permits analysis of the outcome of competitive trading from an endowment point that represents the initial division of commodities. The Edgeworth box can also be used to analyse the allocation of a fixed stock of two inputs between the production of two different goods. The width and height of the box then correspond to the stocks of the two inputs, and a point in the box is an allocation of inputs between the production processes for the two goods. At a Pareto-efficient allocation of the inputs it is not possible to raise the output of one good without reducing the output of the other. *See also* ECONOMIC EFFICIENCY; GENERAL EQUILIBRIUM.

effective demand *Ex ante spending, that is plans to purchase, by people with the means to pay. Effective demand is contrasted with notional demand, the demand that would exist if all markets were in equilibrium. Effective demand thus excludes the extra goods that unemployed workers would buy if they could get jobs, or that credit-constrained entrepreneurs would buy if they could obtain finance.

effective exchange rate A country's exchange rate calculated as a weighted average of its bilateral nominal exchange rates against other currencies. The weights are normally based on the value of trade with other countries. The effective exchange rate is a nominal and not a real exchange rate, but it helps to explain the contribution of exchange rates to changes in a country's competitiveness better than simply looking at its rate against one currency, for example the US dollar, which may be distorted by variations peculiar to the particular foreign currency chosen.

effective protection The effects of a *tariff system on an industry's *value added, taking account of tariffs on imported inputs as well as on output. Defining units of output and imported inputs so that their prices would be 1 under free trade, if the tariff on output is $100t$ percent and the tariffs on imported inputs are $100s$ percent, and a units of imported inputs are used per unit of output, with zero tariffs value added per unit of output is $(1 - a)$. With tariffs value added per unit is $[(1 + t) - a(1 + s)]$. The rate of effective protection e is then defined by

$$(1 + e) = \frac{(1 + t) - a(1 + s)}{(1 - a)}$$

so that $e = (t - as)/(1 - a)$. Effective protection is increased by higher tariffs on output, and decreased by higher tariffs on imported inputs.

efficiency Obtaining the maximum output for given inputs. Efficiency in consumption means allocating goods between consumers so that it would not be possible by any reallocation to make some people better off without making anybody else worse off. Efficiency in production means allocating the available resources between industries so that it would not be possible to produce more of some goods without producing less of any others. Efficiency in the choice of goods to produce means choosing so that it would not be possible to change the set of goods so as to make some consumers better off without others becoming worse off. The concept of *Pareto efficiency is used as a test of efficiency for an economic allocation. *See also* TECHNICAL EFFICIENCY; X-EFFICIENCY.

efficiency audit A process of checking whether an organization is working as efficiently as possible. This may be done internally, as management tries to improve profitability, or externally by regulatory bodies, for example those in the UK responsible for supervising privatized utilities. The two standard methods of efficiency audit are the engineer's approach, of comparing practice with what theory suggests is possible, and the statistician's approach, of comparing performance with that of similar enterprises elsewhere in the economy, or in other countries.

efficiency–equity trade-off The observation that policies designed to achieve economic efficiency often have detrimental effects on distribution. For example, it is efficient to tax commodities with a low elasticity of demand at a high rate, and those with a high elasticity at a low rate. If commodities have a low elasticity because they are necessities the tax burden will fall relatively heavily upon low-income groups for whom necessities are a large part of the budget. If the policy is changed to improve the distributional effects then it will be less efficient.

efficiency frontier *See* PRODUCTION POSSIBILITY FRONTIER.

efficiency wages Wages above the market-clearing level paid by employers in order to increase the productivity, or efficiency, of their employees. The various explanations of efficiency wages include nutritional reasons (especially in developing economies), prevention of shirking, reduction in labour turnover, the adverse selection problem, and traditions.

efficient allocation A feasible allocation of economic resources such that there is no alternative feasible allocation where one economic agent is better off and no agent worse off. *See also* PARETO EFFICIENCY.

efficient asset markets *See* EFFICIENT MARKETS HYPOTHESIS.

efficient estimator An estimator that has the lowest possible variance in the class of all unbiased estimators.

efficient markets hypothesis The theory that where assets are traded in organized markets, prices take account of all available information, so that it is impossible to predict whether some assets will give better risk-adjusted returns than others. This cannot be predicted because it depends on news, that is, information which is not yet available, and cannot be deduced from information which is available. There are several variants of the efficient markets hypothesis. Weak-form efficiency asserts that it is not possible to use historical share prices to construct a trading strategy that yields excess returns. Semi-strong efficiency states that excess returns cannot be earned on the basis of public information. Strong-form efficiency states that excess returns cannot be earned by trading on the basis of private information. Empirical evidence seems to support semi-strong efficiency as a description of markets.

elastic A variable whose *elasticity with respect to another variable has absolute value greater than 1. If demand is price-elastic the proportional fall in quantity is larger than the proportional rise in price. If supply is price-elastic, an increase in price increases supply more than in proportion.

elasticity The ratio between the proportional change in one variable and the proportional change in another. For two variables x and y the elasticity $\varepsilon = (dy/y)/(dx/x)$. The concept is useful because comparisons of proportional changes are independent of the units in which the variables, such as price or quantity, are measured. As $(dy/y)/(dx/x) = d(\log y)/d(\log x)$, elasticity equals the ratio of changes in the logarithms of the two variables. *See also* ARC ELASTICITY; POINT ELASTICITY.

elasticity of demand The ratio between proportional change in quantity demanded and proportional change in price. Counter to the general definition of elasticity, it is common to insert a minus sign in the definition, so where q is quantity and p is price, elasticity of demand is given by

$$\varepsilon_d = -\left(\frac{dq}{q}\right)\bigg/\left(\frac{dp}{p}\right) = -\left(\frac{p}{q}\right)\left(\frac{dq}{dp}\right).$$

This is to make the elasticity of demand positive, to avoid confusion when discussing larger or smaller elasticities. If demand is elastic, $\varepsilon_d > 1$; the proportional rise in quantity is more than a proportional cut in price, so total spent rises as price falls. This is contrasted with inelastic demand, where $\varepsilon_d < 1$, so total spent falls as price falls. *See also* CROSS-PRICE ELASTICITY OF DEMAND; INCOME ELASTICITY OF DEMAND.

elasticity of intertemporal substitution A measure of the willingness of a consumer to move consumption between time periods. The elasticity of intertemporal substitution, ε_s, is defined by

$$\varepsilon_s = -\left(\frac{d\left(c_i/c_j\right)}{c_i/c_j}\right)\bigg/\left(\frac{d\left(U_{c_i}/U_{c_j}\right)}{U_{c_i}/U_{c_j}}\right) = -\frac{d\ln\left(c_i/c_j\right)}{d\ln\left(U_{c_i}/U_{c_j}\right)}$$

where c_i denotes consumption in time period i and U_{c_i} is the marginal utility of consumption in period i.

elasticity of substitution The ratio of the proportional change in the relative quantities of two goods demanded to the proportional change in their relative prices. Let p_x and p_y be the prices of goods X and Y, and q_x and q_y be the quantities demanded. The elasticity of substitution, σ, is defined as

$$\sigma = -\left(\frac{d\left(q_x/q_y\right)}{q_x/q_y}\right) \Big/ \left(\frac{d\left(p_x/p_y\right)}{p_x/p_y}\right) = -\frac{d\ln\left(q_x/q_y\right)}{d\ln\left(p_x/p_y\right)}.$$

The minus sign is included to make σ positive. The better substitutes any two goods are, the higher the σ between them. For perfect substitutes σ is infinite. Where $\sigma > 1$, as a good gets relatively cheaper it takes a larger share of total expenditure. If $\sigma < 1$, as a good gets relatively cheaper it takes a smaller share of total expenditure. If $\sigma = 1$, the two goods take constant shares of expenditure whatever their relative prices. The elasticity of substitution can be written in terms of marginal utility using the relation $p_x/p_y = U_x/U_y$.

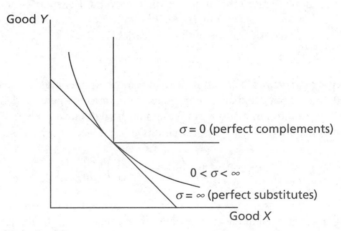

Elasticity of Substitution

elasticity of supply The ratio of the proportional rise in the quantity of a good supplied to a proportional rise in its price. If q is the quantity supplied and p is price, the elasticity of supply is given by

$$\varepsilon_s = \left(\frac{p}{q}\right)\left(\frac{dq}{dp}\right).$$

The concept of an elasticity of supply is only applicable to an industry in which the firms are price-takers: that is, the market sets the price and firms adapt their outputs to it. For any one firm, elasticity of supply will be larger in the long run than in the short run. In the long run more equipment can be installed, and more workers can be taken on and trained, whereas in the short run output can be increased only by taking on more workers who may not be well trained. For the industry, long-run elasticity of supply will depend not only on the elasticity of supply of existing firms, but on entry and exit. Long-run elasticity of supply will be larger, the easier it is for firms to enter the industry as the result of higher prices or to leave as the result of lower prices.

elasticity of technical substitution The ratio of proportional change in the relative quantities of two inputs used by a firm to proportional change in their relative prices, holding total output constant. This elasticity has the same role for the firm as the *elasticity of substitution has for the consumer. If it is high, a small change in the relative cost of two factors leads to a large change in relative quantities used by a cost-minimizing firm. If it is small, a large change in relative factor prices causes a cost-minimizing firm to make only a small change in factor proportions.

electronic trading Trading stocks and shares or commodities through the use of a computer network. The network transmits information on offers to trade by *market-makers and others, and data of trades done. It can also be made to conduct the actual trades, though this part is often still done by telephone. Electronic trading is contrasted with the traditional market organization of having individual dealers meet and proceed by 'open outcry', that is, trade conducted verbally with all offers and trades done out loud so that competitors on both sides of the market can follow what is happening.

eligible liabilities The class of liabilities against which banks are required to hold specified percentages of reserve assets.

eligible paper Securities considered suitable for rediscounting by a central bank. In the UK the Bank of England will rediscount Treasury bills, short-dated gilts, and any first-class security accepted by a British bank or discount house. In the US eligible paper is securities which can be rediscounted with the Federal Reserve. Eligible paper is suitable for bank portfolios as it can quickly be turned into cash.

embargo 1. A prohibition on trading with a country, generally or in some particular goods. A general embargo is intended as an expression of disapproval, for example of practices such as apartheid in South Africa; an embargo on particular products is generally based on defence considerations, to prevent the spread of advanced weaponry, for example during the Iraq–Iran war in the 1980s.
2. A prohibition on releasing or quoting published material until some deadline. This is generally intended to avoid political embarrassment or opportunities for insider trading by synchronizing the release of information through various channels.

embodied technical progress Improvements in technical knowledge which can be exploited only by *investment in new equipment; technical improvements are embodied in the equipment. Embodied technical progress is contrasted with *disembodied technical progress, where new knowledge can be exploited with unchanged equipment. In practice many innovations require partial but not total replacement of equipment for their utilization, so the embodiment of technical progress is a matter of degree. *See also* TECHNICAL PROGRESS.

emerging markets Stock exchanges in countries where investors are unused to trading. These are mainly *newly industrialized countries, such as Taiwan or Brazil, or newly *liberalized economies, such as Hungary or Poland. Because of thin markets and lack of experience of both investors and market regulators, emerging markets are often even riskier than stock exchanges in countries where they have been long established.

emissions Substances given off by the activities of people or by productive processes. Emissions may be solid particles or liquids deposited in rivers or the sea, or solid particles and gases put into the atmosphere. Economic policies related to the environment are concerned with emissions which have adverse external effects on people, animals, or plants. *Pollution can be reduced in the short run by taxing or restricting activities involving harmful emissions, and in the longer run by research on alternative productive techniques involving fewer or less harmful emissions.

emission taxes Taxes designed to reduce damage to the environment by creating incentives to reduce emissions of products such as nitrous oxide or carbon dioxide. Emission taxes can be used as an alternative to, or a supplement for, quantitative controls on emissions. The arguments for using taxes are that they induce reductions in emissions where this can be achieved at least cost, and that they raise revenue so that other distortionary taxes can be reduced. *See also* DOUBLE-DIVIDEND HYPOTHESIS.

employee A person working for somebody else, for wages or salary, rather than working on their own account and selling their product or services. An employee has a contract of employment, and employers are liable for damage caused either by or to employees in the course of their duties. In the UK employers are required to collect income tax and National Insurance contributions from employees liable to them. Similar legislation exists in many countries. Self-employed workers are responsible for their own insurance and for their tax and National Insurance payments.

employee stock ownership plan (ESOP) An arrangement for a US company to provide shares for its employees through a trust fund. Company contributions to ESOPs are tax-deductible. Employee share ownership is believed to make employees better motivated, better informed about their employer's business, and more loyal to the company.

employer An individual, company, or government body that pays somebody wages to work for them. This is distinguished from hiring a self-employed person to do the work.

employers' association A body representing employers in some sector of the economy. Such bodies may conduct collective bargaining with trade unions on behalf of their members, on wages, hours, and working conditions. They often also lobby the government about changes in laws affecting their members, for example concerning security of employment or health and safety measures.

employer's liability The legal liability of employers to compensate their employees for accidents and illnesses due to their work. Employers in the UK are compelled to insure themselves for this. It would be possible to run an economy on the basis that wages reflected the risks to health of various jobs, and employees were responsible for insuring themselves. There are two main arguments for imposing the liability on employers. One is economies of scale: there are far fewer employers than workers in the economy, so insurance by employers is less costly both to carry out and to enforce. The other argument is economy of information: on average employers have a broader experience of occupational risks in their industry, and they are responsible for working practices. They can use their experience to organize work in ways which keep down the risks run, and thus the cost of insurance.

employment 1. Service performed for pay or wages under a contract of hire.
2. The number of people in an economy who provide services for pay under a contract (this includes both full-time and part-time workers in private, public, non-profit, and household sectors), as well as the self-employed. *See also* CONTRACT OF EMPLOYMENT; FULL EMPLOYMENT; OVERFULL EMPLOYMENT.

employment protection Regulations concerning the dismissal of workers by their employers. These concern matters such as the procedures to be followed, the reasons for which employees can be dismissed, and the compensation to which they are entitled in the case of redundancy or wrongful dismissal.

endogeneity problem Simultaneous causality between the *dependent variable and an *endogenous variable that is used as an explanatory variable. Endogeneity renders the *ordinary least squares estimator biased and inconsistent; a consistent estimator can be obtained using regression with *instrumental variables.

endogenous business cycle A model of *business cycles where the sources of fluctuation are random shocks to the beliefs of the economic agents. These beliefs become self-fulfilling due to increasing returns to scale in some sector of the economy or at the aggregate level, or due to the presence of externalities in the agents' choices. *See also* REAL BUSINESS CYCLE.

endogenous growth Economic growth where the growth rate is determined by the choices of economic agents. Firms expend resources on research and development to secure profitable innovations. Consumers invest in education to develop human capital and increase lifetime earnings. Governments increase growth by providing public inputs, encouraging foreign direct investment, and enhancing educational opportunities. All these actions can raise the rate of growth. This is contrasted with exogenous growth, where the long-run growth rate is determined from outside the system by an exogenously given rate of *technical progress. In either case short-run growth can be increased by additional investment. In exogenous growth this increase is only transitory: growth gradually falls towards an exogenously determined long-run rate. In endogenous growth higher investment, or the devotion of more resources to research and development, can increase the rate of growth for an indefinite period.

endogenous preferences Individual preferences that form under the influence of the economic, social, legal, and cultural structure of the environment and may change in response to changes in the environment. For example, consumers' tastes for a particular good can be shaped by advertising, or investors' risk aversion can be affected by market arrangements. Under the assumption of endogeneity of preferences, the environment and the preferences are interdependent and are jointly determined in equilibrium.

endogenous variable A variable whose value is determined by the equilibrium of a system, in contrast to an exogenous variable that is imposed on a system from outside. For example, the resource endowments of an economy are exogenous, whereas equilibrium prices are endogenous. In the context of econometrics, an endogenous variable is correlated with the *error term in the regression.

energy tax A tax on the consumption of energy. An energy tax would slow down exhaustion of the limited world stock of fossil fuels, and it is claimed that it would reduce global warming.

Engel curve A curve showing the relation between income level and consumption of some good, at a given price. In a diagram with income on the horizontal axis and consumption on the vertical, the Engel curve for a good with unit *income elasticity of demand is a ray through the origin. The Engel curve for a necessity with less than unit income elasticity is flatter than a ray through the origin; and that for a luxury with more than unit income elasticity is steeper.

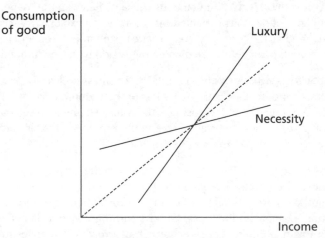

Engel Curve

English auction An auction in which the auctioneer initially announces a low price and takes bids from potential purchasers until no higher bid is forthcoming. The item is then sold to the highest bidder at the price they have bid. *See also* AUCTION.

enterprise 1. A business venture, private or public.
　　2. The combination of initiative, foresight, and willingness to take risks required to make a success of running a business. *See also* PRIVATE ENTERPRISE; STATE ENTERPRISE.

enterprise culture A climate of social opinion favourable to enterprise. This includes a willingness to take risks, a willingness to adopt new ways of doing business, respect for those successful in business, and willingness to allow others the freedom to compete and to retain a large proportion of their profits.

Enterprise Investment Scheme (EIS) A UK scheme to encourage the formation of new small companies, by giving income tax relief to individuals investing up to £400000 (as of 2008) in the equity of new companies. The EIS replaced the *Business Expansion Scheme in 1994.

enterprise zone An area subject to special treatment by the government with the purpose of encouraging investment and employment. The special treatment may include government grants, relaxation of planning regulations, or reduction in taxation. This device has been adopted, for example, in both the UK and the US to try to stimulate recovery in decayed urban areas.

entitlement program A US term for a government spending programme where the rules give recipients a legal right to the payments concerned, such as social security and Medicare. There is thus no government discretion over who should be paid; the cost is open-ended and cannot be capped by policy decisions without getting Congress to change the rules.

entitlements Benefits to which the recipients have a legal right. Such benefits form part of mandatory expenditure for the government. They are contrasted with discretionary benefits, which the donor is empowered but not compelled to pay.

entrepôt A place where goods are imported and re-exported without processing. Entrepôt trade exists because of economies of scale in transport, and because the countries concerned have specialized commodity market institutions.

entrepreneur A person with overall responsibility for decision-taking in a business, who receives any profits, and bears any losses. Entrepreneurs need not necessarily contribute either labour, which can be hired, or financial capital, which can be borrowed; but they must contribute either one of these or a credible guarantee, if their responsibility for possible losses is to be genuine. In a business run by a sole trader it is clear who is the entrepreneur; in incorporated businesses the role is dispersed among directors and shareholders.

entry Access to a market by a new supplier. An entrant may be a new firm, or a firm which has previously been active in other markets. It is possible to enter a new market from scratch, but many firms seeking to broaden their activities by entry to new markets do this by buying up a firm which already has market contacts. *Barriers to entry are factors making entry difficult. Entry is likely to be both most attractive and least subject to restrictions when a market is profitable and growing rapidly. *See also* FREE ENTRY; HIT-AND-RUN ENTRY; INNOCENT ENTRY BARRIERS; STRATEGIC ENTRY DETERRENCE.

entry deterrence The strategic erection of *barriers to entry to deter potential competitors from entering a market and thus preserve monopoly power.

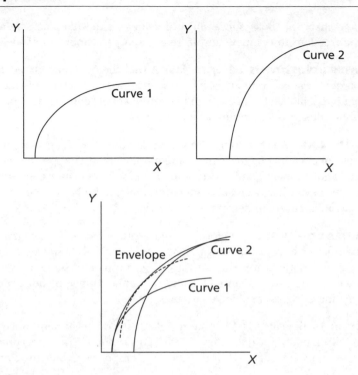

Envelope Curve

envelope curve The outer envelope of a set of curves. For example, the long-run cost function is the lower envelope of the set of short-run cost functions. The figure shows the upper envelope of a set of curves, with curve 1 and curve 2 being two representative members of the set.

envelope theorem A theorem determining the effect of a differential change in a parameter on the outcome of a maximization problem. Formally, consider the problem of choosing x to maximize a function $f(x; a)$, where a is a parameter. Denote the solution to this maximization by $x(a)$ and define the maximum value function $V(a)$ by

$$V(a) = max_{\{x\}} f(x; a) = f(x(a); a).$$

The envelope theorem states that

$$\frac{dV(a)}{da} = \frac{\partial f(x(a); a)}{\partial a}\Big|_{x=x(a)}$$

so that the derivative of the value function is the partial derivative of the objective evaluated at the solution to the optimization.

environment The external conditions and resources which influence human life and development.

environmental economics Study of the economic effects of national or local environmental policies. An example is a *cost–benefit analysis of alternative environmental policies dealing with air pollution, global warming, etc.

Environmental Protection Agency (EPA) A US federal agency for research into pollution and the environment. The EPA is concerned with air and water pollution by solid wastes, pesticides, toxic substances, and radiation; it collaborates with other federal agencies and coordinates the anti-pollution policies of state and local governments.

Equal Employment Opportunity Commission (EEOC) A US federal commission set up by the Civil Rights Act of 1964. The EEOC deals with discrimination in wages, hiring, firing, training, and promotion, on the basis of age, race, sex, religion, or ethnic origin.

Equality and Human Rights Commission An independent non-departmental UK public body, in operation since 1 October 2007, whose objectives are to eliminate discrimination, reduce inequality, protect human rights, and build good relations, ensuring that everyone has a fair chance to participate in society. It replaced and combined the responsibilities of three previous equality commissions: the Equal Opportunities Commission, the Commission for Racial Equality, and the Disability Rights Commission. The Equality and Human Rights Commission also has responsibility for human rights and equality with regard to age, sexual orientation, and religion or belief.

(((⊕))) SEE WEB LINKS
• The official website of the Equality and Human Rights Commission.

equalization grant A grant made by central government to poorer local authorities, to compensate for their lack of local taxable capacity.

equalizing wage differential A wage differential necessary to compensate workers for non-pecuniary disadvantages of a job. Such disadvantages could include danger, dirt, discomfort, an inaccessible workplace, low social regard, or unsocial hours.

equal pay As specified in the UK legislation by the Equal Pay Act of 1970, amended by the Equal Pay (Amendment) Regulations 1983, the principle that provides for equal pay between women and men in the same employment by giving a woman the right to equal pay in her contract of employment where she is employed on like work to that of a man, or work rated equivalent to that of a man, or work of equal value to that of a man; similar legal requirements are in place in many other countries. More generally, a principle that the pay for given work should be independent of the sex, race, religion, age, or other personal characteristics of the worker.

equal sacrifice The principle that the tax burden should be allocated across individuals so that each makes an equal sacrifice. The difficulty with applying this principle is the definition and measurement of sacrifice. One possibility is that there should be an equal sacrifice of consumption but this could be in absolute or proportional terms. An alternative is that the sacrifice is measured in utility terms, but this raises difficult questions about *interpersonal comparisons of utility. *See also* ABILITY TO PAY.

equilibrium An equilibrium can be defined either as a position of balance in the economy or, equivalently, as a situation in which no agent in the economy has any incentive to modify their chosen strategy. The first definition is derived from the perspective of equilibrium occurring when the forces of supply are balanced by the forces of demand. The second definition derives from the theory of games and is illustrated by the equilibrium of an oligopolistic market in which all firms are satisfied with their choice of output level given the choices of their rivals. Proving the *existence of equilibrium and demonstrating the welfare properties of equilibrium are important steps in the analysis of an economic model. Equally important is analysis of the uniqueness and stability of equilibrium, and the determination of how changes in exogenous parameters affect the equilibrium (*comparative statics). There are several explanations for the emphasis upon equilibrium. Historically, the economy was viewed as self-correcting so that if it were ever pushed away from equilibrium forces exist that would move it back towards equilibrium. The present justifications for focusing upon equilibrium are more pragmatic. The analysis of a model must begin somewhere, and the equilibrium is a natural starting point. Alternatively, the focus can be justified by showing that the equilibrium is the outcome of playing the underlying game correctly. In addition, even if the final focus is on disequilibrium, there is benefit from comparing the properties of points of disequilibrium to those of the equilibrium. Finally, no positions other than those of equilibrium have any obvious claim to prominence. *See also* COMPETITIVE EQUILIBRIUM; GENERAL EQUILIBRIUM; MARKET EQUILIBRIUM; MULTIPLE EQUILIBRIUM; NASH EQUILIBRIUM; PARTIAL EQUILIBRIUM; SUBGAME PERFECT EQUILIBRIUM.

equilibrium price A price at which the quantity of a good supplied is equal to the quantity demanded. If the supply curve is upward-sloping and the demand curve is downward-sloping, this price is unique.

equilibrium quantity The quantity of a good supplied and demanded when the price is such that these quantities are equal, so that the market is in equilibrium. With an upward-sloping supply curve and a downward-sloping demand curve, if the price is above the equilibrium price, the quantity supplied is above the equilibrium quantity, which, in turn, is above the quantity demanded.

equities The ordinary shares (UK) or common stock (US) of companies. The owners of these shares are entitled to the residual profits of companies after all claims of creditors, debenture holders, and preference shareholders have been satisfied. Equities thus have a higher variance of expected yield than other shares;

this effect increases with a company's *gearing. *See also* CORPORATE EQUITY; DEBT FOR EQUITY.

equity The concept of distributive justice used in *welfare economics. Equity is a general concept that can be given alternative meanings when formalized. As a general concept it refers to the belief that the distribution of economic welfare matters, and that increasing the equality of distribution is a laudable objective. The degree to which equity should be pursued by a policy-maker depends on the rate at which efficiency has to be sacrificed to achieve equity, and on social preferences as summarized in the welfare function. One formalization is the concept of *horizontal equity: those who are equal should be treated equally. For example, when applied to taxation horizontal equity implies that consumers of equal ability should pay the same amount of tax. A second formalization is *vertical equity: welfare should be transferred from those with high ability (who have the opportunity to earn high incomes) to those with lower ability. For example, high-ability consumers should pay relatively more tax.

equity capital Finance for a company raised in exchange for a share of ownership. Ownership can take the form of a shareholding or of having the right to convert other financial instruments into shares.

equity-linked assurance A system of life insurance where the benefits to be received are linked to the level of an index of equity share prices. The benefits may have some guaranteed minimum, but above this they reflect the behaviour of equity prices up to the time when the policy matures.

equity withdrawal Raising a new or increased *mortgage for some purpose other than buying or improving the mortgaged property. It may be used as a means of raising capital to start or expand a business or as a means of raising a cheaper, secured, loan to pay off unsecured debts already incurred at a higher interest rate.

equivalence scale A method of adjusting household incomes to account for differences in demographic composition. Household incomes that have been adjusted using an equivalence scale can be used directly in welfare comparisons.

equivalent variation The amount of additional income needed to give the level of utility which an individual could have reached if the economic environment had changed. For example, if a price of a good demanded by a consumer were to fall the consumer would be better off. The equivalent variation of this price fall is therefore positive: the consumer would need to be given additional income to make them as well off without the price fall as they would have been with the price fall. Using the *expenditure function, $E(p,U)$, the equivalent variation, EV, is defined by

$$EV = E(p^1,U^1) - E(p^0,U^1)$$

where p^0 denotes initial prices, p^1 final prices, and U^1 final utility. The equivalent variation of a price rise is positive, and the equivalent variation of a price fall is negative. This is an alternative to the *compensating variation, which is the amount of additional income needed to restore an individual's original level of utility if the price of any good consumed changes.

error correction model (ECM) A dynamic model in which the change of the variable in the current time period is related to the distance between its value in the previous period and its value in the long-run equilibrium. This model is frequently used to estimate a short-run dynamic relationship between cointegrated variables and their rate of adjustment to the long-run equilibrium relationship.

errors in variables bias The bias of an estimator caused by measurement errors in the data.

error term In a regression, the difference between the dependent variable and the regression function. It captures the combined effect of any deviation of the true functional form of the relationship between the dependent variable and the explanatory variables from the regression function; any errors in measurement of the variables in the data; and any variables that affect the dependent variable but are omitted from the regression function.

escalator clause A clause in a contract linking the price or wage to be paid to some other price, or to the cost of living. This linkage may apply to all increases in costs, or only to those beyond some threshold level. If escalator clauses are widely used in contracts or wage bargains, they contribute to *cost inflation and make inflation difficult to stop.

estate duty A UK tax formerly levied on the estate of a dead person. It was based on the total value of the estate, with exemption for small estates. Estate duty has been replaced, first by capital transfer tax, and then in 1986 by inheritance tax.

Estimates Proposals on expenditure in the coming financial year included in the UK government's annual budget. These have to be approved by the House of Commons. The Select Committee on Estimates is an all-party parliamentary committee appointed to examine selected items in detail.

estimator A rule for using observed sample data to calculate the unobserved value of a population parameter. For example, a sample average of a variable is an estimator of the population mean of this variable.

Euler's theorem If $f(x_1, \ldots, x_n)$ is homogeneous of degree n then

$$x_1 \frac{\partial f}{\partial x_1} + \ldots + x_n \frac{\partial f}{\partial x_n} = nf(x_1, \ldots, x_n).$$

One use of the theorem is to demonstrate that with constant returns to scale and competitive factor markets the total payment to factors equals the revenue of the firm. Assume there are two factors, capital, K, and labour, L. Constant returns to scale implies the production function is homogeneous of degree one so Euler's theorem gives

$$K \frac{\partial f}{\partial K} + L \frac{\partial f}{\partial L} = f(K, L).$$

If the price of output is p, it follows that

$$Kp\frac{\partial f}{\partial K} + Lp\frac{\partial f}{\partial L} = pf(K,L).$$

Competition on the factor market ensures that $r = p\frac{\partial f}{\partial K}$ and $w = p\frac{\partial f}{\partial L}$. Hence,

$$rK + wL = pf(K, L)$$

so total payment to factors equals revenue. This argument has been used as the basis for a theory of distribution.

Euro The unit of the single European currency, adopted in 1999 as part of *European Monetary Union by eleven members of the European Union: Austria, Belgium, Finland, France, Germany, Italy, Ireland, Luxembourg, the Netherlands, Portugal, and Spain. It had a fixed value in terms of each country's domestic currency: for example, approximately 1.6 Deutschmarks, or 200 Portuguese escudos. Initially the Euro was only a common unit of account, and not a medium of exchange; in 2002 it replaced the domestic currencies of the eleven, plus Greece. Slovenia joined the *Eurozone in 2006, Cyprus and Malta in 2008. Euro notes and coins circulate in all fifteen countries.

Eurobond A bond issued in a Eurocurrency, that is, a European currency held outside its country of origin. Eurobonds are issued in bearer form, and the interest payments are free of withholding taxes. They are thus attractive to investors wishing to remain anonymous, for tax avoidance or other reasons. They may be of various maturities, and at fixed interest rates, or floating rates linked to the *London Inter Bank Offered Rate.

Eurocurrency A currency held in a European country other than its country of origin. Such currencies need not themselves be European: there are large Eurodollar and Euroyen deposits. This market is useful for short- and medium-term international borrowing, mainly by banks and large companies, and for financing international trade and investment. Eurocurrency balances are attractive to those wishing to avoid national taxes or regulations.

Eurodollars *See* EUROCURRENCY.

Euromarket A market dealing in Eurobonds and Eurocurrencies, that is, securities and currencies held in European countries other than their country of origin. There are large Euromarkets in several centres, including Brussels, Frankfurt, London, and Paris.

Europe agreements Agreements between the *European Union and countries applying to become members. These agreements concern changes in the institutional and legal arrangements required before countries can accede, and provision for trade with them in the meantime.

European Bank for Reconstruction and Development (EBRD) An international bank founded in 1990 to assist in the transformation of the countries of Central and Eastern Europe and the former Soviet Union to market economies. The EBRD is empowered to make loans to both private and public sector borrowers. Most Western and Eastern European countries are members.

European Central Bank (ECB) The central institution of the *European Monetary Union (EMU). The ECB was set up in 1998, with power to control interest rates from 1999 and to issue Euro coins and notes from 2002. The ECB's offices are in Frankfurt; it has an executive of six members drawn from member countries of the EMU, and a supervisory board of these plus the central bankers of the fifteen EMU members.

European Coal and Steel Community (ECSC) A European body established in 1952 with France, West Germany, Italy, and the three Benelux countries (Belgium, Luxembourg, and the Netherlands) as members. It established a *common market in coal and steel, abolishing tariffs and quantitative restrictions on trade in these goods between its members. It also provided for the regulation of mergers and restrictive practices, setting up a parliament to lay down the rules and a court to enforce them. The ECSC merged in 1958 into the *European Economic Community, which extended the same principles to all manufactured goods.

European Commission The main executive body of the *European Union (EU). Each of the 27 member country governments appoints a single commissioner. The commission is responsible for initiating action in the EU: it accepts joint responsibility and takes decisions by majority vote.

European Community (EC) The main institution of European unity, formed in 1967 from the European Atomic Energy Community, the European Coal and Steel Community, and the *European Economic Community. In 1993 its title changed to the European Union. Its six founder members were Belgium, France, (West) Germany, Italy, Luxembourg, and the Netherlands. Denmark, Ireland, and the UK joined in 1973, Greece in 1979, and Portugal and Spain in 1986.

European Currency Unit (Ecu) A unit of account introduced by the *European Economic Community when forming the *European Monetary System in 1979. The Ecu was a form of international money used by various official European bodies in their accounting, but very little by other financial markets. Its value was equal to a weighted average of the currencies of several member countries. The Ecu was superseded by the Euro, when this was adopted in 1999.

European Economic Community (EEC) The European common market set up in 1958 by the original six members of the European Coal and Steel Community. These were Belgium, France, (West) Germany, Italy, Luxembourg, and the Netherlands. The EEC was combined with the European Atomic Energy Community in 1967 to form the *European Community. The aims of the EEC included the abolition of tariffs and quota restrictions on trade between members, the adoption of a common tariff on trade with non-members, full mobility of workers and capital between members, harmonization of social and economic legislation, and a *Common Agricultural Policy.

European economic integration The process by which the various countries of Europe are becoming more closely linked, particularly in trade and finance. This is partly the result of natural economic developments: trade has increased mainly because of the rise of intra-industry trade, which is increasingly important in industrialized countries situated close together; financial links have been fostered by the general move to abolition of exchange controls and financial deregulation. Integration has also been promoted by deliberate policy, as shown in the formation of numerous European institutions, of which the main ones are the *European Community, now the *European Union, the *European Free Trade Association, and the *European Monetary Union, with the *Euro as a common European currency.

European Free Trade Association (EFTA) An association of European countries with free trade between them, established in 1959. The original members were Austria, Denmark, Norway, Portugal, Sweden, Switzerland, and the UK. Finland and Iceland joined later; Denmark and the UK left when they joined the *European Economic Community in 1973, as did Portugal in 1986 and Austria, Finland, and Sweden in 1995. EFTA is a *free-trade area and not a *customs union, and the free-trade provisions are restricted to goods originating in member countries. EFTA has an industrial free-trade agreement with the European Union.

European Monetary Institute A European organization that was set up to study the problems of organizing a *European Central Bank.

European Monetary System (EMS) A European organization set up in 1979 to coordinate monetary policy and exchange rates in Europe. Its main activities were running the *Exchange Rate Mechanism and planning *European Monetary Union.

European Monetary Union (EMU) The common monetary system for Europe. This includes coordination of monetary policies, the creation of the *European Central Bank, and the adoption of the single European currency.

European Single Market The target of complete integration of the economies of members of the *European Community, now *European Union. The Single European Act of 1986 ensured that this process was completed by 1992. The single market allows free movement of goods, workers, and capital between member states, and removes discrimination in the award of public contracts, transport, and insurance.

European System of Central Banks (ESCB) The system is composed of the *European Central Bank and the central banks of all 27 European Union member states. Not all member states have adopted the *Euro so the ESCB cannot act as the monetary authority for the *Eurozone. This task is undertaken by the *Eurosystem.

European Union (EU) The name since 1993 of the former *European Community. The EU was formed with twelve members: Belgium, Denmark, France, Germany, Greece, Ireland, Italy, Luxembourg, the Netherlands, Portugal, Spain, and the United Kingdom. Austria, Finland, and Sweden joined in 1995. Ten more countries joined in 2004 (Cyprus, the Czech Republic, Estonia, Hungary, Latvia, Lithuania, Malta, Poland, Slovakia, and Slovenia). Bulgaria and Romania joined in 2007. Croatia, the Republic of Macedonia, and Turkey are currently official candidate countries for membership. Additionally, the western Balkan countries of

Albania, Bosnia and Herzegovina, Montenegro, and Serbia are officially recognized as potential candidates.

Eurosystem The monetary authority of the *Eurozone. The Eurosystem is composed of the *European Central Bank and the central banks of the European Union member states that have adopted the *Euro.

Eurozone The countries that have abolished their national currencies and adopted the Euro. In 2008 there are fifteen: Austria, Belgium, Cyprus, Finland, France, Germany, Greece, Ireland, Italy, Luxembourg, Malta, the Netherlands, Portugal, Slovenia, and Spain. Monaco, San Marino, and Vatican City also use the Euro through agreements with EU member states. Andorra, Kosovo, and Montenegro use the Euro but without any legal agreement with the EU.

evolutionary theory of the firm The view that the survival of firms is an evolutionary process. The specific feature of the evolutionary approach is that it explains the adaptive behaviour of firms to changing market conditions via the interaction between innovation and natural selection.

ex ante Literally translated from Latin: from before. The term describes activities (e.g. actions, decisions, formation of expectations) that are undertaken before the state of nature is revealed. For instance, a firm may make an ex ante plan to invest next year, but when next year arrives market conditions may be poor (the realized state of nature) and the firm may have no incentive to undertake the investment. Ex ante is contrasted with *ex post, meaning as viewed after the event.

excess burden *See* DEADWEIGHT LOSS.

excess capacity A situation in which a firm is producing less than the maximum it is capable of producing. A firm may hold excess capacity to meet random fluctuations in demand. Alternatively, the firm may have undertaken in the past fixed investment to meet a higher level of demand than it is currently facing. Excess capacity may also be a strategic choice: investment in capacity signals a credible commitment to raise output if a potential competitor chooses to enter the market. This is an example of *entry deterrence.

excess demand The difference between demand and supply. If the excess demand for a good is positive then the quantity of a good demanded exceeds the quantity supplied; if excess demand is negative the converse is true. An economy is in equilibrium if excess demand is absent. If there is excess demand price adjustment must take place for equilibrium to be achieved. Walras's law states that the total value of excess demand summed over all goods in the economy is zero. Sonnenschein's theorem shows that for any function satisfying Walras's law there is an economy for which it is the excess demand function.

excess profit Profits which are above the level necessary to retain an entrepreneur in the current line of business. Opinions that profits are excessive are usually based on comparisons, either with the rate of return on capital obtainable in other industries with a comparable degree of risk, or with the past profits of the same company.

exchange **1.** The trade of one good or asset for another. Exchange is the most basic form of economic activity. It requires a double *coincidence of wants between the two parties: each must want what the other possesses. The process of exchange can be represented in an *Edgeworth box. *See also* VOLUNTARY EXCHANGE.

2. A place where trading is carried out: thus shares were traded at the stock exchange, corn was traded at a corn exchange, and workers were hired at a labour exchange. In many cases most of the trade is nowadays done electronically, so that a stock exchange is often an institution rather than a physical place. *See also* COMMODITY MARKET.

exchange control A system under which holders of a national currency require official permission or approval to convert it into other currencies. Exchange control may apply to all holders of a currency, or some holders, usually non-residents, may be exempt. Where non-residents are allowed convertibility, exchange control may be applied to transfers from resident to non-resident domestic currency bank accounts. Exchange controls may have varying degrees of strictness; frequently they are much more stringent on obtaining foreign currency for capital account than for current account purposes.

Exchange Equalization Account A UK government account at the *Bank of England, in which the country's gold and foreign exchange reserves are held. This account is used to intervene in the foreign exchange market.

exchange rate The price of one currency in terms of another. A par exchange rate is that agreed between governments, or registered with a central authority such as the *International Monetary Fund. A market exchange rate is the actual price on foreign exchange markets. Market prices of foreign exchange are liable to fluctuate, between narrow margins in a fixed exchange rate system, and much more widely under a floating or flexible rate system. In countries with exchange controls, there may be *multiple exchange rates: the price of foreign currency varies according to the use the central bank believes a purchaser intends to make of it. In countries with *convertible currencies there is at any one time only a single exchange rate with any given foreign currency. Because of transaction costs and some element of monopoly in dealing with small buyers and sellers of currencies, banks generally charge more to sell foreign exchange than they offer to buy it, particularly in the case of small amounts and low-denomination notes. In the markets used by banks and large commercial organizations the range of prices is much smaller. All this refers to nominal exchange rates: these are contrasted with real exchange rates, which compare the relative prices of different countries' products. A country's real exchange rate may change either through a change in its nominal exchange rate, or through a domestic inflation rate faster or slower than that of its trading partners. *See also* CRAWLING PEG EXCHANGE RATES; EFFECTIVE EXCHANGE RATE; FIXED EXCHANGE RATE; FLOATING EXCHANGE RATE; MISALIGNED EXCHANGE RATE; MULTIPLE EXCHANGE RATES; REALIGNMENT OF EXCHANGE RATES.

exchange rate bands Limits to variations in exchange rates. A country commits itself to hold the exchange rate between its own currency and some foreign currency or currencies within a limited band. Exchange rate bands may be broad or

narrow: under the *Exchange Rate Mechanism, for example, members of the
*European Monetary System agreed to keep their currencies within 2 percent of
parity with the *European Currency Unit, an average of European currencies, while
the UK and Italy only committed themselves to broader bands, of 6 percent each
side of parity.

Exchange Rate Mechanism (ERM) A feature of the *European Monetary
System (EMS), by which EMS members agreed to maintain the relative prices of
their currencies within narrow limits. This was done by keeping each country's
value in *European Currency Units (Ecus) within 2 percent of an agreed parity grid
of par values. Some currencies, including sterling, were allowed a wider range of 6
percent. These values could be realigned only by mutual agreement. The ERM was
founded in 1979, and over the first few years parities were realigned several times.
The UK joined the ERM in 1990, but was forced to leave it in 1992 by speculation
against the pound. The ERM was replaced by the adoption of the Euro in 1999.

exchange rate overshooting An instantaneous adjustment of the exchange
rate to a change in the foreign exchange market such that the initial jump takes the
exchange rate beyond its new equilibrium level, in order to clear the asset markets
when, for example, the speed of adjustment of goods prices is finite. In such a case,
once goods prices begin to adjust to the new environment the exchange rate
proceeds to its new equilibrium level.

exchange rate regime The system by which exchange rates between different
currencies are determined. There are a number of possible systems, ranging from
the *gold standard, under which all countries are permanently committed to
maintaining fixed exchange rates, to a freely floating system in which no effort is
made to stabilize exchange rates, which are left to be determined entirely by market
forces. Under the gold standard each country makes its currency convertible into
gold at a fixed price, or the central bank operates buying and selling prices which
differ only by a small percentage, and trade in gold is not controlled. The exchange
rate between two currencies on the gold standard cannot move far from par, since
this would make it profitable for *arbitrageurs to buy gold from one central bank
and sell it to the other. Under the *Bretton Woods system, which operated from after
the Second World War until 1971, countries registered par values for their
currencies with the *International Monetary Fund, and undertook to keep market
exchange rates within a small margin of variation from these rates. The difference
from the gold standard was that countries retained the right to change their par
rates in the event of 'fundamental disequilibrium', which was never defined. This
'adjustable peg' system meant that government commitment to existing par rates
lacked credibility, so that speculators frequently forced countries with weak
currencies to devalue. Since 1973 the world has been on a flexible exchange rate
system. As governments are worried that speculation might lead to violent
instability in exchange rates, floating is generally not 'pure' or 'clean', but 'managed'
or 'dirty', with considerable intervention by central banks to try to limit fluctuations
in exchange rates, not always successfully. Under a generally adopted fixed
exchange rate system, each country has a choice as to whether to join it or opt for
flexible rates. Under a floating rate system, no country has this choice: if other

currencies are all floating against each other, a single country can choose to peg its exchange rate with some other, usually a larger country with which it does much of its trade. Some smaller countries peg their currencies to the US dollar but their exchange rates with all other currencies still float. Alternatively, they can peg their currencies to a basket of other currencies: the rates with any single currency will still float. It is possible for a group of countries to decide to link their currencies, as was the case with the *Exchange Rate Mechanism of the *European Monetary System. This still leaves them floating relative to the currencies of non-member countries, such as the US dollar. Where a country decides to manage its exchange rate, this can be done either by discretionary action by the central bank, or by setting down rules about the procedure to be followed, for example a *'crawling peg' system, which attempts simply to slow down changes rather than aiming at any fixed target.

exchange restrictions *See* EXCHANGE CONTROL.

excise duty A tax levied on the consumption of particular goods. Excise duties may be levied to raise government revenue, but are often levied at higher rates on goods whose consumption is believed to have adverse effects on public health, public order, or the environment. Excise duties on alcoholic drinks, tobacco, and petrol are widely used for both purposes.

exclusion The legal right and practical ability to prevent others from using a good. If a good is to be a private good it must be possible for its owner to exclude others from using it at reasonable cost. Exclusion is linked to the economic efficiency of competitive equilibrium. A public good has the property of non-excludability and, unless the conditions of the *Tiebout hypothesis are satisfied, will not be supplied efficiently without some form of government intervention.

exclusive dealing An agreement between the producer and a distributor of certain goods that one will trade only with the other. This may apply generally, or within a particular country or district. In some cases this means that a retailer agrees to stock only one manufacturer's brands; in other cases a manufacturer agrees to sell through only one outlet in a given area. It is possible for both forms of restriction to apply. Such practices are criticized as being in restraint of trade.

ex dividend Sale of shares where the vendor retains the right to a dividend already declared but not yet paid. This is contrasted with cum dividend, where the sale includes the right of the purchaser to receive a dividend already declared but not yet paid.

exercise price The price at which an *option gives the right to buy or sell shares, commodities, or currencies. The option will be exercised only if this price is more favourable to the party holding it than the market price. A put option will only be used to sell assets if the exercise price is higher than the market price, and a call option will only be used to buy assets if the exercise price is lower than the market price.

exhaustible resources *See* DEPLETABLE RESOURCES.

existence of equilibrium The demonstration that an equilibrium exists for an economic model or a game. An existence proof requires the demonstration that there is a simultaneous solution to the set of equations that describe the equilibrium. For example, the equations describing equilibrium of the *Arrow–Debreu economy are obtained from the conditions for market clearing. Not all economic models possess an equilibrium: a competitive insurance market with *adverse selection may have neither a pooling nor a separating equilibrium.

exit 1. Departure of a firm from an industry. This will normally occur if a firm is making losses and sees no prospect that the market will recover. Employment protection legislation or other public regulations may hinder a firm wishing to discontinue part of its business while continuing to trade. If a firm is insolvent there is nothing the law can do to prevent it from exiting entirely from the economy, unless the government is willing to carry on the business at the taxpayer's expense. Where an enterprise is actually profitable but the firm owning it is not, due to excessive debt charges, the firm will normally exit but the enterprise will continue under new ownership.

2. The expression of preferences by leaving unsatisfactory situations: this can apply to selling shares, changing jobs, or migration between areas or countries. It is contrasted with 'voice', which is attempting to change the situation one is in by voting, lobbying, or use of complaints procedures or litigation.

exit price The price below which firms will leave an industry. This is likely to be somewhat below the break-even price, as *sunk costs cannot be avoided by exit.

exogenous expectations Expectations that are not determined by the parameters of the economic system and are not systematically revised.

exogenous variable A variable not related to other economic variables in the system under consideration by causal links but determined by factors outside the system. In the context of econometrics, an exogenous variable is uncorrelated with the *error term in the regression.

expectations The forecast or the view of economic agents about the future values of economic variables. Expectations are important in the analysis of economic behaviour as they influence the choices of economic agents. Through these choices expectations affect the time path of an economy, and the time path, in its turn, may affect the expectations of the agents. *See also* ADAPTIVE EXPECTATIONS; EXOGENOUS EXPECTATIONS; EXTRAPOLATIVE EXPECTATIONS; RATIONAL EXPECTATIONS; SELF-FULFILLING EXPECTATIONS.

expectations-augmented Phillips curve A version of the *Phillips curve, relating wage increases to demand pressure, taking account of expected inflation. If the expected rate of price increases is given, the Phillips curve shows wage increases as a decreasing function of the unemployment rate, or an increasing function of demand pressure. Wage increases lead to price increases, so actual inflation is an increasing function of demand pressure. If the expected inflation rate did not respond, and the Phillips curve stayed the same from period to period, it would be possible by the use of monetary or fiscal measures to expand demand to get permanently higher employment at the price of accepting a higher rate of inflation. The expectations-augmented Phillips curve assumes that if actual inflation rises, expected inflation will also increase, and the Phillips curve will move upwards so as to give the same expected real wage increase at each employment level. Under this model there is no long-run trade-off between unemployment and inflation. To achieve an unemployment rate below the *non-accelerating inflation rate of unemployment would involve an ever-increasing rate of inflation. This is thought to be undesirable, since while moderate rates of inflation may do relatively little harm, *hyperinflation seriously interferes with the efficient running of the real economy by impairing the economic functions of money.

expected inflation The rate of inflation that people expect; this may be different for different time horizons. Expected inflation cannot be directly observed, except by surveys in which people are asked to state their expectations. It can be inferred, for example, from the difference between the prices of index-linked and non-indexed government securities with the same maturity dates. The greater the expected rate of inflation, the greater the excess of the prices of indexed securities over those of comparable non-indexed ones.

expected utility The expected value of utility from entering a risky prospect. Assume the risky prospect has n potential outcomes. Let the probability of outcome i occurring be p_i and the pay-off if i occurs be X_i. If the utility derived from pay-off X is $U(X)$, then expected utility is

$$E[U] = p_1 U(X_1) + ... + p_n U(X_n).$$

The expected utility theorem states that if a consumer satisfies a set of axioms describing rationality they should act in risky situations as if they maximize expected utility. If utility is a linear function of X, then $E[U] = U[E(X_i)]$, that is, expected utility is the utility of the expected value of the pay-offs. If utility is a concave function of pay-off, that is, $d^2U/dX^2 < 0$, then the expected utility of a risky prospect is less than the utility of the expected pay-off; $E[U] < U[E(X_i)]$, so the consumer prefers a sure pay-off to a risky prospect of the same expected value.

expected value Given the probability distribution $P[x]$ of a discrete random variable X, the expected value, or the (mathematical) expectation of a function $f(X)$ is defined as

$$E[f(X)] = \Sigma P(x)f(x)$$

where the sum is taken over all possible values that X can take. For a continuous random variable X with probability distribution function $F(x)$ the expected value of $f(X)$ is defined as $\int f(x)dF(x)$ where the integral is taken over all possible values of X. The expected value of $f(X)$ is also referred to as the mean of the distribution of X.

expenditure Spending, by consumers, investors, or the government. Consumer expenditure is restricted to purchasing real goods and services; acquiring assets or making transfers to others by individuals does not count as expenditure. Government expenditure is treated differently: some government expenditure is on real goods and services, but government interest payments and transfer payments to individuals, such as pensions, are counted as government expenditure, and government spending is not clearly divided between current and capital account items, possibly because these are hard to distinguish. National expenditure is what a country spends. *See also* CAPITAL EXPENDITURE; CONSUMER EXPENDITURE; CUTS IN EXPENDITURE; GOVERNMENT EXPENDITURE; TAX EXPENDITURE.

Expenditure and Food Survey (EFS) A continuous survey of household expenditure, food consumption, and income. It replaced the *Family Expenditure Survey and the National Food Survey in April 2001. Its primary aim is to provide information about spending patterns for the *retail price index, and about food consumption and nutrition. Other uses of the EFS include the estimation of consumers' expenditure for the *national income accounts, and as an input in to tax–benefit modelling. It is an important source of economic and social data for government and other research agencies.

(⊕) SEE WEB LINKS
• The home page of the survey.

expenditure-based deflator A price index whose weights reflect the shares of different goods and services in expenditure, rather than shares in production. This includes import prices and excludes export prices.

expenditure changing An economic policy intended to change total expenditure. This may be through fiscal policy, for example a tax cut, or through monetary policy, via a reduction in interest rates. It is contrasted with an *expenditure switching policy, intended to divert expenditure from one outlet to another, for example the use of tariffs or import quotas to switch spending from imported on to home-produced goods.

expenditure function The minimum cost for a consumer of achieving a given utility level. Consider a consumer choosing the quantities, x_1 and x_2, of two goods to minimize expenditure subject to a utility constraint. The cost minimization problem is

$$\min_{\{x_1,x_2\}} p_1 x_1 + p_2 x_2 \text{ subject to } U(x_1, x_2) \geq U.$$

The function $E(p_1,p_2,U)$The solution is described by the two *compensated demand functions $x_1 = h_1(p_1,p_2,U)$ and $x_2 = h_2(p_1,p_2,U)$. Substituting the optimal choices back into the objective gives the minimized level of expenditure as

$$E(p_1,p_2,U) \equiv p_1 h_1(p_1,p_2,U) + p_2 h_2(p_1,p_2,U).$$

The function $E(p_1,p_2,U)$ is the expenditure function. Shephard's lemma states that $\partial E/\partial p_i = h_i(p_1,p_2,U)$, a result that is useful for calculating the welfare consequences of a price change. *See also* INDIRECT UTILITY FUNCTION.

expenditure method The method of calculating domestic product using information on expenditure by various sectors of the economy, including consumers, investors, and the government. This naturally produces a figure at *market prices. The expenditure method is contrasted with the other two methods, the *output method, which proceeds by adding the net outputs of various sectors of the economy, and the *income method, which proceeds by adding up the incomes of various sectors.

expenditure switching A policy intended to divert an existing level of expenditure from one outlet to another. For example, tariffs or import quotas could be used to divert existing spending from imports on to home-produced goods. This is contrasted with *expenditure changing policies, intended to increase or decrease total spending. The distinction applies to the impact effect of the policy concerned: if an expenditure switching policy is successful it will produce multiplier effects which also change total spending. *See also* EXTERNAL BALANCE; INTERNAL BALANCE.

expenditure tax A tax levied on the value of expenditure; also known as consumption tax. Expenditure is an alternative to income as the base for personal taxation. The theoretical distinction between an income tax and an expenditure tax is that the latter does not tax income from savings. An expenditure tax does not, therefore, distort the choice between current and future consumption whereas an income tax does. This has been the basis of claims that the replacement of the income tax by an expenditure tax will increase saving and raise the rate of economic growth. The choice between income and expenditure taxes is not as stark as it may appear: the existence of tax-free saving vehicles removes much of the difference in effect.

experimental economics A field of economics that uses controlled experiments, laboratory as well as field, to test and/or estimate economic models.

exponential distribution A special case of the *gamma distribution with the density function

$$f(x|\beta) = \frac{1}{\beta} e^{-x/\beta}$$

for $0 \leq x < \infty$ and $\beta > 0$. An exponential random variable has mean β and variance β^2. This distribution has the memoryless property and is frequently used to model lifetimes and queuing problems.

exponential smoothing A forecast based on the weighted average of the past values of the variable, in which the weights assigned to the past values decline exponentially with the lag length. This procedure is also used to produce smoothed data by eliminating noise and is a version of the weighted moving average technique.

exportables Goods and services of types which could be exported, whether they are in fact exported or not.

export concentration Concentration of exports on a narrow range of categories of goods and services, or a narrow range of countries. The higher its degree of export concentration, the more liable are a country's balance of trade and national income to disruption by fluctuations in the sectors of the world economy in which it is concentrated. More widely dispersed markets give a lower degree of risk. Export concentration is generally highest in some of the oil-exporting countries, and some of the world's smaller primary commodity exporters. It is generally low in industrial countries.

export control Restriction of exports by governments on the grounds of, for example, defence considerations or promotion of domestic industries in the processing of local raw materials.

export credit The system of selling exports on credit rather than for cash payment. Exports of commodities and consumer goods are frequently financed by trade bills, or short-term credit. These are normally payable in 3 or 6 months, giving the buyer time to ship goods and distribute them for resale, thus providing the money to pay the bills. If the seller needs immediate cash, bills can be discounted, that is sold to discount houses. Producer goods normally need longer-term credit. This may be given by the sellers, or by intermediary financial institutions. The length of credit available is an important factor affecting the marketability of capital goods exports. Many countries promote their exports by providing either subsidized export credit, or guarantees on more favourable terms than can be obtained commercially. Export credits are governed by international agreement between the member countries of the *Organization for Economic Cooperation and Development.

export credit agency A body set up to provide credit to export customers or guarantees of credit granted by exporters. Where the interest charged for credits or the premiums charged for guarantees are below what is available in the market, state subsidies for export credit agencies are a form of export subsidy.

Export Credits Guarantee Department (ECGD) A UK government department responsible for encouraging UK exports by insuring exporters against risks. These include both the risk of default on the part of export customers, and the risk of loss through the imposition of import licensing or exchange controls by the importers' governments. Export credits may be for any period up to 10 years; the premiums charged may constitute an implicit subsidy if they fail to reflect the full cost of risks.

Export–Import Bank (Eximbank) An agency of the US federal government set up to promote US trade. The Eximbank assists US exports by providing finance, or guaranteeing or insuring private loans to finance them.

export incentives Devices used by countries to encourage exports. These can include tax incentives for exporters, allowing them exemptions from the usual provisions of anti-monopoly legislation, preferential access to capital markets, priority allocations of materials in countries where these are controlled, allowing exporters to retain export earnings rather than having to exchange them at the official exchange rate in countries with over-valued currencies, and official honours for successful exporters.

export-led growth Growth in which exports increase faster than other components of national expenditure. This can occur either because foreign incomes are growing faster than at home, or because domestic products are becoming more competitive in world markets, through lower prices, increased variety, or quality improvements.

export promotion **1.** Government activities to help sell exports by providing export incentives at home, and various forms of practical assistance for exporters abroad. These include advice on local trading laws and practices, the provision of export credits or guarantees on favourable terms, and diplomatic pressure, including tying aid to export sales.

2. A strategy for promoting economic development in *less developed countries. This involves running an open economy, relying on foreign markets to allow export-led growth. This strategy has been successfully used by many countries, including the newly industrialized countries of East Asia. It is contrasted with the strategy of import replacement, where countries started to industrialize by protecting local industries against imports.

exports Goods and services produced in a country and sold to non-residents. Visible exports are goods sent abroad; invisible exports are services sold to non-residents. Some invisibles, for example air and sea transport, are services performed abroad. In the case of other invisibles, non-residents come to a country to use the services of hotels, hospitals, universities, or casinos. In the case of services such as insurance the location of the service is not defined. Export of capital means making loans to non-residents or buying real assets located abroad, which is not the same as exporting capital goods. Some countries do both, but it is perfectly possible, as with some oil-exporting countries, to export capital without producing capital goods, and many industrial countries are capital goods exporters while borrowing abroad and so are importers of capital. *See also* NET EXPORTS.

export subsidy A subsidy to exporters, so that the price per unit received by the producers of exports is higher than the price charged to foreign customers. Direct export subsidies are prohibited by international agreement, but other government measures with similar effects are not uncommon. Exporters may be allowed refunds on tariffs on their inputs, subsidized credit, preferential access to ordinary credit in an economy, or assistance with their capital costs or training costs. In economies with either currency or direct controls on imports, exporters can be allowed priority in the allocation of scarce materials or foreign currency. Firms competing with imports which they claim have received export subsidies may be able to obtain countervailing import duties to offset the effects of these subsidies.

export surplus An excess of exports over imports.

ex post Literally translated from Latin: from after. The value of a variable, or of a decision made, as it appears after the outcome of randomness has been realized, that is, what actually occurred. Ex post is contrasted with *ex ante, which means looking at things before the event.

exposure to risk The extent to which lending institutions would lose if particular borrowers or classes of borrower were to default on their obligations. Exposure to risk can be kept down both by choosing relatively safe forms of investment, such as the government debt of countries considered unlikely to default, and by avoiding having too large a percentage of assets invested in the debt of any one borrower or class of borrower.

extensive form The representation of a game as a tree that displays decision nodes, strategies, information sets, and pay-offs. The extensive form permits insight into the play of some games that cannot be obtained from consideration of the pay-off matrix.

extensive margin The margin that is affected by a discrete change in the level to which an activity is undertaken. For example, moving from unemployment to working 40 hours per week is a change at the extensive margin. *See also* INTENSIVE MARGIN.

external balance A sustainable pattern of transactions with the rest of the world. With no capital movements, in a static economy external balance requires a zero balance of payments on current account, since otherwise foreign exchange reserves would become exhausted if there was a current account deficit, and would expand without limit if there was a current account surplus. Without capital movements a growing economy which needs to add to its foreign exchange reserves requires a current account surplus just sufficient for this purpose. With capital movements, external balance means that these are at a sustainable level, at least in the medium run. In an economy with good domestic investment opportunities and low savings, capital inflows and a current account deficit could represent external balance. Conversely, in an economy with high savings and poor domestic investment opportunities, capital outflow and a current account surplus could represent external balance. *See also* INTERNAL BALANCE.

external diseconomies of scale These arise when the entry of new firms into an industry causes the minimum average total cost of all firms in the industry to rise. This occurs when input prices are driven up as the demand for specialized inputs increases. Through this mechanism an expansion of the industry (but not of an individual firm) causes minimum average total cost to rise for all firms in the industry. The industry long-run supply curve therefore slopes upwards.

external economies of scale These arise when the entry of new firms into an industry causes the minimum average total cost of all firms in the industry to fall. This can occur if the prices of inputs fall as suppliers of inputs exploit economies of scale as demand for their products increases. Through this mechanism an expansion of the industry (but not of an individual firm) causes minimum average total cost to fall for all firms in the industry. The industry long-run supply curve therefore slopes downwards.

externality A cost or benefit arising from any activity which does not accrue to the person or organization carrying out the activity. Negative externalities cause damage to other people or the environment, for example by radiation, river or air pollution, or noise, which does not have to be paid for by those carrying out the activity. Positive externalities are effects of an activity which are pleasant or profitable for other people who cannot be charged for them, for example fertilization of fruit trees by bees, or the public's enjoyment of views of private buildings or gardens. Externalities may be technological or pecuniary. Technological externalities affect other people in non-market ways, for example by polluting their water supply; they create a prima facie case for intervention in the interests of efficiency. Pecuniary externalities mean that other people are affected through the market: for example, the emergence of a new industry may raise labour costs for other employers, or reduce the value of their capital by capturing their customers. Pecuniary externalities do not create any prima facie case for intervention, except possibly on grounds of income distribution. *See also* COMPENSATION FOR EXTERNALITIES; CONSUMPTION EXTERNALITY; INTERNALIZING EXTERNALITIES; NETWORK EXTERNALITY; PRODUCTION EXTERNALITY.

external labour market The system by which recruitment for senior appointments in an organization is mainly by open competition. It is contrasted with an *internal labour market, in which senior posts are filled mainly by promoting existing employees in lower-grade jobs. The main merits of an external labour market are that open competition provides a wider choice for senior appointments, and that outsiders may bring new ideas to an organization. The main merits of internal labour markets are that a firm is likely to know more about the strengths and weaknesses of existing employees than outsiders, and that a reputation for internal promotion as its preferred strategy may assist in recruitment and retention of staff.

extrapolation Construction of new data points outside the given set of existing data points. Popular methods are linear and polynomial extrapolation; linear extrapolation uses regression-like techniques and is similar to linear prediction. The reliability of extrapolation is measured by the prediction error or the prediction confidence interval.

extrapolative expectations Expectations about the future values of economic variables constructed using *extrapolation based on the observed current and past values of these variables, under the assumption that observed patterns will continue to hold. Extrapolative expectations are backward-looking.

factor-augmenting technical progress *See* TECHNICAL PROGRESS.

factor cost The value of goods and services at the prices received by sellers. This is the market prices paid by purchasers, minus any indirect taxes, plus any subsidies provided by the government. Factor cost is so called because the value of output at factor cost is the amount available to pay for bought-in inputs and for the services of the factors of production used. Factor cost thus involves treating any profits of the firms concerned as payment for factor inputs.

factor endowment A country's stock of factors of production. This includes the quantities of land, labour, capital, and raw materials. A high factor endowment is a necessary condition for economic prosperity (but successful exploitation of the endowment is also required).

factor incomes Incomes derived from selling the services of *factors of production. In the case of labour, this means wages, plus the part of the incomes of the self-employed which is a reward for their own labour. Income from land is rents, including part of the incomes of the self-employed, and part of the imputed incomes of owner–occupiers of houses. Incomes from capital and entrepreneurship are received as dividends, interest, the retained profits of companies, and the part of the incomes of the self-employed which is a return on their own capital and entrepreneurship.

factor incomes from abroad Incomes received by residents of a country from activities carried out abroad. This includes remittances by migrants working abroad, profits earned by companies operating abroad, and interest received on loans made abroad. Gross factor incomes from abroad are the total amounts so received; net factor incomes from abroad are these receipts minus any expenditure on similar items earned within the country by non-residents. Net factor incomes from abroad can thus be negative.

factoring Buying goods for resale without further processing. Debt factoring is buying debts due from another business's customers and collecting them.

factor intensity The relative proportions of various *factors of production used in producing goods and services. The factor intensity of the techniques of production chosen by a cost-minimizing firm depends on the relative prices of different factors of production. For any given set of relative factor prices, some goods are produced with a low capital–labour ratio: such goods are labour-intensive. Others are produced with a high capital–labour ratio: such goods are capital-intensive. Agricultural goods may be produced using a significant input of land and relatively few other inputs: such products are land-intensive.

factor market The bargaining system in which the prices of the various *factors of production are determined. In most economies there is no one institution in which *factor prices are determined. Wage rates in Europe are typically decided by a series of negotiations between employers or groups of employers and *trade unions. These negotiations are linked in the sense that what happens in one wage bargain has effects on others, but there is no formal organization of this interaction. Collective bargaining over wages is less common in the US. Negotiations over rents of land and the terms on which capital is made available to firms are similarly decentralized.

factor mobility The degree of ease with which productive factors, like labour, capital, land, natural resources, etc., can be reallocated across sectors within an economy (domestic factor mobility) or across countries (international factor mobility).

factor(s) of production Any resource used in the production of goods or services. Factors of production can be broadly classified into three main groups: labour, or human services; capital, or man-made means of production; and land, or natural resources. Each of these broad groups of factors of production can be subdivided in various ways, for example labour with various amounts of human capital, or land with various mineral contents. *See also* FIXED FACTORS; IMMOBILE FACTORS.

factor price equalization A tendency for international trade to reduce international differences in relative *factor prices. In the *Heckscher–Ohlin model explaining *inter-industry trade, countries specialize in the production and export of goods whose production requires relatively large inputs of their more plentiful factors of production, and import part or all of their requirements of goods requiring large inputs of their scarcer factors. Imports of goods intensive in scarce factors lower the demand for them, and therefore their factor prices. Exports raise the demand for, and thus the price of, abundant factors. Trade thus tends to reduce international differences in relative factor prices. If there were no transport costs and no restrictions on international trade, complete factor price equalization would result. In the presence of transport costs and *trade barriers, trade tends merely to reduce international factor price differences.

factor price frontier The combinations of *factor prices that allow a cost-minimizing firm to achieve a given cost per unit of output. Equally, the combinations of factor prices that allow a competitive, profit-maximizing firm to achieve a given level of profit.

factor prices The prices of the services of *factors of production. For labour of various types the factor price is the appropriate wage rate; for land, the rent paid; and for capital, the interest rate. The purchase prices of land and capital goods are not factor prices in this sense. In competitive equilibrium, factor prices would be equal to the marginal revenue product of each factor. If goods or factor markets are not competitive, or the prices of some factors are fixed for some time in advance by contracts, the relation between factor prices and marginal products is less clear-cut.

factor productivity The output of a plant, a firm, or an industry per unit of factor input. The factor concerned may be a particular factor only, such as labour or land. *Productivity is often used to mean labour productivity, that is output per unit of labour employed, which may rise or fall for a variety of reasons. These include changes in effort, in the quality of labour employed, in managerial efficiency, in technical knowledge, in the amount of other factors, such as capital, which are employed with each unit of labour, or in the level of output when returns to scale are not constant. Total factor productivity relates the value of output to total factor inputs, aggregated at some set of relative prices. This can change through changes in effort, managerial efficiency, or available techniques, or through scale effects when the output level varies.

fair gamble A gamble with an expected pay-off of zero. For example, consider a gamble that involves winning £2 with probability 1/3 and losing £1 with probability 2/3. The expected pay-off is $(1/3)2 - (2/3)1 = 0$. A fair gamble is said to have actuarially fair odds. Someone who is strictly *risk-averse will not accept a fair gamble.

fairness The perception that an allocation treats all economic agents fairly. A method of testing for fairness is the no-envy criterion: an allocation satisfies no-envy if there is no economic agent that prefers some other agent's allocation to their own. Fairness is related to, but distinct from, *equity.

fair odds The odds which would leave anybody betting on a random event with 0 expected gain or loss. Thus, if the probability of the occurrence of a random event is p then the fair odds are $(1 - p)$ to p. If, for example, $p = 1/3$, then the fair odds are $(1 - 1/3)$ to 1/3 or 2 to 1. Conversely, if the fair odds for a random event are a to b, then the probability of winning is $b/(a + b)$.

fair rate of return The level of profit that federal and/or state regulators judge is adequate return for a *utility. The fair rate of return is set by public utility commissions at a level that allows the utility to provide an acceptable service to its customers, pay a dividend to shareholders, meet the interest payments on its bonds, and undertake maintenance and investment.

fair trade The purchase of products directly from the producers and retailed to consumers with explicit labelling. Fair-trade products are purchased from farmers at a price above the market price. This is intended to offset the perceived exploitation of product market power by large multinationals and to make the production environmentally sustainable. The products are sold to final consumers at a higher price than non-fair-trade products.

family allowance A UK welfare benefit paid to the parents or guardians of dependent children. The arguments for family allowances are a desire to avoid child poverty, and considerations of horizontal equity, as people with families have more demands on their incomes than childless people with the same income.

Family allowances are contrasted with the use of tax credits as part of the direct tax system: family allowances are more egalitarian, as the poorest parents may lack sufficient income for tax credits to benefit them. Family allowances are a universal benefit; this contrasts with the US position, where *Aid to Families with Dependent Children is a means-tested benefit targeted towards needier families.

Family Expenditure Survey (FES) A continuous survey of household expenditure and income in the UK that ran from 1957 to March 2001. From April 2001 onwards the data continued to be collected in the *Expenditure and Food Survey, formed by combining the FES with the National Food Survey.

Family Income Supplement (FIS) A UK system of state benefit payments to increase the incomes of some lower-paid workers with family responsibilities. It was replaced by Family Credit which in turn was replaced by the Working Families' Tax Credit. The current system is now based on the *Child Tax Credit and the *Working Tax Credit.

fan chart A diagram in which the past history of a variable is plotted against time, but its future is shown as a range of forecast values rather than a point. After the present is passed on the time axis, the graph fans out, hence the name. The fan chart is a useful way of summarizing the uncertainty in economic forecasts.

Farm Credit System (FCS) A US federation of banks and lending associations of farmers formed to provide credit to farmers and ranchers. FCS bonds are guaranteed by the US federal government.

farm subsidies Subsidies to farmers. These may take the form of price support payments, to increase farm incomes per unit of output, or direct payments to farmers, for example as compensation for taking land out of cultivation. Such subsidies are designed to increase farm incomes, and slow down the tendency in modern economies for farmers to leave the land.

F-distribution (Snedekor's F-distribution) A continuous distribution described by the probability density function

$$f(x) = \frac{\Gamma\left(\frac{p+q}{2}\right)}{\Gamma\left(\frac{p}{2}\right)\Gamma\left(\frac{q}{2}\right)} \left(\frac{p}{q}\right)^{p/2} \frac{x^{\frac{p}{2}-1}}{\left(1 + \frac{p}{q}x\right)^{(p+q)/2}}, \quad 0 < x < \infty$$

where p and q are the degrees of freedom. This distribution is used, for example, in finite sample inference in a linear regression model under the assumption that the underlying random error has a *normal distribution.

feasible generalized least squares estimator (FGLS) *See* GENERALIZED LEAST SQUARES ESTIMATOR.

feasible set The set of allocations that satisfies all the constraints in an economic model. For a consumer, for example, the feasible set is all consumption plans that satisfy the budget constraint. For an exchange economy, the *Edgeworth box summarizes the feasible set.

Federal Deposit Insurance Corporation (FDIC) A US regulatory body responsible for chartering banks, and insuring depositors against bank failure. The guarantee covers the first $100 000 of deposits. The FDIC is largely financed by charges on the banks.

federal fiscal system The fiscal system in a federation, with state as well as federal governments. In such a system taxes may be levied, and expenditure incurred, at both levels. Germany and the US are examples of federal systems. *See also* FISCAL FEDERALISM.

Federal Reserve System (Fed) The US system of central banking. This consists of a Board of Governors in charge of twelve District Reserve Banks (a district here means a group of states). The Governors are appointed by the President, with Senate approval. They fix reserve and margin requirements and discount rates through the Federal Open Market Committee, provide discounting facilities, and appoint the directors of the twelve District Reserve Banks. The District Banks supervise member banks in their regions: member banks are subject to stricter reserve requirements than other banks, but in return can obtain cheaper services from the Fed. The Fed acts as agent in collecting taxes and administering federal government debt, and Federal Reserve Notes form the US currency.

Federal Trade Commission (FTC) A US federal agency charged with formulating competition policy and maintaining competitive enterprise. The FTC seeks to prevent restraints on trade and price discrimination, and to ensure disclosure of credit costs. It is empowered to investigate and declare illegal unfair and predatory competitive practices. It acts through voluntary compliance wherever possible, or litigation if this fails.

fiat money Money which has no intrinsic value but has exchange value because it is generally accepted. Originally money was accepted by users because it consisted of materials which were themselves valuable, such as gold or silver. Rulers originally stamped it into coins merely to certify their contents. Later the contents were decreased in value, and the state required coins to be accepted as worth more than their intrinsic value. Later still banknotes originally gave the holder the right to receive coin to the same face value on demand. Present-day money consists of paper notes with negligible intrinsic value, or of book or computer entries. Modern money is fiat money.

fiduciary issue The amount of *high-powered money issued by a central bank in excess of its holdings of gold reserves. In the UK in the 19th century the fiduciary issue was restricted to control the power of the Bank of England to issue money; during banking crises the Bank of England had to be specially authorized, by suspension of the Bank Act, to exceed this limit. In the 20th century nearly all high-powered money has come to consist of a fiduciary issue.

final goods Goods for use by final users, including consumers, investors, the government, and exporters, as distinct from intermediate products. Some products, such as fuel, may be used by consumers as a final good or producers as an input.

Finance Act The UK legislation by which Parliament approves or amends the Chancellor of the Exchequer's budget proposals.

financial assets Money and claims, as distinct from physical assets such as land, buildings, or equipment. Financial assets include money, securities constituting a claim to receive money, such as bills or bonds, and shares giving indirect ownership of the physical and financial assets of companies. The claims held as financial assets include the obligations of individuals, companies, and governments, domestic and foreign. Financial assets include shares in financial institutions, and derivatives such as *options.

financial crisis The collapse, or potential for collapse, of a financial institution that threatens the stability of the financial system. The financial institution may be a bank unable to continue trading or a sovereign nation unable to meet its obligations. The key feature of a financial crisis is its systemic nature. For example, the failure of a single bank is not yet a crisis but may become a crisis if the failure threatens the collapse of other financial institutions. A financial crisis can lead to bank runs, widespread bankruptcy, considerable default on debt obligations, shortage of liquidity, and redundancies in the financial sector.

financial deregulation The removal or relaxation of regulations affecting the type of business financial firms may undertake, the type of firms permitted to deal in particular markets, or the terms on which dealing is allowed. Regulations which have been relaxed include controls on the interest rates at which banks can lend or borrow, controls on operations by banks outside their country of registration, and restrictions on the types of business particular financial institutions can transact.

financial economics The field of economics that analyses the individual allocation of resources between consumption and financial assets, and the equilibrium consequences of individual choices. Financial economics also analyses the behaviour of financial institutions, including banks and investment companies.

financial futures *Futures contracts in currencies, interest rates, or stock indices. Futures contracts, like forward contracts, commit both sides to a transaction on a future date at a pre-arranged price. Futures contracts are traded in *futures markets on organized exchanges. These contracts can be used either for *hedging to reduce the risks traders are exposed to, or for *speculation, taking on extra risk for the sake of expected profits. Financial futures are traded in the UK on the *London International Financial Futures and Options Exchange.

financial innovation Changes in financial institutions, financial instruments, or business practices in the financial sector.

financial intermediary A firm whose main function is to borrow money from one set of people and lend it to another. Financial intermediaries are able to operate profitably because of the economies of scale in collecting savings from many sources and making them available for large loans, and in handling information about large numbers of small debtors or the risks of lending to single large ones. Firms wishing to borrow large amounts do not want the trouble of negotiating with numerous small lenders, and lenders can use financial intermediaries to get a spread of risks in their lending without the high transaction costs of making numerous single small loans to the ultimate users of their money. The use of financial intermediaries reduces risk and transaction costs for both lenders and borrowers.

financial markets The markets in which financial assets are traded. These include *stock exchanges for trading company shares and government debt, the money market for trading short-term loans, the foreign exchange market for trading currencies, and a number of specialized markets trading financial derivatives. Most financial markets now operate minute-by-minute via computer and telephone linkages rather than traders meeting in person, but many participants still prefer to be near to other major market participants, which is why financial markets tend to be concentrated in large business centres such as Frankfurt, London, New York, or Paris.

financial ratios Ratios between various items in a company's accounts and the market value of its shares. These include the *price–earnings (P/E) ratio, that is the ratio of the market price to earnings per share, and the price–dividend (P/D) ratio, that is the ratio of the market price to the latest dividend paid per share. These ratios are used in comparing the merits of investing in different companies.

financial repression The imposition of liquidity constraints through allocation of loans by administrative means rather than use of the market. Financial repression may be adopted through a desire to influence the distribution of investment in the economy, or to facilitate extortion by those responsible for allocating funds.

financial sector The part of the economy concerned mainly with lending and borrowing, long or short term. This includes banks, non-bank financial intermediaries such as building societies (UK) or savings and loan associations (US), as well as merchant banks, insurance companies, pension funds, and a range of financial managers and advisers.

financial security *See* SECURITY.

Financial Services Act The UK legislation governing the regulation of investment business by means of the Securities and Investment Board supervising a system of self-regulating organizations. The functions of the Securities and Investment Board were transferred to the *Financial Services Authority in 1997.

Financial Services Authority (FSA) An independent non-governmental body given statutory powers by the Financial Services and Markets Act of 2000 to regulate the financial services industry in the UK.

(●) SEE WEB LINKS
• Information on the regulatory role of the FSA and training opportunities.

Financial Times Actuaries All-Share Index An index of the prices of shares traded on the London Stock Exchange, including ordinary shares and fixed-interest stocks and covering the financial sector as well as industry. This index covers most trade in the London market.

Financial Times Actuaries Share Indexes Share indexes for various sectors of the London Stock Exchange: the widest coverage is that of the FTA World Share Index, based on 2400 share prices from 24 countries. The widest UK index is the FTA All-Share Index, based on the share prices of 800 companies.

Financial Times Industrial Ordinary Share Index (FT 30) An index of the share prices on the London Stock Exchange of 30 leading UK industrial and commercial companies. This index excludes banking and insurance shares and government stocks. It started from a base of 100 in 1935.

Financial Times Share Indexes A group of share indexes published by the *Financial Times* of London. They include the *Financial Times Industrial Ordinary Share Index, the *Financial Times–Stock Exchange 100 Share Index (Footsie), and a number of other widely used share indexes.

Financial Times–Stock Exchange 100 Share Index (FT–SE 100, Footsie) An index of 100 equities traded on the London Stock Exchange. This index, with a base of 1000 in 1984, covers a list of companies with over £1bn of market capitalization, and is used as the basis for UK futures contracts.

financial year The year used as an accounting period by any organization. This can coincide with the calendar year, but frequently does not.

fine tuning The effort to make precise adjustments in the level of activity via fiscal and monetary policies. Efforts at fine tuning are hampered by lags and minor inaccuracies in the data on which policies are based and the incomplete understanding of the precise mechanisms by which policies affect the economy.

firm The basic unit of organization for productive activities. Economic theory views the firm as transforming inputs into outputs subject to the limitations of its technological knowledge (summarized in the *production set) and guided by its objectives. The theory of the firm models how a firm would behave given assumptions about its objectives, which may include profit maximization, avoidance of risk, and long-run growth, and investigates explanations for the observed firm structures. Many firms are run by sole traders, and others are partnerships; larger firms are usually organized as companies. A single firm may have numerous establishments or branches, such as factories or shops. *See also* DOMINANT FIRM; EVOLUTIONARY THEORY OF THE FIRM; INCUMBENT FIRM; MANAGERIAL THEORIES OF THE FIRM; MARGINAL FIRM; MULTINATIONAL; MULTI-PLANT FIRM; MULTI-PRODUCT FIRM; REPRESENTATIVE FIRM; WORKER-CONTROLLED FIRM.

firm objective The usual assumption is that in a market economy a firm seeks to maximize its profit. Given private ownership, however, the proper objective of the firm has to be the maximization of its value to its shareholders, as represented by the market price of the company's stocks. Alternatively, the objective can be the maximization of the expected present value of cash flow (after-tax profit less depreciation) net of the investment outlays that must be made to generate those cash flows. In certain situations the objectives of management may differ from those of the firm's stockholders, especially in large corporations whose shareholders have little or no influence upon the operations of the company. When the control of a company is separate from its ownership, management may not always act in the best interests of the stockholders. Managers sometimes are said to be 'satisficers' rather than 'maximizers', in the sense that they may seek an acceptable level of performance, being unwilling to take reasonable risks and being more concerned with perpetuating their own existence than with maximizing the value of the firm to its shareholders. However, in order to survive over the long run, management may have to behave in a manner that is reasonably consistent with maximizing shareholders' wealth. *See also* AGENCY THEORY; PROFIT MAXIMIZATION; SATISFICING.

firm-specific human capital Specialized skills, experience, or qualifications which are of value only to one specific employer. Skills may be firm-specific because the equipment the firm operates is unique, or because, while the skills are in principle industry-specific, the firm is a monopolist in the industry.

first-best allocations The set of allocations that can be achieved when the only constraints upon the economic policy-maker involve technology and resources. For example, in a two-consumer exchange economy the set of first-best allocations is given by the *contract curve. First-best allocations are economically efficient, but need not be equitable. If the policy-maker is subject to constraints additional to technology and resources then only second-best allocation can be achieved. The additional constraints could include information restrictions that limit the extent of redistribution of resources that can be achieved.

first-degree price discrimination Price discrimination where consumers are charged the maximum amount they are willing to pay for each unit of a good. This means that the producer obtains all the gains from the good being available, and there is no consumer surplus. Producers generally do not have sufficient information about their customers to be able to practice first-degree price discrimination. In contrast, *second-degree price discrimination, where customers are offered a choice of possible contracts, and *third-degree price discrimination, where different prices are charged to different classes of customer, are relatively common.

first difference For a time series Y_t, the series of increments between two consecutive periods, $Y_t - Y_{t-1}$.

first-in, first-out (FIFO) An accounting convention which assumes that when a firm uses materials it uses first those which it has held in stock longest, so that the first stocks to enter its stores are the first to leave. FIFO is contrasted with last-in, first-out (LIFO), which is the convention that the first stocks to be used are those most recently acquired.

first-mover advantage The argument that there is a strategic advantage to being the first to act. For example, in a *Cournot duopoly with homogeneous products the firm that is the first mover will earn higher profit compared to the level obtained when moves are made simultaneously. *See also* STACKELBERG DUOPOLY.

first-price auction An *auction in which sealed bids are submitted and the item is sold to the highest bidder at the price they have bid. *See also* SECOND-PRICE AUCTION.

fiscal drag The tendency under progressive tax systems for the proportion of incomes collected in taxes to rise under inflation. This results from the fact that the threshold at which income tax becomes payable, and the thresholds for the application of higher tax rates, are fixed in money terms. Inflation thus tends to increase the proportion of incomes collected in direct taxes. The existence of some *specific taxes tends, however, to reduce the proportion of incomes collected in indirect taxes when prices rise, and the fact that many taxes are collected in arrears also tends to reduce fiscal drag.

fiscal federalism The division of revenue collection and expenditure responsibilities among different levels of government. The central, or federal, government is usually free to choose tax instruments, and its responsibilities typically focus on national defence, the provision of law and order, infrastructure, and transfer payments. Local governments are allowed to levy a restricted set of taxes and their responsibilities usually include the provision of education, health care, and local infrastructure. Levels of government are connected by overlapping responsibilities and the transfer payments made between them.

fiscal illusion A systematic misperception of the tax burden by taxpayers when government revenues are unobserved or not fully observed, which may distort democratic decisions on fiscal issues. The fiscal illusion hypothesis is sometimes used to explain the observed substantial increase in government expenditures as a proportion of national income in many countries over the last hundred years.

fiscal neutrality The aim of devising a fiscal system which does not cause distortions in the economy. For example, if the tax system allows firms to write off some types of equipment faster than others with a similar actual life, this tends to divert investment into the types of equipment benefiting from more generous allowances. Fiscal neutrality aims to avoid this type of incentive, and is often proposed as a desirable property of a tax system.

fiscal policy The use of taxation and government spending to influence the economy. This may work via changing tax rates or the rules about liability to tax, or via changes in government spending on real goods and services or transfer payments. Fiscal policy can be used both to influence the level of aggregate demand in the economy, and to change the incentives facing firms and individuals so as to encourage or discourage particular forms of activity. *See also* EASY FISCAL POLICY; TIGHT FISCAL POLICY.

fiscal stance The tendency of the tax and spending policies embodied in a government's budget to expand or contract the economy. The fiscal stance can be found by comparing the full employment budget surplus or deficit with some normal level.

fiscal year The year used for accounting purposes by a government. In the UK, for example, the fiscal year runs from 6 April to 5 April. The US budget year runs from 1 October to 30 September.

Fisher effect A one-for-one change in the nominal interest rate in response to the change in the inflation rate, and vice versa. It follows from the hypothesis that in a country where inflation is expected to be steady the real interest rate is independent of monetary variables, in particular the nominal interest rate.

five-year plan(s) A series of nationwide centralized economic development initiatives, originated in the Soviet Union in 1928 and later adopted by many other countries with high degrees of centralized *economic planning, e.g. Nazi Germany, India, China, and socialist countries of Eastern Europe. Similar methods of setting integrated economic goals for a finite period of time are also used in some capitalist states, adapted for a market economy.

fixed coefficient production function A *production function that describes a process which requires inputs to be combined in fixed proportions. The key economic feature is that a fixed coefficient production function does not allow one factor to be substituted for another when there is a change in the relative prices of inputs.

fixed cost The part of total costs which does not depend on the level of current production. Fixed costs do not affect the profit-maximizing level of output in the short run, though in the longer run a firm which cannot cover its fixed costs will become insolvent and exit.

fixed effects A *panel data regression model in which it is assumed that unobserved heterogeneity is either constant over time for every cross-sectional unit (group-specific fixed effects) or constant across the units at every time period (time-specific fixed effects). This unobserved heterogeneity can be removed by subtracting the mean (over time in the former and across units in the latter case) from each observation, or by introducing binary variables indicating the cross-sectional unit in the former or time period in the latter case. *See also* BETWEEN-GROUPS ESTIMATOR; RANDOM EFFECTS.

fixed exchange rate A system in which a country's exchange rate remains constant. Normally this means that the exchange rate between the country's currency and some other currency or basket of currencies stays within some small margin of fluctuation around a constant par value. Maintenance of a fixed exchange rate requires that a country hold sufficient *foreign exchange reserves which are used for intervention in the foreign exchange market to absorb small variations in willingness to hold its currency, and that monetary and fiscal policies are used sufficiently vigorously to keep these variations small.

fixed factors Factors of production which cannot be withdrawn from a firm even if its output falls. Factors may be fixed because their use is essential if a firm is to stay in business at all. Some are sunk costs, which cannot be recovered even if the firm goes out of business completely.

fixed-interest security A security whose return is fixed, up to some redemption date or indefinitely. The fixed amounts may be stated in money terms, or indexed to some measure of the price level. A fixed-interest security is liable to vary in price with the rate of interest, its price rising as the rate of interest used to find the present discounted value of the fixed receipts falls. This sensitivity to changes in the interest rate increases with the time to maturity of any security.

fixed investment Investment in durable capital equipment, which is expected to last for a long period, and is written off over several years. This is contrasted with investment in stocks and work in progress, which is goods expected to be used up quickly, and not to depreciate at all.

fixprice An economic model in which prices are fixed in the short run, and quantities adjust faster than prices. This is contrasted with a flexprice model, in which quantities are fixed in the short run, and prices adjust faster than quantities. The real world is a mixture of markets where relative prices adjust faster than quantities, for example the foreign exchange market and stock markets, and markets where quantities adjust faster than relative prices, for example the labour market and markets for industrial products.

flag carrier A business which is regarded as contributing to national security and/or national prestige. It is often believed by governments that flag carriers, such as national airlines, should be supported whether or not they are economically viable.

flag of convenience A national registration for a ship which does not correspond to its actual ownership or control. Owners may choose this for tax reasons, to avoid stringent controls on safety and manning prevailing in their own countries, or to allow the use of foreign crew at lower wages than those payable to their own nationals.

flexible exchange rate *See* FLOATING EXCHANGE RATE.

flexible prices Prices that in response to a change in economic environment adjust instantaneously to clear the markets.

flexible wages Wages that in response to a change in economic environment adjust instantaneously to balance supply and demand for labour. In some economic theories it is assumed that while real wages are flexible the nominal wages tend to be fixed in the short run (by wage contracts, unionized bargaining, etc.). This assumption of nominal rigidity in the labour market is used in such theories to explain involuntary unemployment. *See also* EXPECTATIONS-AUGMENTED PHILLIPS CURVE.

flexitime An employment contract that permits a worker to vary the starting and finishing time for work (within limits) provided a given total number of hours is supplied.

flexprice An economic model in which quantities are fixed in the short run, and prices adjust faster than quantities. This is contrasted with a fixprice model, in which prices are fixed in the short run, and quantities adjust faster than prices.

The real world is a mixture of markets where relative prices adjust faster than quantities, for example the foreign exchange market and stock markets, and markets where quantities adjust faster than relative prices, for example the labour market and markets for industrial products.

flight from money The tendency when inflation is very high for people to abandon the use of money, or at least that of their own country. Under *hyperinflation people refuse to accept money, and try to spend any they receive as quickly as possible. They may substitute other goods, such as cigarettes, as a *medium of exchange, revert to barter, or shift to foreign currency if sufficient is available.

floating exchange rate (flexible exchange rate) An exchange rate with no government or central bank action to keep it stable. In a pure or 'clean' float there is no government or central bank intervention at all in the foreign exchange market, and determination of the exchange rate is left to market forces. In a managed or 'dirty' float the monetary authorities of one or both of the countries do intervene in the foreign exchange market, but at their own discretion.

floor In *trade cycle theory, the lowest level of real national product during the slump phase of a trade cycle. *See also* CEILING.

floor price The lowest price that a commodity stabilization scheme is intended to allow. The simplest way to ensure that price does not fall below this floor is to stand ready to buy the commodity at the floor price: this can succeed only if the stabilizing body has sufficient funds to be able to buy all the supplies on offer. A second method is to take measures to restrict supply when the market price approaches the floor level.

flotation The process of making the shares in a public company available for sale to the investing public. Flotation may raise money to finance new company activities, or may enable the owners of existing private companies to realize their assets. It also applies in the case of state-owned businesses. Different methods are used in flotations according to whether likely purchasers of shares are believed to be individual investors or institutions.

flow An economic variable that has a time dimension. For flow variables an indication of the unit of time over which they are measured is essential: for example, output per hour worked, or pay per week. Income, expenditure, and exports are other examples of flow variables. These are contrasted with *stock variables, which are defined as quantities existing at a moment of time. Capital, the labour force, and debt are stocks.

folk theorem The claim that in an infinitely repeated game any outcome in which each player obtains at least their security pay-off can be an equilibrium (in the sense that there are strategies yielding those pay-offs that constitute a *Nash equilibrium). The name of 'folk theorem' was adopted because the result was accepted as true by the community of game theorists before any formal proof was provided, in the way that a folk story is accepted as reporting history without evidence of truth.

Food and Agriculture Organization (FAO) An agency of the United Nations, responsible for problems of agricultural production and nutrition. It conducts research, provides advice, and promotes education and training in productive techniques in agriculture, forestry, and fishing, in the distribution of their products, and in nutritional standards.

food stamps Documents issued to poor families in the US to entitle them to obtain free or cut-price foodstuffs. This is a working example of the use of *vouchers, a method of ensuring the use of public assistance for an approved purpose, in this case the provision of basic foodstuffs, rather than providing assistance in cash which can be used for any purpose.

food subsidies Subsidies to the sale of foodstuffs, which allow the price paid by the consumer to be below the amount received by the vendor. Food subsidies have been adopted in various countries. They increase the incomes of farmers, and decrease the cost of living for the poorest members of society, who spend the largest share of their incomes on food.

footloose industry An industry where there are few advantages in any particular location, so that small differences in cost can lead to large shifts in location.

forecast Also referred to as prediction. In econometrics, a point forecast is the expected value of the variable of interest, or the dependent variable, conditional on the given values of the exogenous and predetermined variables. An interval forecast is the confidence interval for the point forecast. In a dynamic model with lagged dependent variable one needs to distinguish between a dynamic and a static forecast. The dynamic forecast for several periods ahead is computed using the previously forecasted values of the dependent variable in every step, whereas the static forecast for several periods ahead amounts to a series of one-step ahead forecasts always using the actual values of the lagged dependent variable. Therefore, the static forecast requires that the data on exogenous and lagged dependent variables be observed for every point in the forecast sample.

foreclosure Taking over by a lender of a mortgaged property, because of failure by the borrower to comply with the conditions of the *mortgage. This failure usually consists of failure to make interest and amortization payments by the due dates. Foreclosure is usually only resorted to by lenders when considerable arrears have arisen, and normally requires authorization by a court.

foreign aid *See* AID.

foreign currency-denominated borrowing Borrowing denominated in a currency other than that of the debtor's country. If government debt is denominated in foreign currency, this removes the temptation for the government to cause or permit domestic inflation to ease its debt burden. If a country has a record of past inflation, and lenders expect this to continue, foreign currency-denominated borrowing may be cheaper than borrowing in domestic currency, where high interest rates are required to compensate lenders for the risk of further inflation.

foreign direct investment The acquisition by residents of a country of real assets abroad. This may be done by remitting money abroad to be spent on acquiring land, constructing buildings, mines, or machinery, or buying existing foreign businesses. Inward foreign direct investment similarly is acquisition by non-residents of real assets within a country.

foreign exchange Other countries' money. The foreign exchange rate is the rate at which one country's money can be turned into another's. Foreign exchange reserves are stocks of gold or convertible foreign currency held by central banks or governments to enable them to intervene in foreign exchange markets to influence the exchange rate.

foreign exchange control *See* EXCHANGE CONTROL.

foreign exchange markets The markets where foreign exchange is traded. This includes both spot markets, for immediate delivery, and futures markets for delivery on future dates at pre-arranged prices. There is no one place for this market, which operates via computer and telephone connections. The total turnover of world foreign exchange markets is enormous; it is many times total international trade in goods and services. A *Bank of England survey from April 2007 reported the daily turnover on UK foreign exchange markets to be $1359 billion.

foreign exchange rate *See* EXCHANGE RATE.

foreign exchange reserves Liquid assets held by a country's government or central bank for the purpose of intervening in the foreign exchange market. These include gold or convertible foreign currencies, for example US dollars for countries other than the US, or Euros for countries outside the *Eurozone, and government securities denominated in these currencies. Foreign exchange reserves can also include balances with international institutions, notably the *International Monetary Fund. They do not include working balances of foreign currencies or short-dated foreign securities held by a country's banks or other firms. In an emergency some of these could probably be added to a country's foreign exchange reserves.

foreign investment The acquisition by residents of a country of assets abroad. These assets may be real, in the case of foreign direct investment, or financial, in the case of acquisition of foreign securities or bank deposits. Foreign investment may be carried out by the state or the private sector, and foreign securities acquired may represent private or government debt. It is also possible for foreign residents to invest in real or financial assets in a country: this is inward foreign investment. Net foreign investment is the excess of outward over inward foreign investment.

foreign trade Trade in goods and services across national borders. *See also* EXPORTS; IMPORTS.

fortress Europe An expression of worries about European isolationism. The fear was that closer integration will lead not only to fewer obstacles to trade and mobility of capital and labour within Europe, but also to intensified restrictions on trade and factor mobility with the rest of the world. There is currently no evidence to suggest that restrictions are intensifying.

forward To enter into a contract for future delivery of an asset or commodity.

forward and futures Contracts for the future delivery of a commodity, financial asset, or financial index. A *forward contract involves two parties fixing a price to be paid upon delivery at a specified date in the future. For example, it may be agreed that a price of $90 per barrel will be paid for Brent crude to be delivered in six months' time. The party who is 'long' in the forward takes delivery from the party who is 'short'. A forward contract locks in the price for future delivery, and can be used for hedging or for speculation. Futures are similar in concept but are organized, and regulated, by exchanges. A *futures contract also requires the deposit of margin and is settled daily to limit the possibility of default. Very few futures contracts result in delivery taking place. Most positions are closed out by a reversing trade. *See also* CHICAGO BOARD OF TRADE; CHICAGO MERCANTILE EXCHANGE.

forward contract A contract in which a price is agreed for commodities, securities, or currencies to be delivered at a future date. A forward contract is made with an identified counter-party, and the individual or firm entering into a forward contract remains exposed to the risk that the counter-party may fail to carry out their side of the bargain. Forward contracts may be used for hedging, to decrease risk, or as a speculation, taking on risk for the sake of an expected profit.

forward exchange market The market where a contract can be agreed for the delivery of a currency at a future date for a fixed price. *See also* FORWARD AND FUTURES.

forward exchange rate An *exchange rate quoted today for delivery of a currency on a specified future date. The payment for the currency also occurs on the same future date.

forward integration The inclusion in the same firm of 'downstream' activities which use or distribute the products of an 'upstream' activity. An example of this is the ownership of filling stations by oil companies. Forward integration may be adopted to improve efficiency by better coordination of the different levels of production, or to exploit monopolistic advantages at one level to reduce competition at another.

forward-looking behaviour The assumption that economic agents form their expectations with reference to the structure of the economy. Under this assumption an announced policy change can alter the expectations of the agents and, through their response, change the way the economy evolves, provided that this announcement is credible.

forward market A market in which forward contracts are entered into, that is contracts for the delivery at some future date of commodities, securities, or currencies.

forward price The price at which commodities, securities, or currencies are to be delivered in a forward contract. The forward price and the spot price, that is the price for immediate delivery, may differ, and the same commodity may have different forward prices for delivery at different dates. Divergences between these prices are limited by the costs of storage and possibilities of intertemporal substitution.

Fourier analysis An expansion of a periodic function into an infinite sum of sines and cosines, each at a different frequency, also known as harmonic analysis or spectral analysis. Techniques based on Fourier analysis are applied primarily in time series econometrics.

fractional reserve banking A banking system in which banks hold minimum reserves of cash or highly liquid assets equal to a fixed percentage of their deposit liabilities. The minimum percentage of reserves may be adopted voluntarily as a matter of commercial prudence, or required by law or convention. In either case the intention of minimum reserve requirements is to safeguard the ability of banks to meet their obligations.

franc fort The policy of using the foreign exchange rate as an inflation anchor. This policy sought to control inflation by tying the currency to that of a country with an established reputation for low inflation. The franc fort (strong franc) policy was followed in the 1980s and early 1990s by both France and Belgium, who attempted to restrain inflationary expectations by linking their currencies to the German Deutschmark.

franchise 1. The system by which independent firms are authorized to use a common business system. This may include the use of a brand name, designs, patents, and operating systems, and provision of equipment, training, capital, or credit by the franchiser. This system combines the advantages of incentive for the operating firms and economies of scale in research, development, and advertising for the franchiser. The holders of franchises are subject to supervision of their operations in order to maintain the reputation of the franchised product.
2. The civil right to vote. Also known as suffrage. Universal suffrage still remains a relatively recent development. Women were only granted the right to vote in the UK in 1928. Universal suffrage was adopted by the US in 1920 but not enforced until the Civil Rights Act of 1964.

free enterprise A term with political overtones used to describe an economy in which the initiative for production and consumption decisions lies with individuals and companies, and there is limited government regulation.
See also MARKET ECONOMY.

free entry The absence of any obstacle to new entrants to a market. The consequence of free entry is that firms will enter a market until it is not possible for another firm to enter and earn at least *normal profit. The assumption of free entry is often used as justification for concluding that firms act competitively but the two concepts are logically distinct: free entry also occurs in monopolistic competition. *See also* BARRIERS TO ENTRY.

free exchange rate *See* FLOATING EXCHANGE RATE.

free exit The absence of obstacles to leaving a market. If there is free exit no firm will remain in a market in which it is not earning at least *normal profit. *See also* BARRIERS TO EXIT.

free good A good which is not scarce, so that its availability is not an effective constraint on economic activity. A good is not a free good merely because its market price is zero: it may in fact be scarce, but be underpriced by the market because of a lack of enforceable property rights over it. A really free good has an *opportunity cost of zero.

freehold Land or property in the UK held for use by the owner without obligation to any landlord. Freehold is contrasted with leasehold, where a ground landlord is entitled to ground rents and reversion of the property at the end of the lease, and may be entitled to impose restrictions on the use of the property. Freehold property is subject to public controls on its use through planning laws, and to other restrictions such as public rights of way.

free lunch A colloquialism with its root in the expression 'There's no such thing as a free lunch'. A free lunch would be something beneficial obtained for nothing. The expression warns that everything has a price, even if this is not immediately apparent. A *production set satisfies the no free lunch assumption if inputs are required to produce output.

free market A market in which people buy and sell voluntarily, without legal compulsion. Neither the quantities traded nor the price at which trade takes place are subject to control by third parties. This is not to say that such markets operate without legal regulation: the participants have to conform to laws concerning health and safety, weights and measures, labelling requirements, and so on. The essential point about these rules, however, is that they lay down the basis for property rights and contract law. The actual initiative to trade still lies with the market participants, on both sides.

free-market economy An economy in which a substantial majority of economic activity is organized through free markets, in which the parties choose the quantities and prices traded without central direction. This is contrasted with a centrally planned economy, in which a substantial majority of economic activity is carried out through central directions to people and firms as to what they must buy and sell, and at what prices. Very few if any economies are either purely free-market-based or centrally planned; most have substantial elements of each.

free on board (fob) The value of exports when they are placed on a ship, lorry, or aeroplane to leave a country. Fob thus includes costs of production and of transport to the port of embarkation, but does not include the costs of freight and insurance in getting them to their foreign destination. Free on board is contrasted with the value of goods on arrival at a foreign port, which includes freight and insurance.

free port A seaport or airport where national *tariffs are not levied. This is intended to encourage *entrepôt trade, as goods can be shipped in and out without having funds tied up in tariff payments and free from the administrative expenses involved in claiming tariff drawbacks when goods are re-exported. Tariffs are payable when goods are shipped from a free port into the rest of the national territory.

free rider A person or organization who benefits from a *public good but neither provides it nor contributes to the cost of collective provision. They thus free ride on the efforts of others. The free-rider problem means private provision leads to undersupply of a public good. This suggests a role for the government in public good provision. The same problem occurs internationally, when governments prefer to leave others to bear the costs of international institutions to maintain world security, and the expensive measures needed to restrain global warming or reduce destruction of the ozone layer.

free trade A policy of unrestricted foreign trade, with no *tariffs or subsidies on imports or exports, and no *quotas or other trade restrictions. Free trade implies that this regime applies to most goods, though there may be exceptions, for example agricultural goods or military equipment. It has usually been interpreted as applying only to trade in goods and not in services, but a similar policy can be applied to trade in services. A free-trade policy can be adopted unilaterally, or on a multilateral basis by joining a free-trade area. This is a group of countries which have no tariffs or other restrictions on trade between them, but remain free to control their trade with non-members of the area. Again this may apply to most but not all types of goods.

free-trade agreement A treaty between a group of countries setting up a *free-trade area. Such a treaty usually contains exceptions for particular products, and transitional arrangements for the early years of the agreement.

free-trade area A group of countries with free trade between them, but retaining independent systems on trade with non-members. There are several free-trade areas, including those of the *European Free Trade Agreement and the *North American Free Trade Agreement. The free-trade arrangements must apply to a substantial proportion of trade, but some sectors, such as agricultural products or defence equipment, may be exempted from the free-trade provisions. To avoid the country with the lowest external tariff on any good being used as a route for imports to other members, tariff-free trade is confined to goods certified as being produced in member countries. A free-trade area is contrasted with a *customs union which has both free trade between members and a *common external tariff.

free-trade zone An area of a country where national tariffs are not applied. This is intended to encourage industries which rely largely on producing goods for export using large amounts of imported inputs. Having the inputs duty-free saves on the interest costs of having money tied up by tariffs, and avoids the administrative expense of claiming tariff drawbacks on the exports. National tariffs have to be paid on goods shipped from a free-trade zone to the rest of the national economy.

freqency distribution *See* PROBABILITY DISTRIBUTION.

frequency domain analysis An approach in time series econometrics in which the spectral density of a *stochastic process is used to analyse its properties and to estimate its characteristics.

frictional unemployment The unemployment that occurs because, as people change jobs when some sectors of the economy grow and others contract, it is not practicable to dovetail precisely leaving old jobs and starting new ones. At times of fairly full employment, frictional unemployment may form an appreciable fraction of total unemployment.

friendly society A UK institution for small savings and life insurance. Friendly societies are non-profit-making institutions owned by their members. They are regulated under Friendly Society Acts, and have limited power to offer tax-free investments and life insurance.

fringe benefits Benefits, other than pay, bonuses, and pensions, provided for employees by their employers. Such benefits may include company cars, sports facilities, free or subsidized catering facilities, health services or insurance, childcare facilities, and free or subsidized accommodation or cheap mortgages. Employers provide fringe benefits for various reasons: to improve the health, morale, and thus the performance at work of their employees, to stimulate loyalty to the firm, and to reduce their own and their employees' joint tax liabilities.

front-end charge An initial fee by the management of an investment or unit trust, or life insurance policy. This is calculated as a percentage of the initial sum invested, and is distinct from and additional to any annual management fee based on the value of the assets managed.

F-test A test of a *general linear hypothesis based on an F-statistic, that is, a statistic that under the null hypothesis has an *F-distribution. For example, the F-test is used to test whether all the slope coefficients of a regression equation are zero.

full cost pricing The practice of setting prices so as to cover what average cost would be at a normal rate of production, plus a conventional mark-up. At times when output is low, actual average costs exceed those when output is normal, as fixed costs have to be spread over a lower output level. One argument for full cost pricing is that firms frequently have to quote a price for much of their output before they know what total output is going to be, and before they know some of their costs. Under these conditions full cost pricing eliminates some of the risk of pricing below cost.

full employment A situation where the labour market has reached a state of equilibrium, so that those in the active labour force who are willing and able to work at going wage rates are able to find work, and the only remaining unemployment is *frictional unemployment.

full employment national income A concept from Keynesian economics that describes the level of real *gross domestic product that would be consistent with full employment.

full information maximum likelihood (FIML) estimation A method of estimation of nonlinear *simultaneous equations models based on the maximization of a likelihood function, subject to the restrictions imposed by the structure. The FIML estimator estimates all the equations and all the unknown parameters jointly and is asymptotically efficient when the errors are normally distributed. *See also* LIMITED INFORMATION MAXIMUM LIKELIHOOD ESTIMATION.

full line forcing The practice of supplying distributors with goods only on the condition that they carry the full range of a firm's products. This may be used as a monopoly device: for example, if some car spares are highly specific to a make, while others are generic products available more cheaply from rival suppliers, full line forcing protects the manufacturers from being undercut on the spares other people can make as well. Manufacturers defend full line forcing on the grounds that they need to protect their reputations with customers who may not appreciate that spares they are being sold are inferior substitutes.

fully-funded pension A pension that is financed from accumulated saving. A state-operated fully-funded pension scheme will levy a pension tax (in the US, a 'social security' contribution) upon each worker. The tax revenue is then invested by the pension scheme. When the worker retires the investment plus accumulated interest is used to finance pension payments. *See also* PAY-AS-YOU-GO PENSION.

functional income distribution The distribution of income between the owners of the various factors of production. Wages accrue to labour, rent to landlords, and interest, dividends, and retained profits of companies to capital. The incomes of the self-employed pose a problem for functional income distribution, as they often contain elements of the rewards of labour, land, capital, and entrepreneurship; disentangling these is a matter of convention. Functional is contrasted with *personal income distribution, the division of total income between individuals. The relation between functional and personal income distribution depends on the distribution of the ownership of property. Most individuals in a modern economy have both earned and property incomes for part of their lives.

fundamental analysis A method for valuing companies that involves examination of their financial positions and real activities. The starting point for fundamental analysis is that the value of a company is the discounted value of the future flow of profits that it will produce. Fundamental analysis then takes into account data on assets, competitors, debts, earnings, growth, management, and products to predict future profits. *See also* TECHNICAL ANALYSIS.

fundamental disequilibrium The condition of the balance of payments under which the original rules of the *International Monetary Fund (IMF) allowed countries to devalue their currencies. The IMF did not produce a formal definition of fundamental disequilibrium but it was widely assumed that it meant severe balance-of-payments problems which could not be cured without devaluation. In the event the rules proved unenforceable.

fundamentals 1. The determinants of asset prices or exchange rates which are not dependent on the initial expectations of market participants or on the methods of short-run forecasting they employ. Fundamentals are thus the forces of supply and demand which determine the levels to which asset or currency prices will converge after sufficient time for the effects of initial expectations to fade away, assuming that any fluctuations set up by speculative forces are stable. **2.** The endowments, preferences, and technology that describe an economy.

Fundamental Theorems of Welfare Economics The two theorems that describe the efficiency properties of a competitive equilibrium. The First Fundamental Theorem of Welfare Economics states that (in the absence of any *market failure) a competitive equilibrium is *Pareto efficient. The Second Fundamental Theorem of Welfare Economics states that if every consumer has convex *preferences and every firm has a convex *production set then any Pareto-efficient allocation can be decentralized as a competitive equilibrium.

funding The conversion of government debt from short-term forms, or bills, to long-term forms, or bonds. This is regarded as a form of monetary policy, since bills are more liquid than bonds, and form part of the banks' liquid reserves, whereas bonds do not. Funding tends to raise long-term interest rates, as bonds have to be sold, and lower short-term interest rates, as bills become scarcer.

futures *See* FINANCIAL FUTURES; FUTURES CONTRACTS; INTEREST-RATE FUTURES.

futures contract A contract to buy or sell a good, share, or currency on a future date, at a price decided when the contract is entered into. A futures contract entails for each party both the right and the obligation to trade; it is contrasted with an *option which confers the right to trade only on one party and the obligation only on the other. Futures contracts can be used to reduce risk by traders who have to hold a good and want protection against a low price, or who know they are going to have to buy and want protection against a high price. The contract can also be used for speculation by a trader who has a different opinion about expected price movements from that prevailing in the futures market. Futures contracts are traded on an exchange, which balances its buying and selling contracts, and collects margin payments from each side to ensure that they will be able to honour their contracts.

futures market A market organization through which futures contracts are traded. These contracts commit both parties to buy and sell commodities, shares, or currencies on a future date at a price fixed when the contract is made. To ensure that both parties will be able to carry out their side of the bargain, the actual contracts are made between each side and the market organization, which requires both parties to make margin deposits with it of a given percentage of the market price of a contract. In most futures markets no actual delivery is made: the difference between the contract price and the spot price when the contract matures is paid by one party to the market organization, and by the market organization to the other. If the spot price is above the contract price the futures buyer gains and the futures seller loses; the opposite holds if the spot price is below the contract price.

G7 *See* GROUP OF SEVEN.

G8 *See* GROUP OF EIGHT.

G10 *See* GROUP OF TEN.

gains from trade The improvement in welfare possible as the result of countries being able to trade with one another, as compared with a position of *autarchy. Gains from trade arise from two principal sources. One is differences in *factor endowments: countries have different natural resources, and different proportions between labour of various types and stocks of capital. Countries can thus gain from *inter-industry trade, exporting goods which their resources are relatively well adapted to produce, and importing goods where they have no or poor production possibilities. The other source of gains from trade is *economies of scale: *intra-industry trade in differentiated products allows countries to produce on a substantial scale while their consumers enjoy the benefit of having a wide variety of product types available. While the gains from inter-industry trade accrue mainly to a country's plentiful factors of production, and its scarce factors may lose through trade, the gains from intra-industry trade are available to all. Thus where both forms of trade are substantial, it is likely that all factors in an economy gain from trade.

gambling Choosing to enter into a situation with an outcome that is not known with certainty. This can refer to a *fair gamble (or even more than fair odds) but colloquial use implies less-than-fair odds. On the assumption that the gambler understands the odds, there are three possible reasons for being willing to gamble when odds are less than fair. One is that the gambler may have a non-concave *utility function, with marginal utility increasing over some range of incomes. This means that even if the expected value of losses exceeds that of gains, the benefit from the gains exceeds the damage through the losses. A second reason, which may affect businesses, is that to a gambler already insolvent or close to *insolvency, gambling may appear worthwhile because gains can be kept while creditors bear any losses. A third reason for gambling is that people actually enjoy excitement, and gamble for pleasure.

game theory The analysis of strategic situations in which the actions of one agent affect the pay-off received by another. This leads to strategic interaction in decision-making. Game theory provides a means of formally modelling strategic interaction. The key elements of the modelling are the objectives, strategies, and information of each agent, and a concept of equilibrium for the game. Useful distinctions can be made between one-off games and repeated games, where reputation established through earlier games affects the conduct of subsequent ones; and between zero-sum games, where the game affects only the distribution of a given total of resources, positive-sum games, where some players can gain more than others lose, and negative-sum games, such as fighting over resources, where the game itself can decrease the amount available to be shared. Game theory is one of the key tools of economic analysis.

gamma distribution A continuous distribution with a density function of the form

$$f(x|\alpha, \beta) = \frac{1}{\Gamma(\alpha)\beta^{\alpha}} x^{\alpha-1} e^{-x/\beta}$$

for $0 \le x < \infty$ and $\alpha, \beta > 0$. The gamma distribution has mean $\alpha\beta$ and variance $\alpha\beta^2$. Important special cases are the *exponential distribution ($\alpha = 1$) and the *chi-square distribution ($\alpha = p/2$, $\beta = 2$). The gamma distribution is also related to the Poisson distribution: if X is a gamma (α, β) random variable with integer α and Y is a Poisson (x/β) random variable, then $P[X \le x] = P[Y \ge \alpha]$.

gamma stocks Shares of relatively small companies, in which trade on the London Stock Exchange was infrequent. This was part of a system of classification of shares which has now been replaced.

Gaussian process A stationary normally distributed *stochastic process.

Gauss–Markov theorem A theorem stating that under certain assumptions the *ordinary least squares estimator is the best linear unbiased estimator (BLUE) of the regression coefficients, where the best is defined in terms of minimum variance. The assumptions for a regression with fixed (non-stochastic) explanatory variables include the linear regression function being correct and errors being homoscedastic and serially uncorrelated. For stochastic explanatory variables the theorem and its assumptions are formulated in terms of conditional expectations and variances.

gazumping Reneging by the seller of a property on an agreement to sell. This is usually because of a higher offer by an alternative buyer. It is possible because of the existence of delays between an agreement to trade and the signing of a legally binding *contract, and usually occurs when property prices are rising.

GDP *See* GROSS DOMESTIC PRODUCT.

GDP deflator A price index used to assess whether there has been a real rise or fall in *gross domestic product (GDP) from one year to another. GDP at current prices is divided by the GDP deflator to obtain an index of GDP at base-year prices. A GDP deflator is based on a broader class of goods than the *retail price index (RPI), since it needs to take account of the prices of investment goods and goods bought by the public sector as well as consumer goods prices.

gearing The ratio of a company's debt to its equity. Gearing (UK) or leverage (US) is the ratio of a company's debt to the part of its capital owned by shareholders.

High gearing or leverage means high reliance on debt financing. This is risky for the shareholders, as debt service absorbs a large proportion of profits in a normal year, and in a bad year the cost of debt service may exceed total profits. This could lead to dividends being reduced or passed, and possibly to loss of control of the company to creditors or debenture holders.

General Accounting Office (GAO) A US agency responsible to Congress for ensuring that funds voted by Congress are spent as prescribed by law.

General Agreement on Tariffs and Trade (GATT) An agency of the United Nations, based in Geneva, founded in 1948 to promote international trade. By 1995 it had over 100 members, including most leading trading countries. GATT successfully concluded several rounds of multilateral negotiations to reduce world tariffs, but was unable to prevent the spread of *non-tariff barriers to trade such as voluntary export restraints. The latest round of GATT negotiations, the *Uruguay Round, finished in 1994. This included measures affecting trade in agricultural products and services, and intellectual property rights, all of which had been omitted from earlier rounds. It also led to the replacement of GATT by the *World Trade Organization.

General Agreement on Trade in Services (GATS) An international agreement on trade in services, arrived at in 1994 as part of the *Uruguay Round of negotiations under the *General Agreement on Tariffs and Trade (GATT). The GATS is very limited in scope: it is a long way from providing for worldwide market access and 'national', that is non-discriminatory, treatment for foreign providers of services. Its provisions apply only to services included by members in a positive list: this is around half of all services in high-income countries and a very small proportion elsewhere. Even within these positive lists there are numerous exceptions. As with the GATT, a prolonged series of further negotiations seems likely to be needed before anything approaching free trade in services is achieved.

General Agreement to Borrow An agreement made in 1962 by the *Group of Ten countries to extend international credit. The agreement is a misnomer, as the countries actually agreed to lend via the *International Monetary Fund (IMF) to enable each other to borrow extra reserves if this was necessary to defend their currencies. The agreement was later extended to other members of the IMF.

general equilibrium The approach in economics of analysing simultaneous equilibrium on all markets in an economy. For general equilibrium all markets must be in equilibrium, and no change of actions in any market must reward any agent. General equilibrium is contrasted with the *partial equilibrium approach, in which some part of the economy is considered, taking as given what is happening in other markets. *See also* ARROW–DEBREU ECONOMY.

general government The whole of the government sector, including central government, local government, and government at intermediate levels, such as the states in federal countries such as Germany or the US.

general government final consumption The spending of general government, that is, government at all levels, on real goods and services, excluding investment. General government final consumption includes items such as defence spending, the provision of administration, law and order, schools, and hospitals. It excludes government spending on pensions, unemployment benefit, other income maintenance payments, and debt interest. It also excludes government investment spending, for example on road construction or publicly owned housing.

General Household Survey A UK sample survey used to obtain information on the labour force and on household expenditure. The survey has been conducted continuously since 1971, except for breaks in 1997/8 and 1999/2000.

SEE WEB LINKS
• The official website of the General Household Survey.

general human capital Skills and qualifications of value in a wide range of occupations. This clearly applies to general skills such as literacy and numeracy. General human capital is contrasted with forms of human capital, such as medical, legal, or technical skills or qualifications, which are of value only in particular occupations. General human capital improves the outside earnings opportunities of those who acquire it so employers have limited incentive to provide it.

generalized least squares (GLS) estimator A generalization of the *ordinary least squares estimator applicable when the exact form of the error covariance matrix, i.e. heteroscedasticity and/or serial correlation in the error term, is known. A version of GLS that uses the estimate of the error covariance matrix (of restricted structure appropriate for the model under consideration) in place of the unknown true covariance matrix is called feasible GLS (FGLS).

generalized method of moments (GMM) estimator A generalization of the *method of moments estimator applicable when the number of moment conditions exceeds the number of parameters to be estimated. The estimates of the parameters are computed by minimizing the sum of squared differences between the population moments and the sample moments.

Generalized System of Preferences (GSP) Agreements by members of the *General Agreement on Tariffs and Trade (now the *World Trade Organization) to grant market access to the exports of *less developed countries subject to preferentially lower tariffs than the normal level. GSP agreements were made by various European countries and Japan in 1971–2, by Canada in 1974, and by the US in 1976. The GSPs were subject to various exceptions concerning sensitive sectors, such as textiles, and never affected very much international trade. Their value has been eroded by the tariff reductions negotiated over recent decades.

general linear hypothesis A set of linear equality restrictions on the coefficients of a linear regression model. Such restrictions may arise from information on a particular parameter or a linear combination of parameters in the underlying economic model or from previous empirical work.

general linear model A linear statistical model of the form $Y = XB + U$ where Y and X are matrices of multivariate observations, B is a matrix of parameters to be estimated, and U is a matrix of random errors, usually assumed to have multivariate normal distribution.

geometric distribution A discrete distribution with a density function of the form

$$P[X = x|p] = p(1-p)^{x-1}$$

for $x = 1,2,\ldots$ and $0 \le p \le 1$. The geometric distribution has mean $1/p$ and variance $(1-p)/p^2$.

geometric lag model A version of the restricted lag model with an infinite number of lags in which the coefficients on the lagged variable are assumed to decline geometrically. It is used, for example, to model *adaptive expectations. *See also* KOYCK TRANSFORMATION.

German Economic and Monetary Union (GEMU) The reunification in 1990 of East and West Germany. This included the replacement of the East German currency, the Ostmark, by the Deutschmark, at a one-for-one exchange rate, and the setting up of the *Treuhandanstalt* to rationalize and privatize East Germany's state-owned firms.

Giffen good A good for which quantity demanded falls when its price falls. This can in theory occur: a Giffen good must be inferior with limited possibilities for substitution. A fall in the price of a good increases real purchasing power: if the good is inferior the *income effect of this rise in real income is negative. The *substitution effect of a price fall cannot be negative, but it can be small. If the substitution effect is smaller than the negative income effect, the overall effect of a fall in price is a fall in consumption.

gift tax A tax on gifts between the living (or *inter vivos*). This is contrasted with a tax on transfers of wealth by inheritance. A gift tax is designed to counter the loss of revenue from inheritance taxes through people transferring their wealth to their relatives or friends while still alive. A gift tax normally contains some exemptions, for example a certain sum per annum. It may be made progressive, either on the sum given by any one donor to a particular beneficiary, on the total sum transferred, or on the total received in gifts and bequests by a single beneficiary.

gilt-edged security (gilts) A fixed-interest security issued by the UK government. Gilts may be irredeemable Consols; long-dated, with 15 years or more to maturity; medium-dated, with 5 to 15 years to maturity; or short-dated, with under 5 years to maturity. Gilt-edged securities are considered extremely safe from risk of default, but fluctuate in price inversely with current interest rates, long-dated securities being most at risk. Index-linked gilts are also available, reducing the risk from inflation.

Gini coefficient A statistical measure of inequality. For a population of H individuals with mean income μ the Gini coefficient, G, is defined by

$$G = 1 - \frac{1}{H^2 \mu} \sum_{i=1}^{H} \sum_{j=1}^{H} \min\{M^i, M^j\}$$

where M^h is the income of individual h. A value of 0 for the Gini denotes complete equality, and a value of 1 maximal inequality, i.e. all income is received by a single individual. Using the *Lorenz curve diagram, the Gini coefficient can be found as the ratio of the area between the Lorenz curve and the straight line connecting the ends of the Lorenz curve to the total area under this straight line.

Ginny Mae *See* GOVERNMENT NATIONAL MORTGAGE ASSOCIATION.

giro A system of money transfer available even to those without bank accounts. The UK Girobank system works via post office branches, and Bank Giro enables bank customers to make giro payments. The Department of Work and Pensions also makes use of giro cheques for benefit payments.

Glass–Steagal Act A US law passed in 1933 prohibiting banks from acting both as lenders and as investors in companies. This act forbids universal banking in the US, whereas such banking is common in other countries including Germany. The act was passed owing to a belief that universal banking made banks excessively risky, and had contributed to the collapse of the US banking system during the Great Depression.

Glejser test A test for heteroscedasticity in the form of the size of random error increasing proportionally to changes in one or more exogenous variables. The test is performed by regressing the absolute values of *ordinary least squares residuals from the main regression equation on the variables in question. Under the null hypothesis of homoscedasticity the test statistic, NR^2, is asymptotically distributed as $\chi^2(h)$ where h is the number of variables in question, N is the sample size, and R^2 is the coefficient of determination from the test regression. The Glejser test is only valid when the random error is symmetrically distributed; a number of modifications exist for skewed errors.

globalization In a general sense, the increasing worldwide integration of economic, cultural, political, religious, and social systems. Economic globalization is the process by which the whole world becomes a single market. This means that goods and services, capital, and labour are traded on a worldwide basis, and information and the results of research flow readily between countries.

global warming An observed increase in the average temperature of the Earth's near-surface air and oceans in recent decades. Economic costs associated with climate change, as summarized by the United Nations Environment Programme, are related to the risks to farmers and consumers (many of whom are not insured) as well as insurers, reinsurers, and banks of increasingly traumatic and costly weather events; among other economic sectors that are likely to suffer are agriculture and transport. *Less developed countries might be at a greater economic risk than the developed countries. There seems to be compelling evidence that this phenomenon is related to human activity, but it remains possible that it is a part of natural climate variation. Presently, there is ongoing political and public debate worldwide regarding what, if any, action should be taken to reduce or reverse future warming or to adapt to its expected consequences. Most national governments have signed and ratified the *Kyoto Protocol of 1997, aimed at reducing emissions of *greenhouse gases.

glut A situation of unusually large supply of a good. This is likely to drive its price down considerably, particularly if it cannot be stored, or if storage facilities are full.

GNP *See* GROSS NATIONAL PRODUCT.

gold A precious metal, widely used both as a form of money and for jewellery and other ornamental purposes. Gold was already used in these other ways before its use as money and the invention of coinage. Gold coinage was at one time in general circulation, but the monetary use of gold is now confined to holdings of gold bullion by central banks as part of their *foreign exchange reserves. Gold is still widely used as a store of value by individuals who mistrust government-created money because it is vulnerable to inflation. Gold costs real resources to mine, so that its value is not liable to be destroyed by inflation, unlike fiat money. *See also* GOLD STANDARD.

gold and foreign exchange reserves *See* FOREIGN EXCHANGE RESERVES.

golden handshake A provision of an executive's contract giving entitlement to a large bonus on leaving a firm's employment.

golden rule **1.** (in economic theory) In an *overlapping generations model, the relationship between the capital–labour ratio, k, and the population growth rate, n, that maximizes consumption per capita: $f'(k) = n$, where f denotes output per unit of labour as a function of the capital–labour ratio, and hence $f'(k)$ is the marginal product of capital. In a competitive economy it equals the interest rate, r, so that an alternative formulation of the golden rule is $r = n$.
  2. (in British politics) The rule implemented in 1997 by *HM Treasury under Gordon Brown that the government could borrow only to invest, and that the current budget must balance over the economic cycle.

gold exchange standard *See* GOLD STANDARD.

Goldfeld–Quandt test A test for heteroscedasticity applicable when the observations can be ordered according to non-decreasing variance. The test is carried out by omitting r central observations and running two separate regressions on the first and the last $(N - r)/2$ observations. Under the null hypothesis of homoscedasticity the test statistic, $GQ = S_2/S_1$, has an $F((N - r)/2 - K, (N - r)/2 - K)$ distribution, where S_1 and S_2 are the sums of squared residuals from the first and the second test regressions, N is the sample size, and K is the number of explanatory variables in the main regression. The optimum value of r is not known; $r \approx N/3$ is frequently used.

gold parity The official par value in terms of gold of the currency of a country on the gold standard.

gold points The values of exchange rates under the gold standard at which it became profitable to ship gold from one country to another. For example, if the dollar rose relative to the pound sterling, a firm holding sterling with a dollar payment to make could buy gold from the Bank of England, ship it to New York, and sell it to the Federal Reserve Bank for dollars. The gold points were the lowest price of dollars which made this profitable, and the highest price of dollars which made it profitable to ship gold from New York to London. In peacetime conditions modern transport makes shipping gold so cheap that the gold points would be very close together: the possible fluctuations in market exchange rates under a gold standard would thus be very small.

gold standard A system for fixing *exchange rates by the central bank or government of each country making its currency freely convertible into gold at a fixed price. Under this system the par value of exchange rates is set by the amount of each currency that can be obtained for a given quantity of gold. Exchange rates thus cannot shift further from parity than the limits set by the transaction costs of shipping gold between different countries, which is usually a very small percentage of its value. The same applies if gold actually circulates within each country, provided it can be imported and exported freely.

good(s) 1. Things people prefer to consume more of rather than less: thus leisure and security are goods, while pollution is a bad.
   2. Economic assets taking a tangible physical form, such as houses or clothes. These are contrasted with services, such as transport, which cannot be stored, or insurance, which has no physical embodiment. Some economic goods in sense 1, such as restaurant meals, are combinations of services and goods in sense 2. *See also* CAPITAL GOODS; CONSUMER GOODS; FINAL GOODS; FREE GOOD; GIFFEN GOOD; HOMOGENEOUS GOOD; INFERIOR GOOD; INTERMEDIATE GOOD; MERIT GOODS; NORMAL GOOD; PRODUCER GOOD; PUBLIC GOOD.

Goodhart's law The observation by C. Goodhart that when an empirical regularity starts to be exploited as a basis for economic policy, it is liable to break down. This is one application of the *Lucas critique, that the observed behaviour of economic systems is affected by the economic policies in force. If the policy regime changes, the behaviour of the economy is liable to change, so that econometric models fitted during earlier policy regimes become unreliable as a basis for predicting the effects of new policies.

goodness of fit measures Measures of adequacy of the estimated linear regression model. Examples of commonly used measures include the *coefficient of determination and alternative versions of the *information criterion.

goodwill An intangible asset, representing the fact that a business as a going concern is worth more than its tangible assets. This is usually due to the accumulated know-how and trade contacts of its staff. Goodwill is not normally included as an asset in balance-sheets, but is listed if a company has taken over another business for more than the value of its tangible assets. It is then required to be written off over a period.

Gosplan The central planning agency of the former Soviet Union. It was responsible for drawing up successive *five-year plans and annual operational plans, and for auditing enterprises to check whether the plans had been fulfilled.

government Sometimes central government only; on other occasions general government. This is the total of all levels of government, including central and local government, and state governments in federal countries such as Germany or the US. *See also* CENTRAL GOVERNMENT; GENERAL GOVERNMENT; LOCAL GOVERNMENT.

government debt Debt owed by the government at any level. It is necessary to net out any debt owed by one level of government to another, such as central government debt held as financial reserves by local authorities. Government debt may be measured gross or net, when some firms or individuals are indebted to the government, for example through local authority mortgages. The status of debt carrying a government guarantee but issued by other bodies, such as nationalized industries, is ambiguous; such debts may or may not be included in estimates of government debt. Where government securities fluctuate in market value, government debt is normally calculated using their par values.

government expenditure Spending by government at any level. It is necessary to net out payments by one level of government to another, for example central government grants to local authorities. Government expenditure consists of spending on real goods and services purchased from outside suppliers; spending on employment in state services such as administration, defence, and education; spending on transfer payments to pensioners, the unemployed, and the disabled; spending on subsidies and grants to industry; and payment of debt interest.

Government National Mortgage Association (GNMA) A US institution which guarantees securities issued by the Federal Housing Administration and the Veterans Administration. The GNMA is familiarly known as 'Ginny Mae'.

(⊕) **SEE WEB LINKS**
• The official website of the GNMA.

government production The part of the income of government which derives from the services of factors owned by the state or local authorities. This includes rent received from state-owned land and buildings, for example local authority housing. It is also possible for the state to operate productive services such as public utilities, either directly or through public corporations: any profits these make form part of the government's share of the national product. Where the government sector provides services to the public such as administration, defence, law and order, education, and health services, these form part of government production, and are by convention valued at what they cost.

government regulation *See* REGULATION.

government spending on real goods and services Government spending on buying goods, for example military equipment, or employing people, for example police officers. This is contrasted with government spending on transfers or interest payments: spending on real goods and services is part of the gross domestic product, whereas spending on transfers or interest payments is not.

government transfer payments Payments of income by the government which are not made in return for current services rendered. This includes payment of state pensions and unemployment and other social security benefits, by the government itself or the National Insurance Fund. While the state provides most transfer payments, some are also made by charities and individuals.

gradualism The belief that it is preferable to make a series of small changes in economic policy rather than a single large change.

gradualist monetarism The policy of stabilizing *inflation by gradually decreasing the growth rate of the money supply until it approaches the real growth rate of the economy.

Gramm–Rudman–Hollings The sponsors of the US Balanced Budget and Emergency Deficit Control Act of 1985, which attempted to reduce the US fiscal deficit, eventually to zero, by setting legal targets.

Granger causality A set of variables z_t is said to be caused by x_t in Granger's sense, if the information on past and present x_t helps to improve the forecast of z_t. Causality in Granger's sense (or Granger causality) does not imply true causality: the former refers to the concept of predictability, and can be tested using statistical tools; the latter refers to the concept of cause and effect, and is often postulated by economic theory.

granny bond A security with state guarantees on both the interest to be paid and the price at which it can be redeemed at any time. These are thought of as suitable assets for savers with small total wealth and limited financial sophistication, of whom 'grannies' were assumed to be typical examples. Provision of such guarantees cannot be afforded except by the state. Securities of this type have typically been made available only to limited classes of holders, in relatively small amounts. This restriction is partly because the guarantees might be expensive to honour, and partly because if such securities were freely available, it would be difficult for many businesses to borrow at all.

grant in aid A US federal grant to state or local government. These grants are used to ensure that public services can be maintained in poorer states or in times of depression.

gravity model The theory that the contact between different locations is ruled by an inverse square law, similar to that governing gravitation. A consumer's custom, for example, is divided between possible shopping centres in proportion to $1/x_i^2$, where x_i is the distance to centre i. This model has also been applied to explain the patterns of international trade between countries.

Great Depression A worldwide economic downturn beginning in the late 1920s and lasting until the mid-1930s. In the US the Great Depression began on 29 October 1929 with the stock market collapse. The effect of the Great

Depression was to reduce international trade and national incomes. Farming was particularly badly hit with large declines in agricultural product prices. The growth of fascism in Europe is often attributed to a reaction to the Great Depression and the subsequent loss of confidence in less extreme forms of government.

Great Leap Forward An economic and social plan in place from 1958 to 1960 aimed at rapidly transforming mainland China from an agricultural economy into an industrialized communist society. The collectivization of agriculture coincided with poor weather and resulted in a famine that killed an estimated 20 million people. The Great Leap Forward was abandoned in 1960 and private ownership of land reinstated.

greenfield development A factory erected on a previously undeveloped site, as contrasted with extending or converting an existing plant. Greenfield development allows firms to avoid the congestion and pollution problems of the areas around many old sites. It also allows an old plant to continue in use while its successor is being built. A disadvantage of greenfield development is that it may be necessary to invest in providing new sites with power, transport, and other facilities already in place in an old site.

greenhouse gases Gases in Earth's atmosphere (carbon dioxide, methane, nitrous oxide, fluorocarbons, and sulphur hexafluoride) that absorb part of the solar radiation reflected from the Earth's surface and trap the heat in the atmosphere; this is referred to as the greenhouse effect. An increase in the concentration of greenhouse gases is likely to result in rising average temperature of the Earth, or *global warming. Given uncertainty in how the climate system varies naturally and reacts to emissions of greenhouse gases, it is difficult to determine how much of the observed changes can be attributed to human activity.

green issues Policy issues arising from concerns about the *environment. Various environmental problems arise from economic activity and in particular from economic growth. These include climatic change due to excessive usage of fossil fuels, deforestation, soil erosion, extinction of plant and animal species and loss of biodiversity, and health problems due to air and water pollution, radiation, and excessive use of fertilizers and pesticides.

green paper A UK government publication, intended to stimulate public discussion on an issue, without necessarily committing the government to legislation, or to the lines this might take. This is contrasted with a white paper, which is a UK government publication generally intended as a prelude to legislation, and giving some indication of its likely form.

green pound A notional unit of currency, used as part of the European Community's *Common Agricultural Policy (CAP). The green pound was devised when the shift to flexible exchange rates in the early 1970s led to the prices of farm products fixed under the CAP becoming unstable when translated into UK pounds sterling at market exchange rates.

green revolution Large improvements in recent decades in agricultural productivity in *less developed countries, due to improved plant varieties and widespread use of fertilizer and pesticides. This has raised living standards in many countries, and staved off a Malthusian crisis which might otherwise have resulted from persistent high population growth rates.

Gresham's law The observation that 'bad money drives out good'. Bad money was originally interpreted as coins that had been debased and the law was founded on the claim that consumers would prefer to spend bad money and keep good money. The current dominance of *fiat currency has been cited as proof of Gresham's law.

gross An indication that something which could be subtracted has not been. The word appears in economics in a variety of contexts. Gross investment is total investment spending, before making any deduction for *capital consumption, which is subtracted to get net investment. Similarly, *gross domestic product (GDP) is the total of production for consumption, investment, and government use, before making any deduction for capital consumption; net domestic product is GDP minus capital consumption. Gross assets are total assets held, disregarding any liabilities; net assets are gross assets minus liabilities. The gross weight of a product includes packaging; net weight is gross weight minus the weight of any packaging.

gross domestic capital formation A measure of total investment. 'Gross' indicates that it is measured without subtracting any allowance for *capital consumption; 'domestic' that it refers to investment in the country regardless of ownership. It thus includes investment in the country by companies owned by non-residents, and excludes investment abroad by resident firms.

gross domestic fixed capital formation The part of domestic gross investment that consists of durable goods rather than stocks and work in progress. 'Fixed' is contrasted with 'circulating' capital, and does not refer to geographical immobility; thus vehicles, ships, and aircraft are all included in this aggregate.

gross domestic product (GDP) One of the main measures of economic activity. The GDP of a country is defined as the total market value of all final goods and services produced within a country in a given period of time (usually a calendar year). 'Gross' indicates that it is calculated without subtracting any allowance for *capital consumption; 'domestic' that it measures activities located in the country regardless of their ownership. It thus includes activities carried out in the country by foreign-owned companies, and excludes activities of firms owned by residents but carried out abroad. 'Product' indicates that it measures real output produced rather than output absorbed by residents. GDP is reported at both current and constant prices.

gross fixed investment The total spent on fixed investment, before making any deduction for depreciation of the existing capital stock. This is contrasted with net fixed investment, which is gross fixed investment minus an estimate of *capital consumption. The figures for gross fixed investment are relatively reliable, as it is mainly carried out via observable market transactions, whereas capital consumption and thus net fixed investment are estimates, not based on observing market transactions.

grossing up Finding the gross amount of any receipt of income which is actually paid net of income tax. This allows a taxpayer's total gross income to be calculated; for example, if a UK taxpayer receives £78 net of tax and the tax rate is 22 percent, their grossed up income is £100. Any allowances due are then subtracted to find taxable income, and tax payable. The total tax payable is compared with tax already deducted at source: if too little tax has been deducted the taxpayer then gets a demand for the remainder, and if too much tax has been deducted the taxpayer gets a refund.

gross investment Spending on creating new capital goods, before making any allowance for *capital consumption. Gross investment consists of gross fixed investment, plus net investment in stocks and work in progress. Gross investment is distinguished from net investment, which measures the change in the capital stock after allowing for capital consumption. Gross investment is in principle based on observable market transactions; by contrast, capital consumption is based on calculations about the rate at which capital goods wear out or become obsolete. These calculations are not based on market transactions: thus they, and estimates of net investment based on them, are less reliable than measures of gross investment.

gross national product (GNP) One of the main measures of national economic activity. The GNP of a country is defined as the total market value of all final goods and services produced by the residents of this country in a given period of time (usually a calendar year). 'Gross' indicates that it is measured without subtracting any allowance for *capital consumption; 'national' that it includes residents' incomes from economic activities carried out abroad as well as at home, and excludes incomes produced at home but belonging to non-residents. 'Product' indicates that it measures real output produced rather than real output absorbed by residents. GNP is reported at both current and constant prices.

gross profit The profit of a company before deducting depreciation allowances or taxation but after deducting debt interest.

gross trading profit The profit of a company before deducting depreciation allowances, taxation, or debt interest. This is the profit derived from a company's trading activities. Debt interest has to be deducted from it to get gross profit. A company with high *gearing and a large interest bill may make a loss overall, even if its gross trading profits are positive.

Group of Eight (G8) An informal forum for the governments of eight leading economic nations: Canada, France, Germany, Italy, Japan, Russia, the United Kingdom, and the United States.

Group of Seven (G7) An informal group of leading industrial countries, whose leaders meet periodically to discuss economic problems and policies. The G7 nations are Canada, France, Germany, Italy, Japan, the United Kingdom, and the United States.

Group of Ten (G10) An informal group of leading industrial countries, whose leaders meet periodically to discuss economic problems and policies. The G10 is also known as the Paris Club. The G10 nations are Belgium, Canada, France, Germany, Italy, Japan, the Netherlands, Sweden, the United Kingdom, and the United States.

growth *See* ECONOMIC GROWTH.

growth accounting A method used to determine the contribution of each *factor of production to the growth of output. Any growth unexplained by factor growth is viewed as attributable to technical progress. Consider the production function $Y = F(A, K, L)$, where Y is output, A is the level of technical knowledge, K is the quantity of capital employed, and L is the quantity of labour employed. Each of the variables is a function of time, t, so

$$Y(t) = F(A(t), K(t), L(t)).$$

Differentiation with respect to time gives

$$\frac{dY}{dt} = F_A \frac{\partial A}{\partial t} + F_K \frac{\partial K}{\partial t} + F_L \frac{\partial L}{\partial t}.$$

When the markets for factors are competitive the marginal products are equal to factor rewards, so $F_K = r$ and $F_L = w$. Hence

$$\frac{dY}{dt} = F_A \frac{\partial A}{\partial t} + r \frac{\partial K}{\partial t} + w \frac{\partial L}{\partial t} = F_A \frac{\partial A}{\partial t} + rK \frac{1}{K} \frac{\partial K}{\partial t} + wL \frac{1}{L} \frac{\partial L}{\partial t}.$$

Dividing the time derivative of output by Y yields

$$\frac{1}{Y} \frac{dY}{dt} = \frac{rK}{Y} \frac{1}{K} \frac{\partial K}{\partial t} + \frac{wL}{Y} \frac{1}{L} \frac{\partial L}{\partial t} + \frac{F_A}{Y} \frac{\partial A}{\partial t}.$$

Now define the growth rates of output, capital, and labour by

$$g_Y = \frac{1}{Y} \frac{\partial Y}{\partial t}, g_K = \frac{1}{K} \frac{\partial K}{\partial t}, \text{and } g_L = \frac{1}{L} \frac{\partial L}{\partial t}$$

to give

$$g_Y = \alpha_K g_K + \alpha_L g_L + SR$$

where $\alpha_K = rK/Y$ is the share of capital in national income, $\alpha_L = wL/Y$ is the share of labour in national income, and SR is the 'Solow residual'. The Solow residual is the part of growth that cannot be attributed to growth in the stock of capital or labour. This can be interpreted as the underlying growth in productivity due to *technical progress.

growth model *See* ENDOGENOUS GROWTH; HARROD–DOMAR GROWTH MODEL; SOLOW GROWTH MODEL.

growth rate The proportional or percentage rate of increase of any economic variable over a unit period, usually a year. If a variable measured over discrete time intervals grows from 1 to $1 + x$, this is a proportional growth rate of x, or a percentage growth rate of $100x$. If working in continuous time, a continuous constant growth rate g means that a variable grows from 1 at time 0 to e^{gt} at time t. If $y_t = y_0 e^{gt}$, $dy_t/dt = gy_0 e^{gt}$, and $(dy_t/dt)/y_t = g$. As $\ln(y_t) = \ln(y_0) + gt$, $d\ln(y_t)/dt = g$; the rate of change of the natural logarithm of any variable equals its growth rate. *See also* NATURAL GROWTH RATE; WARRANTED GROWTH RATE.

guarantee A promise that if a good is unsatisfactory it will be repaired or replaced, or that if a loan is not repaid the guarantor will repay it. Some guarantees are legally enforceable, which protects the holder of the guarantee provided that the guarantor is solvent. Even if a guarantee is not legally binding, the guarantor risks loss of reputation if the guarantee is not honoured.

g

habit persistence An assumption on preferences such that utility at time t, u_t, is a function of the difference between present consumption, c_t, and consumption in the previous period, c_{t-1}, with some weight, $u_t = u(c_t - \gamma c_{t-1})$. The parameter γ is interpreted as the intensity of habit formation. Under habit persistence an increase in current consumption lowers the marginal utility of present consumption and increases the marginal utility of next period consumption.

Hang Seng index The principal index of Hong Kong share prices.

hard budget constraint A limit to spending by some private or public body, where the consequences of breaching it are expected to be significant. For example, managers whose firms fail to break even, or to achieve the required rate of profit, might expect the result to be loss of their jobs or closure of their firms. The UK *privatization process was based partly on the belief that this was the only way to get people to treat budget constraints as hard. *See also* SOFT BUDGET CONSTRAINT.

hard-core unemployed People of working age who have never worked or have been unable to find work for an extended period of time. The hard-core unemployed often have limited skills and qualifications.

hard currency A currency which is convertible into other currencies, and whose price in terms of other currencies is expected to remain stable or rise. Hard currencies are attractive to hold as private stores of wealth or national foreign exchange reserves. *See also* SOFT CURRENCY.

hard Ecu A proposal for a *European Currency Unit (Ecu) that would initially have been equal in value to a bundle of European currencies, but could not subsequently be devalued relative to any member currency. This would have made the hard Ecu at least as hard as the hardest member currency, and harder than the remainder, and made it, and debt denominated in it, attractive as assets both to private investors and to national authorities as a form of foreign exchange reserves. The concept of the hard Ecu was superseded by the adoption of the *Euro.

hard landing When a *recession follows the end of a period of excess demand and inflation. It is difficult to judge exactly how much fiscal and monetary restraint is needed to stabilize effective demand at a high level and inflation at a low one. Checks applied too little or too late fail to cure excess demand; checks that are too severe are liable to damage business confidence and start a recession. This is known as a hard landing, as contrasted with the ideal of a *soft landing, where the timely use of moderate restraints succeeds in producing a smooth transition to price stability with high employment.

hard loan A loan on normal market terms as regards interest, including a risk premium appropriate to the borrower's credit rating, the maturity date, the currency in which interest is paid, and when repayments are due. This is contrasted with a *soft loan, which may be at a concessional interest rate, with an expectation that interest payments and capital repayments can be easily rescheduled or paid in soft currency.

harmonization The idea that the taxes and regulatory rules in countries belonging to economic blocs should be made to converge over time. Harmonization of tax rates was actively pursued as a policy by the European Union. This resulted in the imposition of a minimum value for the standard rate of *value-added tax in member states. Further harmonization remains an objective of the European Union.

Harrod–Domar growth model A growth model, named after its originators, which considers the consequences of fixed capital–labour ratios and saving propensities. In this model, the labour force, measured in efficiency units to allow for technical progress, grows at an exogenously fixed natural growth rate, n. There is a fixed capital–output ratio, v, and a fixed propensity to save, s. If national income is Y, savings are sY. The desired capital stock is vY, and if this grows at a constant proportional rate g, desired investment is gvY. Ex ante savings and investment are equal only if $sY = gvY$, or $g = s/v$. The only growth rate which makes this possible is $w = s/v$, the *warranted growth rate. If $w = n$, growth is possible with a constant percentage of the labour force employed. If $w < n$, that is, the warranted growth rate is less than the natural rate, equilibrium growth of national income involves steadily increasing unemployment. If $w > n$, equilibrium growth becomes impossible once full employment is reached, and the resulting slowdown in growth produces a slump. The Harrod–Domar growth model is a special case of the *Solow growth model, in which v adjusts to accommodate any combination of s and n.

Harrod-neutral technical progress Technical progress which increases the efficiency of labour, so that the labour force in efficiency units increases faster than the number of workers available. Technical progress of this form is thus labour-saving. It is contrasted with *Hicks-neutral technical progress, where the efficiency of all factors increases in the same proportion. *See also* TECHNICAL PROGRESS.

Hausman test A common name for model specification tests in which one proposed estimator of a parameter is both *consistent and *efficient under the null hypothesis and inconsistent under the alternative, whereas the other proposed estimator of the same parameter is consistent both under the null and under the alternative hypotheses but inefficient under the null. Important applications include the test for *random effects against *fixed effects, and the test for exogeneity (*instrumental variables against *ordinary least squares).

Health and Safety at Work Act The 1974 UK Act of Parliament laying down standards of health and safety at work, and providing for their enforcement through a Health and Safety Commission. The act is designed to protect both workers and the public from hazards to health and safety arising from a variety of causes, including unfenced machinery, toxic and explosive substances, excessive noise, atmospheric pollution, and inadequate heating and lighting of premises. It imposes on employers the duty of providing safety training, and providing safety equipment and ensuring that employees use it.

health economics A field of economics that studies economic aspects of health care provision and management.

health insurance Insurance against medical expenses and loss of earnings due to accident or illness. This may cover individuals only, or extend to their dependants. Health insurance schemes may be compulsory or voluntary, and their cost may fall on individuals or on their employers. Compulsory schemes can cover any form of health risk. Voluntary schemes typically charge premiums related to members' apparent risk, depending on factors such as age, sex, and occupation. A voluntary scheme which did not charge premiums related to apparent risk for members would be subject to *adverse selection: it would attract people with high risks, and would therefore need to charge high premiums. These would make it unattractive to people who appeared to be better risks, who would find that they could get cheaper cover from more selective schemes. Voluntary schemes usually also often exclude the cost of treatment for conditions that members are known to have when they first join. Health insurance may also exclude risks believed to be under a member's own control, for example pregnancy.

Heckscher–Ohlin model The standard model of the theory of *inter-industry trade, named after its originators. In this model countries have the same constant-returns-to-scale production functions for each good, but different amounts of capital relative to their labour supply. In the absence of trade, goods which require large amounts of labour relative to capital would be relatively cheaper in the more labour-abundant countries, and relatively dearer in the more capital-rich countries. If trade becomes possible, countries export goods intensive in the use of their more plentiful factor, and import goods intensive in the use of their scarce factor. This tends to equate relative prices in different countries, and relative factor prices. If there were free trade and no transport costs, complete relative price and *factor price equalization would result. This model does not attempt to explain *intra-industry trade.

hedge fund An investment fund specializing in taking speculative positions in markets for shares or currencies. This may involve selling short, that is, selling forward shares or currency which the fund does not actually possess, in the expectation that the price will fall. Hedge funds also operate in the markets for financial *derivatives. In the US only accredited investors (those judged sufficiently wealthy) are permitted to invest in hedge funds due to the risk involved, and the funds are free from direct regulation.

hedging Activities designed to reduce the risks imposed by other activities. If a business has to hold stocks of a commodity, it runs a risk of making losses if the price falls. This loss can be avoided by hedging, which involves selling the good forward, that is for delivery at an agreed price on a future date, or by going short in *futures contracts. If there is a contract on the specific good the business trades, it may be possible to remove the risk completely by hedging. If there is not, the price of the particular good held may not move in precisely the same manner as the standard commodity traded in forward or futures markets, but provided that there is some correlation between the two prices, hedging reduces the risk. An alternative method of hedging the risk of stock-holding is to buy a *put option, which allows but does not compel the holder to sell at the contract price. Similarly, a firm which knows it will have to obtain supplies of a good at a future date may wish to protect itself against the risk that when the time comes the cost of the goods will be very high. It can hedge this risk by buying forward or buying a futures contract, or by buying a call option, which gives it the right but not the obligation to buy at the contract price.

hedonic pricing The method of pricing a good by estimating the value of the individual *characteristics that form the good. For example, a house would be seen as comprised of a number of rooms, a garden, and a location. The values of the characteristics are summed to derive a price for the good.

Herfindahl index A measure of firm size relative to market size used as an indicator of market power. The Herfindahl index is defined as the sum of the squares of market shares of the firms operating in a market, $H = \Sigma_i s_i^2$, where s_i is the market share of the ith firm. If there are N firms, the lowest value H can take is when all N firms have equal shares, so that $s_i = 1/N$ for all i, and $H = 1/N$. The highest value H can take is 1, which is approached as the market share of the largest firm tends to 1 and the market shares of the rest tend to 0. H thus rises as concentration increases. The advantage of the Herfindahl index over the *N-firm concentration ratio is that it is sensitive to the distribution of market share between firms. *See also* LERNER INDEX.

heteroscedasticity Having different variances. A set, or a vector, of observations is heteroscedastic if the variance is different for different observations. Heteroscedasticity observed in cross-sectional data is typically related to the scale effect: often, larger cross-sectional units are subject to larger erratic values of the disturbance. In time-series data it may take the form of serial correlation in the variance (*autoregressive conditional heteroscedasticity). It may also be introduced by model misspecification. In the presence of heteroscedasticity the *ordinary least squares estimates of the coefficients are consistent but inefficient; those of the standard errors are inconsistent, and hence the standard inference based on the estimated standard errors is invalid. Among the popular tests for heteroscedasticity are the *Breusch–Pagan test, the *Glejser test, and *White's test. Two approaches to estimation with heteroscedastic data are *generalized least squares (both the coefficients and the standard errors are re-estimated) and heteroscedasticity-consistent standard errors (only the estimated standard errors are corrected).

Hicksian demand *See* COMPENSATED DEMAND.

Hicks-neutral technical progress Technical progress where with any given factor proportions the average and marginal products of all factors increase in the same proportion. Thus if $Y = F(K, L)$, where Y is output, K is labour, and L is capital, and the function $F(K, L)$ has constant returns to scale, output after Hicks-neutral technical progress where the productivity of each factor rises to $\lambda > 1$ times its former level is given by

$$Y^* = F(\lambda K, \lambda L) = \lambda F(K, L) = \lambda Y.$$

See also HARROD-NEUTRAL TECHNICAL PROGRESS.

hidden economy Economic activity that is not included in official statistics. The broadest definition of the hidden economy includes legal economic activity that is deliberately concealed from measurement, illegal economic activities (including smuggling, drug dealing, and prostitution), and home production (including subsistence farming). The hidden economy is also known as the shadow economy, black economy, informal economy, and underground economy. The nature of the hidden economy makes it difficult to calculate its size. Estimates place it at around 10 percent of measured *gross domestic product for a typical developed economy and up to 70 percent of gross domestic product for some developing countries. *See also* TAX EVASION.

hidden unemployment Unemployment of potential workers that is not captured in official unemployment statistics. Many countries count as unemployed only those without work who are actively looking for work. Potential workers who have abandoned the search for work, taken early retirement as an alternative to unemployment, or chosen to register as out of work for medical reasons, are not officially unemployed.

high-powered money Money of forms that qualify it to be used as commercial bank reserve assets. Such money is 'high-powered' because if the commercial banking system maintains a reserve ratio of a, an additional £1m of high-powered money allows total deposits to expand by £$(1/a)$m. It is a belief of monetarists that if the central bank controls 'base' or high-powered money, the rest of the money supply will adapt automatically.

hire purchase (HP) The system by which goods are made available to the buyer for immediate use, but payment is made by instalments. HP may or may not require a down payment; instalments are spread over an agreed period, and until the final instalment is paid the goods remain the property of the seller, who can reclaim them if payments are not made on time. Goods being bought on HP cannot legally be sold or given away. The cost of goods bought on HP usually exceeds the price for cash payment. HP is widely used in buying durable goods such as cars, furniture, and household appliances. HP controls were at one time used in the UK as part of government policies to control aggregate demand.

hiring Taking on new employees. This is an important function of the management of a firm. Hiring is less subject to regulation than firing, so far as the number of new workers taken on is concerned. There are, however, various legal restrictions on how new workers are chosen; for example discrimination by race or sex may be illegal, while on the other hand discrimination by nationality may be compulsory.

histogram A graphical representation of a table showing the frequencies or proportions of observations falling in each of several specified categories, usually the sub-intervals (bins) of the range of observed values. It is the simplest non-

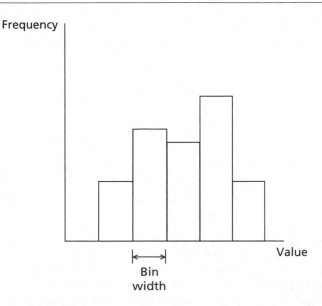

Histogram

parametric, or parameter-free, estimate of the population distribution of the variable under consideration.

historical cost The system of accounting in which assets are valued and depreciation allowances are calculated for firms using the prices paid for assets when they were first bought or built. The merit of this system is that it uses prices based on actual market transactions; any other method of accounting for assets involves using valuations not based on market transactions. Historical cost accounting has the drawback that in a period of sustained inflation it systematically undervalues assets, and calculates depreciation allowances well below the replacement costs of capital goods, so that profits are systematically overestimated.

hit-and-run entry Entry to a market in the expectation of making an immediate profit, possibly followed by withdrawal. This can occur only if the entrant does not incur *sunk costs. If there are sunk costs entry will be profitable only if the entrant expects to stay in the market long enough to recoup them. Absence of sunk costs is probable only through *economies of scope: firms with skills or facilities which can be put to a variety of uses can afford hit-and-run entry to a particular market.

HM Revenue and Customs (HMRC) The UK government department with responsibility for collecting a range of direct and indirect taxes, and for the payment of Child Benefit and Tax Credits. HMRC was formed in April 2005, through the merger of the Inland Revenue and HM Customs and Excise Departments.

(⊕) SEE WEB LINKS
• The official website of HMRC.

HM Treasury (HMT) The UK ministry for economics and finance. HMT is responsible for formulating and implementing financial and economic policy.

(⊕) SEE WEB LINKS
• The official website of HM Treasury.

hog cycle *See* COBWEB.

holding company A company whose sole function is holding shares in other companies.

hold-up A class of contracting problems in which the relative *bargaining power between agents can be affected by actions. Consider two parties that can work together to mutual advantage provided that one of the agents first undertakes an investment. Before the investment is made the two agents are in a symmetric position. After one agent has made the investment the other is in an advantageous position: their bargaining power has increased since the agent that has made the investment has more to lose if no agreement is reached. As a consequence it is possible that neither agent will make the investment, and the potential gains from collaboration will not be realized.

home bias The tendency for consumers to spend relatively more on their own country's products than the world average, and relatively less on the products of other countries. This is due partly to international differences in tastes, partly to government policies concerning *tariffs and *non-tariff barriers to trade, and partly to the cost and difficulty of obtaining full and reliable information on what foreign products are available. A similar effect is shown in international differences in portfolio holdings. Investors tend to hold relatively more of their own country's bonds and shares than the world average, and relatively fewer foreign bonds and shares.

home production *See* HOUSEHOLD PRODUCTION.

homo economicus *See* ECONOMIC MAN.

homogeneous good A good which has uniform properties: every unit of the good is identical. Goods which differ in specifications or quality, or bear different *brand names which convey information to customers, are not homogeneous. Units of money, or securities of the same type, are completely homogeneous. Certain primary products and basic materials are almost homogeneous, apart from their physical location, but many other primary products and most manufactured products are not homogeneous. Economic aggregates invariably involve treating goods as if they were homogeneous when, in fact, they are not.

homoscedasticity Having the same variance. A set, or a vector, of observations is homoscedastic if the variance is the same for all observations. This is one of the classical linear regression assumptions underlying the *Gauss–Markov theorem. Violation of this assumption is called *heteroscedasticity.

horizontal equity The view that people in similar circumstances should be treated equally. Applying this concept to the tax system, for example, horizontal equity requires that two similar workers are taxed at the same rate. Horizontal equity is distinguished from *vertical equity, which is concerned with questions such as how far large differences in income should be moderated by redistributive taxation.

horizontal integration Expanding the product range of a business at the same point in the supply chain. For example, the expansion of supermarkets into non-food items is horizontal integration. Horizontal integration can be achieved within an existing business, by acquisition, or by merger. This may allow cost savings, if there are *economies of scale in any of the processes involved, and it allows more customers to be reached. Horizontal integration is contrasted with *vertical integration, where enterprises at successive stages of production are combined.

horizontal merger A merger between firms at the same stage of production. This may be desired because of cost savings from combined operation, or because a larger firm will be able to use *monopoly power against its customers or *monopsony power against its suppliers and workers. A horizontal merger is contrasted with a *vertical merger, where a firm merges with a supplier or a customer.

hostile bid A *takeover bid whose acceptance is opposed by the directors of a company. A bid may be opposed because the directors feel that the company is better off independent, through concern for their own job security, or because they hope to get a higher offer either from the present or a rival bidder.

Hotelling's law The law of minimal differentiation. Hotelling originally analysed the location choice of two competing suppliers of a product and concluded that the equilibrium would have both competitors located next to each other with minimum differentiation. The law has been widely applied to firm location, product selection, and political economy. Consider two political parties choosing their location on the left–right spectrum. Assume the preferences of voters are distributed evenly along this spectrum. If one party chooses an extreme left position then the other party can secure a majority by locating just to its right. The converse holds for any position except the centre, so the only equilibrium has both parties located at the centre.

hot money Money in bank balances or liquid securities which is liable to rapid removal to other countries if the holders suspect that the currency will depreciate. An inflow of hot money may make a country's balance-of-payments situation look satisfactory, but also makes it subject to sudden deterioration.

hours of work The number of hours per day or per week that a worker is contracted to perform. This may be decided by negotiation, individually or through trade unions, or limited by law. Work in excess of these hours is overtime; work for less is short-time, if temporary, or part-time, if regular.

household A group of people living together in shared accommodation and with common domestic expenses. A household usually but not always contains people who are related or cohabiting. Whereas the individual is the recipient of incomes, the household is the unit through which much consumption expenditure is decided. The *General Household Survey is a source of information on the composition of household expenditure in the UK.

household decision-making A model of collective decision-making on consumption and labour supply inside a household in which a sharing rule specifies how the collective budget is distributed among the household members.

household production Production of goods and services within the household, rather than through formal or informal market organizations. In pre-industrial societies, and in some *less developed countries, a substantial proportion of economic activity takes this form. In modern economies it is less important, though this is partly a matter of accounting conventions. A considerable part of people's time even in advanced economies is taken up with tasks like cookery, cleaning, childcare, gardening, driving and car maintenance, and do-it-yourself building and decorating. All these can in principle be provided commercially, and are performed by employees in some households. These services are generally ignored in national income accounting.

housing association A non-profit-making body providing low-cost housing for people who cannot afford to become owner–occupiers, or cannot competently manage their own housing. Dwellings may be for rent, or for purchase on concessional terms. Housing associations in the UK are financed by a mixture of charitable donations, public funding, and commercial borrowing.

housing benefit Payments under the UK social security system to assist low-income households with housing costs. The reason for having a separate benefit for housing is the existence of wide variations in housing costs between areas and different types of housing tenure.

human capital The present discounted value of the additional productivity, over and above the product of unskilled labour, of people with skills and qualifications. Human capital may be acquired through explicit training, or on-the-job experience. Like physical capital, it is liable to obsolescence through changes in technology or tastes. The training needed to create human capital has to be paid for. Training for firm-specific human capital, which does not improve workers' earning ability outside the firm, can be provided by employers. General or vocational human capital, which can be used by other employers, will increase workers' outside earning power, so employers are in general reluctant to provide this type of training. The cost of creating human capital thus falls mostly on individuals or their families, charitable institutions, or the state. *See also* FIRM-SPECIFIC HUMAN CAPITAL; GENERAL HUMAN CAPITAL.

100 percent gold backing A reserve rule requiring the bank issuing a currency to hold gold of equal value. The only difference between this and a solid gold currency would be the saving in transaction costs from not having to handle the gold. This type of rule is generally regarded as unacceptable for the same reasons as the use of gold coinage itself.

hyperbolic discounting An assumption on the rate of time preference that reflects the observed bias towards present rewards, in the form of the hyperbolic discount function. In contrast to standard exponential discounting, with hyperbolic discounting the discount rate between any two successive periods declines as the time horizon increases, so that the *elasticity of intertemporal substitution depends on the timing of the change in the intertemporal price. A frequently used version of the generalized hyperbolic discount function is the so-called quasi-hyperbolic discount factor; in particular, lifetime utility is modelled as

$$U_t = u(C_t) + \beta\Sigma_{i=1}^{\infty}\delta^i u(C_{t+i})$$

with $0 < \delta < 1$ and $0 < \beta \leq 1$, also referred to as beta-delta preferences. Here β is the degree of self-control which reduces the present bias, and δ is the intertemporal discount factor; $\beta = 1$ is the special case of exponential discounting.

hyperinflation Very rapid inflation; it is sometimes reckoned to set in when price increases exceed 50 percent per month. Such rapid inflation not merely makes money useless as a store of value, but seriously affects its use as a *medium of exchange, and greatly disrupts productive economic activity.

hypothecation Originally a pledge of property as collateral for a mortgage without transfer of possession to the party making the loan. Now hypothecation is also used to describe a tax collected for a specific purpose. *See also* EARMARKING.

hypothesis testing A part of statistical inference; an algorithm for addressing a question of interest, usually put forward by a theory. A typical procedure consists of (1) setting the *null hypothesis and the alternative hypothesis (i.e. formulating the question as a simple claim and the refutation of this claim), as well as the level of significance (the probability of *Type I error); (2) choosing an appropriate test statistic (a quantity whose distribution depends on whether the claim is true); (3) establishing the distribution of the test statistic under the assumption that the null hypothesis is true; (4) computing the value of the statistic from the data and making the decision to reject or not to reject the null hypothesis, usually by comparing the value of the test statistic with the *critical values of the distribution under the null hypothesis.

hysteresis In economics, the property of a dynamic system to retain a memory or lagging effect in which the order of previous events can influence the order of subsequent events. If a system with hysteresis that is initially in equilibrium is subjected to a shock, its new equilibrium position depends on what happens during the process of dynamic adjustment (the *path dependence property). In *behavioural economics, when the disutility from a loss is greater than the utility from an equal gain, the utility of a person going through a cycle of gaining and losing exhibits hysteresis: after subsequent events of a gain and a loss of an item they are worse off than if they had never received the initial gain.

identification problem The problem of estimating the parameters of *structural equations when only equilibrium positions can be observed. For example, in the market for a particular good, if demand conditions vary and supply conditions do not, comparing prices and quantities at different times allows us to determine the supply equation; if supply conditions vary and demand conditions do not, we can estimate the demand equation; but if both supply and demand conditions vary, regressing quantity on price tells us nothing. The identification problem can be resolved only if either theory or the results of other studies inform us that some explanatory variables affect one side of the market but not the other.

idiosyncratic risk Risk of a type which affects each individual case largely independent of others. This could apply to the risk of an individual dying, of a house catching fire, or a car having an accident, during any period. Idiosyncratic risk allows insurance companies, by pooling risks, to insure customers, while keeping their own overall risk exposure relatively small. This is contrasted with market risk, where events such as a slump, a flu epidemic, or a hurricane affect large numbers of individuals in a similar manner.

if and only if (iff) Equivalence between two statements. 'If *A* then *B*' means *A* is a sufficient condition for *B* and *B* is a necessary condition for *A*. 'If *B* then *A*' means *B* is a sufficient condition for *A* and *A* is a necessary condition for *B*. Both statements being true implies '*A* if and only if *B*' (written '*A* iff *B*') which means that each of *A* and *B* is a *necessary and sufficient condition for the other; either both are true or both are false. The two statements are thus equivalent.

illiquidity 1. The property of not being easily turned into money. Some assets are illiquid because there are no markets on which they can easily be traded: for example, unsecured loans to bank customers. Other assets are illiquid because, while they can be traded, the price that can be obtained may be hard to predict, especially if a quick sale is required. This applies to shares in companies, or to houses. This is contrasted with *liquidity, the property of being able to be turned into money rapidly and at a fairly predictable price. Apart from money itself, short-dated securities or bills are the main asset of this form.
2. Having illiquid assets. A business may have problems over meeting its obligations because, although it believes itself to be solvent, its assets are not liquid. If its own view of its solvency were shared by credit institutions it would be able to obtain liquidity on credit, but the information which leads it to feel solvent may be private, for example confidence in new products, and not convincing to creditors. It is possible for businesses forced into liquidation through illiquidity to eventually

pay their creditors in full, that is, for experience to show that they really were solvent. A business which is insolvent, on the other hand, is liable to fail, however liquid its assets may be.

immigration Movement of foreign nationals to reside in a country; this does not include people on short visits, for business or as tourists. Immigrants may arrive with the intention of permanent settlement, arrive with the intention of returning home after a prolonged stay, or be uncertain at the time of arrival how long they will wish to stay. Immigration is motivated by 'push' and 'pull' factors. Push factors could be poverty or persecution in the country migrants are leaving; pull factors could be economic opportunity or freedom in the country they go to.

immiserizing growth Growth of national or regional production which actually decreases welfare. This could occur if the effect of growth of part of the world economy was to worsen its *terms of trade so much that its welfare actually fell. This is unlikely for a single country, as even if growth worsens its terms of trade, much of the resulting loss falls on other countries exporting similar products. It could conceivably apply to a group of countries specializing on exporting a product in *inelastic demand, for example oil exporters. It has been suggested that it could apply to *less developed countries as a group: this seems unlikely given the wide variety of goods they export, many of them manufactures with elastic world demand. It must be remembered that worse terms of trade do not necessarily imply immiserizing growth: if trade accounts for 20 percent of national income, the terms of trade have to worsen by over 5 percent for each 1 percent growth of output for growth to be immiserizing.

immobile factors Factors which do not move readily between sectors, regions, or countries when relative rewards or job opportunities change. Immobility of labour between occupations may be due to lack of qualifications, or to inadequate information on job opportunities. Labour mobility between regions or countries is restricted by social ties, and by housing markets which are often organized so as to favour those who stay put over those who move. Mobility between countries is also hindered by differences of language and social customs, and frequently by legal restrictions. Mobility of capital, while often greater than that of labour, is also limited by lack of information, by differences between countries in law and commercial practices, and in many cases by legal restrictions. *See also* FACTOR MOBILITY.

impact effect The part of the effect of any economic event that acts immediately, or during a short time period. In the *multiplier–accelerator model, for example, the impact effect of an injection of investment, government spending, or exports is 1 unit of further income for each unit spent. After leakages into tax payments, savings, and imports, a second round of k units is created; then a further round of k^2, and so on. The eventual multiplier effect adds up to $1/(1 - k)$, which is larger than the impact effect of 1. Some economic events have impact effects larger than their overall effects: for example, the change in the UK rules on mortgage tax relief for couples is widely seen as having boosted the house price boom of the late 1980s, though the eventual price effect was negligible.

imperfect competition A market situation in which each firm perceives it has the ability to influence the equilibrium price of its own product. *Monopoly is a market with a single seller, *monopsony a market with a single buyer. *Oligopoly arises when there is more than one seller. *Monopolistic competition describes a market where firms produce differentiated products but entry drives equilibrium profit to zero. Imperfect competition is an example of *market failure: the equilibrium of an economy with imperfect competition is generally not *Pareto efficient. *See also* BERTRAND COMPETITION; COURNOT COMPETITION.

implicit contract An understanding between parties on acceptable forms of behaviour that is not part of any formal agreement. Implicit contracts arise in many social situations and have been proposed as an explanation of labour market institutions. Implicit contracts usually develop over time and represent trust between parties. For example, it has been suggested that Coca Cola has an implicit contract with its consumers not to alter the formulation of its standard cola product.

implicit cost The opportunity cost of an action that does not directly involve monetary payment. The choice of an action involves the direct costs for which payments are made plus the implicit cost of forgoing the benefits of an action that could have been chosen. For example, when a firm produces using capital that it owns the implicit cost is the income it could have received by renting that capital to another firm. Implicit costs need to be taken into account when determining *economic profit.

importables Goods of types which could be imported, whether or not they actually are.

import control Administrative restriction and allocation of imports. This may be imposed for balance-of-payments reasons, to reduce spending on imports, or for industrial policy reasons to protect domestic producers of import substitutes. Administrative import controls reduce competition in the economy, and provide opportunities for corruption; programmes of economic liberalization generally include the abolition of import controls, or their replacement by *tariffs.

import deposit A requirement to place a blocked deposit in advance with the central bank as the condition for obtaining foreign currency to pay for imports. Such a deposit has the effect both of imposing a tax on imports, and of reducing the money supply in circulation.

Import Duties Act The UK Act of Parliament passed in 1932 that marked the end of the era during which *free trade was the accepted normal national trading policy. The Import Duties Act imposed a 10 percent tariff on most items from non-Commonwealth countries, excluding food and raw materials, thus marking the end of free trade and the start of the policy of Imperial Preference.

import duty *See* TARIFF.

imported inflation Inflation due to increases in the prices of imports. Increases in the prices of imported final products directly affect any expenditure-based measure of inflation. Increases in the prices of imported fuels, materials, and components increase domestic costs of production, and lead to increases in the prices of domestically produced goods. Imported inflation may be set off by foreign price increases, or by depreciation of a country's exchange rate.

import levy *See* TARIFF.

import licence A permit from the government to import particular goods. The requirement for import licences may be intended to protect domestic producers from competition, to improve the balance of trade by restricting imports, or to facilitate government control over dangerous materials such as explosives.

import penetration The proportion of the market for a particular type of good that is supplied by imports. A rise in import penetration may result from an increase in demand which cannot be met from domestic sources, from worsening of the *competitiveness of domestic suppliers, or from relaxation or removal of restrictions on imports.

import propensity The proportion of the national income that is spent on imports. This can be measured both on average and at the margin. The short-run marginal propensity to import may be higher than the average, particularly at periods of high demand, because of supply constraints in the domestic economy.

import quota A quantitative limit to imports of some type of good. This may be set in terms of value or in physical units. A quota in physical units is liable to lead to a rise in the average price of products imported, as higher-priced products generally carry a higher profit margin.

import restriction *See* IMPORT CONTROL.

imports Goods and services bought by residents of a country but provided by non-residents. Visible imports are goods physically brought into the country. Imports of services, or invisible imports, may involve the supplier entering the country, for example to put out oil-well fires, or residents going abroad to enjoy the services of hotels, or entertainments. For some invisible items, such as payment of royalties on patents, the location of the service is not defined. Capital import means accepting foreign loans or selling real domestic assets to non-residents. This should not be confused with the import of capital goods. Many countries in fact do both, but it is possible to import machinery without borrowing abroad, or to borrow abroad, for example to finance government spending on armaments, without importing capital goods.

import substitution A strategy for the industrialization of *less developed countries (LDCs), of concentrating initially on replacing imports by domestically produced substitutes. This has the advantage that it is already known what markets exist for the products, but the disadvantage that as the imports most easily displaced fall, further progress becomes ever more difficult. If a country is small, its whole domestic market for a product may make it impossible for domestic producers to take full advantage of *economies of scale. The strategy of import substitution is contrasted with that of *export promotion, where LDCs' industrial effort concentrates on products that can be sold in world markets.

import surcharge A temporary additional tax on imports, imposed in addition to normal tariffs, in response to balance-of-payments problems. Such a temporary tax may be very effective in reducing imports, as it creates an incentive to postpone them until it has been removed.

import tariff *See* TARIFF.

impure public good A good that has some of the characteristics of a public good but is not entirely non-rivalrous or non-excludable. An impure public good may be non-excludable but can become congested (*see* COMMON ACCESS RESOURCE), or it may be non-rivalrous but exclusion may be possible (*see* CLUB).

imputation system The system of *corporation tax used in the UK from 1972 until 1999. Dividends distributed to shareholders were subject to tax, but taxes on company profits collected in *advance corporation tax were treated as tax credits at *basic rate for investors receiving dividends. Shareholders had the grossed-up value of their dividends treated as taxable income: if the basic rate of tax was t, the grossed-up value of dividends was the amount received multiplied by $1/(1 - t)$. With basic rate tax already paid, shareholders were liable only for the excess of their own marginal tax rate over basic rate, and could claim refunds if their marginal rate of tax was lower than basic rate or if they were not subject to income tax.

imputed charge for consumption of non-trading capital An estimate of *capital consumption in respect of government assets such as offices, schools, or hospitals which are not run as profit-making businesses. The charge is in principle the amount which would need to be spent on new building to keep the real stock of assets constant.

imputed income Income attributed to the owner of an asset which could have been rented out to somebody else to produce a cash income, where the owner in fact uses the asset themselves. An example of an imputed income is the rental value of *owner-occupied housing: this is included in both the national income and consumption in the UK national income accounts. The argument for this is that without it national income would appear to fall whenever a rented house was purchased by its tenant. In some countries, though not the UK, the imputed income from owner-occupied housing is subject to income tax.

incentive compatibility A mechanism is incentive compatible if it provides an incentive for economic agents to truthfully reveal private information. Consider the implementation of an income tax system. The private information of an individual worker is the level of skill, or productivity, in employment. The public information is the observed income of the individual which is the product of skill and the number of hours worked. The optimum allocation for the economy is defined by an income and consumption level for each level of skill. An income tax system is incentive compatible if it provides an incentive for every individual to earn the income the government desires for their skill level. By earning the required income each individual is implicitly revealing the unobservable level of skill. Incentive compatibility is imposed as a condition that any *incentive contract must satisfy.

incentive contract A contract that incorporates *incentives designed to induce desired behaviour. *See also* AGENCY THEORY.

incentives Rewards or penalties designed to induce one set of economic agents to act in such as way as to produce results that another economic agent wants. As rewards for good results, incentives can include higher pay, better working conditions, better job security, better promotion prospects, or prestige. As penalties for poor results, incentives may take the form of lower pay, worse working conditions, poorer promotion prospects, demotion or sacking, or loss of reputation. Incentives may be applied in response to actual results, such as output or profits, or to management's perceptions of inputs, such as attendance and disciplinary record. Incentives cannot be based on inputs or outputs unobservable by management: to motivate these it is necessary to rely on self-respect or team spirit. *See also* EXPORT INCENTIVES; INCENTIVE CONTRACT; INVESTMENT INCENTIVES.

incidence of taxation The distribution of the burden of taxation. There are two distinct concepts of incidence. The formal incidence of taxation refers to the legal liability to remit taxation. For example, the legal liability of the corporate tax falls upon the corporation. This is distinct from economic incidence which refers to the economic agents who suffer a welfare loss due to the imposition of the tax. For example, the economic incidence of the corporate tax may fall partly on the shareholders who receive a reduced dividend and partly on the customers who pay a higher price. The importance of the distinction is that the economic incidence determines the economic effects of a tax. In a competitive market the economic incidence of a tax on output is determined by the value of the elasticity of supply relative to the elasticity of demand. If demand is perfectly elastic the economic incidence falls on suppliers; if demand is perfectly inelastic the economic incidence falls on consumers. In all other cases the economic incidence is shared. A similar principle applies to the economic incidence of any tax. *See also* TAX SHIFTING.

income 1. The amount an individual can spend in a period while leaving his or her capital unchanged. For an individual with neither assets nor debts, personal income can be defined as receipts from wages, or earned income, plus receipts from transfers, such as pensions. Taxable income is this less any tax allowances. Net or disposable income is income after payment of direct taxes. Real income is money income deflated by a consumer price index, to find its purchasing power at constant prices. For an individual with assets or debts, income from rent, dividends, and interest, or unearned income, has to be added to earned and transfer income. Interest paid out should logically be deducted, though actual tax systems tend to restrict such deductions. For individuals with real or financial assets, the distinction between receipts which are treated as income and those which are treated as *capital gains is a highly technical and often arbitrary matter. For individuals with financial assets consisting of money or securities whose value is denominated in money terms, interest received should logically have losses in real purchasing power due to inflation deducted in measuring their real income. Tax systems, however, generally ignore this point and treat cash receipts as income.

2. The receipts of firms or public corporations from sales or payments of interest and dividends by other firms. These appear as the income side in income and expenditure accounts. Only any net profits in these accounts can be considered to be income in a sense comparable with individual incomes.

3. A macroeconomic aggregate, equal to the sum of individual earned and unearned incomes, the undistributed profits of companies, and property income accruing to the government. *See also* CIRCULAR FLOW OF INCOME; DISPOSABLE INCOME; EARNED INCOME; FACTOR INCOMES; IMPUTED INCOME; PERMANENT INCOME; REAL INCOME; TAXABLE INCOME; UNEARNED INCOME.

income approach to GDP *See* INCOME METHOD.

income distribution The division of total income between different recipients. *Functional income distribution is the division of income between the owners of the different factors of production. *Personal income distribution is the distribution of incomes classified by size. Income distribution can be measured before and after the deduction of direct taxes and the addition of transfers.

income effect The change in demand for a good whose price has altered which would have resulted if prices had stayed the same, but incomes had risen or fallen sufficiently to bring the consumer to the same level of welfare as after the price change. *See also* SUBSTITUTION EFFECT.

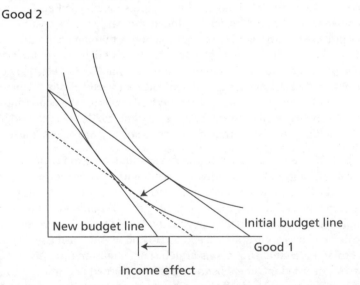

Income Effects

income elasticity of demand The ratio of proportional increase in quantity demanded to proportional increase in income, with all prices held constant. A luxury is a good with an income elasticity of demand in excess of unity: a higher proportion of income is spent on luxuries as income rises. A necessity has an income elasticity of demand which is positive but less than unity: as income rises, spending on a necessity rises, but the proportion of income spent on it falls. An inferior good has a negative income elasticity of demand: as income rises, spending on inferior goods falls. *See also* ENGEL CURVE.

income expansion path A graph (with the axes representing the quantities of two goods) showing how income is divided between different uses, for example importables and exportables, as its total level rises. With unit income elasticity of demand for each, the income expansion path is a ray through the origin; if consumption is biased towards importables as income rises, the income expansion path has a slope between the unit-elasticity ray and the importables axis.

income from employment Income earned working for another person, firm, or government body. It can be measured including or excluding benefits in kind, such as housing, company cars, or free health insurance received from employers. It can also be measured net or gross of deductions by employers, including superannuation contributions, income tax, and National Insurance contributions.

income from self-employment Income of individuals derived from carrying out unincorporated businesses, as sole traders or partners. This is a combination of wages for their own or their family's work, and a return on the capital employed in the business. It can be measured inclusive or exclusive of any imputed income, such as the services of an owner-occupied farmhouse or a flat over a shop. It can also be measured gross or net of depreciation allowances on the capital equipment employed.

income inequality Differences in income between individuals or families, or between different groups, areas, or countries. Inequalities between individuals are accounted for by differences in earning ability, and in property. Individuals who are economically inactive, through age, ill health, or inability to find a job usually have low incomes even after taking account of social security benefits, and those who can work have very varied earning power. Property is also unevenly distributed: inequalities in earned and property incomes are highly correlated and there is also a tendency for high-income earners to intermarry. This means that families or households also show great inequality of incomes. Inequality can be measured either before or after taking account of direct taxes and social security payments: these tend to reduce income inequality but fall far short of eliminating it. Measures of inequality include the *Atkinson index and the *Gini coefficient. Regional and national income differences are similarly caused by differences in earning ability and national capital stocks. *See also* LORENZ CURVE.

income maintenance programme A programme of economic assistance designed to raise the welfare levels of low-income families.

income method The procedure of measuring domestic product by adding the *factor incomes received by various members of the economy. This approach is largely based on information derived from the tax system. Its results are compared with the figures produced by the *expenditure method, which uses information on expenditures by various sectors of the economy including consumers, investors, and the government, and the *output method, which uses information on the net outputs of various sectors of the economy.

income redistribution The use of taxation, government spending, and controls to change the distribution of real incomes. Taxation may be more or less progressive. Government spending programmes may be generally available, or may be targeted or means-tested to try to concentrate benefits on the relatively needy. Controls may be used to alter income distribution: for example, rent controls were originally designed to prevent housing shortages from shifting income from tenants to landlords, and minimum wage legislation aims to benefit low-paid workers at the expense of their employers. The extent of income redistribution through the tax system can be measured by comparing the inequality of income distributions before and after tax. The ability of the state to redistribute incomes is limited by the need to avoid too much damage to the incentives to create income by work, savings, and enterprise.

income support Government payments to maintain individuals' incomes at some prescribed minimum level, in the event of illness, old age, disability, or unemployment making them unable to earn sufficient income. A *negative income tax is a system in which the income support is delivered through a combined tax and social security system, which collects tax if income is above a certain level and pays out if income is below it.

income tax A tax on income. Income tax is normally zero on some range of low incomes, both on equity grounds and because of the expense of collecting tiny amounts of tax. It is then normally proportional up to some upper limit; income beyond this is taxed at higher rates. Thus income tax is usually progressive. An individual's taxable income is calculated after deducting various allowances, in respect of assorted items which may include charitable donations, responsibility for dependants, age allowances, medical insurance, and superannuation contributions. Income for tax purposes may include or exclude imputed items such as the value of the services of owner-occupied houses. *Capital gains may be included as income, excluded, or taxed separately from income. Income tax may be collected from individuals in arrears, or by deduction at source through *pay-as-you-earn in the UK, or a withholding tax on incomes from employment and payment of dividends net of tax by companies, in the US. *See also* CORPORATE INCOME TAX; NEGATIVE INCOME TAX.

income velocity of circulation The ratio of national income to the stock of money, on some definition of money supply. This is considerably smaller than the actual velocity of circulation, as there is a high ratio of total transactions to income in a modern economy: firms buy factor inputs in one set of markets and sell outputs in another, and there is a large quantity of trade in intermediate products. In any case there is a far larger volume of transactions on capital account than on income account.

incomplete contract A contract that specifies the outcome in some but not in all possible *states of the world. A contract may be incomplete through poor drafting or because some distinctions between different states are not publicly verifiable. For example, an employment contract may not be able to make the pay of a worker in a team conditional on the worker's effort because the contribution of individual workers to the team cannot be isolated. Disagreements arising through incomplete contracts are resolved by bargaining or litigation. *See also* AGENCY THEORY.

incomplete information A situation in which economic agents do not know all relevant information. It is helpful to distinguish public information from private information. All agents can be assumed to know, or can learn if they choose to do so, information that is public. Each agent knows their own private information. This cannot be observed by other agents but can only be deduced through observation of actions based on this information. In a game of strategy with incomplete information participants construct a probability distribution over realizations of private information they do not possess in order to compute their optimal strategy. In some cases the lack of knowledge of other agents' private information is not relevant. For example, in a competitive economy a consumer does not need to know the preferences or endowments of other consumers: market prices are the only relevant information for decisions, and these are assumed to be public knowledge.

incomplete markets Situations where certain goods or services cannot be traded because there is no organized market on which to trade. Markets may be incomplete for various reasons. One is that the goods concerned have not yet been invented, so that no contract to trade them can be specified. Another is that while the conditions of a contract to trade could be specified, this would be so complex that the legal bills would outweigh the benefits. Another is that there are too few people interested in trading goods of a given type to make an organized market in them worth the costs of operating it. Incomplete markets are a source of *market failure. *See also* ARROW–DEBREU ECONOMY; COASE THEOREM.

increase in the book value of stocks and work in progress The increase over some period in the value of stocks and work in progress as shown in firms' accounts. This can be decomposed into two parts: the value at current prices of the real increase in stocks and work in progress, and stock appreciation, that is, changes in the value of the original level of stocks due to price increases. The real change in stocks forms part of *gross domestic product; stock appreciation does not.

increasing returns to scale In a productive process, average productivity increasing with output. This means that increasing all inputs in the same proportion results in a more than proportional increase in output. Formally, consider the function $f(x_1, \ldots, x_n)$. If the function satisfies the assumption of increasing returns to scale then

$$f(\lambda x_1, \ldots, \lambda x_n) > \lambda f(x_1, \ldots, x_n)$$

for any $\lambda > 1$.

incumbent firm A firm which is already in position in a market. In a *contestable market, where the goods produced by different firms are homogeneous and there are no *sunk costs, there is complete symmetry between an incumbent firm and would-be entrants. If goods can vary in quality, so that reputation matters, and if there are any sunk costs, the incumbent is in a stronger competitive position than potential entrants: the incumbent has established market contacts, and has already incurred the sunk costs. An incumbent will have a further competitive advantage if cost savings come from *learning by doing: an existing firm has a start on any new entrant in the experience from which cost reductions are derived.

independent risks Risks on projects where there is no relation between the results of one and those of the other. Let the outcomes of a project be represented by the random variables x and y, with means μ_x and μ_y. If the risks are independent then $E[(x - \mu_x)(y - \mu_y)] = 0$.

independent taxation of spouses A system of personal taxation in which individuals are taxed on the basis of their own income only, independent of their marital status and the income of their spouse. The UK in 1990 introduced a system which is not quite independent taxation of spouses, since a married man's allowance is retained, and some taxable items and allowances are transferable between spouses. This system was introduced because the previous system of joint taxation of spouses was felt to involve both breaches of financial privacy for married women, and tax discrimination against marriage, since aggregated incomes made spouses liable to tax at higher marginal rates than under independent taxation.

indexation A system by which wages, prices, or the interest and redemption payments on securities are not fixed in money terms, but are adjusted in proportion to a suitable index of prices, such as the *retail price index. Similarly, pensions can be linked either to prices or to wage rates. Indexation of prices and wages is intended to stabilize real incomes and income differentials; when applied subject to time lags, it does this only approximately.

indexation (funds) A system for making the performance of an investment or unit trust mimic that of a share index. This is done by holding, in proportions approximating to their weights in the index, all the shares concerned or a sufficiently large sample of them.

index-linked An economic variable whose value is linked to an index number. Index-linked government securities have their interest and redemption payments linked to a suitable price index, for example the *retail price index (RPI). Index-linked securities, wage rates, or pensions may be linked either to the RPI or to some index of share prices. The advantage of index-linked securities or incomes is that they protect the holder against the effects of large unforeseen changes in the value of money. A wide spread of index-linking arrangements in an economy may help to make inflation more difficult to stop, as it eliminates the effects of price increases in reducing the real claims on the rest of the economy of those who hold cash and securities with values fixed in cash terms.

index number A number showing the size of some variable, relative to a given base. The base may be assigned any value, and is usually chosen to be either 1 or 100. For a time series, the base may be the value at a given date; for cross-section data, it may be some chosen instance, or the mean of the items covered. Where an index number describes a constructed variable, such as 'the price level', which is an average of prices, or *gross domestic product, which is an aggregate of many different sectors, it is a weighted average of the various components. A *base-weighted or Laspeyres index uses as weights the relative sizes of the different items at the base period; a *current-weighted or Paasche index uses as weights the relative sizes of the component items during the current period.

Index of Industrial Production An index of the volume of production covering the productive sectors of the economy. This is a weighted average of the indexes for manufacturing, mining and quarrying, public utilities, and construction. It is mainly based on measures of physical volume; it excludes private and public services.

indicative planning An attempt to promote economic growth by influencing expectations. Indicative planning attempts to combine the advantages of decentralization and central planning. Growth in an economy may lag because of pessimistic expectations: firms do not expect other firms to invest, and do not feel that market prospects make it profitable for them to invest. Central planning would tell firms to invest, but this is thought to be too rigid. Under indicative planning the government sets out to produce a set of forecasts of activity in various sectors, which if believed would persuade each firm that its own investments would be profitable.

indicator A variable used to determine the employment of *policy instruments. An indicator is used to show when a policy should be introduced, or when the level of an existing policy instrument should be changed. Policy indicators are distinguished from both targets and instruments. Economic policy targets include objectives such as high levels of employment and growth, low and stable levels of inflation, or maintenance of particular exchange rates. Policy instruments are variables the government or central bank can control, or at least influence, such as tax rates or the money supply. Policy indicators may themselves be targets, but frequently are not. They are preferred to targets for use in decision-making because they are available sooner or can be measured more reliably than targets. Policy instruments cannot be indicators for the authority that decides them, but where decision-making is decentralized, one authority's instrument may be used as another's indicator. *See also* ECONOMIC INDICATORS; LEADING INDICATOR.

indifference curve A graphical representation of the set of commodity bundles that are ranked as equally good by a consumer. If commodity bundles x and y are on the same indifference curve then the consumer is indifferent between x and y; and for any *utility function representing the consumer's preferences $U(x) = U(y)$. The indifference curves for any individual cannot cross. The slope of an indifference curve at any point shows the marginal rate of substitution between the goods, and the *elasticity of substitution measures its curvature. Assume the consumer prefers more of every good to less. Then commodity bundles above an indifference curve are preferred to those on it, and these are preferred to those below. The indifference curve will also be downward-sloping. Indifference curves are convex to the origin if the consumer prefers variety (some amount of every good) to either good alone, but this is not a logical necessity. If it is assumed instead that the consumer prefers less of one of the goods, for example labour, then the indifference curves slope upwards. *See also* COMMUNITY INDIFFERENCE CURVE.

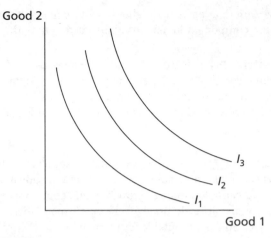

Good 2

I_3

I_2

I_1

Good 1

Indifference Curves

indirect investment The purchase of securities that represent claims on other underlying securities. An indirect investment can be undertaken by purchasing the shares of an investment company. An investment company sells shares in itself to raise funds to purchase a portfolio of securities. The motivation for doing this is that the pooling of funds allows advantage to be taken of diversification and of savings in *transaction costs. Many investment companies operate in line with a stated policy objective, for example on the types of securities that will be purchased and the nature of the fund management. *See also* MUTUAL FUND.

indirect least squares A method for estimating the structural parameters of a single equation in a *simultaneous equations model. It involves estimating the parameters of the system in the *reduced form using *ordinary least squares and solving for the structural parameters in terms of the reduced form parameters.

indirect tax A tax collected by an intermediary (such as a supplier) from the economic agent who bears the formal incidence of the tax (such as the customer). Taxes levied on goods or services, for example value-added tax or excise duties on alcohol and tobacco, are seen as indirect. These taxes are indirect because the tax payment to the revenue service is made by the firm selling the good but the tax is charged to the consumer. The extent to which the tax burden is shared between the supplier and the customer (the economic incidence) depends on the elasticities of supply and demand. *See also* INCIDENCE OF TAXATION; TAX SHIFTING.

indirect utility function The maximum utility level a consumer can achieve expressed as a function of prices and income. Consider a consumer choosing the quantities x_1 and x_2 of two goods to maximize utility subject to a budget constraint. The utility maximization problem is

$$\max_{\{x_1, x_2\}} U(x_1, x_2) \text{ subject to } M = p_1 x_1 + p_2 x_2.$$

The solution is described by the two *Marshallian demand functions $x_1 = d_1(p_1, p_2, M)$ and $x_2 = d_2(p_1, p_2, M)$. Substituting the optimal choices back into the utility function gives the maximized level of utility as

$$V(p_1, p_2, M) \equiv U(d_1(p_1, p_2, M), d_2(p_1, p_2, M)).$$

The function $V(p_1, p_2, M)$ is the indirect utility function. Denote the marginal utility of income by α. Roy's identity states that $\partial V/\partial p_i = -\alpha x_i$, a result that is useful for calculating the welfare consequences of a price change. *See also* EXPENDITURE FUNCTION.

Individual Retirement Account (IRA) A US retirement plan that provides tax advantages on savings for retirement. IRAs were introduced in 1974 to permit saving in tax-privileged form for employees without pension plans. Eligibility for IRAs was expanded by the *Economic Recovery Tax Act of 1981 to permit almost all working taxpayers to contribute, and the IRA limits were increased. This led to a major increase in saving in IRAs. The *Tax Reform Act of 1986 changed the position by excluding higher-income taxpayers with employer-provided pensions.

Individual Savings Account (ISA) A UK scheme designed to encourage saving, by allowing individuals to invest a limited sum annually in assets which are not subject to income tax or capital gains tax. This replaced the personal equity plan scheme in 1999. The permitted limits can vary annually; in 2007–8 they were either a 'mini ISA' of up to £3000 in stocks and shares, a 'mini cash ISA' of up to £3000 in securities such as building society deposits, and a 'mini insurance ISA' of up to £1000 in life insurance, or up to £7000 in a 'maxi ISA' in stocks and shares.

indivisibility **1.** In a productive process, the existence of a minimum scale at which any technique can operate. This applies to all productive techniques. In some cases the minimum scale is so small that it has no economic effects, but in other cases it is sufficiently large to make the technique unavailable to small firms. Indivisibilities in techniques are a major source of both *economies of scale and *economies of scope.

2. A limit on the possible subdivision of a commodity or security. For example, US Treasury Bills are sold in increments of $1000. Indivisibilities limit the extent to which a consumption plan or a portfolio can exactly match the optimal choice. The market offers solutions to some indivisibilities: *indirect investment is a method of overcoming the indivisibility of securities.

induced investment Investment in response to changes in output. This applies at a macro- rather than a microeconomic level. Investment by a firm cannot be a technical response to its own past output, which has already been produced with the capital in place. Investment may, however, be affected by output changes through their effects on profits. When output rises, because overhead costs can be spread more widely profits rise, and this both provides funds for investment directly and makes it easier to borrow. Investment is not determined by future changes in a firm's output: output and investment plans are formed simultaneously. Investment by each firm responds to expectations about market prospects, which are influenced by changes in the incomes of its customers. Induced investment is contrasted with autonomous investment, which is determined by long-run factors independent of short-run changes in income, such as technical innovations.

industrial action Action taken by trade unions or informal groups of workers to bring pressure to bear on employers when *industrial disputes have not been settled by negotiation or arbitration. Such action by workers can include go-slows, 'working to rule', overtime bans, or strikes. Industrial action by employers can include temporary lay-offs or lock-outs.

industrial concentration *See* CONCENTRATION.

industrial countries Countries whose *gross domestic product and exports contain a large share of industrial production. The list of countries which could be described as industrial is continually changing. The *International Monetary Fund uses the name for the group of mainly advanced economies included in the *Organization for Economic Cooperation and Development. This group includes Canada, Japan, Turkey, Australia, New Zealand, the United States, and eighteen European countries: Austria, Belgium, Denmark, Finland, France, Germany, Greece, Iceland, Ireland, Italy, Luxembourg, the Netherlands, Norway, Portugal, Spain, Sweden, Switzerland, and the United Kingdom. This definition omits the *newly industrialized countries, including Brazil, Korea, and Singapore, and the countries of the former Soviet Union and Central and Eastern Europe, of which several, including Russia and the Czech Republic, are heavily industrialized.

industrial democracy The principle that all those employed in a firm should have a say in how it is run. This can take various forms. In cases where capital requirements are relatively small, it is possible that a firm can be owned by those who work in it. In this case the workers can elect the directors and managers, and control all decisions taken. In cases where too much capital is required for this to be possible, or where the workers do not want to accept the risks involved in being owners, they can have a share in decisions, electing some directors. Alternatively, the actual direction of a firm can be by managers appointed by its owners, but workers can be consulted about decisions, either through *works councils elected by the employees, or through their trade unions.

industrial dispute A disagreement between employees and employers concerning pay, hours of work, working conditions, manning levels, or job security. Industrial disputes may be settled by conciliation, that is discussion; by arbitration by some third party agreed on by both sides or prescribed by law; or by industrial action, including overtime bans, go-slows, or in the last resort strikes or lock-outs. The employees may be organized by trade unions; employers may negotiate separately or via employers' associations.

industrial economics The field of economics devoted to the study of decision-making by firms and the interaction between firms in the market place. 'The new industrial economics' was a name given in the 1980s when research in the field began to make extensive use of *game theory.

industrial espionage The illicit acquisition of information by one business about the activities of another. Such information may include formulae, designs, business plans, or information about personnel. The methods of industrial espionage include theft of documents, phone tapping, and computer hacking, with or without help from corrupt employees of the firm being spied on.

industrialization The process of moving resources into the *industrial sector. This is common in the early stages of economic development, when resources move out of primary production. Industrialization was the norm in the now advanced countries earlier in their development, and was energetically pursued by many *less developed countries and by the former planned economies of the former Soviet Union and Central and Eastern Europe. In recent years most of the advanced economies have seen *deindustrialization; this is not really the reverse of industrialization, as it mainly involves a shift of resources from producing goods into service sectors.

industrial licensing *See* LICENSING.

industrial organization A field of economics that studies market structure and the strategic behaviour of firms, with the focus on imperfect competition. It includes the factors determining which activities are coordinated within firms and which through markets; the issues connected with providing incentives within firms to overcome *principal–agent problems; the relation between the structure of industries and their performance; and the public regulation of monopolies, mergers, and competition.

industrial policy Official policies concerning the direction of economic activity to particular parts of the economy. For many years governments were concerned with the division of economies between industry and primary production; the less industrialized countries tried to encourage the growth of local industry, while the more industrial countries protected their native agriculture and mines. In more recent years attention has centred on trying to encourage the rise of high-tech sectors using advanced technology. Policies have included using tax rules and government money to encourage *research and development, intervention in financial markets to direct investment funds into favoured sectors, and intervention in the mergers market to try to obtain firms large enough to gain economies of scale.

industrial relations The relations between the management and workforce of an enterprise, particularly bargaining through *trade unions. This mainly concerns pay, hours and conditions of work, fringe benefits, security of employment, redundancy and redundancy payments, and disciplinary and grievance procedures. These can be determined by economy-wide legislation or, whenever there is scope, by bargaining at the firm or industry level, sometimes through trade unions.

industrial sector The part of the economy concerned with producing goods without much direct input of natural resources. This secondary sector is distinguished from the primary producing sector, that is agriculture, fisheries, forestry, and mining and quarrying, which produces goods with large direct inputs of natural resources, and the tertiary sector, including for example transport, distribution, finance, health, education, and administration, which produces services.

industry 1. A sector of the economy, in which firms use similar factor inputs to make a group of related products. The *Standard Industrial Classification is a partition of industry into sectors and subsectors.
2. A group of sectors, mainly in manufacturing and construction, typically producing physical goods rather than services. The *Confederation of British Industry is a UK organization representing firms in these sectors, and the *Department for Business, Enterprise and Regulatory Reform is the main UK government department responsible for dealing with them. *See also* FOOTLOOSE INDUSTRY; INFANT INDUSTRY; NATIONALIZED INDUSTRY; SERVICE INDUSTRY.

industry demand for labour The demand for labour by an industry as a function of the wage rate. At any given wage rate, industry demand for labour depends on output. If wage rates fall, this can raise industry demand for labour in three ways. First, labour may be substituted for other inputs; second, a reduction in costs may lower price and increase demand for the industry's output; and third, in the longer run a rise in profits may induce new firms to enter the industry and take on additional workers. Industry demand for labour is more elastic the better the opportunities for substitution between labour and other inputs, the more elastic the demand for the industry's output, and the more elastic the supply of potential entrants.

industry supply curve *See* SUPPLY CURVE.

inefficiency Not obtaining the maximum output from the use of resources. Inefficiency is costly to the economy. Formally, inefficiency implies that the economic equilibrium is not *Pareto efficient. Inefficiency can arise at three levels. First, factors of production can be allocated across firms in a manner that does not secure the maximum output from those inputs. Second, inefficiency in the product mix means that inputs are being used to produce the wrong combinations of goods and services. Third, there can be allocative inefficiency in the distribution of goods and services between consumers. In addition to these forms of inefficiency there can also be *X-inefficiency, or organizational slack, which means that enterprises are producing the right outputs, but are using an unnecessarily high level of inputs.

inelastic Lacking in responsiveness. Where one variable, x, can affect another, y, the relation is inelastic if a proportional change in x is associated with a smaller proportional change in y, of whichever sign is appropriate. For example, the demand for a good is inelastic if a fall in price produces a smaller proportional increase in quantity demanded, so that total revenue falls when quantity increases, and marginal revenue is negative.

inelastic demand When the *elasticity of demand is less than 1. If demand is inelastic a proportional fall in price produces a smaller proportional increase in quantity demanded. Total revenue thus falls when quantity increases, and marginal revenue is negative. Therefore, a price on an inelastic part of the demand curve will not be chosen by a profit-maximizing monopolist, but can occur at the equilibrium in a competitive industry.

inelastic supply When the *elasticity of supply is less than 1. The supply of a good or service is inelastic if a given percentage increase in the price at which it can be sold produces a smaller percentage increase in the quantity supplied. Supply is inelastic if a rise in price causes little increase in output by existing firms and little entry to an industry of new firms. If it is easy to expand production in existing firms, or to attract entry of new firms, supply is elastic.

inequality Differences in the distribution of economic stocks or flows among economic agents. For example, wealth inequality refers to the distribution of the stock of wealth, whereas *income inequality refers to the distribution of the flow of income. Inequality can arise among individuals or groups within an economy, or among nations. Inequality can be graphically represented by the *Lorenz curve or measured by a range of indicators including the *Atkinson index and the *Gini coefficient.

infant industry A new industry which during its early stages is unable to compete with established producers abroad, often because of the lack of market reputation and small scale. Governments sometimes support the development of new industries either by direct subsidies, or by protective *tariffs or other trade controls.

inferior good A good of which less is demanded at any given price as income rises, over some range of incomes. An inferior good thus has a negative *income elasticity of demand, over this income range. A good is most likely to be inferior if it has a close substitute of higher quality. It should be noted that a good cannot be inferior at all levels of income otherwise it must be a bad. *See also* ENGEL CURVE.

inflation A persistent tendency for nominal prices to increase. Inflation is measured by the proportional changes over time in some appropriate price index, commonly a consumer price index or a *GDP deflator. Cost inflation is started by an increase in some element of costs, for example the oil price explosion of 1973–4. Demand inflation is due to too much aggregate demand. Once started, inflation tends to persist through an inflationary spiral, in which various prices and wage rates rise because others have risen. *Hyperinflation is extremely rapid inflation, in which prices increase so fast that money largely loses its convenience as a medium of exchange. *See also* CORE INFLATION; COST INFLATION; CREEPING INFLATION; DEMAND INFLATION; EXPECTED INFLATION; HYPERINFLATION; IMPORTED INFLATION; MENU COSTS OF INFLATION; REPRESSED INFLATION; SHOE-LEATHER COSTS OF INFLATION; UNDERLYING RATE OF INFLATION; UNEXPECTED INFLATION.

inflation accounting The production of meaningful company accounts under inflationary conditions. During inflation, *depreciation allowances on capital goods based on historical cost do not provide for their replacement, and thus overstate profits, and increases in the prices of inventories also produce paper profits in excess of real ones. On the other hand, if interest rates increase in response to inflation, counting nominal interest payments as costs but taking no credit for the decrease in the real value of a firm's debts understates true profits. There are also difficulties if the prices of a firm's capital goods, inventories, or output change at different rates from the general price level.

inflation-adjusted budget deficit The budget deficit which would result if government expenditure was reckoned as including the real rather than the nominal interest paid out. For example, consider a government whose budget deficit before adjustment for inflation equals 2 percent of *gross national product (GNP). If net government debt equals half of GNP, and nominal interest rates are 10 percent whereas inflation is 5 percent, then nominal debt interest equals 5 percent of GNP, while real debt interest equals only 2½ percent of GNP. In this case a nominal budget deficit equal to 2 percent of GNP corresponds to an inflation-adjusted budget surplus equal to ½ percent of GNP.

inflationary gap The excess of the actual level of activity in the economy over the level corresponding to the *non-accelerating inflation rate of unemployment. If the inflationary gap is positive, inflation tends to speed up, and the larger the inflationary gap, the faster inflation speeds up. An inflationary gap thus gives rise to *demand inflation.

inflationary spiral The tendency for prices and wages to react in turn to increases in other wages and prices during a *cost inflation. During this process prices rise to pass on increases in costs because of rises in wages and fuel or materials prices, while wages rise because of increases in the cost of living. If cost rises are partially absorbed, the spiral will gradually converge; if nobody consents to absorb cost increases, an inflationary spiral can continue indefinitely once it has started.

inflation rate The rate of increase of a specified *price index. The inflation rate is typically measured in annual terms, though it can be defined over any chosen time period (e.g. monthly or weekly). If p_0 is the price level at time 0 and p_1 the price level at time 1 the inflation rate is defined by $100(p_1 - p_0)/p_1$. In the UK inflation is measured using both the *consumer price index and the *retail price index (RPI). The major difference between these indices is that the RPI includes items related to owner–occupier housing costs, particularly mortgage interest payments.

inflation tax The effect of inflation on the real value of money and government debt denominated in money terms. For example, if the population of a country hold money equal in value to 10 percent of *gross national product (GNP) and government debt equal in value to 30 percent of GNP, annual inflation of 10 percent removes an amount equal to 1 percent of GNP from the real purchasing power of their money balances, and an amount equal to 3 percent of GNP from the real value of their security holdings. This is equivalent to a tax of 4 percent of GNP. The government can incur a nominal budget deficit equal to the yield of the inflation tax without increasing the real value of its debts, including issue of *fiat money.

informal economy *See* HIDDEN ECONOMY.

information 1. The data available to individuals, firms, or governments at the time economic decisions have to be taken. Information in this sense refers to economic statistics and the collection, use, and interpretation of those statistics.
2. The knowledge possessed by economic agents. An economy is described by the preferences and endowments of its consumers, the technology of its firms, and the

prices and characteristics of its products. Consumers, firms, and governments take actions. What matters for the attainment of economic efficiency is who knows which parts of the total description of the economy. The economy has symmetric information if all agents are equally informed about relevant information. What information is relevant changes with the economic environment. In a *competitive economy a consumer only needs to know their own preferences, product characteristics, and prices in order to trade. Information about the preferences of other consumers or about firms is irrelevant. The competitive equilibrium will be *Pareto efficient if there is symmetric information. There is *asymmetric information when some agents are better informed than others about relevant information. For example, a consumer selling a second-hand car may have better knowledge of its qualities than a potential purchaser. Asymmetric information is a cause of *market failure. Contract theory has found it useful to distinguish between public information and private information. Public information is observable and verifiable, so can be a determinant of the pay-off in an incentive contract. Private information cannot be observed but only inferred from actions. An *incentive contract cannot be conditioned on private information. In game theory the distinction is made between games with complete information—all participants know the entire structure of the game—and games with *incomplete information— not all information about the game is known. *See also* PRICE-SENSITIVE INFORMATION.

information agreement An agreement by a number of firms to provide one another with information on their prices, discounts, and conditions of sale. This information is usually provided through a *trade association, either before or after changes are made. While such an exchange of information is not itself a restrictive practice, it could clearly assist in collusion. In the UK such agreements are required to be registered with the *Office of Fair Trading, and may be referred to the *Restrictive Practices Court.

information asymmetry *See* ASYMMETRIC INFORMATION.

information criterion A *likelihood function based statistic used as a model selection criterion. Important examples are the Akaike and the Bayes–Schwarz information criteria. *See also* GOODNESS OF FIT MEASURES.

infrastructure The capital equipment used to produce publicly available services, including transport and telecommunications, and gas, electricity, and water supplies. These provide an essential background for other economic activities in modern economies; the fact that they are not available or reliable is characteristic of *less developed countries, and handicaps their development. Infrastructure services are generally either provided or regulated by the state.

inheritance tax A tax on amounts inherited by particular heirs. The tax rate can vary according to the relation with the deceased; for example spouses may be exempt, or taxed progressively with the amount received. It is possible, as in the UK, to combine an inheritance tax with a tax on gifts *inter vivos*, that is gifts made while the donor is still alive, via a *capital transfer tax.

initial conditions The position from which an economic system is assumed to start. If a system obeys a known system of deterministic difference or differential equations, knowledge of the initial conditions is both necessary and sufficient to calculate its state at any later time. If a system contains a stochastic component, its current state owes less and less to initial conditions as time goes on, and long-term prediction of its state is unreliable, if at all possible. *See also* CHAOS.

initial public offering (IPO) The first sale of stock by a private company to the public. An IPO represents the transition from private ownership to public trading. The public offering is accompanied by a prospectus describing the activities and prospects for the firm and is usually underwritten by investment banks.

injections to the circular flow of income Forms of spending which do not derive from current income. These are investment spending by firms, government spending, and export sales to foreigners. If injections exceed *leakages from the circular flow, the income level rises.

in-kind redistribution Redistribution that takes the form of the gift of commodities rather than cash. The benefit of in-kind redistribution is that it removes choice from the recipient and helps ensure that they consume the commodities. For example, the provision of food to the homeless ensures they eat whereas a gift of cash may be spent on commodities other than food. Underlying these observations are *merit goods arguments.

Inland Revenue *See* HM REVENUE and CUSTOMS.

innocent entry barriers Barriers to entry to an industry which result from natural, technical, or social conditions, but are not deliberately designed to restrict entry. For example, an existing firm may have cost advantages due to accumulated experience of production, or the techniques of production may require large sunk costs before production can start.

innovation The economic application of a new idea. Product innovation involves a new or modified product; process innovation involves a new or modified way of making a product. Innovation sometimes consists of a new or modified method of business organization. *See also* DIFFUSION OF INNOVATIONS; FINANCIAL INNOVATION.

input–output Study of the flows of goods and services between different sectors of the economy. An input–output table lists all flows of goods and services between sectors of origin and factor services, usually denoted by rows, and sectors of destination, including both intermediate and various types of final use, usually represented by columns. Input–output analysis then assumes that each activity has *constant returns to scale, and that the ratio of inputs to production for each sector is constant. On these assumptions it is possible to work out what gross outputs of all sectors are required for any set of final products, and what total factor inputs must be. These totals can then be compared with the available labour force and industrial capacity to see if such a programme is feasible. Input–output has sometimes been advocated as a part of a centralized economic planning mechanism. The results of input–output analysis are limited by the assumptions of constant input proportions, and aggregation into sectors.

input prices The prices at which the services of factors of production, or supplies of fuels, materials, and intermediate products can be obtained. For capital goods, the interest and amortization costs of using them, rather than the prices of the capital goods themselves, are treated as input prices.

inputs The services of factors of production and usage of fuels, materials, and intermediate products necessary for a process of production. The relation of output to the use of various inputs is shown by a *production function. Inputs may be required in fixed proportions, or may be substitutable for one another. Where inputs are substitutable, profit maximization requires using the cheapest set of inputs that will produce any given set of outputs.

inside money Money which is an asset to the person or firm holding it, but is also a liability for somebody else in the economy. Inside money is contrasted with outside money, where the asset of the holder is not balanced by a liability for some other party. Bank balances, for example, are clearly inside money, while gold coinage is outside money. A rise in the real value of inside money does not increase the aggregate wealth of the economy, but redistributes it between the issuers and the holders of money. It is a matter of definition whether money which is a liability of the government counts as inside or outside money.

insider dealing Stock exchange transactions by 'insiders'. These are people who through their positions in or contacts with companies are able to obtain *price-sensitive information, such as profits figures or news of takeover bids, in a more detailed and accurate form, and, in particular, earlier than 'outsiders', who have to rely on published information. Insiders are able to profit by their superior information, buying before share prices rise and selling before share prices fall. Insider dealing is restricted both by stock exchange regulations and by law in many countries.

insiders and outsiders Those currently employed (insiders) and those who are not (outsiders). This distinction is used to help explain the persistence of unemployment in many economies. Wages and working conditions are determined by bargaining, either informally, or via *collective bargaining between trade unions and employers. The workers' representatives are very keen on protecting the jobs of present employees, the insiders, but less keen on providing job opportunities for potential employees, the outsiders. The workers' side have a strong interest in not making wages so high or working conditions so expensive as to handicap employers in competing to retain their existing markets, as losing these would lead to job losses. They have less interest in agreeing to wage levels and working practices which would make profits high enough to induce employers to expand and provide jobs for new workers. The domination of collective bargaining by insiders is believed to help explain why unemployment is so persistent in many countries.

insider trading *See* INSIDER DEALING.

insolvency Inability of an individual or company to pay debts as they fall due. This may lead an individual to become bankrupt, or a company to go into liquidation. In either case a trustee in bankruptcy or liquidator is appointed by a court to realize the available assets and pay off the debts so far as possible. An individual or business may be unable to pay debts because of *illiquidity rather than inadequate assets: if the assets are, in fact, sufficient, creditors may eventually be paid in full. If creditors can be persuaded of this, insolvency can be avoided by rolling over old loans, or taking out new loans to pay off the old ones. It is an offence to trade when insolvent.

Inspector of Taxes A UK *HM Revenue and Customs official who receives tax returns from individuals and companies, and assesses the tax they are due to pay. The actual payment is then made to a different official, a Collector of Taxes.

instalment Payment of a total sum in regular amounts at intervals over a period, instead of making a single payment. Instalment payments are used in credit agreements and can be used to pay utility bills.

institutional economics The analysis of economics from a perspective which stresses the importance of institutions in determining how economies really work. For example, the rules of land ownership are important in economic development in *less developed countries, and the lack of clearly defined and enforced *property rights is proving a handicap in the transformation from planned to market economies. Institutional economics includes the analysis of economic influences on institutional rules themselves.

institutional shareholder A shareholder which is itself a company rather than an individual. Because small amounts of capital can only be used to hold shares either by concentrating on a few securities, which involves high risk, or buying very small holdings, which involves high transaction costs, an increasing proportion of individual investors choose to hold shares via institutions. These may be *unit trusts, investment trusts, pension funds, or insurance companies selling with-profits life policies. Institutional shareholders may act as *relationship investors, seeking a voice in the management of the companies whose shares they own, but usually adopt a passive role and refrain from participation in management decisions.

instrumental variable An *exogenous variable that is correlated with an *endogenous variable used as an explanatory variable in a regression. Instrumental variables are used to obtain consistent estimators when *ordinary least squares suffers from the *endogeneity problem.

insurance The use of contracts to reduce and redistribute *risk. In an insurance contract, the insurer accepts a fixed payment, or premium, from the insured, and in return undertakes to make payments if certain events occur. In life insurance the event insured against is the death of the insured, or his or her survival to some agreed age. In insurance for fire and theft the event insured against is damage by fire or theft to the insured's property. In motor insurance the event insured against is loss by fire, theft, or damage to 'third parties', that is, anybody except the insured and the insurer. In health insurance the event insured against is medical expenses and/or loss of earnings through ill health. In every insurance contract the insured pays to achieve a reduction in risk. Without insurance there is a small chance of a large loss; with insurance there is a certain small loss, that is the premium, and possibly some further loss if the damage done by the event insured against exceeds the sum insured. The insurer makes the reverse exchange, accepting a new risk for the sake of the premium. Insurers are willing to take on risk in this way for two reasons. One is that they may be *risk-neutral, or at least less *risk-averse than the people they are insuring. The other factor which induces insurers to take on risks is that if they take on a number of risks of the same general type which are largely independent, the proportional dispersion of their returns will be smaller than the average of the individual risks they take on. Insurance thus both reduces overall risk, and transfers risk to those with a comparative advantage in risk-bearing. *See also* DEPOSIT INSURANCE; HEALTH INSURANCE; LIFE INSURANCE; THIRD-PARTY INSURANCE.

insurance company A company whose main activity is providing insurance. This may include life, fire, motor, health, and many other varieties of insurance. As the premiums for policies are paid before claims occur, and in the case of life policies the funds collected accumulate for decades, insurance companies hold large stocks of assets. This makes them major participants in the market for government bonds, equity shares, and commercial and household mortgages.

intangible assets Assets of an enterprise which cannot be seen or touched. This includes *goodwill, *patents, *trademarks, and *copyright. In the case of goodwill there is no documentary evidence of its existence. There is in all these cases evidence that intangible assets exist, as they are occasionally bought and sold, but there is no continuing market, and in their nature they are non-homogeneous, so that their valuation is very uncertain.

integration 1. The combination of different economic activities under unified control. This may involve vertical integration, that is, either backward integration, where a business is combined with one supplying its inputs, or forward integration, where a business is combined with one using its outputs. It may also involve horizontal integration, where a business is combined with another which may use the same suppliers or sell in the same markets. *See also* BACKWARD INTEGRATION; FORWARD INTEGRATION; HORIZONTAL INTEGRATION; VERTICAL INTEGRATION.

2. The organization of economic activities so that national boundaries do not matter. The *European Union and the *North American Free Trade Agreement are examples of integration. Complete economic integration would imply *free trade in all goods and services, perfect capital mobility, complete freedom of migration, complete freedom of establishment for businesses, and an unhindered flow of information and ideas. It would also imply the elimination of national differences in taxation, in the financing of social services, in the rules governing competition and monopoly, and in environmental regulation; and arguably a single currency.

3. A property of time series, concerning the number of times they need to be differenced to produce a stationary series. *See also* ORDER OF INTEGRATION.

intellectual property rights Private property rights in ideas. This may take the form of copyright, where material such as books or music can be copied only with permission from the copyright owner, who can charge for this; or *patents, where processes or product designs can only be used with permission from the patentee, who can charge a licence fee. Such property rights originally rest with authors or inventors, or their employers, but can be bought, sold, or inherited.

intensive margin The margin that is affected by changes in the level to which an existing activity is undertaken. For example, increasing work hours from 40 per week to 41 per week is a change at the intensive margin. *See also* EXTENSIVE MARGIN.

interdependent utility An assumption on individual preferences under which the subjective well-being of an individual depends on some measure of well-being of other individuals (a 'reference group'), such as kin, peers, etc. An example is a *consumption externality that can be negative (envy) or positive (*altruism).

interest Payment for a loan additional to repayment of the amount borrowed. The rate of interest is the extra payment per unit of the loan, typically calculated as an annual rate. An interest-bearing security yields interest to the holder; some interest-bearing loans are used as money. Interest payments are made by borrowers to lenders. Simple interest means that, where interest is not actually paid out but is added to the principal of a loan each period, the amount added is the same each period. Compound interest means that, again where interest is not paid out to the lender, the amount to be added to the loan each period is the same percentage of the debt already accumulated: compound interest thus includes interest on past interest. Interest rates can be found for loans of any duration, from those repayable on demand to perpetuities. Rates on loans of under five years are usually termed short-term rates, rates on loans from 5 to 15 years' maturity as medium-term, and rates on loans for over 15 years as long-term rates; but usage is not uniform. Interest rates are commonly quoted in nominal terms. The *real interest rate is the nominal interest rate for any period, corrected for the effects of inflation. *See also* COMPOUND INTEREST; RATE OF INTEREST; SIMPLE INTEREST.

interest-elasticity of the demand for money The proportional change in the quantity of money demanded divided by the proportional change in interest rate. This is a measure of the responsiveness of the demand for money to changes in interest rates. A minus sign is typically inserted into the definition to make the elasticity a positive number. The elasticity, ε, is given by

$$\varepsilon = -\left(\frac{dM}{M}\right) \Big/ \left(\frac{di}{i}\right) = -\left(\frac{i}{M}\right)\left(\frac{dM}{di}\right)$$

where M is the demand for money and i is the interest rate.

interest equalization tax A US tax on foreign portfolio borrowing in the United States. This was intended to reduce capital outflows from the US.

interest payments Payments of interest due on loans. These may be owed by individuals, firms, or the government. Individual interest payments are mostly not tax-deductible, with some exceptions for mortgage interest. Interest payments made by firms have to be subtracted from trading profits to obtain total profits, and interest received has to be added. Interest payments by governments are an important part of government spending, especially in countries with high ratios of government debt to *gross domestic product.

interest rate *See* LONG-TERM INTEREST RATE; NATURAL RATE OF INTEREST; RATE OF INTEREST; REAL INTEREST RATE; TERM STRUCTURE OF INTEREST RATES.

interest-rate futures A form of financial futures where the pay-off from the contract is determined by an interest rate. These futures can be used either to hedge, that is to reduce risks, or to speculate, accepting extra risks for the sake of expected profits. Interest-rate futures are traded in the UK on the *London International Financial Futures and Options Exchange.

interest-rate swaps Transactions in which two financial institutions exchange one flow of interest payments for another. *Swaps can be between fixed and floating rate debt, or between debt denominated in different currencies.

intergenerational equity A concept of fair treatment of individuals who belong to different generations in a given time period. Examples of such issues include fiscal equity, such as debt and tax burden on the young, policy sustainability, and environmental problems.

interim dividend A dividend payment based on interim profit figures for part of a company's financial year. Payment of an interim dividend normally carries a suggestion, but no guarantee, that a final dividend payment will follow.

interim report Any company report other than an annual report. Interim reports are often issued half-yearly. Figures for turnover, profit, or loss included in interim reports are usually not audited.

inter-industry trade Trade between countries where exports and imports consist of different types of goods. Such trade is based on differences in *factor endowments. Countries tend to export goods where they have relatively large amounts of the factors intensively used in producing them, and to import goods which they cannot produce themselves, or which they can only produce at great cost, due to a scarcity of the factors intensively used in producing them. With trade of this type, it is unusual for a country to import and export goods in the same classification. Inter-industry trade is contrasted with *intra-industry trade, which is a consequence of *imperfect competition, and often takes place between countries with very similar factor endowments.

interior solution Also referred to as an interior optimum. In the context of a constrained optimization problem this is a solution that changes in response to any arbitrarily small perturbation to the gradient of the objective function at the optimum. If the optimal solution does not change for at least one direction of such a perturbation it is said to be a corner solution, or a corner optimum.

interlocking directorates The situation where two or more companies are linked by having some members of their *boards of directors in common. This ensures that the firms can be well informed on each other's position without the need for any formal arrangements.

intermediate good A good which is not itself a final good, but is used as an input for production. Some commodities may be used as final or intermediate goods, such as computers, fuels, and man-made materials.

internal balance A situation where the level of activity in an economy is consistent with a stable rate of inflation. At higher activity levels inflation tends to rise, and at lower levels unemployment is unnecessarily high. Maintaining internal balance is one objective of *economic policy. Internal balance is contrasted with *external balance, which is a situation where the economy has a balance of payments, on current and capital account combined, which is sustainable, at least in the medium run. Some combination of monetary and fiscal policies should allow both internal and external balance to be maintained.

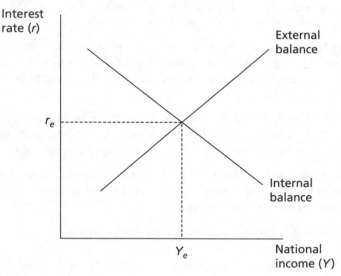

Internal and External Balance

internalizing externalities Any method of getting those producing external costs or benefits to take account of them in their decision-making. Examples include merging agents that are affected into a single entity or imposing taxes so that private costs and benefits reflect social costs and benefits. Internalization is a solution to externality problems that can work even if there are *missing markets. *See also* COASE THEOREM.

internal labour market The system by which recruitment for senior appointments in an organization is mainly from existing employees in lower-grade jobs. The main merits of internal labour markets are that a firm is likely to know more about the strengths and weaknesses of existing employees than outsiders, and that a reputation for internal promotion as its preferred strategy may assist in recruitment and retention of staff. *See also* EXTERNAL LABOUR MARKET.

internal market The territories of all European Union (EU) member states viewed as a single integrated market. The internal market has been a focus of EU policy with the aim of creating an economic area that has free movement of goods, labour, services, and capital.

internal market (health service) The system whereby one section of the UK National Health Service which uses facilities provided by other sections has to pay for them. This is intended to gain the cost-saving benefits of competition, and lead to more efficient utilization of the total resources used. It is independent of the question of whether patients should be required to contribute to the cost of treatment.

internal rate of return (IRR) The interest rate at which the net present value of a project is zero. If the net cash flow on a project starts off negative, and once it becomes positive it remains so, the IRR is unique; but if cash flow at the end becomes negative, as can happen if there are costs of making a plant safe after its useful life is over, the IRR may not be unique. A project is worth investing in if its IRR exceeds the sum of the risk-free rate of interest and an appropriate risk premium.

Internal Revenue Service (IRS) The US federal government organization that assesses and collects personal and business federal taxes. This makes it parallel to *HM Revenue and Customs in the UK.

International Accounting Standards Board (IASB) An independent and privately funded body responsible for developing the International Financial Reporting Standards, and promoting the use and application of these standards. The IASB was founded in April 2001 as the successor to the International Accounting Standards Committee.

International Bank for Reconstruction and Development (IBRD) (World Bank) An international body set up in 1946 after the Bretton Woods conference to promote economic recovery and development. The IBRD was originally intended to assist in the reconstruction of countries in Europe and Asia damaged by the Second World War. It has since become a provider of both funds and technical and economic advice for *least developed countries (LDCs). The IBRD is funded by quota subscriptions of member countries, partly in gold and national currencies, but mainly in uncalled capital, which is, however, available in case of need to back IBRD guarantees of private loans to LDCs. The IBRD's own loans are only available for public sector or state-guaranteed projects, but it has an affiliate, the *International Finance Corporation, which can make and guarantee loans to private sector borrowers. It has another affiliate, the *International Development Association, specializing in loans on less stringent terms to the LDCs.

international cartel A collusion or an explicit agreement among firms from two or more countries on prices, market shares, allocation of customers, division of profits, etc. with the purpose of increasing the profits of individual members by reducing competition. It is more likely to exist in an oligopolistic industry with homogenous output. International competition authorities forbid cartels. *See also* ANTI-COMPETITIVE PRACTICE; ANTITRUST; CARTEL.

international commodity agreement *See* COMMODITY AGREEMENT.

international company *See* MULTINATIONAL.

international competitiveness *See* COMPETITIVENESS.

international debt Debt owing by the government or residents of one country to the government or residents of another, or to an international institution. Such debt takes various forms: it may be long- or short-dated; fixed-interest or floating-rate debt; and denominated in the currency of the lender, the borrower, some third currency such as the US dollar, or an international currency unit such as the Euro. The borrower may be a private sector body, or a government: government or sovereign debt cannot be collected by any legal process unless the government chooses to submit to it. The lenders may be individuals or investment institutions holding bonds, banks making short-term loans, national governments or government-funded institutions, or international bodies such as the *International Bank for Reconstruction and Development (or World Bank). Because lenders prefer varied portfolios, many countries both lend and borrow internationally.

international debt crisis *See* DEBT CRISIS.

International Development Association (IDA) A subsidiary of the *International Bank for Reconstruction and Development (IBRD, or World Bank), established in 1960 to provide development aid and advice to the poorest *least developed countries. The IDA is financed by the IBRD, and is willing to make loans on less stringent terms than the IBRD itself.

international economics The parts of economics concerning the relations between countries. This includes trade in goods and services, factor movements, including migration, capital movements, and technology transfer, and international monetary arrangements, including exchange rates and exchange reserves. It also studies government policies affecting trade, factor movements, and monetary arrangements, international negotiations, regional institutions such as the *European Union and *North American Free Trade Agreement, and international institutions such as the *World Trade Organization and the *International Monetary Fund.

International Finance Corporation (IFC) An international investment bank affiliated to the *International Bank for Reconstruction and Development (IBRD or World Bank), founded in 1956 to make loans to the private sector. The IFC was set up to broaden the scope of the IBRD, which lends directly only for projects in the public sector or with government guarantees, but lends to the IFC to fund loans to the private sector.

International Labour Organization (ILO) A specialized agency of the United Nations that deals with labour issues. It seeks to promote social justice and the international recognition of human and labour rights.

(⊕) SEE WEB LINKS

• The official website of the ILO.

International Monetary Fund (IMF) An agency of the United Nations, founded in 1946 to promote international monetary stability and cooperation. The IMF is financed by *quota subscriptions from member countries, partly in gold or convertible currencies and partly in their own currencies. It was intended to promote international trade through encouraging stable exchange rates and providing additional international liquidity to enable countries to avoid the need for trade restrictions and exchange controls. It administered a system of pegged exchange rates, the *Bretton Woods system, until this collapsed in 1971. It has also made loans to countries with balance-of-payments problems. Extra liquidity was provided by the introduction of *special drawing rights after 1970, and various special facilities have been introduced since. Since the 1980s IMF loans have been mainly to the *least developed countries. The IMF organizes regular meetings to discuss world monetary problems, and provides specialist advice on their balance-of-payments problems to members needing loans, sometimes making these conditional on at least part of this advice being accepted.

international monetary system The system of foreign exchange markets through which international trade and capital movements are financed, and *exchange rates are determined. If there were no national foreign exchange reserves and no world central bank, exchange rates would be entirely determined in the foreign exchange market. In fact most countries have central banks which hold foreign exchange reserves, which can be used to stabilize exchange rates, in the short run at least. In the longer run central banks and governments can use the instruments of monetary and fiscal policy to try to prevent balance-of-payments surpluses and deficits becoming so large that stable exchange rates cannot be maintained. There is no world central bank, but the *International Monetary Fund was intended to act in place of one to provide extra liquidity for national central banks, and to coordinate economic policies so that exchange reserves would not be exhausted. The *General Agreement to Borrow, between the *G10 central banks, also increased the effective size of national exchange reserves.

international payments Payments made between residents of different countries, or between residents and international bodies. These include payments for exports of goods and services, payment of property incomes, and international transfers or gifts; these are current account transactions. They also include sales and purchases of securities, and making and repayment of loans, which are capital account transactions; and transfers of foreign exchange reserves between central banks and governments. International payments may be made in a country's own currency if foreigners are willing to hold it; in a national currency acceptable to both parties, such as the Euro or the US dollar; or in an international money, such as *special drawing rights issued by the *International Monetary Fund.

international reserves *See* FOREIGN EXCHANGE RESERVES.

international trade *See* TRADE.

interpersonal comparisons Comparing the welfare of one individual with that of another. The welfare level of an individual is measured by a *utility function. Utility can be *ordinal* so that it is no more than a numbering of indifference curves.

An ordinal utility function can be subjected to any monotonic increasing transformation, f, without changing its meaning: the initial utility function U and the transformed utility $U^* = f(U)$ are equivalent. Utility is *cardinal* when the initial utility function U is equivalent to the transformed function $U^* = a + bU$ only under affine transformation. An example of cardinal utility is an expected utility function. Non-comparability means that different transformations can be applied to different consumers' utilities. Let U^1 be the utility function of consumer 1 and U^2 the utility function of consumer 2. These utilities are non-comparable if the transformation f^1 can be applied to U^1 and a different transformation f^2 to U^2, with no relationship between f^1 and f^2. With non-comparability a suitable choice of f^1 and f^2 can change the ranking of initial and transformed utilities (i.e., $U^1 > U^2$ becomes $f^1(U^1) < f^2(U^2)$), so the utility information does not provide a welfare ranking. Utility is comparable when the transformations that can be applied to the utility functions are restricted. The only form of comparability with ordinal utility is ordinal level comparability: the same transformation must be applied to the utility functions of all consumers. Denoting the transformation by f, then if $U^1 \geq U^2$ it must be the case that $f(U^1) \geq f(U^2)$: the transformation preserves the ranking of utilities between different consumers. If the underlying utility functions are cardinal, there are two important forms of comparability. For cardinal unit comparability the constant multiplying utility in the transformation must be the same for all consumers, but the constant that is added can differ. For two consumers the transformed utilities are $U^{1*} = a_1 + bU^1$ and $U^{2*} = a_2 + bU^2$. This transformation allows gains in utility for one consumer to be measured against losses to another. Cardinal full comparability further restricts the constant a in the transformation to be the same for both consumers. For all consumers the transformed utility becomes $U^{h*} = a + bU^h$ and it is possible for both changes in utility and levels of utility to be compared. *See also* ARROW'S IMPOSSIBILITY THEOREM.

interpolation Inserting missing data in a sample, usually by calculating the prediction based on the available data.

Interstate Commerce Commission (ICC) A US agency set up to regulate rail traffic across state boundaries. The ICC was intended to regulate both monopolistic pricing and the standard of service provided. Its jurisdiction has since been extended to include transport by inland waterways, roads, and pipelines.

intertemporal budget constraint In a dynamic economy this is the constraint on the flows of spending and income, and the stock of wealth, over two or more periods. For example, a consumer's intertemporal budget constraint in an economy with perfect credit markets requires that the present value of their lifetime consumption does not exceed the present value of their lifetime income plus their initial wealth. The government's intertemporal budget constraint requires that the present value of current and future taxes must be sufficient to cover the present value of current and future government spending plus the initial stock of government debt. In other words, the intertemporal budget constraint reflects the fact that with borrowing and lending current spending need not be restricted by current wealth.

intertemporal substitution The replacement of the consumption of a good or service at one point in time by consumption at a different time. This can be quantified using the *elasticity of intertemporal substitution when the consumer's preferences are described by a *utility function.

intervention in foreign exchange markets Action by central banks or other monetary authorities to influence an exchange rate. A currency will be sold to keep its price relative to other currencies down, or bought to keep its price up. Intervention in the foreign exchange market may be 'unsterilized', meaning that it is allowed to alter the domestic money supply, which rises when foreign exchange is bought and falls when foreign exchange is sold. This is distinguished from 'sterilized' intervention, where the central bank sells securities when it buys foreign currency, so as to keep the domestic money supply constant. *See also* STERILIZATION.

intra-industry trade Trade where goods of the same classification are both imported and exported. Intra-industry trade is a consequence of *imperfect competition: firms with monopoly power sell to every country in which there is a profit margin. Intra-industry trade is contrasted with *inter-industry trade, which arises from differences in resources between countries, so that a type of good is normally exported or imported, but not both.

intra-marginal intervention (in foreign exchange markets) Intervention in the foreign exchange market by the central bank or other monetary authorities before an exchange rate has reached the limit to which it is desired to restrict fluctuations. This is contrasted with intervention when the rate reaches its limit, to prevent it from moving any further.

intrapreneur A manager whose status changes from company employee to proprietor of an independent firm. This change is encouraged and possibly financed by the former employer, in the expectation that increased autonomy and improved incentives for the intrapreneur will raise the parent firm's profits.

invention The idea of a new product, or a new method of producing an existing product. This is distinguished from an *innovation, which is the development of an invention to the stage where its use becomes economically viable.

inventories Stocks of goods held by businesses. These may be fuel, materials, or components awaiting use in production, goods in process, for example cars on assembly lines, or stocks of finished products awaiting sale to distributors or final users.

inverse elasticity rule A rule describing efficient commodity taxation in a single consumer economy when there are no cross-price effects in demand. The inverse elasticity rule is obtained by choosing the set of commodity taxes that maximize the welfare of a single consumer subject to the government achieving a required level of tax revenue. The rule is based on the assumption that the demand for each good depends only on its own price so there are no cross-price effects. The conclusion obtained is that the rate at which a commodity is taxed should be inversely proportional to the absolute value of its elasticity of demand. Thus, goods with low elasticities of demand should be taxed relatively highly. The inverse elasticity rule describes an efficient tax structure, so its conclusions are modified when *equity considerations are introduced. *See also* RAMSEY PRICING.

investment 1. The process of adding to stocks of real productive assets. This may mean acquiring fixed assets, such as buildings, plant, or equipment, or adding to stocks and work in progress. Investment goods are goods designed to be used for investment rather than consumption. Gross fixed investment is spending on new capital equipment; net investment is gross investment minus *capital consumption, an estimate of the loss of value of capital goods through wear and tear, the passage of time, or technical obsolescence. Investment allowances are tax allowances which lower taxation on the profits of firms which invest. *Foreign direct investment is investment spending carried out abroad. Some forms of spending designed to raise future productivity, such as *research and development (R&D) to produce new technical knowledge, and training to improve the skills of the workforce, are conventionally not counted as investment, although as they add to the stock of *human capital they logically could be.

2. The acquisition of financial assets, such as company shares. 'Investors' are the people who own such assets; 'investments' are what they hold. In the sense of a list of assets this is a stock concept. Investment trusts and investment banks are financial institutions which typically hold securities as investments, in this sense, rather than themselves conducting physical investment. Investments in the financial sense are often used to fund investment in the physical sense, for example when companies sell new shares to finance the building of new factories. The two senses of investment are not invariably linked, however: real investment can be paid for from retained profits, without the use of financial intermediaries; and firms can use the proceeds of share issues to pay off debt or to finance the acquisition of other firms, rather than spending the money on physical investment. Investment is often considered in conjunction with *savings. At the world economy-wide level, investment and savings ex post, on some definition, must be equal. At the level of the individual, firm, government, or country, however, there is no reason why savings and investment should be equal either ex ante or ex post. *See also* AUTONOMOUS INVESTMENT; FOREIGN INVESTMENT; INDUCED INVESTMENT; INWARD INVESTMENT; PLANNED INVESTMENT; REPLACEMENT INVESTMENT.

investment bank A US bank similar to a *merchant bank in the UK.

investment incentives Arrangements designed to encourage investment, by increasing its rewards or decreasing its costs. Many such incentives work via the tax system. Accelerated depreciation means that firms are allowed to write off investments faster than the true rate of capital consumption: this lowers measured profits and thus taxes paid in the early years after an investment is made. Initial allowances enable the whole cost of investment goods to be written off when they are purchased. Investment allowances enable part of the cost of investment to be written off when it is made, while still allowing full depreciation allowances to be claimed later; investment allowances are thus a form of investment subsidy. Non-tax incentives for investment include preferential treatment for firms which invest in matters such as allocations of materials, access to financial markets, or planning permission for development.

investment income Income received from the interest on government or commercial bonds, from equity share holdings, or from deposits in building societies and other financial intermediaries. Individuals receive investment income both directly from their own holdings of financial assets, and indirectly in the form of payments from pension funds and insurance companies, which in turn derive their income from holding similar assets.

investment income surcharge Additional income taxes on investment or 'unearned' incomes.

investment in stocks and work in progress The value of the real change in stocks, both of inputs and finished products, and of work in progress, during any period.

Investment Management Regulatory Organization (IMRO) A UK self-regulating organization, that was responsible for regulating any institution which offered investment management. The IMRO drew up and enforced a code of conduct for such institutions; it was recognized by and reported to the *Securities and Investment Board. IMRO was subsumed into the *Financial Services Authority in 2001.

investment trust A company that invests its shareholders' funds in a portfolio of securities. These are normally quoted on a stock exchange; trusts may select from a wide range, or concentrate on securities from particular sectors or countries. They may aim for varying combinations of income and capital growth. Using investment trusts gives investors the benefits of a varied portfolio without excessive transaction costs, and the services of professional management. Investment trusts are distinguished from unit trusts, where a trustee holds the portfolio for the benefit of the unit holders.

invisible balance The balance of trade in invisibles. This is the excess of receipts from sales of services such as transport, tourism, and consultancy over payments for imports of invisible items.

invisible hand An expression introduced by Adam Smith (1723–1790) as an analogy for the way in which the working of *markets allows economic activity to appear to be coordinated without any central organization. Self-interest working through markets induces people to produce goods and services to meet the needs of other people whom they may never meet and for whom they need feel no goodwill. Equally, the market system allows people to satisfy their own wants from the produce of others who are similarly only connected with them through markets. *See also* COMPETITION; ECONOMIC EFFICIENCY.

invisibles International trade in services. Invisible exports are sales of services to non-residents; invisible imports are purchases of services from non-residents. Invisible items include the services of airlines and shipping, hotels and other tourist facilities, banking, insurance, medical services and education, and various forms of consultancy.

involuntary unemployment Unemployment caused by imperfect matching in the labour market between people who want jobs and employers who offer jobs. In other words, an individual willing to take a job at the going wage is unable to do so immediately because of structural problems, or frictions, in the labour market.

inward investment Investment in a country by non-residents. This may be measured gross, or net of capital consumption on existing non-resident-owned assets in the country and disposal of assets by non-residents to residents.

IOU An unsecured promise to pay; it stands for 'I owe you'.

irredeemable security A security with no *redemption date. Interest on an irredeemable security is payable for ever, but the original sum borrowed is never to be repaid. Securities may also be termed irredeemable if the borrower has the right, but no obligation, to redeem them, as is the case with UK 'consols'.

irrigation The use of water pumped from boreholes or diverted from rivers to assist agriculture. This makes it possible to use otherwise uncultivable land, and to produce larger and more reliable crops on land already in use.

IS **curve** The locus of combinations of interest rate, r, and national income, Y, for which *ex ante savings, S, and investment, I, are equal. The equality of ex ante savings and investment is a condition of product market equilibrium in the *IS–LM* model of Keynesian economics. It is usually assumed that when income rises, savings rise considerably and investment changes little. When interest rates rise, investment falls sharply while savings change little. Given these assumptions, to preserve equality between ex ante savings and ex ante investment, if Y rises r must fall; thus the *IS* curve slopes downwards in a diagram with Y on the horizontal axis and r on the vertical axis.

Islamic banking A system of banking that is consistent with the principles of Islamic law. One key principle is the prohibition on usury (the collection and payment of interest) so Islamic banks typically operate using profit-sharing arrangements.

IS–LM **model** A model often used as a representation of the main concepts in *Keynesian economics. The *IS* curve represents combinations of national income, Y, and the interest rate, r, that ensure equilibrium in the commodity market. The *LM* curve represents combinations of Y and r that ensure equilibrium in the money market. The intersection of the *IS* and *LM* curves determines simultaneous equilibrium in the product and money markets. The model can be used to predict the effects of parametric changes (for example, an increase in government spending or in the money supply) on the economy. The *IS* and *LM* curves capture Keynesian ideas by assuming fixed prices and wages. Although the product and money markets are in equilibrium at their intersection, there can be disequilibrium in markets, such as the labour market, not represented in the model.

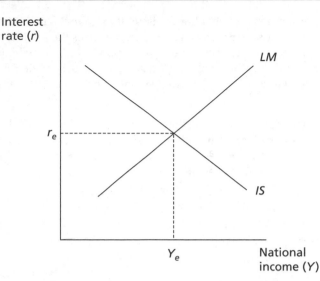

IS–LM Diagram

isocost curve A curve showing the combinations of factor inputs that have constant market cost. If firms are acting as price-takers in factor markets, the isocost curve is a straight line, whose slope represents the relative prices of different factors' services. A profit-maximizing firm will minimize the cost of factors required to produce a given output, corresponding to the *isoquant being tangential to the lowest isocost curve.

isoprofit curve A curve showing the combinations of two or more variables that generate the same level of profit for a firm. For a single firm an isoprofit curve can be constructed for alternative input combinations. In a *duopoly model an isoprofit curve can depict combinations of output levels of the two firms that lead to a constant level of profit for one of the firms.

isoquant A curve showing the various combinations of different inputs which can be used to produce any given output. An isoquant shows only technically efficient combinations: the curve shows the minimum level of each input necessary for given levels of output and other inputs. What points on an isoquant are economically efficient depends on the prices of factor services—shown by an *isocost line—and the economically efficient set of inputs is that at which an isoquant touches the lowest possible isocost line. The curvature of an isoquant shows how readily factor inputs can be substituted: if inputs are perfect substitutes the isoquant is a straight line; if inputs are perfect complements the isoquant is L-shaped. The isoquant becomes less straight as the inputs become poorer substitutes.

issue 1. The amount of shares or stock available, or the amount of banknotes in circulation.
   2. The process by which new shares are distributed. In a *bonus issue (UK) or scrip issue (US) extra shares are given to existing shareholders. In a *rights issue new shares are sold on preferential terms to existing shareholders. New issues of shares

may be sold in various ways: in a *tender issue they go to the highest bidders; in a public issue, offer for sale, or *placing, the company fixes the price and shares are bid for by investment institutions or the general public. An issuing house, usually a merchant bank, may buy the whole issue at an agreed price and then sell it on, or it may underwrite the issue, that is, guarantee that it will buy any shares nobody else takes up.

issued capital The part of the authorized capital of a firm which has actually been issued to shareholders. Any authorized but unissued capital remains available for issue when required, for example to allow executives to take up share options.

i

J-curve A model of the delayed effects of *devaluation on the *balance of trade. Devaluation allows the foreign price of exports to fall and the domestic price of imports to rise immediately. Time is needed, however, for orders to be obtained and contracts negotiated before the quantity of exports rises and the quantity of imports falls. Consequently, an initial worsening of the trade balance can be expected—the downward part of the J—before the trade balance starts to improve—the upward part of the J—following devaluation.

job 1. Paid *employment. Jobs may be full- or part-time, permanent or temporary. The job market is the system through which jobs are filled. This can be formal (such as the markets for economists organized by the *American Economic Association and the *Royal Economic Society) or informal.

2. The term job also has two slang meanings: a. a task; b. a crime.

job acceptance schedule The set of characteristics of jobs that workers engaged in job search are willing to accept. Acceptance depends on pay, prospects, working conditions, and location. If workers are searching while unemployed, their job acceptance schedules are liable to change: typically they become willing to accept lower pay or worse working conditions, and more willing to accept a change in location or type of work, as unemployment lowers both their expectations and their liquidity.

jobber A dealer in shares or commodities who holds a stock of the asset and trades as a principal. Jobbers are distinguished from *brokers, who operate in the same markets, but put people who want to buy and sell in touch with each other, and do not trade for themselves. The modern name for a jobber is a *market-maker.

job quits *See* QUITS.

job search The act of spending time to look for employment. Job search is used to model an imperfect labour market that does not clear instantaneously because of incomplete information, or search frictions. In a typical model an unemployed (or employed) individual encounters sequential job offers and has to decide whether or not to accept an offer, using certain criteria, e.g. comparing the wage and the imperfectly observed working conditions, associated with the offer, with his or her reservation wage (or current wage). This approach is used to explain the observed patterns in labour mobility and persistence in unemployment.

jobseeker's allowance The name for the UK's unemployment benefit, introduced in 1996. The choice of name was selected to reinforce the idea that the recipients should try to find work so that they would cease to need the allowance.

job vacancy *See* VACANCY.

Johansen's approach A *maximum likelihood estimation based approach to estimating a *vector error correction model with several *endogenous variables involving nonstationary as well as stationary variables. The procedure includes testing for and estimating multiple *cointegration relationships among the variables (cointegrating vectors).

joint costs Costs which are shared by two or more products. It may be possible for a firm to measure the *marginal cost of each product separately, but joint costs make it impossible to measure the average cost of each product.

joint probability distribution A *probability distribution of two or more random variables.

joint production Production where the processes giving outputs of different goods are connected. Producing the goods concerned separately would result in increased costs. Where one good would still be economic to produce even if the other had no market or required costly disposal, the other good is a *by-product. Joint production can be a consequence of natural phenomena or it can be undertaken because it offers firms *economies of scope, allowing expensive equipment to be more fully used.

joint profit maximization *See* COLLUSION.

joint-stock bank A bank operated by a joint-stock company. This is contrasted with a private bank, owned by an individual, family, or partnership. The large commercial or 'high street' banks in the UK are all joint-stock banks.

joint-stock company A legal arrangement by which investors pool their funds to carry out a business activity. Investors receive shares in proportion to the funds put in, and the shareholders elect directors to manage the business. Shareholders receive any distributed profits as dividends, proportional to the number of shares they own. Joint-stock companies generally also have *limited liability for their shareholders.

joint supply The supply conditions when outputs are produced jointly. If two or more goods are produced by the same process in completely inflexible proportions, there is no supply curve for each good separately, only for the fixed combination of goods. If the proportions can be varied, the supply curve for each good depends on the extra costs involved in changing the production process so as to obtain more of it.

joint venture A business where the provision of risk capital is shared between two or more firms. This is a method of organization often adopted for projects which are too large or too risky for any one firm to attempt alone. The firms joining in such a venture may provide different forms of expertise: for example, it is common for firms investing abroad to seek local partners. Foreign firms can provide technical expertise, but locals have advantages in familiarity with local conditions and business practices, in marketing, and in dealing with national governments and the labour force.

J-test A test of overidentifying restrictions in the *generalized method of moments (GMM) model. The test statistic is the sum of weighted square deviations of the sample moments evaluated at the GMM estimates, and under the null hypothesis of the restrictions its asymptotic distribution is chi-squared with the number of degrees of freedom equal to the number of restrictions tested.

Juglar cycle *See* BUSINESS CYCLE.

junk bonds Bonds issued on very doubtful security. The finances of the firm issuing them are regarded as so insecure that there is serious doubt as to whether the interest and redemption payments promised will actually be made. Junk bonds are thus risky to hold, and lenders will hold them only if the promised returns are high enough to give an acceptable expected rate of return, after allowing for a non-negligible probability of default.

just-in-time A system of production using minimal inventories and relying on prompt and frequent deliveries of materials and components from suppliers, arriving just before they are needed. This system also relies on prompt and reliable reporting of stock holding. It has the advantages of reducing the space needed to store inventories, and the interest costs of financing them. The just-in-time system may transfer the burden of holding stocks to suppliers, and is easily disrupted if transport arrangements break down.

Kalman filter A recursive algorithm for optimal estimation (minimizing *mean squared error) and prediction of state variables generated by a *stochastic process, that is based on the currently available information and allows the estimate to be updated when new observations become available.

Kennedy Round The round of international *trade talks held under the *General Agreement on Tariffs and Trade in 1964–7. The round was named after US President John F. Kennedy (1917–1963). The agreement arrived at cut tariffs on most world trade in manufactures by about a third, implemented over the following five years. No agreement was reached on agricultural protection, or on *non-tariff barriers to trade.

Keynesian economics An economic theory based on the ideas of John Maynard Keynes (1883–1946), developed in the 1930s, that assigned an important role to the state as well as to the private sector. Central elements of this theory are the failure of prices, especially wages, to adjust to clear markets; and the effect of changes in aggregate demand on real output and employment. Keynesian economics asserts that aggregate demand is the driving force in the economy; in particular, during a recession the government can boost economic activity by increasing its spending, thereby inducing private consumption and investment. Post Keynesian economics, which prevailed in the 1960s and 1970s, emphasized the role of uncertainty, *path dependence, and the effects of money on the real economy. From the early 1990s the ideas of Keynes have been further developed in New Keynesian economics which endeavours to derive them from microfoundations, in particular, assuming *rational expectations for the economic agents. The standard formalization of Keynesian economics is the *IS–LM model and its extensions. The IS–LM model combines the national income identity with simple behavioural rules to determine the values of output and interest rate that imply simultaneous equilibrium on the product and money markets. This equilibrium is obtained assuming fixed real wages, so the labour market can be out of equilibrium. When there is unemployment the IS–LM model predicts that demand management can shift the IS curve and raise output. This view dominated policy-making through the 1950s and 1960s until the combination of high unemployment and inflation experienced in the 1970s revealed the limitations of demand management. From a theoretical perspective Keynesian economics was always criticized for the lack of microeconomic foundations for its assumptions. Macroeconomic models are now much more developed in this respect. From a policy perspective, demand management has been replaced by a more pragmatic view of the supply side of the economy and the use of the interest rate as the major policy tool.

Keynesian unemployment Unemployment due to lack of *effective demand for goods and services which people could have been employed to produce. Keynesian unemployment can be reduced by the use of monetary or fiscal policy to increase effective demand. Keynesian unemployment is distinct from *classical unemployment, where wage rates are too high relative to productivity for employment to be profitable, and *structural unemployment, where the unemployed lack the skills needed by prospective employers, or firms do not have the equipment needed to take on more workers.

Keynes Plan An alternative set of proposals for international monetary institutions proposed by John Maynard Keynes (1883–1946) at the *Bretton Woods negotiations on post-war monetary arrangements in 1944. The Keynes Plan would have involved the creation of an international monetary unit, the 'bancor'. The plan was rejected and the *International Monetary Fund was set up instead, on lines proposed by the United States.

kinked demand curve A *demand curve as it would appear to a firm which expected that if it raised its price, rivals would not follow suit, whereas if it cut its price, rivals would respond by cutting theirs. The demand curve would thus appear more elastic for price rises than price falls. This would lead to a discontinuity in marginal revenue at the existing output, making it likely that small changes in costs would not shift the marginal cost curve enough to make the firm want to change its price. This type of expectations would lead to a tendency for prices to be sticky at their existing levels.

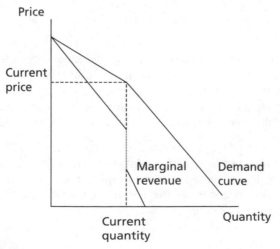

Kinked Demand Curve

know-how Practical economic knowledge, enabling firms to achieve results. Some of this is technical in nature, and can in principle be made into private property by the use of *patents, although these may be difficult to enforce.

Much practical know-how, however, takes forms such as modes of organization, professional standards, or systems of *incentives, which cannot be privatized by patents.

Know-How Fund A UK government agency set up to provide technical assistance to the countries of Eastern Europe and the former Soviet Union in transforming themselves into market economies after the collapse of central planning.

knowledge economy An economy in which the production and management of knowledge is a significant component of total output.

Kondratieff cycle A supposed long cycle in economic activity, with a period of 60 years or more. Economic records in most countries do not go back far enough on a reliable basis to allow this theory to be properly tested. If it is correct, the remarkable spurt of growth in world incomes and trade from 1950 to 1980 may turn out to have been a boom phase in a long cycle.

Koyck transformation A device used to transform an infinite *geometric lag model into a finite model with lagged dependent variable. While this makes estimation feasible, the transformed model is likely to have serial correlation in errors.

kurtosis A measure of how 'humped' a probability distribution is, compared to a *normal distribution with the same mean and variance. The kurtosis of a variable x with mean μ is defined by $K = E\,[(x - \mu)^4]/[E(x - \mu)^2]^2$. A variable with a normal distribution has $K = 3$. A distribution with $K > 3$ is slim and long-tailed, with more weight in its centre and extremes and less at medium distances from the mean than a normal distribution. A distribution with $K < 3$ is fat and short-tailed, with less weight in its centre and extremes and more at medium distances from the mean than a normal distribution.

Kuznets curve A curve depicting the change in *inequality over time during the process of economic development. Kuznets hypothesized that inequality would initially increase in the early stages of development. Eventually, the progress of development would reduce inequality. The evidence was consistent with the hypothesis until the recent growth in inequality in many developed economies.

Kyoto Protocol An international agreement signed in 1997, designed to reduce emissions of *greenhouse gases in the interests of controlling *global warming. Some critics have denounced the protocol as quite inadequate for its declared purpose. It has been ratified by the EU, but not by the US, which considers the reductions proposed to be impracticable.

labour Human beings as *factors of production. The quantity of labour available for an economy consists of all those able and willing to work, including the self-employed and unemployed as well as employed workers. Organized labour refers to the role of *trade unions in negotiating over wages, hours and working conditions, disciplinary procedures and redundancy, and in representing labour interests at the political level. *See also* DIRECT LABOUR; DIVISION OF LABOUR; LABOUR SUPPLY; ORGANIZED LABOUR; SWEATED LABOUR.

labour-augmenting technical progress Technical progress that increases the effective labour input. If production involves the use of labour, L, and capital, K, labour-augmenting technical progress is captured by A increasing with time, t, in the production function $Y = F(A(t)L, K)$. *See also* TECHNICAL PROGRESS.

labour economics The aspects of economics concerned with the supply and demand for labour. This includes factors affecting the participation rate, wage bargaining and organized labour, training, hours and conditions of work, practices concerning hiring, redundancy and labour turnover, migration, and the age of retirement.

labour force The number of people in or available for paid employment, also referred to as the workforce or manpower. According to the formal definition of the *International Labour Organization, the labour force includes the population 15 years old and over who are either employed, unemployed, or seeking employment. The size of the labour force is affected by many factors. The population of working age is determined by the school-leaving age and the size of the further and higher education system, as well as the retirement age and pension system. Among the population of working age, the *participation rate is affected by the social security system. Health standards affect the proportion of the population which is disabled, and family structure affects how many people stay out of the labour market to care for children and the elderly. The availability of childcare facilities affects how many parents are available for part-time work, and the availability of part-time jobs affects how many people can work at all. Past *unemployment affects the number of *discouraged workers who have effectively withdrawn from the labour force. The labour force is also affected by a country's immigration policy.

Labour Force Survey A quarterly sample survey of households living at private addresses in Great Britain. The survey is conducted by the Office for National Statistics and provides information on the UK labour market.

(⊕) SEE WEB LINKS

• The web page of the UK Office of National Statistics with information on the Labour Force Survey.

labour hoarding Retention by a business of more workers than are required to produce the present level of output. This may be based on expectations that output will recover so that the surplus workers will soon be needed again. It may be more efficient to retain workers than to incur redundancy payments by sacking them and then have to meet recruitment and training costs replacing them a few months later. Labour hoarding may, however, simply be a form of organizational *slack. Managers know that redundancies are unpopular and bad for morale, so may be willing to retain unnecessary labour so long as the shareholders in a private firm, or the taxpayers in a state-owned one, are willing to bear the cost.

labour intensity The proportion of labour in the total inputs to a productive process. Labour-intensive processes are those where the ratio of labour to other inputs is relatively large. Where alternative techniques of production are possible, labour intensity can be varied in response to changes in the relation between real wages and the cost of using other inputs.

labour market A place where labour supply is exchanged for a wage. Labour markets can be identified by a combination of such factors as geography (local, regional, national, international), industry, education, licensing or certification, and occupation. More generally, labour market can refer to the processes by which workers and employers are brought into contact, and wages and conditions of work are decided. Some of these involve formal institutions: contacts between workers and employers may be arranged by employment exchanges or agencies, either public or private.

labour standards The proposal that access to markets for imports should be restricted to those made by labour whose pay and working conditions are up to some minimum standard. The reasoning behind the proposal is that it would improve labour conditions in *less developed countries (LDCs). This benefit may be offset by difficulties in policing so that the labour standards would simply serve as an excuse for protectionism in richer countries, and by loss of employment opportunities which would in any case harm workers in LDCs.

labour supply The supply of work effort. This is determined by many factors. The *participation rate is affected by rates of pay, the availability of jobs, and the rules of the social security system, which determine how much income is available without working. The size of the national labour force is also affected by immigration policy. The supply of workers with the specific skills or qualifications needed for particular types of work is affected by a country's education and training systems, and any past restrictions on entry to particular occupations. Given the size of the potential labour force, the number of hours worked per week or weeks worked per year is affected by the *wages offered. Higher pay may induce those in a given occupation to work longer, and may induce entry by people from other occupations. If pay or the ease of getting work varies over time, labour supply at periods of high demand may be boosted by *intertemporal substitution: people work more when the going is good, with the intention of taking time off later.

labour theory of value A statement postulated in *Marxian economics that the *value of goods and services is determined by the amount of direct and indirect labour inputs needed to produce them.

labour turnover The inflow and outflow of labour employed by an enterprise. Some of this is because of fluctuations in total employment over time, either seasonally or cyclically. Some turnover results from geographical mobility of activity, notably in the construction sector. Some results from the ageing of the labour force: older workers retire and young ones enter employment. There is also a large amount of turnover for personal reasons.

Laffer curve A curve showing the relation between tax rates and revenue raised, named after its originator. If any activity is taxed, revenue starts from zero with a zero tax rate, and rises as the rate is increased. The tax tends to discourage the activity, however, so that at some point the total revenue raised turns down. This tendency is accentuated by the effect of higher tax rates in promoting *tax evasion. These properties of the Laffer curve have been used to justify tax cuts as a means of increasing tax revenue.

lag operator A symbol used to denote lags of a variable: $Ly_t \equiv y_{t-1}$, $L^2 y_t \equiv L(Ly_t) = y_{t-2}$, etc. Standard rules of summation and multiplication can conveniently be applied to the expressions containing lag operators.

Lagrange multiplier A variable introduced to solve a problem involving constrained optimization. Suppose that the function $f(x, y)$ has to be maximized by choice of x and y subject to the constraint that $g(x, y) \leq k$. The solution can be found by constructing the Lagrangean function

$$L(x, y, \lambda) = f(x, y) + \lambda[k - g(x, y)]$$

where λ is the Lagrange multiplier. Let f_x denote $\partial f(x, y)/\partial x$, etc. The optimal values of x, y, and λ solve the necessary conditions

$$L_x \equiv f_x - \lambda g_x = 0, \ L_y \equiv f_y - \lambda g_y = 0, \ \lambda[k - g(x, y)] = 0, \text{ and } \lambda \geq 0.$$

If the constraint is not binding, $\lambda = 0$ and the maximum occurs where $f_x = f_y = 0$. If the constraint is binding, $\lambda > 0$ and the optimum is found by solving the three equations $L_x = 0$, $L_y = 0$, and $g(x, y) - k = 0$. The Lagrange multiplier, λ, measures the increase in the objective function ($f(x, y)$) that is obtained through a marginal relaxation in the constraint (an increase in k). For this reason, the Lagrange multiplier is often termed a *shadow price. For example, if $f(x, y)$ is a utility function, which is maximized subject to the constraint that total spending on x and y is less than or equal to income, k, then λ measures the *marginal utility of income— the additional utility provided by one more unit of income.

Lagrange multiplier (LM) test One of the three tests of restrictions on an unknown parameter, or a vector of unknown parameters, θ, based on the *maximum likelihood estimation of θ (along with the *likelihood ratio test and the *Wald test). The null hypothesis is $H_0 : \lambda = 0$, where λ is the vector of Lagrange multipliers of the constrained maximization problem, in which the objective function is the log-likelihood function and the constraint is the set of restrictions. In an equivalent, simpler formulation, the LM test statistic is based on the derivatives of the log-*likelihood function evaluated at $\hat{\theta}^R$, the maximum likelihood estimator of θ obtained under restrictions. Under the null hypothesis the distribution of the LM test statistic in a large sample is chi-square, with degrees of freedom equal to the number of restrictions.

laissez-faire Literally, leave to do. A policy of complete non-intervention by government in the economy, leaving all decisions to the market. If there was no *market failure then laissez-faire would ensure the attainment of *economic efficiency. It would not necessarily secure a distribution of welfare that possessed any desirable properties. The existence of market failure provides justification for government intervention to enhance efficiency, and concern for *equity motivates government intervention to secure redistribution. Either form of intervention represents a move away from laissez-faire. *See also* MINIMAL STATE.

land A natural resource employed as a *factor of production. Land is used in economic activity in a variety of ways: for growing crops and keeping animals; for extracting minerals; and to provide sites for buildings and for transport and leisure facilities. Land as provided by nature can be changed by human activities: agricultural land can be improved by fertilizers and drainage, or ruined by erosion. *See also* MARGINAL LAND.

landlord The owner of land or buildings, entitled to use them or to charge others *rent for their use. The rent received is partly a pure economic rent, and partly a return on capital used in improving land or constructing buildings. A landlord's relation with tenants is governed by contracts and legal controls affecting both rents and security of tenure. A ground landlord is one who has granted tenants a lease, which may fix ground rents in advance, and impose conditions on the tenant.

Laspeyres index *See* BASE-WEIGHTED INDEX.

last-in, first-out (LIFO) The system of accounting for stocks which assumes that any goods withdrawn from inventories will be those most recently acquired. *See also* FIRST-IN, FIRST-OUT.

latent variable Unobserved or not directly measurable variable whose values can be inferred from the observed or measurable variables, for example degree of happiness or confidence, life quality, etc. *See also* PROXY VARIABLE.

law of demand The claim that the level of demand for a good or service is inversely related to its price. The law of demand was originally formulated as an underlying principle of economics until advances in consumer theory showed how income and substitution effects could combine to upset the law. Moreover, *general equilibrium theorists demonstrated that the standard assumptions of economic theory place no limitations on the shape of demand functions. The law has been recently resurrected as a statistical regularity that holds for observed preference and income distributions.

law of diminishing returns A characteristic of a production system with fixed and variable inputs such that, as the amount of any given variable input increases, beyond some point each additional unit of the variable input results in smaller and smaller increases in output (also known as a law of variable proportions).

law of large numbers A number of statistical results related to the idea that as the number of trials of a random experiment increases, the percentage difference between the expected and actual numbers of successful outcomes goes to zero. The weak law of large numbers proves that the sample mean of a sequence of n independent and identically distributed random variables converges to their common mean as n tends to infinity.

law of one price The proposition that where the same good or asset is traded in different *markets, the prices will not diverge. If prices do diverge, a profit can be made by *arbitrage, that is buying in the cheaper market and selling in the dearer. This assumes that information about both prices is available, and that goods or assets can be transferred freely between the markets. By extension, the law of one price can be taken to imply that where there are costs of transferring goods or assets, prices will not diverge by more than the transfer costs; they may of course diverge less than this. The application of this law to goods markets is inhibited by the fact that transfer of goods between markets takes time as well as money.

layoffs Sacking by firms of labour which is not required. This may be permanent, if the firm is ceasing the operations which gave rise to the jobs, or temporary, if demand is low but is thought likely to recover.

leading indicator An economic time series which tends to rise or fall earlier than variables of interest. A series may be a leading indicator either because the activity measured actually changes earlier than the rest of the economy, or because statistics on it are collected more frequently or more promptly, and are processed and published sooner. Leading indicators are useful in economic forecasting.

leads and lags The ability of traders to bring forward or defer the timing of transactions. If a country's currency is expected to be devalued, importers have a strong incentive to buy now before import prices rise, and exporters have a strong incentive to delay selling goods, or delay converting the foreign exchange they get for them, as it is expected soon to be worth more. This ability to make changes in timing means that a country's currency can come under strong speculative pressure, even with apparently stringent *exchange controls.

leakages from the circular flow of income A term from *Keynesian economics that describes uses of income that do not give rise to a further round of incomes. Such uses include saving by individuals or firms, payment of taxes to the government, and purchase of imports from foreigners. If leakages exceed *injections to the circular flow, incomes will decline.

learning by doing A term applied to describe an increase in a worker's productivity through practice. This concept is used in some *endogenous growth models to explain increasing returns to human capital. Except in the case where *spill-overs are worldwide, learning by doing gives a competitive advantage to existing producers, who necessarily have more experience than new entrants. Learning by doing is often characterized by productivity increasing in cumulative total output of a product.

learning curve A relationship between the duration of learning and the amount of accumulated knowledge or skills, or between experience and efficiency. The learning curve effect states that as a task is performed more and more often the cost of doing this task falls.

lease A contract giving the right to use land or buildings for a set period, in return for payment of ground rent to the landlord. The rent payable may be fixed, or subject to periodic review. Leases may be for any period and may impose conditions on the tenant, for example concerning the maintenance of premises or the use to be made of them.

leasehold The form of tenure of land or buildings by which the tenant has a lease.

leasing The practice of hiring items of equipment, rather than buying them outright. This enables firms to manage with less capital than they would need if all their equipment had to be bought. It also shifts to the owners the risk of *obsolescence; this will be reflected in the rentals demanded. Leasing may give tax benefits where a new firm has no profits against which it can set tax allowances on any equipment it buys. It may also enable local authorities to avoid cash limits on their expenditure.

least developed countries The group of least developed countries, as defined by the United Nations General Assembly in 2003, comprises 50 countries, of which 34 are in Africa, 10 in Asia, 1 in Latin America and the Caribbean, and 5 in Oceania. The group includes Afghanistan, Angola, Bangladesh, Benin, Bhutan, Burkina Faso, Burundi, Cambodia, Cape Verde, Central African Republic, Chad, Comoros, Democratic Republic of the Congo, Djibouti, Equatorial Guinea, Eritrea, Ethiopia, Gambia, Guinea, Guinea-Bissau, Haiti, Kiribati, Lao People's Democratic Republic, Lesotho, Liberia, Madagascar, Malawi, Maldives, Mali, Mauritania, Mozambique, Myanmar, Nepal, Niger, Rwanda, Samoa, São Tomé and Príncipe, Senegal, Sierra Leone, Solomon Islands, Somalia, Sudan, Timor-Leste, Togo, Tuvalu, Uganda, United Republic of Tanzania, Vanuatu, Yemen, and Zambia.

least squares A method of estimation of unknown parameters of an econometric (or statistical) model by minimizing the sum of squared differences between the observed values of the variable of interest and the values of this variable predicted by the model. Also referred to as *ordinary least squares.

See also GAUSS–MARKOV THEOREM; GENERALIZED LEAST SQUARES ESTIMATOR; POOLED LEAST SQUARES; TWO-STAGE LEAST SQUARES; WEIGHTED LEAST SQUARES ESTIMATOR.

legal tender Forms of *money which a creditor is legally obliged to accept in settlement of a debt. It is necessary to have some rules on this so that it is clear when debts have been defaulted on. What the rules should be is a matter of convenience. Coin and banknotes are generally legal tender, with some exceptions: small denomination coins are not legal tender in large amounts, and nobody is legally obliged to give change, so that large notes are not legal tender for small amounts. Nobody is obliged to accept cheques. Actual payment is very often accepted in forms that are not legal tender, for example payments by cheque or electronic transfer, but this is at the discretion of the party accepting the payment.

leisure Time spent not working. In many economic models leisure is regarded as a consumption good from which utility is derived. The measurement of leisure raises questions about whether time spent travelling to work if employed, or looking for work if unemployed, should be counted. The provision of leisure facilities, including cultural activities, sport, and entertainments, is a major sector in modern economies.

lemon An unsatisfactory product, where quality cannot reliably be checked before purchase. Even if some goods of the same type are perfectly satisfactory, their market price is lowered by the risk that the purchaser may get a lemon. If customers are *risk-averse, the price will also be lowered by a risk premium. The market for second-hand cars is a typical example of the market for lemons at work.

lender of last resort The function of providing *liquidity for the banking system at times of crisis. This is one of the duties of the *central bank. In the event of a run on the banks or other financial panic, the central bank should be willing to lend to soundly run banks or other financial institutions in order to avoid a general collapse of the financial system. It may be necessary to suspend temporarily the normal limits on the money supply and restrictions on the forms of collateral acceptable. If the institution in difficulties is not believed to have been soundly run, the central bank is left with a difficult decision: lending too easily may encourage other banks to take undue risks in the belief that they are 'too big to fail' and that the central bank will always bail them out, while if central bank assistance is withheld, the collapse of badly run institutions may also bring down good ones.

Leontief paradox The observation by Wassily Leontief (1906–1999) that in spite of being the world's most capital-rich country, the US appeared on average to have exports that were slightly more labour-intensive than its imports. This was thought to be paradoxical because the *Heckscher–Ohlin model of international trade led people to expect that US exports would be capital-intensive and its imports would be labour-intensive. There are two possible explanations for the paradox: first, that the simple Heckscher–Ohlin model ignored the role of natural resources in affecting trade; and second, that because of its large investments in *human capital which gave it a highly skilled labour force, the effective US labour supply was much larger than the mere numbers of workers would suggest.

Lerner index A measure of *monopoly power. The Lerner index is defined by $L = (p-c)/p$, where p is price of the firm's output and c is the marginal cost of production. If the firm operates in a competitive market then $p = c$ and $L = 0$. Conversely, if the firm is a monopolist then $L = 1/|\varepsilon|$ where $|\varepsilon|$ is the absolute value of the elasticity of demand. *See also* HERFINDAHL INDEX; N-FIRM CONCENTRATION RATIO.

less developed countries (LDCs) Also referred to as developing countries, defined as such according to a variety of indicators including income, literacy, and life expectancy. According to the United Nations classification, these are the countries that comprise all regions of Africa, Asia (excluding Japan), Latin America, and the Caribbean, plus Melanesia, Micronesia, and Polynesia. Sometimes this is extended to include the Transcaucasian and Central Asian republics of the former Soviet Union.

level of significance *See* SIGNIFICANCE LEVEL.

leverage The ratio of a company's debt to its equity, that is to the part of its total capital owned by its shareholders. High leverage (US) or gearing (UK) means high reliance on debt financing. The higher a company's leverage or gearing, the more of its total earnings are absorbed by paying debt interest, and the more variable are the net earnings available for equity shareholders.

leveraged buy-out A buy-out of the equity of a firm largely financed by borrowing. This is risky for the purchasers, as interest on the loan will absorb a large proportion of any operating profits. If the firm does badly, this may leave nothing for the equity holders.

liabilities The items on the debit side of a balance-sheet. These include unpaid bills from suppliers, unpaid taxes, and secured and unsecured debts of various sorts. The net equity value of the firm is included as a liability to make the total equal to total assets. *Contingent liabilities are those which may arise, for example if the firm is called upon to honour guarantees. *See also* CURRENT LIABILITIES; ELIGIBLE LIABILITIES.

liability 1. The legal obligation to make some payment. This includes payment of compensation to employees injured at work, or to customers injured by defective products such as unsafe cars, or paying other people's debts if one has guaranteed them and they default. *See also* CONTINGENT LIABILITY; EMPLOYER'S LIABILITY; PRODUCT LIABILITY.

2. The legal obligation to pay debts. *Unlimited liability means that the individual or company concerned must make the payment if their assets permit; if not, they can be made bankrupt or liquidated. Unlimited liability typically applies to individuals, and firms trading as sole traders or partnerships. *Limited liability, which applies only to companies, means that their shareholders are liable for the company's debts only to the extent of losing the money originally put into a business, plus any unpaid portion of the par value of shares purchased.

liberalization A programme of changes in the direction of moving towards a free-market economy. This normally includes the reduction of direct controls on both internal and international transactions, and a shift towards relying on the *price mechanism to coordinate economic activities. In such a programme less use is made of licences, permits, and price controls, and there is more reliance on prices to clear markets. It also involves a shift away from exchange controls and multiple exchange rates, towards a *convertible currency. The extent to which an economy is liberalized can vary greatly since liberalization is a matter of degree. *See also* TRADE LIBERALIZATION.

liberalized economies Economies that have recently passed through a period of *liberalization.

liberal trade policy A trade policy aimed at allowing a country's residents to take part in international trade with the minimum of interference. This involves the reduction of *tariffs, the relaxation or removal of quantitative trade controls, and replacement of discretionary controls by rules, and of quantitative controls by tariffs. It also involves the replacement of multiple exchange rates by a uniform system of exchange rates, and the replacement of exchange controls by sufficient devaluation to allow a satisfactory balance of payments without controls.

licensing Allowing another firm, for payment, to make use of a *patent or *trademark. This is a method of profiting by a patent without investment on the scale necessary to exploit an innovatory idea for oneself. The other possibility would be to sell the patent to somebody who could afford to exploit it, but licensing allows the inventor to retain ownership.

life assurance *See* LIFE INSURANCE.

Life Assurance and Unit Trust Regulatory Organization (LAUTRO) A UK self-regulating organization responsible for regulating organizations offering life assurance and unit trusts as principals. LAUTRO was merged in the Personal Investment Authority in 1994.

life cycle The lifetime pattern of income and consumption. The assumed pattern is that children are supported by their parents, young adults start with low incomes, which rise with age until some time in middle age, after which they fall, possibly quite sharply, on retirement. Little earned income is usually received after retirement. Consumption is generally highest in the early years of adult life when household goods have to be bought and children reared. This results in a pattern of saving, which is generally small in early adult life, large for a period after the children are grown, and negative during retirement. Household assets thus tend to rise before retirement and fall afterwards. Whether assets actually start and finish at zero depends on social habits as regards inheritance: most people leave positive assets at death, if only because they do not know when this will occur. The life-cycle model of savings suggests that the distribution of assets will be uneven between households even if their lifetime incomes and social attitudes are the same.

life insurance A contract providing funds on death or at a certain age. A life insurance (or assurance) policy is a contract whereby, in return for lump-sum or regular premiums, the company provides an agreed sum to the policy-holder's estate in the event of death before some agreed date, or to the policy-holder upon survival to this date. Life policies may be 'without profits', that is, for a fixed sum of money, or 'with profits', in which case the sum paid out reflects the profits the insurance company has been able to make by investing the premiums. Life insurance policies can also be arranged to provide the policy-holder with an annuity income after retirement, and make provision for surviving spouses or other dependants. *See also* WITH-PROFITS LIFE INSURANCE.

likelihood function The probability or the probability density of the occurrence of a sample configuration $(x_1, \ldots, x_n)$, given the joint distribution $f(x_1, \ldots, x_n|\theta)$, expressed as a function of θ conditional on the sample

$$L(\theta|x_1, \ldots, x_n) = f(x_1, \ldots, x_n|\theta)$$

where θ is a parameter or a vector of parameters of the distribution. In many applications the log-likelihood function, $\ell(\theta) \equiv \ln(L(\theta))$, is used.

likelihood ratio test One of the three tests of restrictions (along with the *Lagrange multiplier test and the *Wald test) on an unknown parameter, or a vector of unknown parameters, θ, based on *maximum likelihood estimation of θ. The test statistic is the ratio of the *likelihood functions evaluated at $\hat{\theta}^R$ and $\hat{\theta}^U$, the maximum likelihood estimators of θ obtained with and without restrictions: $\lambda = L(\hat{\theta}^R)/L(\hat{\theta}^U)$. Under certain regularity conditions and under the null hypothesis the distribution of $-2\ln(\lambda)$ in a large sample is chi-square, with degrees of freedom equal to the number of restrictions.

limited company A company whose ordinary shareholders have *limited liability.

limited dependent variable A dependent variable that can take values only from a limited set. Important examples are truncated variable, a random variable whose distribution is truncated above or below some specific value, and censored variable, a variable whose values in a certain range are all transformed to, or reported as, a single value. *See also* CENSORED SAMPLE.

limited information maximum likelihood (LIML) estimation A method of estimation of a single equation in a linear *simultaneous equations model based on the maximization of the likelihood function, subject to the restrictions imposed by the structure. The LIML estimator is efficient among the single equation estimators when the errors are normally distributed. *See also* FULL INFORMATION MAXIMUM LIKELIHOOD ESTIMATION.

limited liability The system by which shareholders in a company are not liable for its debts beyond the nominal value of their shares. Where shares are fully paid up, with limited liability the shareholders cannot be called on for any further funds. If shares are partly paid up, limited liability means that shareholders are liable only to the extent of the unpaid portion of the nominal value of their shares. Limited liability makes it possible to raise capital for purposes considered too risky for investors to be willing to provide funds on the basis of unlimited liability.

limit pricing A policy for an incumbent firm of discouraging entry to its market by charging a low enough price for entry to appear unprofitable to other firms. This is contrasted with a policy of short-run profit maximization, where the price is high enough to attract entry, which will lead to a gradual loss of sales, as customers come to know of alternative suppliers. There is thus a trade-off between large but temporary and smaller but more sustained profits. Limit pricing is not a credible threat: the limit price is not the optimal strategy after entry has occurred.

Lindahl equilibrium A method for determining what quantity of a *public good should be provided and how its cost should be allocated across consumers. The Lindahl equilibrium is obtained by announcing the share of the cost of the public good that each consumer must pay. The consumers respond by announcing the quantity of public good they want given the shares. The shares are adjusted until all consumers demand the same quantity of the public good—this is the Lindahl equilibrium. If consumers report their demands honestly the Lindahl equilibrium achieves a *Pareto-efficient allocation. The theoretical weakness of the Lindahl equilibrium is that a consumer can gain by making a false announcement. The practical weakness is the determination of the equilibrium shares in a large population (where most shares would be close to zero). *See also* SAMUELSON RULE.

linear approximation Approximation of an arbitrary function by a linear function. In economic theory, it is often used to make the solution of a complex equation or a system of equations describing an economic model analytically tractable. A typical example is linearization of a system of dynamic equations describing the behaviour of a model economy in the vicinity of a stationary, or a long-run, equilibrium. Another example is using a linear regression model in numerical data analysis. Mathematically, linear approximation is based on Taylor's expansion of a function when the terms of the order higher than linear are assumed to be negligible.

linear probability model A *discrete choice model in which the regression function is assumed to be linear. The major shortcoming of this model is that the linear functional form does not guarantee that the predicted values of the dependent variable, which have interpretation of probabilities, take values between 0 and 1.

linear programming A mathematical procedure for finding the maximum or minimum value of a linear objective function subject to linear constraints.

linear regression A method in numerical data analysis that models the relationship among variables as a linear function of the unknown parameters. One of the most popular methods of analysing linear regression in econometrics is *least squares; other commonly used methods include least absolute deviation, orthogonal regression, and least median of squares, or robust regression.

liquid assets Assets which are themselves *money, or can be converted into money with minimum delay and risk of loss. Short-dated marketable securities such as Treasury bills are liquid assets. Longer-dated securities, which may change in value as interest rates vary, are not liquid, nor are shares or commodities whose price is liable to vary, even if they are readily marketable. Real assets such as

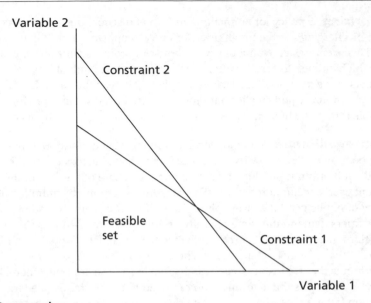

Variable 2

Constraint 2

Constraint 1

Feasible
set

Variable 1

Linear Programming

unincorporated businesses or houses are especially illiquid: they cannot reliably be sold quickly, and the price they will fetch is very uncertain.

liquidation The process of closing down a business and disposing of its assets. This may be done by selling it to a new owner as a going concern, or by selling off the various assets separately. The aim of liquidation is to produce as large as possible a sum of money, which can be used to pay off existing debts of the business, any remaining surplus being available for distribution to the owners or shareholders.

liquidity 1. The property of assets, of being easily turned into money rapidly and at a fairly predictable price. Apart from money itself, and deposits with non-bank financial firms such as building societies, short-dated securities such as Treasury bills are the main assets of this form. This can be contrasted to *illiquidity. Some assets are illiquid because there are no markets on which they can easily be traded: for example, unsecured loans to bank customers. Other assets are illiquid because while they can be traded, the price that can be obtained may be hard to predict, especially if a quick sale is required. This applies to shares in companies, or to houses.

2. The property of having liquid assets. Without these a business may have problems over meeting its obligations because, although it believes itself to be solvent, this view is not shared by credit institutions. The information which leads it to feel solvent, for example confidence in new products, may be private and not convincing to creditors.

liquidity constraint A limit on the ability of an individual or a firm to borrow as much as they would like to. Individuals, given their expectations, may prefer to consume now and pay later, if they expect that in the future their incomes will be higher or their needs will be less than they are now. Firms may believe that it would be profitable to invest in projects they can only finance by borrowing. Where an individual or a firm has *collateral which will make a loan to them safe, or where their reputation inspires lenders to provide loans without collateral, their desired spending plans can be carried out. Individuals and firms without collateral or reputation cannot borrow as much as they would like, or possibly not at all: they are thus liquidity-constrained. Most borrowers are potentially liquidity-constrained: small expenditures can be financed by loans, but for large expenditures a liquidity constraint would apply.

liquidity preference **1.** The preference for holding assets that can most easily be turned into cash. Assets can differ in their degree of liquidity. For example, *common stock in a large established company that trades on a major exchange will be highly liquid. In contrast, *bonds issued to finance a speculative investment project in a less developed country may not be traded on any organized market, so are much less liquid than the stock. Assets that are less liquid must offer a higher expected *return in order to induce investors to hold them.
   2. The factors determining the *demand for money.

liquidity ratio The proportion between a bank or other financial institution's holdings of liquid assets and its total liabilities. Minimum liquidity ratios may be imposed by law or convention, or adopted voluntarily as a matter of commercial prudence.

liquidity trap A situation in which *real interest rates cannot be reduced by any action of the monetary authorities. This is liable to arise if prices are expected to fall. If general price falls are expected, holding money will produce an expected real gain equal to the expected rate of deflation. The real interest rate cannot be reduced beyond the point at which the nominal interest rate falls to zero, however much the money supply is increased. The monetary authorities are thus unable to promote investment by cutting real interest rates, even if investment would be responsive to a real interest rate cut if one should occur.

listing Agreement by a stock exchange to allow a company's shares to be traded. This is conditional on the company complying with the exchange's requirements as regards the information provided to investors. A listed share is included in the exchange's physical and electronic displays of information on dealings.

Lloyd's A London institution whose members provide *insurance of all types on a worldwide basis. In Lloyd's individual investors, or 'names', provide limited cash funds and accept unlimited liability for insurance policies. The policies are arranged by managers on behalf of *syndicates, that is, groups of names. Companies have recently been allowed to join Lloyd's. Lloyd's does not itself provide insurance, but does maintain a central fund to back syndicates which might otherwise default, which would damage the reputation of Lloyd's as a whole. Lloyd's had operated profitably for centuries before the 1980s, but in recent years some syndicates have made losses of billions of pounds. These losses have led to large cash calls on names, which have been followed by allegations of mismanagement and some complex litigation.

LM curve A curve used in *Keynesian economics to represent the conditions for equilibrium in the money market. The *LM* curve shows those combinations of national income, Y, and the interest rate, r, at which the ex ante demand for money holdings, L, equals the ex ante supply of money balances, M. It is usually assumed that the demand for money balances rises when national income rises and falls when interest rates rise, while the supply of money is taken to be exogenous. Under these assumptions, when Y increases r must increase also, so that the *LM* curve slopes upwards, when drawn on a diagram with Y on the horizontal axis and r on the vertical axis. *See also IS–LM* model.

loan Money lent, which has to be returned, usually with interest. Loans may be secured, that is backed by *collateral, which the lender can sell to get their money back if the borrower fails to pay, or may be unsecured. If a debtor cannot pay all debts in full, unsecured creditors rank below secured ones in their claim on such assets as are available. Soft loans are ones where it is expected that if the borrower has problems in paying, the terms will be relaxed, allowing reductions or delay in payments; hard loans are ones where it is expected that the conditions will be strictly enforced. *See also* BANK LOAN; PERSONAL LOAN; REVOLVING LOAN; ROLL-OVER OF LOANS; SECURED LOAN; SOFT LOAN; SYNDICATED LOAN; TERM LOAN; TIED LOANS; UNSECURED LOAN.

loanable funds A theory of the determination of the *rate of interest by the need to equate the demand for funds for investment with the supply of available savings. This was popular in pre-Keynesian thinking, when the level of national income was taken as fixed by long-term supply-side factors. It is contrasted with the Keynesian liquidity preference theory, in which interest rates are determined by the need to equate the supply and demand for money balances. *See also* SUPPLY-SIDE ECONOMICS.

loan-loss reserve A reserve fund held by a financial institution which believes that some of the loans it has made are liable to turn into *bad debts, but does not know, or does not wish to specify, which of its debtors are likely to default.

loan portfolio The collection of loans held as assets by a financial institution. Such institutions hold loan portfolios for two reasons: first, their total assets are often too large for it to be practicable to lend to only one borrower; and second, a number of loans are safer than a single large one, especially if the borrowers have a degree of spread, either geographically or by industry. This makes it safe to expect that even if some borrowers default, the profits on the ones who do not will make the portfolio profitable as a whole.

lobbying Activities devoted to informing politicians of the views of various interest groups, and persuading them to draft legislation or to vote in accordance with these views. Lobbying is conducted by numerous interest groups; the methods vary greatly. Some lobbying is purely informative; no reasonable objection can be made to this, as it is clearly desirable that legislators should know about people's problems, and how any proposed legislation will affect them. At the other extreme lobbyists can use criminal methods such as bribery and blackmail. In between are methods involving financial support for political activities, which many countries believe cannot be prohibited but need to be regulated.

local authority housing State-financed housing for rent, provided in the UK through local authorities. This has for many years been the second largest category of housing in the UK, below owner-occupation but above private rented housing. Local authority housing is allocated on the basis of need, with priority for factors including number of children, and the quality and degree of overcrowding of present accommodation, with top priority for the homeless. Rents are generally held below a market-clearing level. There are usually waiting lists to obtain local authority tenancies.

local content The proportion of inputs to a product supplied from within a country. Minimum levels of local content may be required for a product to qualify for tariff-free movement between the countries of a *free trade area, or for an inward foreign direct investment to qualify for tax concessions.

local government A unit of government which does not claim sovereign powers. Thus the states of federal countries such as Germany or the USA are not local governments, whereas French *départements* and UK counties are. The powers of local governments are entirely delegated from above. Their finance may be provided from the central government, or they may be empowered to levy taxes themselves. They may have discretion over some policies, or be required to administer policies laid down centrally. There may be any number of layers of local government, possibly with overlapping functions. *See also* FISCAL FEDERALISM.

local public good A *public good that is available only within a limited geographical area. Examples include a radio signal that can be received only within a limited distance of the transmitter, and a school that restricts admission to a defined catchment area. Local public goods are important for understanding the economics of *fiscal federalism. The key feature of local public goods is that consumers reveal their preferences when they make a choice of jurisdiction in which to reside. The *Tiebout hypothesis argues that this effect ensures competition between jurisdictions to attract population and can thus achieve economic efficiency. *See also* CLUB.

location The geographical position of a firm's premises, or the marketing position of its product. The aspects of geographical position which matter vary with the business. For example, hotels benefit from the proximity of natural features or man-made attractions. For distribution and commerce, easy access to transport facilities is important. For some financial firms the proximity of other firms is vital: witness the concentration of banks and other financial businesses in Wall Street or the City of London. The location of a firm's product in marketing terms involves the brand image, perception of quality relative to rivals, and pricing strategy. The choice of these characteristics will influence profitability. As changing position is expensive, both geographically and in marketing terms, the location of production is strongly influenced by history.

location-scale family of distributions For any distribution function $f(x)$, a family of distribution functions, indexed by the parameters μ (the location parameter) and σ (the scale parameter), of the form $(1/\sigma)f((x - \mu)/\sigma)$. An example is the normal family: a normal distribution with mean μ and variance σ^2 can be obtained from the standard normal distribution by stretching ($\sigma > 1$) or contracting ($\sigma < 1$) the graph of standard normal probability density function with the scale parameter and then shifting the graph by the location parameter, so that the point that was above 0 is now above μ.

lock-out A form of industrial action by employers, in which workers are excluded from their place of work and their pay, but not dismissed.

locomotive principle The idea that growth in an economy, or in the world economy, depends on growth in some leading sector or leading country. The leader, which may be an industry with favourable investment opportunities, or a country with a strong balance of payments, can by expanding serve as a locomotive to pull the less dynamic parts of the economy or of the world after it.

logarithmic scale A scale on a diagram where distances from the origin represent the logarithm of a variable. Log scales are used particularly in diagrams with time on one, usually the horizontal, axis, and some real or nominal variable such as *gross domestic product or the price level on the vertical axis. The slope of a curve in such a diagram shows the proportional growth rate of the variable, and a constant proportional growth trend is represented by a straight line. If both axes use logarithmic scales, the slope of a curve is proportional to the elasticity of one variable with respect to the other. Neither zero nor negative numbers can be represented on a log scale.

logistic curve A curve showing the behaviour over time of a variable x where $a < x < b$, and the growth of x is governed by the rule $dx/dt = \alpha(x - a)(b - x)$. This type of curve can be fitted as an approximation to economic phenomena such as the proportion of consumers using a new product, or firms using a new technique.

logistic distribution A continuous distribution described by the cumulative distribution function of the form

$$F(x|\mu, \beta) = 1/[1 + \exp(-(x - \mu)/\beta]$$

for $-\infty < x < \infty$ and $\beta > 0$. The distribution has mean μ and variance $\pi^2\beta^2/3$. This function, also known as the logistic function, is used in the logistic regression, or *logit model.

logit model A *discrete choice model in which the population regression function is based on the cumulative logistic distribution function.

log-linear function A function in which the logarithm of the dependent variable is linear in the logarithm of its argument. Thus $\ln(y) = \alpha + \beta \ln(x)$ is log-linear.

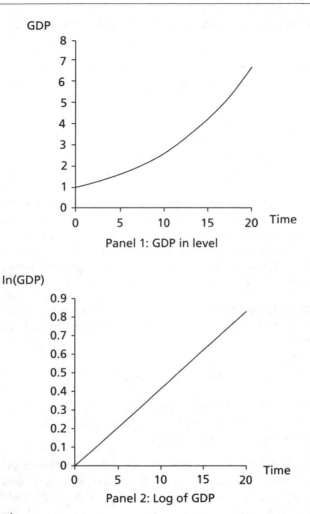

Panel 1: GDP in level

Panel 2: Log of GDP

Logarithmic Scale

log-normal distribution The distribution such that the logarithm of the random variable is normally distributed. This distribution naturally results from the effects of a large number of independent but multiplicative sources of variation. It is contrasted with the *normal distribution, which results when there are numerous independent and additive sources of variation. The log-normal distribution is upward skewed, with a mean larger than its mode, whereas a normal distribution is symmetrical about its mean.

log-rolling Cooperation between representatives in national or local legislatures to support other members' bids for public money in return for support for measures to benefit their own constituents. Log-rolling is blamed for wasteful public expenditures: a coalition formed on this basis may push through a group of measures most of which each member would have opposed if not voting strategically.

Lomé Convention An international agreement reached in 1975 by the *European Economic Community granting associate status to French overseas territories.

London Inter Bank Offered Rate (LIBOR) The rate of interest on short-term wholesale loans in the London money market: this is the rate at which banks are willing to lend to each other. LIBOR is used as a benchmark for variable-rate loans within the UK and internationally.

London International Financial Futures and Options Exchange (LIFFE) A financial futures market opened in London in 1982 to provide for trade in options and futures contracts. These include government bonds, stock indices, currencies, and interest rates. The London Traded Options Market merged with LIFFE in 1992; LIFFE added Options to its title, but kept the acronym unchanged. LIFFE is now part of *NYSE Euronext.

London Stock Exchange (LSE) The major European stock exchange. The LSE began in the coffee houses of 17th-century London and grew to become the most important institution in the *City.

(⊕) SEE WEB LINKS
• The home page of the London Stock Exchange.

long-dated security A security with fifteen or more years to *maturity when first issued. Such securities are particularly liable to fluctuations in their market price when current interest rates change.

long position A situation where dealers in commodity, currency, or security markets are holding a positive quantity of a commodity or asset they have no current arrangements to sell, because they are speculating on a rise in their prices. A long position in a *futures contract describes the party that will take delivery of the asset or commodity.

long rate *See* LONG-TERM INTEREST RATE.

long run A period sufficiently long that all variables can be changed. Some variables that appear fixed in the short run can be changed in the long run. In the long run, for example, a firm can build new premises, carry out research and development programmes to devise new processes and products and apply them, as well as recruit and train managers and skilled workers. In the short run most of these things are impossible: the firm can only buy more fuel and materials, and recruit additional untrained workers. Long-run supply and demand curves are typically more *elastic than the corresponding short-run curves.

long-run average cost *See* AVERAGE COST.

long-run marginal cost *See* MARGINAL COST.

long-run Phillips curve A curve depicting a long-run relation between inflation and unemployment. This is drawn adopting the assumption that the appropriate short-term Phillips curve is that augmented for inflation, and assuming that at each point on the long-run Phillips curve actual and expected inflation are equal. If models featuring a *non-accelerating inflation rate of unemployment (NAIRU) are correct, the long-run Phillips curve is a vertical line at the NAIRU. If such models are not correct, there could be a non-vertical long-run Phillips curve, which while it was steeper than the short-run curves, was still not actually vertical. This would leave some scope for a long-run trade-off between inflation and unemployment, which does not exist if the long-run Phillips curve is vertical.

long-term interest rate The rate of interest paid on government securities with a period to maturity of ten years or above.

long-term unemployment Unemployment for a period exceeding one year. This causes more severe problems than short spells of unemployment because there is evidence that the probability of getting a job decreases, the longer a worker has been unemployed. Long-term unemployment suggests a need for help with retraining or relocation.

Lorenz curve A graphical representation of inequality. Personal incomes in a country, for example, are arranged in ascending order: the cumulative share of total income is then plotted against the cumulative share of the population. The slope of this curve is thus proportional to per capita income at each point of the population distribution. For complete equality of income the Lorenz curve would be a straight line; it becomes more curved as inequality rises. Assume the Lorenz curves for two income distributions with the same mean income have been plotted. If the two Lorenz curves do not cross, the curve closest to being a straight line represents the income distribution with the most equality. If the two Lorenz curves cross, no unambiguous ranking of the inequality of the two income distributions can be given. The *Gini coefficient is equal to half the area between the Lorenz curve for an income distribution and the straight-line Lorenz curve representing the absence of inequality.

loss The result of a business operation where expenditures exceed receipts. Business losses may arise internally, through failure to produce enough of anything the market will buy to cover production expenses, or externally, through failure of others to pay bills due, or to repay debts. The effect of losses is to reduce a business's capital. If losses proceed so far that the total assets of a business become less than its liabilities, the business becomes insolvent, and should be either closed or rescued by a fresh injection of capital. *See also* CAPITAL LOSS; TRIANGLE OF LOSS.

loss leader A good which is priced low, possibly even below cost, to attract customers who are expected to buy other goods which yield a profit. The use of loss leaders can be profitable only if consumers are more conscious of the relative prices of some goods than of others. This may be so, if goods differ in how easily their quality is checked, and how frequently they are bought. Selling cheap goods about which customers are well informed may be used to attract custom for other goods on which they are less well informed, and can therefore be exploited.

Louvre Accord An agreement reached in February 1987 between the G6 industrial countries (Canada, France, West Germany, Japan, the United Kingdom, and the United States) concerning exchange rates of other currencies against the US dollar. At this meeting the countries agreed 'to cooperate closely to foster stability of exchange rates around current levels'.

Lucas critique The argument that the government cannot take the decision rules of private agents as fixed when it chooses policy but instead should take account of how decision rules change as policy changes. An alternative way to describe the critique is as follows. Assume the government conducts an econometric analysis to determine how investment by firms has, in the past, depended upon the corporate tax rate. The Lucas critique then asserts that the results of the econometric analysis will not correctly predict future investment if the government changes its corporate tax policy. This is because firms will adapt to the new policy and the relationship between investment and the corporate tax rate will change.

lumpiness *See* INDIVISIBILITY.

lump of labour The view that there is a fixed total amount of employment available. If this were true, it would be correct to argue that limiting hours worked would create more jobs, and making the elderly retire early would create jobs for the young. This view ignores the possibility that the demand for labour may depend on the relation between wage rates and the value of work to employers. Allowing for this, preventing employers from employing the most experienced workers, or from employing people for longer hours per week, might actually reduce total employment, by lowering the value of the work employers get for the wages they offer.

lump-sum tax A tax whose amount is not affected by the taxpayer's actions. If the lump-sum tax is the same for all taxpayers, it is called a poll tax. Lump-sum taxes can be varied across consumers, and may even be negative for some consumers. A negative lump-sum tax is called a lump-sum subsidy. The differentiation of lump-sum taxes across taxpayers results in redistribution. Lump-sum taxes have a central role in the theory of taxation due to their efficiency in raising revenue and achieving distributional objectives. As taxpayers cannot affect the level of a lump-sum tax by changing their behaviour, there is no distortion in choice. The imposition of lump-sum taxes therefore causes no *deadweight loss. This allows revenue to be raised, and redistribution to be achieved, with no efficiency cost and, hence, permits *decentralization of a *first-best allocation. Unfortunately, the differentiation of lump-sum taxes across taxpayers requires the taxes to be levied on the basis of some unalterable characteristic. There are few characteristics that are both publicly verifiable and relevant for redistribution, which makes this differentiation difficult to implement in practice. *See also* OPTIMAL TAXATION.

luxury A good or service whose consumption at any given price rises more than in proportion to an increase in income. The income elasticity of demand for a luxury is thus more than unity. A luxury is therefore a good on which richer people spend a higher proportion of their incomes than do poorer people. This is contrasted with a *necessity, whose consumption at any given price rises less than in proportion to income. *See also* ENGEL CURVE.

M0 The narrowest definition of the UK money supply. This includes notes and coin in circulation, as well as banks' till money and balances with the Bank of England.

M1 A less narrow definition of the money supply. In the UK M1 includes notes and coin in circulation, private sector current accounts, and deposit accounts transferable by cheque. In the US it includes currency outside the Treasury and Federal Reserve Banks, demand deposits of commercial banks, and other checkable deposits.

M2 A possible definition of broad money. In the UK, M2 includes notes and coin in circulation, non-interest-bearing bank deposits, building society deposits, and National Savings accounts. In the US it includes, in addition to M1, money market deposit accounts, balances in money market mutual funds, and savings and time deposits of under $100000.

M3, M4, and M5 A variety of alternative broader definitions of broad money as M1 and assorted other deposits at banks and other financial intermediaries.

Maastricht Treaty A treaty concluded in 1993 between members of the *European Community. This changed its name to the European Union, and set out a programme for progress towards a *European Monetary Union (EMU) and the creation of a *European Central Bank. The treaty included *convergence criteria, including a 3 percent limit to budget deficits and a 60 percent limit to debt–gross domestic product ratio for members to be eligible to join the EMU. The treaty also included a *Social Chapter, containing various employment protection provisions.

macroeconomic policy A normative counterpart of macroeconomic theory aimed at assessment of the state of the economy and prescription of practical ways of improving its performance. Typical policy objectives of a government, or a central planner, are economic growth, price stability, and full employment of the labour force, and policy tools include *fiscal policy (taxation and government spending), *monetary policy (regulation of money supply and interest rates), debt management policy (trade in government securities), and sometimes prices and incomes policy (regulated prices and minimum wage).

macroeconomics The macro aspects of economics, concerning the determination of aggregate quantities in the economy. Macroeconomics considers what determines total employment and production, consumption, investment in raising productive capacity, and how much a country imports and exports. It also asks what causes booms and slumps in the short run, and what determines the long-term growth rate of the economy, the general level of prices, and the rate of inflation. Macroeconomics considers how these matters can and should be influenced by government through monetary and fiscal policies. It is contrasted with *microeconomics, which is concerned with disaggregated quantities, such as the incentives operating on individuals and firms in the economy, the organization of production, and the distribution of incomes. The emphasis on building macroeconomic models on the basis of microeconomic foundations has lead to an amalgamation of the two in many instances. *See also* MACROECONOMIC POLICY.

majority shareholder A shareholder who owns a majority of the voting shares of a company. This gives control of the appointment of the company's directors, and the final say on company policy.

majority voting A voting method which selects as the winner the option with the majority of votes. When a choice is made from just two options May's theorem states that majority voting is the only decision rule to satisfy the conditions of *Anonymity* (a permutation of the names of any two individuals does not change the outcome), *Neutrality* (all possible options should be treated symmetrically), *Decisiveness* (the decision rule must always pick a winner), and *Positive Responsiveness* (increasing the vote for the winning option should not lead to the declaration of another option as the winner). If there are more than two options the *Condorcet paradox demonstrates how majority voting can fail to produce a successful outcome unless preferences have particular properties. For example, if preferences are single-peaked the outcome of majority voting is described by the *median voter theorem.

Malthusian problem A thesis developed by the economist Thomas Malthus (1766–1834), stating that per capita incomes would be driven down to *subsistence level by a tendency for population to grow faster than output. The argument was that while the population grows exponentially the supply of resources, such as food and shelter, can only grow linearly, which puts a limit on the size of population a given area can support. This, in essence, is the problem of the growth and distribution of resources.

managed currency *See* INTERVENTION IN FOREIGN EXCHANGE MARKETS.

managed floating exchange rate The system under which a country's exchange rate is not pegged, but the monetary authorities try to manage it rather than simply leaving it to be set by the market. This can be done in two ways. Firstly, small fluctuations in the exchange rate can be smoothed out by the authorities buying the country's currency when its price would otherwise fall and selling it when its price would otherwise rise. Secondly, the authorities can also influence the exchange rate through their macroeconomic policies. Higher interest rates tend to bring inward capital flows and improve the trade balance through their effect in depressing domestic activity; lower interest rates have the opposite effects. This type of exchange rate management is sometimes referred to as 'dirty floating'.

managed trade International trade conducted in accordance with plans negotiated by government bodies. This is the natural mode of trade for planned economies, but is not convenient for *market economies. While governments in market economies have sufficient powers to prevent trade they do not approve of, they have no adequate means of inducing private firms to supply exports they have promised that their country will provide or to buy imports they have promised their country will accept.

management 1. The decision-making role in organizations. The role of management is to provide strategic leadership for the organization.
 2. The people who do the managing. This may involve a hierarchy, with junior, branch, or assistant managers exercising limited discretion, and the Managing Director in overall charge of an organization, laying down general lines of policy, and hiring and firing assistant managerial staff to carry out the decisions.
 3. The academic discipline that analyses the decision-making role in organizations. Management aims to understand how decisions are made and to produce managers who can make better decisions. *See also* DEMAND MANAGEMENT.

management accounting The part of accounting devoted to providing information useful to the management of an organization. This is contrasted with the process of producing official accounts, which have to satisfy a company's *auditors and its Inspector of Taxes. Management accounting involves the collection and processing of information which will help in actually running a firm. This includes checking on stocks to ensure that enough are kept to avoid running out, but not so many that they incur excessive interest costs and deterioration from age before items are needed, and ensuring that the staff are not purloining them. Management accounting includes elements of operations research, checking whether the order of operations, or the processes used to deliver products, are efficient. It also includes cost accounting, to discover which operations are profitable and which cost more than they bring in.

management buy-out Acquisition of the equity capital of a firm by its managers. If the managers own or can borrow sufficient capital for a buy-out, this has the advantage of concentrating control in the hands of people with experience of running the firm.

managerial theories of the firm The theory that the conduct of firms must be explained in terms of the motivation of managers. Such theories are alternatives to *profit maximization as explanations of how firms are run. Profit maximization makes sense if there is full information and firms are run in the interests of their shareholders. This is open to two main objections, based on information and motivation. On the information side, *satisficing theories state that firms do not have the information needed to maximize: they run by rules or habits so long as the results are tolerable, and if the current rules give poor results, they use trial and error to search for better ones. On the motivation side, decisions are taken by the directors, who are interested in maximizing their own welfare so long as the shareholders will allow it. This is a typical case of the *principal–agent problem. The interests of top management are best served by growth of the firm, managerial pay and perquisites, and an easy life; the shareholders' interests matter only as a constraint on these. The possible brakes on the directors' autonomy are concentrated ownership, and the threat of *takeovers by rival management groups who offer the shareholders a better deal.

mandatory spending programme The part of government spending which the government is legally obliged to carry out. This is contrasted with *discretionary spending, where the government is empowered to spend in certain ways but is left with discretion as to the detailed composition of spending and possibly its total. For example, spending on pensions or judges' salaries is usually mandatory, while placing contracts for defence equipment is usually discretionary, subject to a limit on the total spent.

margin A deposit a trader has to make with either a stockbroker or an exchange to guarantee that they will complete a transaction. Buying shares on margin means borrowing money from a stockbroker to fund a fraction of the investment. To safeguard the broker, a buyer is required to deposit a margin, that is a fraction of the price sufficient to protect the seller against loss if the buyer cannot complete.

marginal benefit The additional benefit from an increase in an activity. This is the addition to total benefit resulting from a unit increase if it varies discretely, or the addition to total benefit per unit of the increase, if it varies continuously. Marginal private benefit is marginal benefit accruing to the person or firm deciding on the scale of the activity, excluding any external benefits; marginal social benefit includes external benefits as well as private benefit accruing to the decision-taker.

marginal conditions for optimality The equality of marginal benefit and marginal cost as a characterization of an optimal choice. This optimality condition arises throughout economics and is a necessary and sufficient condition when the objective function is strictly concave, the constraint set strictly convex, the functions involved are differentiable, and the optimal choice is interior to the constraint set. The wide applicability is achieved by appropriate definition of marginal benefit and marginal cost. For example, the profit-maximizing output for a monopoly firm occurs where marginal revenue equals marginal cost. In this example, the benefit is measured by revenue.

marginal cost The additional cost from an increase in an activity. This is the addition to total cost resulting from a unit increase if it varies discretely, or the addition to total cost per unit of the increase, if it varies continuously. Marginal cost may be short-run, when only some inputs can be changed, or long-run, when all inputs can be adjusted. Marginal private cost is marginal cost falling on the person or firm deciding on the scale of the activity, excluding any external costs; marginal social cost includes external costs as well as private cost falling on the decision-taker.

marginal cost of abatement The marginal loss in profits from avoiding the last unit of pollution or the marginal cost of achieving a certain pollution target given some level of output. When a pollutant has several sources, each with a different marginal abatement cost curve, the efficient amount of pollution requires equalizing the marginal cost of abatement across sectors. This can be achieved, for example, by using market-based instruments such as emissions charges and tradable permits. *See also* ABATEMENT COST; OPTIMAL LEVEL OF POLLUTION; POLLUTION RIGHTS.

marginal cost pricing The policy of setting the price of a good or service equal to the marginal cost of producing it. The equality of marginal cost to price is one of the conditions that describe *economic efficiency. If the good or service is produced under conditions of increasing returns to scale, however, marginal cost will be below average cost and the firm will make a loss. Paying for this loss requires a subsidy, either from the state or via *cross-subsidization from some profitable activity conducted by the firm. As the taxes required to finance such subsidies impose deadweight costs, marginal cost pricing is not usually adopted in practice in industries with decreasing average costs.

marginal effect The effect of a small increase in A upon the value of B. Formally, the marginal effect is defined as the derivative of B with respect to A, dB/dA.

marginal efficiency of investment (MEI) The highest interest rate at which a project could be expected to break even. This depends on the immediate profits expected from operating the project, and the rate at which these are expected to decline through reductions in the real price of the output, or increases in real wages and fuel and materials costs. If all possible projects in an economy are arranged in descending order of their MEI, theory suggests that investors will proceed with those with an MEI higher than the interest rate plus an appropriate risk premium, and reject those with an MEI lower than this.

marginal firm A firm which would just be induced to enter an industry by a small rise in profitability, or would just be induced to leave the industry by a small worsening in market conditions.

marginal land Land on the margin of cultivation. Such land would become just worth farming if output prices rose slightly, or would go out of cultivation if prices fell slightly.

marginal physical product *See* MARGINAL PRODUCT.

marginal private benefit The increase in *private benefit resulting from a marginal increase in an activity. Marginal private benefit does not take into account any external effects.

marginal private cost The increase in *private cost resulting from a marginal increase in an activity. Marginal private cost does not take into account any external effects.

marginal product The extra output that results from a small increase in an input. Formally, it is the partial derivative of the *production function with respect to the quantity of an input. Hence, for a production function $f(K, L)$, where K is capital and L is labour, the marginal product of capital is $\partial f(K, L)/\partial K$ and that of labour is $\partial f(K, L)/\partial L$. Marginal product is measured in physical terms, disregarding any effects of the change in output on the price at which it can be sold and so is sometimes known as marginal physical product. *Marginal revenue product equals marginal physical product multiplied by marginal revenue per unit of additional output sold. *See also* DIMINISHING MARGINAL PRODUCT.

marginal propensity to consume *See* PROPENSITY TO CONSUME.

marginal propensity to import *See* IMPORT PROPENSITY.

marginal propensity to save *See* PROPENSITY TO SAVE.

marginal rate of substitution The additional amount of one good required to compensate a consumer for a small decrease in the quantity of another, per unit of the decrease. The marginal rate of substitution at a particular level of consumption is given by the negative of the gradient of the *indifference curve. This is the ratio of the marginal utilities for the two goods, so the marginal rate of substitution between goods x and y is

$$MRS_{x,y} = \frac{\partial U}{\partial x} \bigg/ \frac{\partial U}{\partial y}.$$

marginal rate of technical substitution The additional amount of one input required to keep output constant for a small decrease in the quantity of another input, per unit of the decrease. The marginal rate of technical substitution at a particular level of inputs is given by the negative of the gradient of the *isoquant. This is the ratio of the marginal products for the two inputs. For a production function $F(K, L)$ the marginal rate of technical substitution between inputs K and L is

$$MRTS_{K,L} = \frac{\partial F}{\partial K} \bigg/ \frac{\partial F}{\partial L}.$$

marginal rate of transformation The amount by which one output can be increased if another is reduced by a small amount, per unit of the decrease, holding total inputs constant. The marginal rate of transformation can be calculated at the level of the firm, the industry, a country, or the world as a whole. It measures *opportunity costs, and is given by the gradient of the *production possibility frontier. If the production possibility frontier is defined implicitly by $G(K, L) = 0$ the marginal rate of transformation is defined by

$$MRT_{K,L} = \frac{\partial G}{\partial K} \bigg/ \frac{\partial G}{\partial L}.$$

marginal revenue The increase in total revenue when the quantity sold increases by a small amount, measured per unit of the increase in sales. If the seller is a price-taker, marginal revenue is equal to price. Where the seller faces a downward-sloping demand curve, where p is price and y is quantity sold, and the elasticity of demand is defined as $\varepsilon_d = -(p/y)(dy/dp)$, marginal revenue is

$$\text{MR} = \frac{dR}{dy} = \frac{dp}{dy} + p = p\left[1 - \frac{1}{\varepsilon_d}\right].$$

marginal revenue product The addition to total revenue from a small increase in any factor input, per unit of the increase. This takes account of both the effect of the extra input in raising the quantity produced, and the effect of an increase in the quantity sold on the price that can be charged for it. Marginal revenue product equals *marginal product multiplied by marginal revenue per unit of additional output sold. Formally, let revenue be given by

$$R = p(y)y = p(F(K, L))F(K, L)$$

where y is the level of output determined by the production function, $y = F(K, L)$, with K and L as inputs. The marginal revenue product of capital is

$$\text{MRP}_K = \frac{dR}{dK} = \frac{dp}{dy}y\frac{\partial F}{\partial K} + p\frac{\partial F}{\partial K} = \left(\frac{dp}{dy}y + p\right)\frac{\partial F}{\partial K}$$

where $\frac{dp}{dy}y + p$ is *marginal revenue, and that of labour

$$\text{MRP}_L = \frac{dR}{dL} = \frac{dp}{dy}y\frac{\partial F}{\partial L} + p\frac{\partial F}{\partial L} = \left(\frac{dp}{dy}y + p\right)\frac{\partial F}{\partial L}.$$

Positive marginal revenue thus requires that $\varepsilon_d > 1$.

marginal social benefit The increase in social benefit resulting from a marginal increase in an activity. Marginal social benefit includes all external effects. *See also* SOCIAL BENEFIT.

marginal social cost The increase in social cost resulting from a marginal increase in an activity. Marginal social cost includes all external effects. *See* SOCIAL COST.

marginal tax rate The amount by which tax liability increases per unit increase in value of a taxed activity. The statutory marginal tax rate can be obtained from published tax rules. The effect of deductions and exclusions can result in the effective marginal tax rate being different from the statutory marginal tax rate. For example, the phasing-out of tax credits raises the effective marginal rate of tax above the statutory rate of tax. The marginal tax rate is important through the effect that it has upon incentives. For example, a consumer determines labour supply by equating the marginal benefit of additional labour to the marginal cost. The marginal benefit is $w(1 - t)$, where t is the marginal rate of tax.

marginal utility The addition to an individual's utility from a small increase in consumption of any good, per unit of the increase. The information content of marginal utility is dependent on whether utility is *cardinal or *ordinal. If utility is ordinal then positive marginal utility denotes a good and negative marginal utility a bad. The statement that one good has a higher marginal utility than another is meaningful. If utility is cardinal, in addition to the statements for ordinal utility, it is also meaningful to state that the marginal utility of a good declines as more of that good is consumed. The latter property, termed diminishing marginal utility, is connected with the concept of *risk aversion. In both cases the ratio of marginal utilities for two goods (the *marginal rate of substitution) measures the rate at which the consumer will exchange one good for the other.

marginal utility of income The increase in an individual's utility consequent on a small increase in their income, per unit of the increase. If an individual is *risk-averse the marginal utility of income is a decreasing function of income. The marginal utility of income is constant for a *risk-neutral individual, and increasing for a *risk-loving individual. In a single-period analysis there is no distinction between the marginal utility of income and the *marginal utility of wealth. In a multi-period analysis income is a flow and wealth is a stock. Consequently, the two marginal utilities become distinct.

marginal utility of money The amount by which an individual's utility would be increased if given a small quantity of additional money, per unit of the increase. Additional money can increase utility in two ways. First, it is an addition to the wealth that a consumer can allocate to consumption. The marginal utility of money is then derived through the additional consumption it finances. Second, some models of money demand assume that consumers derive utility directly from holding money. The quantity of money held then enters as an argument of the utility function and the marginal utility of money arises from an increase in this argument.

marginal utility of wealth The increase in an individual's utility consequent on a small increase in their total wealth, per unit of the increase. If an individual is *risk-averse the marginal utility of wealth is a decreasing function of wealth. The marginal utility of wealth is constant for a *risk-neutral individual, and increasing for a *risk-loving individual. *See also* MARGINAL UTILITY OF INCOME.

margin requirement The percentage of the value of a transaction that a buyer or seller is required to deposit as a *margin. Margin is required for many financial trades including *short selling, and trading in *derivatives. The margin is needed to protect the broker or exchange against loss if the investor defaults. 'Buying on the margin' is the act of borrowing from a broker to finance part of a security purchase. The investor has to finance part of the investment, and the assets purchased are held as *collateral by the stockbroker.

margin trading An investment in financial assets that is partly financed by borrowed money. A margin account with a broker allows for limited borrowing to purchase assets. The initial margin requirement is the minimum proportion of the investment that has to be provided from the investor's own funds. A margin account is marked to market at the end of each trading day to determine the actual margin. If the actual margin falls below the maintenance margin requirement the investor is obliged to add cash or securities to the margin account. Trading on the margin raises the return on a successful investment compared to a straight cash purchase but also magnifies losses. This increases the risk of the investment.

market A place or institution in which buyers and sellers of a good or asset meet. A market was originally a physical location, and still is for some goods, for example cattle or fish markets, and for some services, for example Lloyd's for insurance. In other cases the market is a network of dealers linked by telephone and computer, and following common trading rules and conventions. Markets facilitate trade in goods, as in a *commodity market; in securities, for example the bond market, the *capital market, or the *stock exchange; in labour services, as in the *labour market; or in foreign exchange, in the *foreign exchange market. Spot markets handle trade in goods or services for immediate delivery. Markets also exist for goods, services, or assets for future delivery, that is trade in forward or futures contracts, and for derivatives, for example options or market indices.

marketable security A security which can be sold in a secondary market. Examples include common stock and bonds. This is contrasted with a non-marketable security, for example National Savings in the UK, which are not marketable, and can only be turned into cash by selling them back to the issuer. Assets such as mortgages which are individually non-marketable may be made marketable by *securitization, combining them into packages which can then be marketed.

market access The freedom to buy or sell in a market. Market access may not be available for natural or institutionally imposed reasons. Natural obstacles include distance and inability to meet the requirements of customers; institutional obstacles include legal restrictions on entry, tariffs and quotas, and public procurement rules excluding possible suppliers. Inability to compete on price may result from nature or policy; in increasing returns industries, lack of access to some markets limits total output and may cause high costs. Similarly, in industries where technical progress is partly due to *learning by doing, past lack of market access contributes to present inability to compete.

market capitalization The market value of a company's issued shares. This is the share price multiplied by the number of shares issued.

market clearing The process of moving to a position where the quantity supplied is equal to the quantity demanded, or the assumption that economic forces always ensure the equality of supply and demand. The process of market clearing involves price adjustment until a market-clearing price is achieved. In some financial markets there is a *market-maker who intermediates between the supply and demand to ensure that trades can always be made. Market clearing is closely connected with the concept of *market equilibrium.

market conduct See STRUCTURE–CONDUCT–PERFORMANCE.

market economy An economy in which a substantial proportion of goods are allocated by the use of markets. This is contrasted with a *planned economy, in which most goods are allocated by a centralized decision-making authority. The advantage of a market economy is that prices fixed by markets convey information about the relative demand for various goods and services and the relative costs of providing them. The prices also provide incentives to increase profitable and decrease unprofitable activities. In the absence of *market failure the equilibrium of a market economy is *Pareto efficient. In practice most economies are based on varying mixtures of markets and government planning.

market entry *See* ENTRY.

market equilibrium The situation when supply and demand in a market are equal at the prevailing price. Market equilibrium refers to a single market, whereas *general equilibrium refers to all markets being in equilibrium simultaneously. When a single market is considered equilibrium occurs at the price and quantity determined by the intersection of the supply and demand curves or, if supply always exceeds demand, at a price of zero with quantity determined by demand. Market equilibrium in the short run can be compatible with firms earning in excess of (or less than) *normal profit. In the long run entry and exit will occur until the *marginal firm earns only normal profit, unless there are *barriers to entry.

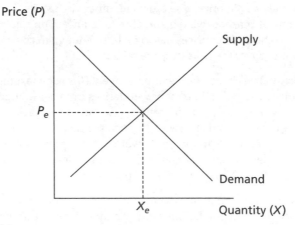

Market Equilibrium

market failure When an economy has an equilibrium that is not *Pareto efficient. The main sources of market failure are *asymmetric information, *externalities, *imperfect competition, *missing markets, and *public goods. The various sources of market failure provide a prima facie case for considering government intervention in the economy. The government may be able to improve on the outcome, but in some instances its actions may also be limited by the same economic features that cause the market failure.

market forces The forces of supply and demand, that determine equilibrium quantities and prices in markets. These are contrasted with the government and monetary authorities, which are able to some extent to influence market forces. In some matters government powers are considerable, but in others the authorities have little power: for example, the total turnover of the *foreign exchange markets is so large compared to the *foreign exchange reserves of most countries that exchange rates can diverge very little from what market forces dictate.

market for lemons *See* LEMON.

marketing The process of getting customers to buy a firm's products. This involves making arrangements for distribution and advertising current products. It also covers market research to discover likely customer reaction to potential new products, and whether possible modifications to existing products would improve their appeal.

market-maker A trader in a goods or securities market who holds a stock of the good or security and is willing to buy or sell at pre-announced prices. These prices only apply up to some limited quantity, but up to this limit they provide *liquidity for other people or firms who want to buy or sell. For larger deals the market-maker will negotiate over price. The market-maker's profits come from the difference between their ask, or selling price, and their bid, or buying price. These prices have to be adjusted over time to keep supply and demand approximately balanced. If demand persistently exceeds supply at the market-maker's offer price, this must rise, otherwise stocks will become exhausted; if supply persistently exceeds demand at the market-maker's bid price, this must fall, otherwise stocks will rise above the level the market-maker is willing and able to finance. The spread between a market-maker's bid and offer prices has to be large enough to cover operating costs and a premium to cover the risks they are taking.

market power The ability of an economic agent (firm or consumer) to affect the equilibrium price in a market. Market power derives from being large relative to the market, so the *N-firm concentration ratio is often used as a proxy. A monopoly supplier of a product has market power: they can set the price that maximizes profit. Similar considerations apply to market power on the demand side of the market. There are several determinants of market power in addition to size. These include *barriers to entry, *brand recognition, and *product differentiation.

market prices 1. The prices at which goods are currently trading in the market.
2. A reference to the method of measuring national income at the prices customers pay. *Gross domestic product or any other national income accounting aggregate at market prices uses the prices customers pay, including any *indirect taxes and subtracting any subsidies. This is contrasted with *factor cost, the prices of goods and services actually received by the sellers. To get from market prices to factor cost indirect taxes are subtracted and consumer subsidies added.

market risk The risk taken by any trader on a market who holds either a long or a short position, that the price will change. The holder of stocks of goods, securities, or currencies not hedged by futures sales runs the risk of losing if the price falls; the seller of futures for goods, securities, or currencies they do not hold runs the risk of losing if the market price rises. Market risk in some markets can be reduced by *hedging. Market risk exists even if the other party delivers fully and promptly; it is contrasted with *counter-party risk, which is the risk that the other party to a deal may fail to deliver punctually, or at all.

market share The share of a market held by a particular firm. The size of this depends largely on the definition of the market: a firm with a small share of a market broadly defined in geographical and industrial terms may have a much larger share of its local market, or the market for a more narrowly defined type of product. This point may be important if monopoly legislation uses market share as a basis for decisions. For example, reference to the *Competition Commission in the UK depends on market share.

market structure The number of firms in a market, and the distribution of market shares between them. Two common measures used in describing market structure are the *N-firm concentration ratio and the *Herfindahl index. The five-firm concentration ratio, for example, shows the total market shares of the largest five firms as a proportion of the whole market. The Herfindahl index works by adding the squares of the proportional shares of all firms. If there are N firms, the largest possible Herfindahl index approaches a maximum of 1 as the biggest firm has nearly all the sales and the rest minute amounts, and a minimum of $1/N$ if all firms have equal market shares.

Markov chain A stochastic process described by a finite number of states and known probabilities of moving from any given state to other states. These probabilities depend only on the current state and do not depend on the previous history.

mark-up The excess of the selling price of a product over the cost of making or buying it. The mark-up on any product has to cover the *overhead costs of the firm, as well as provide a profit margin.

Marshallian demand (ordinary demand, uncompensated demand) Demand for a good expressed as a function of prices and income. *See also* COMPENSATED DEMAND.

Marshall–Lerner condition A condition that ensures *devaluation improves a country's *balance of trade. The Marshall–Lerner condition states that a devaluation will improve the *balance of trade if the sum of the price elasticities of demand for exports and imports (in absolute value) is greater than 1.

Marshall Plan A large programme of US aid to assist recovery of the European economies from the effects of the Second World War. The plan was proposed by the US Secretary of State, George C. Marshall (1880–1959). From 1948 to 1951 the US provided assistance in grants and loans to various European countries, including Austria, France, West Germany, Italy, the Netherlands, and the UK. The main role of this aid in promoting recovery is thought to have been the provision of reserves to restore confidence in financial stability, and the provision of working capital to allow liberalization of production and prices.

martingale A stochastic process in which the expectation of the future value of a variable, conditional on currently available information, including the current value, is equal to the current value of the variable.

Marxian economics An explanation of the functioning of the economy based on the theories of the philosopher Karl Marx (1818–1883). This includes the *labour theory of value, and a theory of exploitation by which surplus value is appropriated by capitalists. The latter argument has been extended to cover exploitation of *less developed countries by more developed countries. The theory predicts the rise of monopolies, the immiserization of the proletariat, an eventual breakdown in capitalist society due to under-consumption, and its replacement by a socialist economy. *See also* SOCIALISM.

massaging statistics Adjusting figures so as to remove apparent discrepancies, which are assumed to be due to miscounting or computational errors. Massaging may also be done to bring the figures into conformity with theories about how the economy works, or to manipulate results for the political convenience of some user, often the government.

mass production Production on a large scale, using mechanized methods to produce standardized goods. This is contrasted with handicraft production, which turns out non-standardized products.

matching In economics, a model of interaction between agents through the market or through social institutions in which the joint productivity of matched agents or, more generally, the pay-offs, depend on the individual characteristics of both sides. Matching models are used, for example, in empirical studies of the labour market.

matching pennies A two-player game that has no pure strategy equilibrium but does have a unique mixed strategy equilibrium. The players simultaneously place pennies on a table. Player 1 receives a payment of £1 from player 2 if the faces on the pennies differ (one being heads and the other being tails). Player 2 receives a payment of £1 from player 1 if the faces match. These pay-offs are shown in the pay-off matrix.

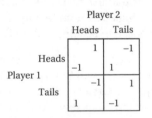

It is easy to see there is no pure strategy equilibrium. Assume there is a pure strategy equilibrium. If the two players choose the same strategy then player 1 will wish to deviate. If the two players choose different strategies then player 2 will wish to deviate. The unique mixed strategy is to play each pure strategy with probability one half.

material resources *See* RESOURCES.

mathematical economics A field of research that is on the boundary between economics and applied mathematics. The research is characterized by the application of mathematical methods to the analysis of the problems of theoretical economics, and the development of mathematical methods for economic analysis.

maturity The date when a security is due to be redeemed. For example, a 91-day Treasury Bill will be redeemed 91 days after issue. Common stocks have no maturity date.

maximin **1.** The maximin principle is a theory of distributive justice proposed by John Rawls (1921–2002). The principle states that the social objective should be the maximization of the utility of the worst-off person (the person with the minimum utility). This objective is represented by the maximin, or Rawlsian, *social welfare function $W = \min\{U^h\}$.
  2. In decision theory and game theory, maximin is the objective of maximizing the minimum gain. The maximin strategy represents a conservative play of a game and need not be a *Nash equilibrium strategy. The terminology first arose in two-player *zero-sum games. In such a game the gain for one player is the loss of another. Hence, the game can be represented by a pay-off matrix that displays only the pay-offs to player 1. Player 1 will choose a strategy to maximize the pay-off while player 2 will choose a strategy to minimize it. The resulting equilibrium is termed maximin.

maximum likelihood estimator (MLE) An estimator of unknown parameters obtained by maximizing the *likelihood function of the sample.

Meade Review A review of the UK tax system chaired by James Meade (1907–1995). The findings of the review were published in the 1978 Meade Report. The major recommendation in the report was for the basis of personal taxation to be changed from income to expenditure. *See also* MIRRLEES REVIEW.

mean In a sample, a measure of central tendency of a set of data points. Most commonly referred to as the mean is the arithmetic mean, that is, the unweighted average of a set of numbers. Other frequently used quantities are the geometric mean, the arithmetic-geometric mean, the harmonic mean, the generalized or power mean, and the root-mean-square. For a *random variable, the mean is the same as the *expected value.

mean squared error (MSE) The MSE of an estimator, $\hat{\theta}$, is defined as $E[(\hat{\theta} - \theta)^2]$ where θ is the estimated parameter. The MSE is equal to the sum of the *variance of the estimator and the square of its *bias. MSE is often used as a criterion for comparing alternative estimators of the same parameter: the one with smaller MSE is preferred.

means test A test applied as a condition of receipt of some benefit, for example a pension. This may be applied to an individual, a family, or a household, and may take account of income, capital, or both.

means-tested benefits Benefits which are available only to claimants whose income or assets fall below some limit. These are contrasted with *universal benefits, which are available to everybody in particular categories, for example based on age, regardless of income or assets. With means-testing, expenditure can be targeted to those in most need, and the level of benefits can be much larger relative to universal benefits for a given expenditure. The argument against means-testing is that means tests are expensive to administer and intrusive.

mean-variance preferences In a model of *portfolio choice with a single-period horizon these represent the preferences of an investor who evaluates alternative portfolios on the basis of their mean return and variance of return. Mean-variance preferences can be obtained from *expected utility if the utility of wealth is a quadratic function or the returns on all assets have normal distributions.

mechanism design The construction of a game of strategic interaction that achieves a specific outcome. Mechanism design chooses the structure of a game so that the players of the game find it in their best interest to behave as the designer of the game intends. When this is achieved the game is described as *implementing* the desired outcome. For example, the Clarke–Groves mechanism succeeds in getting individuals to reveal their true valuations of a *public good, and therefore allows efficient provision of the public good.

median The median of the distribution of a random variable X is the value m such that $P[X \leq m] \geq 1/2$ and $P[X \geq m] \geq 1/2$. A median of a sample is an order statistic that gives the 'middle' value of the data, that is, the value such that there is an equal number of observations below and above it, if the sample size is odd, or the average of the two such central values, if the sample size is even. As a measure of central tendency of the data it is sometimes preferred to the *mean, since it is not affected by *outliers.

median voter theorem A result showing that the outcome of *majority voting is the option most preferred by the median voter. Assume that a choice has to be made from a set of alternatives that differ in only one dimension (such as a left–right spectrum). If all voters have *single-peaked preferences then the alternative that is the most preferred by the median voter will defeat any other alternative in a pairwise majority vote. *See also* VOTING.

Medicaid A US government scheme to pay for medical treatment for individuals with low incomes. Medicaid is funded jointly by the states and the federal government, and administered by the states.

Medicare A US government scheme to pay for medical treatment for those over the age of 65.

medium-dated security A security with between 5 and 15 years to *maturity when first issued.

medium of exchange Any item that is widely acceptable in exchange for goods and services. *Fiat money is the medium of exchange in developed economies but over the course of economic history many other items have played this role. *Gold is one of the most prominent, and there is evidence that seashells were once a medium of exchange in Bengal. Cigarettes are reputed to be a medium of exchange within the economy of prisons. All that is required for a commodity to be a medium of exchange is that it has a significant cost of production and that it is widely acceptable. (The manufacturing cost of fiat money may be very low but the state maintains a monopoly and uses security measures to protect its monopoly, thus raising the production cost for parties other than the state.) The existence of a medium of exchange allows trade to take place without the need for a joint *coincidence of wants: in the absence of a medium of exchange it is necessary to find a person willing to *barter the goods one is selling for the goods one wishes to buy. A medium of exchange facilitates economic transactions.

Medium-Term Financial Strategy (MTFS) The policy adopted by the UK government in 1980 of controlling inflation by embarking on a long-term programme of steady reductions in government borrowing and in the rate of growth of the money supply. This self-imposed constraint on policy-making involved a target range for the growth of sterling *M3 falling by 1 percent each year.

member bank A bank that belongs to a *clearing system. In the US a member bank is one that belongs to the *Federal Reserve System.

menu costs The cost to a firm of revising prices. The term arose out of the literal idea of updating menus, price lists, and any other promotional materials. It is now used to refer to any transaction costs that a firm faces when changing prices. Menu costs are an explanation for price stickiness: the reluctance of firms to change prices in response to minor fluctuations in the economic environment.

menu costs of inflation The part of the real cost of inflation due to the cost of revising prices. The extra costs due to inflation can be significant only for goods not subject to much short-term price variation in the absence of inflation.

Mercado Comun del Sur (MERCOSUR) A Latin American common market agreed in 1991 by Argentina, Brazil, Paraguay, and Uruguay. Bolivia, Chile, Colombia, Ecuador, and Peru currently have associate member status. MERCOSUR contains the majority of the population of Latin America.

mercantilism An economic theory popular in the 16th to 18th centuries that viewed a nation's supply of capital as the determinant of welfare. When this view was coupled with the assumption that the total value of world trade was fixed it implied a policy of seeking balance-of-payments surpluses to increase capital inflow, and advocacy of *protectionism to achieve this.

merchandise account The part of the *balance-of-payments accounts referring to visible trade, or merchandise imports and exports.

merchant bank A bank dealing mainly with other firms rather than the general public. Merchant banks engage in a variety of specialist activities, including: financing foreign trade by accepting bills of exchange; providing hire purchase and industrial finance; underwriting new issues; advising on and arranging finance for mergers and takeover bids; and managing investment for institutions and wealthy individuals.

merger A combination of two or more firms into a single new firm. This takes over all the assets and liabilities of the merging firms; shares in the new firm are divided between the shareholders of the original firms on an agreed basis. Merger procedures in the UK are subject to the *City Code on Takeovers and Mergers.

A merger may allow economies of scale or scope between the firms, which should lead to gains in efficiency. It may, however, also reduce competition, so that mergers in the UK may be referred to the *Competition Commission. *See also* CONGLOMERATE MERGER; HORIZONTAL MERGER; VERTICAL MERGER.

merit goods Goods or services whose consumption is believed to confer benefits on society as a whole greater than those reflected in consumers' own preferences for them. A good may be classed as a merit good if it causes positive *externalities. Education is typically cited as an example. In the absence of government intervention individual choice will lead to under-consumption of a good causing a positive externality. Such merit goods are therefore sometimes subsidized by the government, or directly provided. A good can also be classed as a merit good through *paternalism: the government decides that it is better informed than consumers about what is good for them, and chooses to override *consumer sovereignty to ensure consumption. Examples are compulsory primary education and compulsory vaccination of children in many countries.

method of moments estimator An estimator of the unknown parameters of a distribution obtained by solving a system of equations, called moment conditions, that equate the *moments of distribution to their sample counterparts. *See also* GENERALIZED METHOD OF MOMENTS (GMM) ESTIMATOR.

microeconomics The micro aspects of economics, concerning the decision-making of individuals. Microeconomics analyses the choices of consumers (who can be individuals or households) and firms in a variety of market situations. Its aim is to explore how choices should be made, and to provide an explanation of choices that are made. Microeconomics also considers economies composed of individual decision-makers, and studies the existence and properties of economic equilibrium. The effect of government choices upon consumers and firms is also analysed, with the aim of understanding economic policy. *See also* APPLIED MICROECONOMICS.

mid-market price The mid-point between the lowest price at which any *market-maker is willing to sell a security and the highest price at which any market-maker is willing to buy it.

migrants' remittances Money sent by migrant workers in foreign countries to their former homes. These remittances have three main purposes: to maintain family members still in their old homes; to assist family members to join the migrants in their new homes; and to prepare the way for their own return to their native countries, to retire or set up a business. Migrants' remittances form part of the *invisibles section of the balance of payments on current account, in some countries an important part.

migration Movement of people between regions or countries. Immigration and emigration are usually reserved for migration into and out of countries, respectively. Migration may be temporary, with the intention of returning to the country of origin in the future, or permanent; or migrants may not have decided between these alternatives at the time of migration. Migration is affected by push and pull factors. Push factors include lack of employment opportunities, and fears of disorder or of persecution on grounds of race, religion, or politics in the areas people leave. Pull factors include favourable employment opportunities, good health and educational facilities, public order and freedom, and a favourable climate, particularly for retirement, in the areas people move to.

military–industrial complex An expression used to describe the combination of a country's armed forces and the parts of its industry related to military supply. The phrase is often used in a pejorative way in reference to the accusation that the military–industrial complex in major powers has been motivated by vested interests to influence policy in ways which promote international tension and thus lead to arms races or even war.

Millennium Round The latest series of trade negotiations, under the *World Trade Organization. This started in the Seattle conference of 1999, and in 2008 is still ongoing.

minimal state A government whose intervention in the economy is just sufficient to sustain organized economic activity. The responsibilities of a minimal state would include provision of policing, a judiciary, and defence of the nation. These interventions are necessary to uphold *property rights, enforce contract laws, and defend the gains from trade.

minimax The objective in decision theory of minimizing the maximum loss. *See also* MAXIMIN.

minimax regret In decision theory, a rule for selecting a course of action under uncertainty that minimizes the maximal amount of opportunity loss, or regret, for every possible course of action across different states of nature or different realizations of uncertainty.

minimum efficient scale The minimum level of any activity at which all known economies of scale have been exhausted. In some cases there is no finite level of output at which further cost savings cease: this is the case, for example, when marginal cost is constant and fixed costs can be spread over an ever larger output.

minimum lending rate (MLR) The immediate successor of *bank rate. From 1971 to 1981 MLR was the minimum rate at which the Bank of England would lend to UK *discount houses; it was used as a benchmark for other interest rates. MLR was replaced in 1981 by the *base rate.

minimum wage A minimum level of pay laid down by law, for workers in general or of some specified type. The intention of a minimum wage is to guarantee living standards for the low paid and to prevent exploitation. Both the UK and the US apply minimum wage legislation.

minority shareholder A shareholder who owns only a minority of the voting shares of a company. The vast majority of shares are in fact held by minority shareholders. A minority shareholder can always be voted down by the majority if that majority is united, but usually there is no single *majority shareholder.

mint A factory producing coinage. Coins are produced in the UK by the Royal Mint and in the US by the United States Mint.

Mirrlees Review A review of the UK tax system in 2007/8 organized by the *Institute for Fiscal Studies under the chairmanship of James Mirrlees (b. 1936). The Mirrlees Review follows 30 years after the *Meade Review.

misaligned exchange rate An exchange rate which is inconsistent with a satisfactory *balance of payments. If a country's currency is priced too high, this makes imports excessively attractive and exports hard to sell, which is liable to result in an unsustainable *current account deficit. Equally, if a currency is underpriced it tends to result in a *current account surplus so large as to over-stimulate the economy.

misery index An index of overall economic performance, formed by adding the *unemployment rate and the *inflation rate. The index is based on the assumption that both unemployment and inflation lead to economic and social costs for a country. A rise in the index implies a deterioration in economic performance.

mis-match Differences between the skills and location of unemployed workers and available job vacancies. These help to explain why *unemployment exists at the same time as unsatisfied demand for labour. Mis-match may occur because the location and skill patterns of new entrants to the labour market, those finishing education and immigrants, do not match the pattern of those leaving the labour market through retirement or emigration. It is increased by rapid changes in the pattern of demand for labour through changes in tastes or technology. Methods by which mis-match can be reduced include retraining, regulation of migration, industrial relocation, and changes in the relative wages of different occupations.

missing market The absence of a market on which to trade a good. It is not possible to trade the full range of future and *contingent commodities, and markets are missing for many externalities. Missing markets are a source of *market failure: the equilibrium of a competitive economy will not be *Pareto efficient if there are missing markets. Some future goods cannot be traded because the law forbids contracts for future labour, by which effectively people sell themselves into slavery. Many future goods cannot be traded because the people who would wish to trade in them have not yet been born. Many markets in contingent goods cannot exist because the actual occurrence of the contingencies is private information which cannot be objectively confirmed. Finally, markets may be missing because not enough people would wish to trade in them.

mixed economy An economy with a mixture of state and private enterprises. Some economic activities are carried on by individuals or firms taking independent economic decisions, coordinated by markets; others are carried on by organizations under state ownership and control, with some degree of centralized decision-taking. Most actual economies are mixed, in the sense of having substantial elements of both forms of economic organization.

mixed strategy The use of a random mixture of strategies in a game. The choice between two or more strategies on any particular occasion depends on using some randomizing device, such as tossing a coin or rolling a die. An agent using a mixed strategy does not know what their own actions will be on any particular occasion until the randomizing device has been used, but they do know the probability with which different actions will be chosen. The benefit of adopting a mixed strategy is to make it impossible for any opponent to predict a player's actions with certainty, however well they understand the player's psychology.

mix of policies The use of *policy instruments in combination. If a government has only one objective, it may be possible to achieve it using only one policy instrument. If more than one policy instrument is available, a mix of policy instruments can achieve an outcome that is no worse and will almost always be better. If the government has more than one objective, at least n independent policy instruments are needed to allow n separate objectives to be obtained. This, too, dictates using a mix of policy instruments. If more than n instruments are available, a mix can again do no worse. Using a mix of policy instruments means that each instrument can be smaller. For example, a number of low tax rates can be applied to a broad base rather than one high tax rate to a narrow base. This can have the advantage of mitigating undesirable side-effects.

mobility of labour The ability of workers to change jobs. This may be between different firms, different occupations, different locations, or different countries. There can be a range of obstacles to mobility. Workers changing employers lose seniority, which may affect their pay, vacations, and redundancy rights, and may lose in terms of their pension rights. Workers changing occupations lose in terms of the weight given to their experience and possibly to their formal qualifications. Workers changing location face problems over housing. International mobility of labour is hindered by immigration controls, problems over recognition of the immigrants' qualifications, and language barriers. Governments and supra-national organizations such as the *European Union attempt to improve labour mobility in the interests of economic efficiency, but perfect mobility of labour seems extremely unlikely. *See also* FACTOR MOBILITY.

modal choice models (mode choice models, travel mode choice models) *Discrete choice models used for the analysis of individual choice of mode of transportation.

mode The most frequent or most likely value of a variable. Where the variable is discrete, the mode is the value with the highest share of the distribution. The number of children in a family, for example, may be 0 or any whole number: if the mode is 2 this means there are more families with two children than of any other particular size. Where the variable is continuous, the mode is at the maximum of the probability density function. For example, the mode of the standard normal distribution is at $x = 0$.

model A simplified system used to simulate some aspects of the real economy. Models are used in economics because there are limited possibilities for experimentation and past experience does not always provide an answer. A model is a simplified description of the economy, or the part of the economy, relevant for the analysis. Economic models are distinguished from those in the natural sciences by the incorporation of independent decision-making by firms, consumers, and the politicians and bureaucrats who constitute government. These economic agents do not respond mechanically but are motivated by personal objectives and are strategic in their behaviour. Capturing the implications of this complex behaviour in a convincing manner is the key attribute of a successful economic model.

Modigliani–Miller theorem The theory that in a perfect capital market the value of a firm is independent of the method of financing used. Capital can be raised by borrowing, issuing equity shares, or retaining profits instead of paying dividends. The Modigliani–Miller theorem asserts that in a perfect capital market it does not matter to a firm whether it uses debt or equity, or what dividend policy it follows. The fact that firms do worry about their *leverage and dividend policies reflects the effects of the tax system and imperfection in the capital market.

moments of distribution For every integer n, the nth moment of distribution of random variable X is the *expected value of X^n.

monetarism An economic theory based on the view that the quantity of money is the main determinant of money incomes. This is often combined with the view that markets tend to clear, and that people form *rational expectations. The theory led to the policy recommendation that the best contribution the government can make to stable economic growth is to keep the money supply growing steadily at a rate equal to the growth of aggregate supply plus any target rate of inflation, which may well be zero. In addition, the theory implies that attempts at *demand management on Keynesian lines can do no good, and are liable simply to add one more source of shocks to the economy. *See also* GRADUALIST MONETARISM.

monetary base (base money) The part of the money supply which is eligible to count as reserves in the banking system. Some monetary theorists argue that if the monetary authorities can control the amount of base money the rest of the *money supply will adjust automatically. How far this is true depends on how stable bank reserve ratios are, and on how far base money is also held outside the banking system, for example as notes and coin in general circulation.

monetary control *See* MONETARY POLICY.

monetary economics A field in economics that studies the conduct and institutions of *monetary policy, and its effect on economic variables, such as employment, output, interest rates, prices, consumption, and investment decisions.

monetary overhang That part of the money supply that people are holding merely because they have not been able to spend it. In an economy with *repressed inflation, people hold more money than they really want, because shortages of real goods and services make it impossible to spend it as they would wish. If the controls which kept inflation repressed are removed, monetary overhang tends to produce a burst of open inflation.

monetary policy The use by the government or central bank of interest rates or controls on the money supply to influence the economy. The target of monetary policy may be the achievement of a desired level or rate of growth in real activity, the price level, the exchange rate, or the balance of payments. Methods of monetary policy include setting the interest rate charged by the central bank, sales or purchases of securities to control the money supply, and changes in the required reserve ratios of banks and other financial institutions. The central bank can affect other interest rates both through *open market operations to affect the probability that banks are going to need to borrow at its own lending rate, and by the *announcement effects of changes in the central bank's minimum lending rate, which are regarded by the markets as statements about the authorities' forecasts and objectives. Monetary policy works through the effects of the cost and availability of loans on real activity, and through this on inflation, and on international capital movements and thus on the exchange rate. Central bank and government pronouncements on monetary and other economic questions can be effective in reinforcing practical measures of monetary policy, but do not provide a substitute for them.

Monetary Policy Committee (MPC) A committee set up when the Bank of England was granted independence in 1997 to advise on monetary policy and changes in interest rates. The MPC consists of the Governor of the bank and eight other members, drawn half from the bank's own staff and half from outside. The MPC meets monthly, and its minutes are published, with a short time lag.

monetary system The system by which an economy is provided with money. It is possible for a small country simply to use some other country's money, but most countries choose to provide their own. This is partly for reasons of national prestige, partly because governments derive *seigniorage from providing money, and partly because of a belief that economic stability can be promoted by using *monetary policy to adapt to local shocks, or to insulate the economy from the effects of foreign shocks. An independent monetary system must include a *mint to provide coinage and a central bank to provide base money. It usually includes a system of commercial banks to provide deposit, loan, and payments facilities. It then needs a regulatory body to supervise the banks, to minimize the chance of bank failure, and a *lender of last resort, to prevent failure of any one bank turning into a system-wide crash. These supervisory and last-resort functions may be combined in a single *central bank, as in the UK, or dealt with by separate bodies, as in the US.

monetary union Two or more countries with a single currency. Countries which formerly had independent monetary systems unite to adopt a single currency, or keep separate currencies but enter into a permanent and credible agreement to maintain a constant exchange rate between their currencies. A monetary union requires either a single *central bank or the adoption of effective policy coordination between the central banks of the member countries; the *Eurozone in fact has both.

money **1.** A *medium of exchange and store of value. This may consist of physical objects, that is notes and coin; or of book or computer entries, that is bank deposits. Money was originally a physical substance such as *gold or silver, which was valued for its own sake before it came to be used as coinage. Coins and notes are now usually tokens, whose intrinsic value is below their face value.

2. A verbal shorthand for 'monetary policy'. Thus *cheap money means that loans are cheap and easily available; tight money or *dear money means that loans are expensive and hard to obtain.

3. An expression for wealth in general.

money at call and short notice The most liquid UK bank assets after cash. Money is lent to other banks and non-bank financial institutions such as *discount houses, repayable on demand (call) or at up to 14 days' notice (short notice). These are secured loans bearing interest, usually at low rates.

money illusion Mistaking nominal for real changes. People may interpret rises in their own wages, or the prices of goods and services they sell, or assets that they own, as real gains rather than as part of a general process of price and wage inflation. Money illusion might arise in a society with a history of wage and price stability. The longer inflation persists, the more likely people are to assume that when their wages or prices rise their real position is not improved, as everybody else's prices and wages are probably rising too.

money laundering The use of often complex series of transactions to conceal the ultimate source of money holdings. It is widely used to camouflage receipts from illegal activities, including drug trafficking, *corruption, fraud, and *tax evasion.

money market The market for very short-term loans. In lending money for very short periods, for example overnight, transaction costs are quite large relative to the interest that can be earned, so transactions in the money market are usually for large amounts, and the participants are mainly banks and other financial institutions such as *discount houses, though large firms and a few exceptionally rich individuals also participate.

money multiplier The rate at which an increase in money supply changes national income. In the *IS–LM model an increase in money supply shifts the LM curve and increases national income. In most other economic models an increase in money supply has at most a temporary effect on output and only has a lasting effect on the price level.

money supply The amount of money in an economy. This may be the country's own money, supplied by its banking system, or foreign money, used in preference to domestic money. There is no single accepted definition of what constitutes money: while notes and coin are *legal tender and must be included in any definition, and bank deposits repayable on demand are unlikely to be excluded, there are various types of deposit in non-bank financial intermediaries such as building societies, and various forms of highly *liquid security, which can be included or excluded in various ways. For various definitions applied in the UK see *M0 to *M5.

money wages Wage rates measured in money terms. *See also* REAL WAGES.

monitoring The process of checking whether individuals or firms are actually behaving as they should. This applies to seeing whether laws imposed by the government are being obeyed; whether instructions issued by regulatory agencies to firms are being complied with; whether orders by employers to their employees are actually being carried out; and whether the other party is complying with the terms of a *contract. Monitoring is necessary because it may not be in the private interest of firms to obey laws and regulations, or in the private interests of employees to obey their employers. Monitoring is expensive: in designing laws and issuing private orders there is a trade-off between desirable aims and the level of monitoring costs.

Monopolies and Mergers Commission (MMC) A UK body appointed to investigate monopolies, mergers, and anti-competitive practices referred to it by the Director General of Fair Trading or the Secretary of State for Trade and Industry. The MMC did not initiate its own inquiries, and its reports led to changes only through government action, legislation, or voluntary compliance to avoid these. The MMC was replaced by the *Competition Commission in 1999.

monopolistic competition A market where each firm faces a downward sloping demand curve and acts as a *monopoly in setting price. However, there are many firms selling differentiated versions of the same product and many potential entrants. If *monopoly profit is earned new firms will enter the market. This causes the demand curve of each firm to shift downward and profit to fall. Entry will cease when all monopoly profit is eliminated. In equilibrium all firms will price above marginal cost but earn only normal profit. Models of monopolistic competition are frequently used when the number of firms in an industry is the issue of interest.

monopoly A market situation with only one seller. A natural monopoly exists when the monopolist's solo position is due either to the exclusive possession of some essential input, or to the existence of economies of scale so that no entrant can be profitable once an incumbent firm is established. A statutory monopoly exists when the entry of competitors is forbidden by law. Monopoly is an example of *market failure that leads to economic inefficiency. The extent of inefficiency can be measured by *deadweight loss. The extent of deadweight loss is increased if a monopoly expends resources to sustain *barriers to entry. *See also* STATUTORY MONOPOLY.

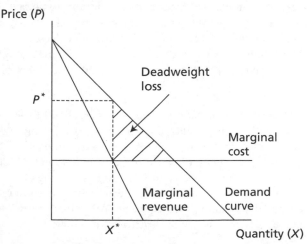

Monopoly

monopoly policy Government policy towards monopolies. This is motivated partly by the fact that monopoly leads to an inefficient use of resources, and partly by a desire to promote a more equal income distribution than the one that tends to result if some firms have monopoly power. The two main approaches to monopoly policy are attempts to control market structure, and attempts to control monopolists' behaviour. Market structure can be tackled by regulating *mergers, forcing monolithic firms to split up, or controlling anti-competitive practices that inhibit entry to monopolized markets by firms established in other markets. Monopolists' behaviour can be controlled through taking them into public ownership by nationalization, or by subjecting them to price controls and other forms of supervision by regulatory bodies such as the UK Office of Telecommunications. *See also* ANTITRUST.

monopoly power The degree of control that a firm can exercise over a market. This is usually measured by the degree of *concentration of the industry.

monopoly profit Profit in excess of *normal profit earned by a firm that is able to exploit monopoly power. A firm earns monopoly profit by pricing above marginal cost. Monopoly profit is therefore indicative of a deviation from *economic efficiency.

monopsony A market situation with only one buyer. Unless the supply is perfectly elastic, a monopsonist has an incentive to exploit the fact that a reduction in the quantity bought will reduce the price. Monopsony is the equivalent on the demand side to *monopoly on the supply side of a market.

monopsony power The degree of control that a firm can exert in a market. This is usually measured by the degree of *concentration of the industry. It is the counterpart of *monopoly power in a market with a single buyer.

Monte Carlo method A method of investigating the behaviour of economic models which are too complicated for analytical solutions to be possible. A system is started off at a large number of initial positions chosen at random, and followed through a numerical simulation to see how it evolves. Monte Carlo methods can be used to check whether a system has an *equilibrium, and whether this is stable for any starting point, or for some limited region of possible starting points.

Montreal Protocol An international agreement reached in 1987 to reduce the production and consumption of *chlorofluorocarbons (CFCs) and halon, substances which deplete the *ozone layer in the upper atmosphere. This was amended in 1990 to target the phasing out of CFCs and halon by 2000. The agreement also provides for trade bans on CFCs and CFC-using products. CFCs and halon are inert and non-toxic substances, and were widely used in refrigeration, foams, aerosols, and dry-cleaning, and halon in fire extinguishers. It has become possible to replace these by less ozone-destructive products.

Moody's One of the main US *credit-rating agencies.

moral hazard The observation that a contract which promises people payment on the occurrence of certain events will cause a change in behaviour to make these events more likely. For example, moral hazard suggests that if possessions are fully insured, their owners are likely to take less good care of them than if they were uninsured. The consequence is that insurance companies cannot offer full insurance. Moral hazard results from *asymmetric information and is a cause of *market failure. *See also* PRINCIPAL–AGENT PROBLEM.

moratorium A suspension of the obligation to repay debts: this may apply to the principal, interest, or both, and may apply to all debts or only to particular types of debt. The payments are only deferred and not cancelled. The objective is usually to give time to make arrangements to refinance the obligations of some particular debtors. It is justified by the fear that their collapse might start a general financial panic. The drawback with a moratorium is that it makes it very difficult for anybody to obtain any new credit, both by freezing the assets of possible lenders and by creating fears of similar measures to intervene in credit markets in the future.

mortgage A loan using a real asset, such as a house or other building, as *collateral. If the interest and redemption payments are not made, the lender or mortgagee can foreclose on the collateral, that is, can take it over and sell it to repay the loan. Mortgages can be for any period: 20 or 25 years is not unusual. With a repayment mortgage the principal is paid off gradually over the life of the mortgage. With an endowment mortgage the principal is paid off at the end of the mortgage from a capital sum built up by an endowment insurance policy.

mortgage interest relief at source (MIRAS) A UK tax allowance by which payers of mortgage interest were allowed to claim part or all of this as a deduction in calculating their taxable income. The relief was given through the lending institutions, so that the borrower paid interest net of tax relief to the lender. The tax allowance was withdrawn in April 2000.

most favoured nation (MFN) A country with rights for equal treatment under a trade agreement. An MFN clause stipulates that imports from the partner country will be treated no less favourably than imports of similar goods from any other country. In the case of *tariffs, this means no other foreign goods face a lower tariff than those from the partner country. With *quota restrictions on trade the meaning of MFN is unclear.

moving average A class of data-smoothing techniques used in the analysis of economic and financial time series. A simple moving average is the arithmetic average of n previous data points. A weighted moving average assigns lower weights to older data points, with the weights declining linearly or exponentially; the latter method is also referred to as *exponential smoothing. *See also* MOVING AVERAGE PROCESS.

moving average process MA(q), of order q A univariate time series process u_t described by

$$u_t = \varepsilon_t - \beta_1 \varepsilon_{t-1} - \cdots - \beta_q \varepsilon_{t-q}$$

where $\beta_1, \ldots, \beta_q$ are constants and ε_t is *white noise. *See also* AUTOREGRESSIVE MOVING AVERAGE MODEL.

multicollinearity In the context of *multiple regression, strong correlations among the explanatory variables, which often result in large estimated standard errors and insignificant estimated coefficients. This is essentially a property of the sample and not a problem with the method of estimation, although sometimes *ridge regression is used as a remedy. Perfect multicollinearity occurs when some of the explanatory variables are perfectly correlated, i.e. linearly dependent; in this case the redundant variable(s) must be removed from the regression.

Multi-Fibre Arrangement (MFA) An international agreement, started in 1973 and renewed several times, between countries exporting and importing textiles and clothing. MFA has restricted exports of these products from *less developed countries (LDCs) to the industrialized countries. This was done to slow down declines in employment in the textile industries in importing countries, and it has substantially increased the cost of clothing in the advanced countries. The MFA is contrary to the guiding principles of the *General Agreement on Tariffs and Trade and the *World Trade Organization. The textile industry has been made an exception through protectionist pressure mainly because the industry combines high labour intensity and relatively simple technology, and has been one of the main entry routes to industrialization in LDCs, which have a comparative advantage in this area. The MFA expired on 1 January 2005.

multilateralism The belief that international economic relations should be conducted on the basis of equal treatment for all non-nationals. This applies both to trade, where multilateralism implies multilateral trade rather than preferential arrangements within trade blocs, and to international capital movements. Multilateralism also implies that negotiations over international trade and investment should be conducted through multinational bodies and not on a bilateral basis.

multilateral trade Trade carried out within a group of countries where there is no need for the trade between any pair of countries to balance. This follows naturally if all countries in the group have *convertible currencies.

multinational A firm conducting business in more than one country, through branches or subsidiary companies. Many large firms are multinationals, and a considerable proportion of international trade is between multinationals and their own foreign branches or subsidiaries. While multinational operation presents some legal and organizational problems, many firms find it worthwhile. It brings them closer to suppliers and markets, they can take advantage of international differences in resources and costs, the benefits of research and development can be spread over wider markets, and it gives a wider spread of risks. Multinational operation also improves their bargaining position in negotiating with national suppliers, governments, and trade unions.

multi-plant firm A firm which operates two or more plants. These may be either branches or run by subsidiary companies.

multiple equilibrium The existence of more than one solution to the equations describing the *equilibrium of an economic model. The multiple equilibria can be locally unique or there can be a continuum of equilibria. If the equilibria are locally unique there is generally an odd number of them. This fact is useful in computing the set of *Nash equilibria for a game: for example, if there are two pure strategy equilbria there must be at least one *mixed strategy equilibrium.

multiple exchange rates The system by which a country's currency has more than one exchange rate with any foreign currency. The rate which applies to any transaction may depend on the holder of the currency, or on the purpose for which it is being used. Multiple exchange rates may discriminate between resident and foreign holders of the currency, between export and import of particular goods, or between current and capital account payments.

multiple regression Linear regression with two or more explanatory variables. Variable y, for example, may be explained by variables x_i, $i = 1, 2, \ldots, K$. The regression equation is then

$$y_t = \alpha + \beta_1 x_{1t} + \beta_2 x_{2t} + \ldots + \beta_K x_{Kt} + \varepsilon_t.$$

multiplier A formula relating an initial change in spending to the total change in activity which will result. The multiplier was central to the argument for *demand management in *Keynesian economics. It is based on the argument that an increase in government spending becomes income for consumers. Some of this income is saved but some is spent. The cycle is then repeated, resulting in the initial increase in expenditure being multiplied. *See also* BALANCED BUDGET MULTIPLIER; MONEY MULTIPLIER.

multiplier–accelerator model A model deriving economic fluctuations from the interaction of the *multiplier and the *accelerator. The multiplier makes output rise following a rise in investment, and the accelerator makes investment increase when output increases. Once expansion starts, if the accelerator is weak the expansion slows down, which lowers investment and causes incomes to decline. A slump follows, during which investment is low and capital wears out. Once capital has fallen sufficiently relative to output, investment starts again and the economy expands. This can produce persistent *business cycles of alternating booms and slumps.

multi-product firm A firm which makes more than one type of product. In the literal sense most firms produce more than one type of good or service, even if the range is not very wide. Some quite small firms such as shops make or trade in a wide variety of products. The term multi-product firm is often reserved for firms which make products which differ significantly in description or construction, especially if they differ sufficiently to come under different categories of the *Standard Industrial Classification.

multivariate data analysis Any statistical technique based on the observation and analysis of more than one variable at a time.

mutual fund A financial institution which holds shares on behalf of investors. In the UK these are called *unit trusts. Investors buy shares, or 'units' in the fund, which uses their money to buy shares in companies. An investor selling back the units gets the proceeds of selling a fraction of the fund's portfolio. A mutual fund's management benefits from appreciation of the shares the fund holds only to the extent that its management charges are a percentage of the market value of its portfolio.

name (at Lloyd's) A member of one or more syndicates at *Lloyd's providing insurance. A name contributes limited cash when joining a syndicate, and accepts *unlimited liability for its obligations. Members share in the profits or losses of syndicates in proportion to the cash they have put in, but are liable for all losses if other members cannot pay. Traditionally, it was assumed that people would only become Lloyd's names if they could afford to lose large amounts. In recent years large losses by some syndicates have led to calls for cash from names. These calls have led to widespread hardship among names who have paid, and extensive litigation involving names who have refused to pay.

narrow-band ERM The relation between members of the *Exchange Rate Mechanism (ERM) of the European Monetary System which agreed to limit fluctuations of their currencies relative to those of other members to 2 percent. This was in contrast to the position of other members, namely the UK and Italy when they were members of ERM, which were allowed 6 percent margins of fluctuation.

Nash bargaining *See* BARGAINING.

Nash equilibrium An equilibrium concept for a game of strategy. A set of strategies (one for each player) constitutes a Nash equilibrium if no player has an incentive to change their strategy given the strategies chosen by the other players. Formally, let s_i be the strategy of player i and s_{-i} the vector of strategies of other players. Then the strategies constitute a Nash equilibrium if, for every player i, $U(s_i, s_{-i}) \geq U(\sigma_i, s_{-i})$ for every alternative strategy σ_i of player i. The Nash equilibrium is the standard equilibrium concept in *game theory. There are some games for which the Nash equilibrium has unusual properties and several 'refinements' of Nash equilibrium have been considered. None of these has seen widespread adoption.

national accounts *See* NATIONAL INCOME ACCOUNTS.

National Association of Securities Dealers Automated Quotation System (NASDAQ) A US securities market, originally for over-the-counter securities not listed on regular stock exchanges. It is now a computer-based market, with a system of market-makers, and is a strong rival to the *New York Stock Exchange.

National Bureau of Economic Research (NBER) A private non-profit US organization founded in 1920 to promote objective quantitative analysis of the

American economy. The NBER is a major provider of high-quality analysis of micro, macro, and international aspects of the US economy.

(🌐) SEE WEB LINKS

• The home page of the NBER.

national debt The debt of a country's government. This may be owed to residents or foreign lenders. In some countries net national debt is smaller than the apparent total, as some government securities are held by other public bodies such as civil service pension funds. In other cases the true national debt is higher than the apparent figures, due to government guarantees of the debts of other bodies such as local governments and state-owned industries. If national debt is held by foreigners, the whole of the interest and redemption payments are claims on national resources. Where the debt is held domestically, the real burden of debt is only the deadweight losses due to the taxes needed to service it.

National Health Service (NHS) The UK system of state-financed medical treatment, covering general practitioner (GP) services, pharmaceuticals, hospitals, and dentistry. NHS treatment is available to all; some forms of treatment are charged for, with exemptions for children, pensioners, and those on very low incomes. The NHS makes some use of an internal market based on fund-holding GP practices and hospital trusts.

national income The total income of residents of a country, measured at *factor cost after deducting *capital consumption. This equals gross national product at factor cost less capital consumption. This sense is used in technical discussions of national income accounting concepts. National income does not include *transfer payments, which merely transfer part of the national income from one set of individuals to another. If transfers are large, personal incomes before taxation can exceed national income. National income is derived from *gross domestic product at factor cost by two main adjustments. First, capital consumption has to be subtracted; this is an estimate of the amount that would have to be spent on *replacement investment to keep the nation's capital stock unchanged. Second, net property income from abroad has to be added, as national income refers to the income of residents, regardless of whether this arises from activities carried on domestically or abroad. The income approach is one of three methods used in national income accounting to measure aggregate economic activity: this approach works by adding the incomes of all sectors of the economy. The other approaches are the *output method, looking at the outputs of various sectors, and the *expenditure method, which adds the expenditures of various sectors of the economy. *See also* FULL EMPLOYMENT NATIONAL INCOME.

national income accounts Accounts showing the main aggregates relating to national income and its components; these include *gross domestic product, *gross national product, national income after deducting *capital consumption, and components including *consumption, *net investment and *gross investment, *government expenditure, *exports, and *imports. National income accounts frequently also include data on *stocks as well as *flows: that is, the domestic stock of productive capital, and external assets and liabilities. National income accounts normally include information on changes in price levels, and show the various aggregates at both current and constant prices, that is, in both nominal and real terms. Data usually refer to whole years; where they are provided for shorter periods, they may or may not be seasonally corrected.

National Institute of Economic and Social Research (NIESR) An independent UK body carrying out research into both macro- and microeconomic aspects of the economy.

(⊕) SEE WEB LINKS

• The home page of the NIESR.

National Insurance contributions (NICs) Charges levied in the UK on employees, employers, and the self-employed to help to pay for social security. These contributions are levied as fixed percentages of wages, with exemptions for very low incomes. NICs form part of the *tax wedge between the cost of labour to employers and the cash benefit of working to their employees.

nationalization Bringing under government ownership and control resources and activities formerly operated by private businesses or local organizations. This is the opposite process to *privatization.

nationalized industry An industry whose ownership has been taken over by the state. Motives for nationalization may vary: in some cases industries are nationalized because they are *natural monopolies, such as public utilities, so that public ownership is expected to enhance economic efficiency by moderating the exercise of monopoly power. Some industries are nationalized because large subsidies are needed to avoid run-downs in output and employment. In other cases the aim is to reduce the power of private capitalists, and take public control of 'the commanding heights of the economy'. Potential drawbacks of nationalization are the absence of a *hard budget constraint leading to overmanning and inefficiency, monopoly power limiting the need to respond to consumer needs, and government interference with management decisions concerning pricing and investment. In many countries formerly nationalized industries have in recent years been privatized, that is, sold off to private owners. *See also* PRIVATIZATION.

national product The total value of income produced by factors of production owned by residents of a country. This includes income from factors owned by residents but operating abroad, and excludes the value of factors operating domestically but owned by non-residents. This is contrasted with *domestic product, which is the value of incomes produced domestically, regardless of ownership. *Gross national product (GNP) is calculated before deducting an estimate of capital consumption; *net national product is GNP minus *capital consumption.

National Savings Bonds carrying a UK government guarantee of both their principal and interest. They may be for fixed sums of money, or index-linked to the retail price index. The National Savings Bank is a UK institution providing safe securities for individuals to hold. These are widely held: they provide a return which is completely safe, but on average somewhat lower than that on other investments. The amount of National Savings bonds any individual can hold is limited.

national treatment The requirement often included in trade agreements that governments treat the products of foreign firms on an equal basis with those of domestic firms. This implies that once goods have been subjected to border measures such as *tariffs and *quotas, they should be treated in the same way as domestic goods in matters such as taxes and excise duties.

natural experiment A natural experiment occurs when an exogenous change allows the derivation of the effect of a change in a single variable. For example, one US state changes a policy while other neighbouring states do not. In the absence of other changes, this allows the identification of the effect of the policy change. The name natural experiment reflects the fact that the policy change is not under the control of the investigator but has the same effect as changing a variable of interest in a controlled experiment. The value to the investigator is that natural experiments are typically conducted on large populations with all reactions natural. The standard terminology is to call the subjects exposed to the policy change the treatment group and those not exposed the control group. Natural experiments also have the benefit that if the change in policy is truly exogenous then there should be no selection bias in the allocation of subjects to the treatment or control groups. The reliability of natural experiments may suffer from correlation among the variables in the system under study.

natural growth rate The growth rate of national income which would just maintain a constant unemployment rate. If there is no technical progress and the labour force grows at rate g, this will be the natural growth rate. If there is also technical progress at rate ρ, the natural growth rate is given by $n = g + \rho$. In a *Solow growth model the actual growth rate converges on the natural rate, whatever the ratio of saving to income. In a *Harrod–Domar growth model, if the warranted growth rate is above the natural rate, the economy will expand until it reaches full employment. At this point growth of actual output must fall below the warranted rate, and there will be a recession. If the warranted growth rate falls below the natural rate, there will be a tendency to ever-increasing unemployment.

natural monopoly A natural monopoly occurs when the production technology is characterized by *increasing returns to scale and the level of demand is such that only a single firm can be profitable. High fixed costs can be an explanation of the increasing returns. For example, it may not be profitable for two electricity suppliers to serve a single town if both have to bear the fixed costs of installing an electricity supply network. The existence of a natural monopoly provides justification for government intervention since efficiency will not otherwise be achieved. This is contrasted with a *statutory monopoly, where the incumbent's position is based on laws to exclude possible rivals. An example of statutory monopoly is sole access to a necessary technology because of the exclusive possession of *patents.

natural rate of interest The rate of interest which would be compatible with a stable level of economic activity in an economy with a constant price level.

Attempts to set a market rate of interest below the natural rate lead in the short run to an expansion of real activity above the level consistent with stable prices, and in the longer run to inflationary rises in prices and money wages.

natural rate of unemployment In *Keynesian economics, the unemployment rate which would prevail in an economy with a constant rate of inflation. This is a function of various man-made institutional factors, including the extent of industrial monopoly, the social security system, minimum wage legislation, restrictions on mobility between occupations, and trade-union organization. All of these can be influenced by policy. At any time the natural rate of unemployment will also be affected by the past history of actual unemployment, if the effect of unemployment is to make people less employable. 'Natural' is used here to indicate that this unemployment rate cannot be permanently reduced simply by *demand management: any attempt to do this will result in ever-rising inflation. It does not imply that this level of unemployment is either desirable or inevitable.

natural resources Factors of production provided by nature. This includes land suitable for agriculture, mineral deposits, and water resources useful for power generation, transport, and irrigation. It also includes sea resources, such as fish and offshore mineral deposits.

natural wastage The proportion of the labour force who quit their jobs each year for reasons other than being sacked by their employer. This includes workers who retire, and those who leave for personal reasons. An appreciable percentage of a firm's labour force may leave in any year and this often makes possible gradual reduction in the labour force without the need for *redundancies.

near money Securities which are very close substitutes for money. Short-dated securities with a government guarantee which are either marketable, or redeemable by the government at short notice, are such substitutes. They are not themselves money, but are so near to being money that their existence reduces the demand to hold money proper.

necessary and sufficient conditions Conditions which must be satisfied for something to be true (necessary) and if satisfied imply that it must occur (sufficient). Consider propositions B and C. 'B is a sufficient condition for C' means that if B is true, C is always true. 'B is a necessary condition for C' means that C cannot be true unless B is true. A condition can be sufficient but not necessary; if B is a sufficient condition for C, C cannot be false when B is true, but C could well be true when B is false. It is possible for the same condition to be both necessary and sufficient; this means that B is true if and only if (written iff) C is true. Thus if B is a necessary and sufficient condition for C, C must likewise be a necessary and sufficient condition for B; the two statements are thus equivalent.

necessity A good or service whose consumption by an individual, at a given price, rises less than in proportion to increases in their income. The *income elasticity of demand for a necessity is less than one. Necessities are thus goods on which poorer people spend a larger proportion of their incomes than richer people. A necessity is contrasted with a *luxury, which is a good or service whose consumption rises more than in proportion to increases in income. *See also* ENGEL CURVE.

negative equity The position of the owner of an asset the value of which is less than the amount of debt secured by a *mortgage on it. For example, a house owner with a mortgage of £100 000 on a house whose market value is only £90 000 has negative equity of £10 000. The providers of mortgage finance do not lend more than they believe the security is worth, but negative equity can occur if house prices fall after a mortgage is taken out, as occurred in the UK in the early 1990s and the late 2000s, or if borrowers get into arrears on their repayments.

negative income tax A proposal to combine *income tax payments and *social security benefits in a single system. Under this system, all citizens would report their pre-tax incomes; they would then pay tax if their income after deducting any allowances to which they were entitled came above some cut-off level, and would receive payments if their income was below the cut-off. The advantage of such a system is that it integrates the tax and welfare systems.

neoclassical economics The analysis of economic activity based on the fundamental premises that all economic agents have rational preferences, all consumers maximize utility, all firms maximize profit, and all choices are made taking into account relevant constraints. These components produce a variety of results, depending upon the assumptions on the economic environment in which the economic agents interact. For example, if all agents are assumed to be price-takers then a model of a competitive economy is obtained. Alternatively, if it is assumed that a firm is the only supplier of a product (and recognizes this fact) then the model is one of monopoly. Neoclassical economics is the accepted orthodox approach to economics.

neoclassical synthesis An approach in economics, predominant in main-stream economics since the 1950s and developed primarily by John Hicks (1904–1989) and Paul Samuelson (b. 1915), that combines neoclassical microeconomics, in particular, consumer theory of individual demand, and Keynesian macroeconomics.

nested models In econometrics, model A is said to be nested in model B if it can be obtained from B by imposing a set of restrictions on the parameters of B.

net An indication that something has been subtracted. The word appears in economics in a variety of contexts. Net price is price after subtracting any discounts, for prompt payment or otherwise. Net weight is the weight of a product excluding packaging. Net investment is total or gross investment less an estimate of *capital consumption. The net national product is similarly equal to gross national product, the total of all value added in the economy, less capital consumption. Net exports are total exports less total imports. The net assets of a firm are its total, or gross, assets less its liabilities.

Net Book Agreement A UK agreement that allowed publishers to fix the retail prices of their books. This was an exception to the general prohibition of *resale price maintenance. It was argued that the agreement helped to keep small and specialized booksellers in business, and was thus good for the reading public. The Net Book Agreement was abandoned in 1995.

net capital formation *See* NET INVESTMENT.

net domestic product The value of incomes produced by factors of production operating in a country, regardless of their ownership, and after subtracting an estimate of *capital consumption.

net economic welfare The concept of a broader measure of economic welfare than income per head. This could include in addition to ordinary measures of income items such as the following: the cost of effort; the value of household production, including services such as childcare and looking after the sick and elderly; any depletion of the stock of natural resources; and the value of changes in the natural environment. While such a measure of overall welfare would be of great interest, the observation and valuation of the components is so difficult that any proposed measure would remain highly subjective.

net exports Exports less imports, either in total, or of any category of goods and services. It is thus negative when imports exceed exports.

net foreign assets The total of assets owned by residents of a country, but situated abroad, less assets located within the country but owned by non-residents. A country's overseas assets include both foreign direct investment and holdings of foreign securities, and foreign holdings of domestic assets include both inward foreign direct investment and foreign holdings of domestic securities. Net foreign assets can thus be either positive or negative.

net investment The net increase in the amount of capital. This equals *gross investment less an estimate of *capital consumption. Net investment is harder to measure than gross, since while gross investment is mainly based on actual market transactions in acquiring capital goods, capital consumption is not based on observing market transactions, but is an estimate of the loss of value of the existing capital stock due to wear and tear, the passage of time, and *obsolescence.

net national product The value of the incomes produced by factors of production owned by residents of a country, whether operating domestically or abroad, measured after deducting an estimate of *capital consumption. Net national product thus includes the earnings of factors owned by residents and operating abroad, and excludes the earnings of factors operating domestically but owned by non-residents.

net present value The present value of a security or an investment project, found by discounting all present and future receipts and outgoings at an appropriate rate of discount. If the net present value calculated is positive, it is worthwhile investing in a project. If the receipts or outgoings are subject to uncertainty, the appropriate rate of discount has to include a risk premium that reflects the degree of risk.

net profit The profits of an organization after all expenses have been taken into account. This can be measured either before or after deduction of taxes payable.

net property income from abroad The excess of property incomes received from abroad over property incomes paid to non-residents. Property incomes include rent, dividends, and interest remitted from abroad plus the retained profits of companies operating direct investment abroad. In practice, company profits earned abroad and reinvested, which should be counted both as receipts of property income and as capital outflows, tend to get omitted from balance-of-payments statistics, so net property income from abroad is subject to error.

net tangible assets The tangible assets of an organization less its current liabilities. This is different from total assets less total liabilities. On the assets side it excludes intangibles such as *goodwill, and on the liabilities side it excludes debts not due for payment within the next financial year.

net transfer income from abroad The excess of transfers from abroad received by the residents of a country over the payments of transfers abroad. Transfers include government grants to overseas bodies, and private charitable donations.

net wealth The wealth of an individual after subtracting any debts owed from their total gross assets.

network In economics, groups of consumers in which the utility derived from consumption of certain goods or services increases as additional consumers purchase the same goods and services. Networks emerge if these particular goods or services have little or no value in isolation, and generate more value when more consumers use the same goods and services. Many products are required to be used with other products at the same time. A market characterized by such properties is called a network market in which there exist positive consumption externalities termed network externalities. A typical example of a network industry is telecommunications.

network externality An *externality derived from being connected to other economic agents, for example through a telephone system or the internet. The concept also applies to social networks. The larger the proportion of the population connected to such a network, the greater the benefits to each of them.

net worth The net value of an organization's assets, after deducting any liabilities. Net worth can only be measured reliably if assets are correctly valued: this cannot usually be done simply by using balance-sheet figures. Where assets are not readily marketed and intangible assets such as *goodwill are important, a figure for net worth can be unreliable.

net yield The interest or dividends on securities, net of tax, that is after deduction of the normal rate of income tax, as a percentage of their price. For taxpayers with a personal marginal income tax rate lower than the normal rate, net yield is

higher than that reported; similarly, for taxpayers with a personal marginal
income tax rate higher than the normal rate, net yield is lower than that reported.

neutrality of money The concept that changes in the quantity of money in
an economy affect only nominal variables, as a change in units, and are irrelevant
to the behaviour of rational economic agents. The neutrality of money was first
identified by David Hume (1711–1776) in the 18th century and developed later
into the *quantity theory of money. Hume's prediction that in the long run nominal
prices grow proportionally to the money supply has been confirmed empirically
using data on different countries in different time periods. The 'neutrality theorems'
derive this result in the framework of dynamic *general equilibrium theory. The
non-neutrality of money in the short run and the potential of monetary policy, in
particular, monetary expansion, to stimulate real economic activity were the
focus of *Keynesian economics after the depression of the 1930s. In the 1970s
the difference between the effects of anticipated and unanticipated money shocks
and the role of *rational expectations were emphasized and tested on both time
series and cross-country data. The main finding was that anticipated changes in
the growth rate of money supply are not associated with changes in employment
and production and only have an inflation tax effect. On the other hand,
unanticipated monetary expansions were found to be associated with economic
booms, and contractions with depressions.

neutral taxes Taxes which do not cause inefficiency by distorting the structure
of incentives. Neutrality is often proposed as a desirable property of a tax system.
*Poll taxes and *lump-sum taxes on economic rents are neutral, but it is hard to
find any other examples. *Direct taxes can avoid discrimination between
occupations, but cannot avoid giving incentives to leisure and do-it-yourself
activity rather than paid employment, and to a shift to the *hidden economy.
*Value-added tax could avoid distorting the choice between different goods and
services if imposed at a uniform rate, but would still distort the choice between
leisure and consumption.

new classical economics A school of economics based on the assumption
that all economic agents hold *rational expectations and that all markets clear.
New classical models also assume utility maximization by consumers and profit
maximization by firms. The consequence of these assumptions is a belief that
unemployment is essentially voluntary, produced by the provision of perverse
incentives by the state, and that discretionary government policies are destabilizing.
This leads to the advocacy of *laissez-faire policies, and to a belief that inflation
can be controlled by strict monetary policy at zero real cost.

New Deal The package of policies adopted in the US in the 1930s under
President Franklin D. Roosevelt (1882–1945) to promote economic recovery from
the Great Depression. This included price stabilization through the National
Recovery Administration, extension of collective bargaining through the *Wagner
Act, promotion of financial stability through the creation of the *Securities and
Exchange Commission and the *Federal Deposit Insurance Corporation, social

security including the creation of *Aid to Families with Dependent Children, and a programme of public works including setting up the *Tennessee Valley Authority.

new economy An economy based on the service sector and financial activities. The name emerged in the 1990s to capture the shift of the US economy away from a manufacturing base. The dotcom boom of the later 1990s was seen as part of the process of moving to the new economy.

New International Economic Order A set of proposals to improve the position of *less developed countries (LDCs) by changing their terms of trade with and their arrangements for borrowing from more advanced economies. These were originated at the United Nations in 1974, and pushed by the *United Nations Conference on Trade and Development. These proposals included measures to improve the terms of trade for exporters of primary products, measures to improve the access of producers from LDCs to markets for industrial exports in the more developed countries, and a reduction in international debt burdens, particularly for the poorer indebted LDCs. These proposals have led to very little action by the advanced economies.

new issues The value of sales of newly issued shares in public companies. This is one of the main sources of finance for companies.

newly industrialized countries (NICs) Countries which were formerly classified as less developed but have recently increased the proportion of industrial production in national income and of industrial exports in trade. The NICs were the most rapidly growing part of the world economy in the last quarter of the 20th century. There is no standard list of NICs: they include the 'East Asian tigers', Hong Kong, South Korea, Singapore, and Taiwan, and various other countries such as Brazil, China, India, Malaysia, Mexico, South Africa, and Thailand, and their number is growing.

new orders The value of orders for goods obtained by firms in those sectors where goods are made to order rather than made first and then sold off the shelf. This is principally the construction industry and those parts of manufacturing industry selling producer goods. Changes in new orders are a leading indicator of changes in economic activity.

new protectionism The revival of *protectionism, with the support of some new arguments. These are based partly on the introduction of strategic considerations, and partly on considering the effects of assuming widespread *increasing returns to scale in industry. The strategic argument for protection is that one country may by protecting its own industry deter others from entering into competition with it. The effect of increasing returns, with resulting imperfect competition, is that protecting a country's home market increases the output of its own industry, thus decreasing its average costs and improving its ability to compete internationally. Protection also cuts rivals' output, thus increasing their average costs and impairing their ability to compete. None of these arguments affects the objection that all forms of protection are *beggar-my-neighbour policies, so that all countries could gain by agreeing to abstain from them.

New York Stock Exchange (NYSE) The oldest and largest US stock exchange. From 2007 the NYSE became part of the combined US and European exchange *NYSE Euronext.

((⊕)) SEE WEB LINKS
• The home page of the NYSE.

N-firm concentration ratio The proportion of total market output produced by the N largest firms in an industry. The concentration ratio is used as a measure of the degree of monopolization of a market. A market with a low value of the N-firm concentration ratio is more competitive than one with a high value of the ratio.

Nikkei index The principal index of Japanese share prices.

1992 The programme of the European Community (EC) aimed at unifying its *internal market by 1992. The target was the elimination of all barriers to the movement of goods, people, and capital within the EC. This involved the removal of border controls, liberalization of financial markets, harmonization of VAT rates, standardization of industrial regulations, and opening up of government procurement to all EC members.

no arbitrage The absence of opportunities to earn a risk-free profit with no investment. The essential idea of *arbitrage is the purchase of a good in one market and the immediate resale, at a higher price, in another market. If both the purchase and sale prices are known then the resulting profit is risk free. The absence of arbitrage ensures that markets are in equilibrium. The concept of arbitrage has been extended to financial markets. In a financial market an arbitrage portfolio involves going short in some assets and long in others, with the portfolio having zero net cost but a positive expected return. No arbitrage means that no such portfolio can be constructed so asset prices are in equilibrium.

nominal anchor A mechanism for determining the general *price level in an economy. The need for equilibrium in markets for goods and factor services determines the structure of relative prices, but this could be achieved with any absolute price level. The monetary authorities may simply proclaim an intention to keep some price index stable, but this promise may lack credibility. A nominal anchor is a way of making such promises credible. Possible methods include using a commodity such as gold or silver as money, or adopting a fixed exchange rate with some other currency, such as the dollar, which already has a reputation for price stability.

nominal protection The proportional price increase in imported goods caused by a tariff. With a proportional tariff rate t, the price of imports inside the country is $(1 + t)$ times their external price. The tariff rate thus measures nominal protection. This is contrasted with *effective protection, the proportional increase in value added in the industry producing a good, taking account of tariffs on any imported inputs used in producing it. The more heavily imported inputs are taxed, the less effective protection is given by any rate of nominal protection.

nominal variable An economic variable measured in money terms. Nominal variables are contrasted with real variables, which are measured in physical units, such as employment or steel production, and variables which are unit-free numbers, such as elasticities and percentage shares.

nominee holding A share holding registered in a name other than that of the real owner. This is sometimes done for sheer convenience, for example when *unit trusts hold shares which are ultimately the property of their own unit-holders. In other cases it is done to avoid revealing the identity of the owner, for example when shares are being acquired prior to a takeover bid.

non-accelerating inflation rate of unemployment (NAIRU) The unemployment rate at which *inflation remains constant. This features in Keynesian models where the rate of inflation depends on demand pressure. In such models, if demand is high, firms aim on average to raise their own prices faster than they expect other prices to increase, which causes inflation to speed up. If demand is low, firms aim on average to raise their own prices more slowly than they expect other prices to increase, which causes inflation to slow down. The NAIRU is the unemployment rate corresponding to a level of demand pressure which causes firms on average to aim to keep their own price increases in line with the price increases they expect elsewhere. This stabilizes the rate of inflation at whatever level it has already reached.

non-contributory pension scheme A pension scheme in which members are not required to contribute to the cost of their pensions, which is entirely met by their employer. This is contrasted with a *contributory pension scheme, in which the members are required to contribute to meet at least part of the cost. *See also* DEFINED CONTRIBUTION.

non-discrimination Equal treatment for comparable cases. This is contrasted with *discrimination, which is differences of treatment on what are considered irrelevant grounds. In employment, for example, non-discrimination implies not choosing employees on grounds of sex, race, or religion, for positions where these grounds are not directly relevant to the duties to be performed. In international trade, non-discrimination means treating all transactions with non-nationals equally. The question of what differences are in fact irrelevant gives rise to problems: the principle of non-discrimination may conflict with actuarial evidence. In pensions, for example, it is an actuarial fact that women on average live longer than men; whether they should therefore receive lower pensions for equal contributions is a subject of controversy.

non-executive director A company director who is not a full-time executive employee of the firm. Non-executive directors are usually chosen either for their expertise in areas relevant to a company's activities, or because they have titles or hold other positions which lend respectability to bodies they join. They may well be executives of other companies.

non-government organization (NGO) An independent voluntary association of people working together for a common purpose that does not include achieving government office, earning profit, or engaging in illegal activities. Oxfam and Médecins Sans Frontières are examples of NGOs. *See also* NON-PROFIT ORGANIZATION.

non-inflationary growth Growth of economic activity without any tendency to inflation of prices.

non-labour income Income from any source other than the supply of labour. Non-labour income includes *capital gains, *dividends, *interest, *transfer payments, gifts, and prizes.

nonlinear least squares estimator An estimator that solves a linearized system of the first-order conditions for *least squares estimation of the parameters, when these conditions are nonlinear functions of the parameters.

non-marketable debt Debt for which there is no secondary market. The holders of such debt may have to wait until it falls due for redemption, or may be able to get it redeemed by the borrower at any time, but possibly on terms involving some penalty. This is the position, for example, with National Savings certificates in the UK. Holders cannot sell their rights to anybody else, though they may be used as collateral for loans from other financial institutions.

non-marketed economic activities Economic activities producing goods and services not distributed through markets. These may be conducted by individuals, organizations, or the state. Individuals perform for themselves or their families activities which can be and often are paid for: these include childcare, looking after the sick and the elderly, housework, driving, gardening, and do-it-yourself home improvements. Many voluntary organizations such as charities and churches produce services which are given free rather than sold. A great many government services, including health, education, and personal social services, are provided free, to some recipients at least. Between them these various forms of non-marketed activity constitute a significant share of a modern economy.

non-monetary job characteristics Job characteristics other than financial. These include hours and working conditions, holidays, training provision, opportunities for promotion, location of the workplace in a pleasant area, and a congenial boss and fellow workers. These are contrasted with purely financial conditions, including pay and bonuses, pension rights, free or subsidized medical insurance, and assistance with house purchase. Some job characteristics have a financial value which is difficult to measure explicitly, such as job security, provision of childcare facilities, or training which improves a worker's outside job opportunities.

non-parametric statistics The branch of statistics concerned with non-parametric statistical models. In non-parametric models the structure is determined from the data, without assuming a priori any particular functional form. For example, a histogram is a non-parametric estimate of a probability distribution. Non-parametric models are also called distribution-free or parameter-free.

non-pecuniary benefits Benefits that are not in a monetary form. The option of working *flexitime is an example of a non-pecuniary benefit of employment.

non-performing debt Debt on which the interest and redemption payments due are not in fact being made. Non-performing debt is an embarrassment to lending institutions: they suffer not merely direct financial loss, but also damage to their reputation for sound judgement in picking borrowers. There is thus a temptation to disguise non-performing debt by making fresh loans to finance repayment of earlier ones.

non-price competition Competition for market share using methods other than price cuts. These include quality of product, quality of advertising, information, and instructions, reliability of promised delivery dates, reliability in use, and after-sales service. Non-price competition is particularly important when there are legal or cartel restrictions on price cutting, and where consumers use price as a signal of quality and assume that cheaper goods must be of lower quality.

non-profit organization A legally constituted group organized for purposes other than generating profit and in which no part of the organization's income is distributed to its members, directors, or officers. Examples of non-profit organizations include churches, public schools, public charities, public clinics and hospitals, political organizations, legal aid societies, volunteer services organizations, labour unions, professional associations, research institutes, museums, and some governmental agencies. *See also* NON-GOVERNMENT ORGANIZATION.

non-satiation The assumption that a consumer will always benefit from additional consumption. The demand for some goods may have a finite limit, but it is likely that there is some good or service a consumer would benefit from having more of.

nonstationary process A *stochastic process whose statistical properties change over time. For example, a process with *trend has a mean that changes over time, and a *random walk has a variance that grows over time.

non-systematic risk *See* IDIOSYNCRATIC RISK.

non-tariff barriers Economic obstructions to international trade other than *tariffs. Non-tariff barriers include: prohibitions and quotas; oppressive and dilatory procedures for the routing and documentation of imports; regulations allegedly for health and safety purposes; requirements for prior deposit of the cost of imports in blocked bank accounts; the requirement of licences or specific foreign currency allocations; and *voluntary export restraint agreements with foreign exporters.

non-tradables Goods and services which cannot be traded internationally.

non-uniqueness of equilibrium A situation where an economic model possesses more than one outcome that satisfies the system of equations describing equilibrium. A model may possess several isolated equilibria or it may have a continuum of equilibria. When the equilibria are isolated there is typically an odd number (an even number can occur but a slight change to the economy will restore an odd number). A continuum of equilibria can occur in economies with *forward-looking behaviour.

non-voting share A share which gives the holder the same right to dividends as a voting *ordinary share, but no vote at company meetings. Non-voting shares are issued to enable a company to raise equity finance without diluting control. They typically have a lower price than voting shares.

norm *See* SOCIAL CUSTOM.

normal distribution (Gaussian distribution) A continuous distribution of a random variable described by a probability density function of the form

$$f(x) = \exp\left[-(x-\mu)^2/(2\sigma^2)\right]/\sqrt{2\pi\sigma^2}, \quad -\infty < x < \infty.$$

The normal distribution has mean μ, variance σ^2, and is symmetric about the mean. The standard normal distribution is defined as the normal distribution with zero mean and unit variance; normal distributions with arbitrary mean and variance form a *location-scale family. The normal distribution plays an important role in statistical inference due to the *Central Limit Theorem.

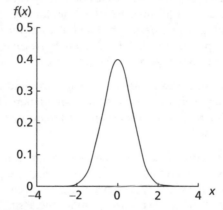

Standard Normal Distribution

normal equations Basic *least squares equations, that is, the first-order conditions for the minimization of the sums of squared residuals, that can be interpreted, when the solution exists, as the (minimized) residuals being orthogonal, or normal, to the matrix of regressors.

normal good A good whose consumption increases with income. Thus any good is normal which is not inferior; this applies to most goods. Normal goods are divided between necessities, with *income elasticities of demand of less than one, and luxuries, with *income elasticities of demand of over one.

normal profit The level of profit equal to the opportunity cost of entrepreneurial effort. Normal profit is regarded as the fair reward for the effort the entrepreneur puts into running a firm and the risk that they take on. Levels of profitability higher than this tend to stimulate entry to an industry, and levels of profits lower than normal tend to cause exit.

normative economics The part of economics that is concerned with how the economy ought to be run. The main considerations are *efficiency and *equity.

On the efficiency side, it asks whether any given objective could be achieved using fewer real resources. If this could be done, it would leave more resources available to achieve other desirable ends. On the equity side, it asks whether the distribution of costs and benefits is desirable, given objectives such as equality, fair rewards for effort, and not disappointing people's reasonable expectations. These aims are not always mutually consistent, and normative economics has to consider the trade-offs between them and between the equity and the efficiency effects of any arrangements.

North American Free Trade Agreement (NAFTA) An agreement reached in 1993 between Canada, Mexico, and the United States making the three countries a *free-trade area.

North Sea oil Oil produced in the North Sea. A combination of advances in oil technology and the rise in oil prices in the 1970s led to a dramatic rise in UK-based oil production. Output rose from approximately nil in 1973 to a level equal to 9 percent of productive sector output by 1979. This dramatically improved the UK's balance of payments: in 1974 net imports of fuel were equal to 3½ percent of *gross domestic product (GDP), while in 1983 net exports of fuel were equal to 4 percent of GDP. Production of North Sea oil peaked in 1999 and has fallen since. It is expected to fall to a third of the peak output by 2020.

no-strike agreement An agreement between a firm and the union(s) representing its employees that in the event of disagreements which cannot be resolved by negotiation, both sides will accept the results of arbitration rather than resorting to strike action.

null hypothesis In statistical inference, a set of restrictions being tested. The null hypothesis is assumed to be true unless the test suggests otherwise, in which case it is rejected in favour of the alternative hypothesis. The test is usually set such that the distribution of the test statistic, under the assumption that the null hypothesis is true, is known (the null distribution). The null hypothesis is rejected in favour of the alternative if the numerical value of the test statistic falls in the region of values that can be generated by a random draw from the null distribution only with a low probability. *See also* ONE-TAILED TEST; TWO-TAILED TEST; TYPE I AND II ERRORS.

numeraire A good used as the standard of value for other goods. The price of the numeraire is defined to be one. Any good can in principle be used as numeraire provided that it can be assured of having a strictly positive equilibrium price.

NYSE Euronext A pan-European stock exchange based in Paris with subsidiaries in Belgium, France, the Netherlands, Portugal, and the United Kingdom. The exchange provided markets for both equities and derivatives. In January 2006 the markets constituting NYSE Euronext had a market capitalization of US $2.9 trillion. NYSE Euronext was formed in 2006 when Euronext merged with NYSE Group.

(⊕) SEE WEB LINKS

• The home page of NYSE Euronext.

Objective 1 region A region with under 75 percent of the average EU per capita income, which is eligible for financial assistance from the EU budget to improve its social overhead capital and employment prospects. Objective 1 also covers the seven most geographically remote regions, areas of Sweden and Finland with very low population densities, and Northern Ireland.

obsolescence Loss of value of equipment due to changes in techniques or tastes. Equipment may become obsolete because consumers no longer want the goods it produces, or because *technical progress in other industries means that intermediate goods it produces are no longer needed. It may become obsolete because new techniques in its own industry allow production with less labour, fuel, or materials, or because it does not comply with improved health and safety regulations. Obsolescence is contrasted with loss of value through *wear and tear or the passage of time.

Occam's razor A principle stating that 'entities should not be multiplied unnecessarily'. A common interpretation of this principle in science is 'between two competing theories which make exactly the same predictions, the one that is simpler is the better'.

occupational pension A pension provided by an employer for former employees. In a *contributory pension scheme employees are required to contribute part of their pay to help meet the cost of the scheme; in a *non-contributory scheme the entire cost is borne by the employer. Fully funded schemes build up sufficient funds to meet the actuarially expected cost of pensions. In unfunded schemes the pensions are paid for out of current revenue by the employer. In partially funded schemes there is a fund, but not one sufficient to meet the full forecasted cost of pensions due. *Defined contribution schemes fix the contributions by employers and employees to the pension fund: pensions depend on the financial peformance of the fund. *Defined benefit schemes fix what the pensioners receive, the employer making up any deficiency in the fund's financial performance. Defined benefit schemes may fix benefits in cash terms, or index-link them, either to prices or current earnings.

off-balance-sheet finance The use of leased rather than owned buildings and equipment. This reduces the capital required to run a business, and reduces the risk of loss due to technical *obsolescence of the equipment. Because the owner of leased equipment bears this risk, the rental on off-balance-sheet items may exceed the interest and amortization costs of owning them, so that use of off-balance-sheet finance lowers current profits.

offer curve The locus of trading plans traced out as relative prices vary. For any set of relative prices there is an optimal trading plan. As relative prices vary the optimal plan changes. The offer curve is the locus of optimal plans and is constructed by considering every feasible set of relative prices. An offer curve can be constructed for a single consumer. A set of relative prices determines a budget constraint and the optimal choice is the consumption plan that maximizes utility given the budget constraint. The offer curve of the consumer is the locus of utility maximizing choices as the budget constraint varies. In an *Edgeworth box an equilibrium for a two-consumer economy occurs at an intersection of the consumers' offer curves. An offer curve can also be constructed for a country. In this case it depicts the international trading plans as relative prices vary. An equilibrium in a two-country model of trade occurs at the intersection of the countries' offer curves.

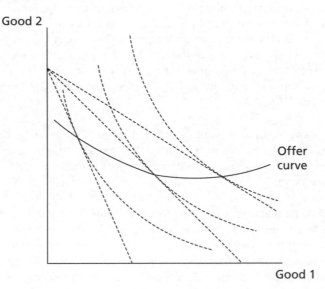

Offer Curve

Office for National Statistics (ONS) The UK government agency responsible for the collection and publication of UK economic statistics. The ONS was formed in 1996 by merging the Central Statistical Office and the Office of Population Censuses and Surveys.

(⊕) SEE WEB LINKS

• The official website of the ONS.

Office of Communications (Ofcom) Ofcom was established by the Office of Communications Act of 2002. Ofcom regulates the UK communications industries and is responsible for television, radio, telecommunications, and wireless communications services.

Office of Fair Trading (OFT) The government body responsible for administering UK competition policy. It is responsible for maintaining the register of restrictive agreements, monitoring restrictive and anti-competitive practices, and regulating consumer credit. It can refer proposed mergers to the *Competition Commission.

(⊕) SEE WEB LINKS

• The official website of the Office of Fair Trading.

Office of Management and Budget (OMB) An office of the US President responsible for preparing the annual federal budget for presentation to Congress. Once the budget is passed, the OMB controls its administration and provides data on the actual performance of federal finances.

Office of Telecommunications (Oftel) The official body set up to regulate the UK telephone industry after the privatization of British Telecom. The functions of Oftel were transferred to the Office of Communications in 2002.

official financing The official element in the *balance of payments. If a country's current and capital account balances do not sum to zero, the difference has to be found by the authorities. If the sum is a deficit, the central bank may meet this by running down its *foreign exchange reserves, or by borrowing from other central banks or from international institutions, particularly the *International Monetary Fund. If the sum of the current and capital accounts is a surplus, the central bank can repay past borrowing, or increase its foreign exchange reserves.

offshore fund A fund operating in a country which is not the residence of the holder. Use of offshore funds may assist in *tax avoidance or *tax evasion.

oil crisis A situation in which there is a sudden fall in the availability and/or a large increase in the price of oil. For the many economies which rely mainly on oil for their energy requirements, a fall in the quantity available would produce a major slump in real output. For countries importing their oil a large price rise produces an immediate and severe balance-of-payments problem. The term usually refers to the oil crisis of 1973–4 when the members of the *Organization of Petroleum Exporting Countries raised the price of oil by a factor of four and some Middle Eastern oil producers threatened a boycott of supplies to countries regarded as sympathetic to Israel in the 1973 Arab–Israeli war.

oil embargo A refusal to supply oil to countries whose policies are disliked. As bulk oil is mainly carried in pipelines and large and easily recognized tankers, an embargo on bulk oil supplies is relatively easy to enforce. Oil is so widely used as a fuel that this can create severe economic problems for the victim of an embargo.

oil price The price of bulk oil, usually quoted in US dollars per barrel. The real oil price drifted downwards in the post-war period, until in 1973–4 the *Organization of Petroleum Exporting Countries (OPEC) increased it by a factor of four. This set off a severe bout of worldwide inflation, and the real price of oil since the 1970s has fluctuated substantially, illustrating the tendency of price-fixing cartels to be unstable: each member has an incentive to raise output and several OPEC members have done precisely this when in need of additional income.

Okun's law The proposition that in cyclical fluctuations, the ratio of actual to potential real output generally rises by a greater percentage than the fall in unemployment. On the basis of data on the US economy from 1960 to 1980 Arthur Okun (1928–1980) put the ratio of proportional changes in output to those of unemployment at around 3. This effect is believed to be due partly to short-run increasing returns to employment, and partly to a tendency for some workers to drop out from the labour force when laid off, rather than appearing as unemployed.

oligopoly A market supplied by a small number of firms in which the choice of one firm affects the profits of the other firms. The firms are linked by strategic interaction, so market equilibrium is determined by the outcome of strategic considerations. In Cournot oligopoly the strategic variable for each firm is output level. In Bertrand oligopoly the strategic variable is price. The firms in an oligopoly can also engage in *non-price competition through product specifications or advertising. The standard analysis of oligopoly represents the market as a game and computes the *Nash equilibrium. The properties of the Nash equilibrium are dependent on the precise specification of the game. *See also* BERTRAND COMPETITION; COURNOT COMPETITION; MONOPOLISTIC COMPETITION.

oligopsony A market with a small number of buyers in which the choice of one buyer affects the pay-offs of the others. This is the equivalent on the demand side of *oligopoly on the supply side of a market.

ombudsman An official responsible for investigating complaints against the administration of institutions. In the UK the use of the ombudsman system started with government bodies, through the Parliamentary Commissioner for Administration; it has since spread to other areas, including banking, finance, and insurance. An ombudsman's conclusions are not usually legally binding, but have considerable moral force, and disregarding them in particular cases can lead to political pressure for changes in the law.

omitted variable bias A *bias of the least squares estimator caused by the omission of a relevant variable from the regression, when this variable is correlated with one or more of the variables included in the regression.

one-tailed test A test of a statistical hypothesis in which this hypothesis is rejected only for sufficiently large values of the test statistic. It is employed when the direction of the effect tested is known a priori. *See also* TWO-TAILED TEST.

on-the-job training Training by working under supervision by an experienced worker. This is contrasted with training by formal courses of instruction, provided by the employer or an outside body. Many employers make use of both training methods.

opaque policy measures Policy measures where it is difficult to discover what they are, who decides on them, and what they cost. These are contrasted with *transparent policy measures, where these points are relatively clear.

open economy An economy which has transactions with the rest of the world. These may include trade in goods and services, movements of capital, transfers of information and technical know-how, and migration of labour. Most economies are at least partially open for some of these forms of contact. *See also* CLOSED ECONOMY.

open-ended fund A form of *mutual fund which has no restriction on the number of shares that the fund will issue. The fund will continue to issue new shares whenever there is demand from investors.

opening prices The bid and offer prices quoted when stock or commodity markets open on any working day.

open market operations The purchase or sale of securities by the central bank as a means of changing interest rates and the money supply. This is one of the major instruments of *monetary policy. If the central bank buys securities their prices rise, interest rates fall, and the money supply increases. If the central bank sells securities their prices fall, interest rates rise, and the money supply decreases.

open outcry The system of trading in commodities, securities, or currencies by traders meeting together and calling out the trades they are offering. Open outcry is a system for trying to ensure that full information is available on an equal basis to all participants in the market. A similar function is performed in many modern markets by having offers and trades continually reported on screen in a computer network.

open position A situation when a trader in securities, commodities, or currencies is at risk if market prices rise or fall. This may involve selling for future delivery items not either held or hedged by contracts to buy, in which case the trader will make a loss if market prices rise, or contracting to buy without hedging by contracts to sell, in which case the trader will make a loss if market prices fall. An open position is contrasted with covered arbitrage, where contracts are balanced and the trader is not exposed to risk of loss through price changes.

operational research The application of mathematical and statistical methods to the practical problems facing businesses. The techniques used include *linear programming, *critical path analysis, and queuing and inventory analysis. These have been applied to problems including finance, purchasing, production, marketing, delivery systems, and inventory control.

opportunism The tendency for one party to a bargain to attempt to change the terms in their favour once the other party has committed itself. For example, if a firm has incurred sunk costs in installing equipment to fulfil an order, the customer faces the temptation to try to negotiate a lower price, knowing that the supplier has bought specialized machinery with no alternative use. Equally, the supplier may be tempted to demand a higher price, knowing that the customer has left it too late to find an alternative source. Opportunism can be countered either by stringent and enforceable *contracts, or by continuing dealings with the same trading partners, where a reputation for fair dealing is valuable, so that fear of losing it acts as a restraint. *See also* HOLD-UP.

opportunity cost The cost of something in terms of an opportunity forgone. Opportunity cost is given by the benefits that could have been obtained by choosing the best alternative opportunity. For example, for a farmer the opportunity cost of growing wheat is given by what they would have earned if they had grown barley, assuming barley is the best alternative.

optimal control A method of solving a dynamic optimization problem formulated in continuous time. Mathematically, it is a solution of a set of differential equations describing the paths of the control variables which minimize the cost functional associated with the control policy. The solution is derived by using Pontryagin's maximum principle (a necessary condition) or by solving the Hamilton–Jacobi–Bellman equation (a sufficient condition).

optimal growth theory The analysis of the best growth path for an economy. An optimal growth path is determined by balancing the loss of current utility as consumption is reduced to finance investment against the future gain in utility as the benefit from greater investment is realized.

optimal level of pollution The level of pollution that maximizes *social welfare by equating the marginal cost of additional pollution with the marginal benefit. The concept of the optimal level recognizes that there may be benefits to allowing pollution which would be lost were pollution to be eliminated.

optimal taxation The structure of taxation that maximizes *social welfare subject to achieving a given level of tax revenue and meeting informational and *incentive-compatibility constraints. *See also* INVERSE ELASTICITY RULE; RAMSEY RULE.

optimism index In the US, an average based on telephone interviews conducted with approximately 1000 adults nationwide each month by the TIPP poll service. The three questions asked are about the possibility of economic conditions improving, the possibility of personal financial situation improving, and the degree of satisfaction with current economic policies. The index can range from 0 to 100, and is derived by comparing the positive and negative responses while disregarding non-responses (such as 'not sure' or 'no answer').

(((⊕)) SEE WEB LINKS)
• The home page of TIPP.

optimization In economics, the choice from all possible uses of resources of that which gives the best result. This is often represented by the maximization of benefits or the minimization of losses; in general, the objective function describes what is to be optimized. The set of potential choices may be unlimited (unconstrained optimization) or limited (constrained optimization) by resource scarcity, budget constraint, or legal barriers.

optimum currency area The number of countries that maximizes the benefits of using a *single currency. The gain from extending a currency area is the reduction in transaction costs in respect of trade and financial transactions between members, and the reduction in currency risk affecting such transactions. This is greater the larger such transactions are relative to national incomes. The loss is that if the countries are affected by asymmetric *shocks, or have different preferences about any trade-off between stable prices and stable real output, having a single currency removes changes in the exchange rate between them as a possible equilibrating mechanism. For any given level of transaction costs, the net advantage of a single currency is larger the more similar the areas are in their preferences and the shocks they are expected to sustain, and is smaller the more their preferences and expected shocks differ. The desirability of a single currency also depends on the effectiveness of the other available means of adjustment. The more prices are flexible and factors of production are mobile, the less need for exchange rate adjustments, so the greater the net benefits of a single currency.

optimum tariff A *tariff which maximizes a country's welfare, trading off improvement in the *terms of trade against restriction of trade quantities. For a small economy which cannot affect world prices in the markets in which it trades, the optimum tariff is zero. For a country with monopoly power in its export markets or monopsony power in import markets, the optimum tariff is positive, but not so large as to eliminate trade entirely.

option A contract giving the holder the right but not the obligation to trade in a commodity, a share, or a currency on some future date at a pre-agreed price. A European option can only be exercised on the agreed date whereas an American option can be exercised at any time until the agreed date. A 'put' option gives the holder the right to sell at a pre-agreed price. This can be used to reduce risk by somebody who has to hold the actual asset and is worried that its price may fall; it can equally be used to speculate on a price fall. A 'call' option gives the holder the right to buy at a pre-agreed price. This can be used to reduce risk by people who expect to need the asset in the future and are worried that its price may rise before they buy; it can equally be used to speculate on a price rise. An options market is a market in which options are traded; these exist for many widely traded goods, shares, and currencies. Share options give a right to buy company shares at a future date at a pre-agreed price; they are used by companies as incentives for their executives. An option is contrasted with a futures contract, which carries the obligation as well as the right to trade. *See also* CALL OPTION; PUT OPTION; SHARE OPTION.

option value The value of being able to put off decisions. If one invests in a project now one's capital is sunk in it. Market conditions may then change to make the project more or less profitable. If the decision is deferred, one can invest next year if the market improves, or abandon the project if the market worsens. Option value is the expected benefit from delaying a decision. The option value of ability to delay investments helps to explain the existence of *liquidity preference, since holding cash does not commit one to any particular form of future expenditure. If a market is expected to improve rapidly, or there is a danger that competitors may enter it first, option value may be negative, in which case it pays to invest now.

order book The value of orders received but not yet carried out by firms in certain sectors, mainly construction and engineering, where output is mainly produced to order, and not sold off the shelf. The size of an industry's order book may be expressed in cash terms, or as months' output. Changes in order books are a *leading economic indicator.

order-driven market An asset market where the role of intermediaries is matching buy and sell orders. In such a market orders to buy at given prices or below, and to sell at given prices or above, are accumulated until a set time, for example noon daily. A *market clearing price is then determined, and orders consistent with this price are executed. This is contrasted with a quote-driven market, where the role of intermediaries is to act as *market-makers, offering to buy and sell at stated prices, up to some quantity limit, and transactions can take place at any time when the market is open.

order of integration The minimum number of times it is necessary to difference a non-stationary time series to produce a *stationary series. A series which has to be differenced n times is integrated of order n, written $I(n)$. The order of integration can be a fraction, in which case the process is said to be fractionally integrated; fractional differencing is a mathematically convenient representation of an infinite series of lags.

ordinal utility A utility function is ordinal if it can be subjected to any positive strictly monotonic transformation without altering the preferences it represents. Consider the preferences of a consumer depicted by a set of indifference curves. A utility function that represents these preferences can be constructed by assigning a number to each curve, with the numbers having the property that if x is preferred to y then the indifference curve on which x lies is assigned a higher number than the indifference curve on which y lies. The constructed utility function is ordinal. The numbers assigned to the indifference curve can be transformed in any way provided that the ranking of the numbers is retained: if one indifference curve has a higher number before the transformation it must have a higher number after the transformation. Ordinal utility conveys no more information than that contained in the indifference curves. The observation that the utility from choice x is greater than the utility from choice y means only that x lies on a higher indiffererence curve than y. *See also* CARDINAL UTILITY; INTERPERSONAL COMPARISONS.

ordinary least squares (OLS) The simplest linear regression technique. OLS involves fitting a linear equation with the coefficients chosen to minimize the sum of squares of residual errors. In estimating systems of simultaneous equations, where the left-hand variable of each equation appears as a right-hand variable in others, OLS produces biased results, and is replaced by *two-stage least squares, or more sophisticated methods of estimation.

ordinary share The UK term for a share in the equity of a company. The US equivalent term is *common stock. The holder of an ordinary share is entitled to share in any distribution of dividends in proportion to the number of shares held. Ordinary shares usually but not invariably entitle their holder to vote at company meetings. They are contrasted with *debentures and *preference shares. Debenture holders usually have a fixed entitlement to interest, but no vote provided the interest is paid and any other conditions are complied with. Preference shareholders have no votes but must be paid their dividends before any distribution to ordinary shareholders is allowed. In the event of winding up a company, ordinary shareholders rank last in any claim to company assets, but get an unlimited part of any residual there is after paying off the others.

organizational slack *See* SLACK.

Organization for Economic Cooperation and Development (OECD) An international organization set up to assist member states to develop economic and social policies to promote sustained economic growth with financial stability. OECD members have been mainly free-market industrialized countries: in Europe this includes Austria, Belgium, Denmark, Finland, France, Germany, Greece, Iceland, Ireland, Italy, Luxembourg, the Netherlands, Norway, Portugal, Spain, Sweden, Switzerland, and the UK. Outside Europe the OECD includes Australia, Canada, Japan, New Zealand, Turkey, and the United States. Mexico became the first of the *newly industrialized countries to join, in 1993, and the Czech Republic the first former planned economy to join, in 1995.

Organization of Petroleum Exporting Countries (OPEC) An organization of oil-producing countries, set up to coordinate their policies in negotiating with the oil companies. Since 1973 OPEC has attempted to operate a world oil-exporting *cartel, setting an agreed price and allocating export quotas. The members of OPEC have included Algeria, Iran, Iraq, Kuwait, Libya, Nigeria, Saudi Arabia, the United Arab Emirates (UAE), and Venezuela. OPEC's members have had difficulties in agreeing and policing a joint monopoly policy, and the real price of oil has fluctuated considerably since the 1970s.

organized labour That part of the labour force that belongs to *trade unions. Trade unions often negotiate pay, hours of work, and working conditions for their members and aim to obtain better terms from employers than workers could obtain by individual bargaining. Trade unions also represent and assist their members in disputes over discipline, sick leave, or redundancy. Organized labour may also engage in political activities, in particular those aimed at ensuring that the legal and social security systems are arranged for the benefit of workers rather than employers. *See also* INSIDERS AND OUTSIDERS.

organized sector Those parts of the economy which operate through institutions which feed figures into official statistics. This includes firms organized as companies, payments made via the banking system, incomes reported to the tax authorities, sales reported to the VAT authorities, and employment reported to the National Insurance authorities. These constitute the vast majority of total economic activity in advanced economies. The organized sector is contrasted with the informal or *hidden economy, in which individuals, voluntary bodies, and criminal organizations engage in trade, mainly for cash, which is not reported to the tax authorities, and employment, also for cash, which is not reported to the tax or social security authorities.

origin principle of taxation An international trade policy according to which goods and services are taxed in the country of production, regardless of the country of consumption. The advantages are a lower potential for tax fraud and an absence of need for border controls on trade flow, since exports do not travel tax-free. The disadvantage is the possibility for the tax system to discriminate between domestically produced goods and imports. *See also* DESTINATION PRINCIPLE OF TAXATION.

outlier An entry in a set of statistical data which lies a long way from any pattern apparent in the rest of the data set. The presence of an outlier suggests two possibilities which warrant further investigation. One is that something really exceptional occurred to cause it; such an occurrence is a shock. The other possibility is that the outlier occurred because of a mistake in recording or processing the data.

output The result of an economic process that has used inputs to produce a product or service that is available for sale or use elsewhere. *See also* DEMAND-DETERMINED OUTPUT; POTENTIAL OUTPUT.

output effect The effect of a rise in output on the use of any particular input, holding input prices constant. Where the most economical proportion in which to combine inputs varies with the level of output, a rise in output causes use of some inputs to increase proportionally more than others.

output method The method of calculating domestic product using information on the net outputs of various sectors of the economy. Two other methods are the *expenditure method, which uses information on the expenditures of various sectors of the economy including consumers, investors, and the government, and the *income method, which proceeds by adding up the incomes of the various factors of production.

output per hour worked A measure of output per unit of labour input. Output may be measured in physical quantities, or in value terms. Output per hour worked is used in comparisons of productivity in different plants, firms, or countries. Variations occur because of differences in the skill and experience of the labour force, the degree of effort, the amount and age of capital equipment, and the level of managerial competence and technical expertise.

outside money Money which is an asset to those who hold it, but is not a liability for anybody else in the economy. This is the case for gold coinage, but not for bank balances. Outside money is contrasted with *inside money, where the asset for the holder is balanced by a liability of the bank issuing the money. It is a matter of definition whether money which is a government liability is outside or inside money.

outsourcing The practice of buying goods and services from outside suppliers, rather than producing them within a firm. This is widespread among both firms and government agencies. Outsourcing may be used because specialist outside suppliers can apply more specialized skills, and can benefit from economies of scale or scope not available within the firm that make the product cheaper. It may also be used because adjusting output to variations in demand and maintaining the quality of inputs may be easier via enforcing contracts with outside suppliers than in dealing with a unionized internal workforce.

over-capacity working Production in a firm or an industry above what is normally regarded as its *capacity. This is possible because capacity itself is calculated on a conventional basis relative to a standard set of working conditions. It is possible to boost output temporarily above normal capacity levels in an emergency, by working more than the normal number of shifts, deferring staff holidays and training and maintenance of equipment, or making use of obsolete equipment which is so expensive to operate that it is not normally counted as part of capacity.

overdraft A negative balance in a bank account, so that the customer owes the bank money. This is often allowed only by prior arrangement, though customers with a good credit record may be allowed to overdraw without prior arangement. Overdrafts are allowed only up to a set limit, and incur interest and possibly extra service charges for the customer.

overfull employment In *Keynesian economics this is a level of employment that is above the *natural rate of unemployment. Difficulty in filling job vacancies causes wages to rise, and labour scarcity results in shortages of goods and services, so prices rise. Overfull employment thus produces and accelerates *demand inflation. Inflation leads to policy reactions designed to slow it; and the effect of inflation on expectations reduces the power of excess demand to elicit higher levels of real activity. Overfull employment is thus not permanently sustainable. Because of *frictional unemployment and *structural unemployment, overfull employment does not imply zero unemployment. The level of demand at which overfull employment sets in is itself a function of the organization of the labour market and social security system, the degree of monopoly in an economy, and the attitudes of its price- and wage-setters.

overhead costs Fixed costs a business must incur for production to be possible. Overheads may be avoidable in the short run, if output is temporarily cut to zero; or they may be avoidable only in the long run, if the possibility of future production is given up. They may include sunk or irrecoverable costs, which cannot be saved even if the firm is permanently closed down.

overheating In *Keynesian economics this is a level of activity leading to excess demand. High output levels relative to capacity, at least in some important sectors, lead to shortages of factor inputs, or unusually high levels of imports.

Overheating produces inflationary pressure internally and a deterioration in the trade balance externally; by causing devaluation of the currency this gives a further boost to inflation.

overlapping generations economy An economic model in which individual agents have finite lives, but each lives for more than one period. In each period there will be a new generation of agents who were not there before, and an old generation for whom this is their final period. If the economy is assumed to continue indefinitely an overlapping generations economy has the special feature that the number of consumers and the number of goods are both infinite when the entire lifespan of the economy is taken into account. As a consequence of this double-infinity the competitive equilibrium of an overlapping generations economy can be Pareto inefficient. Overlapping generations models are widely used in analysing savings behaviour, pension schemes, and security markets. *See also* DYNAMIC INEFFICIENCY; GOLDEN RULE.

overmanning The excessive use of labour in any business. It may be imposed by law, or may result from collective bargaining or from managerial choice. Management may choose overmanning through incompetence, or in the belief that demand is likely to expand in the future, and that it is cheaper to hoard labour for the time being than to lay off redundant workers now and have to recruit and train replacements in the future.

overseas bank The UK term for a foreign bank with a branch or subsidiary in the UK, usually in London.

overseas investment *See* FOREIGN INVESTMENT.

overshooting The possibility that after a *shock to the economy, some variables will move further in the short run than it is necessary for them to adjust in the long run. This occurs because of differences in speeds of adjustment of different variables. *See also* EXCHANGE RATE OVERSHOOTING.

over-stimulation In *Keynesian economics this is the adoption of monetary and fiscal policies that increase the level of *effective demand so far that inflation begins to speed up, or substantial balance-of-trade deficits occur.

over-subscription The situation when the number of shares applied for in a *new issue exceeds the number on offer. This means that some applications have to be refused, and makes it likely that when the market opens the shares will stand at a premium over the issue price.

over-the-counter market A market in securities not regulated by an *exchange.

overtime Work in excess of the working hours per week specified by an employment contract.

overtime ban A refusal by employees to work for more than normal working hours. This is used in *industrial disputes to inconvenience employers, and to press them to increase the numbers employed, in particular to avoid *redundancies.

While an overtime ban reduces workers' pay, it causes a much less severe drop in their incomes than a strike.

overtrading Carrying on business on too large a scale for a firm's capital. This creates a high risk that the firm will be unable to meet its commitments if it encounters temporary problems, for example delay in obtaining payments due from a debtor. Also, it may have to pay high interest rates for credit, since the shortage of capital makes lending to it risky. For a private firm overtrading is harmful to itself, and is discouraged by its bankers and creditors. For banks and some other financial intermediaries overtrading can significantly affect the public, as failure of one institution might be contagious and start a general financial panic. Bank regulators therefore try to prevent overtrading by requiring minimum levels of *capital adequacy.

over-valued currency A currency whose *exchange rate is too high for a sustainable equilibrium in the balance of payments. With no capital movements a currency is overvalued if its exchange rate is too high to produce a balanced current account. With autonomous capital movements a currency is overvalued if its exchange rate is too high to produce a current account deficit that can be financed by a sustainable flow of inward capital movements. A currency can be held for some time at an overvalued rate by using high interest rates to induce inward short-term capital flows, but this causes external debt to rise at a rate which is not permanently sustainable. High interest rates needed to prop up an overvalued currency are also unlikely to be consistent with internal balance in the economy.

owner-occupied housing The system by which a house or flat is owned by its occupants. This is in contrast to *rented housing, where the owner and the occupant are different people. Owner-occupied housing is the largest single form of housing tenure in the UK and many other industrial countries.

ownership The right to exclusive use of an asset. The owner of an asset normally has the right to decide what use shall be made of it, and cannot be deprived of it except by law. The state, however, claims the right to regulate the use of many assets, and to tax income derived from them. The use that can be made of land and buildings is subject to planning permission, and rent from them is subject to income tax. The state also has rights of compulsory purchase of land needed for public works. Other people have contractual rights over assets, such as tenancies; and the general public has some rights, for example public rights of way. The extent to which ownership confers exclusive control over the use of an asset is thus a matter of degree. *See also* PUBLIC OWNERSHIP.

ozone layer A layer of the stratosphere protecting the Earth's surface from harmful radiation. Depletion of this layer is believed to be caused by human activities, the use of chlorofluorocarbons (CFCs), halon, and other chemicals releasing chlorine molecules which, with a delay of around a decade, affect the stratosphere. Control of emissions requires global agreement, since each user of CFCs benefits from its own activities while most of the resulting damage affects the world as a whole. An agreement to replace CFCs and halon was reached in 1987 in the *Montreal Protocol.

Paasche index *See* CURRENT-WEIGHTED INDEX.

package of policies A number of *policy instruments introduced simultaneously. Governments employ packages of policies for two reasons: minimization of side-effects, and uncertainty about the effects of particular policy measures. Any economic policy, such as changing the interest rate, is bound to have side-effects which are not wanted as well as the effects for whose sake the policy is adopted. The use of any single policy measure implies that it must be used strongly. This can produce significant side-effects which are both unwanted and noticeable: for example, sudden large changes in interest rates may destabilize some financial intermediaries. If several measures are used, each at a moderate level, the side-effects may be smaller and less detectable. Also, there is often uncertainty about the size and timing of the effects of particular policy measures. Use of a mixture raises the chance that some at least will produce effects fairly quickly.

paid-up capital The part of the authorized capital of a company that has actually been paid by shareholders. The difference may arise because not all shares authorized have been issued, or because issued shares are only partly paid up.

panel data Data collected over several time periods on a number of individual units. Commonly used methods of analysis of panel data include *pooled least squares, *fixed effects, and *random effects.

paradox of thrift The argument that a rise in the *ex ante propensity to save, that is, the share of incomes that people want to save, may not increase the *ex post level of savings and investment in the economy, which may even decrease. The basis of the argument is that in a depressed economy attempts to save more from present incomes reduce consumption and thus income levels. The fall in incomes then discourages investment, so that ex post savings and investment actually fall: this is the paradox of thrift. The opposing argument says that in a prosperous economy, at any given income level, having more savings available makes it either easier or cheaper to borrow to finance investment; the fall in consumption thus 'crowds in' investment, so that ex post incomes are unchanged and savings and investment rise. The arguments for and against the paradox of thrift each appear to be capable of being correct in some circumstances; which actually applies in any particular situation is a matter of fact.

paradox of voting The observation that the level of voter turnout is inconsistent with rational decision-making on whether or not to vote. The act of voting involves a benefit and a cost to the voter. A benefit is derived if the voter changes the outcome of the election to the one that is desired (in such a case, the voter is said to be pivotal). The probability of this happening is very low so the expected benefit is small. The costs of voting include the use of time and direct travel costs. Calculations show that the cost is typically much larger than the expected benefit. A rational voter should therefore not vote. The paradox is that electoral turnout is relatively high. Possible explanations include irrationality, *social customs, and social duties. *See also* COLLECTIVE CHOICE; MAJORITY VOTING.

parameter In an economic model, a quantity which is taken as given by an economic agent in their decision-making process. Changes in the outcome in response to a small change in some parameter can be analysed using the *comparative statics approach.

Pareto distribution A continuous distribution of the form

$$f(x) = \beta\alpha^{\beta}/(x^{\beta+1})$$

for $\alpha < x < \infty$ and $\alpha > 0$, $\beta > 0$. It is commonly used to model the distribution of wealth across individuals; in this case β is called the Pareto index and is inversely related to the *Gini coefficient, $G = 1/(2\beta - 1)$, so that the smaller values of β correspond to a more unequal distribution. The Pareto distribution has a finite mean if $\beta > 1$ and a finite variance if $\beta > 2$.

Pareto efficiency A form of efficiency for an economic allocation. An allocation is *Pareto efficient if there is no feasible reallocation that can raise the welfare of one economic agent without lowering the welfare of some other economic agent. The concept of Pareto efficiency can be applied to any economic allocation whether it emerges from trade, bargaining, strategic interaction, or government imposition. The First Theorem of Welfare Economics states that the equilibrium of a *competitive economy is Pareto efficient. This is often explained in terms of efficiency in consumption (allocation of commodities between consumers), production (allocation of inputs between firms), and product mix (the composition of output from firms). The outcome of bargaining need not be Pareto efficient if there is *asymmetric information, but Pareto efficiency is usually imposed as a characteristic of a good bargaining mechanism. The *Nash equilibrium of a strategic game also need not be Pareto efficient. This occurs in games such as the *prisoners' dilemma because of the conflict between private and social rationality. It has to be stressed that even if an equilibrium is Pareto efficient it may not be equitable.

Pareto efficient The term applied to describe an allocation that satisfies the conditions required for *Pareto efficiency.

Pareto law (80–20 law, law of the vital few) The law states that 80 percent of the effects are achieved by 20 percent of the causes. Historically, the law originates from the observation made by the economist Vilfredo Pareto (1848–1923) that 80 percent of the land in Italy was owned by 20 percent of the population. The Pareto law has been claimed to have widespread socio-economic applicability. The practical interpretation of the Pareto law is that beyond a certain threshold the marginal cost of improving the situation further becomes prohibitively expensive.

Paris Club *See* GROUP OF TEN.

partial adjustment A process of adjustment where decision-takers aim to remove in any one period only part of any discrepancy between the actual level and their target level of the variables they control. Partial adjustment is adopted for two reasons: costs of adjustment and uncertainty. If costs of adjustment rise more than proportionally with the speed of adjustment, it is cheaper to spread any required adjustment out over several periods. Some adjustment costs do take this form: for example, a gradual fall in the labour force can be achieved through *natural wastage while a rapid fall requires redundancies, which are costly and unpopular; and a gradual rise in the labour force poses fewer problems of recruitment and training than a sudden large increase. The other motive for partial adjustment is uncertainty. The target for any variable has to be based on available information. Gradual adjustment allows time to gather further information to check whether an apparent change in circumstances is permanent or only temporary.

partial autocorrelation coefficient For lag k, the last coefficient in the linear regression of Y_t on $Y_{t-1}, \ldots, Y_{t-k}$.

partial autocorrelation function (PACF) A sequence of the *partial autocorrelation coefficients as a function of the lag length.

partial equilibrium The method of analysis dealing with some part of the economy, deliberately ignoring possible implications of changes in this part for what happens in the rest of the economy. In studying the effects of changes in the supply and demand for a particular good on its equilibrium price and quantity a partial equilibrium analysis ignores changes in the rest of the economy, due, for example, to consequent changes in income distribution. Partial equilibrium analysis is most useful when events in the sector studied have only small effects in the rest of the economy.

participation rate The percentage of the population in any given age group who are economically active, either as employees, self-employed, or unemployed, on the assumption that the unemployed would all work if jobs were available. Participation rates can be calculated for different categories of workers. Participation rates tend to vary with age, being lower among the young, many of whom are still in full-time education, and among the old, who are frequently retired; they are highest among those aged 20–50.

partnership A business which has more than one owner but is not incorporated, the individual partners remaining fully responsible for its debts. Partners need not all be equal: in professional partnerships it is common for senior partners to get a larger share of the rewards and do a smaller share of the routine work than junior partners. The senior partners' contribution is their capital, experience, and reputation. Partners may also be either active participants in the business, or 'sleeping partners', who provide capital, reputation, or guarantees while other partners do most of the work.

part-time work Working for fewer than the number of hours per week normal for full-time workers in the country and occupation concerned. This may suit the preferences of employers or employees. Employers may prefer part-time to full-time work because it fits the time pattern of their need for labour, or offers more flexibility. Employers may also prefer part-time workers if they enjoy less stringent legal protection than full-time workers, or tax and social security contributions for them are lower. Workers may prefer part-time work because this is convenient given other claims on their time: for example, parents with young children, part-time students, or voluntary workers.

par value The stated value or face value of a financial security.

patent A legal device to encourage and reward *invention by giving exclusive rights to inventors. In many countries the inventor of a new product or process can apply for a patent, giving the holder the exclusive right for a number of years to produce the good or use the process. This right can be used either through their own business, or by charging a licence fee to other users. A patent grants monopoly power with the intention that the flow of profit is sufficient to reward the innovator and to provide an incentive to create inventions. The granting of patents trades the static inefficiency of monopoly against the dynamic gains from increased innovation.

paternalism The attitude favouring laws and policies which seek to control people's actions, overriding their preferences for their own good. An example is a central planner whose utility, or welfare function, depends on the decision variables of the individual agents, rather than on their utility levels. In the *overlapping generations economy the paternalistic altruism of a parent is modelled, for example, by including in their utility function the lifetime consumption or income of their offspring, rather than the offspring's utility level; the latter approach is non-paternalistic altruism.

path dependence A concept according to which economic processes do not progress towards a unique predetermined equilibrium but instead reach one of many equilibria, depending on the process of getting there along a particular path. It implies irreversibility of the effect of transitory random shocks, or accidental events, upon the long-run outcome, which is termed *hysteresis.

pay as you earn (PAYE) The UK system of collection of *income tax on earned incomes at source. Employers are required by law to deduct personal income tax and National Insurance contributions from their employees' earnings at the time of payment, and forward the tax and contributions collected to *HM Revenue and Customs (HMRC). This increases the speed and reliability of the government's income tax revenue collection. The PAYE system transfers part of the administrative burden of income taxation from HMRC onto employers.

pay-as-you-go pension A pension scheme where the pensions of the retired are paid from current contributions. A pay-as-you-go pension scheme involves a direct transfer from the working to the retired. The pension scheme does not own any assets and the flow of funds into the scheme must match the flow of funds out. In contrast, with a *fully-funded pension scheme current pensions are paid out of a fund accumulated from the contributions made by the retired during their working lives or by their employers. If a country starts from a pay-as-you-go pension scheme, changing over to a funded scheme is difficult, since those whose working lives fall in the transition period will have to pay twice over, once to pay the pensions of the previous generation and again to build up a fund to pay their own pensions.

pay-back period The time period over which a firm requires that it earns the cost of new equipment in profits if it is to invest. Pay-back period is not an economically rational investment criterion: it passes a project which brings in 101 percent of its cost in the first N years and nothing thereafter, even though the *present discounted value of the expected profits is well below 100 percent, and fails a project which brings in only 99 percent of its cost in the first N years, but is expected to do so well later that its present discounted value is 200 percent of costs.

pay control Control over wage rates, as part of a *prices and incomes policy. As there are many different wage rates, no control body could actually determine them all from first principles: pay control has usually been content with limiting increases, either to some percentage or some flat-rate increase. A *pay freeze is a particularly drastic form of pay control where the target rate of increase is set at zero.

PAYE *See* PAY AS YOU EARN.

pay freeze A total standstill on wage rates imposed as part of a *prices and incomes policy. This can only be temporary. The structure of wage rates at the moment a freeze is imposed is likely to contain anomalies (due to the exact timing of the *wage–price spiral in the period leading up to the freeze) which cause pressure for change. The structure of wages also needs continual adjustment in the face of changes in techniques and tastes in the economy.

payments in kind Payment of employees in goods or services rather than money. Standard arguments of *welfare economics suggest that in the absence of tax-related motives, it is more efficient to pay workers in money and allow them to choose what to buy. If they choose the same goods as they would have received in kind, they are no worse off, and if they choose any other set of goods they are better off with cash payment. In the UK payment of wages in kind is illegal, but many *fringe benefits are provided in kind. Tax rules may make this privately beneficial, if it attracts less tax than a cash payment of equal value.

payments union An arrangement by two or more countries to pool their *foreign exchange reserves. The advantage of this is that it reduces the total reserves they need to hold, and sets them free to trade with one another without worrying about the effects on their reserves. The disadvantage is that they need to entrust their monetary policy to a combined central bank, or to agree on coordinated monetary policies. Unless this is done, there is a potential conflict between individual and group incentives.

pay-off matrix A matrix showing the pay-offs to each player in a two-player game. Usually the strategies available to the 'row player' are shown to the left of the matrix and the strategies available to the 'column player' are shown above the matrix. A choice of strategy for the row player and for the column player uniquely identifies a box in the matrix. Each box in the pay-off matrix contains two numbers. The number to the left is the pay-off of the row player and the number to the right is the pay-off to the column player. A pay-off matrix conforming to this description is shown below.

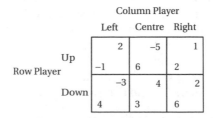

In the special case of a *zero-sum game the pay-offs to one player are equal and opposite to those of the other, so only one set needs to be shown explicitly.

payroll A list of those employed by a given firm, or the amount paid to them.

payroll tax A tax on wage payments. The UK's National Insurance contributions, for example, are a payroll tax. Many other countries have similar taxes, which make up a large part of the *tax wedge between the costs of employment and wages received. Payroll taxes tend to discourage employment by raising the cost of labour relative to the cost of capital.

peace dividend The resources made available for other purposes if a reduction in international tension allows cuts in defence expenditure. In this context 'peace' refers to a reduction in aggressive intentions towards other countries and/or fears of aggressive conduct from them, rather than formal agreements with them.

peak The highest point of a fluctuation. Where an economic variable has a trend, it may be necessary to distinguish between a peak in the sense of an absolute local maximum, and in the sense of a maximum relative to trend, i.e. a peak in the detrended data. If a country's real *gross domestic product (GDP) has a trend growth rate of 3 percent, for example, one may wish to identify as a peak in the business cycle a year following which GDP growth falls below 3 percent, even though it is still rising in absolute terms.

peak-load pricing A price structure in which more is charged for units supplied at peak-load periods than for units supplied at other times. The argument for peak-load pricing is that the total *capacity needed for a power, transport, or telephone system is determined by the maximum output it has to provide. If demand fluctuates daily or seasonally, charging higher prices at times of peak-loading makes prices reflect the extra capacity costs imposed by peak-period users. It also gives an incentive for customers who can avoid the peak period at low cost to themselves to do so.

pecuniary externality An *externality that is felt through prices rather than through quantities. Migration of workers into a country will increase labour supply and lower wages. This is a pecuniary externality for the native workers of the country who suffer from reduced real income. In the presence of competitive markets such an externality does not create an inefficiency, since price mediation leads to a Pareto-efficient outcome.

pendulum arbitration Arbitration in which two sides set out their proposals and the arbitrator is required to choose between them. The parties could be trade unions and employers, or firms involved in a commercial dispute. Frequently arbitrators work by splitting the difference between the parties' claims, so that it pays each party to make exaggerated demands. Pendulum arbitration is designed to avoid this problem by giving each party an incentive to make proposals which the arbitrator will regard as more fair and reasonable than the other side's suggestions.

pension A regular income paid by the state to people above pensionable age, by former employers to people who have retired from employment, or by a personal pension fund to a contributor. State pensions may be conditional on having made contributions to an insurance fund during one's working life. Occupational pensions may be contributory or non-contributory. Pension schemes normally give members pensions for their own lives; they vary in their provision for surviving spouses and other dependants. The self-employed can purchase personal pensions via insurance companies. *See also* OCCUPATIONAL PENSION; PAY-AS-YOU-GO PENSION; PORTABLE PENSION.

pensionable age The age at which a pension becomes payable, from the state or an occupational pension scheme. This varies between occupations and countries, and in the UK, as well as in many other countries, between men and women.

pension crisis A forecast deficit in existing pension systems, mostly in developed countries, caused by demographic and social changes resulting in the ageing of the population and an increase in the *dependency ratio. Three factors in the pension crisis are the fall in the birth rate, increased longevity, and a tendency for the retirement age to fall.

pension fund A fund from which pensions are paid. Pension funds receive contributions from employers, employees, or both. The funds are then invested to generate income and accrue capital gains until the pensions are paid. Pension schemes may be fully funded, when the fund is actuarially solvent; or partially funded, when the fund relies on the employers to make up the sums necessary to pay for the promised pensions. Pension funds are held by trustees, but these are usually nominated by the employers, and often invest part or all of the accumulated funds in the employer's business.

pension rights Rights to receive pensions, from the state or from former employers. The value of pension rights refers to the actuarial value of expected pension receipts, given the age and other individual characteristics of the pensioner; what is received in any individual case depends on how long they survive to draw the pension. Pension rights are one of the main forms of personal wealth in modern societies. They are, however, a rather illiquid form of wealth: it is not easy to use them as collateral for borrowing.

pension scheme *See* CONTRIBUTORY PENSION SCHEME; NON-CONTRIBUTORY PENSION SCHEME; UNDER-FUNDED PENSION SCHEME; UNFUNDED PENSION SCHEME.

PEP *See* PERSONAL EQUITY PLAN.

per capita income The national income of a country, or region, divided by its population. Per capita income can be calculated per person, counting everybody; per adult; or per 'adult equivalent', using weights to count children of various ages as equivalent to fractions of an adult. Countries or regions with a high proportion of children rank lower when per capita income is compared using a measure which gives more weight to children than using income per adult.

per capita real GDP A country's real *gross domestic product per member of the population. This may be calculated using the total population, adults only, or 'adult equivalents', giving children of various ages weights equal to a fraction of an adult. Per capita real GDP is lower than per capita income in a country with net external assets which yield an income, and greater than per capita income in a country with a lot of inward investment, so that net property income payments have to be made abroad.

percentile *See* QUANTILE.

perestroika A system of economic reforms, or restructuring ('perestroika' in Russian), initiated in the Soviet Union in 1987 by the newly appointed leader Mikhail Gorbachev (b. 1931) and his economic advisers, that aimed at relaxing strict centralized planning of production and distribution and allowed private ownership of enterprises.

perfect capital mobility A situation when capital is able to move without cost between countries. If this occurred, the risk-adjusted returns to capital, net of tax, would be equal in all countries. Perfect capital mobility is prevented partly by controls on capital movements, and partly by lack of information about foreign countries, which makes the risks of investment or lending abroad appear greater than those for home country activities.

perfect competition An idealized market situation in which all information is known to all market participants, and both buyers and sellers are so numerous that each is a price-taker, able to buy or sell any desired quantity without affecting the market price. It was once thought that these were the assumptions necessary to describe a *competitive economy. This is not the case. Provided all market participants have symmetric information and act as if they were price-takers then the competitive equilibrium will emerge. Perfect competition is now an outdated concept since it invokes untenable and unnecessary assumptions.

perfect foresight The correct prediction of future events. If there is no uncertainty then an agent can have perfect foresight if they know all relevant information and have a correct model to use for prediction. When there is uncertainty it is not possible to have perfect foresight. Instead, the relevant concept is that of *rational expectations.

perfect market A market in which the conditions for *perfect competition are satisfied and a homogeneous commodity is traded.

perfect substitute A good which is indistinguishable in use from another. If two goods are perfect substitutes, their prices (per comparable unit) must be the same if both are to be used: the *elasticity of substitution between them is infinite, and any price difference will lead to all consumers choosing the cheaper. An *indifference curve between them is a straight line. Goods may be perfect substitutes in some but not all uses.

performance-related pay Pay related to the output or profits of the employer. This typically takes the form of bonuses over some agreed rate if the firm does well. Pay may be related to the performance of the firm as a whole, to that of a division or part of a firm, or to team or individual results if these can be measured. The argument for performance-related pay is that it provides motivation for effort and cooperation to maximize results for the firm, and that it is good for morale if staff get more when profits are good. An argument against it is that it transfers part of the risks of a firm to its workers, who if they are risk-averse might prefer incomes which were smaller on average, but safer.

peril point A point where any further reduction in US tariffs would, in the opinion of the US Tariff Commission, lower import prices to a level threatening the continued existence of the US domestic industry.

period of gestation The period between the start of an investment project and the time when production using it can start. Because this period is usually quite long, particularly for major investment projects, expectations about market conditions when the project is complete may be uncertain; long gestation periods make investment both riskier and more difficult to predict.

periphery An outlying region of an economy, with poor communications and sparse population, which hinder its prosperity. The periphery is contrasted with the *core, central regions with good communications and high population density. Poor facilities in the periphery provoke outward *migration and deter investment which causes the differences between the periphery and the core to increase unless there is offsetting policy intervention. Small populations also give peripheral regions low voting power, which causes government policies to be less responsive to peripheral than to core needs.

permanent income The component of lifetime income that is anticipated and planned by a consumer. It is determined by a consumer's physical and human capital, as both of these affect the consumer's ability to earn income during his or her lifetime. Any part of income that is not anticipated and/or planned is *transitory income. The *permanent income hypothesis suggests that consumption constitutes a constant proportion of permanent income (the process of 'consumption smoothing'), and that transitory changes in income do not affect long-run spending behaviour.

permanent income hypothesis The hypothesis that the level of consumption depends upon the level of *permanent income. The implication of the permanent income hypothesis is that the flow of consumption over time will be smooth even if the flow of income is not. Expressed alternatively, income can be viewed as having a permanent component and a transitory component. Consumption will only respond to changes in the permanent component and not to changes in the transitory component.

permit to pollute A permit allowing the emission of a given quantity of pollution to the atmosphere, rivers, or the sea. One possible method of restricting pollution is to issue a limited quantity of permits to pollute, and forbid pollution without a permit. If the permits are tradable this means that the limited amount of pollution allowed will be allocated to those firms for which the costs of avoiding it are greatest. If permits are not tradable, the limited amount of pollution will be less efficiently allocated, and the permits will act as restrictions on entry to the industries concerned. Permits to pollute are an alternative to a tax per unit of pollution. If pollution standards are tightened, allocating tradable permits to pollute to firms in proportion to their past emissions gives them some compensation for the tightened standards. *See also* COASE THEOREM; POLLUTION CONTROL.

perpetual inventory method The method of estimating a country's total *capital stock, starting from the level of real investment in each past year. Investment is classified by type of capital goods, such as buildings, plant and machinery, and vehicles. An appropriate rate of *write-off each year, based on the estimated lives of the various goods, is applied to each type of capital. The present capital stock is taken to be equal to the sum of past investments, written down in this way. The perpetual inventory method is contrasted with attempts to measure directly the actual levels of different types of capital goods in the economy.

perpetuity A security which yields an income for ever.

perquisites Payments in kind attached to jobs. These may be of various forms; company cars, company sports facilities, and company medical facilities or insurance are common, and there are some idiosyncratic ones, such as company boxes at the opera. These perquisites are provided openly and some are taxed; others are subject to periodic attempts by *HM Revenue and Customs to tax them.

personal disposable income Personal income after deduction of income tax and National Insurance contributions. This is the sum available to be divided between personal consumption and saving.

personal equity plan (PEP) A UK system, established in 1986, by which individuals could invest a limited sum each tax year in shares and unit trusts, through a financial intermediary. PEP investments were then free from both income and capital gains tax, subject to a minimum holding period. The financial intermediaries charged for their services in managing PEPs. PEPs were introduced to encourage savings, and to promote individual involvement in the company sector. They were replaced by *Individual Savings Accounts in 1999.

personal income distribution The distribution of income across individuals. This can be measured before or after the deduction of *direct taxes and receipt of income transfers. Personal income distribution is distinguished from *functional income distribution, which is concerned with the division of total incomes between the owners of different factors of production.

Personal Investment Authority (PIA) A UK self-regulating organization under the *Securities and Investment Board, responsible for regulating the branches of the investment business dealing mainly with private investors. The PIA was formed in 1994 by merging the Financial Intermediaries, Managers and Brokers Regulatory Association and the Life Assurance and Unit Trust Regulatory Organization. The functions of the PIA were taken over by the *Financial Services Authority in December 2001.

personal loan A loan, usually from a bank, to an individual, who is not necessarily required to produce any specific collateral for it. Personal loans are widely used to finance the purchase of expensive items such as cars and furniture, and are usually a cheaper method of financing than *hire purchase. Repayment is usually at an agreed rate over a period of months or years. Personal loans are riskier for the lenders than *secured loans such as *mortgages, and normally bear higher interest rates.

personal preferences Individual tastes, as regards both consumption and work. Personal preferences determine the *indifference curves of an individual, and differences in preferences among individuals are reflected in differences in their indifference curves. Personal preferences combine with the *budget constraint to determine choices.

personal sector The part of the UK economy consisting of households, unincorporated businesses, life assurance and pension funds, and private non-profit-making bodies serving persons, such as charities. This is distinguished from the corporate sector, consisting of companies, financial institutions and public corporations, and the government sector.

peso problem The tendency in countries with a past history of high inflation for interest rates to remain higher than abroad. This problem occurs where experience of inflation and currency depreciation in the past has led to expectations that the future will be similar. Even if such a country succeeds in stabilizing its price level and exchange rate, until market expectations adjust to this new stability, interest rates remain higher than in countries whose currencies are expected to remain stable. An interest premium is needed to compensate both domestic and foreign investors for the risk they feel exposed to when holding a currency whose stability they mistrust. The name 'peso problem' links it to Mexico, but many other countries, including the UK, have suffered from the same problem.

petro-currency The currency of a country heavily dependent on oil exports. The exchange rate of a petro-currency is strongly influenced by the world price of oil.

petro-dollars Balance-of-payments surpluses of oil-exporting countries which were invested abroad, often in securities denominated in US dollars.

Phillips curve An inverse relationship between inflation and unemployment. The original Phillips curve depicted the rate of increase of nominal wages against unemployment. The model has been extended to take account of inflationary expectations: inflation is considered low or high relative to *expected inflation, whereas unemployment is considered low or high relative to the *natural rate of unemployment, at which inflation equals expected inflation. The short-run *expectations-augmented Phillips curve plots actual inflation against unemployment, with given inflation expectations. In the long run it is assumed that *rational expectations lead the expected inflation rate to equal the actual rate, so that the long-run Phillips curve is very steep or even vertical at the *non-accelerating inflation rate of unemployment (NAIRU).

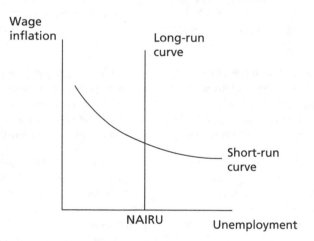

Phillips Curve

physical capital Capital in the form of physical goods, either fixed capital or stocks and work in progress. Physical capital is contrasted with both financial and human capital. Financial capital includes both cash holdings of firms, and net trade credit extended to customers. *Human capital includes both technical know-how, whether or not embodied in *patents, and the skills of the workforce. The ability of economies to recover rapidly after wars and natural disasters is thought to indicate that physical capital is less important than human capital as a long-run determinant of productivity.

phytosanitary measures Restrictions on trade designed to protect the health of humans, animals, or plants. While some restrictions on trade are necessary to prevent the spread of diseases such as BSE or foot-and-mouth disease, there is a danger that restrictions purporting to be phytosanitary will be used to protect domestic producers of the goods concerned.

picketing The procedure during *strikes of placing strikers outside workplaces to inform other workers that they are in dispute, and to attempt to persuade other employees, and those of suppliers and customers, not to enter the premises. Actual picketing can vary between peaceful demonstrations by small numbers of strikers outside their own workplaces, and violent intimidation by large numbers at the premises of firms not involved in a strike ('secondary picketing'). UK law prohibits secondary picketing.

picking winners The idea that governments can promote economic development by selecting particular projects for financial and technical support. This form of industrial strategy only promotes economic growth if the government is better than private investors at picking projects likely to succeed. The strategy runs two risks: the government may support projects which would have been adopted anyway, so that its support merely makes them more profitable; or it may pick too high a proportion of unsuccessful projects. The alternative is for governments to concentrate on providing general technical education to produce a skilled labour force, and promoting efficient financial markets to provide capital, and leave private businesses to select the most suitable particular projects for development.

piecework The system of pay by which a worker's wages are proportional to output produced. This system is suitable only when a worker's output can be reliably measured, and when variations do not arise from factors over which the worker has no control, for example late delivery of materials. It is contrasted with time rates, where pay simply depends on hours worked.

Pigou effect The argument that a fall in prices increases real wealth (the *real balance effect) and raises aggregate demand. The Pigou effect implies that if prices fell sufficiently in a slump, full employment would be restored because of the resulting real balance effect. There are several shortcomings with this argument. In an economy with money debts, large falls in prices would damage the solvency of many firms, and probably cause the collapse of some financial institutions. Perfectly flexible prices and wages might ensure real stability in the economy; if prices and wages fell gradually, however, the prospect of further falls to come would bring the *liquidity trap into play, with adverse effects on real spending, so the short-term effects of greater price and wage flexibility might well make slumps worse.

Pink Book *United Kingdom Balance of Payments*, the annual publication of the *Office for National Statistics, formerly the Central Statistical Office. This is a source of data on UK visible and invisible trade, capital movements, and overseas assets and liabilities.

placing Sale of shares by a UK company to selected individuals or institutions approached directly, rather than by an issue open to the general public. A placing may be preferred on grounds of lower costs, or because it gives the company a chance to choose its new shareholders.

planned economy An economy in which the government takes all major production and distribution decisions. The former Soviet Union and its associated countries provided large-scale examples of planned economies. The results proved unsatisfactory, mainly for two reasons: insufficient individual incentives for productivity, and insufficient (and sometimes distorted) information for taking decisions and controlling performance. Many world economies contain elements of planned economy: in the UK, for example, the government directs several large sectors, including defence, roads, education, and health.

planned investment The amount of investment that firms, individuals, or public bodies intend to make during some period. Actual investment may not correspond to planned investment for various reasons. Fixed investment plans may not be met because the required investment goods or finance cannot be obtained. Investment in stocks may fall short of planned levels because of unforeseen increases in demand, or may exceed planned levels because goods cannot be sold, so that stocks accumulate until production can be cut back.

planned savings The amount that individuals, firms, or governments plan to save. Savings plans may not be carried out for two main reasons. Income may be larger or smaller than expected, and emergencies may arise which require unanticipated spending or prevent spending plans from being carried out. Planned savings should be distinguished from *contractual savings, such as mortgage repayments or life insurance premiums.

planning (land-use) Controls by central or local government over the use of land. These are common, because of the importance of *externalities resulting from land use. Land-use planning is intended to keep activities causing negative externalities, such as noise or visual intrusion, away from places where they are believed to be particularly harmful. Land-use controls typically operate more strictly on changes of use and new activities than on continuation of existing activities.

planning permission Permission granted by local or central government for the owners of land to use it for specific purposes. Typically, permission has to be sought for changes in land use, for example from agriculture to residential use, or from residential to shops or offices. Planning permission for a transfer of land from a less to a more profitable use may increase land values.

player The term used in *game theory for any participant in a strategic situation being modelled. A player is any individual, firm, or government that has to make a choice between different *strategies.

PLC *See* PUBLIC LIMITED COMPANY.

plough-back The system of financing investment in firms by retaining profits. This is contrasted with financing investment by borrowing or issuing new *equity capital. The advantage of plough-back is that it retains control, and reduces *gearing if the firm has borrowed in the past. The disadvantage is that complete reliance on internal finance limits a firm's possible growth rate, and it cannot be applied in new firms.

point elasticity The ratio of a proportional change in one variable to that of another, measured at a point. For example, if p is price and q is quantity, the price elasticity of demand, ε_d, is defined as $\varepsilon_d = (p/q)(dq/dp)$. The point elasticity is the limit of the *arc elasticity as the length of the arc tends to zero.

points (change in index) The change in an index in terms of the units in which it is measured. If a stock exchange index, for example, moves from 500 to 505, it rises by 5 points. This is contrasted with the percentage increase, which is $5/500 = 1$ percent.

polarization The rule introduced by the UK Securities and Investment Board that bodies such as banks and building societies must choose either to give independent advice on all brands of *life insurance and *unit trusts, or confine themselves to selling the products of only one company. The intention was to ensure either that advice was truly independent, or that customers were aware that it was not. The actual effect may have been to reduce the amount of information available to consumers of investment products.

policy coordination The collaborative choice of policy by two or more policy-makers. Policy coordination between countries can be justified by the argument that national fiscal and monetary policies would produce better results if countries collaborated. This is because the fiscal and monetary policies followed in each country have effects abroad as well as at home. These *externality effects are ignored in the choice of policy if countries act independently. Policy coordination produces better results by taking the externalities into account.

policy instrument A policy measure under the control of the monetary or fiscal authorities. This could be a measure such as a change in the money supply or in tax rates, or the imposition of price or quantitative controls. Policy instruments are distinguished from policy targets and policy indicators. Policy targets are aims such as high employment and low inflation; the authorities cannot decide these, but can only try to influence them through policy instruments. Policy indicators are used in taking policy decisions; the indicators are not necessarily themselves targets, but may be used in deciding policy in preference to targets, because the indicators can be measured more reliably or earlier than the targets. *See also* ECONOMIC POLICY.

political business cycle The theory that some economic fluctuations are due to governments seeking political advantage by expanding the economy in advance of elections. Governments may also choose to make painful reforms immediately after elections, to give the electorate a chance to forget the pain and start reaping the benefits in time for the next election.

political economy The original name of what is now known as economics. The name has resurfaced in the 'new political economy' that draws attention to the political motivation of economic policies: policy-makers and lobbyists are often more concerned with the income distribution of their electorate than with the efficiency effects of policies.

poll tax A *lump-sum tax levied on every citizen at the same rate regardless of income. A poll tax is necessarily regressive, taking a larger proportion of small incomes than of large ones. The UK *community charge of 1989–93, though it was labelled 'the poll tax' by its critics, was not a true poll tax, as it had exemptions for some citizens and lower rates for some taxpayers taking account of their lower incomes.

polluter pays principle The principle according to which the polluter should bear the cost of measures to reduce pollution according to the extent of either the damage done to society or the exceeding of an acceptable level (standard) of pollution.

pollution Damage to the environment by the emission of noxious substances, which may be dirty, toxic, radioactive, or pathogenic. This may affect water, air, or land surfaces, in some cases over wide areas. Pollution resulting from economic activities is a major source of negative externalities. *See also* PERMIT TO POLLUTE.

pollution control Methods of reducing pollution. These include taxation of polluting activities and the imposition of quantitative restrictions on pollution. Quantitative restrictions may take the form of a ban on polluting activities, the imposition of pollution standards, which limit the permissible amount of pollution per unit of an activity, or the issue of a restricted number of *permits to pollute, which may or may not be tradable. A ban on pollution may not be possible if there is no alternative production method available. Long-term policies to reduce pollution include research into alternative less- or non-polluting technologies.

pollution rights A government-issued permit that entitles a firm to emit a specified quantity of polluting waste; an instrument allowing the regulatory authority to control the amount of pollution by limiting the number of certificates. Trade in pollution rights provides incentives to reduce emissions. *See also* COASE THEOREM; POLLUTER PAYS PRINCIPLE.

pollution standards The maximum acceptable level of pollution imposed by the government. Firms may, for example, be required to clean waste products up to some minimum standard before discharging them into rivers or sewers, or there may be standards of maximum tolerated emissions from road vehicles. Standards are an alternative to the use of the price mechanism to control pollution, by taxing emissions of polluting substances. A disadvantage of emission standards is that having reached this, a standard gives firms no incentive to reduce pollution further. Also, the costs of avoiding pollution are higher for some firms than others: a tax will reduce emissions where they are most cheaply avoided, whereas under a standard the marginal cost of reducing pollution to the permitted level may vary widely between firms.

pooled least squares Least squares regression analysis that ignores possible group structure of the data. For example, in the context of panel data this means stacking the observations, i.e. assuming that the covariance matrix is diagonal and all regression coefficients are the same for all cross-sectional units.

pooling equilibrium An equilibrium in which agents with differing characteristics choose the same action. For example, in an insurance market a pooling equilibrium involves high-risk and low-risk agents choosing the same insurance contract. *See also* SEPARATING EQUILIBRIUM.

population census *See* CENSUS.

population trap A situation where no increase in living standards is possible, because the population is growing so fast that all available savings are needed to maintain the existing *capital–labour ratio. This is the position of some *less developed countries, especially in Sub-Saharan Africa. Escape from the trap requires an increase in savings, a cut in population growth, or both.

portable pension An *occupational pension which allows a person to change employers without loss of *pension rights. A pension may be made portable in two ways when an employee leaves a firm. One method is for the employee's accrued pension contributions to be frozen in the former employer's pension fund until the employee reaches pensionable age, when the fund will pay part of their pension. The other method is for the former employer to transfer an agreed capital sum equal to the present discounted value of accrued pension rights either to the new employer's pension fund, or to a personal pension scheme, operated by an insurance company independent of any employer.

portfolio A collection of different *assets owned by an individual or firm. A variety of assets may be preferred to holding a single type of asset for several reasons. Holding a variety of assets can reduce risk, and allows a combination of some assets with higher income but poor *liquidity, and others with lower income but more liquidity. Large institutions may also hold a variety of assets because there is not enough of some attractive assets to absorb all their funds or, more likely, if they invested all they could in any one asset their holding would be too large relative to the market to be liquid. *See also* LOAN PORTFOLIO; PROPERTY PORTFOLIO.

portfolio selection The choice of the proportions of different assets which should be held in order to obtain the maximum expected benefit from any given stock of wealth. The chosen proportions depend on both the characteristics of various assets and the objectives of the person or institution holding them. Assets differ in their *return and in their riskiness. The variance of expected returns, and covariance with other assets, are often used in portfolio selection, but these are not the only possible measures of risk. If variance is taken as the appropriate measure of risk, an efficient portfolio is one which gives the minimum variance available with any given expected mean returns, or the maximum returns available accepting any level of variance. As the returns on various securities are not perfectly correlated, the variance of returns on a portfolio can be reduced by holding more different securities. However, after a quite limited number the increased transaction costs of smaller holdings means that further diversification does not pay. The choice of which efficient portfolio to hold depends on the degree of *risk aversion of the investor. An individual pensioner, or a pension fund, may have a strong preference for a safe income, without much concern about short-term fluctuations in capital value. A bank or other financial intermediary may have a much stronger preference for stable capital values, even at the cost of a variable income.

portfolio theory The analysis of how individual assets should be selected for a portfolio to achieve the most preferred combination of risk and return. Portfolio theory studies how the returns and risks of individual assets interact when combined into a portfolio. The fundamental results of the theory are the characterization of the portfolio frontier (the set of portfolios that maximize return for a given level of risk) and the identification of the minimum variance portfolio (the portfolio with the least variance). Any risk-averse investor will select a portfolio from the efficient frontier according to their degree of risk aversion. The higher the degree of risk aversion, the closer will be the chosen portfolio to the minimum variance portfolio. *See also* MEAN-VARIANCE PREFERENCES.

position *See* LONG POSITION; OPEN POSITION; SHORT POSITION.

positive economics A branch of economics that describes and explains economic processes and predicts the outcomes of institutional or policy changes, without making value judgements. *See also* NORMATIVE ECONOMICS.

posterior In *Bayesian econometrics, the revised belief, or the distribution of a parameter obtained by Bayesian updating of the *prior, or the initially assumed distribution of the parameter, given the sample of the data. *See also* BAYESIAN INFERENCE.

Post Office Savings *See* NATIONAL SAVINGS.

potential competition Competition from possible as well as actual rivals. If an industry has *constant returns to scale and freedom of entry, potential competition is a powerful deterrent to monopolistic conduct by existing firms, even if the industry currently has a highly concentrated structure. This argument is explored in the theory of *contestable markets.

potential output The output which could be produced with the available labour, capital, and technology. For an individual firm, potential output is the output that could be produced with present capital and technology, allowing for recruitment of labour. Potential output for the economy as a whole is not necessarily the sum of potential output for all firms, since while any one firm could obtain extra inputs of fuel and labour, it might not be feasible for them all to expand at once.

pound (£) The UK currency unit; this is often referred to as the pound sterling. The name is also used for the currency units of several other countries, including Cyprus, Egypt, Lebanon, and Syria. If no type of pound is specified, the reference is normally to sterling, unless the context suggests that it is the local currency unit.

poverty Inability to afford an adequate standard of consumption. What this standard is once actual starvation is avoided is very much subject to variation between countries and over time. Economists have differed as to whether poverty should be considered in absolute terms, as falling below some fixed minimum consumption level, or whether it should be defined in relative terms, so that poverty means inability to afford what average people have. If an absolute standard is accepted it is at least conceivable that technical progress will eventually lift everybody above the poverty line. If poverty is relative, the poor will persist. *See also* POVERTY LINE; POVERTY TRAP.

poverty line An income level supposed to be just enough to avoid less than adequate consumption. The poverty line can be defined as an absolute or as a relative concept. Absolute poverty assumes that there is some fixed minimum level of consumption that constitutes poverty and is independent of time or place. Such a minimum level of consumption, often called the *subsistence level, can be a diet that is just sufficient to maintain health, and limited housing and clothing. The cost of this minimum consumption level defines the poverty line. If the incomes of all households rise, there will eventually be no poverty. Relative poverty is defined in terms of the standards of a given society at a given time and, as the income of that society rises, so does the level that represents poverty. With a relative concept, it becomes much more difficult to eliminate poverty. Relative poverty has also been defined in terms of the ability to 'participate' in society. Poverty then arises whenever a household possesses insufficient resources to allow it to participate in the customary activities of its society.

poverty trap A situation in which poverty outcomes reinforce themselves, acting as causes of poverty. The poverty trap can be defined at individual or household level, or at national level. An example of a poverty trap at the individual level is the situation where an unemployed person refrains from taking a job because their earnings will disqualify them from claiming unemployment benefits or raise their tax liability, and, as a result, their net income will fall. At the national level, poverty trap refers to the all-pervasive poverty in many *less developed countries where the available resources are barely sufficient to meet the basic needs of the population, and the lack of resources for investment acts as the major constraint for economic growth.

power Strength in arranging the terms of one's dealing with other firms or people. *See also* BARGAINING POWER; COUNTERVAILING POWER; MONOPOLY POWER.

power of a test *See* TYPE I AND II ERRORS.

PPP *See* PURCHASING POWER PARITY.

Prebisch thesis A claim that the terms of trade between primary products and manufactured goods deteriorate over time, so that countries that export primary commodities should establish manufacturing industry to avoid the adverse effect of the change in terms of trade.

precautionary motive The motive to hold money to provide for the unexpected. *See also* DEMAND FOR MONEY.

pre-commitment *See* COMMITMENT.

predatory pricing Pricing low with the intention of driving rivals out of a market or preventing new firms from entering. This is good for consumers in the short run, but may be bad in the long run if a firm which has used predatory pricing to establish a *monopoly position then raises its prices.

predetermined variable In a dynamic econometric model, a variable whose current and lagged values, but not necessarily future values, are uncorrelated with the current disturbance. More generally, a variable whose value is determined prior to the current period. Predetermined variables are often used as *instrumental variables to tackle the *endogeneity problem.

predictor An estimator of the value of the *dependent variable given by the estimated regression equation.

preference(s) *See* AXIOMS OF PREFERENCE; LIQUIDITY PREFERENCE; PERSONAL PREFERENCES; REVEALED PREFERENCE; SINGLE-PEAKED PREFERENCES; TIME PREFERENCE.

preference share A company share which carries no vote, but ranks before *ordinary shares for dividends.

premium 1. The price paid for an insurance policy. This may be a monthly or annual payment, or it is possible to take out a single-premium policy by a lump-sum payment.
2. A share price higher than the issue price. A share traded at a price higher than its issue price stands at a premium.
3. An addition to interest rates required to compensate lenders for risk. *See also* RISK PREMIUM.

premium bond A UK government security where the interest goes into a fund which provides for lotteries held at regular intervals, in which all bond-holders are entered. In the UK premium bond scheme the prizes are tax-free.

prescriptive statement A statement about what ought to be, as opposed to a positive statement which is concerned only with facts. In many cases statements which are formally of one type carry strong implications of the other. 'Smoking can seriously damage your health', for example, is in form purely positive, but carries the prescriptive implication 'so don't smoke'.

present discounted value The present value of a payment due to be received in the future. If a payment of amount A is due t periods into the future and the proportional interest rate remains constant at r per period, the present discounted value is given by $V = A/(1 + r)^t = A(1 + r)^{-t}$. The present discounted value of a stream of receipts spread over time is the sum of the present discounted values of the various parts of the stream. *See also* DISCOUNTED CASH FLOW.

pressure group An organization trying to bring about changes in laws or policies. These may be in the interests of its members, or of some wider cause such as the environment. Pressure groups may work via various forms of propaganda or public demonstration, or via *lobbying of national and local governments.

pre-tax profits The profits of a company before deduction of *corporation tax, or of an unincorporated business before deduction of *income tax. In each case pre-tax profit is calculated after deduction of other taxes the business has to pay, including *value-added tax, *business rates, and employers' *National Insurance contributions.

price The amount of money paid per unit for a good or service. This is easy to observe for many goods and services: in any ordinary shop, customers will find displayed a price at which as many or few units as they wish can be purchased. For some goods and services, however, price is less easy to observe. Special terms may be available for large orders, for repeat orders, or for particular types of customer. In some markets buyers and sellers negotiate over the price of each item. The price of similar goods varies over time and place, and goods with the same name vary in quality. A price index is an aggregate measure of the prices of goods in some specified category: for example, consumer goods, raw materials, or exports. Wholesale prices are the prices charged by wholesalers; factory gate prices are the prices charged by manufacturers. The price mechanism refers to the role of prices in organizing the production and distribution of goods and services in an economy: the prices people are willing to pay convey information about the valuation they put on different goods and services, and the prices charged by suppliers convey information on how they value the effort and inputs needed for production. *See also* ADMINISTERED PRICE; CEILING PRICE; CLOSING PRICES; CURRENT PRICES; DISTORTED PRICES; EXERCISE PRICE; EXIT PRICE; FACTOR PRICES; FLEXIBLE PRICES; FLOOR PRICE; FORWARD PRICE; LAW OF ONE PRICE; MARKET PRICES; MID-MARKET PRICE; OPENING PRICES; RELATIVE PRICE; SHADOW PRICES; SHUT-DOWN PRICE; SPOT PRICE; STICKY PRICES; STRIKE PRICE.

price control The setting of maximum or minimum prices by law. This may affect particular markets, for example domestic rents, or apply in an economy overall.

price discrimination Charging different prices to different customers for the same good or service. This is possible only if the supplier has some monopoly power and can identify the customer, and if the customer cannot resell the good, or it is expensive to do so. Price discrimination is profitable for a monopolist if different customers have different *elasticities of demand, so that marginal revenue in different markets is equal only if price is not. *First-degree price discrimination involves selling every unit at the maximum the purchaser would pay, so that there is no consumer surplus and the producer takes all potential benefits from a good. First-degree price discrimination defines an upper limit to what producers can gain but producers usually lack the information needed to discriminate this much. *Second-degree price discrimination occurs when producers cannot tell which group customers belong to, but offer alternative contracts which induce consumers to identify themselves. *Third-degree price discrimination occurs when sellers can identify different groups of customers, and offer different prices to each group.

price–earnings ratio (P/E ratio) The ratio of the current market price of a company's *ordinary shares to its most recently published earnings for equity per share. A relatively high price–earnings ratio may mean that earnings are expected to grow rapidly, or that they are regarded as relatively safe. A low price–earnings ratio indicates either that earnings are expected to grow slowly or fall, or that the company is regarded as relatively risky.

price effect In consumer theory, change in consumption in response to a change in the commodity prices. The effect of change in price on consumption can be decomposed into an *income effect and a *substitution effect.

price elasticity The ratio of a proportional change in quantity supplied or demanded to a proportional change in price. The price elasticity of supply is $\varepsilon_s = (p/q)(dq/dp)$, where p is price and q is quantity. The price elasticity of demand is often defined as $\varepsilon_d = -(p/q)(dq/dp)$ so that it is positive, but the minus sign is not universally used.

price fixing Agreement between two or more firms about the prices they will charge. This is considered to be anti-competitive, and is forbidden by monopoly legislation in many countries.

price floor A minimum price for a certain good or service imposed by the government.

price index An index number, or an aggregate measure, of the prices of goods in some given category. Consider good i. Let period 0 be the base period, period t the current period, and $p_{i\tau}$ the price in period τ. The price index for good i is given by p_{it}/p_{i0}. This gives the index in ratio form and has a value of 1 in the base period. It is often multiplied by 100 to give a value of 100 in the base period. If a class of goods $i = 1, 2, \ldots, N$ is concerned, the price index is a ratio of the weighted average of their prices. The weights are the values of the goods purchased in some period. If $q_{i\tau}$ is the quantity of good i in period τ, the *base-weighted or Laspeyres price index is defined as

$$p_B = \sum_{i=1}^{N} p_{it} q_{i0} \bigg/ \sum_{i=1}^{N} p_{i0} q_{i0}$$

and the *current-weighted or Paasche price index is defined as

$$p_C = \sum_{i=1}^{N} p_{it} q_{it} \bigg/ \sum_{i=1}^{N} p_{i0} q_{it}.$$

Again these are in ratio form but can be multiplied by 100. Price indices can also be found for security prices or wage rates. *See also* CONSUMER PRICE INDEX; RETAIL PRICE INDEX.

price leader A firm whose price changes tend to be followed by other sellers in its markets. This may be by agreement, which is illegal under monopoly legislation in many countries, or by collusion, which is considered anti-competitive but is difficult to prevent. A price leader may be a particularly large firm, or one with particularly aggressive management.

price level The general level of prices in an economy. This may refer to consumer goods prices, in which case it is measured by a *retail price index, or to all goods produced, including investment and government purchases as well as consumer goods, in which case it is measured by a *GDP deflator.

price-maker *See* PRICE-SETTER.

price mechanism An expression referring to the role of prices in a *market economy in conveying information, providing incentives, guiding choices, and allocating resources. The 'market mechanism' is an alternative phrase making the same point. The prices people are willing to pay for goods and services convey information about how much they value them, and the prices producers ask convey information about how their inputs are valued. The price mechanism provides incentives to allocate resources where their value is highest, and to satisfy wants from the cheapest sources.

price reform In a transition from a centrally planned to a *market economy this is the shift from arbitrary controlled prices towards a system in which prices reflect opportunity costs. If the systems of *price control had fixed some prices too low relative to opportunity costs, which has led to excess demand, the price reform helps eliminate shortages, often at the cost of rapid *inflation, as was observed in the former Soviet Union and other countries during the transition. The merit of price reform is that it helps to lead to more efficient production, and to end perpetual shortages and the waste involved in queuing.

prices and incomes policy Attempts by government to control prices and incomes directly, by persuasion or law. Such policies are distinguished from influencing prices and wages through monetary and fiscal policies, or setting prices by acting as a buyer or seller in particular markets. The existence of administrative costs cause prices and incomes policies to either set some important prices and leave others to the market, or set limits on price increases. Either alternative produces distortions in the structure of relative prices, and becomes increasingly difficult to enforce as time passes.

price-sensitive information Information about a company which, if publicly known, could affect its share price. This includes figures on profits, employment, turnover, innovations, mineral finds, changes in senior management, or takeover bids. Preferential access to price-sensitive information is what makes 'insider traders' insiders. *See also* INSIDER DEALING.

price-setter A firm which sets the price of a good or security. Only a firm with some degree of *monopoly power can be a price-setter. A price-setter is contrasted with a *price-taker, which is a competitive firm or individual who has to treat the market price as given.

price squeeze An anti-competitive practice when a firm with *monopoly power on the wholesale level engages in a prolonged price increase that drives competitors out of the retail level, and thereby extends its monopoly power to the retail market.

price stability An objective of *economic policy aimed at avoidance of both prolonged *inflation and *deflation. It amounts to maintaining the rate of increase or decrease in an aggregate price index, usually the *consumer price index, within tolerable limits. For example, the *European Central Bank defines price stability as 'a year-on-year increase in the Harmonized Index of Consumer Prices for the Euro area of below 2%' over the medium term.

price stickiness Resistance or failure of price to change instantaneously in response to a change in an economic environment. Possible causes of price stickiness are *monopolistic competition and *menu costs, *money illusion, *imperfect information with regards to price changes, and *fairness concerns.

price support Government policies to keep the producer prices of commodities above some minimum level. This applies mainly to agricultural products, to raise the incomes of producers. Price support works either by buying the product to prevent the market price from falling, or by paying the producer a subsidy to cover any shortfall of market price below the support price.

price-taker An individual or firm trading on a market where they do not believe that their own transactions will affect the market price. As a consequence a price-taker makes decisions on the basis that prices are given exogenously.

price volatility The extent to which a price fluctuates. Fluctuations may be measured on any time-scale, from year-by-year to minute-by-minute. The quantitative measure of volatility of the price in period $t - 1$ is defined as the standard deviation of the natural logarithm of the ratio of prices in period t and $t - 1$ (log returns). Price volatility tends to be higher when supply, demand, or both are liable to large random shocks, and when the elasticity of both supply and demand is low. Price volatility tends to be higher for commodities, shares, and exchange rates than for industrial products.

price–wage spiral *See* WAGE–PRICE SPIRAL.

price war Charging low prices to harm competitors' profits. In a price war one or more firms charge prices below those that would maximize their own profits, to inflict losses on rivals. A price war may aim to punish competitors for breaking a *cartel agreement, to weaken their finances in order to force acceptance of a takeover bid, or to drive them out of business completely.

pricing *See* AVERAGE COST PRICING; COST-PLUS PRICING; FULL COST PRICING; LIMIT PRICING; MARGINAL COST PRICING; PEAK-LOAD PRICING; TRANSFER PRICING.

primary market A market on which new *financial securities are initially traded.

primary sector The sector of an economy making direct use of natural resources. This includes agriculture, forestry and fishing, mining, and extraction of oil and gas. This is contrasted with the secondary sector, producing manufactures and other processed goods, and the tertiary sector, producing services. The primary sector is usually most important in *less developed countries, and typically less important in industrial countries.

prime rate A reference interest rate used by banks. Traditionally, this was the interest rate offered to the most creditworthy borrowers. *See also* LONDON INTER BANK OFFERED RATE.

principal **1.** A person or firm employing another to act as their agent. A person using an estate agent to sell a house, for example, is a principal; the estate agent is the agent. The *principal–agent problem is concerned with how agents can be induced to act in the interests of their principals rather than their own.
 2. The amount lent at the start of a loan.

principal–agent problem The problem of how person A can motivate person B to act for A's benefit rather than following self-interest. The principal, A, may be an employer and the agent, *B*, an employee, or the principal may be a shareholder and the agent a director of a company. The problem is how to devise incentives which lead agents to report truthfully to the principal on the facts they face and the actions they take, and to act for the principal's benefit. Incentives include rewards such as bonuses or promotion for success, and penalties such as demotion or dismissal for failure to act in the principal's interests. *See also* CONTRACT THEORY; MECHANISM DESIGN.

principal components analysis A technique based on the linear transformation of a multivariable data set into a smaller set of uncorrelated variables, called principal components. The first principal component accounts for as much of the variability in the data as possible, and each succeeding component accounts for as much of the remaining variability as possible.

prior The initial value or probability distribution attached to a parameter in *Bayesian econometrics. *See also* BAYESIAN INFERENCE.

prisoners' dilemma A two-player game that illustrates the conflict between private and social incentives, and the gains that can be obtained from making binding commitments. The name originated from a situation of two prisoners who must each choose between the strategies 'Confess' and 'Don't confess' without knowing what the other will choose. The important feature of the game is that a lighter penalty follows for a prisoner who confesses when the other does not. The game is summarized in the pay-off matrix where the negative pay-offs can be interpreted as the disutility from imprisonment.

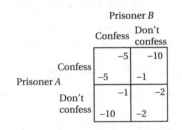

The *Nash equilibrium of the game is {Confess, Confess}. The interesting feature is that this equilibrium is not *Pareto efficient: the pay-off of both players would be higher if they played {Don't confess, Don't confess}. However, if one player chose Don't confess then it is individually rational for the other player to choose Confess. Without a device for making a binding commitment it is not possible for {Don't confess, Don't confess} to be an equilibrium.

private benefit The benefit arising to a single individual from an economic activity. The maximization of private benefit is the guiding principle of economic decision-making. When all economic agents follow this principle then market equilibrium will be *Pareto efficient if there is no *market failure. If an externality is present, private benefit is not equal to *social benefit and inefficiency can result.

private company A *limited liability company in the UK restricted to between 2 and 50 shareholders, not counting present and past employees. Shareholders cannot transfer their shares without the consent of other members, and shares cannot be offered to the general public.

private cost The cost of providing goods or services as it appears to the person or firm supplying them. This includes the cost of any factor services or inputs bought by the supplier, the value of work done, and the use of land, buildings, and equipment owned by the supplier. Private cost excludes any external harm caused to other people or the environment, such as noise or pollution, unless the supplier is legally obliged to pay for it. *See also* SOCIAL COST.

private enterprise The system by which economic activity is undertaken by independent individuals or firms, rather than under central direction. The concept of private enterprise has political connotations beyond the purely economic meaning. In the political sphere, support for private enterprise follows from the claim that it is generally beneficial not so much because it is private, as because it is enterprising, which makes for greater efficiency and more technical improvements than centrally controlled firms would produce.

private good Any good or service which is rivalrous (if used by one individual or firm it is not available to others) and excludable (the owner can costlessly prevent other individuals or firms from consuming it). Most ordinary consumer and capital goods are private goods. *See also* PUBLIC GOOD.

private property Things which the law recognizes as belonging exclusively to particular individuals or organizations. This is contrasted with things which are owned by the government, such as public highways, and things which are held to be available for use by anybody, for example the works of authors whose copyright has expired. Things which are private property can be legally transferred only with the owner's consent, or by due legal process, for example compulsory purchase of land needed for *public works. There are often restrictions on the use which can be made of private property, to avoid danger or inconvenience to other people: for example, *planning permission is required for building on private land.

private sector The parts of the economy not run by the government. This includes households, sole traders and partnerships, companies, and non-profit organizations.

private sector balance The excess of savings over investment spending by the private sector. It is a national income accounting identity that the private sector balance, government sector balance, and current account deficit of the economy must sum to zero. Thus, for any given government balance, an increase in the private sector balance must reduce the current account deficit.

privatization The transfer to private ownership and control of assets or enterprises which were previously under *public ownership. Privatized assets may have been under direct state ownership, or owned by local authorities, for example council houses in the UK, or by state-owned public corporations. Privatization may be adopted because of a belief that assets will be used more efficiently under private ownership, to reduce the power of central authorities, to raise revenue for the government, or to attempt to spread property ownership more widely in society.

probability (of a random event) A quantitative measure of the chance that a random event will occur, expressed by a number between 0 and 1. The probability is 0 if the event is certain not to occur, and 1 if it is certain to occur.

probability distribution (of a random variable) Specification of the probabilities with which the random variable can take any particular value or a range of values.

probit model A *discrete choice model in which the population regression function is based on the cumulative normal distribution function.

process innovation Innovation where an existing product is made in a new and cheaper way. *See also* PRODUCT INNOVATION.

procurement Government purchase of goods and services. The large scale of government purchases makes inefficiency in procurement a potential drain on government finances, and *corruption may lead to the misallocation of resources. It is also common for government procurement to favour domestic supplies over foreign suppliers: unless this is necessary on the grounds of national security, it is a form of *protectionism which is an important source of inefficiency.

producer good A good intended for use as a capital good or intermediate product by producers, rather than for direct use by consumers. Some goods are both consumer and producer goods: cars, for example, are bought by individuals as well as firms, and fuel is used both privately and commercially.

producer surplus The excess of total sales revenue going to producers over the area under the *supply curve for a good. If the supply curve is perfectly elastic there is no producer surplus, but if the supply curve is upward-sloping, those productive resources which would have stayed in the industry at a lower price earn quasi-rents.

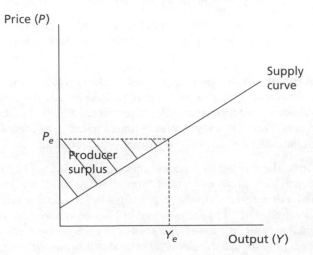

Producer Surplus

product What is produced, by an individual firm, an industry, or the economy as a whole. *See also* GROSS DOMESTIC PRODUCT; MARGINAL PRODUCT; NATIONAL PRODUCT; PRODUCT DIFFERENTIATION; PRODUCT INNOVATION; PRODUCT LIFE CYCLE; STAPLE PRODUCT.

product differentiation A form of *non-price competition between firms under which products that fulfil the same needs but are not necessarily identical are offered under different *brand names. Differentiated products can also be produced within the same firm and targeted to different groups of consumers. The differentiation is vertical if the products can be ordered according to their quality (low to high). The differentiation is horizontal if the feature along which the products differ does not allow ordering, such as different colours.

product innovation Innovation where a new or improved product is introduced. Product innovation is a source of *economic growth. *See also* PROCESS INNOVATION.

production The use of resources to make goods or services. Production can be organized within firms or within the household. In both cases inputs are employed to produce outputs. Firms produce the outputs to sell and earn profit. The household produces the output to meet the needs of the family. The relationship between inputs and outputs is determined by the production technology. Production and *exchange are the two basic components of economic activity. *See also* BATCH PRODUCTION; CENSUS OF PRODUCTION; FACTOR OF PRODUCTION; GOVERNMENT PRODUCTION; HOUSEHOLD PRODUCTION; JOINT PRODUCTION; MASS PRODUCTION.

production externality An external effect of production that harms or benefits someone else than the producer. An example of negative production externality is noise or air pollution; an example of positive production externality is pollination of nearby crops and orchards by the bees kept by a beekeeper for their honey. Typically, a negative production externality results in over-provision of the good produced, whereas a positive production externality leads to under-provision, relative to the *social optimum.

production function A function showing the maximum output possible with any given set of inputs. The expression of production possibilities by a production function assumes that inputs are used efficiently, so the production function is the upper boundary of the *production set. A production function satisfies the 'Inada conditions' if the marginal product of each input tends to infinity as the quantity of input tends to zero, and tends to zero as the quantity of input tends to infinity. These conditions are frequently imposed in models since they imply a positive quantity of every input is used whenever input prices are finite.

production possibility frontier (PPF) A locus of points showing the maximum outputs of goods and services possible with the available resources. For an economy with two goods the PPF can be displayed in a two-dimensional diagram. Let the output of one good be measured on the horizontal axis and the output of the other good on the vertical axis. The PPF then usually slopes downwards: its slope shows the *opportunity cost of each good in terms of the other. Limited supplies of specific factors of production and differences in factor proportions between industries tend to make the PPF concave to the origin. Increasing returns in one or both industries tend to make it convex to the origin. A PPF can be defined for a firm, an industry, a country, or the world as a whole. *See also* PRODUCTION POSSIBILITY SET; PRODUCTION SET.

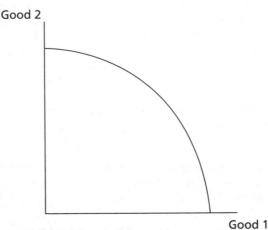

Production Possibility Frontier

production possibility set The set of all non-negative outputs of goods and services that can be produced using the economy's available factor inputs. The output combinations on the frontier of this set correspond to the *Pareto-efficient allocation of factor inputs, i.e. the allocation at which it is not possible, given the total factor endowment, to increase the production of one good without decreasing the production of some other good.

production set The set of technologically feasible input–output combinations for an individual firm or for an economy as a whole. The *production function is the upper boundary of the production set and represents efficient input–output combinations. Points inside the production set are inefficient. A convex production set represents a technology with non-increasing returns.

production subsidy A payment by the government to producers of a good or service, at a fixed sum per unit produced. This is available only to domestic producers and not to importers. An important example of a production subsidy is the support for farmers provided by the EU under the *Common Agricultural Policy.

productive efficiency *See* EFFICIENCY.

productivity The amount of output per unit of input achieved by a firm, industry, or country. This may be per unit of a particular factor of production, for example labour employed, or per unit of land in agriculture, or 'total factor productivity' may be measured, which involves aggregating the different factors. Productivity is determined by the level of output if *returns to scale are not constant.

product liability Liability for damage caused by a product of the original producer, as well as the immediate vendor.

product life cycle A model of how products go through a series of phases over time. In this model, new products start as small-scale specialities produced by innovators. Prices are initially high, both because of high costs due to small-scale production and because initially the innovators have cost advantages of *know-how, equipment, and possibly *patents, which give them a quasi-monopoly position. As knowledge of the new product spreads, costs fall through increased scale and greater experience, other producers enter the market, and prices come down. Once the product becomes mature, with large-scale production by techniques now regarded as standard, production tends to shift to areas with low labour costs, often in newly industrialized countries. Eventually the product is replaced by something new and drops out of the economy.

product proliferation Marketing of many varieties of the same product by a producer. It is sometimes regarded as a waste of resources and a *barrier to entry, as the incumbent firm may use it to occupy the gaps in the market that could potentially be used by an entrant firm.

professional body An organization of people with particular professional qualifications. Such an organization may seek to set standards of professional competence, to control entry in order to ensure that its members are able to maintain professional standards, to monitor the conduct of members to ensure that they maintain these standards, and to exclude them if they do not. Professional bodies may also lobby for legal restrictions on the right of non-members to provide professional services. This is designed to protect the public from possible damage by incompetent or dishonest practitioners; it is also possible to use entry requirements to keep down numbers so as to keep up the price of professional services, and to use codes of conduct to restrict competition between members of the profession.

profit An excess of the receipts over the spending of a business during any period. This includes credit transactions and asset revaluations as well as cash transactions and changes in holdings of real assets. Profit for a period includes dividends and profits taxes as well as the excess of net assets at the end of the period over net assets at its start. So long as a business is a going concern, its profits are a matter of judgement rather than objective fact. Only when a business has been finally wound up and its assets converted to cash can profits be objectively measured. Until then, judgement is required as to the valuation of physical and financial assets, particularly if they are not traded on liquid markets, and as to the quality of debts due from credit customers. *See also* EXCESS PROFIT; GROSS PROFIT; MONOPOLY PROFIT; NET PROFIT; NORMAL PROFITS; PRE-TAX PROFITS; SUPERNORMAL PROFIT; UNDISTRIBUTED PROFITS.

profit-and-loss account An account of an organization's receipts and spending over a period. Both sides of the account include credit transactions and asset revaluations as well as cash transactions and changes in holdings of real assets. An excess of receipts over spending is profit; an excess of spending over receipts is loss. The profit-and-loss account is contrasted with the other part of the accounts, the *balance-sheet, which records the composition of assets and liabilities on a particular date.

profit maximization The act of making as much profit as possible for a business. It is standard in economic theory to assume that the actions of firms are guided by profit maximization. This applies equally to firms operating in competitive markets and to firms with monopoly power. These differ with respect to scenarios the variables that are under the control of the firm and the form of *strategic interaction with other firms. The assumption of profit maximization is justified if firms are run to meet the interests of their shareholders: the share price is equal to the discounted value of the flow of profits. If the separation between ownership and control in a firm creates an *agency problem then profit maximization may not be the firm's objective.

profit motive The desire for gain as a motive in economic activity. The profit motive can mean no more than the assumption that firms aim to maximize profit, but it can also be used in a derogatory sense to imply selfish justification for socially damaging actions. In economic theory it is the profit motive that ensures the choices of competitive firms satisfy the conditions required for *Pareto efficiency. This was the insight of Adam Smith (1723–1790): when mediated by the *price mechanism choices that are individually rational are also socially efficient.

profit-related pay The system of making pay a function of the employer's profits. This usually takes the form of additional payments when profits are good, either as a rise in pay scales or as *bonuses. Bonuses are more common, since the level of profits continually varies, and is not usually known until well after normal pay is received. Employers hope that relating pay to profits will make workers more cooperative in trying to increase profits, decrease labour turnover, and improve morale generally. Employees who are *risk-averse may prefer smaller but safer incomes.

profit-sharing Giving employees a share in a firm's profits. This may be done either by profit-related pay, or by enabling employees to become shareholders, by giving them either shares or options to buy shares on preferential terms. Profit-sharing is intended to improve motivation by giving employees an interest in the firm's profitability. It is more frequently adopted for management than for other employees, possibly because managers have more influence on profitability than other workers, and may be less *risk-averse, so that profit-sharing incentive schemes are relatively attractive to them.

profit-sharing arrangement A formal agreement between two or more parties on the distribution of profit from a business venture. The parties may be partners in the venture, or be an entrepreneur and a provider of finance.

profit-taking Selling an asset in order to realize an accrued *capital gain. The holder of any asset has to decide whether to hold on to it or sell it. A sale means that capital gains are realized, which may mean paying *capital gains tax. Holding on involves the risk that the price may fall, so that accrued capital gains are never realized at all. This applies to all assets, whether traded on a market, like shares, or subject to ad hoc negotiation, like houses and takeovers. Knowing when to take profits is part of the art of successful *speculation.

progressive tax A tax where the revenue collected rises more than proportionally to the taxable amount. The UK *income tax is made progressive by having an exemption for low incomes, a low rate for the first slice of taxable income, and higher rates for the largest incomes. This structure is fairly typical. *Indirect taxes can be progressive if there are exemptions or low tax rates for goods heavily consumed by the poor, for example the UK's zero VAT on food, and higher rates on luxury items more heavily consumed by the rich.

prohibitive tariff A tariff set at a rate so high that no trade in the good concerned can take place.

propensity to consume The proportion of disposable income which individuals desire to spend on consumption. The average propensity to consume is total desired spending as a proportion of total disposable income; the marginal propensity to consume is the proportion of additional income that an individual desires to consume. The marginal propensity to consume is typically less than 1. The size of both the average and marginal propensities may be affected by factors such as the consumer's total assets, liquidity, and expectations of inflation.

propensity to save The proportion of disposable income which individuals do not desire to spend on consumption. The average propensity to save gives total desired saving as a proportion of total disposable income; the marginal propensity to save is the proportion of additional income an individual desires to save. The sum of the propensity to save and the propensity to consume, average or marginal, is always 1. The size of the average and marginal savings propensities may be affected by factors such as a person's total assets, liquidity, and expectations of inflation.

property 1. Land and buildings; the UK legal term for these is real property. Property forms an important part of a country's capital stock.
   2. Ownership of assets by private individuals or organizations. These assets may include property in sense 1, but may also include securities and intellectual property such as patents. Property incomes are incomes derived from such assets. *See also* INTELLECTUAL PROPERTY RIGHTS; PRIVATE PROPERTY.

property company A company whose principal activity is owning and developing property. This may be industrial, commercial, or residential. Property companies may specialize in letting existing properties, or in new developments and conversion of properties with a view to selling them.

property developer An individual or firm which buys property with a view to changing its use, making significant improvement, or constructing new property. Property development is inherently risky: this is partly because of the liability of the property market to large price changes, and partly because of uncertainty about obtaining planning approval for changes of use and new building.

property income Income derived from the ownership of property of any sort. This includes rents, dividends, and interest. This is a component of unearned income; it is contrasted with income from employment. Income from self-employment is a mixture of earned and property income.

property income from abroad Incomes of residents of a country derived from rents, dividends, and interest received from abroad. Net property income from abroad is these receipts less similar items of property income paid by residents to non-residents.

property lending Lending to finance purchases of property. Such lending commonly uses the property concerned as collateral, via mortgages on it. Property lending can be very risky if the loans cover a high percentage of the property's valuation: if property prices fall the collateral may be worth less than the loan, leaving the borrower with *negative equity.

property market The system by which land and buildings are bought and sold. There is no central institution for this market, which works through an informal network of estate agents and other specialized intermediaries.

property portfolio A collection of properties held by a company. Such a portfolio may be held for income or with a view to development. Property companies hold portfolios rather than single properties partly to reduce risk, since any particular property may be refused *planning permission for proposed developments, or may fail to find a tenant.

property rights The rights of an owner over property. These generally include rights to use property, and to exclude others from it. Property rights are not absolute: the use of assets may be subject to legal controls, such as the need for *planning permission for changes in the use of land and buildings. The law also restricts the methods owners may use to exclude others from their property: for example, in the UK dwellings can only be reoccupied by their lawful owners through the courts and not by force. The existence of property rights is a basic requirement for organized economic activity to take place. If it is not clear who owns property, and what their rights over it are, there is a disincentive to acquire property and resources will be wasted defending from theft property that is accumulated. *See also* INTELLECTUAL PROPERTY RIGHTS.

proportional tax A tax where the revenue collected rises proportionally with the taxable amount. A tax system is proportional if it has a uniform rate of tax and no exemptions.

prospect theory A theory of choice in the presence of *risk. Prospect theory embodies the empirical observations that individuals place excessive weight on outcomes that occur with low probability and place greater emphasis on small losses than on small gains. The pay-off function in prospect theory is convex for losses and concave for gains, where losses and gains are measured relative to a reference point. Prospect theory is an alternative to *expected utility theory.

prospectus A document provided by a company wishing to sell newly issued *shares or *debentures to the public. A prospectus must provide information on the aims, past financial history, and capital structure of the venture, and may contain profit forecasts. Prospectuses in the UK have to be lodged with the Registrar of Companies, and there are penalties for making false claims in a prospectus.

protection 1. The use of trade policy to raise profits and employment in industries liable to competition from imports. Protection may be via *tariffs, *import quotas, or *voluntary export restraints and other *non-tariff barriers to trade. *See* CONTINGENT PROTECTION; EFFECTIVE PROTECTION; NOMINAL PROTECTION.

   2. Government policies aimed at safeguarding the interests of consumers, producers, or the environment. *See* AGRICULTURAL PROTECTION; CONSUMER PROTECTION.

protectionism A policy of restriction of international trade, with the aim of preventing unemployment or capital losses in industries threatened by imports, promoting particular types of industrial development, affecting the internal distribution of incomes, or improving a country's terms of trade by exploiting its international monopoly power. *See also* COST OF PROTECTION; NEW PROTECTIONISM.

proxy variable A variable used instead of the variable of interest when that variable of interest cannot be measured directly. For example, per capita GDP can be used as a proxy for the standard of living. *See also* LATENT VARIABLE.

proxy vote A vote exercised by one person on behalf of another. At company meetings proxy votes are commonly allowed. Usually shareholders can nominate some other person to cast their vote, either in some specified manner or at the proxy-holder's discretion. It is common for proxies to be entrusted to the Chairman of a company meeting. In many cases the majority of votes cast are proxies, rather than those of shareholders attending a meeting.

PSBR *See* PUBLIC SECTOR BORROWING REQUIREMENT.

public choice 1. An approach to the analysis of economic policy that emphasizes the motivations of bureaucrats and politicians. The public choice literature stresses that the ability of the government to improve on the market outcome has to be proved rather than asserted. This follows from the assumption that bureaucrats and politicians are economically rational and enter government for their own advantage. The pursuit of self-advantage is constrained imperfectly by the electoral mechanism. Only when the objectives of those in government are consistent with the needs of broader society will government action be generally beneficial.

   2. An alternative name for *social choice.

public company *See* PUBLIC LIMITED COMPANY.

public corporation The UK form of organization for nationalized industries. Public corporations were supposed to operate in the public interest, using capital provided by the government, but with managerial autonomy in day-to-day business. In fact there was considerable government intervention in their management, particularly in relation to investment spending and pricing policy.

public debt Money or credit owed by a government to domestic (internal debt) or foreign (external debt) lenders. When a government borrows by issuing securities (bonds) the public debt is equal to the total value of government bonds outstanding at any particular time.

public economics A field of economics that studies economic efficiency, distribution, and government economic policy. In particular, it deals with the analysis of the *public sector and its interaction with the economy, responses to *market failure in the presence of *externalities, *public goods, taxation, social security systems, etc.

public expenditure *See* GOVERNMENT EXPENDITURE.

Public Expenditure Survey Committee (PESC) A UK government interdepartmental committee that reviewed expenditure plans in the process leading to the annual Public Expenditure White Paper. The plans referred both to the coming financial year and to forward projections for the following four years. The PESC has now been abolished.

public finance A branch of economics concerned with the study of the financing of government. This includes taxation, spending by public bodies on real goods and services, provision of transfer incomes by the government, government property incomes, government borrowing and debt, and the financial relations between various levels of government.

public good A good that no consumer can be excluded from using if it is supplied, and for which consumption by one consumer does not reduce the quantity available for consumption by any other. The first property is referred to as non-excludability, whereas the latter is termed non-rivalry. As a consequence of these properties public goods cause *market failure. In practice, it is difficult to find a pure public good, i.e. one that satisfies these two conditions exactly. Public goods that are excludable, but at a cost, or suffer from *congestion when too many consumers try to use them simultaneously, are called *impure public goods; examples are parks and roads. Public goods are not necessarily desirable; undesirable ones are sometimes called public bads, e.g. polluted air.

public interest The good of the general public, as contrasted with the particular individuals or firms involved in a decision. The instructions for managers of publicly owned enterprises, or bodies appointed to regulate monopolies, often contain phrases such as 'operate in the public interest'. In the absence of any objective method of determining what the public interest is, those given such instructions must necessarily use their own judgement, or rely on precedents set by similar bodies.

public limited company (PLC) A UK company registered under the Companies Act. Its name must end in 'PLC'. The act lays down minimum capital requirements, and sets the form for its memorandum. Such companies can offer shares and securities to the public with *limited liability. The rules governing public companies are stricter than those for private companies.

public ownership Ownership of enterprises by the government, or a government-controlled body. This may include direct operation by the central government, as for example with military establishments or the civil service; operation by local authorities, as with many public amenities, and in the UK local authority housing; and operation by government-appointed bodies, as with the UK National Health Service. It is also possible for the government to own part or all of the shares of companies.

public procurement The purchase of goods and services by the public sector, at all levels of government. This may include providing defence, law and order, health, education, and other public services.

public sector Those parts of the economy which are not controlled by individuals, voluntary organizations, or privately owned companies. The public sector thus includes government at all levels, national and local; government-owned firms; and *quasi-autonomous non-government organizations. Where government money is provided to bodies such as charities or housing associations, or privately owned public utilities are subject to close regulation by government-appointed bodies, the distinction between the public and private sectors is not clear-cut.

Public Sector Borrowing Requirement (PSBR) The amount the UK government has to borrow each year, when the government's expenditure exceeds its income. The PSBR must lead either to sales of securities to the public, which may raise interest rates and crowd out private investment, or borrowing from the banking system, leading to inflationary increases in the money supply. The PSBR has been regarded as an important indicator of the government's fiscal stance. It does not include the proceeds of selling off privatized industries, which are thus effectively treated as current government income.

public sector debt *See* GOVERNMENT DEBT.

Public Sector Debt Repayment The amount of debt the UK government is able to repay in any period. This is the converse of *Public Sector Borrowing Requirement, and occurs if there is a budget surplus, that is, the government's total revenues exceed its expenditure.

public spending *See* GOVERNMENT EXPENDITURE.

public utility *See* UTILITY.

public works Construction projects paid for by the government. These can include both new construction and improvements to roads, bridges, schools, hospitals, government offices, and publicly owned housing.

pump priming The theory that it is possible for the government to bring about permanent recovery from a slump by a temporary injection of purchasing power into the economy. The argument is that if incomes are low because lack of confidence in the future prevents investment, a temporary rise in government spending, financed by borrowing rather than taxes, can raise incomes through its multiplier effects, which will allow investment to recover. Once a cumulative recovery process gets going, it will be possible to remove the extra government spending. The government may even eventually receive sufficient extra tax revenue to restore government debt to its original level.

punishment strategy A strategy used in a *repeated game to secure an outcome which is not a *Nash equilibrium for a single play of the game. Consider the *prisoners' dilemma. The outcome {Don't confess, Don't confess} is not a Nash equilibrium if the game is played only once. If the game is repeated an infinite number of times the strategy {Play Don't confess if opponent played Don't confess in last round, Play Confess in every future play of the game if opponent ever plays Confess} is a punishment strategy that secures the equilibrium {Don't confess, Don't confess} if played by both players. The strategy rewards good behaviour (the play of {Don't confess}) by responding in like manner and ensuring a high pay-off, but punishes bad behaviour (the play of {Confess}) by driving the pay-off down to the Nash equilibrium level.

purchase tax A UK tax on consumer goods, at rates varying between goods and over time. It was replaced by *value-added tax in 1973.

purchasing power The amount of real goods and services each unit of money will buy. Purchasing power is thus the reciprocal of a suitable *price index: if prices go up, the purchasing power of money goes down.

purchasing power parity (PPP) The theory that *exchange rates between currencies are determined in the long run by the amount of goods and services that each can buy. In the absence of transport costs and *tariffs, if the price of tradable goods were lower in one country than another, traders could gain by buying goods in the country where they are cheaper and selling in the other one: relative price levels thus determine the equilibrium exchange rate. Not all goods are tradable, and even for tradables transport costs and tariffs mean that prices need not be equal, but the same forces of arbitrage limit their differences, and thus limit the deviations of exchange rates from PPP. An alternative form of PPP says that changes in the equilibrium exchange rate are determined by changes in *relative price levels.

pure floating exchange rate (clean floating exchange rate) A *floating exchange rate which is set by the market without any intervention by central banks or governments. Under pure floating the exchange rate is whatever private speculators believe it should be. There is thus a risk of extreme fluctuations in exchange rates, and for this reason very few countries allow a completely clean float for their currencies. Most countries attempt some degree of official intervention intended to stabilize the foreign exchange markets. *See also* MANAGED FLOATING EXCHANGE RATE.

put option A contract giving the right but not the obligation to sell a good, security, or currency on some future date at a price fixed when the contract is first taken out. A put option will be exercised when the date arrives only if the spot market price is below the option price; if the market price is higher than the option price it will pay better to sell on the spot market. A put option can be used to reduce risk by somebody who has to hold the good, or as a speculation by somebody who expects a low spot market price.

pyramid scheme A financial scheme in which investors are offered a high rate of return paid out of investments made by a large number of newly joined members, attracted by these high rates, rather than from real production or investment activities. Such schemes are inherently fraudulent; they can pay the promised return only as long as total membership rises fast enough, and once new entry slows down or falls they are bound to default on their promises.

p

qualification of accounts A report by *auditors that they are not, for some specified reasons, able to certify that its *accounts give a true and fair view of an organization's affairs. This may reflect either serious financial misconduct, or deficiencies in the organization's bookkeeping.

qualitative choice models *See* DISCRETE CHOICE MODELS.

quality-adjusted life years (QALYs) A method used to measure the benefit of medical intervention. Each additional year of life attributed to the medical intervention is given a value reflecting the quality of life in that year. A value of 1 is given to a year lived in perfect health and a lower value, down to a minimum of 0, is given to any years with illness. Hence, a year lived with mild discomfort may be rated 0.75 but a year with serious illness rated 0.25. The benefit of medical intervention is measured by the QALYs it generates which are defined as the sum of the additional years of life with each year weighted by its value. In a *cost–benefit analysis the benefit of treatment is equal to the number of QALYs multiplied by the financial valuation of a year of life (the UK Department of Health uses a value of approximately £30000). The resulting benefit can be compared to the cost of the treatment to judge whether treatment is economically justified.

quality control The system for checking the quality of a product. This may be done before it is sold, and/or at earlier stages of production. Where the checking itself destroys or is liable to damage the product, quality control has to work via sampling batches of products chosen so that they are expected to have common properties, for example those processed on a given date by the same machine. The level of spending on quality control is affected both by commercial considerations of maintaining a reputation for quality, and by legal sanctions imposing penalties or awarding damages for defective products.

quality ladder A model of product development in which firms steadily upgrade the quality of their products. Movement up the quality ladder includes making products more reliable and improving their specifications and design. In the process a product changes from being a cheap line aiming at the lower end of the market, to being a superior article aimed at more sophisticated and better-off consumers. This process is associated with the development of *newly industrialized countries. The quality ladder is a key element in some models of *endogenous growth.

quality standards Minimum standards for goods, set by government bodies or trade associations. These standards are designed to protect consumers, by ensuring satisfactory levels of durability, and hazard safety.

quango *See* QUASI-AUTONOMOUS NON-GOVERNMENT ORGANIZATION.

quantile For any number p between 0 and 1, the pth population quantile is the number x such that the probability of a value below x occurring equals p; in other words, population quantile is the inverse cumulative distribution function. In a sample of size N, the pth quantile is the observation such that approximately Np of the observations are less than this observation and $N(1 - p)$ of the observations are larger. The pth quantile is also referred to as the $(100p)$th percentile. The 0.5th quantile is the median; the 0.25th and the 0.75th quantiles are called the lower and the upper quartiles. The distance between the lower and upper quartiles, called the interquartile range, is sometimes used as a measure of *dispersion.

quantity demanded The quantity of a good demanded at a given price. The quantity demanded traces out the *demand curve as the given price is changed. The *equilibrium price is that at which quantity demanded is equal to quantity supplied.

quantity discount A price reduction available only to purchasers of at least some minimum quantity. Such reductions may be publicly advertised, or available by negotiation. Quantity discounts may be due to lower costs made possible by economies of scale in supplying larger orders, to the monopsonistic advantage possessed by large-scale buyers, or to *second-degree price discrimination.

quantity equation The equation $MV = PT$ relating the *price level and the *quantity of money. Here M is the quantity of money, V is the velocity of circulation, P is the price level, and T is the volume of transactions. The quantity equation is the basis for the *quantity theory of money.

quantity of money The amount of money in circulation in a country. There are several possible definitions of money: for details, *see* M0; M1; M2; M3, M4, AND M5.

quantity supplied The quantity of a good supplied at a given price. The quantity supplied traces out the *supply curve as the given price is changed. The *equilibrium price is that at which quantity supplied is equal to quantity demanded.

quantity theory of money The theory that the *price level is proportional to the *quantity of money. This is expressed by the *quantity equation, $MV = PT$, where M is the quantity of money, V is the *velocity of circulation, P is the price level, and T is the volume of transactions. The quantity theory assumes that T is determined by supply-side forces, which determine the level of real output, and institutional factors, which determine the ratio of total transactions to output; and V is determined by the legal status and operating habits of the financial system. These assumptions allow T and V to be treated as fixed. The quantity equation then implies that P must be proportional to M. This reasoning supports the assertion of Milton Friedman (1912–2006) that inflation is caused by increases in the money supply. If T and V are not taken as fixed the direct link between money and prices is lost and a broader range of economic considerations enters the analysis.

quarterly data Data recorded for each of the four quarters of each year (that is, January–March, April–June, July–September, and October–December). Quarterly data are produced for many components of the *national income accounts. They are often presented both before and after *seasonal adjustment, that is, the removal of the estimated effects of seasonal factors.

quartile *See* QUANTILE.

quasi-autonomous non-government organization (quango) A form of organization used when it is desired to provide government finance for an activity without making the day-to-day details of its operations subject to direct political control, and without making government ministers responsible for them. Governments appoint the governing bodies of quangos, and lay down their general objectives, but then entrust detailed decisions to their discretion. In the UK, for example, quangos include the Arts Council and the various research councils.

quasi-fixed factors Factors of production that are subject to *adjustment costs when their levels are changed.

quasi-rent A payment for the services of a factor of production which in the medium term is similar to *rent. Whereas rent is paid for the services of land, which is provided by nature, quasi-rent is paid for the services of factors which owe their qualities to past sunk investment. It behaves like rent because in the short run the factors would not disappear if the payments were decreased. These payments are not true rents, since in the long run they have to be sufficient to induce new investment, for example, renewing buildings or paying for professional training.

queue A number of customers for a good or service waiting to be served. Queue discipline describes the order in which customers are served: this may be first-come first-served, random order, or last-in first-out, or some system of priorities may be used. Queuing models analyse the behaviour of queues, often using numerical simulation, and explore efficient ways of handling queues.

quits Termination of employment, for whatever reason. Quits may be initiated by the employee leaving voluntarily, for example to take a better job, or by the employer if an employee is unsatisfactory or redundant. Quits initiated by employees tend to be more common in booms than in slumps; quits initiated by employers tend to be higher in slumps than in booms.

quota A quantitative allocation. This may be set as a minimum or a maximum. A quota for jobs for disadvantaged groups, or for compulsory deliveries by former *planned economy farmers to state marketing organizations, would be a minimum. A limit on imports of cars, or the quantity of milk sold under the *Common Agricultural Policy, would be a maximum. In each case it can be argued that any objective achieved by a quota system could be achieved at lower cost by use of the *price mechanism, through an appropriate tax or subsidy. The use of quotas tends to inhibit competition, directly if quotas are allocated to individual producers, and indirectly if they are fixed en bloc, as this encourages the formation of organizations to share out the market.

quota (IMF) The share of each member of the *International Monetary Fund (IMF) in its total funds. The quota allocated to each IMF member determines its voting power, the amount of gold or international currency and of its own currency that it initially subscribes, and its access to various borrowing facilities. A large quota is attractive to any IMF member in terms of prestige and borrowing power: the price of this is a large initial subscription and large liability to extend credit to countries that need to borrow. National quotas are periodically revised.

quota (OPEC) The maximum level of international oil sales allocated to each member of the *Organization of Petroleum Exporting Countries (OPEC) at its periodic meetings. There is an incentive for each OPEC member to exceed its quota, as the resulting increase in revenue accrues to the individual member, while any resulting decrease in world oil prices affects all producers.

quota sample A sample including representatives of different sections of the population being sampled in fixed proportions, but not necessarily the same proportions as the overall population. This applies, for example, to choosing people from different sex and age groups. This is intended to ensure that particular groups are represented in the sample, although the sample may not be representative of the population. *See also* RANDOM SAMPLE; STRATIFIED SAMPLE.

quotation Acceptance of a company's shares to be traded on a *stock exchange. This is normally conditional on providing an acceptable level of information to investors. Market-makers are allowed, but not compelled, to quote prices at which they will buy or sell such shares, up to some quantitative limit.

quoted company A company whose shares have been accepted for trading on a *stock exchange. This makes it easier to raise capital, as shares once issued are made more marketable by being quoted on an organized exchange.

quote-driven market A securities market which operates by *market-makers quoting prices at which they will buy or sell, up to some quantitative limit. Prices are adjusted by the market-makers increasing their prices if they run short of stock, or cutting prices if they start accumulating excessive stocks. This is contrasted with an *order-driven market, where orders to buy at or below given prices, and to sell at or above given prices, are accumulated until at intervals, for example daily, a market-clearing price is found and buying and selling orders consistent with this price are executed.

racial discrimination *See* DISCRIMINATION.

rainforest The zone of tropical forests, with high rainfall. The rainforest is of concern to environmentalists because of its role as a source of biodiversity, and as a sink for large volumes of carbon dioxide. Scientific evidence suggests that the destruction of rainforests may lead to a rise in atmospheric carbon dioxide and thus to the *greenhouse effect and *global warming. Destruction also causes severe erosion, and increased run-off of rain leading to flooding downstream on rivers draining rainforest areas.

Ramsey pricing A pricing policy that maximizes economic welfare subject to firms achieving given profit targets. If all firms produce with *constant returns to scale and must break even then Ramsey pricing reduces to *marginal cost pricing. If firms have *increasing returns to scale and must break even then the mark-ups of the Ramsey prices over marginal cost are inversely related to the elasticity of demand. Ramsey pricing has been investigated in the context of public sector monopoly and regulated private sector *natural monopoly. Ramsey pricing is closely related to the *Ramsey rule for *optimal taxation of commodities. *See also* INVERSE ELASTICITY RULE.

Ramsey regression equation specification error test (RESET) A general specification test for a *linear regression model. It tests whether non-linear combinations of explanatory variables, in particular, their powers, help explain the dependent variable. The test is performed by regressing the predicted value of the dependent variable, $\hat{y}$, on the explanatory variables as well as the powers of $\hat{y}$, and then testing the joint significance of the coefficients on the latter. If these are significant, the linear model is misspecified.

Ramsey rule The formula that characterizes optimal commodity taxes in an economy with a single consumer. The Ramsey rule is derived by assuming that the government sets commodity taxes to maximize the utility of a single consumer subject to the chosen taxes generating a required level of tax revenue. This optimization determines the most efficient set of commodity taxes (they are efficient because the assumption of a single consumer implies there are no *equity considerations). The Ramsey rule states (approximately) that the optimal taxes cause every good to have the same proportional reduction in *compensated demand. *See also* INVERSE ELASTICITY RULE.

R&D *See* RESEARCH and DEVELOPMENT.

random effects A *panel data regression model in which it is assumed that unobserved heterogeneity is uncorrelated with the included variables. This unobserved heterogeneity is treated as a component of the disturbance term and can be group-specific (a single draw for each cross-sectional unit that enters the regression identically in each period) or time-specific (a single draw for each time period that enters the regression identically for every unit). *See also* FIXED EFFECTS.

random error A discrepancy between the observed value of a variable and its true value that is due to chance or an imprecise measurement. In a regression model, the random error is a component of the regression function that combines the unobserved effects of omitted variables, measurement error, any deviation of the assumed functional form from the true model, and chance.

random sample A sample of a population, chosen by some method which ensures that every member of the population has an equal chance of being picked. *See also* QUOTA SAMPLE.

random variable A function that maps the outcomes of a random experiment onto the real numbers. For example, one can define a random variable X as taking value 0 when a tossed coin shows 'heads' and value 1 when the coin shows 'tails'. A random variable is characterized by a *probability distribution, i.e. the set of all possible values that it can assume and the corresponding probabilities. A random variable is continuous, or has a continuous distribution, if it can take any values from an interval, bounded or unbounded; and it is discrete, or has a discrete distribution, if it can only take a countable, finite or infinite, number of separate values.

random walk A *stochastic process described by equation $y_t = y_{t-1} + \varepsilon_t$ where ε_t is *white noise. It is a prototypical example of *unit root process. A frequently considered version is the random walk with drift, $y_t = y_{t-1} + \delta + \varepsilon_t$.

range The difference between the largest and the smallest observed or possible values of a variable. The sample range is not usually a good measure of dispersion, as it makes use of only two observations, which may each be *outliers.

rank correlation *See* SPEARMAN RANK CORRELATION COEFFICIENT.

ratchet effect A tendency for a variable to be influenced by its own largest previous value. For example, consumption from any given income may be higher, the higher the previous peak consumption level; or the *real wages demanded by trade unions may be an increasing function of the highest real wage previously attained. The ratchet effect implies that variables are more sticky in one direction than the other. A ratchet effect may make inflation hard to stop, if varying speeds of adjustment have led to a situation where the sum of past peak real incomes of all sections of the community is considerably greater than the present total available.

rateable value The value placed on buildings in the UK for purposes of local taxation. Rateable values were originally supposed to be estimates of the rent which would be paid on a property, but over time have come to bear little relation to this.

Rateable values are still used for the *business rate and as a basis for domestic water rates, but have been replaced by the *council tax as the tax on residential property.

rate of exchange *See* EXCHANGE RATE.

rate of growth *See* GROWTH RATE.

rate of interest The charge made for the loan of financial capital expressed as a proportion of the loan. A borrower usually has to repay the lender more than the value of the loan originally granted. The excess of repayment over loan is the interest charge. The rate of interest is the amount of the charge paid over a given period of time expressed as a proportion of the loan. For example, if a loan of £100 is granted for two years and an interest charge of £10 per year is made, the rate of interest per year is $10/100 = 0.1$. Typically, the rate of interest is expressed as a rate per annum but it can equally be semi-annually, monthly, weekly, daily, or even continuous. If a loan is certain to be repaid, the pure rate of interest compensates the lender for loss of liquidity. If a loan is not certain to be repaid, the rate of interest is higher than the pure rate of interest, including a *default premium to compensate the lender for the average loss expected through default, and a *risk premium to compensate a *risk-averse lender for uncertainty about how large such losses will be. *See also* COMPOUND INTEREST.

rate of return The increase in the value of an asset expressed as a proportion of the asset's initial value over a given time period (the 'holding period'). For example, if a share costs £2.00 to purchase and a year later is worth £2.10, the return over the holding period of a year is $(2.10 - 2.00)/2.00 = 0.05$. A rate of return can be calculated before or after the deduction of tax, and over any length of holding period. *See also* INTERNAL RATE OF RETURN; REQUIRED RATE OF RETURN.

rate of return regulation A system for controlling the prices charged by regulated monopolists. Rate of return regulation sets prices at a level that allows the monopolist to earn the market return on its capital. Rate of return regulation has the adverse consequence of encouraging increases in costs since these define the capital base on which the return is calculated (the *Averch–Johnson effect). Rate of return regulation has mostly been superseded by price-cap regulation. *See also* UTILITY.

rates A system of local taxation in the UK. The rateable value of properties is decided by District Valuers, and is used as the basis of *business rates and charges to domestic premises by water companies. Domestic rates, which were paid only by households, were at levels per pound of rateable value, the rate in the pound being set by local authorities. Domestic rates were replaced in 1990 in England and Wales (1989 in Scotland) by the *community charge. A *uniform business rate is now charged on business premises, at a level determined by the central government.

rate support grant A UK system of grants from central government to local authorities. As the name implies, these grants were used to supplement the revenues of local authorities, which were not able to raise enough local taxation from rates to pay for their expenditure.

rational expectations Expectations which are model-consistent, leading to behaviour consistent with the model of the economy used in forming them. If there is uncertainty a rational expectation need not coincide with the actual outcome (it is not *perfect foresight), but on average it cannot be improved by the use of any available information. When obtaining and analysing information is costless, the use of rational expectations can be based on the argument that individuals, firms, or governments will make losses in terms of utility, profits, or achievement of policy objectives if they do not use all available information including the best available model of the economy. If accessing and manipulating information is expensive in terms of resources or effort, it becomes rational to trade accuracy of expectations against cost.

rationality *See* BOUNDED RATIONALITY; CONSUMER RATIONALITY.

rationalization Reorganization of production in the interests of efficiency or profits. It generally includes non-marginal changes: for example, production may be concentrated in fewer factories where it was previously scattered, or may be dispersed where it was previously concentrated.

rationing Allocation of scarce commodities by administrative decision rather than price. Many countries, for example, ration food and clothing in wartime. The argument for rationing is based on considerations of both equity and efficiency: governments want nobody to starve, and fit workers are needed for war production. Rationing is typically inefficient, especially in dealing with goods where tastes differ widely. If quantity is rationed and the price is kept low, users who get little benefit from a scarce good have little incentive to economize on it, and producers have no incentive to increase the supply. If goods are needed irregularly, and rationing prevents enough being bought on those occasions when the need arises, every user has an incentive to take up their ration regularly to form an emergency stockpile. Thus, since more may be needed in dispersed small stocks than in one central reserve, rationing may actually encourage consumption and make shortages worse. The administration of rationing schemes itself also uses scarce resources. *See also* CREDIT RATIONING.

Rawlsian social welfare function The *social welfare function that uses as its measure of *social welfare the utility of the worst-off member of society. The following argument can be used to motivate the Rawlsian social welfare function. Imagine a group of individuals who have not yet entered the economy (they are 'behind the veil of ignorance') so do not yet know what position they will occupy. That is, they may become rich members of the economy or poor members. If asked what form of social welfare function they would wish the economy to have an extremely risk-averse individual would propose the Rawlsian.

raw materials The products of *primary sector industries, intended for use as inputs to production. The main groups of raw materials are plant crops such as cotton, animal products such as wool and leather, and assorted mineral products such as bauxite ore, used to make aluminium. Raw materials form a decreasing proportion of international trade, but are still very important for many *less developed countries.

reaction curve The optimal strategy of one player in a game expressed as a function of the strategy choices of other players. For example, in a *Cournot competition the reaction curve of one firm describes the profit-maximizing output as a function of the output level of the other firms. A *Nash equilibrium occurs where the reaction curves of the players intersect.

Reaganomics The policy combination of tight monetary policy to discourage inflation, and lax public finance to encourage real growth. This policy mix is named in recognition of its use in the United States during the presidency of Ronald Reagan (1911–2004). It led to large deficits in both the US government budget and the US balance of payments on current account.

real balance effect The effect on spending of changes in the real value of money balances. During inflation, as prices rise, the real purchasing power of the money people already hold goes down. This is expected to make people more likely to save and less likely to spend their incomes. With a constant nominal money supply, this should eventually bring inflation to a halt. The *Pigou effect refers to a real balance effect during a depression: as prices fall, the real purchasing power of the stock of money rises, which should eventually lead to increased spending.

real balances The *money supply divided by a suitable *price index. This determines the quantity of real goods and services that can be purchased. Changes in real balances are a function of changes in the money supply and changes in the price level: real balances rise if the money supply increases proportionally faster than the price level. The amount of real balances people wish to hold is an increasing function of their real incomes, and may be a decreasing function of interest rates and/or the rate of inflation.

real business cycle (RBC) A theory of the *business cycle where the source of fluctuations is persistent random shocks to the technology, or to total factor productivity in the production function. *See also* ENDOGENOUS BUSINESS CYCLE.

real costs The real resources used up in producing a good or service, or the *opportunity cost in terms of other possible outputs forgone. The real costs of a good differ from private costs if the inputs are taxed or subsidized, or if there are external costs which do not fall on the person or organization responsible for production.

real exchange rate The rate at which one country's real goods and services can be changed into those of another. If the home price level is p_h, the foreign price level is p_f, and the nominal exchange rate, measured as the home price of a unit of foreign currency, is e, the real exchange rate, r, is defined as $r = ep_f/p_h$. If each country produced only one type of good, so that home and export sales were at the same price, the real exchange rate would be the same as the *terms of trade. As home sales typically include non-traded goods, and the composition of exports and home sales of exportables usually differs, the real exchange rate can deviate from the terms of trade.

real GDP *Gross domestic product divided by a suitable *price index, to express it in real terms. The price index used for this purpose is usually the *GDP deflator; as this covers the prices of investment goods and government purchases as well as consumer expenditure, it is more suitable than the *retail price index.

real GNP *Gross national product divided by a suitable *price index, to express it in real terms. The price index used for this purpose is usually the *GDP deflator. Since this covers the prices of investment goods and government purchases as well as consumer expenditure, it is more suitable than the *retail price index.

realignment of exchange rates A package of changes in exchange rates, negotiated by agreement between the countries concerned. Under the *European Monetary System from 1979 onwards there were a series of realignments. These raised the relative par values of the currencies of countries with low inflation and balance-of-payments surpluses, and lowered the relative parities of countries with high inflation and balance-of-payments problems.

real income Income measured at constant prices. This is found by deflating money income by a suitable *price index. Because of continuous changes in the types and quality of goods and services available, measurements of changes in real income become steadily less reliable as comparisons over longer time periods are considered.

real interest rate The real rate of interest received on the loan of financial capital. This is the money return, adjusted for *inflation. If the nominal interest rate is i and the rate of inflation is ρ, the real rate of interest of r is defined by

$$(1 + r) = (1 + i)/(1 + \rho).$$

For low interest and inflation rates, the approximation $r \cong i - \rho$ is fairly accurate and is frequently used.

real money supply *See* REAL BALANCES.

real national income The *national income deflated by a suitable *price index. This shows the level of real spending the country can afford. The value of real national income is affected both by changes in real productivity and by changes in the *terms of trade.

real terms A way of measuring economic variables to remove or minimize the effect of nominal changes, such as changes in the level of prices. Because of continual changes in the type and quality of goods and services available, measurement of changes in real terms becomes increasingly unreliable as longer time intervals are considered. *See also* REAL BALANCES; REAL GDP; REAL INCOME; REAL INTEREST RATE; REAL WAGES.

real variable A variable in economics which is measured in physical units of some sort: for example, the level of employment, or the volume of oil extracted in a year. *See also* NOMINAL VARIABLE.

real wage resistance Difficulty in reducing *real wages. This can be explained by the opposition of *trade unions to accepting wage settlements that do not at least compensate for price increases since the last agreement, and through employers knowing that workers dislike accepting reductions in their real incomes: wage offers involving real reductions are thought to be bad for morale, so employers are reluctant to make them. Real wage resistance obstructs adjustments in the structure of relative wages when these are necessary, and makes it difficult to bring an inflationary spiral to an end.

real wages *Money wages deflated by a suitable *price index. From an employee's point of view, the relevant price index is a consumer price index such as the *retail price index; real wages show what workers can consume. From the employer's point of view, the relevant price is the price of the firm's output: a rise in wages relative to prices decreases profitability and discourages employment.

receivership The situation when a company has defaulted on its obligations, and a receiver is appointed to use the company's assets to pay off the creditors.

recession An overall decline in economic activity mainly observed as a slowdown in output and employment. It is not as severe or prolonged as a *depression. A recession is often defined as *real GDP falling for two successive quarters, but the *National Bureau of Economic Research defines a recession as 'a significant decline in economic activity spread across the economy, lasting more than a few months, normally visible in real GDP, real income, employment, industrial production, and wholesale-retail sales'. A recession begins just after the economy reaches a peak of activity and ends as the economy reaches its trough. Between trough and peak, the economy is in an expansion.

reciprocity The principle of international economic relations by which a country treats the nationals of any foreign country in the same way as its residents are treated in that country. This is contrasted with *multilateralism and the *most favoured nation principle, by which all non-residents are treated equally. Supporters of reciprocity argue that it is both fair and likely to promote market access for one's own exporters; opponents argue that insisting on reciprocity is futile, because imports promote competition and lower prices, so that every country loses by its own trade restrictions. Reciprocity is difficult to interpret when countries are not symmetric.

recommended retail price A price that the producer of a good recommends should be charged to final customers. In the UK such recommendations are not in general legally enforceable.

recovery The phase of a *business cycle when output and employment are moving back from their lowest point towards normal levels.

recursive model A version of the *simultaneous equations model in which the matrix of coefficients of the current *endogenous variables is triangular and there is no *contemporaneous correlation of random errors across equations. These conditions ensure that all parameters in all equations in the system can be computed recursively, i.e. all equations are identified.

recycling The reuse of goods which have served their original purpose: for example, empty bottles or worn-out motor vehicles. Recycling is advocated on both cost-saving and environmental grounds, as it reduces both the need for extractive industries and the dumping of waste products.

redeemable security A security which the borrower is due to redeem at some date. This is contrasted with an irredeemable security, where the borrower has no obligation to repay the loan. As a redeemable security approaches maturity, its price converges to its redemption value, that is the amount which is due to be repaid.

redemption date The date on which a security is due to be redeemed by the borrower. This may be a single date, or a range of dates within which the borrower has discretion to choose when repayment will take place.

redemption value The price at which a security is due to be redeemed when it reaches *maturity.

redemption yield The interest rate at which receipts of interest and repayment on a security held until it matures need to be discounted to make their present value equal to its market price.

redeployment Shifting of factors of production from one use to another. When labour is redeployed, this can mean that workers no longer needed in one part of a firm are found jobs in another part. In many cases, however, new jobs are not available within the firm, and redeployment is sometimes used as a euphemism for *redundancy, with no definite prospect of any alternative job.

rediscount To buy a *bill of exchange from the holder before it reaches *maturity. The original holder will have discounted it, that is, received less for it than its face value. If the holder needs to obtain cash before the bill comes to maturity, it has to be sold on to another firm, again at a discount on its face value.

redistributive tax A tax designed to alter the distribution of income or wealth. In practice, the redistribution is usually in the direction of greater equality, but history has recorded rulers who have used taxation to redistribute in their own favour and hence to increase inequality. A system of lump-sum taxation under which some consumers pay positive taxes while others receive subsidies is redistributive: it reduces income inequality if the subsidies are received by low-income consumers and positive taxes are paid by high-income consumers. The redistributive effect of the tax system can only be found by considering the net effect of all taxes; the redistributive effect of government intervention in total must take into account all transfers and taxes.

redlining Refusal by banks to make loans or by insurance companies to issue policies to individuals or firms in particular areas. This was justified by banks as the result of bad experience with loans or policies in these areas. The practice was criticized as being a form of discrimination against ethnic groups concentrated in such areas. In the US redlining based on race, religion, gender, family status, disability, or ethnic origin was prohibited by the Fair Housing Act of 1968.

reduced form A formulation of the *simultaneous equations model in which all current *endogenous variables are expressed in terms of *exogenous and *predetermined endogenous variables. The corresponding parameters are called the reduced form parameters. *See also* INDIRECT LEAST SQUARES.

reducing balance depreciation The method of depreciating fixed assets by writing off a constant percentage of their remaining value each period. The remaining fraction is then written off when they are finally scrapped. This is contrasted with straight line depreciation, where an equal sum is written off each period for a predetermined number of years.

redundancy Termination of employment without any fault on the part of the employees concerned, because of a fall in the employer's need for labour. Some UK workers have a legal right to compensation for redundancy. Employers may make redundancy payments in excess of legal requirements to induce workers to accept offers of voluntary redundancy and so avoid the need for compulsory redundancies.

reform *See* CURRENCY REFORM; PRICE REFORM.

refusal to supply Refusal by producers to sell their goods to all applicants. This is believed to inhibit competition between distributors. Firms may wish to restrict their outlets because they believe that some distributors would undermine the reputation of their products by selling them without proper storage facilities, advice to customers, and installation services, or in some cases simply by trading in sordid premises that would impair their prestige. Refusal to supply may also take place when a producer prefers to sell through outlets which do not stock rival products. Refusal to grant trade credit on the usual terms may be due to doubts about a distributor's solvency.

regional aid Help by central government for regions with low per capita incomes or high unemployment. This may take the form of state funds for *infrastructure investment, subsidies, or tax allowances to induce private firms to invest in depressed regions, or special assistance with projects such as technical education, designed to make the areas in need of aid more attractive to investors. The European Union also provides regional aid to depressed regions in member countries, through the European Regional Development Fund and the European Social Fund. In spite of large amounts of regional aid, some regional differences in per capita incomes have been highly persistent.

regional policy Policies concerning the distribution of income and employment between different geographical regions of a country, or in the case of the European Union, a group of countries. Regional policies usually seek to bring regions with exceptionally low per capita incomes up towards the national average, and to lower the unemployment rates of regions with exceptionally high unemployment. They may also be concerned with relieving the social problems and congestion caused by over-concentration of activities in the most crowded regions. Regional policy works by seeking to direct both private and public sector investment into the more depressed regions. This may be done both by the direct use of government funds, and by tax concessions to encourage private investment in peripheral regions.

regional trade agreements (RTAs) Agreements between groups of countries to trade with each other more freely than with the world in general. There are numerous RTAs, and most world trade is affected by one or more of them. RTAs differ greatly in their effectiveness. Some have major effects, notably the Common Market of the European Union, and the North American Free Trade Agreement, including Canada, Mexico, and the US. Many RTAs unite developing countries, for example *Mercado del Sur, whose members are Argentina, Brazil, Paraguay, and Uruguay. It is thought that regional arrangements are preferred to full multilateral liberalization because of the extreme difficulty in reaching worldwide agreement; they are preferred to unilateral trade liberalization because of a desire to get improved access to foreign markets and worries about the effects of unilateral liberalization on the balance of payments. It is unclear whether RTAs are a step towards more general world free trade, or an obstacle to achieving it.

registered unemployed Unemployed persons in receipt of unemployment-related benefits. This means that they are unemployed in the view of the official agencies responsible for administering benefits. This definition of unemployment is contrasted with that based on labour force surveys, which record the numbers of those who consider themselves to be unemployed. In the UK the registered unemployed figure is usually around 1 percent of the labour force below that produced by labour force surveys.

Registrar of Companies A UK official responsible for registering companies, issuing certificates of registration, maintaining a register of companies, and receiving annual returns. One Registrar covers England and Wales; Scotland has a separate Registrar.

regression A tool for numerical data analysis that summarizes the relationship among the variables in a data set as an equation, where the variable of interest, or the dependent variable, is expressed as a function of one or several explanatory variables. The name regression originates from the phenomenon of regression to the average in heights of children compared to the heights of their parents, described by Francis Galton (1822–1911) in the 1870s. *See also* LINEAR REGRESSION; MULTIPLE REGRESSION.

regressive tax A tax where the ratio of tax paid to the taxable amount falls as the taxable amount rises. A regressive tax system redistributes from the poorer members of society to the richer members. There are many ways a tax system can be made regressive. Two examples are by having a maximum direct tax charge irrespective of income, or by having *indirect taxes levied at relatively high rates on goods heavily consumed by the poor.

regret theory A theory of choice based on the premise that people anticipate regret if a wrong choice is made, and take this anticipation into account when making decisions. Regret theory is an alternative to *expected utility and can explain some economic *anomalies. *See also* BEHAVIOURAL ECONOMICS; MINIMAX REGRET.

regulation A rule individuals or firms are obliged to follow; or the procedure for deciding and enforcing such rules. Modern economies are subject to numerous forms of regulation. These may be designed to promote public health and safety: for example, rules on food hygiene and the coding of electrical wiring. They may be designed to promote competition and prevent unfair trading practices: for example, *monopolies and *mergers are controlled in most societies, and *insider dealing is forbidden in many countries. Regulations may be set and enforced by government bodies, or by *quasi-autonomous non-government organizations (quangos). In the last resort regulation relies on legal sanctions, but the largest proportion of effective regulation is done by the regulators setting standards which organizations then try to comply with as a matter of self-discipline. *See also* BANK REGULATION; SELF-REGULATION.

regulatory agency A body set up to decide on and enforce *regulations. In some cases the government does this itself; in the UK, for example, town planning and weights and measures regulations are decided by the central government and enforced by local authorities. In many cases a *quasi-autonomous non-government organization (quango) is set up and the task of regulation deputed to it. This is largely because of the vast amount of detail involved, and also in an attempt to remove the influence of politicians from deciding on details, and to relieve them of responsibility for the results. In the UK, regulatory quangos include the *Competition Commission and the various bodies, such as the *Office of Telecommunications, set up to regulate the pricing and other policies of the privatized public utilities. Regulatory agencies may be set up from outside an industry, or use may be made of *self-regulation, by bodies representing firms in an industry. The advantage of self-regulatory organizations is that practitioners in an industry can be expected to be aware of its problems; the danger is that they may tend to identify the public interest with protection of existing firms in an industry.

regulatory capture The tendency of regulators to identify with the interest of the industry they are supposed to regulate. This occurs when a public authority charged with regulating an industry in the public interest comes to identify the public interest with the interests of producers in the industry, rather than the interests of its customers, or the general public.

reinsurance The system by which the issuers of *insurance policies pass on part of the risk to others, by themselves taking out further insurance policies. Reinsurance generally applies only to claims on a policy or group of policies in excess of some minimum amount. This limits the insurer's maximum possible losses if claims on the policies turn out to be higher than expected: it is thus a method of risk-spreading.

relationship banking Banking on the basis that there is a continuing relation between a bank and a customer. The bank is expected to take an interest in the customer's business, offering advice and support when in difficulties. This is contrasted with the view that a bank should simply operate a customer's account, and that the customer should take each type of transaction to whatever bank will handle it most cheaply.

relationship investor An investor who is an active participant in a business, as well as providing capital. Such participation may vary between appointing some members of the board of directors and informal consultation on a continuing basis. It involves a long-term connection between the investor and the company; a relationship investor is not in the business of selling out to make short-term speculative gains. Relationship investment is contrasted with the view that investors should merely hold shares, and let the existing management undertake the task of running a company.

relative income hypothesis The theory that *savings behaviour is affected by a person's relative position in the income distribution. Thus at a given level of *real income, a person may be a relatively poor member of a rich community, or a relatively rich member of a poor community. The member of the richer community is expected to consume more and save less, as ideas of what constitutes a socially acceptable minimum level of consumption are influenced by what is habitual to their friends and neighbours. This analysis also applies to comparisons between different countries or regions, or the same country at different times.

relative price The price of good i relative to the price of good j is given by p_i/p_j. This ratio measures the rate at which good i can be exchanged for good j and is what matters for economic choices. For example, the real wage is the wage paid for labour relative to the price of consumption and determines the trade-off between consumption and labour for a consumer. Two sets of prices represent the same set of relative prices if it is possible to change one set to the other by multiplying each price by a constant λ. This observation motivates the use of a *numeraire commodity to allow all prices to be expressed relative to the price of the numeraire.

relief *See* DEBT RELIEF; MORTGAGE INTEREST RELIEF AT SOURCE.

reneging Going back on a promise, contract, or bargain. This may be motivated by *opportunism: once the other party is committed to an irrevocable action there is a temptation to renege if it is profitable. In judging whether to renege it is necessary to weigh the short-term gains against the long-term losses (from retaliation, punishment, or loss of reputation). General freedom to renege would make impossible many economically efficient contracts, for example those concerning loans and career choice. One role of the legal system is to reduce the extent of reneging. The legal system aims to ensure that the terms of contracts are satisfied, and when they can be verified to have been broken, to ensure that compensation is paid to the injured party.

renewable energy Energy produced by methods which do not involve using up *depletable resources. These are solar, geothermal, wind, wave, hydroelectric, and tidal energy, and energy from biomass. Energy produced from nuclear fusion or fission is not regarded as renewable.

renewable resources Natural or man-made resources that are replenishable at least as fast as they are consumed or used up. Natural resources such as fresh water or timber may become non-renewable if used up at a faster rate than they are replenished by natural processes, unlike solar or tidal energy. Examples of man-made renewable resources include food, paper, and leather. *See also* DEPLETABLE RESOURCES.

rent 1. A payment made for the use of land or buildings. If land is productive purely on account of its natural features or its location, rent is a pure surplus accruing to the owner, who contributes no inputs into creating it. The rent on buildings, or on land which has been improved, for example by drainage, is often termed *quasi-rent, as it is partly rent and partly payment for the services of the capital invested in buildings or improvements. Payment for the hire of consumer durables or productive equipment is referred to as rental payments. Rent of ability describes payments for the work of people with exceptional and scarce talents, such as artists or footballers, whose fees often exceed what they could earn in other occupations combined with a normal rate of return on the cost of special training needed for their professions.

2. A general term for payment in excess of *opportunity cost. Rent can be created by monopoly power, by legislation, or by *network externalities. *See also* ECONOMIC RENT.

rental payment A payment for the use of hired equipment. This may be productive equipment, such as cranes or scaffolding, or consumer durables. Such payments are in the nature of *quasi-rents: in the long run equipment will only be replaced when it is worn out if the rental payments are sufficient to cover interest and amortization.

rent control Government control of rents for houses and flats. This may involve setting the levels of rents, or restricting increases. It has been widely adopted, mainly for motives of income distribution, based on the assumption that landlords are richer than tenants, so that controlling rents produces a more equal distribution of real incomes. During inflationary periods lags in adjustment tend to make controlled rents fall below market-clearing levels: this produces excess demand, and necessitates protection of security of tenure for tenants. In the long run rent controls discourage investment in housing for rent, and also discourage maintenance work on rented housing, so that its quality deteriorates. A general situation of excess demand for housing impairs labour mobility, as sitting tenants are unable or unwilling to move.

rented housing Housing owned by somebody other than the occupant, who is a tenant and pays rent to occupy it. Rented housing may be owned by private individuals, by companies, by public bodies such as local authorities or HM services, or by *housing associations. *See also* OWNER-OCCUPIED HOUSING.

rentier A person whose main income comes from interest on assets, normally gilt-edged. This is contrasted with forms of property income connected with entrepreneurial activities.

rent-seeking Spending time and money not on the production of real goods and services, but rather on trying to get the government to change the rules so as to make one's business more profitable. This can take various forms, including seeking subsidies on the outputs or the inputs of a business, or persuading the government to change the rules so as to keep out competitors, tolerate or promote collusion between those already engaged in an activity, or make legally compulsory the use of professional services.

repeated game A game that is repeated a number of times into the future. The number of repetitions may be finite or infinite. The number may be known in advance, or there may be an expectation that the game will be repeated. Participants in repeated games have an incentive to choose their *strategies taking into account how their actions in each play of the game will affect their reputation, that is, how other participants will expect them to behave in future rounds of the game. It may thus pay in a repeated game to adopt strategies which would not be chosen in a one-off game, where reputation does not matter. In any game that is repeated a finite number of times *backward induction can be used to find the equilibrium strategy: the *Nash equilibrium for the one-shot game will be played in every repeat of the game. *See also* FOLK THEOREM.

replacement cost The system of accounting in which the assets of firms are valued and their depreciation allowances are calculated using the costs of replacing their buildings and equipment. Where buildings and equipment can be replaced exactly, this might seem an ideal accounting method. However, particularly in the case of equipment, owing to technical progress, exact replacements are frequently not available, and would not be worth installing even if they were. In such cases calculating the cost of appropriate replacements for equipment is very much a matter of judgement.

replacement investment Purchase of machinery and equipment by a producer to maintain the output capacity that is lost through deterioration (ageing or *obsolescence) and scrapping (complete withdrawal) of the existing machinery. It is essentially a problem of economic choice for the producer, rather than a technological necessity.

replacement ratio 1. The pension of a retired person as a proportion of income when in employment. The higher is the replacement ratio the stronger is the incentive to retire. Conversely, a worker may postpone retirement if the current replacement ratio is too low. A target replacement ratio is used as a guide in pension planning.
    2. The income of an unemployed worker as a proportion of income when in work. If this ratio is too high it gives a disincentive to accept job offers: allowing for the cost of travel to work and other working expenses, and the value of leisure, a replacement ratio below 1 is needed to maintain incentives to work. Too high a replacement ratio may perpetuate unemployment, while too low a ratio inflicts suffering on the unemployed and their families. In practice replacement ratios vary widely, as income support for the unemployed is based on family size while wages are not.

representative firm A single firm whose choices are representative of its industry. Assume all the firms in an industry have the same constant returns to scale technology and every firm acts as a *price-taker. In equilibrium each firm must make zero profit and hence is indifferent to the level of output it produces. In contrast, the optimal *capital–labour ratio is uniquely defined. The industry can therefore be modelled by a representative firm that has the same technology, chooses the same capital–output ratio, and produces the same output as the entire industry.

repressed inflation A situation in which price and wage increases are restrained by official controls. This can lead to an increase in inflation when the controls are relaxed, unless policies to remove the excess demand are adopted.

reputational policy A policy which relies on other people believing the policy-maker's promises. For example, it is possible to attempt to control inflation by cutting the money supply immediately, or by promising to cut it steadily over some future period. The policy of promising a gradual cut in the money supply can only work if people believe the future cuts will actually be made: that is, the authorities' promises must be credible. If their past conduct has led people to regard official promises as worthless, a reputational policy is not available, and inflation can be controlled, if at all, only by immediate cuts in the money supply, possibly at a severe cost in unemployment. Reputational policies are only made possible by building up a reputation for keeping one's word, even in circumstances when immediate pain could be avoided by breaking it. *See also* CREDIBILITY.

required rate of return The minimum rate of return on an investment needed to make it acceptable to a business.

resale price maintenance (RPM) The fixing by manufacturers of minimum prices at which their products may be resold by distributors. While RPM does not necessarily imply a price-fixing *cartel of producers, it does make such a cartel easier to organize. RPM was stopped in the UK by the Retail Prices Act of 1964 and the Restrictive Practices Act of 1966, with some exceptions, including the Net Book Agreement, until that system collapsed in 1995. Manufacturers can still set a *recommended retail price, but cannot legally enforce this.

reschedule debt Revise a debt contract, by which interest and/or redemption payments are deferred to later dates than those originally agreed. This has been applied both to the private debts of companies in difficulties and the *sovereign debts of nations, especially *less developed countries. Rescheduling is accepted by lenders because the alternative may be outright *default on the debt, and the consequent requirement to write it off in their own accounts.

research and development (R&D) The use of resources to create new knowledge, and to develop new and improved products or more economical methods of production. Research is the part of this devoted to discovering new knowledge; development is the part devoted to bringing new ideas to the stage where production for the market can start. This includes devising methods of making the products, and testing that they work reliably and do not create hazards for health or safety. In many models of *endogenous growth R&D is the engine of growth.

reservation price The maximum price that a buyer is willing to pay for a good or the minimum price that a seller will accept.

reservation utility The minimum level of utility that must be guaranteed by a *contract to make it acceptable to an agent. *See also* PRINCIPAL–AGENT PROBLEM.

reservation wage The minimum wage that a worker engaged in search for a new job is willing to accept. A worker will not accept an offer if the wage is below their reservation wage.

reserve asset ratio A required minimum proportion between banks' reserve assets and their deposits and other liabilities. This may be imposed or varied as part of a central bank's monetary policy, to enable it to control total bank lending by using *open market operations to control the amount of reserve assets, or as part of the *regulations imposed to safeguard the solvency of the banking system. It is not very useful for this latter purpose, as banks with unsatisfactory non-reserve assets are liable to become insolvent, however strong their reserve position.

reserve currency A currency used as *foreign exchange reserves by other countries. To be suitable for use as reserves, a currency needs to be *convertible, and to belong to a large country with a reputation for low inflation. The principal currency currently used as reserves is the US dollar. In the past the pound sterling was used as a reserve currency, mainly by *sterling area countries, and the French franc has been used, mainly by francophone countries. The Euro is becoming increasingly popular as a reserve currency. Opinions differ as to whether countries gain by having their currencies used as reserves. Reserve currency countries receive cheap loans from the holders while the system lasts, but their currencies are exposed to severe speculative pressure if confidence in them declines, which inhibits independence in monetary policy.

reserve ratio The proportion of the total assets of a bank or other financial institution held as reserves, that is as money balances or some form of highly liquid asset. Minimum reserve ratios have been used both as instruments of monetary policy, and as regulatory methods of attempting to ensure solvency.

reserve requirements The minimum percentage of their total assets which banks or other financial institutions are required to hold in money balances, or in some form of highly *liquid assets. Minimum reserve requirements may be used as instruments of monetary policy, or as methods of trying to ensure the institutions' solvency. They are not satisfactory as guarantees of solvency, as they take no account either of the riskiness of the institutions' other assets, or of the adequacy of their capital. A financial institution whose assets depreciate so that they are worth less than its debts will be insolvent, regardless of the high liquidity of its remaining assets.

reserves *See* CAPITAL RESERVES; FOREIGN EXCHANGE RESERVES; LOAN-LOSS RESERVES.

reserve tranche (IMF) The first quarter of the *quota of any member of the *International Monetary Fund, which is available to the member unconditionally if required. This corresponds to the part of each member's quota originally deposited in gold or *convertible currency.

RESET *See* RAMSEY REGRESSION EQUATION SPECIFICATION ERROR TEST.

residual In a *regression, the difference between the observed value of the variable and its value predicted by the estimated regression equation.

residual unemployment Unemployment remaining during times of full employment, made up of people unwilling to work or unable to work because of a disability.

residual variation Variation in the dependent variable that is not explained by the regression model and is represented by the *residuals of the regression.

Resolution Trust Corporation (RTC) A US federal agency set up in 1989 to wind up bankrupt *thrifts. The RTC was funded by the federal government, and supervised by the *Federal Deposit Insurance Corporation (FDIC). In 1995 its duties were transferred to the Savings Association Insurance Fund of the FDIC.

resources Any factor endowments that can contribute to economic activity. This includes natural resources, including both those located on land and those in or under the sea; human resources, including labour of various skills and qualifications; and capital goods, or man-made means of production. Economics can be defined as the study of how resources are, or should be, allocated. *See also* DEPLETABLE RESOURCES; EFFICIENT ALLOCATION; NATURAL RESOURCES; RENEWABLE RESOURCES.

Restart A UK scheme to assist the long-term unemployed to re-enter the labour market.

restraint of trade A term in a *contract that restricts a person's right to exercise a trade or carry on business. Such a term is common, for example, in the sale of a business, where the seller agrees not to set up in competition with the purchaser. Contracts of employment often include a term restraining employees from working for the firm's rivals for some period after they leave: this is to protect confidential commercial or technical information gained in the previous employment being passed to competitors. Agreements in restraint of trade are void in the UK unless the party relying on them can show that the restrictions are not unreasonable or contrary to public policy.

restricted least squares estimator An estimator obtained by minimizing the sum of squared residuals subject to the set of constraints that constitute a hypothesis to be tested. The test of the hypothesis then amounts to establishing whether assuming the hypothesis leads to a significant loss of fit, and is based on the comparison of the sums of squared residuals from the restricted and unrestricted regressions.

restrictive practices 1. Practices which affect the ability of firms to compete freely in markets for their products and inputs. This includes discrimination between customers by suppliers, exclusive dealing arrangements, and agreement or collusion to share out markets, either geographically or by products. Agreements embodying restrictive trade practices may be made illegal, or may require registration, so that they can be referred to a regulatory body.

2. Practices which affect the efficient use of labour. This may include demarcation of work between different employees, minimum manning levels on the workforce required for any given task, or refusal to cooperate with temporary or unqualified workers. Such practices are often justified as being necessary for the health and safety of workers, or of the general public: difficulties clearly can arise from having work done by staff who are insufficiently qualified, or too few to cope if anything goes wrong. However, they are criticized as being motivated by a desire to create more and safer jobs for 'insiders', and to restrict competition by 'outsiders'. The reduction or elimination of restrictive labour practices is frequently part of productivity agreements. *See also* INSIDERS AND OUTSIDERS.

Restrictive Practices Court (RPC) A UK court set up under the Restrictive Trade Practices Acts to judge whether restrictive trading agreements were in the public interest. The RPC was abolished in 1998, when its functions were transferred to the *Competition Commission.

retail banking Banking involving transactions with the general public. Retail banks collect deposits from individuals and small businesses, and make loans to them. In both cases the sums concerned may be small. Retail banking is distinguished from wholesale banking, which concentrates on large-scale transactions with other financial institutions.

retail price index (RPI) The official UK *cost of living index. The RPI is based on a monthly survey of the prices of UK consumer goods and services, and is used as the basis for payments on *index-linked government securities, and pensions and allowances. 'RPI' is in fact a misleading description, as it covers many forms of consumer expenditure such as rents, mortgage interest, and public utility charges which do not pass through retail outlets. The RPI measures prices inclusive of *value-added tax and other *indirect taxes, and so may change as the result of changes in indirect taxation. In many countries a similar index is referred to as a *consumer price index.

retail sales The part of total consumption expenditure which passes through retail outlets, that is shops. This excludes many parts of consumer spending: for example, rent, mortgage interest, public utility charges, and insurance.

retained earnings The part of company profits which is not paid out in taxes or dividends, but is ploughed back into a business. Retained earnings may be used to finance fixed investment, to finance takeovers of other firms, to extend credit to customers, to pay off loans, or to increase liquid assets. Retention of earnings is an alternative to borrowing or raising equity capital through share issues for financing new investment.

retaliation A policy change made to punish another firm or country for its actions. In a *trade war, for example, country *A* retaliates to *quotas on its exports to country *B* by imposing quotas on *B*'s goods. It is difficult in practice to distinguish between deliberate retaliation and policy changes which are simply a reaction to a worsening in country A's position. If a fall in exports to country B worsens country A's balance of payments, A may restrict imports for balance-of-payments reasons; while a fall in its exports injures country B, this is a side-effect rather than an objective of country A's policy.

return *See* RATE OF RETURN; TAX RETURN; VAT RETURN.

returns *See* CONSTANT RETURNS TO SCALE; DECREASING RETURNS TO SCALE; INCREASING RETURNS TO SCALE; RETURNS TO SCALE.

returns to scale In a productive process, the relation between an equal proportional change in all inputs and the resulting proportional change in output. If a proportional increase of λ in all inputs produces a proportional increase of λ in output, there are constant returns to scale. If output rises by a larger proportion than inputs, there are increasing returns to scale. If output rises by a smaller proportion than inputs, there are decreasing returns to scale.

revaluation 1. A change in the basis of valuing a company's assets in its accounts. This may be necessary because of general inflation, or because of changes in the real value of particular assets.
    2. A rise in the value of a country's currency. *See also* CURRENCY APPRECIATION.

revealed preference Information about preferences revealed by economic choices. As prices and income change a consumer will make different choices. The observed choices can be used to construct a preference order for the consumer. Consider three bundles of goods, A, B, and C. An individual, who could have afforded something preferred to B (for example, an alternative with more of all goods), chooses A: A is thus strictly preferred to B. If the consumer chooses A but could not afford C, it can in some cases still be shown that A is preferred to C. This occurs if B is chosen when something preferred to C could have been afforded: B is thus preferred to C. With transitive preferences, if A is preferred to B and B is preferred to C, then A is established to be revealed preferred to C, even though the consumer has not been observed making a direct comparison between A and C.

revenue 1. Receipts from sales. Total revenue is total receipts; average revenue is revenue per unit sold; and marginal revenue is the addition to total revenue from a small increase in quantity sold, per unit increase in the quantity.
    2. The total received by the government from the imposition of taxation.

revenue tariff A tariff imposed principally as a source of government revenue. This is contrasted with a protective tariff, imposed mainly as a means of assisting domestic producers to compete with imports. Many actual tariffs have effects in both ways, though a tariff on goods a country does not produce is clearly for revenue purposes only, while a prohibitive tariff can only be protective as it raises no revenue. Revenue tariffs are important for many *less developed countries, which find difficulty in collecting taxes from a largely informal internal economy.

reverse takeover A situation where a smaller company takes over a larger company, or where a private company takes over a public company. In the latter case the ownership is transferred to the company that is taken over, allowing a private company a possibly easier route to *public ownership.

reverse yield gap An excess of returns on *gilt-edged securities above those on *equities. This is likely to occur during periods of high inflation because equities are expected to provide capital gains to compensate for inflation while gilt-edged securities are not. During periods of stable prices the yield gap is usually positive: a greater yield on equities is needed to compensate investors for their relative riskiness.

revolving loan A loan which is formally for short periods, but which is habitually renewed. Such a loan would be made, for example, by a bank to a shopkeeper financing stocks on credit: sales allow the repayment of loans, but it is profitable for both parties to renew the loans to finance the purchase of further stocks. It is not easy to distinguish such loans from loans renewed because the borrowers cannot repay them.

Ricardian equivalence The argument that a change in government policy can be offset by a change in individual behaviour so as to leave equilibrium unchanged. For example, assume the government introduces a *fully-funded pension scheme under which each individual is taxed an amount τ to pay for a pension. If the return on the pension scheme and on private saving is the same, then a reduction of private saving of amount τ will offset the effect of the pension scheme and leave equilibrium unchanged. Moreover, if the level of saving was optimal for each individual before the pension scheme was introduced then it must be optimal to reduce saving exactly by the amount needed to offset the pension. Ricardian equivalence arises in many areas of economics. The original application was to debt. Assume the government gives bonds to individuals. Will spending rise because wealth has increased? The Ricardian equivalence arguments says not: the bond must eventually be redeemed which implies a future tax liability. The discounted value of the tax liability is exactly equal to the value of the bond. Net wealth does not increase and the equilibrium does not change. The range of policies that can be offset is extended if there are links between individuals in the economy. If every parent cares about the utility of their children then individuals are linked across generations and a range of intertemporal government policies can be offset by changes in bequests. Alternatively, if individuals are linked within a generation, say through marriage, then policies that attempt to redistribute within the generation can be offset by changes in transfers.

ridge regression A practical approach to estimating a regression with *multicollinearity in explanatory variables. The resulting estimator is biased but has a smaller variance than the *least squares estimator.

right-hand-side variable A jargon name for an explanatory variable in a regression equation.

rights issue An issue of new shares in a company which are first offered to existing shareholders in proportion to their present holdings: shareholders are entitled but not obliged to take up their rights. Where the issue price is below the market price of the shares, it may be possible to sell the rights. If rights are not taken up, the shares are sold in the market, and shareholders receive the excess if the shares fetch more than the issue price. The advantage of a rights issue as a means of raising capital is that the register of present shareholders provides a ready-made list of people who have already shown some interest in a company.

risk A form of uncertainty where, while the actual outcome of an action is not known, probabilities can be assigned to each of the possible outcomes. This permits application of the *expected utility function to represent preferences over alternatives. The *variance of the distribution of possible outcomes is frequently used as a measure of risk, particularly in financial theory. *See also* COUNTER-PARTY CREDIT RISK; CURRENCY RISK; DOWNSIDE RISK; EXPOSURE TO RISK; IDIOSYNCRATIC RISK; INDEPENDENT RISKS; MARKET RISK; SETTLEMENT RISK; SYSTEMATIC RISK.

risk-adjusted return on capital (RAROC) A method of comparing returns on different investments taking account of *risk. The actual return is adjusted by measuring how the assets held are exposed to risk, and adjusting downwards the returns on riskier assets. How useful RAROC is depends on how accurately the riskiness of different assets can be assessed, and on how well the penalties on riskier assets reflect the degree of risk aversion of any given investor. For new types of assets, such as *derivatives, risk assessment is highly uncertain in advance of experience of how their prices will actually behave.

risk-averse An individual is risk-averse if they prefer a certain pay-off of M to a risky prospect with an expected pay-off of M. This will be true whenever the *marginal utility of wealth is decreasing, so the *utility function is strictly concave. A risk-averse individual will not accept an actuarially *fair gamble, and will pay a *risk premium to avoid randomness of pay-offs.

risk aversion The preference for a certain pay-off rather than a risky pay-off with the same expected value.

risk bearing Having or sharing responsibility for accepting the losses if projects go wrong. Most economic activities are capable of resulting in losses under some circumstances, however good the expected results may be. Somebody has to bear the risk of meeting any losses. The first risk bearer for any project is the *entrepreneur in a private firm, or the equity shareholders in a company. If the losses are sufficiently bad, other people connected with a firm are also at risk, including creditors, the tax authorities, customers who have paid deposits on goods, and workers left unpaid when a business collapses.

risk capital Capital which the owners are willing to invest in equity in new and untried projects, where there is a recognized chance that they will lose it. Venture capitalists are willing to take these risks if they expect that their successes will make sufficiently large profits to keep their average return positive, in spite of some losses. *Venture capital may be provided by individuals who are almost or entirely *risk-neutral, or by investment banks and other organizations which are large enough to be able to spread their investments sufficiently to reduce risk to acceptable levels by *risk pooling.

risk-free security A security which is free of the various possible sources of risk. One is the risk that the debtor may default; this is thought to be absent in the case of UK, US, and many other countries' *government debt. A second risk is that the market price may be low at the time when a security has to be sold; this risk is high for securities with a long time to *maturity, and shrinks steadily as the maturity date gets closer. In money terms, a government obligation is risk-free if the holder has the option to have it redeemed at any time. In *real terms, so long as there is uncertainty about inflation no security is risk-free, unless it is suitably indexed. From any individual's point of view, the suitable index would have weights corresponding to his or her own tastes, and be kept fully up to date. Actual UK government indexed securities use the *retail price index with a lag of several months, so are not entirely risk-free in real terms. A third source of risk derives from currency fluctuations. US treasury bills are usually seen as the closest practical equivalent to a risk-free security, provided that the holder ultimately wishes to purchase commodities denominated in dollars.

risk-loving An individual is risk-loving if they prefer a risky prospect with an expected pay-off of M to a certain pay-off of M. This will be true whenever the *marginal utility of wealth is increasing, so the *utility function is strictly convex. A risk-averse individual will be willing to pay a fee to enter an actuarially *fair gamble.

risk-neutral An individual is risk-neutral if they are indifferent between a risky prospect with an expected pay-off of M and a certain pay-off of M. This will be true whenever the *marginal utility of wealth is constant, so the *utility function is linear. A risk-neutral individual will be indifferent between entering and not entering an actuarially *fair gamble.

risk-neutral valuation A method for valuing financial assets. Risk-neutral valuation calculates the value of an asset by discounting the expected value of its future pay-offs at the risk-free *rate of return. The expected value is not obtained using the actual probabilities of each pay-off. Instead, risk-neutral valuation calculates the expected value of future pay-offs using constructed probabilities that have the property of rationalizing observed asset prices if all investors were risk-neutral.

risk pooling Combining two or more risky projects, with returns which are not perfectly correlated. The expected sum of the returns to such projects is less dispersed than the expected returns on the separate projects. Insurance companies work by pooling the risks on a number of separate projects, for example the chance that any one of many houses will catch fire. Risk pooling also applies to *portfolios of investment and *unit trusts, which hold a number of different shares whose behaviour is at least partly independent. Risk pooling is one source of advantage for larger organizations relative to smaller ones.

risk premium 1. The amount that a *risk-averse individual is willing to pay to avoid a risk. Consider an individual with initial wealth W and facing a risky prospect that will lead to a final wealth, $\widetilde{W}$, that is random. The risk premium, ρ, is defined by

$$U(W - \rho) = E[U(\tilde{W})]$$

so that it equates the utility of the certain wealth level, $W - \rho$, to the *expected utility of the risky wealth level, $\tilde{W}$. If $E[\tilde{W}] = W$ then $\rho > 0$ when the utility function is strictly concave.

2. The additional return that a risky asset must pay over that paid by the *risk-free security in order to induce *risk-averse investors to purchase it. The risk premium is endogenously determined by the equilibrium in financial markets. For example, in the *Capital Asset Pricing Model the risk premium on asset i is given by $\beta_i(\bar{r}_m - r_f)$, where β_i is the *beta coefficient of asset i, $\bar{r}_m$ is the expected return on the market portfolio, and r_f is the return on the risk-free security.

risk sharing The sharing of risk between economic agents. Suppose a firm wishes to finance a risky project. If it uses its own money, it bears all the risk itself. If it issues *equity capital to finance x percent of the project, x percent of the risk is borne by whoever buys the shares. Similarly, the government shares risks among taxpayers. Consider the government investing in a risky project. If the project performs badly any losses (or costs in excess of budget) are met by the taxpayers. This ability of the government to share risk has been used to argue that the government should act as if it were *risk-neutral. Efficient risk sharing arises when the risk is allocated to the least *risk-averse agents. Hence, efficient risk sharing between a risk-averse worker and a risk-neutral firm will allocate all the risk to the firm.

risk taking Engaging in any risky activity when a safer alternative was available. This applies to many situations, for example trading on one's own account rather than working for an employer, making unsecured loans rather than secured ones, betting, or failing to insure one's home. Even *risk-averse individuals are prepared to take many risks: they would prefer a safer alternative if the mean expected return were the same, but believe that the risky alternative offers a higher return than the safe one.

robustness of policies The property of economic policies that their merits are relatively insensitive to the exact specification of the underlying model of the economy.

roll-over of loans Allowing borrowers to renew loans when they fall due for repayment, rather than actually paying them off. This is common in two cases. In many cases the loans have been used to finance profitable transactions, such as buying goods for resale: the borrower could repay the loan, but has good prospects of profit from similar further transactions if the loan is renewed. In other cases the borrower cannot repay the loan, and the lender has the choice of rolling over the loan or writing it off as a bad debt, with adverse effects on their own accounts. In such cases there is a strong temptation to roll over the loan, especially if there is some prospect that the borrower will eventually be able to repay it.

rounding error The error introduced by rounding numbers in the intermediate steps of calculation, with the final result being different from what would have obtained using the exact values.

Royal Economic Society An economic association formed in the UK in 1890. The Royal Economic Society has over 3000 members, with 60 percent living outside the UK. It promotes the study of economic science in academic life, government service, banking, industry, and public affairs.

(⊕) **SEE WEB LINKS**

• The home page of the Royal Economic Society.

royalties Payments to the owners of *natural resources such as minerals or oil, made by mine operators. Royalties are so called because the owner is frequently a sovereign, or a state. Royalties are governed by agreements, which may specify them in amounts per unit extracted, or as a percentage of revenue. The term is also used for payments by publishers to authors, and by recording companies to composers.

RPIX A retail price index excluding mortgage interest payments. This is contrasted with the UK's *retail price index (RPI) which includes mortgage interest. In many other countries the commonly used retail price index is calculated excluding mortgage interest, so is already an RPIX. The main argument for using an RPIX is that under the UK system, if rising prices provoke a rise in interest rates to suppress demand, the *impact effect is an increase in the measured rate of inflation. The main argument for including mortgage interest in the RPI is that people with mortgages do in fact have to pay it, and it absorbs a substantial proportion of personal incomes.

R-squared *See* COEFFICIENT OF DETERMINATION.

rules-based policy A policy regime formulated as a set of certain rules that are not supposed to change over time or in response to a change in the economic environment. An example of a rule-based monetary policy is mandating constant growth of the money supply. *See also* DISCRETIONARY POLICY.

rules of origin Rules applied in *free-trade areas to determine whether goods qualify for duty-free admission. Usually such rules specify a minimum percentage of inputs which have to come from member countries.

r

rules of the game A historical name for the rules under which the *gold standard was supposed to operate. Under the 'rules of the game', countries losing gold were supposed to raise their interest rates and cut their money supply; countries gaining gold were supposed to cut interest rates and increase their money supply. These rules were intended to restore equilibrium in the balance of payments fairly quickly. However, the incentive to obey these rules was much greater for the countries losing gold, who were in danger of running out of *foreign exchange reserves, than for the countries gaining gold. The countries gaining gold could afford to insulate their domestic economies from its inflationary effects by sterilizing the increase in their exchange reserves, and often did so; the countries losing reserves could not afford to sterilize the effects for long. This imparted a deflationary bias to the gold standard system as a whole. *See also* STERILIZATION.

running yield The income on a portfolio as a percentage of the current market value of the portfolio. For example, if a portfolio yields £800 per annum income and its value is currently £8000 the running yield is 800/8000 = 10 percent.

rustbelt The area of the USA stretching from Pittsburgh to St Louis, containing a large concentration of traditional heavy industries. The rustbelt suffers from high *obsolescence and relatively strong unionization of the labour force, which have both encouraged a tendency for economic activity to shift to the South and the West.

Rybczynski theorem A proposition concerning the results of increasing only one factor of production. The proposition, named after its originator, concerns a two-good, two-factor economy with *constant returns to scale, and economic growth due to an increase in one factor of production, holding other factors and techniques constant. This leads at constant *relative prices to an increase in the output of the good intensive in the factor which has increased, but a decrease in the output of the industry using the factor which has not. This result at first sight seems surprising: the argument behind it is that with constant prices the techniques used in each industry must stay the same. To employ the extra supply of the growing factor, output rises in the industry using it intensively; but this also uses some of the other factor, so that less is left for the second industry, whose output therefore declines. *See also* FACTOR INTENSITY.

r

sacking Dismissal of labour by an employer. This may be 'for cause', where some form of misconduct by the employee is given as the reason; in some cases UK employees may have rights to compensation for *unfair dismissal if this cannot be substantiated. Dismissal may also be due to *redundancy, when the work an employee was hired to perform is no longer required, and the employer has no other suitable job available. In such cases no misconduct on the worker's part is alleged, and such redundant workers may be entitled to compensation. Sacking is distinguished from voluntary quitting of employment, where it is the employee who takes the initiative.

sacrifice ratio In *Keynesian economics, the ratio between the amount of unemployment needed to reduce inflation and the reduction achieved. According to *demand inflation models, an increase in demand when activity is high has more effect in increasing inflation than an equal fall in demand has in decreasing inflation when activity is low. This implies that the sacrifice ratio for any economy will be lower if disinflationary pressure is applied steadily than if the economy varies between spells of expansionary policy and occasional bursts of severe cuts in *effective demand. The sacrifice ratio is likely to be lower if the authorities' commitment to reducing inflation is regarded as credible.

saddle point A point at which a function of several variables is at a maximum for movement in some directions and a minimum for movement in the remaining directions. Assume $f(x)$ is to be maximized subject to $g(x) \geq 0$, where $x = (x_1, \ldots, x_n)$. Then the maximum occurs at a saddle point of the Lagrangian function $L \equiv f(x) + \lambda g(x)$, with L maximized for each x_i and minimized for λ.

safety at work *See* HEALTH and SAFETY AT WORK ACT.

St Petersburg paradox The observation that experimental subjects will only offer to pay a small fee to enter a coin-tossing game with an expected pay-off that is infinite. Consider being offered the chance to play in a game in which a fair coin is repeatedly tossed until a tail appears. If the first tail appears on the tth toss the pay-off is 2^{t-1}. The expected pay-off from entering the game is

$$EP = \frac{1}{2}2^0 + \frac{1}{4}2^1 + \frac{1}{8}2^2 + \ldots = \frac{1}{2} + \frac{1}{2} + \frac{1}{2} + \ldots = \infty.$$

The fact that most subjects are willing to pay only a small fee to enter the game can be explained by the diminishing marginal utility of money. There are stronger paradoxes that can be explained only by bounded utility or *behavioural economics. *See also* ANOMALIES.

salary Fixed compensation for the supply of labour services paid on a regular basis. Traditionally salaried workers in the UK were paid monthly, often into a bank account, and were not eligible for overtime pay. This made salaries distinct from *wages, which were paid weekly, in cash, to workers who received overtime if they worked more than normal hours. In modern economies the spread of bank accounts, less frequent pay days, and bonuses has blurred the distinction between wages and salaries, which have essentially the same economic function.

sales tax A tax on the sales of a business. A sales tax is normally a fixed percentage of total sales of some classes of goods and services. Sales taxes are used to raise revenue, for example, by some states of the US. While in principle a *value-added tax is better for economic efficiency, a sales tax is much simpler to administer when much of the business being taxed is done by firms whose business spreads over several states.

sample A selection of examples of a class of objects, whose characteristics are used to infer those of the whole class or population. Sampling is used where it would be impossible, too slow, or too costly to examine the entire population. Inference from sample to population constitutes the subject matter of statistics. *See also* QUOTA SAMPLE; RANDOM SAMPLE; STRATIFIED SAMPLE.

sample selectivity bias A problem that occurs when the available data sample is truncated according to the value of some variable correlated with the dependent variable. For example, pupils in private schools are likely to come from wealthy families. Suppose post-school earnings are used as a measure of quality of a given school. If people with wealthy family backgrounds tend to have higher earnings for reasons other than their schooling, then ignoring this selection leads to the confounding of the effect of family background with the effect of training received at a particular private school. In such cases the *ordinary least squares estimator is biased and inconsistent. *See also* TRUNCATED SAMPLE.

Samuelson rule An equation describing the set of *Pareto-efficient allocations in an economy with a *public good. In an economy with one public good, one private good, and H consumers, the Samuelson rule requires that

$$\sum_{h=1}^{H} MRS_{G,x}^{h} = MRT_{G,x}$$

where $MRS_{G,x}^{h}$ is the *marginal rate of substitution for consumer h between the public good, G, and the private good, x, and $MRT_{G,x}$ is the *marginal rate of transformation between G and x. The marginal rate of substitution should be interpreted as a measure of marginal benefit and the marginal rate of transformation as a measure of marginal cost. The marginal benefits are summed since an additional unit of the public good benefits all consumers.

satisficing A decision-making strategy that aims to reach an adequate outcome rather than an optimal outcome. Examples of satisficing are charging a fixed mark-up over costs, and purchasing the same bundle of commodities each week. Satisficing is often justified on the grounds that optimizing involves costly information collection and processing. As an economic theory it fails to explain why optimization is not undertaken incorporating these additional costs.

saving(s) Saving is a flow and refers to the excess of *income over *consumption in a given period. Savings are a stock and refer to the quantity of *assets held. The stock of savings is accumulated from the flow of saving over a number of periods. The average propensity to save is the ratio of saving to income; the marginal propensity to save is the proportion of any addition to income that is saved. The interest-elasticity of saving measures the proportional response of saving to changes in interest rates. *See also* CONTRACTUAL SAVINGS; PLANNED SAVINGS; PROPENSITY TO SAVE.

saving ratio Household *saving expressed as a proportion of household gross *disposable income.

savings and loan association (S&L) A US institution borrowing from the general public to provide housing finance. S&Ls are the nearest US equivalent to the UK's *building societies. During recent years S&Ls have encountered major financial problems through financing fixed-interest mortgages with short-term deposits, whose cost responds rapidly to changes in market interest rates.

savings function A function relating saving to its determinants. For an individual these include income (both actual and permanent), age, family status, assets, and possibly *liquidity. At the aggregate level the savings function includes the effects of income, the age distribution of the population, and total assets.

Say's law Typically summarized as the proposition that 'supply creates its own demand'. The argument behind Say's law is that the supplier of a product will spend the income received, thus the supply creates a demand. In the words of Jean-Baptiste Say (1767–1832), 'It is worthwhile to remark that a product is no sooner created than it, from that instant, affords a market for other products to the full extent of its own value. When the producer has put the finishing hand to his product, he is most anxious to sell it immediately, lest its value should diminish in his hands. Nor is he less anxious to dispose of the money he may get for it; for the value of money is also perishable. But the only way of getting rid of money is in the purchase of some product or other. Thus the mere circumstance of creation of one product immediately opens a vent for other products' (J. B. Say, 1803, *A Treatise on Political Economy, or the Production, Distribution and Consumption of Wealth*, pp. 138–9).

scarce currency clause A provision in the original rules of the *International Monetary Fund (IMF), to deal with the problem that its stocks of any one particular currency might run out. The clause provided that if the IMF ran out of stocks of a country's currency, this could be declared a 'scarce currency', upon which members would be entitled and expected to discriminate against the country's goods in their trade policies. It was widely expected during the late 1940s that the US dollar would become scarce, though due to the *Marshall Plan and other US bilateral aid programmes this did not in fact occur. *See also* DISCRIMINATION.

scarcity The property of being in excess demand at a zero price. This means that in equilibrium the price of a scarce good or factor must be positive.

scatter diagram A diagram depicting the relation between two characteristics of a set of observations. Each point marked on the diagram shows an observation of the two characteristics, for example age and the income of an individual, measured on the two axes. This is often helpful in suggesting whether it is likely to be possible to find any significant statistical relation between the two characteristics, and what type of function it is worth trying to fit. It also draws attention to any outlying observations which may merit special investigation.

scenario A set of assumptions on policy choices and the values of *exogenous variables that will be used to determine the future developments of an economy. The assumptions, for example about government tax and spending policies, can be varied to produce alternative scenarios. The construction of alternative scenarios is employed to consider the effects of different policies and the robustness of conclusions to alternative values of exogenous variables.

Schedule A tax A former section of the UK income tax, levied on the imputed rent of owner-occupied land and houses. This tax was used before the Second World War; during the war the tax assessments were not revised, which reduced its real yield, and it was subsequently abolished.

screening A process implemented by an uninformed party to induce other parties with private information to act so as to reveal it. In equilibrium both the uninformed and the informed are aware of the informational consequences of their actions. In the case where the uninformed party takes the initiative, screening is employed. In the case where the informed takes the initiative to identify himself as a particular type, then it is considered to be *signalling. Thus the difference between screening and signalling lies in whether the informed or uninformed party moves first. *See also* ASYMMETRIC INFORMATION.

scrip issue *See* BONUS ISSUE.

search In economics, a model of the optimal decision-making of an agent facing a choice of options with random pay-offs when delay is costly. In this setting an agent is confronted with a trade-off between the cost of delaying the choice and a potential opportunity of a better option arriving in the future. The most common applications of search theory include *job search in labour economics and product search in *consumer theory.

search unemployment Unemployment which occurs while an unemployed worker searches the job market for an acceptable job offer. In some occupations workers may leave one job voluntarily because search for another is more efficiently conducted while not working. In many professional occupations this does not happen, because being unemployed is itself a handicap in attracting offers: workers who want better jobs can search more efficiently while employed. If they lose their jobs involuntarily, however, search unemployment occurs if they do not simply apply for any job and accept any offer. Unemployed workers seeking jobs have *reservation wages, that is, minimum acceptable pay offers, and cut-offs for the type of work they are willing to perform. If they do not receive acceptable job offers, their reservation wage and minimum job specifications change, probably falling as lack of income reduces their liquidity and failure to find acceptable jobs depresses their expectations about the distribution of potential offers.

seasonal adjustment Adjustment to correct for seasonal patterns in *time-series data performed by estimating and removing seasonal effects in economic activity that exist due to natural factors such as weather, administrative measures such as school year dates, and social or religious traditions such as Christmas and other fixed holidays.

seasonal unemployment Unemployment due to seasonal variations in the demand for labour. Some occupations have large seasonal variations, for example agriculture and tourism. How far this leads to seasonal variations in aggregate unemployment depends on how far such variations are mutually offsetting.

secondary market The market for resale of shares. This is distinct from the market for new issues: the vast majority of dealings in shares is in secondary markets. The existence of a liquid secondary market for shares is an important factor in making them saleable as new issues. If people intending to buy newly issued shares knew they could not sell them readily, but had to retain them permanently, they would be much more reluctant to risk buying them in the first place.

second-best A situation in which a policy-maker is subject to one or more constraints in addition to those relating to technology and endowments. When a policy-maker is constrained only by technology and endowments a *first-best outcome can be achieved which satisfies the full set of efficiency conditions for the economy. If there are additional constraints, such as *asymmetric information or unavoidable *monopoly power, the situation is one of second-best. The Lipsey–Lancaster theory of second-best shows how to choose policies optimally in these circumstances. The key result of the theory is that if there is even only one efficiency condition that cannot be satisfied it may be optimal to choose an allocation that satisfies none of the efficiency conditions. In other words, if there is a distortion away from efficiency in one market it may be optimal to counter this by offsetting distortions in all other markets. The policy implication is that piecemeal satisfaction of efficiency conditions is not generally an optimal policy.

second-degree price discrimination A form of *price discrimination in which different units of a product are sold at different prices. A discount for buying in bulk is an example of second-degree price discrimination. Another form of second-degree price discrimination is commodity-bundling. Two products (such as a computer and the operating system) can be sold separately or as a bundle. Selling the bundle for less than the sum of prices of the two products is second-degree price discrimination. The benefit for the seller of bundling is that it may attract additional consumers who would not have purchased the separate products.

See also FIRST-DEGREE PRICE DISCRIMINATION; THIRD-DEGREE PRICE DISCRIMINATION.

second-order approximation Approximation of an arbitrary function by its expansion in a Taylor's series keeping only linear and quadratic terms and assuming that the terms of the higher order are negligible. It is used, for example, in models of individual choice under uncertainty to capture risk aversion, or in welfare models to capture the effect of income distribution. *See also* LINEAR APPROXIMATION.

second-price auction An *auction in which sealed bids are submitted and the item is sold to the highest bidder at the price bid by the second-highest bidder. *See also* FIRST-PRICE AUCTION.

sector A part of the economy. Sectors can be delimited in a number of different ways. One way is by the bodies organizing expenditures: thus the economy is divided between the *public sector, that is, the government at various levels and government-controlled bodies; the *corporate sector, which is companies; and the *private sector, which is individuals, and unincorporated businesses. For national income accounting purposes the rest of the world is sometimes regarded as a sector. Sectors may also be distinguished by the type of product: a *primary sector, that is, agriculture and mining; a secondary, or manufacturing, sector; and a tertiary, or services, sector. *See also* INDUSTRIAL SECTOR; ORGANIZED SECTOR; SENSITIVE SECTORS.

secured loan A loan where the creditor has a claim on some particular part of the debtor's assets in the event of default. This is contrasted with an *unsecured loan, where the lender has no right to take over any particular asset if payments are not made when due. In the event of the borrower going bankrupt or becoming insolvent, after the tax authorities secured creditors rank before unsecured creditors for any available assets. Secured loans, such as *mortgages, are thus safer than unsecured loans, and command lower rates of interest.

Securities and Exchange Commission (SEC) The main government agency responsible for supervising trade in securities and takeovers in the US.

Securities and Investment Board (SIB) A regulatory body set up to oversee UK financial markets. Its aim was to prevent fraud and *insider dealing. The SIB worked via the system of each financial sector, for example the stock exchange, having a self-regulating organization which reported to the SIB. The SIB was empowered to recognize investment institutions, and to finance itself by fees charged for recognition. In 1997 the functions of the SIB were transferred to the *Financial Services Authority. *See also* SELF-REGULATION.

securities market *See* STOCK EXCHANGE.

securitization The packaging of several non-marketable assets, such as mortgage loans, into bundles which are marketable. Individual mortgages are not generally marketable because there is too much *idiosyncratic risk in dealing with any one of them. A package of several similar mortgages reduces the riskiness, which allows the package to be marketed. The fact that mortgages are made marketable may enable them to be financed at lower interest rates.

security A paper asset. Securities include government debt, both long- and short-term, company shares, and company debt. Securities may be registered, where legal ownership depends on the entry in a register, usually run by a bank, and the paper is merely evidence of ownership; or may be in bearer form, where ownership is conferred by possession of the document. *See also* BEARER BOND; BLUE CHIP; COLLATERAL; FIXED-INTEREST SECURITY; GILT-EDGED SECURITY; IRREDEEMABLE SECURITY; LONG-DATED SECURITY; MARKETABLE SECURITY; REDEEMABLE SECURITY; RISK-FREE SECURITY; SHORT-DATED SECURITY; UNDATED SECURITY.

security of tenure The right of some tenants renting or leasing houses, flats, or business premises to continue as tenants, so long as they pay the agreed rent and abide by the conditions of tenancy. Security of tenure is clearly beneficial to existing tenants, as it protects them against the trouble and expense of moving if they do not want to, and the danger that they might not be able to find anywhere else to rent. Security of tenure may, however, discourage investment in property, and make the owners of existing property reluctant to let it; this harms those who are not currently tenants but would like to rent housing or business premises.

segmented market A market where there is restricted contact between different customers, or different suppliers. If different customers either do not know what prices others are paying, or are unable to resell goods and services to them, it is possible to discriminate in the prices charged or level of service offered to different parts of the market. Similarly, if different suppliers are isolated from each other, it is possible to buy at discriminatory prices. The same applies in labour markets: if minority groups are segregated by social or language differences, for example, employers can pay separate groups different wages for similar work.

seigniorage The profits made by a ruler from issuing money. Originally this referred to the profits from the issue of coinage with a face value greater than its cost of production. Nowadays seigniorage refers to the ability of governments to obtain goods and services in return for newly created money. A growing economy needs some extra money, but if governments issue too much this produces inflation, which reduces the real *purchasing power of the money they have already issued.

self-assessment (tax) The system of tax assessment where the taxpayer reports all items of income and all allowances due, and works out how much tax is payable. The tax authorities then check this calculation. The alternative is the system where the taxpayer reports income and claims allowances, but the calculations leading to the tax assessment are made by the authorities. The disadvantage of self-assessment is that it demands both knowledge of the tax system and arithmetic competence: this is realistic for companies whose *tax returns are prepared by professional accountants, but less so for small businesses and individuals, who are amateurs where the tax authorities are professionals.

self-correcting system A system where deviations from any initial position lead to reactions which tend to return the system to equilibrium. A self-correcting, or self-stabilizing, economic system will return to equilibrium without any assistance from the monetary or fiscal authorities. It may still be possible for the authorities to speed up the return to equilibrium by policy measures.

self-employment Work carried out as a business, rather than as an employee. The self-employed are responsible for their own tax, National Insurance, and insurance, whereas those employed by others can leave these matters to their employer. The self-employed are also responsible for their own health and safety. Income from self-employment is a mixture of rewards for work, returns on private capital employed, and rewards for entrepreneurship.

self-financing Financing a business without recourse to borrowing or share issues. A business can only be started on a self-financing basis by those with some initial capital. The business can then expand only by the *plough-back of retained profits. The advantage of self-financing is that it combines safety with control: a self-financed business can be run without any regard for the opinions of creditors or shareholders. The main disadvantage is that an entrepreneur's initial capital and profits may not be large enough to allow full advantage to be taken of possible *economies of scale.

self-fulfilling expectations *Expectations which induce people to take actions which bring about the situation that is expected. This is the case, for example, with expectations about the future prices of assets and durable goods. If prices are expected to rise, this gives an incentive to bring forward purchases and to postpone sales, which tends to produce excess demand and leads to price increases. If prices are expected to fall, this gives an incentive to bring forward sales and postpone purchases, which leads to excess supply and price cuts. Thus, in the short run prices in speculative markets are dominated by expectations. If a shortage of a good is anticipated, this gives an incentive to lay in stocks while they are available, so that rumours of a shortage tend to produce one. Self-fulfilling expectations are contrasted with self-frustrating expectations: for example, producers who expect a high price increase output, which tends to drive the price down, and producers who expect a low price cut output, which tends to drive the price up.

self-regulation A system where the approach of government to regulating a sector of the economy is to lay down general objectives, but entrust the task of devising and enforcing detailed rules to a body representing those engaged in the sector. The merit claimed for this is that people within the sector are better able than outsiders to diagnose problems and devise realistic methods of control. The limitation of self-regulation is that it will operate too much for the protection of established firms in the sector, and too little in the interests of consumer protection or opportunities for innovators and new entrants to an industry.

seller concentration The number of sellers in a market and their market shares. *See also* N-FIRM CONCENTRATION RATIO.

seller's market An informal term referring to a market in which conditions are much better for sellers than for buyers. If sellers are scarce and are in no hurry to dispose of their assets, while buyers are numerous and are under strong pressure to satisfy their requirements quickly, it is likely that the current trading price will be high relative to the average price in the past, and that conditions of sale will be favourable for sellers.

selling costs Costs incurred in the process of selling products. This covers items such as the cost of advertisements on hoardings or in the media, exhibiting at trade fairs, or employment of representatives or door-to-door salespeople. It does not normally cover the costs of design and quality control, though these may be more important than selling costs in making products marketable.

sensitive sectors Sectors of an economy which are particularly concerned about loss of markets and jobs through competition from imports. This applies particularly to sectors where *less developed countries have a comparative advantage. Agriculture, textiles and clothing, iron and steel, and basic chemicals fall in this category. Sensitive sectors in advanced economies have lobbied, usually successfully, for exemption from general *trade liberalization measures.

separable utility function A utility function is separable if it can be written in the form

$$u = U(v_1(x^1), v_2(x^2), \ldots, v_m(x^m))$$

where $x^1, \ldots, x^m$ form a partition of the available products. (Assume three goods are available and denote the consumption of good i by x_i, $i = 1, 2, 3$. Then $x^1 = (x_1, x_2)$, $x^2 = (x_3)$ is an example of a partition.) The implication of separability is that the marginal rate of substitution between any two goods in x^j is unaffected by the consumption level of any good not in x^j. If a consumer has separable preferences then the demand for a good in x^j depends on the expenditure allocated to all goods in x^j and the prices of goods in x^j. This is a form of two-stage budgeting: the consumer first decides how much to spend on each category of goods (meaning, for each element of the partition), and then allocates the expenditure between goods within a category. A utility function is additively separable if

$$u = v_1(x^1) + v_2(x^2) + \ldots + v_m(x^m).$$

This is a special case of separability. Additive separability is frequently used to represent preferences over consumption at different points in time.

separating equilibrium An equilibrium in which agents with different characteristics choose different actions. For example, in an insurance market high-risk agents and low-risk agents will choose different insurance contracts in a separating equilibrium. *See also* POOLING EQUILIBRIUM.

separation of ownership and control *See* CONTROL (OF A COMPANY).

sequestration **1.** A UK procedure by which assets can be temporarily frozen by court order.
   2. The US term for mandatory spending cuts in the budget proposed under the *Gramm–Rudman–Hollings law on the deficit.

serial correlation Same as *autocorrelation.

service contract A *contract for the provision of services. These may be routine services, such as inspection, regular maintenance, or cleaning, or emergency services such as repair after breakdowns, or provision of temporary staff to cover absence of permanent employees. Service contracts are useful where firms require services involving specialized labour, management skills, or equipment, but do not need them regularly enough to make it economic to provide them in-house.

service flows The services rendered by *consumer durables. These count as consumption when they are bought, but items such as furniture, refrigerators, cars, or boats give services over years and often decades. Only in the case of housing do *national income accounts follow the procedure of treating their purchase as investment when it occurs and the flow of services as *imputed income in later years. This means that when individual or national consumption expenditure falls during depressions or in wartime, the figures exaggerate the immediate fall in utility, which builds up gradually as stocks of consumer durables wear out. Similarly, the real standard of living does not rise as fast as consumption spending during a recovery.

service industry The parts of the economy providing services. These may be to individual consumers, for example medical treatment or entertainment, or to businesses, for example architectural, cleaning, computing, engineering, or legal work. In some cases, such as restaurants, a combination of goods and services is provided. Service industries are collectively referred to as the tertiary sector, and are an increasing part of total activity in advanced economies. *See also* NEW ECONOMY.

services Economic goods which do not take a tangible and storable form. In some cases these require the physical presence of the customer, as for example with hairdressing, medical treatment, or live entertainment. In other cases services can be performed at a distance: for example, legal representation or insurance.

set-aside Removal of land from agricultural production. Farmers may be either compelled or paid to set aside part of their land. Set-aside is part of agricultural policy, in particular the *Common Agricultural Policy of the European Union. Set-aside land may be allowed to lie fallow, or may be diverted to forestry, or, subject to *planning permission, to amenity or residential use.

settlement The act of completing the trade required in a *contract to pay for or deliver goods, securities, or currency. Because of the documentation involved, and postal and clerical delays, many bargains are not carried out immediately, but some time is allowed. This may take the form of having a set date for completion of all contracts made during a given period, or of 'rolling settlement', where each bargain is allowed a number of days for settlement. Prompt and reliable settlement is a major attraction of goods and securities markets. Failure to settle by a major financial institution could trigger a chain reaction of failures among other firms; one of the major reasons for financial *regulation is to prevent this from happening.

settlement risk The risk that other parties may fail to fulfil their side of bargains. Delay in settlement may merely cause inconvenience, but complete failure to settle could cause severe losses. To reduce *counter-party risk many commodity and stock exchanges act as counter-parties for the actual traders, making payments to sellers and collecting payment from buyers.

shadow economy *See* HIDDEN ECONOMY.

shadow prices Prices of goods, services, and resources that are proportional to true *opportunity costs for the economy, taking account of any *externalities. If individuals and firms all made choices to maximize their pay-offs subject to a set of prices proportional to the shadow prices for the economy, the resulting equilibrium would be *Pareto efficient. In a competitive economy with no market failure, market prices and shadow prices would be equivalent. In an economy with *market failure, such as *monopoly, legal price regulation and externalities, actual and shadow prices do not coincide. The *Lagrange multipliers appearing in constrained optimization problems can be interpreted as shadow prices. *See also* PARETO EFFICIENCY.

shake-out The process of removing resources from some sector of the economy. This may occur within firms, or in industries by a reduction on the number of firms. Shake-out is liable to be set off by bad times: cuts in demand induce firms to reduce both their capacity and their labour force, and cuts in profits induce firms to make more effort to remove organizational *slack and may compel them to leave an industry.

Shapley value A process for determining a fair allocation in a cooperative game. The Shapley value is computed by first determining what each player adds to every possible coalition they may potentially join. The player is viewed as adding the difference between the pay-off to the coalition with the additional player and the pay-off to the coalition without. Second, the weighted sum of these pay-offs is computed with the weights being the probability that each coalition may form. The weighted sum is the Shapley value.

share A part of the ownership of a *company. Shares may be held by individuals or other companies. Company law requires companies to treat all shareholders of any given type alike as regards dividends, or division of the assets on liquidation. *Ordinary shares normally carry voting rights, though it is possible to have some non-voting shares. In some countries there may be limits on the total votes cast by any one shareholder. *Preference shares rank before ordinary shares for dividends, but have no vote, and *debentures rank before preference and ordinary shares for dividends. Debentures carry fixed interest, but the holders have the right to take over control of a company if these are not paid. A share register is an official list of the names and addresses of shareholders; a share certificate is a document proving ownership. In some countries, but not the UK, companies can have bearer shares, where there is no central share register, and the holder of share certificates is deemed to own the shares. *See also* A-SHARE; DEFERRED SHARE; NON-VOTING SHARE; VOTING SHARE.

share buybacks The practice of companies returning capital to their shareholders by buying in some of their own shares. Buybacks benefit shareholders by reducing their income tax bills. Share buybacks tend to raise the price of the remaining shares whereas distribution of the same amount in dividends tends to reduce it. This may benefit directors and other employees holding share options as part of their remuneration. The theoretical motivation for a buyback is that the deductibility of interest payments from profit before tax leads to a preference for debt finance over equity finance. It may be profitable for a firm to reduce its outstanding equity and finance new investment by borrowing.

share capital The authorized or nominal value of a company's shares as established in the memorandum of association. When a company becomes public the memorandum of association states the number of shares it can issue and the nominal price of each share. The issued share capital is that part of the share capital that the firm has sold to the market.

sharecropper A tenant who pays rent fixed as a share of crops produced rather than an agreed amount of money. This system is relatively common in backward regions and *less developed countries. Sharecropping has the effect of sharing risk between landlord and tenant, but discourages tenants from investing in fertilizers, irrigation, and other permanent improvements.

shareholder A person or company holding shares in a company. The ultimate say over control of a company lies with its equity shareholders, who can change the management either by using their votes at company meetings, or by accepting a *takeover bid. A majority shareholder is one who holds a majority of voting shares; a minority shareholder holds fewer than half the shares. *See also* INSTITUTIONAL SHAREHOLDER; MAJORITY SHAREHOLDER; MINORITY SHAREHOLDER.

share option An option to buy shares at a pre-arranged price, granted as an incentive to company directors or employees. Share options will only be exercised if the option price is below the market price at the time. They are offered as incentives: the better a company performs the higher its share price will be, and the more holders of share options gain from exercising them.

share price The price at which a share can be traded. This is not any single amount: even for widely traded shares the offer price at which market-makers are willing to sell shares is higher than the bid price at which they are willing to buy. The average of these, the *mid-market price, is frequently quoted in the financial press. In the case of shares which are little traded, the reported price may simply be the last one at which any transactions were reported, and may give little guidance on the terms on which they can now be traded.

share price index An index of the prices of shares of some specific type. Share price indexes are published in all countries with stock exchanges. They vary in the range of industries they cover, and the number of companies whose shares are included. For US shares see the *Dow Jones index; for the UK see the *Financial Times Stock Exchange indexes; for Japan see the *Nikkei index; for Hong Kong, the *Hang Seng index.

share register The register kept by a limited company recording the names and addresses of shareholders, and the type and number of shares held. Entry in the register is proof of ownership: shareholders whose share certificates are lost or destroyed can obtain replacements on production of proof of identity.

shark repellent Contracts entered into to make a company unattractive to potential takeover bidders. Contracts may be made with directors, for example, entitling them to large payments on loss of office, or giving them options to buy critical parts of company assets, or the company's shares, at low prices.

shell company A company which does not trade, but has a legal existence, and possibly some non-trading assets. These may include a credit rating, and the right to carry forward losses for tax purposes. For anybody who needs a company to trade through, acquiring a shell company may be cheaper and quicker than registering a new company.

sheltered monopoly A monopoly protected from competition in some way. This could include legal restrictions on entry by competitors, or tariffs and *non-tariff barriers restricting foreign competition.

Sherman Act The original US federal antitrust legislation. In 1890 this act prohibited 'all contracts, combinations and conspiracies in restraint of trade', and monopoly in interstate and foreign trade. The Sherman Act required subsequent amendment, including the *Clayton Act of 1914.

shift work Work scheduled so that the same equipment can be used by more than one set of workers in a day, typically with additional compensation for work in very late or very early hours. It is worth incurring these costs in capital-intensive industries where equipment is too expensive to be kept idle for much of the time. Shift working is also necessary in some industries using continuous processes and in organizations such as the police, fire, and ambulance services, providing round-the-clock cover.

shock In economics, an unexpected and unpredictable event that has a positive or a negative effect on the economy. A shock is said to be permanent if it has a long-run effect, for example, economic effects of major geographical discoveries or major technical developments; otherwise it is said to be transitory: for example, monetary or fiscal policy changes may have no long-run effect on real income. *See also* ADVERSE SUPPLY SHOCK.

shoe-leather costs of inflation The suggestion that one of the real costs of *expected inflation is that it increases transaction costs by inducing people to economize on their money holdings. The shoe-leather concerned was worn out making more frequent trips to the bank to avoid carrying large stocks of cash. A similar effect applies to other *transaction costs.

shop steward A worker elected at shop-floor level to represent fellow-workers in discussions with management. Shop stewards are not trade-union officials, though they are usually union members. They can catch *industrial relations problems early and help to prevent them from escalating into *industrial disputes.

shortage A situation when the demand for a good or service exceeds the available supply. This can only occur if price is not adjusted to clear the market. If there is a sudden rise in the demand or fall in the supply of a good, law or social convention may prevent the price from rising far enough to clear the market, thus creating a shortage. When this occurs, available supplies of the good must be allocated by some non-price method, such as formal or informal *rationing, or queuing.

short-dated security A security with under 5 years to *maturity when first issued.

short position A contract to sell, for future delivery, goods or securities in excess of the amount a firm or individual actually holds. The holder of a short position relies on eventually being able to produce or buy sufficient goods or securities to be able to fulfil the contract, or to enter a reversing trade. When the time for delivery arrives, if spot market prices are lower than the contract price, the holder of the short position will be able to buy the goods at this lower price, and will make a profit. If the spot market price is higher than the price agreed in the contract, however, the result can be a loss, with no finite limit to its size. A short position is therefore risky with the potential for considerable loss.

short run A period in which some things cannot be changed, but which could be changed given more time. In the short run, for example, a firm can buy more materials or fuel, and can hire more unskilled workers, but does not have time to build new plant or to recruit and train more skilled workers or managers. The short run is contrasted with the medium run, in which more things, but not everything, can be changed, and with the *long run, in which everything can be changed that can ever be changed at all. Short-run supply and demand curves typically have lower *elasticity than the corresponding long-run curves.

short-run capital movements Movements of capital between countries which can be quickly reversed. This usually means holding *liquid assets, such as bank deposits or short-dated financial assets such as bills. It is possible to move funds short-term and buy shares or longer-dated bonds, but this adds to the risks. Short-run capital movements may be caused by differences in interest rates, where investors shift funds to countries with higher interest rates; or by expectations of exchange rate changes, where speculators shift funds out of currencies they expect to depreciate into currencies they expect to appreciate. Short-run capital movements may also be provoked by fears of persecution or breakdown of public order, or be part of the processes of *money laundering. It is believed that large-scale short-run capital movements contribute to the instability of exchange rates when exchange rates are flexible.

short-run cost curve See COST CURVE.

short-run marginal cost See MARGINAL COST.

short-run Phillips curve See PHILLIPS CURVE.

short selling Selling an asset or commodity that you do not own. This can be achieved by borrowing the asset or commodity from an existing owner. In financial and commodity markets stockbrokers are able to arrange the loan of the asset or commodity. Short selling is equivalent to holding a negative quantity of the asset or commodity, and permits a gain to be made from a fall in price.

short-termism The conduct of a business with too much regard to short-run relative to longer-run results. For industry, this means spending too little on *research and development, staff training, and investment in projects with a long lag in bringing in profits; for financial institutions, it means putting too much weight on short-term capital gains. Short-termism thus means *discounting the future too heavily. The concept is necessarily subjective, as there is no objective way of deciding the correct rate at which future costs and benefits should be discounted.

short-time working Cutting a firm's use of labour by reducing hours of work below a normal working week rather than laying some workers off. The merit of this is that it keeps the firm in contact with all its workers, so that more labour can be obtained very easily when it is needed. It is likely to be more acceptable to the workers than *redundancies if alternative jobs are difficult to obtain. Short-time working also keeps workers in practice, so that their skills are maintained. It is normally only used when the demand for labour is expected to recover.

shut-down price A price so low that at this or any lower price a firm prefers to shut its plant down rather than continue production. At prices just above the shut-down price the firm will usually be making a loss, but provided that the market is expected to recover, so that the firm is not planning to leave the industry permanently, this is preferred to the loss of contact with both workers and customers involved in a complete shut-down. The shut-down price is thus typically below marginal cost.

sickness benefit Benefits paid to workers temporarily unable to work because of illness.

side-effects Unintended results of policies. These are frequently undesirable; for example, governments attempting to make essentials available cheaply to the poor by imposing maximum prices below the cost of production have found that the goods cease to be available at all. Side-effects can sometimes be beneficial; for example, local councils which cut down on spraying roadsides with weed killer to save money have incidentally encouraged the return of wild flowers.

side-payment A payment made by one or more parties in an agreement to other parties, to induce them to join the agreement. Suppose, for example, that in a group of firms, each has a profitable plant. They calculate that if one plant were closed and its output shifted to the remaining plants, total costs for the group would be lower and thus total profits would rise. If each firm gets its profits solely by selling the output from its own plant, no agreement can be reached, since the firm whose plant closes loses all its profits. The firms can thus only be induced to agree to a plan which includes side-payments, by which the firms whose plants remain open use part of their increased profits to compensate the firm whose plant closes down.

signalling Actions taken not for the sake of their direct results, but to inform prospective customers or employers. For example, students may seek qualifications through formal examinations even though they have no interest in a subject, and it is well known that it will be of no use to them in actually doing a job. This is rational conduct if they believe that prospective employers will regard success in examinations as signalling ability, so that such success helps obtain a good job. Signalling is a consequence of *asymmetric information and involves the informed party actively trying to reveal information. A signal will be believed only if it is costly to transmit, so that in equilibrium it is optimal for some types to transmit the signal but not optimal for other types. For example, an educational qualification works as a signalling device only if it is costly to obtain, and worth obtaining only by individuals with high ability.

significance level (of a test) (size of a test) The probability that the test statistic will reject the null hypothesis when the latter is true, in other words, the probability of committing a *type I error.

significance test For the individual significance of a parameter in a *linear regression, a *two-sided test of the null hypothesis $H_0 : \theta_i = 0$ against the alternative $H_1 : \theta_i \neq 0$, or a *one-sided test of $H_0 : \theta_i \leq 0$ against $H_1 : \theta_i > 0$ (or $H_0 : \theta_i \geq 0$ against $H_1 : \theta_i < 0$). This is a particular case of a *t-test where the null hypothesis is interpreted as showing that the corresponding exogenous variable x_i has no explanatory power in the regression. For the joint significance of a subset of parameters, a test of the null hypothesis that all parameters in the subset are zero against the alternative hypothesis that at least one of these parameters is not zero; this is a particular case of an *F-test.

Silicon Valley The area of southern California containing a major concentration of computer and information technology businesses. This is a frequently cited example of the tendency to geographical *specialization, caused by external economies resulting from the proximity of similar businesses.

simple interest The system by which repayment of a loan after n periods requires payment of a sum equal to the principal plus n times the interest payable for a single period. If the principal is P and the interest rate per period is r, at the end of n periods payment of $P(1 + nr)$ is required. As n increases, the proportional rate of return to the lender goes down, as the proportional return for the $(n + 1)$th period is $rP/[(1 + nr)P]$, which is a decreasing function of n. Simple interest is very rarely used, except for loans of very short duration.

simulation The use of quantitative models to represent the working of an economy. Given assumptions about how an economy works, simulation is used to see how models respond to changes in these assumptions, changes in the distribution of stochastic shocks, or changes in economic policy. Simulation models normally use numerical methods, as their structure is too complicated for analytical conclusions about their behaviour to be obtainable. *See also* MONTE CARLO METHOD.

simultaneous equations model (SEM) An econometric model of a relationship among two or more *endogenous variables and a set of *exogenous or *predetermined variables, formulated as a system of equations. *See also* STRUCTURAL EQUATION; REDUCED FORM.

single currency A currency used by two or more countries. The decision on the amount to be issued may be determined by agreement between two or more national central banks, or by commissioning a single supra-national institution to issue the currency. If a single currency is issued independently by more than one national authority, without any agreement between them, it is likely that too much of it will be issued. This is because the initial gains from additional currency accrue to the nation that issues it, while the losses resulting from inflation following excessive issue of a currency are spread between all countries using it. *See also* OPTIMUM CURRENCY AREA.

Single European Act A 1986 amendment to the *Treaty of Rome, governing the conduct of the *European Community. This made a large number of changes arising from the Cockfield Report (1985), *Completing the Internal Market*. These included permitting decisions by majority voting, an increase in the powers of the European Parliament, and recognition of the *European Monetary System.

single market The unified European market created in 1992 by the *Single European Act. This was achieved through the removal of all barriers to movements of goods, labour, and capital between member countries of the *European Community.

single-peaked preferences Preferences that have a single maximum over a linearly ordered set of alternatives. A set of alternatives can be linearly ordered if it is possible to arrange them along a one-dimensional axis. For example, the location of shops on one side of a street is linearly ordered. Preferences are single-peaked if there is a unique most-preferred point on the axis, and the valuation of other alternatives declines monotonically away from the most-preferred point in either direction. This means that any individual asked to choose or vote will always prefer the most-valued level to any other, and, of any two alternatives on the same side of the most preferred value, will vote for that nearer the preferred value.

size distribution of firms The number of firms of various sizes. Size can be measured in various ways: employment, turnover, and stock exchange capitalization are commonly used measures of size. On any measure the distribution tends to be skewed, with many small firms and relatively few large ones in any industry or area, or a country as a whole.

skewness A measure of the degree of asymmetry of the distribution of a random variable; the standardized third *moment of the distribution, defined as

$$\gamma = E[(X - \mu)^3]/\sigma^3$$

where μ is the *mean and σ is the *standard deviation. For a symmetrical distribution $\gamma = 0$ and the *median of the distribution equals its mean. In a distribution with positive skewness the median is below the mean, and with negative skewness the median is above the mean. For example, the empirical distribution of income across the population in both developed and less developed countries exhibits positive skewness: a large proportion of income accrues to a small proportion of the population.

skilled work Work that can be satisfactorily performed only by somebody with appropriate technical qualifications, experience, or both. Skilled workers are usually paid more than unskilled, and their jobs are typically more secure, because they would be difficult to replace, so that employers do not lay them off in the face of temporary falls in demand.

skills The ability to perform various tasks satisfactorily. Skills may involve physical dexterity, mental ability, or both. They can be learned either through formal instruction or through the apprenticeship system, working under the supervision of somebody who already has them. Individuals appear to differ in their ability to acquire skills. Workers with scarce skills can generally obtain better paid and more secure jobs than those without them.

slack Unused or under-used resources. Organizational slack occurs when firms or government bodies have more employees, equipment, or buildings than they really need. Most organizations contain some slack: when demand varies, it is difficult to distinguish slack from necessary *spare capacity.

slump *See* DEPRESSION.

Slutsky equation The equation showing how the effect on demand for a good of a change in a price can be decomposed into a *substitution effect, which is the effect of a change in relative prices at an unchanged level of *utility, and an *income effect, which is the effect of a change in real income holding prices constant. Denote the demand for good i by x_i, the price of good j by p_j, income by M, and utility by U. The Slutsky equation is

$$\frac{\partial x_i}{\partial p_j} = \frac{\partial x_i}{\partial p_j}\Big|_U - x_j \frac{\partial x_i}{\partial M}$$

where $\frac{\partial x_i}{\partial p_j}\big|_U$ is the substitution effect and $-x_j \frac{\partial x_i}{\partial M}$ the income effect.

Smithsonian Agreement An agreement reached in 1971 to try to restore a *Bretton Woods-style system of pegged exchange rates. The agreement was so named from the location of the conference at which it was reached, in the Smithsonian Institute in Washington, DC. The new *Smithsonian parities lasted only a few months.

Smithsonian parities New parities for the world's major currencies agreed at the Smithsonian conference in 1971. These were intended to replace the *Bretton Woods system, which had broken down. The new parities agreed were rapidly found to be unsustainable.

smog Classic smog results from the burning of coal and is caused by a mixture of smoke and sulphur dioxide. Photochemical smog is caused by emissions of hydrocarbons and nitrous oxides from vehicle exhausts. Named for its similarity to a cross between smoke and fog, smog is damaging to health. The Great Smog of 1952 in London was directly responsible for approximately 4000 deaths, and possibly several thousand more from the damage to health it caused. Smog occurs particularly in heavily urbanized areas subject to temperature inversion which traps emission products near the surface. Smog is an obvious and conspicuous example of a negative *externality.

Smoot–Hawley Tariff Act A US act of 1930 establishing a protectionist tariff regime. It is widely believed that this act and similar measures in other major trading countries including Germany and the UK helped to produce the *Great Depression of the 1930s.

snake in the tunnel An expression for an agreement by a group of countries in a flexible exchange rate system to intervene in the foreign exchange market to hold their currencies closer to each other than the generally permitted maximum deviation. The general limit is the tunnel; the closer limit is the snake. This system was operated by some European countries before the adoption of the *European Monetary System in 1979.

social benefit The total benefit from any activity. This includes benefits accruing directly to the person or firm conducting the activity, as well as external benefits outside the price system accruing to other people or firms.

social capital The networks, institutions, relationships, and *social customs that determine the quality of social interactions. It has been argued that a high stock of social capital leads to many desirable outcomes including lower crime rates, better health, increased longevity, improved educational achievement, and less corrupt government. Social capital has proved a difficult concept to define precisely and has defied direct measurement.

Social Chapter A chapter of the *Maastricht Treaty of 1993, dealing largely with social questions, including *employment protection and *works councils. The UK government chose originally to opt out of this section of the treaty, but has since accepted it.

social charges Taxes on employment, whether levied on employers or employees. Social charges are levied in many countries to pay for various social benefits such as unemployment insurance and pensions. In the UK social charges take the form of *National Insurance contributions. Social charges make the cost of labour to employers higher than the earnings of their employees.

social choice Choices made collectively by an entire society. This is a special case of *collective choice.

social cost The total cost of any activity. This includes *private costs which fall directly on the person or firm conducting the activity, as well as external costs outside the price system which fall on other people or firms.

social custom An accepted, established, or expected pattern of behaviour. Social customs guide behaviour and can replace the need to make choices. For example, it is a social custom in many countries that a man should open a door for a woman. When two people meet at a door this custom solves the decision problem of who should open it approximately half of the time. The concept of social custom has been used to explain observations of behaviour that are otherwise not individually rational. Examples include the membership of a trade union when non-members also benefit from the gains secured by the union, and the decision not to evade tax even when the expected return from evasion is positive.

socialism The idea that the economy's resources should be used in the interests of all its citizens, rather than allowing private owners of land and capital to use them as they see fit. A socialist economy requires voluntary cooperation and *central planning. The idea was implemented by the USSR and allied countries between the 1930s and the 1990s when it was abandoned in favour of *market economy, primarily because of lack of individual incentives, among other factors, having gradually led these countries to economic collapse.

social opportunity cost The amount of other goods which has to be forgone because resources are used to make some particular good. When any goods or services are produced, the resources used to make them are not available for other purposes. Social opportunity cost takes account of any *externalities, as well as direct costs to the producers. It is contrasted with private opportunity cost, which takes account only of direct opportunity costs to the producers, disregarding any externalities.

social optimum The point on the *utility possibility frontier that maximizes *social welfare. The social optimum is the allocation chosen by a benevolent *social planner who is constrained only by the endowment of resources. If there are restrictions upon the policy instruments of the social planner the social optimum will not, in general, be achievable.

social overhead capital Capital goods of types which are available to anybody, hence social; and are not tightly linked to any particular part of production, hence overhead. Because of their broad availability they often have to be provided by the government. Examples of social overhead capital include roads, schools, hospitals, and public parks.

social planner A benevolent decision-maker who chooses economic policy either to maximize a *social welfare function or to attain a *Pareto efficient allocation.

social returns to education *Externalities generated by education of individuals, or *human capital externalities. Increases in the overall level of education can benefit society in ways that are not fully reflected in the wages of educated workers. In particular, aggregate productivity may increase far beyond the direct effect of education on individual productivity due to human capital spillovers. Furthermore, increases in education also may result in better health of educated individuals and their children, reduce criminal participation, and improve voters' political behaviour.

social safety net A system of available payments in cash or in kind which will keep people's incomes from falling below some socially accepted minimum level. This needs to cover old age, sickness and disability, and unemployment. It may include *benefits in kind for people with special requirements: for example, health care, and publicly provided housing for those without the means or competence to house themselves privately.

Social Security Act A US act of 1935 that established a federal system of social security. Prior to the act benefits had been organized at a state, or lower, level. The act provided old-age benefits for workers, benefits for victims of industrial accidents, unemployment insurance, and aid for dependent mothers and children, the blind, and the physically handicapped.

social security benefits State payments designed to assure all residents of a country of minimum living standards. These benefits are typically provided to those over retirement age, and those unable to support themselves because of disability, illness, or inability to find work. The benefits cover the recipient and any dependants, especially children. Social security benefits may be paid for by contributions from workers or their employers, or by general taxation. National insurance schemes, such as that in the UK, are usually not actuarially solvent, and have to be subsidized from general taxation. Social security benefits may or may not be means tested, where the recipients have any private income or occupational pensions. *See also* MEANS-TESTED BENEFITS.

social security contributions Charges levied on individuals or their employers to pay for the costs of social security benefits. The argument for having specific charges for this purpose rather than simply paying for social security through the tax system is possibly the hope that such charges will be less resented than taxes and that calling the benefits system an insurance scheme will remove stigma from accepting benefits, and the political freedom it confers to raise additional revenue without 'raising taxes'. Social security systems are generally not true insurance schemes: in the UK, for example, *National Insurance contributions are not sufficient to make the National Insurance system actuarially solvent.

social services The parts of social security requiring individual contact rather than cash payments. People's minimum consumption needs can be met by cash payments to those without sufficient incomes, through pensions and other benefits. Some citizens, however, need personal assistance with managing their lives as well as cash handouts. Personal social services cover matters such as home help for the disabled, advice and supervision for those on probation, advice and assistance in dealing with children and adults with behavioural problems, and supervision of parents thought to be in danger of harming their children.

social time preference The value that society places on present consumption relative to future consumption. The rate of social time preference can be used in *cost–benefit analysis to discount future benefits and costs. In a competitive equilibrium with no *market failure the rate of social time preference is equal to the equilibrium interest rate.

social welfare The well-being of society. This can be measured by a *social welfare function.

social welfare function 1. The level of welfare in an economy or society expressed as a function of economic variables. This is the Bergson–Samuelson sense. Social welfare can be expressed as a function $W(X_1, \ldots, X_n)$ of the aggregate consumption levels X_i of goods $i = 1, \ldots, n$. Alternatively, an *individualistic* social welfare function is a function of individual utility levels. If there are H consumers in the economy, then an individualistic social welfare function is written $W(U^1, \ldots, U^H)$, where U^h is the utility of h. Two special cases are the *Rawlsian social welfare function $W = \min\{U^h\}$ and the utilitarian social welfare function $W = \Sigma U^h$. These functions capture different philosophies concerning the desirability of *equity in distribution.

2. A process for aggregating individual preferences into social preferences. This is the Arrow sense. *Arrow's impossibility theorem addresses the difficulties of finding an acceptable aggregation process that works in all circumstances.

socio-economic class (NS-SEC) The UK National Statistics classification that groups together people with similar social and economic status. The version used for most analyses has 8 classes with the first one subdivided. These classes are as follows: 1 Higher managerial and professional occupations: 1.1 Large employers and higher managerial occupations; 1.2 Higher professional occupations; 2 Lower managerial and professional occupations; 3 Intermediate occupations; 4 Small employers and own account workers; 5 Lower supervisory and technical occupations; 6 Semi-routine occupations; 7 Routine occupations; 8 Never worked and long-term unemployed; and Not classified. This classification replaced the previously used classification of socio-economic groups (NS-SEG), along with the classification of social class (NS-SC).

soft budget constraint A limit to spending by some public body where those supposed to be subject to it believe that the consequences of breaching it will not be serious. For example, the managers of state-owned firms may believe that if they run at a loss, or make smaller profits than they have been instructed to, the state will meet the firm's losses, and not sack them. *See also* HARD BUDGET CONSTRAINT.

soft currency A currency which is not convertible into other currencies, or whose value in terms of other currencies is expected to fall. *See also* HARD CURRENCY.

soft landing A successful stabilization programme which restores price stability after a period of excess demand and inflation without provoking a *recession in the process. The problem with achieving this is that if restrictive monetary and fiscal policy are not tight enough, the economy will not land at all, and inflation will continue; while if policies are too restrictive there will be a fall in demand before stability is restored. A *hard landing occurs when there is a recession before stability is restored.

soft loan A loan on terms less onerous than prevailing market rates. This may take various forms. A loan may carry a low rate of interest, the start of interest payments may be deferred, repayment may be spread over an unusually long period, it may be easy to arrange deferment of interest or redemption payments, or the debtor may be allowed to make interest or redemption payments in soft currency. With a *hard loan interest is at market rates, and interest and redemption payments have to be made promptly in hard currency.

sole proprietor A person running a business without partners or incorporation. The advantage of sole proprietorship is unity of control, as the owner and management are the same. The drawback of sole proprietorship is that in many industries *economies of scale are such that the minimum efficient scale of a business is well beyond the capacity of a single individual to provide sufficient capital and manage the functioning of the business.

sole trader *See* SOLE PROPRIETOR.

Solow growth model A model that explains *economic growth through the accumulation of capital. The Solow growth model assumes that output is produced using capital and labour with *constant returns to scale. Output is either saved or consumed. The capital stock is the accumulated saving of previous periods less depreciation. Labour supply is fixed, and saving is a fixed fraction of output. Assume the economy is in an initial position with a low capital stock. In every period saving will increase the capital stock until the steady state is reached in which saving is equal to depreciation. Along the path to the steady state consumption per capita will increase and the economy will experience growth. Once the steady state is reached consumption per capita remains constant so growth ceases. Further growth can only occur if there is some exogenous change, such as technological improvement, that raises the level of output for any given inputs.

Solow residual The part of the growth of national income which cannot be explained by the growth of labour and capital. The Solow residual is calculated by assuming that labour and capital are rewarded an amount equal to their marginal revenue products. The residual that remains after subtracting payments to factors from the value of output is ascribed to *technical progress. *See also* GROWTH ACCOUNTING.

solvency Possession of assets in excess of a person or a firm's liabilities. Where the assets are either cash or marketable securities it may be obvious that a person or firm is solvent. It is an offence to trade knowing oneself to be insolvent, but if the assets are non-marketable solvency is largely a matter of judgement. Individuals can and do obtain *unsecured loans, which they rely on future earnings to repay. Companies frequently trade successfully and pay off all their debts, when they would have been insolvent if forced into premature liquidation. In such cases the assets consist of *patents, *know-how, or contacts which could not be sold but were able to yield an income if kept together as a going concern.

sound money Money which preserves stable *purchasing power. This will only happen if the authorities issuing the money give priority in their policies to maintaining its value, and have an established reputation for such policy priorities, which in turn leads to market expectations of price stability. A sound money policy is in conflict with the Keynesian view that the primary responsibility of the monetary authorities should be maintaining a stable level of *effective demand. While a policy of priority for *demand management does not directly lead the authorities to promote inflation, it does mean that the authorities tend to tolerate any inflation that does occur by *accommodatory monetary policy, which in turn leads to market expectations that inflation is likely.

sources of capital The sources from which businesses, whether private, corporate, or state-owned, obtain their capital. One major source is the savings of the owners of private businesses, and the undistributed profits of companies. A second major source is borrowing, either by selling bonds or borrowing from banks and other financial intermediaries. A further source of capital is selling equity shares. A large amount of fixed investment is financed from the depreciation allowances on existing equipment. Stocks of material are often financed by trade credit from suppliers. The government is also a major source of finance. Some businesses are publicly owned, and their capital is provided by the government. Governments make some capital transfers to finance investment, for example by housing associations. They also frequently tax businesses under rules which decrease business taxes if investment is undertaken: companies which invest pay less tax, or are allowed to pay later, than companies with equal profits but less investment.

sovereign debt Debt of the governments of independent countries. With the debt of an individual or corporation, it is generally possible to use legal procedures compelling them to pay the interest and redemption payments due, or to hand their assets over to the creditor if they do not pay. Such legal sanctions are not available against governments, unless they choose to submit voluntarily to legal procedures. There is thus a risk that sovereign debt may be subject to repudiation, interest reductions, or compulsory rescheduling. The only protection for the creditors of sovereign debtors is the borrowers' concern about loss of reputation: default makes it difficult or expensive for them to borrow in the future.

spare capacity Capital equipment which is not currently needed for production. Firms like to have some spare capacity available, to meet sudden increases in demand for their products, and to be able to maintain production if equipment breaks down. Spare capacity is costly to purchase and maintain, however, so there is a limit to the amount that is wanted. Where firms have equipment which is too unlikely to be needed to be worth maintaining, this is *excess capacity.

spatial model A model of *product differentiation in which the producers are located in a single- or multi-dimensional *characteristics space, with consumers' locations, i.e. their ideal points of consumption, distributed over this space. In particular, this could be a physical space, with the distance from a consumer, and related transportation cost, being the characteristic of the product. Examples are the linear city and the circular city models. In spatial models each firm competes for customers only locally, that is, only with the firms offering similar products. A particular case is spatial monopoly. *See also* GRAVITY MODEL; SPATIAL PRICE DISCRIMINATION.

spatial price discrimination In a spatial model with imperfect competition, a firm's choice of price for each location maximizing its profit from that location. *See also* SPATIAL MODEL.

Spearman rank correlation coefficient A distribution-free statistic measuring the degree of monotone association between two variables defined by

$$r = 1 - 6\sum\nolimits_{i=1}^{N} d_i^2/(N(N^2 - 1))$$

where N is the number of pairs of observations and d is the difference in statistical ranks of the two variables in every pair.

special deposits Additional deposits that other banks are required to make with the *central bank. These may carry low or no interest, and do not count towards any normal minimum *reserve requirements. Special deposits reduce bank profits, and their ability to extend credit.

special drawing rights (SDRs) A form of international money, created by the *International Monetary Fund (IMF) and defined as a weighted average of various *convertible currencies. The IMF's official accounts are kept in terms of SDRs as units of account. Members have holdings of SDRs which can be used to settle balance-of-payments deficits between them, subject to rules governing the average amount to be held over any five-year period.

specialization Concentration on providing particular types of goods and services, and relying on others to provide what one does not produce. This occurs at all levels: individuals acquire particular skills or professional qualifications; firms concentrate on particular industries; districts, regions, or whole countries specialize in particular activities. Specialization may be total or partial. With total specialization, most activities are not carried on at all, and the goods and services concerned are entirely provided by others. This is very common at the individual and the firm level. With partial specialization, some but not all of particular goods and services are acquired from others. This is common at the regional and national level: many countries, for example, provide some but not all of their own food or fuel.

specific tax A tax levied as a fixed sum on each physical unit of the good taxed, regardless of its price. This is in contrast to an *ad valorem tax, where the tax is proportional to the price of the good. Specific taxes have administrative advantages where measuring quantities is simple, for example in licensing cars or television sets. The disadvantage of specific taxes is that the real yield of specific taxes is eroded by inflation.

speculation Economic activity aimed at profiting from expected changes in the prices of goods, assets, or currencies. In a world of uncertainty, most transactions are capable of being interpreted as speculative, but the term speculation is reserved for transactions where expected *capital gains provide a major motive. Speculators may buy goods or assets they do not want but whose prices they expect to rise, or buy call options on such assets. They can contract to buy assets they do not have the funds to pay for. Speculators may sell goods, assets, or currencies they do not really want to part with, but whose prices they expect to fall, so that they will be able to buy them back more cheaply; or they may buy put options on such assets. It is also possible to contract to sell assets one does not actually possess. The introduction of new forms of financial *derivative have extended the possibilities for speculation.

speculative bubble *See* BUBBLE.

speculative demand for money The demand for money to take advantage of an investment opportunity. In *Keynesian economics an investor can hold money or bonds. If it is felt that the interest rate is going to rise (meaning the price of bonds will fall) the investor will hold money until the fall in the price of bonds is realized.

speculative motive The component of the *demand for money that arises from the aim of gaining from expected changes in interest rates. In Keynesian monetary theory such expectations are important. If it is believed that interest rates are likely to rise, and thus that bond prices are likely to fall, this makes bonds less and money more attractive to hold. This gives an incentive to sell bonds and hold money, or to defer buying bonds and hold on to money which would otherwise have been put into bonds to earn interest. Similarly, if interest rates are expected to fall, and bond prices to rise, this makes bonds more and money less attractive. This gives an incentive to reduce money holdings and buy bonds.

speculator An individual or firm taking *risks for the sake of expected profits. Speculators may be willing to do this because they believe they have better information and ability to forecast future prices than other market participants, or because they are *risk-neutral, or less *risk-averse than other market participants, who are willing to pay to transfer risks to somebody else. Speculation has been seen as a cause of economic instability. This possible disadvantage has to be set against the claims that speculators provide *liquidity for other people's assets, that on average their activities smooth price fluctuations rather than increasing them, and that without speculators many innovations could not have been financed.

spill-over A connection between different parts of the economy. Spill-overs may be pecuniary or non-pecuniary. A pecuniary spill-over occurs, for example, when changes in one industry affect factor supplies to another: if a new factory bids up the wages of unskilled labour so that local people find cleaners or gardeners more expensive, this is a pecuniary spill-over. Pecuniary spill-overs produce their effects through markets. A non-pecuniary spill-over occurs when one industry inflicts a negative *externality on another: there is usually no market through which they can be paid not to do so. Non-pecuniary spill-overs provide a prima facie case for government intervention, by regulation or taxation, whereas pecuniary spill-overs do not, except on grounds of income distribution.

spot market A market for immediate delivery (in some cases a short time is allowed for delivery). Spot markets exist for goods, securities, and currencies. They are distinguished from *forward and futures markets, in which delivery of the items traded is due at an agreed future date. The terminology arose from the practice of unskilled labourers gathering at a meeting point, or 'spot', early in the morning for possible selection by employers needing additional (and immediate) labour.

spot price The price of goods, securities, and currencies for immediate delivery.

spread The difference between the bid and offer prices quoted by a *market-maker. The prices of securities at which market-makers are willing to sell are higher than those at which they are willing to buy. The spread has to cover the market-makers' operating costs and provide profits, and includes a premium against the risk that any particular customer has insider knowledge about the security being traded. Spreads tend to be smaller on more widely traded securities.

spurious correlation Statistically significant correlation between two random variables observed in a sample when the true correlation between these variables is zero. The most common cause of spurious correlation between two uncorrelated and possibly independent time series is the presence of a *trend in both.

stability conditions The conditions for a system to tend to revert to its original position after a disturbance. The process of convergence may involve fluctuations, and the *equilibrium state to which a system reverts may itself be a stationary state, a steady-state growth path, or some form of limit cycle. Where a system can be described by a set of linear equations, the stability conditions for a linear difference equation system are that all characteristic roots be less than 1 in absolute value; in a linear differential equation system the stability conditions are that all characteristic roots have negative real parts.

stabilization policy The use of economic policies to reduce fluctuations. This may be applied at the macroeconomic level, to reduce fluctuations in real incomes, unemployment, inflation, or exchange rates, or at the microeconomic level, to reduce fluctuations in the prices of particular goods. Where a system is subject to stochastic *shocks, to the extent that these can be predicted, stabilization policy can work by either preventing or offsetting them. If the shocks cannot be forecast or offset without time lags, some fluctuations are inevitable, and stabilization policy can seek only to reduce them.

Stackelberg duopoly A *duopoly in which one firm is the leader and the other is the follower. The leader is assumed to choose its optimal *strategy taking into account the follower's expected reaction. The follower has to choose its optimal strategy given the choice of the leader.

stag To subscribe to new issues of shares in the hope of selling immediately at a profit. A stag is an investor who acts in this way.

stages of economic growth The theory that countries develop through a series of modes of economic organization, each leading to the next. Various such sequences have been proposed: for example, feudalism–capitalism–socialism; or hunting-gathering–herding animals–agriculture–industry–service-based economy. In each case several economies can be observed to have followed such a sequence; whether all economies must do so, or whether the order can be changed or some stages omitted, is a matter of debate.

stagflation The situation where a country persistently suffers from both high *inflation and high *unemployment.

stagnation A situation in which there is little or no change in techniques or income levels. This is contrasted with development, when techniques are advancing and income levels increasing.

stakeholder Anybody with some form of interest in a business. As well as *shareholders, this includes directors, managers, other employees, customers, subcontractors, and even the general public in cases where the firm's activities impact on the environment. A stakeholder is thus anybody who stands to lose if a business is run badly. While formally directors are supposed to run companies in the interests of the shareholders, in many cases they are expected by others, and often claim themselves, to consider the interests of the other stakeholders as well.

stamp duty A tax on transactions, levied by requiring that documents bear an official stamp to be legally valid. In the UK at one time there was a small stamp duty on cheques; it is now levied on some sales of property and on share transfers.

Standard and Poor's (S&P) One of the main US *credit-rating agencies. It produces the S&P 500 stock price index, based on the prices of 500 principal shares traded on the New York Stock Exchange (NYSE). This covers about 80 percent of the total value of stocks traded. The S&P 100 index covers many of the larger corporations' stocks, representing about 60 percent of the NYSE market.

((⊕)) SEE WEB LINKS
• Access to the credit rating services and other products of Standard and Poor's.

standard deviation In a sample of observations, a commonly used measure of *dispersion, defined as the square root of the average of squared deviations of the observations from the sample mean. In a population, the square root of the *variance of the distribution.

standard error (of a statistic) An estimated *standard deviation of a statistic; a measure of the reliability of this statistic as an estimator of the population parameter from the sample.

Standard Industrial Classification (SIC) The method of classifying types of economic activity used in UK official statistics. This is consistent with the International Standard Industrial Classification issued by the United Nations, and the Nomenclature des Activités établies dans les Communautés Européennes used by the European Union. The advantage of a similar classification of industries is that it facilitates international comparisons of the composition and the efficiency of industries.

Standard International Trade Classification (SITC) The system used to classify international *visible trade. The main sections are denoted by single digits; for example, 0 is food and live animals, 1 is beverages and tobacco, etc. More detailed classifications are denoted by further digits, down to the five-digit level.

standardized commodity A commodity produced to uniform specifications, so that different units are interchangeable. Standardized goods make possible lower costs of production through *economies of scale, but place some restriction on consumer choice. Only standardized commodities are suitable for being traded on *forward and futures markets.

standard of living The economic component of people's welfare. This is often measured by consumption per head, or by consumption per equivalent adult, counting children as fractions of adults. This is not in fact a perfect welfare measure: it disregards some important factors contributing to overall welfare. First, it does not count services such as health care and education, which are sometimes provided free or at subsidized prices by governments, and sometimes have to be provided by consumers for themselves. Second, it takes no account of environmental *externalities such as pollution, traffic congestion, or crime. Third, it can be argued that income saved contributes to welfare as well as income consumed, since the assets accumulated make their owners safer.

standard rate A now obsolete name for the rate of UK income tax applied to most incomes. This is now called *basic rate. There are usually lower rates for the first slice of *taxable income, below some lower limit, and higher rates for income in excess of some upper limit. In the UK the standard rate applied to the bulk of taxable incomes.

standby arrangement An arrangement by central banks to lend one another reserves if necessary to resist speculative pressure on their exchange rates. The existence of standby arrangements between a group of central banks decreases the total of *foreign exchange reserves that they need to hold between them, if speculative capital movements are likely to occur between their currencies.

staple product The most important product of an area or country. Domination of an economy by a single product is unusual except for some major oil-producing countries, such as Kuwait, and a number of *less developed countries. Most modern economies have no single staple product, though some local areas are heavily dependent on particular industries.

State Earnings-Related Pension Scheme (SERPS) A UK government scheme to provide earnings-related pensions in addition to the basic flat-rate pension. Workers were required to belong to this unless they opted for a recognized occupational pension scheme or personal pension scheme. The SERPS scheme has been discontinued, but pensions from it are still being paid.

state enterprise A firm founded on the initiative of the state and run by it. A state enterprise is likely to exist when there are activities which would be socially beneficial but are not attractive to private entrepreneurs, or activities which would be profitable but involve *natural monopolies. An example of the first category would be factories to employ disabled people; of the second, provision of essential public services such as sewers. The drawback with state enterprise is that as an owner the state provides a too *soft budget constraint, and that the running of state enterprises is liable to capture by their management and workers, who run the business for their own benefit rather than that of the public. In the UK many state enterprises have been privatized, subsidized where necessary, and regulated.

state-owned company A company whose shares are owned by the state. This may be during the prelude to *privatization. If a company is privatized in stages, it is possible to have part of its shares state-owned, while the remainder are held privately.

states of the world The possible future outcomes for an economy with uncertainty. Viewed from today the economic situation tomorrow (or at any time in the future) is uncertain. A state of the world is a complete summary of one possible economic situation tomorrow. The full set of states of the world includes every possible future situation. It is usually assumed that an individual economic agent knows the set of possible states, but does not know which will arise.

static equilibrium An equilibrium in which the values of economic variables do not change in the absence of external forces; an example is the Walrasian market equilibrium. *See also* DYNAMIC EQUILIBRIUM; TEMPORARY EQUILIBRIUM.

stationary process *See* COVARIANCE STATIONARY PROCESS; STRONGLY STATIONARY PROCESS.

statistic A function of the sample of observations. Various statistics can be constructed to summarize the properties of the sample (descriptive statistics), to estimate an unknown parameter of the population (estimators), or to test a statistical hypothesis (test statistics).

statistical adjustment *See* BALANCING ITEM.

statistics A branch of mathematics dealing with the methods of collection and analysis of samples of data, used to infer the properties, or the unobserved characteristics, of the population.

statutory monopoly A *monopoly protected by law from entry by rivals. Such monopolies are sometimes set up as a quid pro quo for an obligation to provide a universal service; the UK Post Office is an example of this.

steady state In economics, a state of an economy that does not change over time. In *neoclassical economics this is the state with a constant *capital–labour ratio. In particular, this implies that per capita quantities of output and consumption are also constant, whereas the levels of capital stock, output, and consumption in the steady state grow at the rate of population growth.

sterilization The method by which a central bank prevents *balance-of-payments surpluses or deficits from affecting the domestic *money supply. If there is a surplus in the balance of payments on current and capital account combined, this leads to a rise in the *foreign exchange reserves, and an increase in the money supply. If the central bank does not want the money supply to increase, it can prevent this by selling securities so as to sterilize the cash inflow. Similarly, if there is a deficit in the balance of payments on current and capital accounts combined, this leads to a loss of foreign exchange reserves and a shrinkage in the money supply. If the central bank does not want the money supply to fall, it can sterilize the cash outflow by buying securities. The central bank can choose to sterilize some proportion rather than the whole of the monetary effects of changes in foreign exchange reserves.

sterling The UK currency. The name originated from the pound Easterling, formerly used in trade with the Baltic. The sterling area was an arrangement under which a number of *Commonwealth countries pegged their exchange rates to sterling and held their foreign exchange reserves in London: this system declined after 1950. *Sterling M3 was a measure of the UK money supply excluding balances held in London but in other currencies.

sterling area A group of countries, mainly in the *Commonwealth, which linked their currencies to sterling and held their foreign exchange reserves in London. This group was very important in the inter-war years and immediate post-war period, but declined in importance in the 1950s, mainly because of the UK's decreasing share in world trade and finance.

sterling M3 A former measure of broad money, including the following components: (1) M0, that is, currency, plus banks' till money, plus banks' balances at the Bank of England; (2) UK private sector sight bank deposits; and (3) UK private sector time deposits plus public sector sterling deposits. This measure is now known simply as M3.

sticky prices Prices which do not vary in the face of small changes in costs or demand conditions. Sticky prices can be rationalized by administrative costs in changing prices, and through uncertainty about which way costs or demand conditions will move next. Firms may also believe that raising prices risks losing customers if competitors do not follow suit, while cutting prices runs the risk of starting a *price war.

sticky wages Wage rates that are not readily changed in the face of changes in market conditions. This frequently takes the form of either nominal wage resistance (an unwillingness to accept lower money wages), or *real wage resistance (an unwillingness to accept real wage cuts, that is, wage increases less than the rate of inflation). Employers are also unwilling to increase wages in the face of temporary labour shortages, because of anticipated difficulty in lowering them again; and trade unions have been known to oppose their members accepting wage increases not negotiated through them.

stochastic process A family, or a collection of random variables, indexed by time. It is said to be a discrete process, or a discrete time process, if the time index only takes integer values (typically, $0, \pm 1, \pm 2, \dots$), and a continuous process, or a continuous time process, if the time index takes a continuous range of real values (finite or infinite).

stock **1.** The total quantity accumulated at a point in time. This is contrasted to a *flow, which refers to the change in the stock over a given period. For example, the quantity of capital is a stock while investment is a flow.
   2. A synonym for stocks, a collection of goods held by an enterprise. *Stock appreciation is an increase in the value of stocks held due to price changes. A stockpile is a large holding of commodities, held, for example, by a government as a strategic reserve. *See also* BUFFER STOCK; INVESTMENT IN STOCKS AND WORK IN PROGRESS.
   3. A synonym for share. Common stock is the US term for ordinary share. Government stock is government debt instruments. *See also* ALPHA STOCKS; BETA STOCKS; COMMON STOCK; GAMMA STOCKS; OVER-THE-COUNTER MARKET.

stock appreciation The part of the change in the value of the stocks held by a business over any period which is due to price changes. Rising commodity prices cause this to be positive; falling commodity prices cause it to be negative. During inflationary periods stock appreciation causes real profits to be overestimated: firms may be allowed to subtract it in calculating their taxable profits, since without this adjustment they could be paying tax on nominal profits while real profits were in fact negative.

stockbroker A dealer in securities who acts only as an agent for others. A stockbroker sells stocks and shares for ultimate vendors at the highest available price, and buys for ultimate purchasers at the lowest available price. Stockbrokers may advise clients, or operate on the basis of simply executing orders, without giving advice. Brokers are contrasted with *jobbers, or *market-makers, who buy and sell securities on their own account.

stock dividend The situation when shareholders take their dividends in the form of new shares in a company rather than cash. This is a cheaper way of selling new shares than organizing an issue on the stock exchange, if only a small amount of new capital is required.

stock exchange An institution through which company shares and government stock are traded. Originally the exchange would be a building, where traders gathered and trade proceeded either by individual negotiation or by *'open outcry', where prices bid and offered were announced out loud so as to inform all traders within earshot. Modern stock exchanges are institutions with traders linked by computer networks and telephones. Stock exchanges have rules about the information companies have to provide for their shares to be listed, the individuals or firms allowed to trade, the notification of trades carried out, and the procedure for settlement, that is, actual delivery of shares and money payments. There are stock exchanges in all major world commercial centres, such as Frankfurt, London, New York, Paris, and Tokyo.

Stock Exchange Automated Quotation System (SEAQ) A screen-based dealing system allowing the buying and selling prices of all *market-makers for a given security to be displayed to all traders simultaneously. This system was introduced in London after deregulation in 1986.

stock exchange listing The right of a company to have its shares traded on a *stock exchange. Listing is usually conditional on the company providing a satisfactory level of information on its activities, and may be conditional on its size, or on making a sufficient proportion of shares open to the general public.

stock market *See* STOCK EXCHANGE.

stock market crash A sudden and drastic general fall in security prices on a stock exchange. For example, on 'Black Monday', 19 October 1987, the *Dow Jones index in New York fell 23 percent in a single day, and major falls occurred in London and other stock exchanges worldwide. A stock market crash is always possible, since the present price of shares is heavily dependent on opinions about future changes. A crash is most likely when a prolonged *bull market has pushed shares to high *price–earnings ratios.

stock option *See* SHARE OPTION.

stockpile A large stock of a commodity. Stockpiles of goods such as wheat or tin may be held as strategic reserves, for use in emergencies such as wars or natural disasters. They may also be held to try to stabilize commodity prices, or more usually as the result of trying to hold commodity prices above a market-clearing level.

stock split *See* BONUS ISSUE.

Stolper–Samuelson theorem A result stating that in a competitive world economy with *constant returns to scale and two factors of production, a rise in the *relative price of a good will lead to an increase in the return to the factor which is used most intensively in the production of that good, and to a fall in the return to the other factor. The theorem, named after its originators, is used to explain the consequences of opening an economy to trade, or of introducing trade protection. In either case, the relative prices of goods will change, and the theorem predicts the consequences of this change for income distribution.

stop–go cycle Terminology from *Keynesian economics that refers to a sequence of alternations of official policy between trying to expand and contract *effective demand. If the economy, when left alone, tended to produce alternating spells of depressed and excessive demand, stop–go policies could be defended as stabilizing. The suggestion of critics of 'stop–go' policies in the UK in the 1950s and 1960s was that the monetary and fiscal authorities applied the brakes and the accelerator alternately, in each case vigorously but too late. This set up tendencies to overshoot in each direction, destabilizing the economy. Stop–go policies were thus blamed for irregular growth.

store of value One of the functions of money. If asset prices are stable, money is unattractive as a store of value, as it brings in no income, but if asset prices are unstable, it may be worth holding some part of total assets in money, as a safeguard against *risk. Money is particularly attractive as a store of value if it is believed that prices generally will fall, and is less so the more inflation is thought likely.

straight-line depreciation The system of accounting for *depreciation on an asset by taking an assumed life, say n years, and charging depreciation at the rate of $(1/n)$ of its cost each year until it is fully written down. The system is so named because if the remaining value is plotted against time on a graph the result is a downward-sloping straight line.

strategic entry deterrence Actions undertaken by a firm to deter competitors from entering their markets. Such actions could include making a large investment of sunk capital, which makes it unlikely that rivals could drive it out, or offering long-term low-price contracts to customers. For any given entry decisions by rivals, these policies do not maximize profits, but they may pay by discouraging entry. *See also* BARRIERS TO ENTRY.

strategic interaction A situation in which the pay-off of one economic agent is dependent upon the choices of others. For example, in a duopolistic industry the profit of each firm is dependent on the choice (quantity or price) of the other firm. The outcome of strategic interaction is analysed using *game theory.

strategic trade policy A trade policy intended to influence the trade policies of other countries. A policy is said to be strategic if, while it would not be beneficial to adopt it if the policies of all other countries were taken as given, adopting it may be beneficial if it caused other countries to change their trade policies. For example, an export subsidy on a particular good might involve making losses if all other exporting countries continued to supply the world market, but might be beneficial if announcing the subsidy induced some or all foreign competitors to withdraw from the market.

strategic trade retaliation Retaliation to foreign trade restrictions which is imposed mainly to deter further restrictions. If country A raises its *tariffs or cuts its *quotas on B's goods, B has to decide whether to retaliate. If B could assume that A would take no further action, the best reaction might be to do nothing, on the argument that while A's action was harmful, retaliation would just make matters worse. However, B may believe that this would be interpreted by A as a signal that further restrictions would not be resisted, so B may take some form of retaliatory action simply to signal to A that they should go no further.

strategic voting Voting for an alternative other than own most preferred choice in the expectation that a better outcome will obtain. Strategic voting can arise whenever votes are cast over more than two alternatives. *See also* COLLECTIVE CHOICE.

strategy In *game theory, a plan detailing the action that a player will take at each decision node during the play of a game. A *dominant strategy exists if one choice of action by a player is always best whatever actions are chosen by other players. A *mixed strategy uses a randomizing device, such as tossing a coin, to choose between two or more actions: this has the advantage of making it impossible for other players to predict the randomizing player's choice of action, as the latter does not know what it will be until after the randomizing device has been used. An open loop strategy is one where the rules to be followed are laid down at the start and do not change; a closed loop strategy includes 'feedback', that is, rules about changing the rules in the light of experience. *See also* PUNISHMENT STRATEGY.

stratified sample A sample obtained by taking a sample from each subgroup of population when the population is not homogeneous and can be classified into subgroups according to some factor(s). Each subgroup is then represented in the same proportion in the sample as in the entire population. Stratified sampling is appropriate when the measurement of interest is expected to vary across subgroups. *See also* QUOTA SAMPLE; RANDOM SAMPLE.

strengthening of a currency A rise in the price of one currency in terms of others. This is caused by an increase in the demand to hold it, which may be due either to an improvement of the country's current account, or to shifts into it from other currencies on capital account. *See also* CURRENCY APPRECIATION.

strike Withdrawal of labour by a group of employees, typically members of a *trade union. An official strike is one called or recognized by a union; an unofficial strike is one started without union authorization. *See also* NO-STRIKE AGREEMENT.

strike ballot A vote of the members of a *trade union as to whether or not to resort to strike action. This may be required before a strike either by a union's own rules or by the law.

strike price The pre-arranged price at which an *option to buy or sell can be exercised.

strongly stationary process A *stochastic process x_t is said to be strongly stationary if the joint distribution of $X_{t_1}, X_{t_2}, \ldots, X_{t_n}$ is the same as the joint distribution of $X_{t_1+k}, X_{t_2+k}, \ldots, X_{t_n+k}$, i.e. is invariant under translation. Strong stationarity implies weak stationarity; the converse in general does not hold.

structural equation In a *simultaneous equations model, an equation that describes the behaviour of economic agents, or an economically meaningful relationship among economic variables, and typically has endogenous variables on both sides. An example is a demand equation or a supply equation, where prices and quantities are endogenous. The parameters of a structural equation are called structural parameters. *See also* REDUCED FORM.

Structural Funds Funds operated by the *European Union (EU) to improve economic conditions in the poorest regions of member countries. Objective 1 funding, for example, is directed to regions whose per capita *gross domestic product is under 3/4 of the EU average. The intention of the funds is to reduce regional inequality in the EU.

structural transformation A process of major change in a country's economy. This can involve a large-scale transfer of resources from primary to industrial sector activity, as in many *newly industrialized countries. It can also involve a shift in methods of economic organization, from a mainly planned to a largely market-based economy, as in many previously planned economies of the former Soviet Union and Central and Eastern Europe.

structural unemployment Unemployment due to a lack of capital equipment which unemployed workers could use, or lack among unemployed workers of the skills necessary to produce anything for which there is a market. This can occur because investment has failed to keep pace with growth in the labour force: this is common in *less developed countries. It can also occur because of changes in demand, leading to the decline of industries which previously provided jobs. Structural unemployment cannot be cured by increasing *effective demand, which would remedy *Keynesian unemployment, or by cutting wages, which would cure *classical unemployment; its cure requires major investment in new industries, or large-scale migration from depressed areas.

structure–conduct–performance The dominant paradigm of *industrial organization in the 1950s to 1970s. The structure of a market is the degree of monopoly power, often measured by the *N-firm concentration index. Conduct refers to the behaviour of firms and the ways in which they compete. Structure combines with conduct to produce an outcome. The performance of the outcome can be judged against the efficient outcome. The paradigm faded from use when it was found not to be supported by empirical evidence.

Student's t-distribution A continuous distribution of the form

$$f(x) = \frac{\Gamma((v+1)/2)}{\sqrt{\pi v}\,\Gamma((v/2))}\left[1 + \frac{x^2}{v}\right]^{-(v+1)/2}$$

for $-\infty < x < \infty$ and $v = 1, 2, \ldots$. The parameter v is called the number of degrees of freedom. It has mean zero for $v > 1$ and variance $v/(v-2)$ for $v > 2$. As v gets large the t-distribution converges to the standard normal. The square of a variable with a t-distribution with v degrees of freedom has an *F-distribution with $(1, v)$ degrees of freedom.

stylized facts Empirical observations used as a starting point for the construction of economic theories. A stylized fact must be true in general, but not necessarily in every case. For example, it is a stylized fact that the shares of capital and labour in national income have been constant over time. This is true approximately for most countries, but is not exactly true for any country, nor approximately true for all countries.

subcontracting The practice of the principal suppliers of goods and services buying in some of their inputs from independent firms, rather than using employees to produce them in-house. Subcontracting may be used because the work concerned needs specialized skilled labour or equipment which the principal producer does not need full-time. It also allows more flexibility in employment, if the principal's own employees are protected by employment laws or a strong trade union.

subgame A subset or part of a sequential game that begins at a node where each player knows every action of the players that moved previously at every point.

subgame perfect equilibrium A refinement of *Nash equilibrium used in sequential games. A subgame perfect equilibrium is a set of strategies (one for each of the players) with the property that the strategies constitute a Nash equilibrium for every *subgame of the original game. A subgame perfect equilibrium is usually found using *backward induction.

subsidiarity The principle that decisions on policy should be taken at the most decentralized level consistent with making them effective. Decisions affecting the global atmosphere, for example restrictions on the use of chlorofluorocarbons, need to be taken at an international level. Decisions on safety standards for vehicles need to be taken at a national or possibly supranational level. There is a tendency in modern economies for an increasing proportion of policy decisions to be centralized, from local authorities to national governments, and from national governments to supranational bodies such as the *European Union. The main arguments for subsidiarity are, first, that there are so many decisions to be taken that the centre should not be swamped in detail; and, second, that there are national and local variations in income levels, traditions, and social attitudes, so that common rules which are hardly noticed in one area, where they merely formalize established habits, would be regarded as so unusual as to be unenforceable in others.

subsidiary A firm which is owned or controlled by another. There are wide variations in the extent to which subsidiary companies are allowed to make decentralized decisions about matters such as investment projects, and choices between trading with other firms in the same group or with outsiders.

subsidized credit Credit provided on terms below normal market rates. Subsidized credit may be granted to encourage particular forms of activity, including, for example, exports, provision of affordable rented housing by *housing associations, or the growth of entrepreneurship among minority groups. It may also be granted as a corrupt favour to people or firms with political influence. Credit may be subsidized by governments, or lending institutions may cross-subsidize some borrowers out of the profits on other loans.

subsidy A payment by the government to consumers or producers which makes the factor cost received by producers greater than the market price charged to consumers. Subsidies may be given on grounds of income distribution, to improve the incomes of producers, or the welfare of consumers. They are not usually efficient for either purpose: even goods consumed heavily by the poor are also consumed by the better-off, so that much of the benefit of a subsidy goes to those who do not need it. *See also* EXPORT SUBSIDY; FARM SUBSIDIES; FOOD SUBSIDIES.

subsistence level The minimum level of consumption on which people can survive.

subsistence wages The lowest level of wages that allows workers to survive.

substitute At an informal level, one good or service is a substitute for another if it can be used to satisfy the same need, or at least a similar need. A pair of goods are said to be substitutes if, holding the utility level constant, a rise in the price of one of them increases demand for the other. Hence, the *substitution effect is negative. (If there are only two goods then with *convex preferences they must be substitutes, so the definition only has substance when there are three or more goods.) This relation between a pair of goods is contrasted with that of complements where, holding the utility level constant, a rise in the price of one good decreases demand for the other. This is a negative substitution effect. *See also* PERFECT SUBSTITUTE.

substitution The switching of consumption from one good or service to another in response to a change in the ratio of prices. Holding utility constant, the *elasticity of substitution between two goods or services is the ratio of the proportional change in relative quantities consumed to the proportional change in relative prices. If the price of one good changes, the prices of all other goods being held constant, the change in demand can be divided into a *substitution effect and an *income effect. The substitution effect is the change in consumption holding the utility level constant: it shows how consumption would have changed if consumers had been compensated for the change in prices. *See also* ELASTICITY OF SUBSTITUTION; IMPORT SUBSTITUTION; MARGINAL RATE OF SUBSTITUTION; SUBSTITUTION EFFECT.

substitution effect The effect on the demand for good i of an increase in the price of good j when the consumer is compensated sufficiently to remain at the same level of utility. The substitution effect is determined by a move around an indifference curve. Hence, the substitution effect of an increase in a good's own price is always non-positive, and is strictly negative whenever any substitution is possible. *See also* SLUTSKY EQUATION.

sunk costs Those parts of the costs of an enterprise which cannot be recovered if it ceases operations, even in the long run. These include items such as the construction costs of mines or tunnels, or the development costs of industrial processes. The existence of sunk costs tends to produce *hysteresis in the economy, and helps to explain the rarity of *contestable markets.

sunspot theory A theory that predicts that economic activity can be coordinated with events outside the economic system. Sunspot theory was originally proposed by William Jevons (1835–1882), who provided evidence that economic cycles could be linked to the regular occurrence of solar flares or spots. Sunspot theory now refers to the proposition that it is possible for the economic activity of individuals to be endogenously coordinated and hence appear correlated with some outside activity (such as a sunspot) that has no real economic effect.

superannuation Payments to retired employees. Superannuation contributions are deductions from the pay of employees still working, to help to finance payments to those retired.

supernormal profit (economic rent, abnormal profit, pure profit, excess profit) Any profit in excess of *normal profit, that is, above the level necessary to retain entrepreneurial effort in its current activity.

Supplementary Benefit A UK social security benefit that was available on a means-tested basis to pensioners or others whose total income would otherwise be below some target level. Supplementary Benefit has now been replaced by *Income Support.

supply 1. The amount of a good or service offered for sale. The supply function relates supply to the factors which determine its level. These include the price of the good, the prices of factor services and intermediate products employed in producing it, the number of firms engaged in producing it, and their levels of capital equipment. *See also* ADVERSE SUPPLY SHOCK; AGGREGATE SUPPLY; ELASTICITY OF SUPPLY; INELASTIC SUPPLY; JOINT SUPPLY; LABOUR SUPPLY; MONEY SUPPLY; REFUSAL TO SUPPLY.

2. The act of providing a good or service.

supply curve A curve showing the amount that firms in an industry are willing to supply at each possible price. A supply curve is defined only if the firms are price-takers, who do not consider the effects of their own output on the price they can charge. With price on the vertical axis, the supply curve at any price is the horizontal sum of the marginal cost curves of the firms in an industry. The industry supply curve is at least as elastic as the supply of individual firms, and is more elastic if a rise in price induces more firms to enter the industry, or if a fall in price induces some existing firms to leave. *See also* BACKWARD-BENDING SUPPLY CURVE.

supply-side economics The view that real growth in the economy depends to a considerable extent even in the short run, and almost completely in the long run, on factors affecting supply rather than on *effective demand. Supply-side proposals to increase economic growth could include measures such as the reform of tax systems to encourage investment and innovation, the reform of restrictive practices, improvements in the infrastructure of transport and communications, better training and more assistance with mobility for unemployed workers, and reforming social security systems to encourage labour supply. This is contrasted with the view in *Keynesian economics that the main factor affecting economic growth is the level of effective demand.

supply-side policy A policy intended to increase the aggregate supply available in an economy. Supply-side policies could include reform of the social security system to encourage the supply of effort; improvement of education and training to improve the productivity of the labour force; reform of restrictive practices and restrictions on market entry to improve efficiency; or reform of the tax system to encourage the devotion of more effort to production and less to tax avoidance and evasion. Such policies are contrasted with *demand management policies, which seek to increase and stabilize aggregate output by controlling *effective demand.

surplus *See* BUDGET SURPLUS; CONSUMER SURPLUS; CURRENT ACCOUNT SURPLUS; EXPORT SURPLUS; PRODUCER SURPLUS.

surplus value The excess of what workers can produce over what they need to consume. As pointed out by Karl Marx (1818–1883), surplus value is essential if economies are to be able to afford either investment or 'unproductive' workers, producing goods or services which are not part of essential consumption. Political economists, including Marx, were concerned with the division of surplus value between various members of society. Marx believed that it would be appropriated by capitalists. In modern economies surplus value is divided between many sections of society, including consumption by workers of considerably more than their minimum needs.

surtax An additional income tax levied on high incomes.

survey data Data collected by surveys of individuals or firms. Surveys may be total in their coverage, as with *censuses, or may be based on samples of the relevant population. They may be conducted by government bodies, either specifically set up for the purpose, for example the Office for National Statistics in the UK, or in the course of their normal work. Data on UK incomes, for example, are collected by *HM Revenue and Customs, and data on trade by the *Department for Business, Enterprise and Regulatory Reform. Surveys are also conducted by private commercial bodies such as market research firms, by private bodies such as the *Confederation of British Industry, and by academic institutions.

Survey of Current Business A monthly publication of the *Bureau of Economic Analysis providing information on economic activity in the US and internationally.

(((⊕))) SEE WEB LINKS

• The home page of the *Survey of Current Business.*

sustained yield A level of output which can be continued indefinitely, without impairing the future productivity of any *natural resources used. This is contrasted with overcropping or resource mining, which reduces or destroys the productive capacity of the resources involved. Examples are found in agriculture, where good practice can improve the soil whereas overcropping or overgrazing damage it; in forestry where a regular cycle of felling and replanting can be sustainable; or in fisheries, where a limited harvest can continue indefinitely whereas overfishing destroys breeding stocks. *See also* DEPLETABLE RESOURCES; RENEWABLE RESOURCES.

swap A financial derivative in which two counter-parties agree to exchange one stream of cash flows for another stream. In an interest rate swap a flow of payments at a fixed interest rate is swapped for a flow at a variable interest rate. A currency swap involves the initial exchange of principal denominated in two different currencies, payments of interest in the currency received over the lifetime of the swap, and a final re-exchange of principal. *See also* DERIVATIVE.

sweated labour Workers employed for low pay and often for long hours under poor working conditions. In many poor countries this is true of almost everybody who is employed at all. In more advanced countries, where such treatment is exceptional, workers treated in this way are often separated from the main labour markets by factors such as poor education and language differences, and sometimes by their status as illegal immigrants.

symmetrical distribution A distribution of a random variable that is characterized by a probability mass function (for a discrete variable) or a probability density function (for a continuous variable) that is symmetric about the mean of this variable. Examples are the *uniform distribution and the *normal distribution.

syndicate (at Lloyd's) A group of *Lloyd's names who combine to provide insurance. Each member of a syndicate provides a stated amount of capital; if the syndicate makes a profit on the policies it has issued, all members of the syndicate gain in proportion to their share of the capital employed. If a syndicate makes a loss, each member is liable in proportion to his or her share in the capital, with unlimited liability as to the extent of the loss. Every member of a syndicate is also responsible to an unlimited extent for the losses if other members default on their share of the liabilities.

syndicated loan A loan provided by a syndicate of banks or other lending institutions. Such loans, often to *less developed countries, are usually arranged by one or a small group of leading banks negotiating the terms and persuading a large number of other lenders to take up small parts of the loan. Participating in a number of syndicated loans gives lenders a less risky portfolio than negotiating loans for themselves with particular borrowers: borrowers can negotiate terms with a single body which they can trust to be able to raise the money by recruiting other lenders to join a syndicate.

synergy Benefits from combining different businesses. For example, if company *A* has a large stock of good ideas ripe for development but few production facilities or funds, and company *B* has a large fund of accumulated reserves and factories whose products face declining markets, the two can both benefit by combining their businesses. Benefits from synergy are frequently claimed by the promoters of *mergers.

systematic risk (systemic risk) Risk arising from disturbances which affect all projects in a class. This type of risk cannot be reduced by diversification. This is contrasted with non-systematic or *idiosyncratic risk, where the disturbances affecting different projects are independent, so that the overall risk of a *portfolio of assets can be reduced by dividing it between a number of projects. In the stock market, for example, risk is partly systematic: there are market-level factors that affect most share prices in the same direction. It is also partly idiosyncratic: every industry and every company is affected by different random disturbances.

S

Taft–Hartley Act The US Labor-Management Relations Act of 1947. This act restricted the rights of US *trade unions in various ways, including a ban on the *closed shop and authorizing states to enact 'right-to-work' laws.

take-off A stage of economic development at which an economy becomes capable of sustained growth in per capita income. An economy which has not reached take-off has saving and investment inadequate to do more than keep pace with population increase at low and stagnant levels of per capita income. Take-off requires sufficient saving for investment in infrastructure and productive equipment, as well as adequate credit and banking systems, and institutions capable of providing education and public order.

takeover The acquisition of a company by new owners. The shares of the company are acquired by new owners, usually another company. They may be paid for in cash, or in the purchaser's shares.

takeover bid An offer to purchase all the shares of a company, thereby acquiring *control of it. Payment may be offered in cash, in the shares of the purchaser, or a mixture. A takeover bid becomes effective only if the holders of a majority of existing shares accept it. As ownership of a controlling interest by a single party leaves *minority shareholders at a disadvantage, stock exchange rules usually require that all shares be purchased on the same terms, and that no party or group can buy more than a certain proportion of the shares (30 percent in the UK) without making a takeover bid for the remainder.

take-up rate The proportion of those entitled to a benefit who actually claim it. This may be restricted by lack of information, a cumbersome claims procedure, or social embarrassment if the benefit is felt to carry some stigma. In spite of information campaigns by welfare authorities and voluntary bodies, the take-up rate for most benefits is significantly below 100 percent.

talk down The attempt to bring down the value of an economic variable through persuasion by the authorities. The variable concerned could, for example, be inflation or the exchange rate. Talking down works via policy announcements by influential people such as central bank governors or finance ministers. As a substitute for substantive policy measures such persuasion is likely to be most successful when the authorities have *credibility. As a complement to the use of practical *policy instruments, talking down may help to bring about adjustment faster and at lower cost in terms of real activity than just using monetary or fiscal policy without explaining what results this is intended to achieve.

tangency optimum A solution to an optimization problem that can be represented as a position of tangency between two curves. For example, a tangency optimum for a consumer occurs at the point where an *indifference curve is tangential to the *budget line.

tangible assets Assets that can be physically touched. This should literally include only physical objects like plant and equipment, but it is often also used to include leases and company shares, as these are mainly titles to tangible assets. *See also* INTANGIBLE ASSETS.

tap issue An issue of UK *Treasury bills to other government departments. This is done at a fixed price, and does not go through the market; it is a piece of internal government bookkeeping. It is contrasted with a *tender issue, by which Treasury bills are sold to non-government purchasers at a competitively determined price.

target An aim of policy. Economic policy targets include objectives such as high levels of employment and growth, low and stable levels of inflation, or maintenance of particular exchange rates. Policy targets are distinguished from both instruments and indicators. *Policy instruments are variables the government or central bank can control, or at least influence, such as tax rates or the money supply. Policy instruments can themselves be targets, but often are not, and targets such as the rate of inflation are clearly not instruments. Policy *indicators are variables used in deciding on the use of policy instruments; indicators which are not themselves targets may be preferred to targets for this task because they are available sooner or can be measured more reliably than targets. *See also* MACROECONOMIC POLICY.

targeting Making benefits available to a particular group of people who are identified by certain characteristics. For example, child benefit in the UK is paid to all mothers with children aged under 16. Targeting is intended to focus the benefit on the most deserving people and to keep down the total cost of attaining a policy objective. Targeting can be done in two ways: providing *benefits in kind which appeal only to particular groups, or administrative restriction of the availability of benefits in cash or in kind.

target zone (exchange rates) A range within which a country seeks to keep its *exchange rate. The range may be broad or narrow, and may be specified in terms of some single foreign currency or some suitable basket of foreign currencies. A target zone can be interpreted in a strict or relaxed manner. With a strict target zone the country's central bank is committed to intervening to prevent the market rate moving outside the target zone, while retaining discretion over intervention when the market rate is within the zone. With a relaxed target zone, the central bank promises to adopt policies calculated to bring the market rate back within the target zone if it strays outside, but not necessarily to intervene in the market to achieve this result immediately.

tariff A scale of charges. In economics a tariff was originally a schedule of taxes on imports; it now refers to the actual import duties. An ad valorem tariff is set as a percentage of the price of the goods imported. A specific tariff is set in money terms per physical unit of the good imported, and does not depend on its price. A non-discriminatory tariff taxes imports from all countries equally; tariff preferences mean that similar imports from different countries are taxed at different rates. *See also* OPTIMUM TARIFF; PROHIBITIVE TARIFF; REVENUE TARIFF; TWO-PART TARIFF.

tastes An alternative, and less formal, terminology for *preferences. Differences in tastes can explain why two consumers who are identical in all observable characteristics do not make identical purchases.

tax A payment compulsorily collected from individuals or firms by a government (central, state, or local) or by the functional equivalent of a government. In modern societies taxes are paid in money but payment in the form of commodities has occurred in the past. Current tax legislation requires that the level of tax payment is defined by objective criteria so is not set arbitrarily by the tax collector. This has not always been the case. In principle, taxes can be levied on any identifiable characteristic (such as eye colour) though most taxes are based on economic characteristics or transactions. A recent exception is the UK *community charge that was levied from 1990 to 1993. This was a fixed tax payable by all adults, so was essentially a tax on existence. Taxes are employed by governments to raise revenue. As a consequence, the increase in the size of government relative to the economy over the past 100 years has caused the average level of taxation to rise.

taxable income That part of income which is liable to tax. Taxable income differs from total cash receipts in several ways. Some receipts are regarded as being of a capital nature: these may be liable to *capital gains taxes, but are not liable to income tax. Taxable income may include *imputed income, such as the rental value of owner-occupied houses (not in the UK). Total income may be reduced for tax purposes by various allowances, either personal allowances for all taxpayers, or allowances for particular categories, for example in respect of dependants, charitable donations, or pension contributions.

tax allowance A deduction from gross income allowed under the tax laws to reduce the *taxable income of an individual or firm. Tax allowances may be given to encourage certain forms of activity: for example, firms are given tax allowances to encourage investment, and both individuals and firms receive tax allowances in respect of some charitable donations. This may be on grounds of *equity, because having to pay the deductible item lowers ability to pay relative to a taxpayer with the same gross income but no comparable liability. Every tax concession reduces the *tax base, which raises the tax rates needed to obtain any given total tax revenue.

tax assessment The determination of the amount of tax any individual or company is liable to pay. This may be done in one of two ways. One is that the taxpayers make *tax returns, listing their income from various sources and any facts affecting their entitlement to tax allowances. The tax authorities then make the actual assessment. The alternative method is *self-assessment: besides supplying information on their income and entitlement to allowances, taxpayers produce their own assessments, applying the tax rules to their own figures; these self-assessments are then checked by the tax authorities. In the UK the assessment is made by an

Inspector of Taxes if a tax return is made within a time limit; after this taxpayers have to produce a self-assessment.

tax avoidance Arranging one's affairs so that tax is not legally payable. Tax avoidance is legal, as contrasted with *tax evasion, which means not paying tax that is in fact legally due, for example by making false tax returns. While in theory tax avoidance and tax evasion are entirely distinct, in many practical cases it requires a court to rule which description applies to any specific set of transactions.

tax base The set of incomes on which *direct taxes are levied, and transactions on which *indirect taxes are levied. The tax base is lowered by all allowances and exemptions: for example, the tax base in the UK is lowered by exempting pension contributions from income tax, and by not including food and children's clothing in the tax base for *value-added tax. The broader the tax base, the lower are the tax rates required to raise any given total of tax revenue.

tax-based incomes policy A policy of using the tax system to reduce *inflation through its incentive effects. This is distinguished from the macroeconomic effect of higher taxes in cutting *effective demand. The reasoning behind such policies is that if sudden increases in incomes attract punitively large tax rates, firms will choose smaller wage and price increases. The shortcomings are that firms with monopoly power will choose even larger price increases to enable them to pay the taxes, and that such tax policies will encourage *creative accounting, and drive economic activity into hidden and untaxed channels.

tax burden The total cost to the economy of having to pay taxes. This includes not only the actual amount collected in taxes, but also administrative costs, compliance costs, and deadweight loss. Administrative costs are incurred by the revenue collection agency including, for example, the cost of employing tax inspectors. *Compliance costs are the costs imposed upon firms and consumers in complying with the rules of the tax system. These include the costs of additional record-keeping required because of liability to tax, and the extra accounting costs of devising methods of tax avoidance. *Deadweight loss arises through the economic distortions caused by taxation. Total deadweight loss is the sum of the loss of *consumer surplus and *producer surplus. The deadweight loss of taxation can be negative if the taxes are imposed upon activities that cause *externalities.

tax credit A payment from the government to an individual or a family. The payment of a tax credit is conditional on certain characteristics. The UK government currently offers a *Child Tax Credit, which is payable to any person over 16 below a certain income level with at least one child and the primary care responsibility for that child, and the *Working Tax Credit, which is paid to anyone below a certain income level working over 16 hours per week. The level of payment for both of these credits is contingent upon income.

tax evasion Failure to pay taxes legally due, for example by making a false tax return or failing to make a return at all. Tax evasion is thus illegal; it is contrasted with *tax avoidance, which means arranging one's affairs so that tax is not legally payable. An individual choosing whether to engage in tax evasion has to weight the gains from a reduced tax payment against the punishment if caught evading. This is a standard example of the economics of choice with *risk.

Tax Exempt Special Savings Account (TESSA) A UK system, intended to encourage small savers, by which individuals could invest a limited amount each year with a building society, the interest being tax-free. This system has now been closed to new investors, being replaced by *Individual Savings Accounts (ISAs), but the capital part of maturing TESSAs can be reinvested in an ISA which does not count against an individual's permitted annual total.

tax expenditure A means by which the government can encourage particular activities without formally making expenditures. If the government wants taxpayers, for example, to take out private medical insurance, it can either make specific grants for the purpose, which will appear as government expenditure, or it can pay implicitly by giving a *tax allowance which reduces net tax paid by an equal amount. The real economic effects of the two systems are exactly the same, except for those too poor to pay any income tax. Under the tax expenditure system, however, total government revenue and expenditure are both lower than under the grant system. Tax expenditures allow the government to influence the economy while reducing the apparent size of the state sector.

tax haven A country which provides foreign residents with opportunities to reduce their tax payments by doing business there. Tax havens can be used for *tax avoidance, when tax liabilities can legally be reduced by using foreign financial intermediaries. They can also be used for *tax evasion, for example by the use of confidential bank accounts to facilitate concealment of income and *money laundering.

tax holiday A limited period of tax-free operation, or of specially reduced taxation. This may be used to induce foreign firms to invest in a country, or domestic firms to invest in an industry or area which the government especially wishes to encourage. A tax holiday scheme may be very expensive in terms of lost revenue if firms which take advantage of it would have invested in any case even without it.

Tax Reform Act A US federal statute of 1986 reforming the federal tax system. The purpose of the act was to simplify the US income tax code, broaden the *tax base, and eliminate many *tax shelters and other preferences. The notable features were a reduction in the top rate of tax from 50 percent to 28 percent accompanied by an increase in the bottom rate from 11 percent to 15 percent.

tax refund A repayment by the tax authorities of excess tax previously collected. This may occur because of mistakes in the original *tax assessment which are corrected on appeal. It may also occur when tax is deducted at source and the taxpayer is subsequently found to be liable for less tax than has been withheld. With a *pay-as-you-earn income tax scheme, as in the UK, a taxpayer who becomes unemployed partway through a tax year may qualify for a tax refund.

tax return A report by a taxpayer to the tax authorities of his or her income, and of any facts affecting their entitlement to *tax allowances. Tax returns may be demanded by the tax authorities, with legal penalties for failing to make returns. Alternatively, where a *withholding tax system is in force, it may be left to taxpayers to make tax returns as a condition for reclaiming any tax refunds to which they are entitled.

tax schedule The relationship between taxable activity and tax liability. *See also* PROGRESSIVE TAX.

tax shelter An arrangement by which part of a person's income is protected from taxes. In the UK, for example, *Individual Savings Accounts enable savers to enjoy some tax-free income.

tax shifting The passing of the *tax burden from one economic agent to another. For example, the burden of a sales tax that is formally levied on a firm may be passed on to consumers in the form of higher prices. Generally, the tax burden is shared between economic agents with the precise allocation determined by elasticities of demand and supply.

tax threshold The value that determines the limit of tax-free activity. In most income tax systems no tax is payable until income reaches a tax threshold. Income above the threshold is then subject to tax. Thresholds apply to many other taxes such as *capital gains tax and *inheritance tax.

tax wedge A summary of the distortion in choices caused by a tax. The tax wedge measures the extent to which taxation causes the relative prices of two commodities to deviate from the efficient value. For example, a tax on income causes a wedge between the price of consumption relative to the wage rate and the marginal rate of transformation between consumption and labour. It does not cause a wedge between the price of one commodity relative to the price of another and the corresponding marginal rate of transformation. As a second example, a tax on the interest from savings causes a wedge in the choice between consumption today and consumption tomorrow, but not in the choice between labour today and consumption today.

t-distribution *See* STUDENT'S T-DISTRIBUTION.

technical analysis The use of past information on security prices to predict future security prices, often by using charts to reveal patterns in prices. Market practitioners who use technical analysis are sometimes referred to as *chartists. Despite its use being fairly common, technical analysis has limited empirical justification. *See also* EFFICIENT MARKETS HYPOTHESIS.

technical efficiency Those aspects of *efficiency concerned with obtaining the largest possible level of output for a given quantity of inputs, or using the smallest possible quantity of inputs to obtain a given output. This is efficiency in production. It is distinguished from efficiency in exchange, which is concerned with the distribution of outputs between different users, and the efficient choice of the set of outputs to produce. Technical efficiency is a necessary condition for the overall efficiency of the economy but it is not sufficient since an economy could be better off producing the right mix of goods by technically inefficient methods, than producing an unsuitable set of goods with complete technical efficiency.

technical progress Improvement in knowledge about techniques for production. Such progress may allow more output to be obtained from unchanged inputs, the same output to be obtained from fewer inputs, or new forms of output to be produced which were not previously possible. Technical progress may be embodied or disembodied. If it is disembodied, improvements in productivity are purely due to new knowledge or improved skills, without the need for any new equipment. If it is embodied, exploitation of the new techniques requires investment in new capital equipment or new intermediate products. *See also* DISEMBODIED TECHNICAL PROGRESS; EMBODIED TECHNICAL PROGRESS; HARROD-NEUTRAL TECHNICAL PROGRESS; HICKS-NEUTRAL TECHNICAL PROGRESS.

technical standard A specification of the design of particular goods or components. Examples range from the gauges of screw on nuts and bolts to the voltages of electronic equipment. Technical standards are needed to ensure compatibility. The use of technical standards is an example of *network externalities, where everybody gains from their equipment being compatible with everybody else's. In the early days of a new product, there is a considerable competitive advantage to a firm that can get its own design accepted as the technical standard.

technical substitution *See* ELASTICITY OF TECHNICAL SUBSTITUTION; MARGINAL RATE OF TECHNICAL SUBSTITUTION.

technological unemployment Unemployment due to technical progress. This applies to particular types of worker whose skill is made redundant because of changes in methods of production, usually by substituting machines for their services. Technical progress does not necessarily lead to a rise in overall unemployment. New methods of production are economic to adopt only if they lower costs, which allows a larger output to be sold at a lower price. If the elasticity of demand is high enough, overall employment in the industry concerned may rise, as will employment in the industry producing the machines. It is still possible, however, for technological unemployment to afflict workers with old skills, if the new jobs created are either lower-grade operative jobs, or require skills they do not possess.

technology 1. The body of knowledge about materials, techniques of production, and operation of equipment, based on the application of science.
2. A summary of what determines the possibilities in an economy for turning inputs into outputs as described by the *production set.

technology gap The difference between two countries in the techniques available for production. Technology gaps are based on differences in the level of scientific knowledge, the education, training, and motivation of the labour force, the availability and quality of infrastructure, such as reliable power supplies and telecommunications, and market size.

technology transfer The transfer of techniques from countries where they are more advanced to other countries where they are less advanced. Technology transfer may involve *foreign direct investment, transfers of skilled personnel from more advanced countries, training of workers from less advanced countries, or licensing of patents. Technology transfer is of great importance to *less developed countries but it is useful to all countries.

Temporary Assistance to Needy Families (TANF) The US federal assistance programme introduced in 1997 to succeed the *Aid to Families with Dependent Children programme. TANF provides cash assistance to families with dependent children through the United States Department of Health and Human Services.

temporary equilibrium In a model of a dynamic economy consisting of a sequence of short single periods, such as the *overlapping generations model, a *static equilibrium in a given single period, with agents having expectations about the values of economic variables in the future periods. These expectations may be correct (*perfect foresight) if there is no uncertainty about the future. If there is uncertainty, the expectations will typically be modelled as forward-looking *rational expectations.

tender A bid to undertake a project. The bid will consist of information on the company or individual placing the tender, an outline of how the project will be approached, and a price for completing the project. *See also* COMPETITIVE TENDERING.

tender issue An issue of *Treasury bills by inviting bids or tenders for a stated quantity, and accepting the bids from those offering the highest price. The actual sales are at the market-clearing price, bids at or above which are sufficient to take up the supply of bills on offer. *See also* TAP ISSUE.

Tennessee Valley Authority (TVA) A US public corporation set up in 1933 as part of the *New Deal. Its functions include power supply, flood control, development of natural resources and tourism, and training. Its power supply activities are self-financing; its remaining functions are funded by the federal government.

term loan A loan due to be repaid on a definite date. This is a US usage.

term premium The amount by which the return on a long-term bond is above the rate predicted by the *unbiased expectations hypothesis. The term premium has been interpreted as a measure of *liquidity preference.

terms of trade The ratio of an index of a country's export prices to an index of its import prices. The terms of trade are said to improve if this ratio increases, so that each unit of exports pays for more imports, and to deteriorate if the ratio falls, so that each unit of exports buys fewer imports. This terminology can be misleading: if a country's terms of trade improve because of increased foreign demand for its exports, this is an improvement in its economic position. If the terms of trade improve because domestic inflation exceeds that abroad, however, the result may be problems with the *balance of trade, which cannot sensibly be regarded as an improvement in the economy. The commodity or 'barter' terms of trade are contrasted with the 'factoral' terms of trade, which are the amount of imports that can be obtained via trade per unit of factor services. A country's factoral terms of trade may improve either because of improvements in the barter terms of trade, or because of increased productivity. 'Terms of trade' with no adjective normally refers to the barter terms of trade.

term structure of interest rates The relation between the rate of interest paid by a financial security and the time until *maturity of the security. The term structure is generally upward-sloping so securities with longer maturities pay higher rates of interest. This slope may be reversed if on average interest rates are expected to fall.

test discount rate The real rate of return used in *cost–benefit analysis by the UK government. The standard rate is 3.5 percent per annum, though a lower rate is used for costs and benefits occurring more than 30 years into the future.

Thatcherism A shorthand for the economic principles underlying the policies of the Thatcher government in the UK from 1979 to 1990. These included promotion of competition to strengthen economic incentives, reduction of the role of government by deregulation and privatization, reliance on monetary policy to eliminate inflation, widening of individual choice, for example through the sale of council houses to their tenants, and a reduction in the powers of trade unions.

third-degree price discrimination Price discrimination where sellers can identify different types of customer, and offer each type a different contract. Special prices may be offered, for example, to students or pensioners. This type of discrimination is possible only when the resale of goods or services is costly or impossible; if resale were costless, every customer would buy through the type that offered the lowest price. *See also* FIRST-DEGREE PRICE DISCRIMINATION; SECOND-DEGREE PRICE DISCRIMINATION.

third-party insurance Insurance against the cost of compensating third parties, that is individuals or companies other than the insurance company and the policy-holder, for death, injury, or damage to property. UK drivers are legally obliged to hold third-party insurance, whereas they are left to decide for themselves whether to insure against fire, theft, and accident.

third world Poor or *less developed countries. The term originated to cover countries which were not part of the *Organization for Economic Cooperation and Development, the advanced capitalist bloc, or the former Soviet bloc.

thrift Willingness to save and economy in spending. *See also* PARADOX OF THRIFT.

thrifts United States non-banking financial institutions which collect savings from the public and finance mortgages. A thrift (a term used interchangeably with *savings and loan asssociation) is the nearest US equivalent to a UK *building society. Many thrifts ran into severe financial problems in the 1980s, and had to be rescued with US government money.

Tiebout hypothesis The hypothesis asserts that economic efficiency will be attained in an economy with *local public goods. Charles Tiebout (1924–1968) observed that market failure arises with *public goods because of the difficulties of information transmission that prevent the true valuation of a public good by a consumer being observed. If there are a number of alternative communities (or jurisdictions) in which a consumer can choose to live and these differ in their provision of local public goods, then the consumer's choice of location provides a very clear signal of preferences. The chosen location is the one offering the provision of local public goods closest to the consumer's ideal, and through community choice preference revelation takes place. It follows that if there are enough different types of community and enough consumers with each kind of preference, then all consumers will allocate themselves to a community that is optimal for them and each community will be optimally sized. This ensures that the market outcome is efficient. It can be said that consumers reveal their preferences by 'voting with their feet' and this ensures the construction of efficient communities. The practical relevance of the Tiebout hypothesis has been much debated. One perspective is that it is another demonstration of the success of markets in allocating resources. An alternative perspective is that it is simply an empty demonstration of what is possible under unrealistic assumptions. The hypothesis has received some empirical support through evidence that there is partial sorting of similar consumers into communities. In any case, the hypothesis has been very influential in shaping discussion of decentralization of public good provision.

tied aid Assistance to other countries, normally *less developed countries, which has to be spent on goods and services from the donor. This is contrasted with *untied aid, which can be spent in any way. Tied aid may be of less value than untied aid of an equal amount, as tying restricts the choices open to the recipient, though where the recipient imports large quantities from the donor in any case tying may not be effective. As tied aid reduces the possibility that giving aid may cause balance-of-payments problems for the donor, more aid may be available if it is given on a tied basis.

tied loans Foreign loans, typically to *less developed countries, which have to be spent on goods and services from the lender. This is contrasted with an untied loan, which can be spent in any way. A tied loan may be of less value than an untied loan of equal size, as the tying restricts the choices open to the borrower, though where the borrower imports large quantities from the lender in any case, tying may not be effective. Tied loans reduce the chance that making them may cause balance-of-payments problems for the lender, so more loans may be available if they are made on a tied basis.

tight fiscal policy Fiscal policy which tends to restrict *effective demand. This may include high taxes or low public spending. In both cases 'high' and 'low' are relative terms, comparing the current levels with whatever has come to be regarded as normal for the current level of real activity.

tight monetary policy A restrictive monetary policy. This is intended to restrict the level of effective demand by making loans expensive and difficult to obtain.

time deposit A deposit in a US bank or other financial institution where the depositor is required to give notice of withdrawal, or is subject to an interest penalty in lieu of notice. The UK equivalent is *deposit account.

time discounting Placing a lower value on receipts or payments due in the future than on equal payments occurring immediately. This may be on account of pure time preference, uncertainty as to whether one will survive to benefit from receipts or make payments, or an expectation that higher incomes will make the marginal utility of money lower in the future than it is at present.

time horizon The most remote future period taken into account in making economic decisions, such as investment. While in principle *expectations about conditions in all future periods could affect present decisions, there are practical reasons for adopting a limited time horizon. First, uncertainty increases rapidly as decision-makers look into the future. Second, discounting implies that future values become small relative to current values.

time-inconsistency A policy is time-inconsistent if the policy-maker has an incentive to act in a manner counter to an earlier commitment. For example, a government may announce that it will not tax income from capital in order to encourage increased investment. Once the additional investment has taken place and the capital is installed the government has an incentive to tax capital income to raise revenue. The announced policy is therefore time-inconsistent and the firms should not believe the initial announcement. A policy-maker that has *credibility can announce a time-inconsistent policy and will be believed. The incentive to keep to the announcement is driven by a desire to retain the reputation which makes time-inconsistent policies possible. Where the policy authorities have no credibility, a time-consistent policy is the only one available to them; there is no point in making promises that nobody expects to be kept. *See also* REPUTATIONAL POLICY.

time lags The delay between an action and the event which is believed to have caused it. Time lags arise in several ways. First, there are lags in the collection, collation, and dissemination of economic data. Second, even when the data are available, economic decision-makers often defer action while they wait for more data, to try to assess whether changes are temporary or permanent, or because of disagreement about what the response should be. Third, even when decisions have been taken, it takes time to put them into effect: in some cases, for example opening a new factory in response to a rise in demand, this delay may be considerable.

time preference The preference for immediate consumption over an equal amount of consumption at a time in the future. Time preference in this sense is a consequence of an individual's (or society's) preferences over allocations of consumption at different points in time. *See also* DISCOUNTING THE FUTURE; SOCIAL TIME PREFERENCE.

times covered The ratio of a company's earnings for equity to its dividends to ordinary shareholders. A company with high *dividend cover may be retaining most of its profits to invest in expansion, leading to future growth in dividends, or it may be building up financial reserves or paying off debt to safeguard its ability to keep up dividends if business conditions become less profitable. A company with low or negative dividend cover may be a poor growth prospect, or a poor risk in a recession.

time-series data Data for the same variable at different times, usually at a regular frequency, for example annual, quarterly, weekly, daily, or even minute-by-minute for stock prices. Econometric theory has developed a range of special techniques to analyse time-series data. *See also* CROSS-SECTION DATA; PANEL DATA.

tit for tat A strategy for playing a *repeated game that is founded on the principle of retaliation. In a repeated *prisoners' dilemma game the tit for tat strategy is to play {Don't confess} while your opponent plays {Don't confess}, but to play {Confess} the period after your opponent plays {Confess}. If the opponent switches back to {Don't confess}, so will the tit for tat strategy in the subsequent play. The strategy is very simple but has proved very successful in contests between different strategies. *See also* TRIGGER STRATEGY.

Tobin's q The ratio of the valuation shareholders put on a firm to the market value of its assets. At the margin the shareholders' valuation is shown by the share price multiplied by the number of shares. The theory is that if $q > 1$ a firm should invest; if $q < 1$ the firm should run down or sell off its capital equipment.

Tobit model A regression model used to estimate the unknown parameters from a *censored sample, where the explanatory variables are observable whereas the dependent variable is only observed when some *latent variable takes values in a certain range.

Todaro model In development economics, a model of rural–urban *migration in the presence of high urban unemployment. The decision to migrate is economically rational for an individual migrant, if modern urban sector wages are sufficiently high relative to earnings in agriculture, even when the probability of finding a job is low. The Todaro model has strong policy implications regarding development strategies. In particular, efforts to reduce urban unemployment by stimulating job creation in the urban modern sector are likely to induce a greater flow of rural migrants, resulting in even higher urban unemployment, and therefore rural development should be encouraged instead.

token money Money for which the face value of notes or coin is unrelated to the value of the material they are produced from. Money is now mostly token money if it has any physical existence at all, and consists mainly of book or computer entries.

Tokyo Round The round of international trade talks under the *General Agreement on Tariffs and Trade held in 1973–9. The round was named from its opening conference in Japan. It reached agreement on tariff cuts on most world trade in manufactures by about a third, implemented over the following five years. It failed to reach any agreement on *agricultural protection or *non-tariff barriers to trade.

total cost *See* COST(S).

total domestic expenditure The total of consumer expenditure, general government final consumption, and gross domestic capital formation. This is calculated without deducting either imports or *capital consumption.

total final expenditure The total of consumer expenditure, general government final consumption, gross domestic capital formation, and exports. Thus total final expenditure includes both total domestic expenditure and exports. This is measured before deducting anything for imports or capital consumption.

total revenue *See* REVENUE.

tradable emission permit Emission permits (licences that allow a given level of pollution) that can be traded between polluters. Allowing permits to be traded ensures that they are eventually used by those who benefit most from being allowed to pollute. This ensures efficient allocation of pollution rights and constitutes a market-based solution to the control of an *externality.

tradables Goods and services of types which can be traded internationally. This applies whether or not the particular goods concerned actually are traded. Given the ability of tourists, students, and foreign customers for health care to buy goods and services in foreign countries, most goods are to some extent tradable; whether goods are tradables or non-tradables is thus a matter of degree.

trade **1.** The exchange of goods between two individuals or nations. Trade is the basic component of economic activity and is undertaken for mutual advantage.
 2. A type of skill, such as that of a carpenter or a plumber. A *trade union was originally a combination of workers with similar skills.
 3. The process of distribution, for example the motor trade. *See also* BALANCE OF TRADE; BILATERAL TRADE; FAIR TRADE; FREE TRADE; GAINS FROM TRADE; INTER-INDUSTRY TRADE; INTRA-INDUSTRY TRADE; INVISIBLES; MANAGED TRADE; MULTI-LATERAL TRADE; RESTRAINT OF TRADE; TERMS OF TRADE; TRADE DEFICIT.

trade association A voluntary body representing the firms engaged in a particular type of business. Trade associations promote the collection and exchange of information and discussion of technical standards; they also lobby government concerning legislation affecting the industry, and possible subsidies to it.

trade barriers Laws, institutions, or practices which make trade between countries more difficult or expensive than trade within countries. Some are deliberately designed to discourage trade: *tariffs, that is special taxes on imports, come under this heading. In many countries tariffs have been greatly reduced under the *General Agreement on Tariffs and Trade, and various groups of countries including the *European Union (EU) and the *North American Free Trade Agreement between Canada, Mexico, and the United States have reduced or removed tariffs on trade between member countries. Other *non-tariff barriers, such as quota restrictions and *voluntary export restraint agreements, however, have become increasingly common in recent years. Barriers to trade are also imposed by national differences in matters such as health and safety standards, labelling requirements, and weights and measures regulations. While these are not necessarily intended to act as barriers to trade, the need to modify products to conform to local requirements, and the documentation required to certify that this has been done, tend to impose costs and delays on international trade in excess of those experienced in domestic trade. Effective trade barriers are also imposed by public *procurement policies, which often give preferential treatment to domestic over foreign suppliers, as the result of legal requirements, through acts of policy, or simply through better information about domestic sources. The EU attempts to prevent this domestic bias in public procurement, so far as member countries are concerned, but with limited success.

trade bill *See* BILL OF EXCHANGE.

trade creation The effect of a *customs union in creating or increasing trade between member countries. This new trade results from the reduction in tariffs between the members and is generally welfare-increasing. Trade creation is distinguished from *trade diversion, which is the replacement of trade with non-members by trade between members. Trade diversion is generally welfare-decreasing. A customs union is beneficial to its members in the short run if their gains from trade creation exceed their losses from trade diversion.

trade credit The provision of credit by suppliers to their customers. It is common for customers to be required to pay for goods delivered not immediately, but within some normal grace period, varying from weeks for consumer goods to years for some capital goods. The need to provide trade credit accounts for a significant part of the capital needed in many industries.

trade cycle A model by John Hicks (1904–1989) of cycles in economic activity. Modern usage has seen the term replaced by *business cycle.

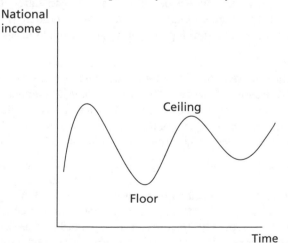

Trade Cycle

trade deficit trade gap The excess of imports over exports.

trade diversion The effect of a *customs union in replacing trade with non-members by trade between members. This occurs because the tariff-free prices of goods from members are lower than the tariff-inclusive prices of non-members who formerly supplied them. Trade diversion involves shifting sourcing of imports from lower to higher cost suppliers, and is generally welfare-decreasing. It is distinguished from *trade creation, where new or increased trade between member countries resulting from the elimination of tariffs is generally welfare-increasing. A customs union is beneficial to its members in the short run if their losses from trade diversion are less than their gains from trade creation.

trade gap *See* TRADE DEFICIT.

trade liberalization The process of reducing or removing restrictions on international trade. This may include the reduction or removal of *tariffs, abolition or enlargement of import *quotas, abolition of *multiple exchange rates, and removal of requirements for administrative permits for imports or allocations of foreign exchange, or at least simplification of the process of applying for them. The main argument for trade liberalization is that exposing a country's economy to international competition leads to greater efficiency.

trademark A symbol, logo, or name used to enable the public to identify the supplier of goods. In the UK and many other countries trademarks can be registered, which gives the holder exclusive right to use them. Trademarks may be registered by manufacturers, distributors, or importers. They can be sold, and are an important form of commercial property.

trade not aid A slogan epitomizing the view that industrial countries could facilitate the progress of *less developed countries (LDCs) more by liberalizing their treatment of LDC exports than by *aid payments. The argument is that aid may be spent inefficiently whereas better access to *Organization for Economic Cooperation and Development markets for LDC products such as textiles would promote sustainable development consistent with countries' *comparative advantage.

trade-off The requirement that some of one good or one objective has to be given up to obtain more of another. The need to trade off goods or objectives against one another is a sign of economic *efficiency; if it is possible to get more of one good without accepting less of another, or to achieve one objective without sacrificing another, the economy is not *Pareto efficient.

trade policy *See* LIBERAL TRADE POLICY; STRATEGIC TRADE POLICY.

Trade-Related Intellectual Property Rights (TRIPS) An agreement reached in 1995 as part of the *Uruguay Round, concerning countries' respect for other countries' *copyright, *patents, and *trademarks. The *Organization for Economic Cooperation and Development countries, which own most of these, were very keen on TRIPS; many *less developed countries were very suspicious of it, but some of the *newly industrialized countries, which are developing their own patents, supported it.

Trade-Related Investment Measures (TRIMS) An agreement reached in the *Uruguay Round to attempt to control national policies such as investment subsidies which have significant effects on international trade.

trade sanctions A restriction or prohibition by one country of trade contacts with another country of whose actions or policies it disapproves. Sanctions may be general, or applied to particular goods, especially armaments and oil. While it is difficult to enforce sanctions completely, as trade can be conducted by smuggling or the use of indirect routes, sanctions increase the costs involved in trade and so can bring some pressure to bear on the victims.

Trades Union Congress (TUC) The UK national organization representing *trade unions. Its main functions are to lobby the government on issues concerning workers, particularly legislation affecting employment and social security, and to settle disputes between member unions. The TUC has a fair amount of moral influence but no legal authority over its member unions.

trade talks Discussions on the arrangements for international trade. These may be conducted bilaterally between countries, by limited groups of countries, or on a world scale. Bilateral talks are common, in efforts to resolve minor disputes. Groups of countries hold talks to discuss the setting-up and running of trade blocs such as the *European Union or the *North American Free Trade Agreement. World trade talks have been held under the *General Agreement on Tariffs and Trade. The last series, the *Uruguay Round, ended in 1994 with the setting up of the *World Trade Organization, which is now holding the *Millennium Round. The participants in trade talks are usually governments, but proposals for *voluntary export restraint agreements may involve private trade associations as well.

trade union An organization of employees, formed for the purpose of *collective bargaining with employers over wages, hours, conditions of service, job security, and manning levels. They collect subscriptions from which to fund services for members such as legal advice about unfair dismissal, and pay during strikes. Trade unions have in the past provided *friendly society facilities for their members, including sick and unemployment pay, and may also negotiate price concessions for their members. They may engage in political activity to promote their members' interests, particularly over issues such as legislation affecting security of employment and the social security system. A union's membership may be confined to a narrowly defined group of skills, or may be spread widely over the workforce in general unions. In the UK most unions belong to the *Trades Union Congress, an organization representing unions at the national level. Many US unions belong to the *American Federation of Labor and Congress of Industrial Organizations. The rights and duties of both UK and US trade unions are governed by extensive legislation.

trade war A situation when countries try to damage each other's trade. The tools of a trade war include tariffs, quota restrictions, or outright bans on imports from the other country; and subsidies or subsidized credit for exports to the other country, or for exports to third countries where the opponent is a rival. During a trade war such methods may be intensified in a series of tit-for-tat reprisals for measures taken by the opponent.

trade-weighted index number An index number with weights proportional to the shares of various other countries in a country's trade. Such an index number is used to calculate a country's *effective exchange rate, when the other countries have variable exchange rates with one another. The weights may be based on imports, exports, or the sum of the two.

trading currency A currency used to invoice international trade transactions. While the currency of either the buyer or seller is frequently used, in some cases transactions are invoiced in the currency of a third country; this is common where neither party's own currency is widely used. The US dollar and the Euro are often used as trading, or vehicle, currencies.

tragedy of the commons A *common access resource will be over-utilized when users do not take into account the social impact of their actions. Consider a lake that can be used for fishing. The catch of each fisherman will be set to maximize profit by equating private marginal cost (equipment, time, etc.) to private marginal benefit (revenue from the sale of fish). This calculation does not take into account that the catch reduces the quantity of fish available for other fishermen which reduces their revenues. Consequently private marginal benefit is larger than social marginal benefit and the profit-maximizing catch is in excess of what is socially efficient. This over-utilization occurs whenever there is a negative externality between users of the resource and no control over access.

training The process of improving workforce skills. This may be done by formal instructional courses, provided by employers or by educational institutions, either before or during employment. Such courses may be full- or part-time. Training can also be provided on the job by working under the supervision of more experienced workers. Most firms which provide any training at all make some use of both methods. Training may lead to some type of formal qualification, but need not do so. *See also* ON-THE-JOB TRAINING.

transaction cost economics An approach to the economic explanation of institutions. This considers the relative merits of conducting transactions within firms and between different firms using markets. It takes account of bounded rationality, information problems, the costs of negotiating contracts, and opportunism.

transaction costs The cost incurred in undertaking an economic exchange. Practical examples of transaction costs include the *commission paid to a stockbroker for completing a share deal and the booking fee charged when purchasing concert tickets. The costs of travel and time to complete an exchange are also examples of transaction costs. The existence of transaction costs has been proposed as the explanation for many of the economic institutions that are observed. For example, it has been argued that production occurs in firms rather than through contracting via the market because this minimizes transaction costs. Transaction costs have also been used to explain why the market does not solve *externality problems. *See also* COASE THEOREM; TRANSACTION COST ECONOMICS.

transaction motive The desire to hold money in order to finance transactions. The transactions to be financed include both current and capital account payments. The amount of money required seems certain to be an increasing function of each type of transaction. There is no fixed ratio between transactions and money balances; use of *credit allows the timing of cash settlements to be deferred, and it is possible to economize on money holdings, at some cost of organizing cash budgeting and careful record-keeping. The desired ratio of cash to transactions may also be affected by interest rates and expectations of inflation. *See also* DEMAND FOR MONEY.

transfer earnings The amount any *factor of production could expect to earn in its best alternative use. To obtain factor inputs, an industry needs to pay factors at least their transfer earnings. If demand for factors is high, competition may force employers to pay factors more than their transfer earnings; the additional payments are an *economic rent.

transfer payments Payments of income which are not a return for the provision of current factor services. In many countries the state makes large-scale transfer payments, particularly to retired, disabled, and unemployed people. Countries also make transfer payments abroad. Some transfer payments are also made by private charities. Transfer payments are not part of the *national product; as the name implies, they simply transfer spending power from one group of people to another.

transfer pricing The prices of goods and services provided by one part of any organization to another. This applies particularly to transactions between firms and their branches, subsidiaries, or affiliates in other countries. It is possible by using suitable transfer prices to shift overall profits between different parts of the same business. This may be advantageous when tax rates and rules differ across countries. It may also be politically advantageous if profits in one country are more likely to attract criticism, or the attention of regulators, than equal profits in another. Where there is a competitive market in similar products, an appropriate transfer price can be defined and used by a regulator to detect transfer price manipulation. When there are no *arm's-length prices for comparable transactions the determination of fair transfer prices is a real problem.

transfers in kind *See* BENEFITS IN KIND.

transformation *See* MARGINAL RATE OF TRANSFORMATION; STRUCTURAL TRANSFORMATION.

transformation curve *See* PRODUCTION POSSIBILITY FRONTIER.

transitional economy An economy in the process of major changes in its mode of economic organization. This may be from a centrally planned economy to a market-based economy, as in the former Soviet Union and many countries of

Eastern Europe. It may also be from a highly dirigiste policy regime to a more liberalized one, as in many developing countries. Transitional economies face special microeconomic difficulties, as they may need to reform their institutions, for example by creating clear property laws and introducing bankruptcy procedures. They also face special macroeconomic problems, as they may need to reform their tax systems, and their monetary authorities may lack relevant experience on which to base their policies. Many transitional economies have experienced slumps in real output and bursts of inflation in the early stages of transition.

transitional unemployment Unemployment due to a major change in the way an economy is organized. This could apply to conversion from a wartime to a peacetime economy, industrialization of *less developed countries, or a shift from central planning to a market economy. In any major change it is likely that managers and skilled workers will be needed to set up new systems and production facilities earlier than less skilled workers are needed to operate them. The less skilled are thus liable to suffer from unemployment during the transitional period.

transitive relation A relation, denoted by R, such that $A\ R\ B$ and $B\ R\ C$ imply $A\ R\ C$. The relations of equality, denoted =, and greater than, denoted >, are transitive. The transitivity of the relation 'at least as good as' is usually adopted as an *axiom of consumer theory.

transitory income The difference between the actual (current) income of an individual and their permanent income.

transmission mechanism The ways in which changes in incomes, prices, interest rates, etc. are spread between sectors, regions, or countries. This involves the working of both goods and capital markets, and the relation between them. A boom in industrial countries, for example, affects *less developed countries (LDCs) through several channels: higher output increases the volume of LDC exports, and raises commodity prices so that their *terms of trade improve, but higher interest rates worsen the balance of payments of indebted countries.

transnational corporation *See* MULTINATIONAL.

transparent policy measures Policy measures whose operation is open to public scrutiny. Transparency includes making it clear who is taking the decisions, what the measures are, who is gaining from them, and who is paying for them. The setting of the official UK interest rate by the Monetary Policy Committee is a transparent policy: the minutes of the meetings and the voting patterns are publicly released.

transplant In economics, a product which was imported in the past but is currently produced within a country. Transplants are normally made either by foreign firms, or by domestic firms in association with foreign suppliers. They are common, for example, in the car industry, with US and European firms producing in Brazil and other *less developed countries, and Japanese firms producing in the US and Europe.

transport costs The costs of moving goods from place to place. These tend to be higher for goods which are bulky or heavy relative to their value, and for goods which are fragile and thus require careful handling, or which are perishable and thus require rapid transport. Where transport costs are high, it is economic to produce near to the market, and inter-regional and international trade are relatively unimportant. Where transport costs are low, production tends to be footloose. Transport costs have fallen considerably during the last century, which has contributed to an increasing ratio of trade to incomes. The development of cheap air freight has allowed rapid growth of international trade in perishable products such as fresh flowers and vegetables. On average transport costs between countries amount to well under 5 percent of the total value of world trade.

trap *See* LIQUIDITY TRAP; POVERTY TRAP.

Treasury *See* HM TREASURY.

Treasury bill A short-dated UK government security. Treasury bills bear no formal interest, but are promises to pay in 91 (occasionally 61) days' time, issued at a discount on their redemption price. They are regarded as a highly liquid financial asset by banks and other financial institutions.

Treaty of Rome A treaty signed in Rome in 1957 that established the *European Economic Community. A second treaty signed at the same time established the European Atomic Energy Community. The treaties were signed by representatives of Belgium, France, the Federal Republic of Germany, Italy, Luxembourg, and the Netherlands. *See also* EUROPEAN UNION.

trend In *time-series data, a long-term movement, with an upward or downward tendency. In an *econometric model, a deterministic trend is introduced by including time as an exogenous variable, whereas a stochastic trend means that the model is an integrated process of some order, that is, it needs to be differenced to obtain stationarity.

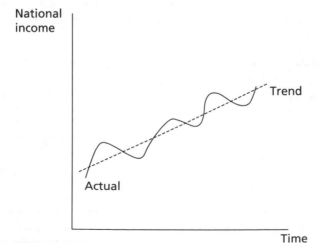

Trend and Cycles

Treuhandanstalt A German institution set up after *German economic and monetary union in 1990 to rationalize and privatize East German state-owned firms. This was done by handing them back to former owners or their heirs, or by sale of their assets to new or existing companies.

triangle of loss A measure of the loss attributable to setting an output level so that marginal cost and marginal benefit are not equal. In a market with an upward-sloping supply curve and a downward-sloping demand curve, if output is below the level at which the curves intersect, the triangle of loss is the area between actual output and the output at the intersection above the supply curve and below the demand curve. If the units between the actual and the intersection had been produced the marginal benefit to consumers would have been greater than the cost to producers. If output is above the equilibrium level, the triangle of loss is the area between equilibrium and actual output above the demand curve and below the supply curve. If these units are produced, the marginal benefit to consumers is less than the cost to producers.

trickle-down theory A claim that accumulation of wealth by the rich eventually results in the improvement of the life quality of the poor. An example of the mechanism through which wealth may trickle down to the poor is borrowing and lending in the capital market: when the capital market is imperfect, as more capital is accumulated in an economy more funds become available to the poor for investment purposes.

trigger strategy A strategy in a non-cooperative *repeated game in which a player cooperates until the opponent is observed not to cooperate. The observation of non-cooperation triggers a switch to punishment of the opponent. For example, in a repeated *prisoners' dilemma the trigger strategy is to play {Don't confess} provided the opponent plays {Don't confess}, and then to punish by playing {Confess} in every subsequent round if the opponent is ever observed to confess. *See also* TIT FOR TAT.

trillion A thousand billion = a million million = 10^{12} in the US and modern British systems; 10^{18} in the traditional British system.

triple-A rating The highest grading available from *credit rating agencies. A triple-A rating (AAA) means that delay or default in payments of principal or interest on the security concerned is regarded as extremely unlikely. Any institution with a triple-A rating on its securities can borrow easily and on favourable terms.

trough The lowest period for real incomes or activity in a *business cycle. In a severe cycle the trough may be a minimum in absolute terms. In a mild cycle in an economy with a positive trend rate of growth of output, the trough may be a minimum relative to trend rather than in absolute terms.

true and fair view The idea that *accounts should provide a correct impression of the state of a company. It is the role of *auditors to check and certify that accounts offer a true and fair view. Accounts should not contain false statements; this is the true part. Neither, however, should they mislead by omission; this is the fair part. It requires more information to be sure that accounts are fair than that they are true.

truncated sample A sample from which some observations have been systematically excluded, in other words, a sample drawn from a restricted part of a population, rather than from the entire population. An example is a sample of households with income below a certain level: the households with income above that specified level are systematically excluded. In this case, if the dependent variable is income, applying *ordinary least squares to the truncated sample renders the estimators inconsistent.

trust 1. An arrangement through which one set of people, the trustees, are the legal owners of property which is administered in the interests of another set, the beneficiaries. Trusts may be set up to provide support for individuals or families, to provide pensions, to run charities, to liquidate the property of bankrupts for the benefit of their creditors, or for the safe keeping of the securities bought by *unit trusts with their investors' money. The assets which trusts may hold are regulated by law. These must be administered in the interests of the beneficiaries, and not for the profit of the trustees.
2. A US term for a large or monopolistic business formed by amalgamation. This is why US anti-monopoly policy is called antitrust. *See also* INVESTMENT TRUST.

trustee An individual or company who is the legal owner of property which he or she administers on behalf of a beneficiary. The beneficiary in turn may be an individual, a charity, the creditors of a bankrupt, or the investors in a *unit trust. Trustees may be paid for their services, but are bound to administer the trust in the interests of the beneficiaries and not for their own profit.

t-test In a *linear regression, a test of a simple linear hypothesis $H_0 : f(\theta_1, \ldots, \theta_K)$ = 0 against the alternative $H_1 : f(\theta_1, \ldots, \theta_K) \neq 0$ (*two-sided test) or $H_1 : f(\theta_1, \ldots, \theta_K)$ < 0 (*one-sided test), where θ is a $(K \times 1)$ vector of regression parameters and $f(\cdot)$ is a scalar linear function. Under the null hypothesis, assuming normally distributed random errors, the test statistic, $t = f(\hat{\theta})/s.e.(f(\hat{\theta}))$, has *Student's t-distribution with $(N - K)$ degrees of freedom. Here $\hat{\theta}$ is the *least squares estimator of θ and *s.e.* is the *standard error.

turnkey project An investment project where a foreign firm contracts to build a factory, install equipment, and train local labour, and hand it over as a going concern ready to start production. This system means that the supplier's experience of similar plants elsewhere is made available, and unexpected problems have to be resolved before the host country takes over responsibility for the project. The name comes from the notion that the supplier simply hands over the keys when the project is completed.

turnover The value of total sales of goods and services by any organization during a given period, or the total value of transactions in a given market. *See also* LABOUR TURNOVER.

turnover tax A tax proportional to a firm's turnover. This gives an incentive for *vertical integration, as the tax may make it cheaper to produce an intermediate product within a firm than to buy a similar input produced more efficiently by an outside supplier. *Value-added taxes have been very widely adopted in preference to turnover taxes because they do not provide this artificial inducement to vertical integration.

turnpike theorem In growth theory, a characterization of the optimal, or welfare-maximizing, growth path for the economy. A turnpike was the name given to roads in medieval England. It was derived from the fact that access to the road was controlled by soldiers with pikes (a form of spear) which were turned aside to allow a traveller to progress; the name was adopted for major highways in the US that provided the quickest route between cities.

two-gap model The proposition that development of *less developed countries is constrained by two gaps: that between domestic savings and the investment required for take-off, and that between export revenues and the imports needed for development. *National income accounting theory suggests that these gaps are not independent.

two-part tariff A pricing system by which customers pay more per unit for their purchases up to some given quantity, with a lower price per unit for further purchases. Such a system is only practicable when the customer can be identified, and resale is difficult. The argument for two-part tariffs is that the higher price for the first n units bought reflects the *overhead costs of supplying a particular customer: for example, gas, electricity, and water suppliers incur costs in connection to the mains, however much or little is then bought. The simplest two-part tariff involves a fixed access fee followed by a constant charge per unit of consumption. In the context of a *club, the fixed fee can be seen as a membership charge. Two-part tariffs are a special case of *second-degree price discrimination designed to secure some of the customer's *consumer surplus.

two-sector endogenous growth model A model where two kinds of capital goods, physical capital and human capital, are produced in different sectors. In a standard set-up with a Cobb–Douglas production function in each sector the two production activities each exhibit constant returns to scale in the quantities of the two capital inputs. Hence, the model displays endogenous steady-state growth, where consumption, output, the stock of physical capital, and the stock of human capital all grow at the same constant rate.

two-stage least squares (2SLS) (instrumental variable (IV) estimation) An extension of *ordinary least squares (OLS) estimation of a linear regression in the presence of endogeneity, that is, when the *disturbance term is correlated with explanatory variables. In the first stage, the endogenous explanatory variables are regressed on appropriately chosen *instrumental variables, using OLS. In the second stage, the original regression is estimated, using OLS, with the endogenous explanatory variables replaced by their fitted values from the first stage. Under certain conditions the 2SLS (or IV) estimator is *consistent and *efficient. *See also* HAUSMAN TEST.

two-tailed test A test of a statistical hypothesis in which this hypothesis is rejected when the test statistic is either sufficiently large or sufficiently small. It is used when the direction of the effect tested is not known a priori. *See also* ONE-TAILED TEST.

two-tier board A system of company organization in which there are two *boards of directors. Overall policy is decided by a supervisory board, on which employees as well as the shareholders are represented, and day-to-day management decisions are taken by a management board. The object of this division is to promote information and goodwill among employees by having their representatives on the supervisory body, while retaining the authority necessary for the managers to execute policies effectively through the management board. This system is relatively common in Germany.

type I and II errors The two types of mistake that can be made when deciding whether or not to reject the *null hypothesis. A type I error is rejecting a true null hypothesis; the probability of committing a type I error can be controlled by choosing the level of significance of the test. A type II error is failing to reject a false null hypothesis; the probability of committing a type II error, in general, cannot be computed. The probability of not committing a type II error, that is, of correctly rejecting a false null hypothesis, is called the power of the test.

t

unanimity rule A voting rule in which unanimous approval is required for an alternative to be selected. The unanimity rule is employed when it is felt desirable to have no disagreement. Examples are the requirement for unanimity among juries for some court cases and in the admission of new members to private clubs. *See also* COLLECTIVE CHOICE; MAJORITY VOTING.

unbiased estimator An estimator with *bias equal to zero.

unbiased expectations hypothesis The hypothesis that the *forward rate is an unbiased predictor of the future *spot market rate. The empirical observation that the *term structure is upward-sloping more often than it is downward-sloping is usually given as evidence that the hypothesis is not a perfect explanation.

unbundling The sale of peripheral parts of a business to concentrate on its core activities. This may be because it is believed that the outlying parts of a business empire could operate more profitably if they became independent or joined different groupings, or to raise money to pay off debt.

uncertainty A consciousness of limited knowledge about present facts or future possibilities. A distinction is sometimes drawn between *risk and uncertainty: risk applies when probabilities can be assigned to the likely occurrence of future outcomes; uncertainty applies when probabilities cannot be assigned. Used in this sense, decisions with risk permit the application of *expected utility. In contrast, expected utility does not apply in the case of uncertainty so a more general theory of choice has to be constructed. More commonly, risk and uncertainty are used interchangeably.

uncompetitive Unable to realize potential profit. Goods or services may be uncompetitive because their prices are too high relative to alternative suppliers, or may be unsaleable because of defects in quality, where other suppliers offer better products. Inability to compete may apply to a firm, a region, or a country. High costs may be due to dear or poor quality inputs of labour or materials, or to obsolete equipment and poor management. Products may be unsaleable at any price because of poor design, unreliability, failure to meet promised delivery dates, or failure to comply with health and safety regulations in possible markets.

unconditional grant A grant made from central government to local government that can be spent in any way the local government wishes. In contrast, a conditional grant must be used for a specified purpose.

uncovered interest parity A relationship between domestic and foreign interest rates derived under the assumption that the *forward currency market is not used to hedge exchange rate risk. Uncovered interest parity requires

$$(1 + r_a) = (1 + r_b)e_0 / E(e_1)$$

where r_a is the domestic interest rate, r_b is the foreign interest rate, e_0 the current exchange rate, and $E(e_1)$ the expected future exchange rate. *See also* COVERED INTEREST PARITY.

undated security A security with no set *redemption date. With such a security the borrower has only the obligation to pay interest as agreed, and need not redeem it. An undated security may be irredeemable, in which case the borrower has no right to redeem it, or it may be redeemable at the borrower's discretion, as in the case of UK 'consols' (Consolidated Fund Annuities), where the government has the right but no obligation to redeem them at par at any time.

under-capitalized Having too little capital in relation to the business carried on or intended. If a business has insufficient capital, it is liable to become insolvent too easily in the face of the risks normal in its line of activity, such as delays in payment by customers. It is risky to lend or extent credit to an under-capitalized business, and being charged premium rates or refused credit is bad for its profits. For most businesses, under-capitalization is discouraged simply by being unprofitable, but in the case of banks and other financial institutions there is public regulation of *capital adequacy, to prevent the insolvency of one institution from causing a general financial panic.

under-developed countries *See* LESS DEVELOPED COUNTRIES.

under-funded pension scheme A pension scheme with accumulated funds insufficient to meet the actuarially expected costs of pensions payable. The adequacy of funding is a matter of judgement, as it depends both on demographic forecasts of the expected lives of pensioners, and financial forecasts of the expected yield on the fund's assets.

underground economy *See* HIDDEN ECONOMY.

underlying rate of inflation The rate of inflation as measured by a retail price index excluding mortgage interest payments (*RPIX). This is contrasted with the 'headline' rate of inflation, in the UK measured by the *retail price index (RPI), which includes mortgage interest payments. The RPI in most other countries excludes mortgage interest, so this distinction is peculiar to the UK.

under-subscription Failure of applications for shares in a new issue to match the number on offer. This means that some shares will be unsold, or bought by underwriters, which makes it probable that when the market opens the newly issued shares will sell at a discount relative to the issue price. *See also* UNDERWRITING.

under-valued currency A currency whose exchange rates with other currencies are lower than is necessary for *external balance. This tends to improve the country's *balance of payments on current account, as relatively low prices make exports easy to sell and imports easy to compete with. It should also make it possible to borrow easily, if the market expects the exchange rate to rise. It is not easy to judge whether a currency is under-valued: for example, the current account may be in surplus during a recession even though the exchange rate is too high to be consistent with external balance once activity recovers.

underwriting The provision by merchant banks of a guaranteed market for a *new issue of shares. Firms making new issues cannot know in advance whether there will be sufficient demand for the shares they offer at the issue price, from the public or institutional investors. An underwriter removes the uncertainty as to whether shares will sell by promising to buy any the market does not take up. These shares then have to be sold, which may involve accepting a low price or a long wait. A commission is charged for this service.

undistributed profits Profits of a business which are neither paid out in taxes nor paid to the shareholders or owners. Undistributed profits are ploughed back into the business. While they may be kept as cash balances or marketable securities, they are usually invested in buying physical equipment, acquiring other companies, or extending *trade credit to customers. They are a major source of finance for new investment in the economy.

unearned income Personal income derived from sources other than work. It thus consists of rent, dividends, interest, and transfer payments. *See also* PROPERTY INCOME.

unemployable People who are difficult or impossible to employ. A person can be unemployable in this sense because of ability, attitude, or behaviour. Being unemployable is not a permanent or unchangeable characteristic but is partly under the control of the person and is relative to a specific set of labour market conditions and employment opportunities.

unemployment Inability to obtain a job when one is willing and able to work. This can be measured in two ways: official registration with a state agency, which carries some form of income support, and through the self-assessment of a *random sample of the population. Self-assessment generally produces higher figures. *See also* CLASSICAL UNEMPLOYMENT; CYCLICAL UNEMPLOYMENT; DEMOGRAPHIC UNEMPLOYMENT; DISGUISED UNEMPLOYMENT; FRICTIONAL UNEMPLOYMENT; INVOLUNTARY UNEMPLOYMENT; KEYNESIAN UNEMPLOYMENT; LONG-TERM UNEMPLOYMENT; NATURAL RATE OF UNEMPLOYMENT; NON-ACCELERATING INFLATION RATE OF UNEMPLOYMENT; RESIDUAL UNEMPLOYMENT; SEARCH UNEMPLOYMENT; SEASONAL UNEMPLOYMENT; STRUCTURAL UNEMPLOYMENT; TECHNOLOGICAL UNEMPLOYMENT; TRANSITIONAL UNEMPLOYMENT; VOLUNTARY UNEMPLOYMENT.

unemployment benefit Income support payments to the unemployed. Countries differ in the level of such payments, which may be at a fixed rate or an amount related to previous wages, and in the length of time for which they are available. Eligibility for unemployment benefit may be related to previous contributions to an unemployment insurance fund.

unemployment rate The total number of unemployed (for an economy, region, or subgroup) as a percentage of the corresponding total labour force (the sum of the total persons employed and unemployed in the economy, region, or subgroup). The standard definition of the unemployment rate is provided by the *International Labour Organization (ILO). The ILO defines the labour force as the economically active portion of the population, not the total population, and the unemployed as those individuals without work, seeking work in a recent past period, and currently available for work. This definition of unemployment excludes people who are not currently in the labour market, who want to work but do not actively seek work. There can be a variety of reasons for not seeking work, including the belief that job opportunities are limited and restricted labour mobility.

unexpected inflation *Inflation at a higher or lower rate than had been expected. If the expected rate of inflation has been taken into account in arriving at wage agreements and loan contracts, inflation higher than expected transfers purchasing power from workers to employers or from lenders to borrowers; inflation lower than expected transfers purchasing power from employers to workers or from borrowers to lenders.

unfair competition Business practices complained of by firms whose rivals offer prices or use methods with which they are unable or unwilling to compete. For example, they may allege that foreign competitors receive help from their governments in the form of subsidies or cheap loans, which their own government does not provide; or that rivals are unhampered by laws on health and safety which they have to obey.

unfair dismissal Dismissal of an employee that the employer cannot show to be fair. Fair grounds for dismissal include the employee's conduct, lack of capacity or qualifications, or laws prohibiting their employment; or that while the employee is satisfactory, the need for their services no longer exists, so that they are redundant. Employees in the UK who believe they have been unfairly dismissed can apply to an industrial tribunal for reinstatement or compensation; not all groups of employees have this right.

unfunded pension scheme A pension scheme with no pension fund. The pensions of current beneficiaries are paid by a former employer out of current revenue or contributions by present employees, on a pay-as-you-go basis. Such pensions are safe only if the employer cannot become insolvent or cease to trade; this normally requires either state ownership or a state guarantee.

unified budget The system by which the UK Parliament is presented with a *budget covering both government spending and tax plans, to be considered together. In 1993 this replaced the previous system, under which the government's tax plans were presented to Parliament in the spring and its spending plans were considered in the autumn.

uniform business rate The UK system of property taxes on business premises in force since 1990. This replaced *rates set at varying levels by individual local authorities. *Business rates are now charged at a uniform percentage of valuation throughout England, so that local variations reflect differences in the valuation of property, rather than differences in local tax policies; Scotland and Wales have separate rates. Since 1 April 2005 there has been a lower rate for small businesses and a standard rate for larger businesses.

uniform distribution A discrete uniform distribution is described by the probability function $P[X = x_i] = 1/N$, where the random variable X can take values $x_1, \ldots, x_N$. A continuous uniform distribution is described by the probability density function $f_X(x) = 1/(b - a)$ where random variable X can take values $x \in [a,b]$.

union *See* CUSTOMS UNION; PAYMENTS UNION; TRADE UNION.

unionized An occupation or workplace where the workers are organized in a *trade union, which is recognized as representing them in negotiations with employers over pay and working conditions. Workers may or may not all be union members.

union/non-union wage differential The excess of wages of workers in unionized firms over those of workers with similar skill levels in non-unionized firms. A positive differential is prima facie evidence that unions are beneficial for their members.

unique equilibrium Occurs when an economic model or a game of strategy has a single equilibrium. This is an advantageous situation for an economic analyst since it eliminates debate about which equilibrium will emerge (a tricky question when there are multiple equilibria) and permits the application of *comparative statics techniques.

unitary taxation A system of taxing firms operating in several countries on the basis of a country's share in their total operations. If taxation of a *multinational firm operating in a country is based purely on its profits made in that country, tax can be avoided by accounting procedures. Measures to shift apparent profits out of the country include *transfer pricing, that is, overvaluing purchases by branches of the firm from its branches in other countries, or undervaluing sales to them. Under unitary taxation a multinational firm is taxed on the basis of its worldwide profits multiplied by some measure of the proportion of its operations carried out in a country; such a measure could be employment or turnover. The adoption of unitary taxation would require changes in *double taxation agreements.

United Nations Conference on Trade and Development (UNCTAD) A United Nations organization, established in 1964, which is intended to represent the *less developed countries (LDCs), and which acts as a pressure group for increased *aid and an international regime for trade and investment more favourable to LDCs. Proposals for a *New International Economic Order (NIEO) came from UNCTAD.

United Nations Development Programme (UNDP) A United Nations body formed to give technical assistance and make *soft loans to *less developed countries.

unit elasticity The case where a proportional change in one variable causes an equal proportional change in another. In the case of a unit price elasticity of demand, a proportional rise in price produces an equal proportional fall in quantity demanded: total revenue is thus constant, and marginal revenue is zero. In the case of the *income elasticity of demand, unit elasticity means that at any given price the proportion of income spent on a good remains constant as income changes.

unit-free measure A quantity that has no units of measurement. Examples of unit-free measures are percentages, market shares, and elasticities. Interest rates and growth rates are not unit-free measures, as while they are independent of the units in which prices and quantities are measured, they are measured in units per unit of time (e.g. per month or per annum) and so do depend on the units used to measure time.

unit of account A standard monetary unit to measure the costs of goods and services. One of the roles of *money is to be the unit in which contracts are expressed and individual incomes or firms' profits are measured. High and fluctuating rates of inflation interfere with the performance of money as a unit of account, which is believed to be bad for the efficient and equitable running of the economy.

unit root process In time series, a non-stationary process whose first difference is stationary, also referred to as an integrated of order one or (1)-process. An example of a unit root process is a *random walk. The name 'unit root' is related to the roots of the polynomial equation derived from the lag polynomial representation of an autoregressive process: $A(L)y_t = \varepsilon_t$. The process y_t is stationary if all roots of equation $A(z) = 0$ exceed 1 in absolute value, and is non-stationary if at least one root is less than or equal to 1 in absolute value; the latter is called a unit root.

unit trust A UK system by which small investors can benefit from diversified *portfolios. Unit trusts sell units to investors, and use the funds to hold a portfolio of securities managed by the trust and held by a bank as *trustee. Unit trust shareholdings may be widely spread, or concentrated on a particular sector or country. They may aim at varying combinations of income and capital growth. Investors receive professional management and a diversified portfolio without high transaction costs. They can buy more units or sell their units back to the trust at published prices at any time. Unit trusts are distinguished from investment trusts, where investors buy shares in the trust company.

universal benefit A benefit available to all citizens of a country regardless of income. Universal benefits may be conditional on other criteria, such as age for pensions, or disability. The argument for making benefits universal rather than *means-tested is that means-testing is expensive and open to abuse, and is an invasion of privacy. The objection to making benefits universal is that this is extremely expensive, and may involve most of the money going to people who are not in severe need. The alternative is to use means-testing to target the available funds towards those in greatest need. In economies where the bulk of the labour force receives occupational pensions, state pensions could be larger if they were means-tested. This, however, would create *disincentives both to saving before retirement age and to continuing work after it; pensions which are universal benefits have neither of these side-effects. *See also* TARGETING.

unlimited liability Liability for the debts an individual or business has incurred, without limit. This is contrasted with *limited liability, where shareholders in a limited liability company are not liable for its debts provided they hold fully paid-up shares. Unlimited liability for the debts of a business makes it difficult to raise capital for large and complex ventures, as without the protection of limited liability small investors are reluctant to put money into a business they do not fully understand and cannot control. The recent experience of some members of *Lloyd's illustrates the dangers of unlimited liability. Larger investors sometimes choose to operate with unlimited liability, as their reputation enables businesses run on this basis to get credit relatively easily and to borrow relatively cheaply.

Unlisted Securities Market (USM) A part of the *London Stock Exchange that dealt in the shares of smaller companies. The USM had less stringent requirements and traded shares in far fewer companies than the main market. It was abolished in 1995.

unofficial economy *See* HIDDEN ECONOMY.

unsecured loan A loan where the creditor has no claim on any particular asset of the debtor in the event of default. This is contrasted with a *secured loan, where the lender has a right to take over some particular asset if repayments are not made at the due dates. In the event of the borrower going bankrupt or becoming insolvent, unsecured creditors normally rank below secured creditors for any available assets. Unsecured loans are thus riskier than secured loans, and require higher interest rates to compensate the lenders for this.

unskilled work Work not demanding formal qualifications or much experience. Such work is generally poorly paid.

unsterilized intervention *See* INTERVENTION IN FOREIGN EXCHANGE MARKETS.

untied aid Assistance to other countries, usually *less developed countries, which can be spent on goods and services from any country. This is contrasted with *tied aid, which has to be spent on goods and services from the donor country. Untied aid may be of greater value than tied aid of an equal amount, as tying restricts the choices open to the recipient, though where the recipient imports a lot from the donor in any case tying may not be effective. As untied aid may cause balance-of-payments problems for the donor, less aid may be available if it is given on an untied basis.

upstream *See* BACKWARD INTEGRATION.

urban economics The study of the economics of urban areas. This includes the factors making for the growth first of towns and then of metropolitan areas, including *complementarity between industries and the attraction of proximity to markets. It also covers the special problems of conurbations, including congestion and pollution.

Uruguay Round The last round of trade talks under the *General Agreement on Tariffs and Trade; this round started in 1986 and finished in 1994. The round managed for the first time to include some modest steps to restrict *agricultural protection, and arrived at a new *General Agreement on Trade in Services. It also covered reform of the *Multi-Fibre Arrangement on international trade in textiles, and the question of *intellectual property rights.

US deficit The United States *government deficit. This grew vastly during the 1980s and continued in the 1990s in spite of repeated political pledges to reduce it and an attempt, via the *Gramm–Rudman–Hollings Act, to do this by legislation. The deficit disappeared in the late 1990s due to growth in the US economy but increased again with a record deficit in 2004. It is now declining once more. 'The deficit' is not the same as the deficit in the US balance of payments on current account, though the budget deficit has been a major cause of the external deficit.

U-shaped average cost curve A shape that is often assumed for the average cost curve. The U-shape can be justified by arguing that the productive process has some overheads or fixed costs that ensure at low levels of output average cost is high, and that there are some inputs which cannot be increased indefinitely, at least in the short run. When output is high, shortages of these inputs restrict the efficiency with which they can contribute to increased output. Thus at high levels of output marginal costs tend to be high, leading to increasing average costs. At some medium level or possibly range of output, average costs reach a minimum.

US Trade Representative An office set up to formulate US trade policy and conduct trade negotiations. The US Trade Representative forms part of the Executive Office of the President.

((⊕) SEE WEB LINKS)

• The official website of the US Trade Representative.

usury Charging excessive *interest on loans. The term was formerly applied to charging any interest, but now refers to interest rates regarded as excessive given the market rate for other loans with similar risk characteristics.

usury laws Laws restricting the level of *interest that could be charged or paid for loans. The intention of such laws was to restrain exploitation of those in need by money-lenders. If the highest permitted interest rate is too low to compensate for inflation and the risk of default or delay in payment, it creates excess demand for loans. This leads to their being rationed to the safest risks, so those without *collateral cannot get loans when they need them.

util A rarely used name for the unit in which *utility would be measured, if any device were to be discovered that could measure it.

utilitarianism An ethical doctrine that judges the value of an action by its contribution to overall utility. 'The greatest good of the greatest number' was a slogan of the originator of this school of thought, Jeremy Bentham (1748–1832). A utilitarian attempts to tackle the question of to what extent the state should control and to what extent respect *private property by considering its usefulness and defects as a framework for economic activity, rather than asking how rules are related to either divine commandments or 'natural rights'. The utilitarian *social welfare function captures this doctrine by expressing welfare as the sum of individual utilities

$$W = \sum_{h=1}^{H} U^h$$

where U^h is the utility of individual h, and H is the number of individuals in the population.

utility **1.** A synonym for individual *welfare. Utility can be interpreted literally as a measure of an individual's happiness or, more functionally, as an economist's summary of what guides individual choice. In the first interpretation the writings of 19th-century economists suggest an expectation that a device for measuring utility would eventually emerge from psychological research. This has not yet been realized, but monitoring of brain activity is increasingly part of joint neurological, psychological, and economic research. In the second interpretation utility is used as a tool for constructing a model of individual choice based on the argument that a rational individual will act as if decisions are made to maximize utility. *See also* CARDINAL UTILITY; EXPECTED UTILITY; MARGINAL UTILITY; ORDINAL UTILITY.

2. A public utility, that is, a company that maintains the infrastructure for a public service, and often provides the service using that infrastructure. The public services involving utilities include electricity, water, gas, and transport. *See also* PUBLIC UTILITY.

utility function A function that can either be the actual evaluation of an individual's *utility or an economist's convenient representation of an individual's *preferences. There is in principle no reason why an individual cannot evaluate the utility of different outcomes using a utility function. If they do, then the first interpretation applies. Note that 'an individual' can be broadly interpreted to include organizations, and an organization may employ a utility function to guide its decision-making. Economists employ utility functions as a convenient representation of preferences that permits mathematical analysis. A utility function represents a set of preferences if the function has a higher value for consumption bundle x than for consumption bundle y if, and only if, x is preferred to y. The restrictions that must be placed on preferences to ensure a utility function exists that represents them are very weak. Moreover, a rational

individual will act as if they maximize the utility function. *See also* INDIRECT
UTILITY FUNCTION; SEPARABLE UTILITY FUNCTION.

utility maximization The method of modelling choice by assuming that an
individual's preferences can be represented by a *utility function which they seek
to maximize. Where choices have to be made under conditions of risk the objective
becomes that of maximizing *expected utility. Utility maximization can be used
to model individual consumers, organizations, and (by replacing the utility function
by a *social welfare function) governments. Utility maximization has widespread
applicability throughout economics and has been the basis of the formalization
of the theory of choice.

utility possibility frontier The maximum attainable levels of utility for the
consumers in an economy given the economy's endowment and technology.
The utility possibility frontier can be constructed by taking each *Pareto-efficient
allocation and plotting the utility levels of the consumers at that allocation. Varying
the allocation traces out the frontier. A point below the frontier is not Pareto
efficient. The *social optimum is the point on the frontier that maximizes a
chosen *social welfare function.

u–v curve *See* BEVERIDGE CURVE.

vacancy A post which an employer intends to fill if a suitable applicant appears. The total number of job vacancies in an economy at a given time is difficult to measure, as there is no one standard method of advertising or filling them. Job information is circulated by official and private employment agencies, public advertisement, and word of mouth among present and past employees.

vacancy rate The number of unfilled jobs expressed as a proportion of the *labour force.

value **1.** Value = price × quantity. For example, if between two years prices quadruple and quantities in the economy increase by 25 percent, the money value of *gross domestic product rises to 4 × 1.25 = 5 times its former level.
　2. A synonym for price. Valuables are goods which sell for high prices.
　3. A general term of praise, used in a phrase such as 'good value'. Value in this sense refers to something similar to price but more important and more permanent. Advertisers claim that their goods represent 'value for money'; politicians claim the same for their policies.
　4. The magnitude of a variable or parameter.

value added The total sales of a firm less purchases of inputs from other firms. What is left is available for the wages of its employees and the profits of its owners. *National income is the sum of value added in all enterprises in the economy. Trying to calculate national income by adding the outputs of all firms would involve massive *double counting.

value-added tax (VAT) An *indirect tax levied on goods or services as a percentage of their value added. The customer pays VAT on purchases in addition to the normal price; the seller then pays the government VAT collected on sales less the VAT they have paid on purchased inputs. VAT is levied in many countries: it was introduced in the UK in 1973. Goods may bear VAT at different rates. Some goods, for example food in the UK, are exempt, and VAT is not payable by businesses with turnover below some minimum level. In January 2008 the minimum limit stood at £64000.

value index An index number of the total value of any economic aggregate at current prices: if p_t is the price and q_t the quantity concerned at time t, the value index is given by

$$V_t = p_t q_t / p_o q_o$$

where 0 is the base date. Where p_t and q_t are themselves index numbers, as is the case when dealing with aggregates, for example consumption, the value index V_t can be found as the product of a price and a quantity index; one of these must be base-weighted and the other current-weighted. Thus where there are n goods,

$$V_t = \sum_{i=1}^{n} p_{it}q_{it} / \sum_{i=1}^{n} p_{i0}q_{i0} = \left(\sum_{i=1}^{n} p_{it}q_{it} / \sum_{i=1}^{n} p_{i0}q_{it} \right) \left(\sum_{i=1}^{n} p_{i0}q_{it} / \sum_{i=1}^{n} p_{i0}q_{i0} \right),$$

that is, the product of a *current-weighted or Paasche price index and a *base-weighted or Laspeyres quantity index; or alternatively

$$V_t = \left(\sum_{i=1}^{n} p_{it}q_{it} / \sum_{i=1}^{n} p_{it}q_{i0} \right) \left(\sum_{i=1}^{n} p_{it}q_{i0} / \sum_{i=1}^{n} p_{i0}q_{i0} \right),$$

that is, the product of a base-weighted price index and a current-weighted quantity index.

value judgement An opinion about the relative merits of two or more states of the economy that is based on morals or aesthetics rather than logical argument. For example, consider a proposed change which will affect individuals A and B. If each gains a logical argument can be made, based on the concept of a Pareto improvement, in favour of implementing the change. Suppose instead that the change benefits A but harms B. Whether or not it should be made then involves a value judgement on how society should assess the benefit for A against the harm to B. The presence of value judgements is a defining feature of *normative economics, and their absence a characteristic of *positive economics.

value of the physical increase in stocks and work in progress That part of the total increase in the value of stocks and work in progress which is due to changes in their quantities. This is distinguished from the part of the change in the total value of stocks and work in progress which is due to revaluations of the existing volume of stocks because of price changes. The value of the physical increase is part of the real *national product, whereas the increase due to revaluation of stocks is not.

valuer A professional who estimates what price goods would fetch if they were sold. The stock of a shop or firm is transferred from one proprietor to the next 'at valuation', that is, for an amount set by a valuer.

value-subtracting industry An industry where the value of output is less than that of purchased inputs, so that *value added is negative. This situation can arise in two ways: when the industry concerned is heavily subsidized, either by the government or by *cross-subsidization from profitable parts of the same firms; alternatively, when inputs and outputs are valued at prices other than those actually prevailing.

variable A quantity which is liable to change. Economic variables may measure prices, interest rates, income levels, quantities of goods, etc. An exogenous variable is one where the changes originate from causes outside the scope of a given model; an endogenous variable is determined within the model. *See also* RANDOM VARIABLE.

variable cost That part of cost which varies with the level of output. *See also* FIXED COST.

variable factor proportions A production process that permits substitution of one factor of production for another. Factor proportions are not variable for some production processes. For example, if a production process always requires two units of labour for each unit of capital then the factor proportions are fixed at 2 to 1. Where factor proportions are variable, if the *elasticity of technical substitution between inputs is high a small change in relative factor prices causes a cost-minimizing firm to shift its use of factors strongly towards whichever has become relatively cheaper. If factor proportions are not easily variable, the elasticity of technical substitution is low, and firms change their relative use of factors very little as relative factor prices change.

variance A measure of dispersion. The sample variance of a set of N numbers is found by adding the squares of their deviations from their mean value, and dividing by N. Thus if the numbers are x_i, $i = 1, 2, \ldots, N$, and their mean is μ, their sample variance is given by

$$V = \frac{1}{N} \sum_{i=1}^{N} (x_i - \mu)^2 .$$

The population variance of a random variable X is

$$\text{Var}(X) = E[(X - E[X])^2]$$

where E denotes *expected value. *See also* COVARIANCE MATRIX.

variance–covariance matrix *See* COVARIANCE MATRIX.

variation *See* COEFFICIENT OF VARIATION; COMPENSATING VARIATION; EQUIVALENT VARIATION.

variety 1. A particular good differentiated by specification or *brand name from other similar goods.
   2. The existence of a large number of varieties in sense 1.

VAT *See* VALUE-ADDED TAX.

VAT registration The procedure by which firms are added to the *value-added tax (VAT) register. This is the list of firms required to make VAT returns, and to pay VAT on their sales if these exceed the VAT exemption level.

VAT return A regular report of a firm's sales of goods and services subject to *value-added tax (VAT), which is required of firms registered for VAT.

vector autoregressive (VAR) model A generalization of the univariate model of an *autoregressive process to a system of equations describing multivariate time series, where all variables are treated equally as *endogenous variables and the evolution of each variable is modelled as a linear function of its own lags and of all other variables and their lags.

vector error correction model (VECM) A generalization of the *error correction model to a system of equations describing multivariate non-stationary time series.

vehicle currency *See* TRADING CURRENCY.

velocity of circulation The ratio of some aggregate of transactions, for example *gross domestic product, to some measure of the *money supply, for example M1. *See also* QUANTITY EQUATION; QUANTITY THEORY OF MONEY.

venture capital Capital whose owners are willing to invest in new or small businesses, where the risk of losing it is high. Venture capital is necessary if people without sufficient capital of their own are to be able to start new businesses.

vertical equity The view that people in an advantageous position should make a greater contribution to society. The difficulty with applying this concept is in defining what is an advantageous position. Applied to taxation vertical equity has the implication that the amount of tax paid should increase with income, if income is viewed as an appropriate measure of advantage. However, an alternative perspective that is equally valid is that advantage should be measured by the ability to earn income. Vertical equity would then seek greater contributions from high-ability individuals than from low-ability individuals regardless of individual decisions on whether or not to apply ability to earn income. Vertical equity is distinguished from *horizontal equity, which is concerned with considerations of *fairness between people with roughly equal incomes.

vertical integration The combination in one firm of two or more stages of production usually operated by separate firms. Vertical integration may be beneficial for firms if it assists in coordination over the quality and reliability of intermediate goods which one independent firm would have sold to the other. On the other hand, it may inhibit entry to and competition in an industry.

vertical merger A merger between two firms where one is a major supplier of the other. Examples would be a brewery and a chain of public houses, or a publisher and a bookshop. This is contrasted with a *horizontal merger, which combines two firms operating at the same stage of production.

visible balance *See* BALANCE OF TRADE.

visible trade *See* TRADE.

voice The expression of preferences by attempting to change unsatisfactory situations: this may be by voting, lobbying, or use of complaints procedures or litigation. It is contrasted with 'exit', which means leaving an unsatisfactory situation: this may involve selling shares, changing jobs, or migrating to a different area or country.

volatility Same as *dispersion. In finance, volatility usually refers to the rate at which a financial variable, such as stock price, moves up or down over time. Volatility is measured by the *standard deviation or, sometimes, by the *variance. The (absolute) empirical volatility of a stock price is usually calculated as the annualized standard deviation of daily change in price. A measure of the relative volatility of a stock to the market is its *beta coefficient.

volume index An index of the real level of production or consumption, in the whole economy or some part of it. A volume index is a weighted average of the production or consumption of some suitably chosen bundle of goods. The weights are the prices in some period. Where 0 is the base period and t the current period, p_{it} the price and q_{it} the quantity of good i produced or consumed in period t, a *base-weighted, or Laspeyres, volume index is defined by

$$q_B = \sum_{i=1}^{n} p_{i0} q_{it} / \sum_{i=1}^{n} p_{i0} q_{i0}$$

and a *current-weighted, or Paasche, volume index is defined by

$$q_C = \sum_{i=1}^{n} p_{it} q_{it} / \sum_{i=1}^{n} p_{it} q_{i0}.$$

voluntary exchange Exchange between two parties where each is free to refuse to trade. Under these circumstances both parties will gain, or at least not lose, from the exchange: support for a *market economy rests on this point. The argument need not apply if there is *asymmetric information between the two parties.

voluntary export restraint (VER) An agreement by a country's exporters or government to limit their exports to some other country. The limit set may be in terms of quantity, value, or market share. VERs may be 'voluntary' only in the sense of being accepted under duress, to avoid the threat of tariffs or other trade barriers. They may, however, be genuinely voluntary if exporting firms expect to make more profits from fewer export sales at higher prices. VERs were widespread in the 1970s and 1980s, but are being phased out following an international agreement achieved in 1992.

voluntary unemployment Unemployment which is deliberately chosen by the person unemployed. An unemployed person may refrain from applying for jobs which they could have got had they applied, or may apply in such a way as to be refused the offer of a job. This could be because they do not want to work at all, at least at the present time, or because they do want work, but are searching for a better job opportunity.

voting A method of group decision-making. There are many voting mechanisms that differ in the number of votes each participant in the mechanism can cast, and in how these votes are aggregated to reach a decision. For example, the *majority voting mechanism allocates each participant a single vote, and the alternative that receives the most votes is chosen. *See also* BORDA COUNT; COLLECTIVE CHOICE; PARADOX OF VOTING.

voting share An *ordinary share in a company giving the owner the right to vote at the company's general meetings. This is distinguished from a non-voting share, which gives the holder equal rights to information about the company and to dividends, but no vote. In some countries companies can set a maximum on the number of votes which can be cast by any one shareholder, regardless of the number of shares held.

voucher A certificate usable in place of money, but only for a specific purpose. For example, in some school districts in the US parents or guardians receive education vouchers to cover the cost of educating their children in the school of their choice. Such a system is aimed at combining the advantages of universal state funding of education with competition in its provision.

V

wage(s) Payment for work performed as an *employee. Wages and *salaries were once distinguished: wages were paid weekly, or more frequently for casual work, in cash, while salaries were paid monthly into bank accounts. In recent years the growth of payments of wages by cheque has blurred the distinction, and wages and salaries are best regarded as a single total. Payments for work performed by the self-employed as independent contractors are not classed as wages.

wage differential A difference in wage rates between two types of worker. Wage differentials may be on account of different levels of *skill or different formal qualifications, between *unionized and non-unionized firms, or between workers of different age, sex, or ethnic group. In the UK wage differentials based on age are legal, while those based on sex or ethnic group are not.

wage drift The tendency for the average level of wages actually paid to rise faster than *wage rates. This may be due to increases in *overtime, increases in special allowances, the operation of age-based salary scales, or upgrading of job descriptions. Wage drift is particularly likely during *booms when labour is relatively scarce, and during periods of attempted wage control, which firms try to evade.

wage flexibility *See* FLEXIBLE WAGES.

wage freeze A ban on changes in *wages, imposed as part of a *prices and incomes policy. As a temporary measure a wage freeze may help to cut inflation. It is very unlikely to be a practical long-term policy: the pattern of *wage rates in force at the time the policy starts is unlikely to equilibrate labour markets even at the time, and will become steadily less suitable. A wage freeze is difficult to enforce, as job descriptions can be changed, and operates unequally between workers on static wage rates and others on progressive salary scales.

wage–price spiral The tendency during inflation for wage increases to lead to price increases and for price increases to lead to wage increases, thus creating an *inflationary spiral. Wage increases tend to raise prices in their own industry by increasing costs, and in other industries by increasing demand. Price increases tend to lead to wage increases by increasing both the cost of living and the ability of employers to afford to pay higher wages. This makes *cost inflation hard to stop once it has begun.

wage-push inflation *See* COST INFLATION.

wage rate The rate per hour paid for work of a given type. This applies where time rates are in force; some types of work are paid for at piece rates. The wage rate is taken as that applying to normal hours of working: special rates, usually higher, tend to apply to overtime, or work at night, weekends, holidays, or other unsocial times. Wage rates may be laid down by law, or decided by *collective bargaining or individual agreement. Wage rates are generally quoted exclusive of bonuses or allowances and before deduction of *income tax, *superannuation, or *National Insurance contributions.

wage resistance Difficulty in cutting wages. *Real wage resistance applies to cuts in real wages, and nominal wage resistance to cuts in money wages.

wage restraint Decisions by *trade unions not to demand wage increases, or to moderate their demands. Wage restraint is often urged on unions by governments trying to restrain inflation.

wage rigidity The tendency of wage rates to be 'sticky', and not to adjust so as to clear the market in the short run. Wages may be rigid because of long-term contracts. Alternatively, if wage rates are decided by *collective bargaining, neither side may be keen to disturb an agreement which cost much effort to reach.

wage round An annual sequence of pay negotiations. There is a tendency for later settlements to follow precedents set in earlier ones by major *trade unions.

wages council A body set up by law to fix minimum wages for particular forms of work. In the UK wages councils operated from 1911 to 1994 in various industries, for example catering and agriculture. Wages councils tended to be set up in industries where wages were low, and *collective bargaining was weak or non-existent, possibly because of dispersion of employment and low educational qualification of workers.

Wagner Act The National Labour Relations Act of 1935, known informally as the Wagner Act, gave workers in the US the right to form unions and engage in collective bargaining. The act also created the National Labour Relations Board to oversee union certification and investigate violations of the law.

Wagner's law An observation made in the 19th century by Adolph Wagner (1835–1917) that the share of the public sector in *gross domestic product had increased over time. Wagner's law was the prediction that this trend would continue. The law is based on three claims: economic growth results in an increase in complexity requiring continued introduction of new laws and development of the legal structure; urbanization increases negative *externalities, such as congestion and crime, which necessitate intervention; and the goods supplied by the public sector have a high income elasticity of demand. If the elasticity of demand exceeds one, public sector expenditure will consequently rise as a proportion of income. It is the third claim that has received most attention but empirical evidence has failed to convincingly demonstrate that the elasticity of demand is above one. Wagner's law has some compelling features but by concentrating solely on the demand for public sector services it overlooks the supply side and the politics of provision.

Wald test One of the three tests of restrictions (along with the *Lagrange multiplier test and the *likelihood ratio test) on an unknown parameter, or a vector of unknown parameters, θ, based on the *maximum likelihood estimation of θ. The test statistic is a quadratic form involving the restriction vector and the covariance matrix of the parameter vector, evaluated at $\hat{\theta}^U$, the unrestricted maximum likelihood estimator of θ. Under the null hypothesis it has asymptotic chi-square distribution with the number of degrees of freedom equal to the number of restrictions.

Wall Street The main financial area in Manhattan, New York. It is symbolic of high finance in the United States.

Walras's law The law states that the value of excess demand is zero. The excess demand, z_i, for good i is the difference between demand, x_i, and the sum of supply from firms, y_i, and the initial endowment, ω_i; hence $z_i = x_i - y_i - \omega_i$. Noting that demand and supply are both functions of prices, Walras's law states that for an economy with n goods

$$\sum_{i=1}^{n} p_i z_i = \sum_{i=1}^{n} p_i (x_i - y_i - \omega_i) = 0$$

for any prices p_i, $i = 1, \ldots, n$. The law implies that in an economy with n markets there are only $n - 1$ independent demand–supply equations. Hence, when the *general equilibrium for an economy with n goods is studied only $n - 1$ markets need to be analysed. If a set of prices can be found that place these $n - 1$ markets in equilibrium then the prices also ensure the nth market is in equilibrium.

warrant A security giving the holder the right but not an obligation to buy shares in a company on some future date at a pre-arranged price. A warrant will be valuable if, when the date arrives, the market price is above the *exercise price. Warrants can be traded: a warrant is thus a traded option.

warranted growth rate The rate at which growth must occur in a *Harrod–Domar model if it is to be sustainable. If national income is Y, saving is S, and investment is I, saving is assumed to be a constant proportion of income so that $S = sY$. Investment is assumed to be given by an accelerator model, where investment is given by $I = v(dY/dt)$, where t is time. For *ex ante saving and investment to be equal requires that $sY = v(dY/dt)$. This implies that the growth rate of Y must be

$$w = \left(\frac{1}{Y}\right)\left(\frac{dY}{dt}\right) = \frac{s}{v}.$$

This is the only rate at which equilibrium growth is possible, so long as the saving ratio s and the capital–output ratio v are taken as fixed.

warranty A guarantee by the provider of goods or services as to their quality. A manufacturer's warranty is only of value to customers if it goes beyond the minimum properties of the good or service required by law. A warranty does not curtail the customer's statutory rights.

wasting asset An asset which diminishes over time. This wastage may be due to gradual destruction through use, for example the depletion of ore reserves by mining them. Alternatively, it may be due to the passage of time: for example, a *patent will expire on some future date, which draws closer as time passes.

Ways and Means Advances Advances to the government made by the central bank. These are made when necessary if government expenditure runs in advance of receipts from taxation plus borrowing from the public. They have the effect of increasing the *money supply.

weak convergence *See* CONVERGENCE IN DISTRIBUTION.

weakening of a currency A fall in the price of a currency in terms of other currencies. This is caused by a reduction in the demand to hold it, which may be due either to a worsening of the country's *current account, or to shifts into other currencies on *capital account. *See also* CURRENCY DEPRECIATION.

weak stationarity *See* COVARIANCE STATIONARY PROCESS.

wealth The total value of a person's net assets. Wealth may be held in various forms: these include money, shares in companies, debt instruments, land, buildings, intellectual property such as *patents and *copyrights, and valuables such as works of art. From this any debts owed are subtracted. The valuation put on these assets is liable to uncertainty and fluctuations, as many of the assets are not marketed, and those that are may have volatile market prices. It is disputable whether wealth should include prospective accessions of assets: the actuarial value of pension rights can be calculated, but what pensioners will actually receive depends on how long they survive. Similarly, prospective legacies have incentive effects comparable to actual wealth, but what will actually be received depends on how long testators survive, whether their assets change, and whether they change their minds about how to bequeath them. *See also* NET WEALTH.

wealth effect The effect of an increase in the total wealth of an individual upon the level of expenditure. It is generally expected that an individual with a higher value of net assets will spend a larger proportion of current income, and save less, than somebody with the same income but lower value of net assets. It is also expected that an individual with a higher value of net assets will hold more money balances relative to income than somebody with a lower value of net assets.

wealth tax A tax based on the personal wealth of individuals. Collection of such a tax involves regular valuation of the individual's assets. This raises problems where the assets are not traded in regular markets, or where their market prices are subject to rapid fluctuations. It is also difficult to measure assets which are easily concealed, such as jewellery, bearer securities, or bank deposits in foreign *tax havens. Actual wealth taxes tend to be levied at low rates on conservative valuations of restricted classes of assets.

wear and tear The cumulative damage done to equipment through regular use. Normal wear and tear is not insurable, unlike accidental damage which can usually be insured against. Its effects are also excluded from cover by manufacturers' warranties. Wear and tear is one of the major causes of *capital consumption, the others being accidents and *obsolescence.

weighted average An average giving weights to different numbers in proportion to their importance. The weighted average of n numbers $x_1, x_2, \ldots, x_n$ is found by taking the sum of the numbers times their weights $w_1, w_2, \ldots, w_N$, divided by the sum of the weights, so

$$\mu_w = \sum_{i=1}^{n} w_i x_i \bigg/ \sum_{i=1}^{n} w_i.$$

The unweighted average has $w_i = 1$, $i = 1, \ldots, n$.

weighted least squares estimator A version of the *generalized least squares estimator used when the *covariance matrix of the random error is known to be diagonal. This estimator minimizes the sum of squares of residuals weighted by the inverse of the standard deviation for each observation. Thus, the more reliable observations (those with relatively lower variance) are weighted more heavily in estimation than the less reliable ones.

weights in index numbers The relative importance attached to various components entering into any index number. The weights are chosen according to the purpose for which it is expected that an index number will be used. The weights in a *consumer price index, for example, are chosen so that the bundle of goods and services whose prices are measured corresponds to what an average consumer would buy. These weights are based on surveys of consumer behaviour.

welfare 1. The state of well-being of an individual or a society. The level of welfare measures the degree of contentment of an individual or a society. For an individual this is represented by a *utility function and for a society by a *social welfare function.
2. Welfare is US terminology for an income support programme.

welfare criterion A method of deciding whether a proposed change in the economy should be made. The Pareto criterion says that a change should be made if somebody gains and nobody loses. This is uncontroversial, but fails to answer the much more common question of whether or not to make changes with both gainers and losers. The Hicks–Kaldor criterion says that changes should be made if the gainers could afford to compensate the losers. If such compensation is actually paid, the criterion becomes similar to the Pareto criterion. The Scitovsky criterion says that a change should be made if, after it has occurred, the losers could not afford to compensate the gainers for changing back. Differences between the Hicks–Kaldor and Scitovsky criteria arise if the change brings about alterations in relative prices. The Hicks–Kaldor criterion treats the pre-change distribution of real incomes as the status quo, the Scitovsky criterion is based on the post-change distribution. There is no general reason for preferring either distribution to the other. A number of difficulties have been identified in the application of welfare criteria based on compensation, so only the Pareto criterion remains in use. *See also* PARETO EFFI- CIENCY.

welfare economics The part of economics concerned with the effects of economic activity on welfare. This includes the modelling of individual or household behaviour by *utility functions; criteria for *efficiency, including *Pareto efficiency and theories of the *second-best; criteria for judging whether changes in the economy are beneficial; consideration of how income distribution affects *social welfare; and *cost–benefit analysis. Welfare economics has both positive and normative components.

welfare state A state committed to ensuring for all its citizens at least some minimum standard of living, including housing, education, and medical services. The size of the welfare state varies across economies. Economies in Northern Europe tend to have larger welfare systems than those in Southern Europe, North America, and Asia. The welfare state also represents the ideal of a state that provides universal comprehensive support. The term can be used in a derogatory sense to describe over-dependence on welfare benefits and the stifling of individual initiative.

white knight A purchaser for a company, willing to rescue it from an unwanted *takeover bid by another buyer. A company threatened with takeover may welcome a competitive bid by a white knight as a means of improving the terms offered by the first bidder, whether or not the alternative bid is ultimately accepted.

white noise A *stochastic process with zero *mean, constant *variance, and zero *autocorrelation.

white paper A UK government publication, generally intended as a prelude to legislation. The eventual legislation may differ from the white paper's proposals in some respects. A white paper is contrasted with a *green paper, a UK government publication intended to stimulate public discussion of an issue, without committing the government to legislating at all, or to the lines any legislation might take.

White's test A test of the null hypothesis of *homoscedasticity against the alternative of *heteroscedasticity, based on the fact that under heteroscedasticity the ordinary least squares estimator of the covariance matrix is inconsistent. The test is performed by regressing squared OLS residuals from the main regression on all *explanatory variables, their squares and cross-products, and a constant. The test statistic is given by NR^2, where N is the sample size and R^2 is the coefficient of determination from the test regression. Under the null it has an asymptotic chi-square distribution with the degrees of freedom equal to the number of regressors in the test regression, excluding the constant.

wholesale banking Banking by institutions which specialize in dealing with other financial institutions, large firms, and wealthy individuals. Wholesale banks do not need the dense network of branches which characterizes *retail banking.

W

wholesale prices The prices of goods which are dealt with wholesale, mainly bulk goods, which are mostly inputs to production rather than finished commodities. A wholesale price index, for example, includes wheat and sheet steel, where a *retail price index includes bread and cars. Because they involve goods that are dealt in before the production of final goods, and are held as stocks of inputs, wholesale price indexes tend to be *leading indicators, moving earlier in economic cycles than the retail price index.

wholesaling The sale of goods to distributors, rather than the general public. Wholesale traders usually deal in larger quantities than retailers: they break bulk and sell in smaller quantities than their purchases from manufacturers. Wholesalers are able to compete with direct sales by manufacturers to retailers through *economies of scale and scope in stock-holding and transport.

widget In economic texts the term widget is used as a generic word for a manufactured good.

wildcat strike A strike embarked on by groups of employees without being organized or supported by their trade union.

willingness to pay The maximum amount that an economic agent is willing to pay to acquire a specified good or service. The willingness to pay is private information but may be obtained by using *revealed preference techniques or the *contingent valuation method.

windfall gain An unexpected addition to income, for example, receiving an inheritance from a distant relative or winning a lottery. Similarly, windfall profit is an unexpected increase in profit for a firm. It is often argued that windfall gains/ profits are a good target for taxation since a tax upon them is not distortionary.

winding up Closing down a business, paying off its debts, and distributing any remaining assets to its *shareholders. Winding up or liquidation may be voluntary, when owners decide to retire or cut their losses, or may be imposed by the courts if the business has defaulted on its debts.

winner's curse The danger that the winner of a *contract will lose money on it. Where contracts are awarded by *competitive tendering, the winner is usually the firm offering the lowest price. Estimates of costs (and revenues) are subject to error, and there is a danger that the winner will be a firm which has made a large underestimate of the true cost (or overestimate of revenue), and will thus lose money on the contract. The same argument applies in *auctions when the winner pays the value of the highest bid.

W

Wirtschaftswunder Literally translated from German: economic miracle. A term referring to the remarkable recovery of the West German economy after the Second World War. In 1945 West Germany was devastated by the war, and had to absorb millions of refugees from the East. By the 1960s West Germany had some of the world's most prosperous and productive industries, and a remarkably strong currency.

withholding tax A tax levied at a standard rate on all receipts of income from wages or dividends, regardless of the individual's tax liability. Taxpayers then make *tax returns so that their tax liability can be determined. Those liable to pay less than the withholding tax, for example because of low total incomes, then receive *tax refunds, while those liable to pay more get tax demands for the excess. This system helps the tax authorities as they ensure the receipt of revenue, and taxpayers entitled to refunds have a strong incentive to file their tax returns promptly. It is disadvantageous for taxpayers, who get their refunds in arrears: it does however protect them from the danger that they may have spent too much of their income before the tax bill arrives. The US income tax system makes use of withholding taxes.

within-groups estimator An estimator of the vector of the parameters in a model with *panel data, computed as an *ordinary least squares estimator using the deviations from the time averages of the data for each cross-section unit (deviations from group means). It is equivalent to estimating a model with dummy variables for each unit (the least squares dummy variable, or LSDV, model). *See also* BETWEEN-GROUPS ESTIMATOR.

with-profits life insurance *Life insurance where benefits to the policy-holders depend on the financial performance of the fund accumulated from their premiums. This is in contrast to without-profits life insurance, where a policy-holder receives a guaranteed level of benefits regardless of the financial perform-ance of the fund. As with-profits policies involve far less risk for the insurance company than without-profits policies, premiums on with-profits policies are less than those on without-profits policies giving the same level of expected benefits at maturity. However, with equal premiums a without-profits policy offers more *cover during the early years of a policy. A with-profits policy offers much better protection against inflation over the life of the policy than a without-profits policy.

Wold's decomposition theorem A result stating that every zero-mean *covariance stationary stochastic process Y_t can be decomposed into a deterministic part and a non-deterministic part; the deterministic part is the optimal linear *predictor of Y_t based on its lagged values and is uncorrelated with the non-deterministic part, which, in its turn, can be represented as an infinite *moving-average process.

work Activities involving physical and/or mental effort. While a large part of this is in paid employment, or working for economic gain while self-employed, there are other forms of work. This is recognized in the terms voluntary work, where people perform for charities or political parties tasks other people are paid for, and housework, where people work for the welfare of their families. *See also* HOURS OF WORK; PART-TIME WORK; SHIFT WORK; SKILLED WORK; UNSKILLED WORK.

worker-controlled firm A firm which is owned and managed by its workers, or a producers' cooperative. In an industry with low *capital intensity, the workers may provide the firm's capital themselves; in more capital-intensive industries, it is possible for them to borrow capital, or to lease buildings and equipment. The advantage claimed for workers' control of firms is that it removes the conflict between owners and workers. It does not, however, eliminate conflicts of interest between the more skilled and senior workers and the less skilled. There are relatively few successful worker-controlled firms. Many worker-controlled firms have failed after being tried as a last resort when other forms of organization had already been tried, and failed.

worker participation Participation by workers in the process of decision-making in a firm. This varies widely between firms. At the one extreme are producers' cooperatives, or *worker-controlled firms, where the workers are the owners and elect the directors. At the other are firms with no worker participation except for any informal contacts between owners and workers, though in very small firms this may be quite effective. In between are firms with *works councils, where matters of general policy like manning levels and redundancies can be discussed, though management makes the final decisions. There are also firms with arrangements for workers to become ordinary shareholders, sometimes on concessional terms. It is possible for firms to co-opt directors nominated by workers, though this is uncommon. It is also possible, as in Germany, to have a *two-tier board: workers elect representatives to the upper tier, which decides general policy, but not to the lower tier, which takes operational decisions. Many firms consider that some degree of worker participation is in the interests of shareholders, as it is expected to reduce feelings of alienation, promote loyalty to the firm, and induce workers to take a more sympathetic view of its problems.

workfare A system making income support for the unemployed conditional on their performing some form of work for which they are suitable.

workforce *See* LABOUR FORCE.

working capital The part of the capital of a business that is not tied up in land, buildings, or fixed equipment. Working capital is used to hold liquid balances, pay for wages and materials, and extend credit to customers.

working conditions The conditions under which employees have to work. This includes matters such as permitted breaks, the state of heating, lighting, and ventilation of workplaces, the safety and comfort of machinery, vehicles, and other equipment, normal manning levels, and disciplinary procedures. These conditions are affected by legislation, for example under the *Health and Safety at Work Act, by *collective bargaining between employers and trade unions representing workers, and by voluntary improvements by employers who believe that better working conditions pay for themselves in terms of staff morale and loyalty, as well as productivity.

working practices The ways in which the members of the labour force in an enterprise carry out their tasks. Working practices may be set by formal agreement between employers and workers' representatives, or by customs which have emerged and are followed without any formal agreement. They are concerned with who undertakes what functions, and how many people a given task is expected to occupy. Unnecessarily restrictive working practices, however, can seriously impair efficiency.

Working Tax Credit A UK *tax credit paid to low-income workers aged over 25 and working in excess of 30 hours per week. *See also* CHILD TAX CREDIT.

work in progress *See* INVESTMENT IN STOCKS AND WORK IN PROGRESS.

works council A body where representatives of the management and workers of an establishment or a firm meet to discuss matters of mutual interest. These typically exclude wages, but include *working conditions, health and safety, and individual or group grievances. Many managements find works councils useful in settling problems before they escalate into *industrial disputes. They may also be used as a convenient occasion for briefing workers on the firm's prospects and profits. Works councils generally do not have the power to make executive decisions, but unless management takes considerable notice of their proceedings, discussion not followed by action is liable to make problems worse rather than better. In some countries, and under the *Social Chapter of the *Maastricht Treaty, works councils are compulsory for larger firms.

work study The study of working procedures with a view to improving their efficiency, safety, or comfort. This includes looking at the order of operations to see whether rearranging them could save time or effort, and looking at the physical processes to see whether changes in equipment or in environmental features such as lighting could reduce fatigue or improve accuracy and reduce defects in the products.

World Bank *See* INTERNATIONAL BANK FOR RECONSTRUCTION and DEVELOPMENT.

World Trade Organization (WTO) An international body to supervise and encourage international trade. An international trade organization was proposed following the *Bretton Woods conference in 1944, but was never set up; the *General Agreement on Tariffs and Trade (GATT) was started instead. GATT organized the Uruguay Round trade talks, which concluded in 1994 by setting up the WTO to take over its functions in encouraging multilateral trade in goods and services.

write off To reduce the value put on an asset in a company's accounts. *Depreciation is the process of writing off assets gradually over time. 'Write-off' is also used to describe the status of an asset after an accident severe enough to reduce the value of the asset to zero.

wrongful dismissal Termination of employment by the employer contrary to the employee's contract of employment. Dismissal may be wrongful because the grounds given are not justified, or the procedure laid down by the contract of employment has not been followed.

w

X-efficiency That part of overall *efficiency which consists of getting the maximum output technically possible from any given inputs, or producing a given output with the fewest possible inputs. X-efficiency thus implies the complete absence of *slack in production. Evidence for X-efficiency can take two forms. One is theoretical, showing that in principle better results are not obtainable. The other is empirical, showing that no other firm or organization is observed to do better.

X-inefficiency Failure of a firm or other organization to get the maximum possible output from the inputs it uses, or to produce its output with the minimum use of inputs. X-inefficiency implies that there is *slack in the organization. Its existence can be shown in two possible ways. One is the engineer's method, producing a plan of operations which is expected to do better. The other is the statistician's or benchmark approach, showing that other firms or organizations manage to get more output from equal inputs, or the same output from fewer inputs.

Y

Yaoundé Convention An international agreement by which many former French colonies became associates of the *European Community.

year *See* BUDGET YEAR; FINANCIAL YEAR; FISCAL YEAR.

yen (¥) The Japanese currency unit.

yield The income from a *fixed-interest security as a percentage of its price. The nominal yield is the interest per annum divided by the *par value. The running yield is the interest divided by the market price. The yield to maturity is the interest equivalent to the actual interest payments plus capital gains (or minus capital losses) if the security is held to *maturity. A *yield curve plots the yield on fixed-interest securities against their time to maturity. *See also* NET YIELD; REDEMPTION YIELD; RUNNING YIELD; SUSTAINED YIELD.

yield curve A graph plotting the yield on *fixed-interest securities against their years to *maturity. As longer-dated securities are more subject to price fluctuations if interest rates change, and are thus less liquid than shorter-dated securities, it is usually expected that if interest rates are equally likely to rise or fall the yield curve slopes upwards; that is, longer-dated securities will have higher yields than shorter-dated ones. This slope may be temporarily reversed if interest rates are generally expected to fall, as the expectation of higher *capital gains on longer-dated securities makes them relatively attractive to hold. *See also* LIQUID ASSETS; TERM STRUCTURE OF INTEREST RATES.

yield gap The difference between the average dividend yield on *equities and the average yield on long-dated *gilt-edged securities. During periods of stable prices the yield on equities usually needs to be greater to compensate investors for their relative riskiness, so the yield gap is positive. During periods of high inflation the fact that equities are expected to provide *capital gains to compensate for inflation, while gilt-edged are not, can lead to a reverse yield gap, with returns on gilt-edged above those on equities. *See also* REVERSE YIELD GAP.

Yule–Walker equations Difference equations relating the *autocorrelation coefficients of an autoregressive process to the coefficients on the lags.

zero-base budgeting The proposal that the *budgets of governments and other organizations should be designed starting from first principles, defining the aims of the organization and adopting the best method of achieving them. This is contrasted with the usual budgetary procedure, which starts from the previous period's budget and makes marginal changes. As real world organizations are committed to contracts with their employees and suppliers, and are affected by the public's expectations about the prices they should charge and the services they should provide, zero-base budgeting is difficult to achieve.

zero coupon bond A bond that does not make any periodic *coupon payments. A zero coupon bond is sold at a discount from its face value but pays the face value at *maturity. For example, a zero coupon bond with a face value of £1000 and one year to maturity may sell for £909. The return to the investor is determined by the discount. For the example, £909 invested in the bond is rewarded with the face value of £1000 a year later, which is an annual return of 10 percent.

zero growth The state of an economy without further expansion of activity. This term occurs in two contexts: in some poor and backward economies where it is a fact, it is called *stagnation and is rightly regarded as a problem; in some very advanced and wealthy economies, however, worries about *pollution and the exhaustion of *natural resources lead to zero growth being propounded as an ideal. This raises two problems: first, if resources really are exhaustible then no positive rate of depletion is permanently sustainable, and advanced economies must evolve to survive; second, the vast majority of the world's inhabitants are far poorer than the advocates of zero growth. They would have to become far richer than they now are, consume vastly more resources, and produce far more pollution, before they would be in the least likely to join in advocating zero growth as an ideal.

zero-rated (VAT) Goods or services included in the *value-added tax system, with a value-added tax (VAT) rate of zero. Firms can reclaim VAT on inputs to zero-rated goods. These are distinguished from VAT-exempt goods and services which are outside the VAT system, so that VAT on inputs cannot be reclaimed.

zero-sum game A game in which the sum of the pay-offs to players is zero for every outcome. In a two-player zero-sum game a positive pay-off for one player implies a negative pay-off (of equal absolute value) for the other player. Zero-sum games represent direct opposition between the interests of the players and are used to model conflict. *See also* MAXIMIN.

zoning The system of specifying that certain activities can only be carried on in particular areas. Some activities cause harmful *externalities, by emitting noise, smells, or dust, or by attracting heavy traffic. Zoning tries to minimize the harm done by such activities, by concentrating them where they do least damage, and separating them from residential, commercial, or amenity areas.

Appendix 1. Institutional Acronyms

(⊕) SEE WEB LINKS

This is a web-linked dictionary. To access the websites listed below, go to the dictionary's web page at http://www.oup.com/uk/reference/resources/economics, click on the **Web links** in the Resources section and click straight through to the relevant websites.

AACB/ABCA Association of African Central Banks/Association des Banques Centrales Africaines, Dakar, Senegal
- The official website of the AACB

ACAS Advisory, Conciliation and Arbitration Service, London, UK
- The home page of ACAS

AFDB African Development Bank, Abidjan, Côte d'Ivoire
- The official website of the AFDB

AFL–CIO American Federation of Labor and Congress of Industrial Organizations, Washington DC, USA
- The official website of the AFL–CIO

AIM Alternative Investment Market, London, UK
- The home page of the AIM

AMEX American Stock Exchange, New York, USA
- The home page of the AMEX

APEC Asia-Pacific Economic Cooperation, Singapore
- The home page of APEC

CBI Confederation of British Industry, London, UK
- The home page of the CBI

CBOT Chicago Board of Trade, Chicago, USA
- The home page of the CBOT

CC Competition Commission, London, UK
- The official website of the Competition Commission

CCC Commodity Credit Corporation, Washington DC, USA
- The home page of the Commodity Credit Corporation

CFTC Commodity Futures Trading Commission, Washington DC, USA
- The official website of the CFTC

CME Chicago Mercantile Exchange, Chicago, USA
- The home page of the CME

EBRD European Bank for Reconstruction and Development, London, UK
- The official website of the EBRD

ECB/BCE European Central Bank/Banque Centrale Européenne, Frankfurt am Main, Germany
- The official website of the European Central Bank

ECGD Export Credits Guarantee Department, London, UK
- The official website of the ECGD

EEOC Equal Employment Opportunity Commission, Washington DC, USA
- The official website of the EEOC

EFTA European Free Trade Association, Geneva, Switzerland
- The official website of the EFTA

EPA Environmental Protection Agency, Washington DC, USA
- The home page of the EPA

ESRC Economic and Social Research Council, Swindon, UK
- The home page of the ESRC

ESRI Economic and Social Research Institute, Dublin, Ireland
- The home page of the ESRI

EU/UE European Union/Union Européenne, Brussels, Belgium
- A website with information about the initiatives of the European Commission maintained by the EU

FAO Food and Agriculture Organization, Rome, Italy
- The official website of the FAO

FCC Federal Communication Commission, Washington DC, USA
- The official website of the FCC

FCO Foreign and Commonwealth Office, London, UK
- The official website of the Foreign and Commonwealth Office

FDIC Federal Deposit Insurance Corporation, Washington DC, USA
- The official website of the FDIC

FSA Financial Services Authority, London, UK
- The official website of the FSA

FSA Financial Services Agency, Tokyo, Japan
- The official website of the Financial Services Agency of Japan

FTC Federal Trade Commission, Washington DC, USA
- The official website of the FTC

HMRC HM Revenue and Customs, London, UK
- The official website of HMRC

IADB Inter-American Development Bank, Washington DC, USA
- The home page of the IADB

IASB International Accounting Standards Board, London, UK
- The home page of the IASB

IATA International Air Transport Association, Montreal, Canada
- The home page of the IATA

IBRD International Bank for Reconstruction and Development, Washington DC, USA
- The official website of the World Bank

IDA International Development Association, Washington DC, USA
- The home page of the IDA

IEA Institute of Economic Affairs, London, UK
- The home page of the IEA

IEA International Energy Authority, Paris, France
- The home page of the IEA

IFC International Finance Corporation, Washington DC, USA
- The home page of the IFC

IFS Institute for Fiscal Studies, London, UK
- The home page of the Institute for Fiscal Studies

ILO International Labour Organization, Geneva, Switzerland
- The official website of the ILO

IMF International Monetary Fund, Washington DC, USA
- The official website of the IMF

INSEE Institut National de la Statistique et des Études Économiques, Paris, France
- The home page of the INSEE

IOM International Organization for Migration, Geneva, Switzerland
- The official website of the IOM, an inter-governmental organization providing services and advice to governments and migrants

IOSCO International Organization of Securities Commissions, Madrid, Spain
- The home page of the IOSCO

IRS Internal Revenue Service, Washington DC, USA
- The official website of the IRS

LIFFE London International Financial Futures Exchange, London, UK
- The home page of LIFFE

LSE London School of Economics, London, UK
- The home page of the LSE

LSE London Stock Exchange, London, UK
- The home page of the London Stock Exchange

MERCOSUR/MERCOSUL Mercado Común del Sur/Mercado Comum do Sul, Montevideo, Uruguay
- The official website of MERCOSUR

NAFTA/ALÉNA/TLCAN North American Free Trade Agreement/Accord de libre-échange nord-américain/Tratado de Libre Comercio de América del Norte, USA/Canada/Mexico
- The official website of NAFTA

NASDAQ National Association of Securities Dealers Automated Quotations, New York, USA
- The home page of the NASDAQ

NATO North Atlantic Treaty Organization, Brussels, Belgium
- The official home page of NATO

NBER National Bureau of Economic Research, Cambridge, USA
- The home page of the NBER

NHS National Health Service, London, UK
- The official website of the NHS

NIESR National Institute of Economic and Social Research, London, UK
- The home page of the NIESR

NYSE New York Stock Exchange, New York, USA
- The home page of the New York Stock Exchange

OECD/ODCE Organization for Economic Cooperation and Development/ Organisation de Coopération et de Développement Économiques, Paris, France
- The official website of the OECD

Ofcom Office of Communications, London, UK
- The official website of the Office of Communications

OFT Office of Fair Trading, London, UK
- The official website of the OFT

OMB Office of Management and Budget, Washington DC, USA
- The official website of the OMB

ONS Office for National Statistics, Newport, Wales
- The official website of the ONS

OPEC Organization of Petroleum Exporting Countries, Vienna, Austria
- The official home page of OPEC

SEC Securities and Exchange Commission, Washington DC, USA
- The official website of the SEC

SEIU Service Employees International Union, Washington DC, USA
- The official website of the SEIU, the North American union of workers in hospital systems, long-term care, property services, and public services

SWRDA South West of England Regional Development Agency, Exeter, UK
- The official home page of the SWRDA

3i Investors in Industry, London, UK
- The home page of 3i

TUC Trades Union Congress, London, UK
- The official website of the TUC

UAW United Automobile, Aerospace and Agricultural Implement Workers of America, Detroit, USA
- The official home page of the UAW

UNCTAD United Nations Conference on Trade and Development, Geneva, Switzerland
- The official website of UNCTAD

UNDP United Nations Development Programme, New York, USA
- The official website of the UNDP

USAID US Agency for International Development, Washington DC, USA
- The official website of USAID

WHO World Health Organization, Geneva, Switzerland
- The official home page of the WHO

WTO World Trade Organization, Geneva, Switzerland
- The official website of the WTO

Appendix 2. Nobel Prize Winners

The 'Nobel prize in economics' is more accurately called the Sveriges Riksbank Prize in Economic Sciences in Memory of Alfred Nobel. The prize was established in 1968 by Sveriges Riksbank (the central bank of Sweden) in memory of Alfred Nobel, founder of the Nobel Prize. The first prize in economics was awarded in 1969. The prize amount for 2007 was set at Swedish kronor (SEK) 10 million per full prize.

1969   Ragnar Frisch and Jan Tinbergen for having developed and applied dynamic models for the analysis of economic processes.

1970   Paul A. Samuelson for the scientific work through which he has developed static and dynamic economic theory and actively contributed to raising the level of analysis in economic science.

1971   Simon Kuznets for his empirically founded interpretation of economic growth which has led to new and deepened insight into the economic and social structure and process of development.

1972   Sir John R. Hicks and Kenneth J. Arrow for their pioneering contributions to general economic equilibrium theory and welfare theory.

1973   Wassily Leontief for the development of the input–output method and for its application to important economic problems.

1974   Gunnar Myrdal and Friedrich August Von Hayek for their pioneering work in the theory of money and economic fluctuations and for their penetrating analysis of the interdependence of economic, social, and institutional phenomena.

1975   Leonid Vitaliyevich Kantorovich and Tjalling C. Koopmans for their contributions to the theory of optimum allocation of resources.

1976   Milton Friedman for his achievements in the fields of consumption analysis and monetary history, and theory, and for his demonstration of the complexity of stabilization policy.

1977   Bertil Ohlin and James E. Meade for their pathbreaking contribution to the theory of international trade and international capital movements.

1978   Herbert A. Simon for his pioneering research into the decision-making process within economic organizations.

1979   Theodore W. Schultz and Sir Arthur Lewis for their pioneering research into economic development research with particular consideration of the problems of developing countries.

1980   Lawrence R. Klein for the creation of econometric models and the application to the analysis of economic fluctuations and economic policies.

1981 James Tobin for his analysis of financial markets and their relations to expenditure decisions, employment, production, and prices.

1982 George J. Stigler for his seminal studies of industrial structures, functioning of markets, and causes and effects of public regulation.

1983 Gerard Debreu for having incorporated new analytical methods into economic theory and for his rigorous reformulation of the theory of general equilibrium.

1984 Sir Richard Stone for having made fundamental contributions to the development of systems of national accounts and hence greatly improved the basis for empirical economic analysis.

1985 Franco Modigliani for his pioneering analyses of saving and of financial markets.

1986 James M. Buchanan Jr. for his development of the contractual and constitutional bases for the theory of economic and political decision-making.

1987 Robert M. Solow for his contributions to the theory of economic growth.

1988 Maurice Allais for his pioneering contributions to the theory of markets and efficient utilization of resources.

1989 Trygve Haavelmo for his clarification of the probability theory foundations of econometrics and his analyses of simultaneous economic structures.

1990 Harry M. Markowitz, Merton M. Miller, and William F. Sharpe for their pioneering work in the theory of financial economics.

1991 Ronald H. Coase for his discovery and clarification of the significance of transaction costs and property rights for the institutional structure and functioning of the economy.

1992 Gary S. Becker for having extended the domain of microeconomic analysis to a wide range of human behaviour and interaction, including non-market behaviour.

1993 Robert W. Fogel and Douglass C. North for having renewed research in economic history by applying economic theory and quantitative methods in order to explain economic and institutional change.

1994 John C. Harsanyi, John F. Nash, and Reinhard Selten for their pioneering analysis of equilibria in the theory of non-cooperative games.

1995 Robert Lucas for having developed and applied the hypothesis of rational expectations, and thereby having transformed macroeconomic analysis and deepened our understanding of economic policy.

1996 James A. Mirrlees and William Vickrey for their fundamental contributions to the economic theory of incentives under asymmetric information.

1997 Robert C. Merton and Myron S. Scholes for a new method to determine the value of derivatives.

1998 Amartya Sen for his contributions to welfare economics.

1999 Robert A. Mundell for his analysis of monetary and fiscal policy under different exchange rate regimes and his analysis of optimum currency areas.

2000 James J. Heckman for his development of theory and methods for analysing selective samples and Daniel L. McFadden for his development of theory and methods for analysing discrete choice.

2001 George A. Akerlof, A. Michael Spence, and Joseph E. Stiglitz for their analyses of markets with asymmetric information.

2002 Daniel Kahneman for having integrated insights from psychological research into economic science, especially concerning human judgement and decision-making under uncertainty, and Vernon L. Smith, for having established laboratory experiments as a tool in empirical economic analysis, especially in the study of alternative market mechanisms.

2003 Robert F. Engle for methods of analysing economic time series.

2004 Finn E. Kydland and Edward C. Prescott for their contributions to dynamic macroeconomics: the time consistency of economic policy and the driving forces behind business cycles.

2005 Robert J. Aumann and Thomas C. Schelling for having enhanced our understanding of conflict and cooperation through game-theory analysis.

2006 Edmund S. Phelps for his analysis of intertemporal trade-offs in macroeconomic policy.

2007 Leonid Hurwicz, Eric S. Maskin, and Roger B. Myerson for having laid the foundations of mechanism design theory.

2008 Paul Krugman for his analysis of trade patterns and location of economic activity.

Appendix 3. The Greek Alphabet

Lower case	Upper case	Letter
α	A	Alpha
β	B	Beta
γ	Γ	Gamma
δ	Δ	Delta
ε	E	Epsilon
ζ	Z	Zeta
η	H	Eta
θ	Θ	Theta
ι	I	Iota
κ	K	Kappa
λ	Λ	Lambda
μ	M	Mu
ν	N	Nu
ξ	Ξ	Xi
o	O	Omicron
π	Π	Pi
ρ	P	Rho
σ	Σ	Sigma
τ	T	Tau
υ	Y	Upsilon
φ	Φ	Phi
χ	X	Chi
ψ	Ψ	Psi
ω	Ω	Omega

Appendix 4. Additional Websites

(⊕) SEE WEB LINKS

This is a web-linked dictionary. To access the websites listed below, go to the dictionary's web page at http://www.oup.com/uk/reference/resources/economics, click on the **Web links** in the Resources section and click straight through to the relevant websites.

Conference announcements

Conference Calls at INOMICS
- Conference calls listing provided by INOMICS, an internet site for economists

Dr.T's Econlinks Conferences
- Conference listing provided by Dr.T's Econlinks.com

Econometric Conferences
- Conferences with interest in econometrics, provided by the *Econometrics Journal*

Economic Conferences and Calls for Papers
- List of conference announcements provided by the European University Institute

Economic Conferences Worldwide
- List of upcoming conferences in economics, business, and related fields

Economics Bulletin
- Conference listing provided by the *Economics Bulletin*

QM&RBC Calls for Papers, Conferences, and Workshops
- Calls for papers, conferences, and workshops, provided by quantitative macroeconomics and real business cycle home page

RFE Future Conferences
- List of future conferences provided by Resources for Economists on the Internet

Data sources

UK sites
- Bank of England
- HM Treasury

National statistics
- Census data
- Time-series data

International sites
- AEA Web Links to Data Sources
- European Central Bank
- European Commission
- Federal Reserve Economic Data

- IMF Data and Statistics Website
- NBER Data and Data Links
- OECD Statistics Portal
- UNCTAD Statistical Databases On-Line
- World Bank Data Website
- WTO Statistics Database

Market data

- BBC Market Data
- Energy Information Administration
- HBOS House Prices Database
- Yahoo Finance (UK)
- Yahoo Finance (US)

data availabale to UK HE staff and students

- Economic and Social Data Services
- INTUTE Statistics and Data for Social Sciences

Employment opportunities

American Agricultural Economics Association (AAEA) Employment Services

- Job openings list provided by the AAEA

Chronicle of Higher Education: Career Network

- Jobs and employment information for administrators and faculty, from the *Chronicle of Higher Education*

EconJobMarket

- A central repository for the files of job-market candidates (including papers, reference letters, and other materials) accessed online, provided by a non-profit organization

Economic Research Network (ERN) Placement Forum

- Job openings list provided by the ERN

Financial Economics Network (FEN) Placement Forum

- Job openings list provided by the FEN

Job Market for Economists

- Job listing for economists provided by the European Economic Association

Job Openings for Economists (JOE)

- Job openings list provided by the American Economic Association

Jobs at INOMICS

- Worldwide job listing provided by INOMICS, an internet site for economists

The QM&RBC Job Market

- Job market links from the quantitative macroeconomics and real business cycle home page

UK Academic Jobs

- List of research and faculty job vacancies in the UK and abroad

UK Job Openings for Economists (UK JOE)

- Job openings list provided by the Royal Economic Society

UK Jobs in Economics
- Job opportunities for economists in the UK

Walras
- A free job market resource for PhDs in economics and related fields

Media

Barron's
- *Barron's* is a US financial newspaper and the website provides in-depth economic and financial stories

CNBC
- The CNBC home page with breaking economic and financial news

CNN
- The home page of the CNN television news channel carrying the latest news

Investors' Chronicle
- Magazine for UK investors with daily share tips

New York Times
- The home page of the *New York Times* carrying news from a US perspective and links for US market data

Sky News
- The home page of Sky News with links to UK and world news

The Economist
- A UK weekly newspaper that provides worldwide coverage of economics and politics

The Financial Times
- The *Financial Times* is a UK daily newspaper that focuses on economic and financial news

The Times
- The *Times* newspaper is a respected UK daily newspaper

Wall Street Journal
- The *Wall Street Journal* provides US financial news and access to extensive market data

Washington Post
- The *Washington Post* is a source of US and world news